Hierarchical Linear Models

Second Edition

Advanced Quantitative Techniques
in the Social Sciences

Hierarchical Linear Models

Applications and Data Analysis Methods

Second Edition

Stephen W. Raudenbush
Anthony S. Bryk

Advanced Quantitative Techniques **1**
in the Social Sciences Series

Sage Publications
International Educational and Professional Publisher
Thousand Oaks ▪ London ▪ New Delhi

For information:

Sage Publications, Inc.
2455 Teller Road
Thousand Oaks, California 91320
E-mail: order@sagepub.com

Sage Publications, Ltd.
6 Bonhill Street
London EC2A 4PU
United Kingdom

Sage Publications India Pvt. Ltd.
M-32 Market
Greater Kailash I
New Delhi 110 048 India

Printed in the United States of America

Library of Congress Cataloging-in-Publication Data

A catalog record for this book is available from the Library of Congress

06   10   9   8   7   6

Acquiring Editor:	C. Deborah Laughton
Editorial Assistant:	Veronica Novak
Production Editor:	Sanford Robinson
Typesetter/Designer:	Technical Typesetting

Contents

To our loving wives Stella Raudenbush and Sharon Greenberg

Acknowledgments for the Second Edition

The decade since the publication of the first edition of this book has produced substantial growth in knowledge about hierarchical models and a rapidly expanding range of applications. This second edition results in part from the sustained and enormously satisfying collaboration between its authors, and also from collaboration and discussion with many colleagues too numerous to mention. Nevertheless, certain persons deserve special thanks for making this work possible.

Ongoing methodological discussions involving Darrell Bock, Yuk Fai Cheong, Sema Kalaian, Rafa Kasim, Xiaofeng Liu, and Yasuo Miyazaki have challenged our thinking. Yeow Meng Thum's work helped inspire the multivariate applications found in Chapters 6 and 11. Mike Seltzer provided an extremely useful critique of the Bayesian approaches described in Chapter 13 and generously gave us permission to reproduce the last example in that chapter. Meng-Li Yang and Matheos Yosef were essential in developing the maximum likelihood estimation methods used for hierarchical generalized linear models (Chapter 10). Young-Yun Shin provided careful reviews and many helpful comments on the entire manuscript. Guang-lei Hong's critique of an earlier draft helped shape Chapter 12 on cross-classified models. The work of Richard Congdon, applications programmer extraordinaire and long-time friend, shows up in every chapter of this book. Stuart Leppescu also assisted with preparation of data and new analyses for the second edition.

Colleagues with the Project on Human Development in Chicago Neighborhoods (PHDCN), including Felton Earls, Rob Sampson, and Christopher Johnson, have had an important impact on the second edition, as revealed in examples of neighborhood effects in Chapters 10 and 11. Indeed, we thank the MacArthur Foundation, the National Institute of Justice, and the National Institute of Mental Health for grants to PHDCN, which supported key methodological work reported in the new chapters of this volume.

Special thanks go to Pamela Gardner who helped proof, edit, and type this entire volume. Her amazing productivity and good humor were essential in this enterprise.

Anonymous reviewers provided many helpful suggestions on the new chapters in this edition. And C. Deborah Laughton, methodology editor for Sage, showed admirable patience and moral support. We again thank the series editor, Jan De Leeuw, for his encouragement.

Series Editor's Introduction to Hierarchical Linear Models

In the social sciences, data structures are often hierarchical in the following sense: We have variables describing individuals, but the individuals also are grouped into larger units, each unit consisting of a number of individuals. We also have variables describing these higher order units.

The leading example is, perhaps, in education. Students are grouped in classes. We have variables describing students and variables describing classes. It is possible that the variables describing classes are aggregated student variables, such as number of students or average socioeconomic status. But the class variables could also describe the teacher (if the class has only one teacher) or the classroom (if the class always meets in the same room). Moreover, in this particular example, further hierarchical structure often occurs quite naturally. Classes are grouped in schools, schools in school districts, and so on. We may have variables describing school districts and variables describing schools (teaching style, school building, neighborhood, and so on).

Once we have discovered this one example of a hierarchical data structure, we see many of them. They occur naturally in geography and (regional) economics. In a sense, one of the basic problems of sociology is to relate properties of individuals and properties of groups and structures in which the individuals function. In the same way, in economics there is the problem of relating the micro and the macro levels. Moreover, many repeated measurements are hierarchical. If we follow individuals over time, then the measurements for any particular individual are a group, in the same way as the school class is a group. If each interviewer interviews a group of interviewees, then the interviewers are the higher level. Thinking about these hierarchical structures a bit longer inevitably leads to the conclusion that many, if not most, social science data have this nested or hierarchical structure.

The next step, after realizing how important hierarchical data are, is to think of ways in which statistical techniques should take this hierarchical structure into account. There are two obvious procedures that have been somewhat discredited. The first is to disaggregate all higher order variables to the individual level. Teacher, class, and school characteristics are all assigned to the individual, and the analysis is done on the individual level. The problem with this approach is that if we know that students are in the same class, then we also know that they have the same value on each of the class variables. Thus we cannot use the assumption of independence of observations that is basic for the classical statistical techniques. The other alternative is to aggregate the individual-level variables to the higher level and do the analysis on the higher level. Thus we aggregate student characteristics over classes and do a class analysis, perhaps weighted with class size. The main problem here is that we throw away all the within-group information, which may be as much as 80% or 90% of the total variation before we start the analysis. As a consequence, relations between aggregated variables are often much stronger, and they can be very different from the relation between the nonaggregate variables. Thus we waste information, and we distort interpretation if we try to interpret the aggregate analysis on the individual level. Thus aggregating and disaggregating are both unsatisfactory.

If we limit ourselves to traditional linear model analysis, we know that the basic assumptions are linearity, normality, homoscedasticity, and independence. We would like to maintain the first two, but the last two (especially the independence assumption) should be adapted. The general idea behind such adaptations is that individuals in the same group are closer or more similiar than individuals in different groups. Thus students in different classes can be independent, but students in the same class share values on many more variables. Some of these variables will not be observed, which means that they vanish into the error term of the linear model, causing correlation between disturbances. This idea can be formalized by using variance component models. The disturbances have a group and an individual component. Individual components are all independent; group components are independent between groups but perfectly correlated within groups. Some groups might be more homogeneous than other groups, which means that the variance of the group components can differ.

There is a slightly different way to formalize this idea. We can suppose that each of the groups has a different regression model, in the simple regression case with its own intercept and its own slope. Because groups are also sampled, we then can make the assumption that the intercepts and slopes are a random sample from a population of group intercepts and slopes. This defines random-coefficient regression models. If we assume this for the intercepts only, and we let all slopes be the same, we are in the variance-component situation discussed in the previous paragraph. If the slopes vary randomly as well, we have a more complicated class of models in which the covariances of the disturbances depend on the values of the individual-level predictors.

In random-coefficient regression models, there is still no possibility to incorporate higher level variables, describing classes or schools. For this we need multilevel models, in which the group-level model is again a linear model. Thus we assume that the slope of the student variable SAT depends linearly on the class variables of class size or teacher philosophy. There are linear models on both levels, and if there are more levels, there are more nested linear models. Thus we arrive at a class of models that takes hierarchical structure into account and that makes it possible to incorporate variables from all levels.

Until about 10 years ago, fitting such models was technically not possible. Then, roughly at the same time, techniques and computer programs were published by Aitkin and Longford, Goldstein and co-workers, and Raudenbush and Bryk. The program HLM, by Bryk and Raudenbush, was the friendliest and most polished of these products, and in rapid succession a number of convincing and interesting examples were published. In this book, Bryk and Raudenbush describe the model, the algorithm, the program, and the examples in great detail. I think such a complete treatment of this class of techniques is both important and timely. Hierarchical linear models, or multilevel models, are certainly not a solution to all the data analysis problems of the social sciences. For this they are far too limited, because they are still based on the assumptions of linearity and normality, and because they still study the relatively simple regression structure in which a single variable depends on a number of others. Nevertheless, technically they are a big step ahead of the aggregation and disaggregation methods, mainly because they are statistically correct and do not waste information.

I think the main gain, illustrated nicely in this book by the extensive analysis of the examples, is conceptual. The models for the various levels are nicely separated, without being completely disjointed. One can think about the possible mechanisms on each of the levels separately and then join the separate models in a joint analysis. In educational research, as well as in geography, sociology, and economics, these techniques will gain in

Series Editor's Introduction
to the Second Edition

The first edition of this book has been a bestseller. The book turned out to have just the right level of technical detail for many social and behavioral scientists. It also contained just enough practical suggestions and worked-out examples, and, in combination with the corresponding software HLM, it functioned for many people as a handbook and a user's guide for multilevel analysis. After 10 years, however, it is time for an update.

Multilevel analysis has developed a great deal over this 10 year period. In the social and behavioral sciences the technique caught on like wildfire, and many applications have been published. In some areas, HLM has become the norm for good data analysis, and the basic software packages have been generalized and otherwise perfected. Perhaps even more importantly, mixed models (of which multilevel models are an important special case) have become very dominant in statistics. This is true, in particular, for nonlinear mixed models and generalized linear mixed models (GLMM), which are the basis of two of the most active research areas in statistics and biostatistics. This research has lead to many exciting theoretical and computational developments.

If we compare the first and second editions, the most obvious change is the addition of four completely new chapters. Chapter 10 covers hierarchical generalized linear models, an important subclass of GLMM models. These models allow the researcher to deal with integer-valued outcome variables (counts, frequencies, rates, proportions). Chapter 11 adds hierarchical models for latent variables, including measurement error and item response models. In Chapter 12, the standard multilevel nesting assumption is generalized to allow for more complicated cross-classified design. Chapter 13 gives a Bayesian perspective on hierarchical models and discusses Markov chain Monte Carlo computations. All four chapters correspond with the most active research areas in multilevel analysis over the last decade and with the recent addition to the basic computer software packages (HLM and MLWin). Each chapter relaxes some of the key assumptions in the first chapters (and in the first edition), which means that, in the end, we are dealing here with an enormously larger class of models and techniques.

The Technical Appendix in the first edition has been replaced by a new Chapter 14 on estimation theory. This chapter discusses Bayesian and maximum likelihood estimation techniques and corresponding computational problems in considerable technical detail. Again, this addition covers the latest developments such as the use of Laplace approximations to the likelihood function. If we compare both editions in detail, we find hundreds of corrections and additions to the earlier chapters as well.

I have remarked elsewhere, in fact, on many occasions, that the use of hierarchical linear models may be very well established, but that many aspects of these models are not yet well understood. Thus routine application is still not here, and maybe it should never come at all. This new edition goes much deeper than the old one into questions of power, sample size, data preprocessing such as centering, and so on, which provides us with much more understanding of the basic techniques. Of course, by adding (many/much) more complicated models with equally complicated computational procedures in the new chapters, the dividing line between research and data analysis is changed again, and many more options that are even less routine are introduced. Reading this book will not make you an expert in all these different areas, but hopefully it will teach you what these options are, where to find your expert, and which questions to ask her or him.

In comparing the editions, we also note that the authors felt that their balance of work and contribution had tipped in such a way that changing the order of authorship became necessary. Thus the standard text in behavioral and social science multilevel analysis is no longer Bryk and Raudenbush (1991), but Raudenbush and Bryk (2001). For the practicing statistician in these areas, the most important question is perhaps, "Should I upgrade?" The answer is a resounding yes. You get twice as much material, from a more modern and integrated perspective, and you are introduced to some of the most exciting areas of statistical research. Moreover, many exotic and promising tools are added to your toolbox. We, the editors, are proud to have this upgrade in our series.

JAN DE LEEUW
SERIES EDITOR

Section I

Logic

1

Introduction

- Hierarchical Data Structure: A Common Phenomenon
- Persistent Dilemmas in the Analysis of Hierarchical Data
- A Brief History of the Development of Statistical Theory for Hierarchical Models
- Early Applications of Hierarchical Linear Models
- New Developments Since the First Edition
- Organization of the Book

Hierarchical Data Structure: A Common Phenomenon

Much social research involves hierarchical data structures. In organizational studies, researchers might investigate how workplace characteristics, such as centralization of decision making, influence worker productivity. Both workers and firms are units in the analysis; variables are measured at both levels. Such data have a hierarchical structure with individual workers nested within firms.

In cross-national studies, demographers examine how differences in national economic development interact with adult educational attainment to influence fertility rates (see, e.g., Mason, Wong, & Entwistle, 1983). Such research combines economic indicators collected at the national level with household information on education and fertility. Both households and countries are units in the research with households nested within countries, and the basic data structure is again hierarchical.

Similar kinds of data occur in developmental research where multiple observations are gathered over time on a set of persons. The repeated

3

measures contain information about each individual's growth trajectory. The psychologist is typically interested in how characteristics of the person, including variations in environmental exposure, influence the shape of these growth trajectories. For example, Huttenlocher, Haight, Bryk, and Seltzer (1991) investigated how differences among children in exposure to language in the home predicted the development of each child's vocabulary over time. When every person is observed at the same fixed number of time points, it is conventional to view the design as occasions crossed by persons. But when the number and spacing of time points vary from person to person, we may view occasions as nested within persons.

The quantitative synthesis of findings from many studies presents another hierarchical data problem. An investigator may wish to discover how differences between studies in treatment implementations, research methods, subject characteristics, and contexts relate to treatment effect estimates within studies. In this case, subjects are nested within studies. Hierarchical models provide a very general statistical framework for these research activities (Berkey et al., 1995; Morris & Normand, 1992; Raudenbush & Bryk, 1985).

Educational research is often especially challenging because studies of student growth often involve a doubly nested structure of repeated observations within individuals, who are in turn nested within organizational settings. Research on instruction, for example, focuses on the interactions between students and a teacher around specific curricular materials. These interactions usually occur within a classroom setting and are bounded within a single academic year. The research problem has three foci: the individual growth of students over the course of the academic year (or segment of a year), the effects of personal characteristics and individual educational experiences on student learning, and how these relations are in turn influenced by classroom organization and the specific behavior and characteristics of the teacher. Correspondingly, the data have a three-level hierarchical structure. The level-1 units are the repeated observations over time, which are nested within the level-2 units of persons, who in turn are nested within the level-3 units of classrooms or schools.

Three-level hierarchies also arise frequently in cross-sectional research. For example, Nye, Hedges, and Konstantopoulos (2000) reanalyzed data from the Tennessee class size experiment, which involved students nested within classrooms within schools. Raudenbush, Cheong, and Fotiu (1999) analyzed the U.S. National Assessment of Educational Progress, which involves students nested within schools within states.

Persistent Dilemmas in the Analysis of Hierarchical Data

Despite the prevalence of hierarchical structures in behavioral and social research, past studies have often failed to address them adequately in the data analysis. In large part, this neglect has reflected limitations in conventional statistical techniques for the estimation of linear models with nested structures. In social research, these limitations have generated concerns about aggregation bias, misestimated precision, and the "unit of analysis" problem (see Chapter 5). They have also fostered an impoverished conceptualization, discouraging the formulation of explicit multilevel models with hypotheses about effects occurring at each level and across levels. Similarly, studies of human development have been plagued by "measurement of change" problems (see Chapter 6), which at times have seemed intractable, and have even led some analysts to advise against attempts to directly model growth.

Although these problems of unit of analysis and measuring change have distinct, long-standing, and virtually nonoverlapping literatures, they share a common cause: the inadequacy of traditional statistical techniques for modeling hierarchy. In the past, sophisticated analysts have often been able to find ways to cope at least partially in specific instances. With recent developments in the statistical theory for estimating hierarchical linear models, however, an integrated set of methods now exists that permits efficient estimation for a much wider range of applications.

Even more important from our perspective is that the barriers to use of an explicit hierarchical modeling framework have now been removed. We can now readily pose hypotheses about relations occurring at each level and across levels and also assess the amount of variation at each level. From a substantive perspective, the hierarchical linear model is more homologous with the basic phenomena under study in much behavioral and social research. The applications to date have been encouraging in that they have both afforded an exploration of new questions and provided some empirical results that might otherwise have gone undetected.

A Brief History of the Development of Statistical Theory for Hierarchical Models

The models discussed in this book appear in diverse literatures under a variety of titles. In sociological research, they are often referred to as *multilevel linear models* (cf. Goldstein, 1995; Mason et al., 1983). In biometric applications, the terms *mixed-effects models* and *random-effects models* are common (cf. Elston & Grizzle, 1962; Laird & Ware, 1982; Singer, 1998).

They are also called *random-coefficient regression models* in the economet-rics literature (cf. Rosenberg, 1973; Longford, 1993) and in the statistical literature have been referred to as *covariance components models* (cf. Demp-ster, Rubin, & Tsutakawa, 1981; Longford, 1987).

We have adopted the term *hierarchical linear models* because it conveys an important structural feature of data that is common in a wide variety of applications, including studies of growth, organizational effects, and research synthesis. This term was introduced by Lindley and Smith (1972) and Smith (1973) as part of their seminal contribution on Bayesian estimation of linear models. Within this context, Lindley and Smith elaborated a general frame-work for nested data with complex error structures.

Unfortunately, the Lindley and Smith (1972) contribution languished for a period of time because use of the models required estimation of covariance components in the presence of unbalanced data. With the exception of some very simple problems, no general estimation approach was feasible in the early 1970s. Dempster, Laird, and Rubin's (1977) development of the EM algorithm provided the needed breakthrough: a conceptually feasible and broadly applicable approach to covariance component estimation. Dempster et al. (1981) demonstrated applicability of this approach to hierarchical data structures. Laird and Ware (1982) and Strenio, Weisberg, and Bryk (1983) applied this approach to the study of growth, and Mason et al. (1983) applied it to cross-sectional data with a multilevel structure.

Subsequently, other numerical approaches to covariance component esti-mation were also offered through the use of iteratively reweighted generalized least squares (Goldstein, 1986) and a Fisher scoring algorithm (Longford, 1987). A variety of statistical computing programs are available for fitting these models, including HLM (Raudenbush et al., 2000), MIXOR (Hedeker, & Gibbons, 1996), MLWIN (Rasbash et al., 2000), SAS Proc Mixed (Littel et al., 1996), and VARCL (Longford, 1988). Fully Bayesian methods have also been developed by Gelfand et al. (1990) and Seltzer (1993) and are now widely available through software packages such as BUGS (Spiegelhalter et al., 1994).

Early Applications of Hierarchical Linear Models

As noted above, behavioral and social data commonly have a nested struc-ture, including, for example, repeated observations nested within persons. These persons also may be nested within organizational units such as schools. Further, the organizational units themselves may be nested within communi-ties, within states, and even within countries. With hierarchical linear models, each of the levels in this structure is formally represented by its own sub-model. These submodels express relationships among variables within a given level, and specify how variables at one level influence relations occurring at another. Although any number of levels can be represented, all the essential statistical features are found in the basic two-level model.

The applications discussed below address three general research purposes: improved estimation of effects within individual units (e.g., developing an improved estimate of a regression model for an individual school by borrowing strength from the fact that similar estimates exist for other schools); the formulation and testing of hypotheses about cross-level effects (e.g., how varying school size might affect the relationship between social class and academic achievement within schools); and the partitioning of variance and covariance components among levels (e.g., decomposing the covariation among set of student-level variables into within- and between-school components). Early published examples of each type are summarized briefly below.

Improved Estimation of Individual Effects

Braun, Jones, Rubin and Thayer (1983) were concerned about the use of standardized test scores for selecting minority applicants to graduate business schools. Many schools base admissions decisions, in part, on equations that use test scores to predict later academic success. However, because most applicants to most business schools are white, their data dominate the estimated prediction equations. As a result, these equations may not produce an adequate ordering for purposes of selecting minority students.

In principle, a separate equation for minority applicants in each school might be fairer, but difficulties often arise in estimating such equations, because most schools have only a few minority students and thus little data on which to develop reliable predictions. In Braun et al.'s (1983) data on 59 graduate business schools, 14 schools had no minorities, and 20 schools had only one to three minority students. Developing prediction equations for minorities in these schools would have been impossible using standard regression methods. Further, even in the 25 schools with sufficient data to sustain a separate estimation, the minority samples were still small, and as a result, the minority coefficients would have been poorly estimated.

Alternatively, the data could be pooled across all schools, ignoring the nesting of students within schools, but this also poses difficulties. Specifically, because minorities are much more likely to be present in some schools than others, a failure to represent these selection artifacts could bias the estimated prediction coefficients.

Braun et al. (1983) used a hierarchical linear model to resolve this dilemma. By borrowing strength from the entire ensemble of data, they were able to efficiently use all of the available information to provide each school with separate prediction equations for whites and minorities. The estimator for each school was actually a weighted composite of the information from that school and the relations that exist in the overall sample. As one might intuitively expect, the relative weights given each component depend on its precision. The estimation procedure is described in Chapter 3 and illustrated in Chapter 4. For a related application, see Rubin (1980), and for a statistical review of these developments, see Morris (1983).

Modeling Cross-Level Effects

The second general use of a hierarchical model is to formulate and test hypotheses about how variables measured at one level affect relations occurring at another. Because such cross-level effects are common in behavioral and social research, the modeling framework provides a significant advance over traditional methods.

An Example from Social Research. Mason et al. (1983) examined the effects of maternal education and urban versus rural residence on fertility in 15 countries. It has been well known that in many countries high levels of education and urban residence predict low fertility. However, the investigators reasoned that such effects might depend on characteristics of the countries, including level of national economic development, as indicated by gross national product (GNP), and the intensity of family planning efforts.

Mason et al. found that higher levels of maternal education were indeed associated with lower fertility rates in all countries. Differences in urban versus rural fertility rates, however, varied across countries with the largest gaps occurring in nations with a high GNP and few organized family planning efforts. The identification of *differentiating effects,* such as this rural-urban gap, and the prediction of their variability is taken up in Chapter 5.

An Example from Developmental Research. Investigators of language development hypothesized that word acquisition depends on two sources: exposure to appropriate speech and innate differences in ability to learn from such exposure. It is widely assumed that innate differences in ability are largely responsible for observed differences in children's vocabulary development. However, the empirical support for this assumption is weak. Heritability studies have found that parent scores on standardized vocabulary tests account for 10% to 20% of the variance in children's scores on the same tests. Exposure studies have not fared much better. Most of the individual variation in vocabulary acquisition has remained unexplained.

In the past, researchers have relied primarily on two-time-point designs to study exposure effects. Children's vocabulary might first be assessed at, say, 14 months of age, and information on maternal verbal ability or language use also might be collected at that time. Children's vocabulary size then would be reassessed at some subsequent time point, say 26 months. The data would be analyzed with a conventional linear model with the focus on estimating the maternal speech effect on 26-month vocabulary size after controlling for children's "initial ability" (i.e., the 14-month vocabulary size).

Huttenlocher et al. (1991) collected longitudinal data with some children observed on as many as seven occasions between 14 and 26 months. This permitted formulation of an individual vocabulary growth trajectory based on the repeated observations for each child. Each child's growth was characterized by a set of parameters. A second model used information about the children, including the child's sex and amount of maternal speech in the home environment, to predict these growth parameters. The actual formulation and estimation of this model are detailed in Chapter 6.

The analysis, based on a hierarchical linear model, found that exposure to language during infancy played a much larger role in vocabulary development than had been reported in previous studies. (In fact, the effects were substantially larger than would have been found had a conventional analysis been performed using just the first and last time points.) This application demonstrates the difficulty associated with drawing valid inferences about correlates of growth from conventional approaches.

Partitioning Variance-Covariance Components

A third use of hierarchical linear models draws on the estimation of variance and covariance components with unbalanced, nested data. For example, educational researchers often wish to study the growth of the individual student learner within the organizational context of classrooms and schools. Formal modeling of such phenomena require use of a three-level model.

Bryk and Raudenbush (1988) illustrated this approach with a small subsample of longitudinal data from the Sustaining Effects Study (Carter, 1984). They used mathematics achievement data from 618 students in 86 schools measured on five occasions between Grade 1 and Grade 3. They began with an individual growth (or repeated measures) model of the academic achievement for each child within each school. The three-level approach enabled a decomposition of the variation in these individual growth trajectories into within- and between-school components. The details of this application are discussed in Chapter 8.

The results were startling—83% of the variance in growth rates was between schools. In contrast, only about 14% of the variance in initial status was between schools, which is consistent with results typically encountered in cross-sectional studies of school effects. This analysis identified substantial differences among schools that conventional models would not have detected, because such analyses do not allow the partitioning of learning-rate variance into within- and between-school components.

New Developments Since the First Edition

As interest in hierarchical models has grown, the pace of methodological innovation has accelerated, with many creative applications in social science and medicine. First, methodologists have expanded the range of outcome variables to which these models apply. Second, models have been extended to include cross-classified as well as purely nested data structures. Third, the applications to multivariate outcome problems have become more prominent. Fourth, latent variable models have been embedded within hierarchical models. Fifth, Bayesian inference for hierarchical models has increased in accessibility and popularity. When combined with the vast increases in computational power now available, this expansion in modeling has inspired a whole array of new applications.

An Expanded Range of Outcome Variables

The first edition of this book confined its attention to continuously distributed outcomes at level 1. For outcomes of this type, it is often reasonable to assume that model errors are normally distributed. Statistical inference proceeds within comparatively tractable normal distribution theory. Inference is much more challenging when outcomes are discrete. Prominent examples include binary outcomes (e.g., employed versus unemployed), counted data (e.g., the number of crimes committed in a given neighborhood per year), ordered categorical outcomes (e.g., low, medium, or high job satisfaction), and multicategory nominal scale outcomes (e.g., occupation type as manual, clerical, service, or professional). For these outcomes, it is implausible to assume linear models and normality at level 1. Embedding such nonnormal outcomes within a hierarchical model makes the task of developing appropriate statistical and computational approaches much more challenging.

Stiratelli, Laird, and Ware (1984) and Wong and Mason (1985) were among the first to tackle these problems using a first-order approximation to maximum likelihood (ML) estimation. Goldstein (1991) and Longford (1993) developed software that made these approaches accessible for several types of discrete outcomes and for two- and three-level models. However, Breslow and

Clayton (1993) and German and Rodriguez (1995) showed that such approximations could be quite inaccurate under certain conditions. Goldstein (1995) developed a second-order approximation. Hedeker and Gibbons (1993) and Pinheiro and Bates (1995) developed accurate approximations to ML using Gauss-Hermite quadrature, and these are now implemented, respectively, in the software packages Mixor and SAS Proc Mixed. An alternative approximation that is typically accurate and computationally convenient uses a high-order Laplace transform (Raudenbush, Yang, & Yosef, 2000) and is implemented in the program HLM.

As a result of these statistical and computational innovations, researchers can now apply the logic of hierarchical models to a vastly expanded array of outcome types. Rumberger (1995) used a two-level model to study the predictors of students' dropping out of school. He identified a number of student-level and school-level risk factors for early drop-out. The level-1 model was a logistic regression model in which the log-odds of early drop-out depended on student background characteristics. Level-1 coefficients varied over schools as a function of school characteristics. Horney, Osgood, and Marshall (1995) provide an interesting application in the context of repeated measures. The aim was to study whether the propensity of high-rate offenders to commit crimes changes with life circumstances such as employment and marital status. The outcome was binary, where each participant either did or did not commit a crime during the prior month. Some explanatory variables also varied with time (e.g., employed versus unemployed), whereas others varied over participants but were invariant with respect to time. The level-1 model was a logistic regression model for individual change in the log-odds of committing crime. Parameters of individual change varied at level 2. Sampson, Raudenbush, and Earls (1997) provide an example with count data as the outcome (the number of homicides per neighborhood), whereas Reardon and Buka (in press) consider a survival model to study the age of onset of substance use of youth nested within neighborhoods.

Chapter 10 considers applications of hierarchical models in the case of binary outcomes, counted data, ordered categories, and multinomial outcomes.

Incorporating Cross-Classified Data Structures

All the examples in the first edition of this book involved "pure" hierarchies. For example, if students are nested within classrooms within schools, we can reasonably assume that each student is a member of one and only one classroom and that each classroom is located in one and only one school. Often, however, nested structures are more complex. Consider, for example, a study of children attending a set of schools and living in a set of neighborhoods. The data do not form a pure hierarchy, because a school will typically draw students from multiple neighborhoods while a neighborhood will also send students to multiple schools. We may view the students as cross-classified by neighborhoods and schools. Raudenbush (1993) developed methodology for this kind of setting. A level-1 model describes the association between student-level predictors and the outcome with each "cell" defined by the cross-classification of neighborhoods and schools. The coefficients of that model can then vary over the neighborhoods and schools. Neighborhood-level and school-level predictors may be of interest and two-way interactions between neighborhood- and school-level characteristics may also be of interest. A second example involves the cross-classification of students by primary school and secondary school attended (Goldstein, 1995).

Crossed classifications can also arise in the context of repeated-measures data. In Chapter 12, we consider the growth of math achievement during the elementary school years. Each year, a student attends a new classroom. In principle, experience in that classroom could "deflect" the student's growth curve in a positive or negative direction. The variance of these deflections is the classroom variance. The data involve the cross-classification of repeated measures by student and classroom. Under certain specified assumptions, the results show that part of the variation in growth curves that would otherwise have been attributable to individual differences among children is instead associated with differences in teacher effectiveness. Taking classroom effects into account also reduces the estimate of temporal instability in student outcomes.

Chapter 12 describes cross-classified random-effects models, illustrating the approach with several examples.

Multivariate Models

The first edition of this book considered univariate outcomes at level 1. Since then, hierarchical models for multivariate outcomes have become more common. Perhaps the most prominent application involves repeated-measures data. Suppose that a longitudinal study uses a fixed data-collection design for every participant. That is, the plan is to collect data on the same set of occasions for every participant. If there are no missing data, such a design will produce a balanced set of data: The number of measures per person will be invariant, as will the time elapsed between occasions. In this setting, classical models for multivariate repeated measures will apply. These approaches make possible a generous array of models for the variances and covariances of the time-series data, including autocorrelated errors and randomly varying slopes, as well as an unrestricted model, which allows a distinct variance for each time point and a distinct covariance for each pair of time points. Jennrich and Schluchter (1986) were among the first to propose methods and software that would apply even in the presence of missing time points. Goldstein (1995) incorporated this idea into a hierarchical model. SAS (1996) implemented a similar approach in its program Proc Mixed as did Hedeker and Gibbons in Mixor (1996) and Raudenbush et al. (2000) in HLM. This second edition considers multivariate growth models in Chapter 6, providing a comparison with results obtained from a standard hierarchical model having a univariate outcome. It also considers extension of this approach to the case in which the repeatedly observed participants are nested in organizations.

Latent Variable Models

A second class of multivariate outcome models becomes extremely useful in missing data problems. Using a variant of Jennrich and Schluchter's (1986) approach, one can estimate the joint distribution of a set of continuous variables from incomplete data. This enables an elegant approach for estimating regressions when predictors are missing at random. The "complete data" are regarded as the observed data augmented by unobserved, latent variables. The observed, incomplete data are used to estimate the associations among these latent variables (cf. Little & Rubin, 1987; Little & Schenker, 1995). The method uses a similar strategy to take into account the measurement error of predictors in estimates of multiple regression models. The first level of the hierarchical model represents associations between the fallible observed data and the latent "true" data. The approach extends nicely to the case in which the fallibly measured variables are characteristics of groups such as schools or neighborhoods. Another natural extension is to estimate the direct and indirect effects of fallibly measured predictors in the context of a hierarchical model. These topics are taken up in Chapter 11.

Item response models, long used in educational testing, are increasingly applied in other domains of social science. Such models represent the probability of a given response as a function of characteristics of the item and "ability" or "latent trait" of the person. The person's trait is the latent variable of interest. Such models can be represented as two-level models where item responses are nested within persons. Chapter 11 also shows how such models can be formulated and then extended to incorporate the nesting of persons within groups.

Bayesian Inference

In the first edition of this book, all statistical inferences were based on the method of maximum likelihood (ML). The ML approach has many desirable properties: Parameter estimates are consistent and asymptotically unbiased and efficient. These estimates have large-sample normal distributions, and statistical tests for comparing models are readily available. These desirable properties are based, however, on large-sample theory. In the case of hierarchical models, the number of higher-level units (e.g., the number of level-2 units in a two-level model) is usually key in determining whether these large-sample properties will apply. If, in fact, the sample size at the highest level is small, statistical inferences may not be trustworthy, depending on the degree to which the data are unbalanced and the particular type of inference sought.

Bayesian methods provide a sensible alternative approach in these cases. Standard errors will tend to be more realistic than under ML. Moreover, by supplying the posterior distribution of each parameter of interest, the Bayesian approach affords a variety of interesting graphical and numerical summaries of evidence about a research question.

The appeal of the Bayesian approach is not new. What is new is the availability of convenient computational methods, particularly in the context of hierarchical data and models. The advances underlying these new approaches involve a family of algorithms using Monte Carlo methods to approximate posterior distributions in settings that were previously regarded as intractable. These methods include data augmentation (Tanner & Wong, 1987) and Gibbs sampling (Gelfand et al., 1990; Gelfand & Smith, 1990). Software implementing these approaches is now available (Spiegelhalter et al., 1996; Rasbash et al., 2000). An interesting example is Seltzer's (1993) reanalysis of the vocabulary data originally published by Huttenlocher et al. (1991) and studied in the first edition of this book. This example involved the vocabulary growth of 22 children during the second year of life. ML inference is at risk in this instance because the number of second-level units (children) is small. The analysis produces the posterior distribution of level-1 coefficients, most notably, the acceleration rates for each child, and of the key level-2 coefficients specifying the association between maternal speech and acceleration. Chapter 13 provides a brief introduction to the logic of Bayesian inference, with applications to hierarchical data.

Organization of the Book

The book is organized into four main sections. The first two sections include Part I, "Logic," and Part II, "Basic Applications." These two sections consist of nine chapters and closely parallel the first edition but with some significant expansions and technical clarifications.

We have added a new section to Chapter 6 on multivariate growth models, expanded the number of illustrative examples throughout Part II, and added further data analytic advice on centering of level-1 predictors. We also introduce some new statistics—plausible value intervals and robust standard errors—not in use when the first edition was published.

Part III, "Advanced Applications," is entirely new. Part IV provides a technical discussion of the methods and computational approaches used in the book.

Part I includes three additional chapters beyond this introductory chapter. Chapter 2 introduces the logic of hierarchical linear models by building on simpler concepts from regression analysis and random-effects analysis of variance. In Chapter 3, we summarize the basic procedures for estimation and inference used with these models. The emphasis is on an intuitive introduction with a minimal level of mathematical sophistication. These procedures are then illustrated in Chapter 4 as we work through the estimation of an increasingly complex set of models with a common data set.

Part II, "Basic Applications," includes five chapters. Chapters 5 and 6 consider the use of two-level models in the study of organizational effects and individual growth, respectively. Chapter 7 discusses research synthesis or meta-analysis applications. This actually represents a special class of applications where the level-1 variances are known. Chapter 8 introduces the three-level model and describes a range of applications, including a key educational research problem—how school organization influences student learning over time. Chapter 9 reviews the basic model assumptions, describes procedures for examining the validity of these assumptions, and discusses what is known about sensitivity of inferences to violation of these various assumptions.

Part III, "Advanced Applications," consists of four chapters. Chapter 10 presents hierarchical models for applications with discrete outcomes. It considers binary outcomes, counts, ordered categorical outcomes, and multi-category nominal outcomes. It provides detailed examples in each case, and considers the distinction between population-average models, also called marginal models (Heagerty & Zeger, 2000), and unit-specific models. Chapter 11 considers latent variable models. Topics of interest include estimating regressions from missing data, estimating regressions when predictors are measured with error, and embedding item response models within the framework of the hierarchical model. Chapter 12 presents cross-classified random effects models. Chapter 13 concerns Bayesian inference for hierarchical linear models.

Part IV provides the statistical theory and computations used throughout the book. It considers univariate linear models with normal level-1 errors, multivariate linear models, and hierarchical generalized linear models.

2

The Logic of Hierarchical Linear Models

- Preliminaries
- A General Model and Simpler Submodels
- Generalizations of the Basic Hierarchical Linear Model
- Choosing the Location of *X* and *W* (*Centering*)
- Summary of Terms and Notation Introduced in This Chapter

This chapter introduces the logic of hierarchical linear models. We begin with a simple example that builds upon the reader's understanding of familiar ideas from regression and analysis of variance (ANOVA). We show how these common statistical models can be viewed as special cases of the hierarchical linear model. The chapter concludes with a summary of some definitions and notation that are used throughout the book.

Preliminaries

A Study of the SES-Achievement Relationship in One School

We begin by considering the relationship between a single student-level predictor variable (say, socioeconomic status [SES]) and one student-level outcome variable (mathematics achievement) within a single, hypothetical school. Figure 2.1 provides a scatterplot of this relationship. The scatter of points is well represented by a straight line with intercept β_0 and slope β_1. Thus, the regression equation for the data is

$$Y_i = \beta_0 + \beta_1 X_i + r_i. \qquad [2.1]$$

The intercept, β_0, is defined as the expected math achievement of a student whose SES is zero. The slope, β_1, is the expected change in math achievement associated with a unit increase in SES. The error term, r_i, rep-

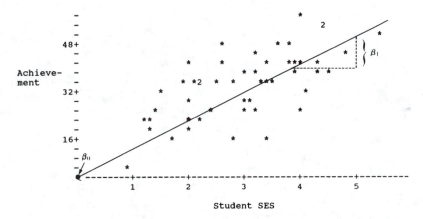

Figure 2.1. Scatterplot Showing the Relationship Between Achievement and SES in One Hypothetical School

resents a unique effect associated with person i. Typically, we assume that r_i is normally distributed with a mean of zero and variance σ^2, that is, $r_i \sim N(0, \sigma^2)$.

It is often helpful to scale the independent variable, X, so that the intercept will be meaningful. For example, suppose we "center" SES by subtracting the mean SES from each score: $X_i - \overline{X}$, where $\overline{X}$ is the mean SES in the school. If we now plot Y_i as a function of $X_i - \overline{X}$. (see Figure 2.2) with the

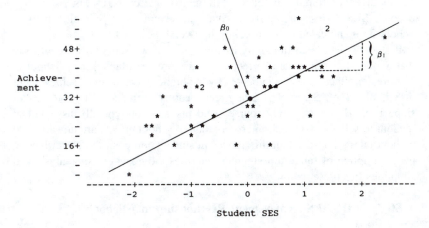

Figure 2.2. Scatterplot Showing the Relationship Between Achievement and SES (Centered) in One Hypothetical School

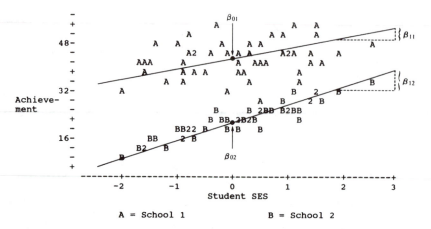

Figure 2.3. Scatterplot Showing the Relationship Between Achievement and SES Within Two Hypothetical Schools

regression line superimposed, we see that the intercept, β_0, is now the mean math achievement while the slope remains unchanged.

A Study of the SES-Achievement Relationship in Two Schools

Let us now consider separate regressions for two hypothetical schools. These are displayed in Figure 2.3. The two lines indicate that School 1 and School 2 differ in two ways. First, School 1 has a higher mean than does School 2. This difference is reflected in the two intercepts, that is, $\beta_{01} > \beta_{02}$. Second, SES is less predictive of math achievement in School 1 than in School 2, as indicated by comparing the two slopes, that is, $\beta_{11} < \beta_{12}$.

If students had been randomly assigned to the two schools, we could say that School 1 is both more "effective" and more "equitable" than School 2. The greater effectiveness is indicated by the higher mean level of achievement in School 1 (i.e., $\beta_{01} > \beta_{02}$). The greater equity is indicated by the weaker slope (i.e., $\beta_{11} < \beta_{12}$). Of course, students are not typically assigned at random to schools, so much interpretations of school effects are unwarranted without taking into account differences in student composition. Nevertheless, the assumption of random assignment clarifies the goals of the analysis and simplifies our presentation.

A Study of the SES-Achievement Relationship in *J* Schools

We now consider the study of the SES-math achievement relationship within an entire *population* of schools. Suppose that we now have a random sample of J schools from a population, where J is a large number. It is no longer practical to summarize the data with a scatterplot for each school. Nevertheless, we can describe this relationship within any school j by the equation

$$Y_{ij} = \beta_{0j} + \beta_{1j}(X_{ij} - \overline{X}_{.j}) + r_{ij}, \qquad [2.2]$$

where for simplicity we assume that r_{ij} is normally distributed with homogeneous variance across schools, that is, $r_{ij} \sim N(0, \sigma^2)$. Notice that the intercept and slope are now subscripted by j, which allows each school to have a unique intercept and slope. For each school, effectiveness and equity are described by the pair of values (β_{0j}, β_{1j}). It is often sensible and convenient to assume that the intercept and slope have a bivariate normal distribution across the population of schools. Let

$$E(\beta_{0j}) = \gamma_0, \qquad \text{Var}(\beta_{0j}) = \tau_{00},$$
$$E(\beta_{1j}) = \gamma_1, \qquad \text{Var}(\beta_{1j}) = \tau_{11},$$
$$\text{Cov}(\beta_{0j}, \beta_{1j}) = \tau_{01},$$

where

γ_0 is the average school mean for the population of schools;

τ_{00} is the population variance among the school means;

γ_1 is the average SES-achievement slope for the population;

τ_{11} is the population variance among the slopes; and

τ_{01} is the population covariance between slopes and intercepts.

A positive value of τ_{01} implies that schools with high means tend also to have positive slopes. Knowledge of these variances and of the covariance leads directly to a formula for calculating the population correlation between the means and slopes:

$$\rho(\beta_{0j}, \beta_{1j}) = \tau_{01}/(\tau_{00}\,\tau_{11})^{1/2}. \qquad [2.3]$$

In reality, we rarely know the true values of the population parameters we have introduced $(\gamma_0, \gamma_1, \tau_{11}, \tau_{00}, \tau_{01})$ nor of the true individual school means and slopes $(\beta_{0j} \text{ and } \beta_{1j})$. Rather, all of these must be estimated from the data. Our focus in this chapter is simply to clarify the meaning of the parameters. The actual procedures used to estimate them are introduced in Chapter 3 and are discussed more extensively in Chapter 14.

Suppose we did know the true values of the means and slopes for each school. Figure 2.4 provides a scatterplot of the relationship between β_{0j} and

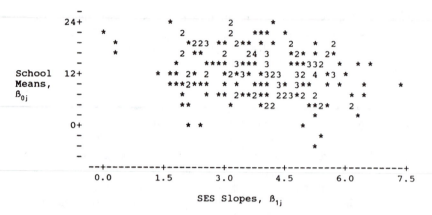

Figure 2.4. Plot of School Means (vertical axis) and SES Slopes (horizontal axis) for 200 Hypothetical Schools

β_{1j} for a hypothetical sample of schools. This plot tells us about how schools vary in terms of their means and slopes. Notice, for example, that there is more dispersion among the means (vertical axis) than the slopes (horizontal axis). Symbolically, this implies that $\tau_{00} > \tau_{11}$. Notice also that the two effects tend to be negatively correlated: Schools with high average achievement, β_{0j}, tend to have weak SES-achievement relationships, β_{1j}. Symbolically, $\tau_{01} < 0$. Schools that are effective and egalitarian—that is, with high average achievement (large values of β_{0j}) and weak SES effects (small values of β_{1j})—are found in the upper left quadrant of the scatterplot.

Having examined graphically how schools vary in terms of their intercepts and slopes, we may wish to develop a model to predict β_{0j} and β_{1j}. Specifically, we could use school characteristics (e.g., levels of funding, organizational features, policies) to predict effectiveness and equity. For instance, consider a simple indicator variable, W_j, which takes on a value of one for Catholic schools and a value of zero for public schools. Coleman, Hoffer, and Kilgore (1982) argued that W_j is positively related to effectiveness (Catholic schools have higher average achievement than do public schools) and negatively related to the slope (SES effects on math achievement are smaller in Catholic than in public schools). We represent these two hypotheses via two regression equations:

$$\beta_{0j} = \gamma_{00} + \gamma_{01}W_j + u_{0j} \qquad [2.4a]$$

and

$$\beta_{1j} = \gamma_{10} + \gamma_{11}W_j + u_{1j}, \qquad [2.4b]$$

where

γ_{00} is the mean achievement for public schools;

γ_{01} is the mean achievement difference between Catholic and public schools (i.e., the Catholic school "effectiveness" advantage);

γ_{10} is the average SES-achievement slope in public schools;

γ_{11} is the mean difference in SES-achievement slopes between Catholic and public schools (i.e., the Catholic school "equity" advantage);

u_{0j} is the unique effect of school j on mean achievement holding W_j constant (or conditioning on W_j); and

u_{1j} is the unique effect of school j on the SES-achievement slope holding W_j constant (or conditioning on W_j).

We assume u_{0j} and u_{1j} are random variables with zero means, variances τ_{00} and τ_{11}, respectively, and covariance τ_{01}. Note these variance-covariance components are now *conditional* or *residual* variance-covariance components. That is, they represent the variability in β_{0j} and β_{1j} remaining after controlling for W_j.

It is not possible to estimate the parameters of these regression equations directly, because the outcomes (β_{0j}, β_{1j}) are not observed. However, the data contain information needed for this estimation. This becomes clear if we substitute Equations 2.4a and 2.4b into Equation 2.2, yielding the single prediction equation for the outcome

$$Y_{ij} = \gamma_{00} + \gamma_{01}W_j + \gamma_{10}(X_{ij} - \overline{X}._j) + \gamma_{11}W_j(X_{ij} - \overline{X}._j)$$
$$+ u_{0j} + u_{1j}(X_{ij} - \overline{X}._j) + r_{ij}. \qquad [2.5]$$

Notice that Equation 2.5 is not the typical linear model assumed in standard ordinary least squares (OLS). Efficient estimation and accurate hypothesis testing based on OLS require that the random errors are independent, normally distributed, and have constant variance. In contrast, the random error in Equation 2.5 is of a more complex form, $u_{0j} + u_{1j}(X_{ij} - \overline{X}._j) + r_{ij}$. Such errors are dependent within each school because the components u_{0j} and u_{1j} are common to every student within school j. The errors also have unequal variances, because $u_{0j} + u_{1j}(X_{ij} - \overline{X}._j)$ depend on u_{0j} and u_{1j}, which vary across schools, and on the value of $(X_{ij} - \overline{X}._j)$, which varies across students. Though standard regression analysis is inappropriate, such models can be estimated by iterative maximum likelihood procedures described in the

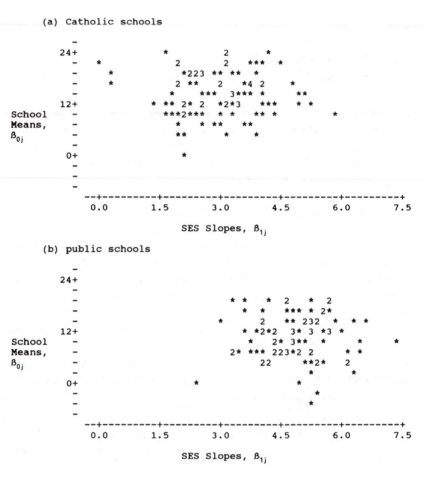

Figure 2.5. Plot of School Means (vertical axis) and SES Slopes (horizontal axis) for 100 Hypothetical Catholic Schools and 100 Hypothetical Public Schools

next chapter. We note that if u_{0j} and u_{1j} were null for every j, Equation 2.5 would be equivalent to an OLS regression model.

Figure 2.5 provides a graphical representation of the model specified in Equation 2.4. Here we see two hypothetical plots of the association between β_{0j} and β_{1j}, one for public and one for Catholic schools. The plots were constructed to reflect Coleman et al.'s (1982) contention that Catholic schools have both higher mean achievement and weaker SES effects than do the public schools.

A General Model and Simpler Submodels

We now generalize our terminology a bit so that it applies to any two-level hierarchical data structure. Equation 2.2 may be labeled the *level-1* model; Equation 2.4 is the *level-2* model, and Equation 2.5 is the *combined* model. In the school-effects application, the level-1 units are students and the level-2 units are schools. The errors r_{ij} are the level-1 random effects and the errors u_{0j} and u_{1j} are level-2 random effects. Moreover, Var(r_{ij}) is the level-1 variance, and Var(u_{0j}), Var(u_{1j}), and Cov(u_{0j}, u_{1j}) are the level-2 variance-covariance components. The β parameters in the level-1 model are level-1 coefficients and the γs are the level-2 coefficients.

Given a single level-1 predictor, X_{ij}, and a single level-2 predictor, W_j, the model given by Equations 2.2, 2.4, and 2.5 is the simplest example of a full hierarchical linear model. When certain sets of terms in this model are set equal to zero, we are left with a set of simpler models, some of which are quite familiar. It is instructive to examine these, both to demonstrate the range of applications of hierarchical linear models and to draw out the connections to more common data analysis methods. The submodels, running from the simpler to the more complex, include the one-way ANOVA model with random effects; a regression model with means-as-outcomes; a one-way analysis of covariance (ANCOVA) model with random effects; a random-coefficients regression model; a model with intercepts- and slopes-as-outcomes; and a model with nonrandomly varying slopes.

One-Way ANOVA with Random Effects

The simplest possible hierarchical linear model is equivalent to a one-way ANOVA with random effects. In this case, β_{1j} in the level-1 model is set to zero for all j, yielding

$$Y_{ij} = \beta_{0j} + r_{ij}. \qquad [2.6]$$

We assume that each level-1 error, r_{ij}, is normally distributed with a mean of zero and a constant level-1 variance, σ^2. Notice that this model predicts the outcome within each level-1 unit with just one level-2 parameter, the intercept, β_{0j}. In this case, β_{0j} is just the mean outcome for the jth unit. That is, $\beta_{0j} = \mu_{Y_j}$.

The level-2 model for the one-way ANOVA with random effects is Equation 2.4a with γ_{01} set to zero:

$$\beta_{0j} = \gamma_{00} + u_{0j}, \qquad [2.7]$$

where γ_{00} represents the grand-mean outcome in the population, and u_{0j} is the random effect associated with unit j and is assumed to have a mean of zero and variance τ_{00}.

Substituting Equation 2.7 into Equation 2.6 yields the combined model

$$Y_{ij} = \gamma_{00} + u_{0j} + r_{ij}, \qquad [2.8]$$

which is, indeed, the one-way ANOVA model with grand mean γ_{00}; with a group (level-2) effect, u_{0j}; and with a person (level-1) effect, r_{ij}. It is a random-effects model because the group effects are construed as random. Notice that the variance of the outcome is

$$\mathrm{Var}(Y_{ij}) = \mathrm{Var}(u_{0j} + r_{ij}) = \tau_{00} + \sigma^2. \qquad [2.9]$$

Estimating the one-way ANOVA model is often useful as a preliminary step in a hierarchical data analysis. It produces a point estimate and confidence interval for the grand mean, γ_{00}. More important, it provides information about the outcome variability at each of the two levels. The σ^2 parameter represents the within-group variability, and τ_{00} captures the between-group variability. We refer to the hierarchical model of Equations 2.6 and 2.7 as *fully unconditional* in that no predictors are specified at either level 1 or 2.

A useful parameter associated with the one-way random-effects ANOVA is the intraclass correlation coefficient. This coefficient is given by the formula

$$\rho = \tau_{00}/(\tau_{00} + \sigma^2) \qquad [2.10]$$

and measures the proportion of the variance in the outcome that is between the level-2 units. See Chapter 4 for an application of the one-way random-effects submodel.

Means-as-Outcomes Regression

Another common statistical problem involves the means from each of many groups as an outcome to be predicted by group characteristics. This submodel consists of Equation 2.6 as the level-1 model and, for the level-2 model,

$$\beta_{0j} = \gamma_{00} + \gamma_{01} W_j + u_{0j}, \qquad [2.11]$$

where in this simple case we have one level-2 predictor W_j. Substituting Equation 2.11 into Equation 2.6 yields the combined model:

$$Y_{ij} = \gamma_{00} + \gamma_{01} W_j + u_{0j} + r_{ij}. \qquad [2.12]$$

We note that u_{0j} now has a different meaning as contrasted with that in Equation 2.7. Whereas the random variable u_{0j} had been the deviation of unit j's mean from the grand mean, it now represents the residual

$$u_{0j} = \beta_{0j} - \gamma_{00} - \gamma_{01} W_j.$$

Similarly, the variance in u_{0j}, τ_{00}, is now the residual or conditional variance in β_{0j} after controlling for W_j. The advantages of estimating Equation 2.12 rather than performing a standard regression using sample means-as-outcomes are discussed in Chapter 5.

One-Way ANCOVA with Random Effects

Referring again to the full model (Equations 2.2 and 2.4), let us constrain the level-2 coefficients γ_{01} and γ_{11} and the random effects u_{1j} (for all j) equal to 0. The resulting model would be a one-factor ANCOVA with random effects and a single level-1 predictor as a covariate. The level-1 model is Equation 2.2, but now the predictor X_{ij} is centered around the grand mean. That is,

$$Y_{ij} = \beta_{0j} + \beta_{1j}(X_{ij} - \overline{X}..) + r_{ij}. \qquad [2.13]$$

The level-2 model becomes

$$\beta_{0j} = \gamma_{00} + u_{0j}, \qquad [2.14a]$$

$$\beta_{1j} = \gamma_{10}. \qquad [2.14b]$$

Notice that the effect of X_{ij} is constrained to be the same fixed value for each level-2 unit as is indicated by Equation 2.14b.

The combined model becomes

$$Y_{ij} = \gamma_{00} + \gamma_{10}(X_{ij} - \overline{X}..) + u_{0j} + r_{ij}. \qquad [2.15]$$

The only difference between Equation 2.15 and the standard ANCOVA model (cf. Kirk, 1995, chap. 15) is that the group effect here, u_{0j}, is conceived as random rather than fixed. As in ANCOVA, γ_{10} is the pooled within-group regression coefficient of Y_{ij} on X_{ij}. Each β_{0j} is now the mean outcome for each level-2 unit adjusted for differences among these units in X_{ij}. Specifically, $\beta_{0j} = \mu_{Y_j} - \gamma_{10}(\overline{X}._j - \overline{X}..)$, where μ_{Y_j} is the mean outcome in school j. We also note that the $\text{Var}(r_{ij}) = \sigma^2$ is now a residual variance after adjusting for the level-1 covariate, X_{ij}.

An extension of the random-effects ANCOVA allows for the introduction of level-2 covariates. For example, if the coefficient γ_{01} is nonnull, the combined model becomes

$$Y_{ij} = \gamma_{00} + \gamma_{01} W_j + \gamma_{10}(X_{ij} - \overline{X}..) + u_{0j} + r_{ij}. \qquad [2.16]$$

This model provides for a level-2 covariate, W_j, while also controlling for the effect of a level-1 covariate, X_{ij}, and the random effects of the level-2 units, u_{0j}. Interestingly, all of the parameters of Equation 2.16 can be estimated using the methods introduced in the next chapter. This is not the case, however, for a classical fixed-effects ANCOVA. Also, the classical ANCOVA model assumes that the covariate effect, γ_{10}, is identical for every group. This homogeneity of regression assumption is easily relaxed using the models described in the next three sections (for randomly varying and nonrandomly varying slopes). We illustrate use of the random-effects ANCOVA model in Chapter 5 in analyzing data on the effectiveness of an instructional innovation on students' writing.

Random-Coefficients Regression Model

All of the submodels discussed above are examples of *random-intercept models*. Only the level-1 intercept coefficient, β_{0j}, was viewed as random. The level-1 slope did not exist in the one-way ANOVA or the means-as-outcomes cases. In the random-effects ANCOVA model, β_{1j} was included but constrained to have a common effect for all groups.

A major class of applications of hierarchical linear models involves studies in which level-1 slopes are conceived as varying randomly over the population of level-2 units. The simplest case of this type is the random-coefficients regression model. In these models, both the level-1 intercept and one or more level-1 slopes vary randomly, but no attempt is made to predict this variation.

Specifically, the level-1 model is identical to Equation 2.2. The level-2 model is still a simplification of Equation 2.4 in that both γ_{01} and γ_{11} are constrained to be null. Hence, the level-2 model becomes

$$\beta_{0j} = \gamma_{00} + u_{0j}, \qquad [2.17a]$$

$$\beta_{1j} = \gamma_{10} + u_{1j}, \qquad [2.17b]$$

where

γ_{00} is the average intercept across the level-2 units;

γ_{10} is the average regression slope across the level-2 units;

u_{0j} is the unique increment to the intercept associated with level-2 unit j; and

u_{1j} is the unique increment to the slope associated with level-2 unit j.

We formally represent the dispersion of the level-2 random effects as a variance-covariance matrix:

$$\text{Var}\begin{bmatrix} u_{0j} \\ u_{1j} \end{bmatrix} = \begin{bmatrix} \tau_{00} & \tau_{01} \\ \tau_{10} & \tau_{11} \end{bmatrix} = \mathbf{T}, \qquad [2.18]$$

where

$\text{Var}(u_{0j}) = \tau_{00} =$ unconditional variance in the level-1 intercepts;

$\text{Var}(u_{1j}) = \tau_{11} =$ unconditional variance in the level-1 slopes; and

$\text{Cov}(u_{0j}, u_{1j}) = \tau_{01} =$ unconditional covariance between the level-1 intercepts and slopes.

Note that we refer to these as unconditional variance-covariance components because no level-2 predictors are included in either Equation 2.17a or 2.17b. Similarly, we refer to Equations 2.17a and 2.17b as an *unconditional* level-2 model.

Substitution of the expressions for β_{0j} and β_{1j} in Equations 2.17a and 2.17b into Equation 2.2 yields a combined model:

$$Y_{ij} = \gamma_{00} + \gamma_{10}(X_{ij} - \overline{X}._{j}) + u_{0j} + u_{1j}(X_{ij} - \overline{X}._{j}) + r_{ij}. \qquad [2.19]$$

This model implies that the outcome Y_{ij} is a function of the average regression equation, $\gamma_{00} + \gamma_{10}(X_{ij} - \overline{X}._{j})$ plus a random error having three components: u_{0j}, the random effect of unit j on the mean; $u_{1j}(X_{ij} - \overline{X}._{j})$, where u_{1j} is the random effect of unit j on the slope β_{1j}; and the level-1 error, r_{ij}.

Intercepts- and Slopes-as-Outcomes

The random-coefficients regression model allows us to estimate the variability in the regression coefficients (both intercepts and slopes) across the level-2 units. The next logical step is to model this variability. For example, in Chapter 4, we ask "What characteristics of schools (the level-2 units) help predict why some schools have higher means than others and why some schools have greater SES effects than others?"

Given one level-1 predictor, X_{ij}, and one level-2 predictor, W_j, these questions may be addressed by employing the "full model" of Equations 2.2 and 2.4. Of course, this model may be readily expanded to incorporate the effects of multiple Xs and of multiple Ws (see "Generalizations of the Basic Hierarchical Linear Model").

A Model with Nonrandomly Varying Slopes

In some cases, the analyst will prove quite successful in predicting the variability in the regression slopes, β_{1j}. For example, it might be found that the level-2 predictor W_j in Equation 2.4b does indeed predict the level-1 slope β_{1j}. In fact, the analyst might find that after controlling for W_j the residual variance of β_{1j} (i.e., the variance of the residuals, u_{1j} in Equation 2.4b) is very close to zero. The implication would be that once W_j is controlled, little or no variance in the slopes remains to be explained. For reasons of both statistical efficiency and computational stability (as discussed in Chapter 9), it would be sensible, then, to constrain the values of u_{1j} to be zero. This eliminates τ_{11}, the residual variance of the slope, and τ_{01}, the residual covariance between the slope and the intercept, as parameters to be estimated.

If the residuals u_{1j} in Equation 2.4b are indeed set to zero, the level-2 model for the slopes becomes

$$\beta_{1j} = \gamma_{10} + \gamma_{11} W_j, \qquad [2.20]$$

and this model, when combined with Equations 2.2 and 2.4a, yields the combined model

$$Y_{ij} = \gamma_{00} + \gamma_{01} W_j + \gamma_{10}(X_{ij} - \overline{X}_{\cdot j})$$
$$+ \gamma_{11} W_j (X_{ij} - \overline{X}_{\cdot j}) + u_{0j} + r_{ij}. \qquad [2.21]$$

In this model, the slopes do vary from group to group, but their variation is nonrandom. Specifically, as Equation 2.20 shows, the slopes β_{1j} vary strictly as a function of W_j.

We note that Equation 2.21 can be viewed as another example of what we have called a random-intercept model, because β_{0j} is the only component that varies randomly across level-2 units. In general, hierarchical linear models may involve multiple level-1 predictors where any combination of random, nonrandomly varying, and fixed slopes can be specified.

Section Recap

We have been considering a simple hierarchical linear model with a single level-1 predictor, X_{ij}, and a single level-2 predictor, W_j. In this scenario, the level-1 model (Equation 2.2) defines two parameters, the intercept and the slope. At level 2, each of these may be predicted by W_j and each may have a random component of variation, as in Equations 2.4a and 2.4b. The resulting full model, summarized by Equation 2.5, is the most general model we have considered so far. If certain elements of the full model are constrained to be null, we are left with a submodel that may be useful either as preliminary to a full hierarchical analysis or as a more parsimonious summary than the full model.

The six submodels we have considered may be classified in several different ways. We have distinguished between random-intercept models and randomly varying slope models. The one-way random-effects ANOVA model, the means-as-outcomes model, the one-way ANCOVA model, and the model with nonrandomly varying slopes are all random-intercept models. In such models, the variance components are just the level-1 variance, σ^2, and the level-2 variance, τ_{00}. We noted that in the ANOVA and means-as-outcomes models, no level-1 slope exists. In the ANCOVA model, the level-1 slope exists but is constrained or fixed to be invariant across level-2 units. In the nonrandomly varying slope model, slopes were allowed to vary strictly as a function of a known W_j with no additional random component. In contrast, the random-coefficients model and the slopes- and intercepts-as-outcomes models allowed random variation for both the intercepts and slopes.

Another distinction is whether models include *cross-level interaction terms* such as $\gamma_{11} W_j (X_{ij} - \overline{X}._j)$. In general, the combined model will include such cross-level interaction terms whenever we seek to predict variation in a slope. Such terms appear in two of our submodels: the intercepts- and slopes-as-outcomes model and the nonrandomly varying slope model.

Generalizations of the Basic Hierarchical Linear Model

Multiple *X*s and Multiple *W*s

Suppose now that the analyst wishes to use information about a second level-1 predictor. Let X_{1ij} denote the original X discussed above and let X_{2ij} denote the second level-1 predictor. For now, assume that there is still just a single level-2 predictor, W_j. The level-1 model, assuming group-mean centering for both X_{1ij} and X_{2ij}, becomes

$$Y_{ij} = \beta_{0j} + \beta_{1j}(X_{1ij} - \overline{X}_1._j) + \beta_{2j}(X_{2ij} - \overline{X}_2._j) + r_{ij}. \qquad [2.22]$$

Again, we have three options for modeling β_{2j}. One option is that the effect of X_{2ij} is constrained to be invariant across level-2 units, implying

$$\beta_{2j} = \gamma_{20},$$

where γ_{20} is the common effect of X_{2ij} in every level-2 unit. We say that the effect of β_{2j} is *fixed* across level-2 units.

A second option would be to model the slope β_{2j} as a function of an average value, γ_{20}, plus a random effect associated with each level-2 unit:

$$\beta_{2j} = \gamma_{20} + u_{2j}. \qquad [2.23]$$

Here β_{2j} is *random*. Notice that Equation 2.23 specifies no predictors for β_{2j}. Suppose, however, that this slope depends on W_j. One might then formulate the slopes-as-outcomes model:

$$\beta_{2j} = \gamma_{20} + \gamma_{21} W_j + u_{2j}. \qquad [2.24]$$

According to this model, part of the variation of the slope β_{2j} can be predicted by W_j, but a random component, u_{2j}, remains unexplained. On the other hand, it may be that once the effect of W_j is taken into account, the residual variation in β_{2j}—that is, $\text{Var}(u_{2j}) = \tau_{22}$—is negligible. Then a model constraining that residual variation to be null would be sensible:

$$\beta_{2j} = \gamma_{20} + \gamma_{21} W_j. \qquad [2.25]$$

In this third case, β_{2j} is a *nonrandomly varying* slope because it varies strictly as a function of the predictor W_j.

So far we have been interested in just a single level-2 predictor, W_j. The introduction of multiple W_js is straightforward. Further, the level-2 model does not need to be identical for each equation. One set of W_js may apply for the intercept, a different set be used for β_{1j}, another set for β_{2j}, and so on. When nonparallel specification is employed, however, extra care must be exercised in the interpretation of the results (see Chapter 9).

Generalization of the Error Structures at Level 1 and Level 2

The model specified in Equations 2.2 and 2.4 assumes homogeneous errors at both level 1 and level 2. This assumption is quite acceptable for a broad class of multilevel problems. Most published applications have been based on this assumption, as are most of the examples discussed in Chapter 5 through 8.

The model can easily be extended, however, to more complex error structures at both levels. The level-1 variance might be different for each level-2 unit and denoted σ_j^2, or it might be a function of some measured level-1 characteristic. (The modeling framework for this extension appears in Chapter 5.) Similarly, at level 2, a different covariance structure might exist for distinct subsets of level-2 units. This would result in different T matrices estimated for different subsets of level-2 units.

Extensions Beyond the Basic Two-Level Hierarchical Linear Model

The core ideas introduced in this chapter in the context of two-level models extend directly to models with three or more levels. These extensions are described and illustrated in Chapter 8. A common feature of the basic hierarchical linear model, regardless of the number of levels, is that the outcome variable at level 1, Y, is continuous and assumed normally distributed, conditional on the level-1 predictors included in the model. Over the last decade, extensions beyond the basic hierarchical linear model framework have been advanced to include dichotomous level-1 outcomes, count data, and categorical outcomes. Models for missing data, latent variable effects, and more complex data designs, including crossed random effects, have also appeared. Although the estimation methods are more complex for these extensions, the basic conceptual ideas and modeling framework extend quite naturally. In general, the range of modeling possibilities is now much richer than when we authored the first edition of this book. Part III, which is new to the second edition, introduces these new developments.

Choosing the Location of X and W (*Centering*)

In all quantitative research, it is essential that the variables under study have precise meaning so that statistical results can be related to the theoretical concerns that motivate the research. In the case of hierarchical linear models, the intercept and slopes in the level-1 model become outcome variables at level 2. It is vital that the meaning of these outcome variables be clearly understood.

The meaning of the intercept in the level-1 model depends on the location of the level-1 predictor variables, the Xs. We know, for example, that in the simple model

$$Y_{ij} = \beta_{0j} + \beta_{1j} X_{ij} + r_{ij}, \qquad [2.26]$$

the intercept, β_{0j}, is defined as the expected outcome for a student attending school j who has a value of zero on X_{ij}. If the researcher is to make sense of models that account for variation in β_{0j}, the choice of a metric for all level-1 predictors becomes important. In particular, if an X_{ij} value of zero is not meaningful, then the researcher may want to transform X_{ij}, or "choose a location for X_{ij}" that will render β_{0j} more meaningful. In some cases, a proper choice of location will be required in order to ensure numerical stability in estimating hierarchical linear models.

Similarly, interpretations regarding the intercepts in the level-2 models (i.e., γ_{00} and γ_{10} in Equations 2.4a and 2.4b) depend on the location of the W_j variables. The numerical stability of estimation is not affected by the location for the Ws, but a suitable choice will ease interpretation of results. We describe below some common choices for the location of the Xs and Ws.

Location of the Xs

We consider four possibilities for the location of X: the natural X metric, centering around the grand mean, centering around the group mean, and other locations for X. We assume that X is measured on an interval scale. The case of dummy variables is considered separately.

The Natural X Metric. Although the natural X metric may be quite appropriate in some applications, in others this may lead to nonsensical results. For example, suppose X is a score on the Scholastic Aptitude Test (SAT), which ranges from 200 to 800. Then the intercept, β_{0j}, will be the expected outcome for a student in school j who had an SAT of zero. The β_{0j} parameter is meaningless in this instance because the minimum score on the test is 200. In such cases, the correlation between the intercept and slope will tend toward -1.0. As a result, the intercept is essentially determined by the slope. Schools with strong positive SAT-outcome slopes will tend to have very low intercepts. In contrast, schools where the SAT slope is negligible will tend to have much higher intercepts.

In some applications, of course, an X value of zero will in fact be meaningful. For example, if X is the dosage of an experimental drug, $X_{ij} = 0$ implies that subject i in group j had no exposure to the drug. As a result, the intercept β_{0j} is the expected outcome for such a subject. That is, $\beta_{0j} = \mathrm{E}(Y_{ij}|X_{ij} = 0)$. We wish to emphasize that it is always important to consider the meaning of $X_{ij} = 0$ because it determines the interpretation of β_{0j}.

Centering Around the Grand Mean. It is often useful to center the variable X around the grand mean, as discussed earlier (see "One-Way ANCOVA with Random Effects"). In this case, the level-1 predictors are of the form

$$(X_{ij} - \overline{X}..). \tag{2.27}$$

Now, the intercept, β_{0j}, is the expected outcome for a subject whose value on X_{ij} is equal to the grand mean, $\overline{X}..$. This is the standard choice of location for X_{ij} in the classical ANCOVA model. As is the case in ANCOVA, grand-mean centering yields an intercept that can be interpreted as an adjusted mean for group j,

$$\beta_{0j} = \mu_{Y_j} - \beta_{1j}(\overline{X}._j - \overline{X}..).$$

Similarly, the $\text{Var}(\beta_{0j}) = \tau_{00}$ is the variance among the level-2 units in the adjusted means.

Centering Around the Level-2 Mean (Group-Mean Centering). Another option is to center the original predictors around their corresponding level-2 unit means:

$$(X_{ij} - \overline{X}._j). \tag{2.28}$$

In this case, the intercept β_{0j} becomes the unadjusted mean for group j. That is,

$$\beta_{0j} = \mu_{Y_j} \tag{2.29}$$

and $\text{Var}(\beta_{0j})$ is now just the variance among the level-2 unit means, μ_{Y_j}.

Other Locations for X. Specialized choices of location for X are often sensible. In some cases, the population mean for a predictor may be known and the investigator may wish to define the intercept β_{0j} as the expected outcome in group j for the "average person in the population." In this case, the level-1 predictor would be the original value of X_{ij} minus the population mean.

In applications of two-level hierarchical linear models to the study of growth, the data involve time-series observations so that the level-1 units are occasions and the level-2 units are persons. The investigator may wish to define the metric of the level-1 predictors such that the intercept is the expected outcome for person i at a specific time point of theoretical interest (e.g., entry to school). So long as the data encompass this time point, such a definition is quite appropriate. Examples of this sort are illustrated in Chapters 6 and 8.

Dummy Variables. Consider the familiar level-1 model

$$Y_{ij} = \beta_{0j} + \beta_{1j}X_{ij} + r_{ij}, \qquad [2.30]$$

where X_{ij} is now an indicator or dummy variable. Suppose, for example, that X_{ij} takes on a value of 1 if subject i in school j is a female and 0 if not. In this case, the intercept β_{0j} is defined as the expected outcome for a male student in group j (i.e., the predicted value for student with $X_{ij} = 0$). We note in this case that $\text{Var}(\beta_{0j}) = \tau_{00}$ will be the variance in the male outcome means across schools.

Although it may seem strange at first to center a level-1 dummy variable, this is appropriate and often quite useful. Suppose, for example, that the indicator variable for sex is centered around the grand mean, $\overline{X}_{..}$. This centered predictor can take on two values. If the subject is female, $X_{ij} - \overline{X}_{..}$ will equal the proportion of male students in the sample. If the subject is male, $X_{ij} - \overline{X}_{..}$ will be equal to minus the proportion of female students. As in the case of continuous level-1 predictors centered around the respective grand means, the intercept, β_{0j}, is the adjusted mean outcome in unit j. In this case, it is adjusted for differences among units in the percentage of female students.

Alternatively, we might use group-mean centering. For females, $X_{ij} - \overline{X}_{.j}$ will take on the value equal to the proportion of male students in school j; for males, $X_{ij} - \overline{X}_{.j}$ will take on a value equal to minus the proportion of female students in school j. The fact that X_{ij} is a dummy variable does not change the interpretation given to β_{0j} when group-mean centering is employed. The intercept still represents the average outcome for unit j, μ_{Y_j}.

In sum, several locations of dichotomous predictors will produce meaningful intercepts. Again, it is incumbent on the researcher to take this location into account in interpreting results. Care is especially needed when there are multiple dummy variables. For example, in a school-effects study with indicators for whites, females, and students with preprimary education, the intercept for school j might be the expected outcome for a non-white male student with no preprimary experience. This may or may not be the intercept the investigator wants. Again we offer the general caveat—be conscious of the choice of location for each level-1 predictor because it has implications for interpretation of β_{0j}, $\text{Var}(\beta_{0j})$, and by implication, all of the covariances involving β_{0j}.

In general, sensible choices of location depend on the purposes of the research. No single rule covers all cases. It is important, however, that the researcher carefully consider choices of location in light of those purposes; and it is vital to keep the location in mind while interpreting results.

In addition, the choice of location for the level-1 predictors can, under certain circumstances, also influence the estimation of the level-2 variance-covariance components, $\mathbf{T}$, and random level-1 coefficients, β_{qj}. Complications can occur in the context of both organizational research and growth curve applications. The reader is referred to Chapters 5 and 6, respectively, for a further discussion of these technical considerations.

Location of Ws

In general, the choice of location for the Ws is not as critical as for the level-1 predictors. Problems of numerical instability are less likely, except when cross-product terms are introduced at level 2 (e.g., a predictor set of the form W_{1j}, W_{2j}, and $W_{1j}W_{2j}$). All of the γ coefficients can be easily interpreted whatever choice of metric (or nonchoice) is made for level-2 predictors. Nevertheless, it is often convenient to center all of the level-2 predictors around their corresponding grand means, for example, $W_{1j} - \overline{W}_1..$

Summary of Terms and Notation
Introduced in This Chapter

A Simple Two-Level Model

Hierarchical form:

$$\text{Level 1 (e.g., students)} \quad Y_{ij} = \beta_{0j} + \beta_{1j}X_{ij} + r_{ij},$$

$$\text{Level 2 (e.g., schools)} \quad \beta_{0j} = \gamma_{00} + \gamma_{01}W_j + u_{0j},$$

$$\beta_{1j} = \gamma_{10} + \gamma_{11}W_j + u_{1j}.$$

Model in *combined form:*

$$Y_{ij} = \gamma_{00} + \gamma_{10}X_{ij} + \gamma_{01}W_j + \gamma_{11}X_{ij}W_j + u_{0j} + u_{1j}X_{ij} + r_{ij},$$

where we assume:

$$E(r_{ij}) = 0, \qquad \text{Var}(r_{ij}) = \sigma^2,$$

$$E\begin{bmatrix} u_{0j} \\ u_{1j} \end{bmatrix} = \begin{bmatrix} 0 \\ 0 \end{bmatrix}, \qquad \text{Var}\begin{bmatrix} u_{0j} \\ u_{1j} \end{bmatrix} = \begin{bmatrix} \tau_{00} & \tau_{01} \\ \tau_{10} & \tau_{11} \end{bmatrix} = \mathbf{T},$$

$$\text{Cov}(u_{0j}, r_{ij}) = \text{Cov}(u_{1j}, r_{ij}) = 0.$$

Notation and Terminology Summary

There are $i = 1, \ldots, n_j$ level-1 units nested with $j = 1, \ldots, J$ level-2 units. We speak of student i nested within school j.

β_{0j}, β_{1j} are level-1 coefficients. These can be of three forms:

fixed level-1 coefficients (e.g., β_{1j} in the one-way random-effects ANCOVA model, Equation 2.14b)

nonrandomly varying level-1 coefficients (e.g., β_{1j} in the nonrandomly-varying-slopes model, Equation 2.20)

random level-1 coefficients (e.g., β_{0j} and β_{1j} in the random-coefficient regression model [Equations 2.17a and 2.17b] and in the intercepts- and slopes-as-outcomes model [Equations 2.4a and 2.4b])

$\gamma_{00}, \ldots, \gamma_{11}$ are level-2 coefficients and are also called fixed effects.

X_{ij} is a level-1 predictor (e.g., student social class, race, and ability).

W_j is a level-2 predictor (e.g., school size, sector, social composition).

r_{ij} is a level-1 random effect.

u_{0j}, u_{1j} are level-2 random effects.

σ^2 is the level-1 variance.

$\tau_{00}, \tau_{01}, \tau_{11}$ are level-2 variance-covariance components.

Some Definitions

Intraclass correlation coefficient (see "One-Way ANOVA with Random Effects"):

$$\rho = \tau_{00}/(\sigma^2 + \tau_{00}).$$

This coefficient measures the proportion of variance in the outcome that is between groups (i.e., the level-2 units). It is also sometimes called the *cluster effect*. It applies only to random-intercept models (i.e., $\tau_{11} = 0$).

Unconditional variance-covariance of β_{0j}, β_{1j} are the values of the level-2 variances and covariances based on the random-coefficient regression model.

Conditional or residual variance-covariance of β_{0j}, β_{1j} are the values of the level-2 variances and covariances after level-2 predictors have been added for β_{0j} and β_{1j} (see, e.g., Equations 2.4a and 2.4b).

Submodel Types

One-way random-effects ANOVA model involves no level-1 or level-2 predictors. We call this a *fully unconditional* model.

Random-intercept model has only one random level-1 coefficient, β_{0j}.

Means-as-outcomes regression model is one form of a random-intercept model.

One-way random-effects ANCOVA model is a classic ANCOVA model, except that the level-2 effects are viewed as random.

Random-coefficients regression model allows all level-1 coefficients to vary randomly. This model is *unconditional at level 2*.

Centering Definitions	**Implications for β_{0j}**
X_{ij} in the natural metric	$\beta_{0j} = \mathrm{E}(Y_{ij}\|X_{ij} = 0)$
$(X_{ij} - \overline{X}..)$ called grand-mean centering	$\beta_{0j} = \mu_{Y_j} - \beta_{1j}(X_{ij} - \overline{X}..)$ (i.e., adjusted level-2 means)
$(X_{ij} - \overline{X}._j)$ called group-mean centering	$\beta_{0j} = \mu_{Y_j}$ (i.e., level-2 means)
X_{ij} centered at some theoretically chosen location for X	$\beta_{0j} = \mathrm{E}(Y_{ij}|X_{ij} = $ chosen centering location for X)

Principles of Estimation and Hypothesis
Testing for Hierarchical Linear Models

- Estimation Theory
- Hypothesis Testing
- Summary of Terms Introduced in This Chapter

Our goal in Chapter 2 was to clarify the meaning of the basic parameters found in hierarchical linear models. In this chapter, we introduce the statistical theory that undergirds estimation of inference for these models. We elucidate the key principles at work here through a series of simple models. An actual application of these procedures follows in Chapter 4. The more applied reader may want to read Chapter 4 first, and use Chapter 3 more as a reference guide. For the more technical reader, this chapter should provide a useful background to the full statistical theory presented in Chapter 14.

Estimation Theory

Three types of parameters can be estimated in a two-level hierarchical analysis: fixed effects, random level-1 coefficients, and variance-covariance components. In actuality, estimation of each of these depends on the others. To clarify basic principles, however, we consider first the estimation of the fixed effects and random coefficients in the case where the variance-covariance components are assumed known. We then consider the estimation of the variance-covariance components themselves. Chapter 14 presents a more rigorous account of the estimation theory and computational approaches used throughout this book.

Estimation of Fixed Effects

We consider fixed-effects estimation for three simple models. First is the one-way random-effects ANOVA model. This involves a single fixed effect, the overall mean, which is estimated as an optimally weighted average of the sample means from the J level-2 units. Second, we examine the means-as-outcomes model, which includes a level-2 regression coefficient. Again, the optimal weighting principle applies. Third, we consider the random coefficient regression model. The optimal weighting principle applies here too, but the weighting is now multivariate and requires matrix notation. For those unfamiliar with such notation, the first two examples should suffice to convey the essential idea.

One-Way ANOVA: Point Estimation. As in Chapter 2, we begin with the one-way random-effects ANOVA. Recall from Equation 2.6 that the level-1 model was

$$Y_{ij} = \beta_{0j} + r_{ij} \qquad [3.1]$$

for level-1 units $i = 1, \ldots, n_j$ and level-2 units $j = 1, \ldots, J$, where we assume $r_{ij} \sim N(0, \sigma^2)$.

Averaging across the n_j observations within school j yields a level-1 model with the sample mean as the outcome

$$\overline{Y}_{\cdot j} = \beta_{0j} + \bar{r}_{\cdot j}, \qquad [3.2]$$

where

$$\bar{r}_{\cdot j} = \sum_{i=1}^{n_j} r_{ij}/n_j.$$

Equation 3.2 shows that the sample mean, $\overline{Y}_{\cdot j}$, is an estimate of true school mean, β_{0j}. The error of estimation is $\bar{r}_{\cdot j}$, which has a variance

$$\mathrm{Var}(\bar{r}_{\cdot j}) = \sigma^2/n_j = V_j. \qquad [3.3]$$

We refer to V_j as the *error variance*, that is, the variance of $\overline{Y}_{\cdot j}$ as an estimator of β_{0j}.

The level-2 model is

$$\beta_{0j} = \gamma_{00} + u_{0j}, \qquad [3.4]$$

where we assume $u_{0j} \sim N(0, \tau_{00})$. Notice that τ_{00} is the variance of the true means, β_{0j}, about the grand mean, γ_{00}. We shall refer to τ_{00} as *parameter variance*.

Substituting Equation 3.4 into Equation 3.2 yields the combined model for $\overline{Y}_{\cdot j}$:

$$\overline{Y}_{\cdot j} = \gamma_{00} + u_{0j} + \bar{r}_{\cdot j}. \qquad [3.5]$$

The variance of $\overline{Y}_{.j}$ has two components:

$$\text{Var}(\overline{Y}_{.j}) = \text{Var}(u_{0j}) + \text{Var}(\bar{r}_{.j})$$

$$= \tau_{00} + V_j$$

$$= \text{parameter variance} + \text{error variance}$$

$$= \Delta_j. \qquad [3.6]$$

Notice that although the parameter variance, τ_{00}, is constant across level-2 units, the error variance, $V_j = \sigma^2/n_j$, varies depending on the sample size, n_j, for each level-2 unit.

If every level-2 unit has the same sample size, every V_j will be equal to a common V and every Δ_j will be equal to a common Δ, that is, $\Delta = \tau_{00} + V$. Then the unique, minimum-variance, unbiased estimator of γ_{00} would be just the average value of $\overline{Y}_{.j}$:

$$\tilde{\gamma}_{00} = \sum \overline{Y}_{.j}/J. \qquad [3.7]$$

If the sample sizes are not equal, however, the statistics, $\overline{Y}_{.j}$, have unequal variances $\Delta_j = \tau_{00} + V_j$. Viewing each $\overline{Y}_{.j}$ as an independent, unbiased estimator of γ_{00} with variance Δ_j, we define the *precision* of $\overline{Y}_{.j}$ as the reciprocal of its variance—that is,

$$\text{Precision}(\overline{Y}_{.j}) = \Delta_j^{-1}. \qquad [3.8]$$

Then, assuming Δ_j is known, the unique, minimum-variance, unbiased estimator of γ_{00} is the *precision weighted average*:

$$\hat{\gamma}_{00} = \sum \Delta_j^{-1}\overline{Y}_{.j}/\sum \Delta_j^{-1}. \qquad [3.9]$$

Equation 3.9 is commonly called the weighted least squares estimator of γ_{00}. (This is also the maximum likelihood estimator.) Note that the values of Δ_j must be known (or estimated) to compute γ_{00}, which was not true in the equal-sample-size case (see Equation 3.7). Clearly, the precision weighted average applies generally. When all the precisions are equal, the precision weighted average (Equation 3.9) reduces to the simple average (Equation 3.7).

One-Way ANOVA: Interval Estimation. The precision of $\hat{\gamma}_{00}$ is the sum of the precisions, that is,

$$\text{Precision}(\hat{\gamma}_{00}) = \sum \Delta_j^{-1}. \qquad [3.10]$$

The variance of $\hat{\gamma}_{00}$ is the inverse of its precision:

$$\text{Var}(\hat{\gamma}_{00}) = \left(\sum \Delta_j^{-1}\right)^{-1}. \tag{3.11}$$

Therefore, the 95% confidence interval for $\hat{\gamma}_{00}$ is given by

$$95\% \text{ CI}(\gamma_{00}) = \hat{\gamma}_{00} \pm 1.96 \left(\sum \Delta_j^{-1}\right)^{-1/2}. \tag{3.12}$$

Regression with Means-as-Outcomes: Point Estimation. Again paralleling the presentation in Chapter 2, we now consider an analysis in which the level-1 mean is predicted by a level-2 variable. That is, the model at level 1 remains as in Equation 3.1. The level-2 model now expands to include a predictor, W_j. As a result, the combined model (formerly Equation 3.5) now expands to

$$\overline{Y}_{\cdot j} = \gamma_{00} + \gamma_{01} W_j + u_{0j} + \bar{r}_{\cdot j}, \tag{3.13}$$

and the variance of $\overline{Y}_{\cdot j}$, given W_j, is

$$\text{Var}(\overline{Y}_{\cdot j}) = \tau_{00} + V_j = \Delta_j, \tag{3.14}$$

where $V_j = \sigma^2/n_j$. Note that Δ_j is now the residual variance of $\overline{Y}_{\cdot j}$, that is, the conditional variance of $\overline{Y}_{\cdot j}$, given W_j. Again, we assume that u_{0j} and r_{ij} are independent and normally distributed.

If every group had the same sample size, Δ_j would be identical in each group and the unique, minimum-variance, unbiased estimator of γ_{01} would be the ordinary least squares (OLS) estimator

$$\tilde{\gamma}_{01} = \frac{\sum (W_j - \overline{W}_{\cdot})(\overline{Y}_{\cdot j} - \overline{Y}_{\cdot\cdot})}{\sum (W_j - \overline{W}_{\cdot})^2}, \tag{3.15}$$

where

$$\overline{W}_{\cdot} = \sum W_j / J \quad \text{and} \quad \overline{Y}_{\cdot\cdot} = \sum \overline{Y}_{\cdot j} / J.$$

The OLS estimator of γ_{00} is

$$\tilde{\gamma}_{00} = \overline{Y}_{\cdot\cdot} - \tilde{\gamma}_{01} \overline{W}_{\cdot}. \tag{3.16}$$

If the sample sizes n_j are unequal, however, the statistics, $\overline{Y}_{\cdot j}$, will have unequal variance $\Delta_j = \tau_{00} + V_j$. In this case, assuming every Δ_j is known, the unique, minimum variance, unbiased estimator of γ_{01} will be the weighted least squares estimator in which each group's data is weighted proportional to its precision, Δ_j^{-1}:

$$\hat{\gamma}_{01} = \frac{\sum \Delta_j^{-1}(W_j - \overline{W}_{\cdot}^*)(\overline{Y}_{\cdot j} - \overline{Y}_{\cdot\cdot}^*)}{\sum \Delta_j^{-1}(W_j - \overline{W}_{\cdot}^*)^2}, \tag{3.17}$$

where $\overline{W}^*_{\cdot}$ and $\overline{Y}^*_{\cdot\cdot}$ are now also precision weighted averages:

$$\overline{W}^*_{\cdot} = \sum \Delta_j^{-1} W_j / \sum \Delta_j^{-1}, \qquad [3.18a]$$

$$\overline{Y}^*_{\cdot\cdot} = \sum \Delta_j^{-1} \overline{Y}_{\cdot j} / \sum \Delta_j^{-1}. \qquad [3.18b]$$

The weighted least squares estimator of γ_{00} is

$$\hat{\gamma}_{00} = \overline{Y}^*_{\cdot\cdot} - \hat{\gamma}_{01} \overline{W}^*_{\cdot}. \qquad [3.19]$$

Regression with Means-as-Outcomes: Interval Estimation. The sampling variance of the statistic $\hat{\gamma}_{01}$, given Δ_j, is

$$\text{Var}(\hat{\gamma}_{01}) = \left[\sum \Delta_j^{-1} (W_j - \overline{W}^*_{\cdot})^2 \right]^{-1}. \qquad [3.20]$$

Thus, a 95% confidence interval for $\hat{\gamma}_{01}$ is given by

$$95\% \text{ CI}(\gamma_{01}) = \hat{\gamma}_{01} \pm 1.96[\text{Var}(\hat{\gamma}_{01})]^{1/2}. \qquad [3.21]$$

More General Models: Point Estimation.[1] The extension of these basic principles to more general cases is straightforward. The general level-1 model with Q predictor variables can be expressed in matrix notation as

$$\mathbf{Y}_j = \mathbf{X}_j \boldsymbol{\beta}_j + \mathbf{r}_j, \qquad \mathbf{r}_j \sim \text{N}(\mathbf{0}, \sigma^2 \mathbf{I}), \qquad [3.22]$$

where $\mathbf{Y}_j$ is an n_j by 1 vector of outcomes, $\mathbf{X}_j$ is an n_j by $(Q+1)$ matrix of predictor variables, $\boldsymbol{\beta}_j$ is a $(Q+1)$ by 1 vector of unknown parameters, $\mathbf{I}$ is an n_j by n_j identity matrix, and $\mathbf{r}_j$ is an n_j by 1 vector of random errors assumed normally distributed with a mean vector of $\mathbf{0}$ and a variance-covariance matrix in which all diagonal elements are equal to σ^2 and all off-diagonal elements are 0.

Assuming $\mathbf{X}_j$ to be of full column rank $Q+1$, the OLS estimator of $\boldsymbol{\beta}_j$ is

$$\hat{\boldsymbol{\beta}}_j = (\mathbf{X}_j^T \mathbf{X}_j)^{-1} \mathbf{X}_j^T \mathbf{Y}_j, \qquad [3.23]$$

and its dispersion matrix is given by

$$\text{Var}(\hat{\boldsymbol{\beta}}_j) = \mathbf{V}_j = \sigma^2 (\mathbf{X}_j^T \mathbf{X}_j)^{-1}. \qquad [3.24]$$

Premultiplying Equation 3.22 by $(\mathbf{X}_j^T \mathbf{X}_j)^{-1} \mathbf{X}_j^T$ yields the model for $\hat{\boldsymbol{\beta}}_j$:

$$\hat{\boldsymbol{\beta}}_j = \boldsymbol{\beta}_j + \mathbf{e}_j, \qquad \mathbf{e}_j \sim \text{N}(\mathbf{0}, \mathbf{V}_j), \qquad [3.25]$$

where $\mathbf{V}_j$ is the error-variance matrix, indicating the error dispersion of the $\hat{\boldsymbol{\beta}}_j$ as an estimate of $\boldsymbol{\beta}_j$.

At level 2, the general model for $\boldsymbol{\beta}_j$ is

$$\boldsymbol{\beta}_j = \mathbf{W}_j \boldsymbol{\gamma} + \mathbf{u}_j, \qquad \mathbf{u}_j \sim N(\mathbf{0}, \mathbf{T}), \qquad [3.26]$$

where $\mathbf{W}_j$ is a $(Q+1)$ by F matrix of predictors, $\boldsymbol{\gamma}$ is an F by 1 vector of fixed effects, $\mathbf{u}_j$ is a $(Q+1)$ by 1 vector of level-2 errors or random effects, and $\mathbf{T}$ is an arbitrary $(Q+1)$ by $(Q+1)$ variance-covariance matrix. Note that $\mathbf{T}$ is the residual variance-covariance matrix, indicating the dispersion of $\boldsymbol{\beta}_j$ about the expected value $\mathbf{W}_j \boldsymbol{\gamma}$. The $\mathbf{W}_j$ matrix involves a stacking of the $Q+1$ row vectors of predictors in a block diagonal fashion. Each row in the matrix corresponds to one of the $Q+1$ outcome variables, β_{qj}, in the level-2 model. (For a simple illustration of this block diagonal $\mathbf{W}_j$, see Equation 3.86.)

Substituting Equation 3.26 into Equation 3.25 yields the single, combined model

$$\hat{\boldsymbol{\beta}}_j = \mathbf{W}_j \boldsymbol{\gamma} + \mathbf{u}_j + \mathbf{e}_j, \qquad [3.27]$$

where the dispersion of $\hat{\boldsymbol{\beta}}_j$, given $\mathbf{W}_j$, is

$$\text{Var}(\hat{\boldsymbol{\beta}}_j) = \text{Var}(\mathbf{u}_j + \mathbf{e}_j) = \mathbf{T} + \mathbf{V}_j = \boldsymbol{\Delta}_j$$

$$= \text{parameter dispersion} + \text{error dispersion}. \qquad [3.28]$$

If the data were perfectly balanced such that each group had the same number of observations, the same values of the predictor matrix $\mathbf{X}$, and the same set of level-2 predictors for each component of $\boldsymbol{\beta}_j$, each $\hat{\boldsymbol{\beta}}_j$ would have the same dispersion $\boldsymbol{\Delta}$, where

$$\boldsymbol{\Delta} = \mathbf{T} + \mathbf{V} = \mathbf{T} + \sigma^2 (\mathbf{X}^T \mathbf{X})^{-1}. \qquad [3.29]$$

In this case, the unique, minimum-variance, unbiased estimator of $\boldsymbol{\gamma}$ would be the OLS regression estimator

$$\tilde{\boldsymbol{\gamma}} = \left(\sum \mathbf{W}_j^T \mathbf{W}_j \right)^{-1} \sum \mathbf{W}_j^T \hat{\boldsymbol{\beta}}_j. \qquad [3.30]$$

However, given that the data are not perfectly balanced, the $\boldsymbol{\Delta}_j$ values will differ from group to group, and, assuming each $\boldsymbol{\Delta}_j$ is known, the unique, minimum-variance, unbiased estimator of $\boldsymbol{\gamma}$ will be the *generalized least squares* (GLS) estimator

$$\hat{\boldsymbol{\gamma}} = \left(\sum \mathbf{W}_j^T \boldsymbol{\Delta}_j^{-1} \mathbf{W}_j \right)^{-1} \sum \mathbf{W}_j^T \boldsymbol{\Delta}_j^{-1} \hat{\boldsymbol{\beta}}_j. \qquad [3.31]$$

The GLS estimator weights each group's data by its precision matrix, that is, $\mathbf{\Delta}_j^{-1}$, which is the inverse of the variance-covariance matrix. Notice the close parallel between the GLS estimator and the weighted least squares estimator (Equation 3.17) in the case of means-as-outcomes. We note that, given the normality assumptions of Equations 3.22 and 3.26, Equation 3.31 is also the maximum likelihood estimator for $\mathbf{\gamma}$.

More General Models: Interval Estimation. Confidence regions for $\mathbf{\gamma}$ are based on $\mathbf{V}_{\hat{\gamma}}$, the dispersion matrix of the estimates $\hat{\mathbf{\gamma}}$, where

$$\mathbf{V}_{\hat{\gamma}} = \text{Var}(\hat{\mathbf{\gamma}}) = \left(\sum \mathbf{W}_j^T \mathbf{\Delta}_j^{-1} \mathbf{W}_j\right)^{-1}. \qquad [3.32]$$

For example, a 95% confidence interval for a particular element, say γ_h, is given by

$$95\% \text{ CI}(\gamma_h) = \hat{\gamma}_h \pm 1.96(V_{hh})^{1/2}, \qquad [3.33]$$

where V_{hh} is the hth diagonal element of $\mathbf{V}_{\hat{\gamma}}$.

Deficient Rank Data. The formulas for $\hat{\mathbf{\gamma}}$ (Equation 3.31) and $\mathbf{V}_{\hat{\gamma}}$ (Equation 3.32) are useful for purposes of exposition but are rather limited in application. Specifically, they require (a) that all level-1 coefficients are random, and (b) that every level-2 unit contains an adequate sample to allow computation of the OLS estimate, $\hat{\mathbf{\beta}}_j$ (Equation 3.23).

Both of these conditions are easily relaxed. To do so, consider the combined model, created by substituting Equation 3.26 into Equation 3.22:

$$\mathbf{Y}_j = \mathbf{X}_j \mathbf{W}_j \mathbf{\gamma} + \mathbf{X}_j \mathbf{u}_j + \mathbf{r}_j. \qquad [3.34]$$

Note that all of the level-1 variables contained in $\mathbf{X}_j$ have associated fixed effects, contained in $\mathbf{\gamma}$, and random effects, contained in $\mathbf{u}_j$. However, we can readily rewrite the model in a way that allows some level-1 variables to have fixed effects but not random effects:

$$\mathbf{Y}_j = \mathbf{X}_j \mathbf{W}_j \mathbf{\gamma} + \mathbf{Z}_j \mathbf{u}_j + \mathbf{r}_j. \qquad [3.35]$$

In Equation 3.35, $\mathbf{Z}_j$ is typically a subset of $\mathbf{X}_j$, that is, $\mathbf{Z}_j$ may contain in its columns those level-1 variables having random effects, and the columns of $\mathbf{X}_j$ not found in $\mathbf{Z}_j$ have only fixed effects. However, it is also possible that some level-1 variables have random effects (and are therefore found in $\mathbf{Z}_j$) but not fixed effects (and are therefore not found in $\mathbf{X}_j$). An example appears in Chapter 6. Either way, the marginal variance of $\mathbf{Y}_j$ is

$$\text{Var}(\mathbf{Y}_j) = \mathbf{V}_{y_j} = \mathbf{Z}_j \mathbf{T} \mathbf{Z}_j^T + \sigma^2 \mathbf{I}_j, \qquad [3.36]$$

where $\mathbf{I}_j$ is the n_j by n_j identity matrix. Then the generalized least squares estimator of the fixed effects becomes

$$\hat{\boldsymbol{\gamma}} = \left(\sum_{j=1}^{J} \mathbf{W}_j^T \mathbf{X}_j^T \mathbf{V}_{y_j}^{-1} \mathbf{X}_j \mathbf{W}_j \right)^{-1} \sum_{j=1}^{J} \mathbf{W}_j^T \mathbf{X}_j^T \mathbf{V}_{y_j}^{-1} \mathbf{Y}_j \qquad [3.37]$$

with variance-covariance matrix

$$\text{Var}(\hat{\boldsymbol{\gamma}}) = \left(\sum_{j=1}^{J} \mathbf{W}_j^T \mathbf{X}_j^T \mathbf{V}_{y_j}^{-1} \mathbf{X}_j \mathbf{W}_j \right)^{-1}. \qquad [3.38]$$

If $\mathbf{Z}_j = \mathbf{X}_j$ and if $\mathbf{X}_j$ is full rank,

$$\mathbf{X}_j^T \mathbf{V}_{y_j}^{-1} \mathbf{X}_j = \boldsymbol{\Delta}_j^{-1}. \qquad [3.39]$$

Therefore, the general expression of Equation 3.38 reduces to Equation 3.32. The key step in deriving Equation 3.39 is the matrix identity (Smith, 1973)

$$[\text{Var}(\mathbf{Y}_j)]^{-1} = (\mathbf{X}_j \mathbf{T} \mathbf{X}_j^T + \sigma^2 \mathbf{I}_j)^{-1}$$
$$= \sigma^{-2} \mathbf{I}_j - \sigma^{-2} \mathbf{X}_j (\sigma^{-2} \mathbf{X}_j^T \mathbf{X}_j + \mathbf{T}^{-1})^{-1} \mathbf{X}_j^T \sigma^{-2}. \qquad [3.40]$$

Using this identity, we write

$$\mathbf{X}_j^T \mathbf{V}_{y_j} \mathbf{X}_j = \sigma^{-2} \mathbf{X}_j^T \mathbf{X}_j$$
$$\qquad - \sigma^{-2} \mathbf{X}_j^T \mathbf{X}_j (\sigma^{-2} \mathbf{X}_j^T \mathbf{X}_j + \mathbf{T}^{-1})^{-1} \sigma^{-2} \mathbf{X}_j^T \mathbf{X}_j$$
$$= \mathbf{V}_j^{-1} - \mathbf{V}_j^{-1} (\mathbf{V}_j^{-1} + \mathbf{T}^{-1})^{-1} \mathbf{V}_j^{-1}$$
$$= \mathbf{V}_j^{-1} [\mathbf{I} - (\mathbf{V}_j^{-1} + \mathbf{T}^{-1})^{-1} \mathbf{V}_j^{-1}]$$
$$= \mathbf{V}_j^{-1} (\mathbf{V}_j^{-1} + \mathbf{T}^{-1})^{-1} \mathbf{T}^{-1}$$
$$= [\mathbf{T}(\mathbf{V}_j^{-1} + \mathbf{T}^{-1}) \mathbf{V}_j]^{-1}$$
$$= (\mathbf{T} + \mathbf{V}_j)^{-1} = \boldsymbol{\Delta}_j^{-1}.$$

Estimation of Random Level-1 Coefficients

In the examples provided thus far, we have formulated a level-1 model in which the outcome depends on certain coefficients (e.g., a mean or a regression coefficient) that vary across level-2 units. The question now arises: What is the "best estimate" of these level-1 coefficients?

The One-Way ANOVA Case: Point Estimation. In our simplest example, we had the two-level model of Equations 3.1 and 3.4. Expressing the level-1 model in terms of the sample mean as the outcome (see Equation 3.2), we have

$$\overline{Y}_{.j} = \beta_{0j} + \bar{r}_{.j}, \qquad \bar{r}_{.j} \sim N(0, V_j), \text{ for } V_j = \sigma^2/n_j$$

and, at level 2,

$$\beta_{0j} = \gamma_{00} + u_{0j}, \qquad u_{0j} \sim N(0, \tau_{00}).$$

This model suggests two alternative estimators of β_{0j}. First, based on the level-1 model, we see that $\overline{Y}_{.j}$ is an unbiased estimator of β_{0j} with variance V_j. However, $\hat{\gamma}_{00} = \sum \Delta_j^{-1} \overline{Y}_{.j} / \sum \Delta_j^{-1}$ could also be viewed as a common estimator of each β_{0j}. A Bayes estimator (Lindley & Smith, 1972), call it β_{0j}^*, is an "optimal" weighted combination of these two:

$$\beta_{0j}^* = \lambda_j \overline{Y}_{.j} + (1 - \lambda_j)\hat{\gamma}_{00}. \qquad [3.41]$$

The weight λ_j is equal to the *reliability* of the least squares estimator, $\overline{Y}_{.j}$, for the parameter, β_{0j} (Kelley, 1927), that is,

$$\lambda_j = \text{Var}(\beta_{0j}) / \text{Var}(\overline{Y}_{.j}) = \tau_{00}/(\tau_{00} + V_j)$$

$$= (\text{parameter variance})/(\text{parameter variance} + \text{error variance}). \quad [3.42]$$

In the language of classical test theory, $\overline{Y}_{.j}$ is a measure of the true, unknown parameter β_{0j}. We refer to λ_j as a *reliability* because it measures the ratio of the *true score* or parameter variance, relative to the *observed score* or total variance of the sample mean, $\overline{Y}_{.j}$. The reliability λ_j will be close to 1 when (a) the group means, β_{0j}, vary substantially across level-2 units (holding constant the sample size per group); or (b) the sample size n_j is large.

When the sample mean is a highly reliable estimate, β_{0j}^* puts substantial weight on $\overline{Y}_{.j}$. However, if the sample mean is unreliable, the estimated grand mean γ_{00} will be given more weight in composing β_{0j}^*.[2]

The weighted average, β_{0j}^*, can also be understood by noting that

$$\lambda_j = V_j^{-1}/(V_j^{-1} + \tau_{00}^{-1}) \qquad [3.43a]$$

and

$$1 - \lambda_j = \tau_{00}^{-1}/(V_j^{-1} + \tau_{00}^{-1})^{-1}. \qquad [3.43b]$$

These expressions show that λ_j, the weight accorded to $\overline{Y}_{.j}$ in composing β_{0j}^*, is proportional to V_j^{-1}, which is the precision of $\overline{Y}_{.j}$ as an estimate of β_{0j}. The weight of $1 - \lambda_j$ accorded $\hat{\gamma}_{00}$ is proportional to τ_{00}^{-1}, which represents the concentration of the β_{0j} parameters around their central tendency γ_{00}. Thus, the more precise $\overline{Y}_{.j}$ is as an estimate of β_{0j}, the more weight it is accorded. Alternatively, the more concentrated the β_{0j} values are around their central tendency γ_{00}, the more weight $\hat{\gamma}_{00}$ is accorded.

We say that the weighted average, β_{0j}^*, is optimal in that no other estimator of β_{0j} has a smaller expected mean-squared error (Lindley & Smith, 1972).[3] Actually, β_{0j}^* is biased toward γ_{00}. When the true value of β_{0j} is greater than γ_{00}, β_{0j}^* will be negatively biased; when β_{0j} is less than γ_{00}, β_{0j}^* will be positively biased. However, on average, β_{0j}^* will tend to be closer to β_{0j} than will any unbiased estimator (e.g., $\overline{Y}_{.j}$). The efficiency of $\overline{Y}_{.j}$ relative to β_{0j}^* is approximately λ_j, which cannot exceed unity (Raudenbush, 1988). Because β_{0j}^* "pulls" $\overline{Y}_{.j}$ toward γ_{00}, β_{0j}^* is called a *shrinkage estimator*. Similar shrinkage estimators were derived by James and Stein (1961), who proved their advantageous properties. The estimate β_{0j}^* has also often been labeled a Bayes estimate (Lindley & Smith, 1972). When the variances are unknown and β_{0j}^* is based on substituting an estimate of λ_j into Equation 3.41, the estimates have been termed *empirical Bayes estimates* (Morris, 1983).

One-Way ANOVA Case: Interval Estimation. A confidence interval for β_{0j} may be constructed based on V_j^* where[4]

$$V_j^* = (V_j^{-1} + \tau_{00}^{-1})^{-1} + (1 - \lambda_j)^2 \, \text{Var}(\hat{\gamma}_{00}). \qquad [3.44]$$

A 95% confidence interval for β_{0j} is therefore given by

$$95\%\text{CI}\,(\beta_{0j}) = \beta_{0j}^* \pm 1.96 V_j^{*1/2}. \qquad [3.45]$$

This confidence interval is exact when the variances σ^2 and τ_{00} are known. However, it is only an approximation when these variances are unknown, and in this case, the confidence intervals will be shorter than they should be. Unless J is large, these intervals should be used with caution.[5]

Regression with Means-as-Outcomes: Point Estimation. Suppose now that we are interested in using information about a level-2, variable, W_j, to predict β_{0j}. What is the "best" estimator of β_{0j}? Our level-1 model remains as in Equation 3.2, but the level-2 model becomes

$$\beta_{0j} = \gamma_{00} + \gamma_{01} W_j + u_{0j}, \quad u_{0j} \sim \text{N}(0, \tau_{00}). \qquad [3.46]$$

Again, we are confronted with two estimators of β_{0j}. First, we have the sample mean $\hat{\beta}_{0j} = \overline{Y}_{.j}$. Second, we have the predicted value of β_{0j} given W_j:

$$\hat{\beta}_{0j} = \hat{\gamma}_{00} + \hat{\gamma}_{01} W_j. \qquad [3.47]$$

Again, we can optimally combine these two estimators in a composite estimator

$$\beta_{0j}^* = \lambda_j \overline{Y}_{\cdot j} + (1 - \lambda_j)(\hat{\gamma}_{00} + \hat{\gamma}_{01} W_j).$$ [3.48]

β_{0j}^* is again an empirical Bayes or shrinkage estimator. However, now $\overline{Y}_{\cdot j}$ is shrunk toward a predicted value rather than toward the grand mean. We refer to this estimate as a *conditional shrinkage estimator* because the amount of shrinkage is now conditional on W_j. The weight accorded $\overline{Y}_{\cdot j}$ is still proportional to its precision V_j^{-1}, but now the weight accorded the predicted value is proportional to τ_{00}^{-1}, which is the concentration of the β_{0j} values around the regression line, $\hat{\gamma}_{00} + \hat{\gamma}_{01} W_j$. This means that if a substantial proportion of the variation in β_{0j} is explained by W_j, the residual variance around the regression line, τ_{00}, will be small. As a result, the concentration, τ_{00}^{-1}, of the β_{0j} around the regression line will be large.

Corresponding to the empirical Bayes estimator β_{0j}^* is the *empirical Bayes residual*, u_{0j}^*. This is an estimate of the deviation of β_{0j}^* from its predicted value based on the level-2 model. In terms of Equation 3.45,

$$u_{0j}^* = \beta_{0j}^* - \hat{\gamma}_{00} - \hat{\gamma}_{01} W_j.$$ [3.49]

It is useful to compare these to the *least squares residual*, $\hat{u}_{0j}$. The latter is an estimate of the deviation of the OLS estimator of β_{0j} from its predicted value based on the level-2 model. In this instance,

$$\hat{u}_{0j} = \overline{Y}_{\cdot j} - \hat{\gamma}_{00} - \hat{\gamma}_{01} W_j.$$ [3.50]

It can be shown easily that u_{0j}^* is a value of $\hat{u}_{0j}$ "shrunk" toward zero:

$$u_{0j}^* = \lambda_j \hat{u}_{0j}.$$ [3.51]

Thus, if the reliability λ_j is unity, no shrinkage occurs. In contrast, if $\lambda_j = 0$, shrinkage toward the predicted value (e.g., Equation 3.45) is complete.

Regression with Means-as-Outcomes: Interval Estimation. A confidence interval for β_{0j} may be constructed based on V_j^* and the predictor W_j, where now

$$V_j^* = (V_j^{-1} + \tau_{00}^{-1})^{-1} + (1 - \lambda_j)^2 [\text{Var}(\hat{\gamma}_{00} + \hat{\gamma}_{01} W_j)].$$ [3.52]

A 95% confidence interval for β_{0j} is therefore given by

$$95\% \text{ CI}(\beta_{0j}) = \beta_{0j}^* \pm 1.96 V_j^{*1/2}.$$ [3.53]

As in the one-way ANOVA case, such confidence intervals will be spuriously short when J is small.

More General Models: Point Estimation.[6] Again we can extend the basic principle of shrinkage to the more general model represented by Equations 3.22 and 3.26. Our goal is to find the best estimator of $\boldsymbol{\beta}_j$. Again we are confronted with two alternatives. The first estimator is simply the OLS regression estimator, $\hat{\boldsymbol{\beta}}_j$, based on data from group j:

$$\hat{\boldsymbol{\beta}}_j = (\mathbf{X}_j^T \mathbf{X}_j)^{-1} \mathbf{X}_j^T \mathbf{Y}_j. \qquad [3.54]$$

The second estimator is the predicted value of $\boldsymbol{\beta}_j$ given group characteristics captured in $\mathbf{W}_j$:

$$\hat{\hat{\boldsymbol{\beta}}}_j = \mathbf{W}_j \hat{\boldsymbol{\gamma}}, \qquad [3.55]$$

where $\hat{\boldsymbol{\gamma}}$ is estimated by means of GLS as in Equation 3.31.

The optimal combination of these two estimators is

$$\boldsymbol{\beta}_j^* = \boldsymbol{\Lambda}_j \hat{\boldsymbol{\beta}}_j + (\mathbf{I} - \boldsymbol{\Lambda}_j) \mathbf{W}_j \hat{\boldsymbol{\gamma}}, \qquad [3.56]$$

where

$$\boldsymbol{\Lambda}_j = \mathbf{T}(\mathbf{T} + \mathbf{V}_j)^{-1} \qquad [3.57]$$

is the ratio of the parameter dispersion matrix for $\boldsymbol{\beta}_j$ (i.e., $\mathbf{T}$) relative to the total dispersion matrix for the $\hat{\boldsymbol{\beta}}_j$, which contains both error dispersion and parameter dispersion (e.g., $\mathbf{T} + \mathbf{V}_j$). We may view $\boldsymbol{\Lambda}_j$ as a *multivariate reliability matrix*. In general, the more reliable $\hat{\boldsymbol{\beta}}_j$ is as an estimate of $\boldsymbol{\beta}_j$, the more weight it will be accorded in composing $\boldsymbol{\beta}_j^*$. If the $\hat{\boldsymbol{\beta}}_j$ values are unreliable, $\boldsymbol{\beta}_j^*$ will pull $\hat{\boldsymbol{\beta}}_j$ toward $\mathbf{W}_j \hat{\boldsymbol{\gamma}}$. We note that in the general case this shrinkage is fully multivariate. Since covariances may exist in both the error dispersion and the parameter dispersion matrices, all of the $Q + 1$ elements of $\hat{\boldsymbol{\beta}}_j$ and of $\mathbf{W}_j \hat{\boldsymbol{\gamma}}$ combine to estimate each element of $\boldsymbol{\beta}_j^*$. As a result, a well-estimated level-1 random coefficient can help improve the estimates of other less precisely estimated level-1 random coefficients.

More General Models: Reliability of the OLS Level-1 Coefficients. The diagonal elements of $\mathbf{T}$ and $\mathbf{V}_j$ denoted by τ_{qq} and ν_{qqj}, respectively, can be used to form reliability indices for each of the $Q + 1$ OLS level-1 coefficients. Analogous to Equation 3.42,

$$\text{reliability}(\hat{\beta}_{qj}) = \tau_{qq}/(\tau_{qq} + \nu_{qqj})$$

$$\text{for each } q = 0, \ldots, Q. \qquad [3.58]$$

Because the sampling variance v_{qqj} of $\hat{\beta}_{qj}$ will in general be different among the J units, each level-2 unit has a unique set of reliability indices. The overall reliability across the set of J level-2 units can be summarized as

$$\text{reliability}(\hat{\beta}_q) = \frac{1}{J} \sum_{j=1}^{J} \tau_{qq} / (\tau_{qq} + v_{qqj})$$

for each $q = 0, \ldots, Q$.   [3.59]

We explicitly note that Equation 3.59 is not the same as the diagonal elements of Λ_j in Equation 3.57.

More General Models: Residual Estimation. Estimation of residuals at each level can be extremely useful in assessing the adequacy of the model assumptions (see Chapter 9). The OLS estimates of level-2 residuals are functions of the OLS estimates of the level-1 coefficients β_j and therefore, exist only for units that have full rank data. Thus, we have

$$\hat{\mathbf{u}}_j = \hat{\boldsymbol{\beta}}_j - \mathbf{W}_j \hat{\boldsymbol{\gamma}}.$$ [3.60]

The empirical Bayes residuals, at level 2,

$$\mathbf{u}_j^* = \boldsymbol{\beta}_j^* - \mathbf{W}_j \hat{\boldsymbol{\gamma}},$$ [3.61]

exist for every unit, j.

Like the level-2 residuals, level-1 residuals can be estimated either by least squares or by empirical Bayes. These estimates can be useful in examining distribution assumptions for the level-1 data. The least squares residuals, of course, will exist only for those cases whose level-2 units having full rank $\mathbf{X}_j$. In terms of the general model of Equation 3.35, the estimated least squares residuals are

$$\hat{r}_{ij} = Y_{ij} - \mathbf{X}_{ij}^T \mathbf{W}_j \hat{\boldsymbol{\gamma}} - \mathbf{Z}_{ij}^T \hat{\mathbf{u}}_j.$$ [3.62]

Here $\mathbf{X}_{ij}^T$ and $\mathbf{Z}_{ij}^T$ contain elements of the ith row of $\mathbf{X}_j$ and $\mathbf{Z}_j$, respectively. The empirical Bayes residual estimates, which exist for every unit, have the same form

$$r_{ij}^* = Y_{ij} - \mathbf{X}_{ij}^T \mathbf{W}_j \hat{\boldsymbol{\gamma}} - \mathbf{Z}_{ij}^T \mathbf{u}_j^*.$$ [3.63]

More General Models: Interval Estimation. A confidence interval for $\boldsymbol{\beta}_j$ may be constructed based on the conditional variance-covariance matrix, $\mathbf{V}_j^*$, given the data, where

$$\mathbf{V}_j^* = (\mathbf{V}_j^{-1} + \mathbf{T}^{-1})^{-1} + (\mathbf{I} - \boldsymbol{\Lambda}_j)[\text{Var}(\mathbf{W}_j\hat{\boldsymbol{\gamma}})](\mathbf{I} - \boldsymbol{\Lambda}_j)^T. \qquad [3.64]$$

For example, a 95% confidence interval for β_{qj} is given by

$$95\% \ \text{CI}(\beta_{qj}) = \beta_{qj}^* \pm 1.96(V_{qqj}^*)^{1/2}, \qquad [3.65]$$

where V_{qqj}^* is the qth diagonal element of $\mathbf{V}_j^*$.

Deficient Rank Data. Equations 3.54 and 3.56 are useful for exposition, but they require that (a) all elements of $\boldsymbol{\beta}_j$ are random and (b) every group j has sufficient data to allow computation of $\hat{\boldsymbol{\beta}}_j$ by means of OLS. Suppose that all elements of $\boldsymbol{\beta}_j$ are indeed random, but that a level-2 unit j does not have sufficient data to compute OLS estimates of $\boldsymbol{\beta}_j$. The empirical Bayes estimator will still exist as

$$\boldsymbol{\beta}_j^* = (\mathbf{X}_j^T\mathbf{X}_j + \sigma^2\mathbf{T}^{-1})^{-1}(\mathbf{X}_j^T\mathbf{Y}_j + \sigma^2\mathbf{T}^{-1}\mathbf{W}_j\hat{\boldsymbol{\gamma}}). \qquad [3.66]$$

If $\mathbf{X}_j$ does have full rank so that $\mathbf{X}_j^T\mathbf{X}_j$ has an inverse, Equation 3.66 will reduce to Equation 3.56. We can think of $\mathbf{X}_j^T\mathbf{X}_j$ as the information contained in group j about $\boldsymbol{\beta}_j$. Equation 3.66 shows how this information is supplemented by information, based on all of the units, in $\mathbf{T}^{-1}$ so that $\mathbf{X}_j^T\mathbf{X}_j + \sigma^2\mathbf{T}^{-1}$ will have an inverse as long as $\mathbf{T}^{-1}$ is nonsingular, allowing empirical Bayes estimation for all level-2 units.

Estimation of Variance and Covariance Components

So far we have assumed that the variance and covariance components are known. Although this assumption clarifies understanding of estimation of the fixed and random effects, the variances and covariances must nearly always be estimated in practice.

Past use of hierarchical models has been limited by the fact that only in cases of perfectly balanced designs are closed-form mathematical formulas available to estimate the variance and covariance components. To achieve balance, not only must each level-2 unit have the same sample size ($n_j = n$ for every j), but the distribution of predictors within each level-2 unit must be identical ($\mathbf{X}_j = \mathbf{X}$ for every j). When designs are unbalanced (as is typically true), iterative numerical procedures must be used to obtain efficient estimates, usually via maximum likelihood.

Three conceptually distinct approaches to this problem have come into use. They are *full maximum likelihood* (Goldstein, 1986; Longford, 1987), *restricted maximum likelihood* (Mason et al., 1983; Raudenbush & Bryk, 1986), and *Bayes estimation*. Full details on maximum likelihood methods for estimating the variances and covariances are presented in Chapter 14 (Bayes methods are detailed in Chapter 13). We limit our remarks here to a conceptual introduction.

Full Maximum Likelihood (MLF). For any set of possible values of the parameters γ, $\mathbf{T}$, and σ^2 in Equations 3.22 and 3.26, there is some likelihood of observing a particular sample of data $\mathbf{Y}$, where $\mathbf{Y}$ is an N by 1 vector containing the outcomes for the N level-1 units of the study. (Note: $N = \sum n_j$ where n_j is the sample size per level-2 unit.) The basic idea of maximum likelihood is to choose estimates of γ, $\mathbf{T}$, and σ^2 for which the likelihood of observing the actual data $\mathbf{Y}$ is a maximum.

Estimates based on this approach have certain desirable properties. Under quite general assumptions, these estimates are *consistent* (i.e., they will be very near the true parameter with high probability if enough data are collected) and asymptotically *efficient* (i.e., given a large sample of data, the maximum likelihood estimators are approximately unbiased with minimum variance). Another advantage is that if one wants to estimate a function of parameters, one simply plugs in maximum likelihood estimates of the parameters. The resulting function will itself be a maximum likelihood estimator.

For example, we mentioned earlier that the estimator of γ_{00} in a one-way unbalanced ANOVA with random effects was

$$\hat{\gamma}_{00} = \sum \Delta_j^{-1} \overline{Y}_{.j} / \sum \Delta_j^{-1},$$

under the assumption that Δ_j is known. If each Δ_j is not known, but a maximum likelihood estimate of Δ_j is substituted, the resulting estimator $\hat{\gamma}_{00}$ will itself be a maximum likelihood estimator with its desirable statistical properties.

Another useful feature of maximum likelihood estimators is that as sample sizes increase, their sampling distributions become approximately normal with a variance that can readily be estimated. Thus, even if the method for obtaining the MLF estimator is iterative (because no closed-form analytic expression is available), the large-sample distribution of the estimator is well defined.

Restricted Maximum Likelihood (MLR). One shortcoming of MLF is that estimates of variances and covariances are conditional upon point estimates of the fixed effects. Consider a simple regression model

$$Y_i = \beta_0 + \beta_1 X_{1i} + \beta_2 X_{2i} + \cdots + \beta_Q X_{Qi} + r_i, \qquad [3.67]$$

where the errors $r_i, i = 1, \ldots, n$, are normally distributed with a mean of zero and a constant variance, σ^2. Imagine for a moment that the $Q + 1$ regression coefficients $\beta_0, \beta_1, \ldots, \beta_Q$ were known. Then the maximum likelihood estimator of σ^2 would be

$$\hat{\sigma}^2 = \sum r_i^2/n. \qquad [3.68]$$

Now suppose that the regression parameters were unknown (which is typically the case) and therefore must be estimated. The residuals will be

$$\hat{r}_i = Y_i - \hat{\beta}_0 - \hat{\beta}_1 X_{1i} - \hat{\beta}_2 X_{2i} - \cdots - \hat{\beta}_Q X_{Qi}, \qquad [3.69]$$

where each $\hat{\beta}_q$ is the OLS estimate. In this case, the usual unbiased estimator of σ^2 will be

$$\hat{\sigma}^2 = \sum \hat{r}_i^2/(n - Q - 1). \qquad [3.70]$$

Notice that the denominator, $(n - Q - 1)$, corrects for the degrees of freedom used in estimating the $Q + 1$ regression parameters. Often, Q is small, so the correction will have little effect.[7] However, as Q increases, use of Equation 3.68 can lead to a serious bias in estimating σ^2. The bias will be negative, so the σ^2 estimate will typically be too small, leading to artificially short confidence interval and overly liberal hypothesis tests. This distinction between Equations 3.68 and 3.70 is precisely the difference between MLF and MLR.[8]

For hierarchical linear models, the difference between variance-covariance estimates based on MLF versus MLR is not expressible in simple algebraic form. However, the MLR estimates of variance components do adjust for the uncertainty about the fixed effects, and the MLF results do not. For the two-level model, MLF and MLR will generally produce very similar results for σ^2, but noticeable differences can occur in the estimation of **T**. In cases where the number of level-2 units, J, is large, the two methods will produce very similar results. However, when J is small the MLF variance estimates, $\hat{\tau}_{qq}$, will be smaller than MLR by a factor of approximately $(J - F)/J$, where F is the total number of elements in the fixed-effects vector, γ.

Illustration of ML Estimation Using the EM Algorithm. The reader may wonder how algorithms used to compute variance-covariance estimates actually work. The puzzle that has to be solved is that the estimates we have presented for level-1 and level-2 coefficients require knowledge of the variance components, whereas estimates of the variance components require knowledge of the coefficients. The mutual dependence of these estimates suggests some kind of an iterative algorithm. The first procedure widely used for hierarchical models was the EM algorithm (Dempster, Laird, & Rubin, 1977; Dempster, Rubin, & Tsutakawa, 1981). We illustrate application of EM to full maximum likelihood estimation below in the case of the one-way ANOVA model, leaving a discussion of other algorithms and more complex models to Chapter 14. For simplicity we drop the subscript 0 on u_{0j}, γ_0, τ_{00}.

EM is based on the idea that the random effects, u_j, for level-2 units j constitute "missing data," whereas the observed data include the outcomes Y_{ij} for all level-1 and level-2 units. Suppose that the missing data, u_j, were actually observed. Then maximum likelihood estimates of all parameters (γ, τ, σ^2) would be easy to compute. To estimate γ, we would simply subtract u_j from both sides of the combined model, $Y_{ij} = \gamma + u_j + r_{ij}$. Then the OLS estimator of γ would be

$$\hat{\gamma} = \sum_{j=1}^{J}\sum_{i=1}^{n_j}(Y_{ij} - u_j)\Big/\sum_{j=1}^{J}n_j. \qquad [3.71]$$

ML estimators of the variance components would also be simple:

$$\hat{\tau} = \sum_{j=1}^{J} u_j^2/J, \qquad [3.72]$$

$$\hat{\sigma}^2 = \sum_{j=1}^{J}\sum_{i=1}^{n_j}(Y_{ij} - \hat{\gamma} - u_j)^2\Big/\sum_{j=1}^{J}n_j. \qquad [3.73]$$

Inspection of Equations 3.71 to 3.73 reveal that, given the missing data, three statistics are sufficient for estimating the three parameters (the sum in Equation 3.71 and the two sums of squares in Equations 3.72 and 3.73). These are called "complete data sufficient statistics" or "CDSS" for short. Of course, these CDSS cannot be observed because they depend on the missing values u_j, $j = 1, \ldots, J$. However, the CDSS can be estimated, given the data Y and initial guesses of the parameters. That is, given the data Y and $(\gamma^{(0)}, \tau^{(0)}, \sigma^{2(0)})$, where the superscript $^{(0)}$ denotes an initial estimate, each u_j is normal with mean u_j^* and variance V_j^* where

$$u_j^* = \lambda_j^{(0)}(\overline{Y}_j - \gamma^{(0)}), \qquad V_j^* = \tau^{(0)}(1 - \lambda_j^{(0)}). \qquad [3.74]$$

Therefore, the CDSS can be estimated as

$$E\left[\sum_{j=1}^{J}\sum_{i=1}^{n_j}(Y_{ij} - u_j)|Y, \gamma^{(0)}, \tau^{(0)}, \sigma^{2(0)}\right] = \sum_{j=1}^{J}\sum_{i=1}^{n_j}(Y_{ij} - u_j^*) \qquad [3.75]$$

and

$$E\left[\sum_{j=1}^{J} u_j^2 \,\middle|\, Y, \gamma^{(0)}, \tau^{(0)}, \sigma^{2(0)}\right] = \sum_{j=1}^{J}(u_j^{*2} + V_j^*),\qquad [3.76]$$

$$E\left[\sum_{j=1}^{J}\sum_{i=1}^{n_j}(Y_{ij} - \hat{\gamma} - u_j)^2 \,\middle|\, Y, \gamma^{(0)}, \tau^{(0)}, \sigma^{2(0)}\right]$$

$$= \sum_{j=1}^{J}\sum_{i=1}^{n_j}[(Y_{ij} - \gamma^0 - u_j^*)^2 + V_j^*].\qquad [3.77]$$

The "E step" of the algorithm estimates the CDSS by means of its conditional expectation given the data Y and current parameter estimates (Equations 3.75 to 3.77). The M-step substitutes these estimated CDSS into the formulas for the ML estimates given complete data (Equations 3.71 to 3.73). Dempster, Laird, and Rubin (1977) proved that each step of an EM algorithm increases the likelihood and that the estimates will converge to a local maximum.

The formulas above clarify how the empirical Bayes estimators u_j^* and V_j^* are essential in the iterations of EM for hierarchical models. Estimates based on Fisher scoring are also a function of the EM step estimates and also therefore depend on the empirical Bayes residual estimates (see Chapter 14 for details).

Confidence Intervals for Variance Components Based on Maximum Likelihood. It is possible to compute standard error estimates for each variance and covariance term contained in **T**, as well as for σ^2. Chapter 14 of this book presents formulas for both MLF and MLR cases. Difficulties arise, however, in using such standard error estimates. The key problem is that the sampling distribution of the variance estimates, $\hat{\tau}_{qq}$, is skewed to a degree that is unknown. As a result, symmetrical confidence intervals and statistical tests based on these may be highly misleading. Alternative approaches to hypothesis testing are presented later in this chapter.

Bayes Estimation. Both MLF and MLR have a weakness that is corrected by a Bayesian approach to estimation of variances and covariances. Inferences about the fixed effects—that is, confidence intervals and hypothesis tests—are conditional on the accuracy of point estimates of the variance-covariance parameters. For example, the 95% confidence interval for $\hat{\gamma}_{01}$ in the means-as-outcomes example was

$$95\% \text{ CI}(\gamma_{01}) = \hat{\gamma}_{01} \pm 1.96(V_{\hat{\gamma}_{01}})^{1/2},$$

where

$$V_{\hat{\gamma}_{01}} = \text{Var}(\hat{\gamma}_{01}) = \left[\sum \Delta_j^{-1} (W_j - \overline{W}_.^*)^2 \right]^{-1}.$$

Suppose that estimates of $\hat{\Delta}_j = \hat{\tau}_{00} + \hat{V}_j$ were substituted into this formula. If τ_{00} were poorly estimated, the confidence interval could be quite inaccurate. Note also that using 1.96, the critical value of a unit normal variate at the .025 level, would not be exact, because the sampling distribution of $(\hat{\gamma}_{01} - \gamma_{01})/(V_{\hat{\gamma}_{01}})^{1/2}$ is exactly normal only if $V_{\hat{\gamma}_{01}}$ is known.

Fotiu's (1989) simulation study found that more appropriate confidence intervals use the critical t value as the multiplier, yielding

$$95\% \ \text{CI}(\hat{\gamma}_{01}) = \hat{\gamma}_{01} \pm t_{.025} (\widehat{V}_{\hat{\gamma}_{01}})^{1/2},$$

where $\widehat{V}_{\hat{\gamma}_{01}}$ is based on substituting estimates of τ_{00} and σ^2 into the formula for $V_{\hat{\gamma}_{01}}$.

Bayesian estimation in contrast to MLF and MLR allows the researcher to make inferences about γ that are not conditional on specific point estimates of $\mathbf{T}$ and σ^2. Using the Bayesian approach, inferences about γ are based on its posterior distribution given only the data.[9] See Chapter 13 for a full discussion of these methods.

Hypothesis Testing

In the previous section, we discussed estimation of three kinds of parameters: the fixed effects, the random level-1 coefficients, and the variance-covariance components. We now consider hypothesis tests.

To place our discussion in a reasonably general framework, let us consider a level-1 regression model having the form

$$Y_{ij} = \beta_{0j} + \beta_{1j} X_{1ij} + \beta_{2j} X_{2ij} + \cdots + \beta_{Qj} X_{Qij} + r_{ij}$$

$$= \beta_{0j} + \sum_{q=1}^{Q} \beta_{qj} X_{qij} + r_{ij} \quad \text{where } r_{ij} \sim N(0, \sigma^2). \qquad [3.78]$$

Equation 3.78 has $Q + 1$ coefficients, any one of which could be viewed as fixed, nonrandomly varying, or random. In the level-2 model, each coefficient β_{qj} can be modeled as

$$\beta_{qj} = \gamma_{q0} + \gamma_{q1} W_{1j} + \gamma_{q2} W_{2j} + \cdots + \gamma_{qS_q} W_{S_q j} + u_{qj}$$

$$= \gamma_{q0} + \sum_{s=1}^{S_q} \gamma_{qs} W_{sj} + u_{qj} \qquad [3.79]$$

TABLE 3.1 Type of Hypothesis Testable in Hierarchical Models

Type of Hypothesis	Fixed Effect	Random Level-1 Coefficient	Variance Component
Single-parameter			
H_0	$\gamma_h = 0$	$\beta_{qj} = 0$	$\tau_{qq} = 0$
H_1	$\gamma_h \neq 0$	$\beta_{qj} \neq 0$	$\tau_{qq} > 0$
Multiparameter			
H_0	$\mathbf{C}'\boldsymbol{\gamma} = 0$	$\mathbf{C}'\boldsymbol{\beta} = 0$	$\mathbf{T} = \mathbf{T}_0$
H_1	$\mathbf{C}'\boldsymbol{\gamma} \neq 0$	$\mathbf{C}'\boldsymbol{\beta} \neq 0$	$\mathbf{T} = \mathbf{T}_1$

for some set of level-2 predictors W_{sj}, $s = 1, \ldots, S_q$. Because each β_{qj} can have a unique set of predictors in Equation 3.79, there are $S_q + 1$ fixed effects for each β_{qj}, and the total number of fixed effects in the level-2 model, F, is equal to $\sum_q (S_q + 1)$. We assume that each random component, u_{qj}, is multivariate normally distributed, such that for any q

$$\text{Var}(u_{qj}) = \tau_{qq} \qquad [3.80]$$

and for any pair of random effects q and q'

$$\text{Cov}(u_{qj}, u_{q'j}) = \tau_{qq'}. \qquad [3.81]$$

Hypotheses may be formulated and tested about the fixed effects (each γ_{qs}), the random level-1 coefficients (each β_{qj}), and the variance-covariance parameters. The tests may be either single-parameter tests or multiparameter tests. Hence, there are six types of hypotheses that can be tested, as displayed in Table 3.1. The corresponding test statistics commonly employed in these models are displayed in Table 3.2. Each is described and illustrated below.

Hypothesis Tests for Fixed Effects

Single-Parameter Tests. The typical null hypothesis here is

$$H_0: \gamma_{qs} = 0, \qquad [3.82]$$

which implies that the effect of a level-2 predictor, W_{sj}, on a particular level-2 parameter, β_{qj}, is null. In Chapter 4, for example, we shall test the hypothesis that school sector (Catholic versus public) is unrelated to school mean achievement in U.S. high schools. The tests for such hypotheses have the form

$$t = \hat{\gamma}_{qs} / (\widehat{V}_{\hat{\gamma}_{qs}})^{1/2}, \qquad [3.83]$$

where $\hat{\gamma}_{qs}$ is the maximum likelihood estimate of γ_{qs} and $\widehat{V}_{\hat{\gamma}_{qs}}$ is the estimated sampling variance of $\hat{\gamma}_{qs}$. Formally this statistic is asymptotically unit normal. It will often be the case, however, that a t statistic with degrees of freedom equal to $J - S_q - 1$ will provide a more accurate reference distribution for testing effects of level-2 predictors.

Multiparameter Tests. Consider now a simple example that we shall elaborate in Chapter 4. Within each U.S. high school, we model student mathematics achievement as a function of student SES plus error:

$$Y_{ij} = \beta_{0j} + \beta_{1j}(\text{SES})_{ij} + r_{ij}, \qquad [3.84]$$

where Y_{ij} is the math achievement of student i in school j, $(\text{SES})_{ij}$ is the SES of that student, r_{ij} is a random error, and β_{0j}, β_{1j} are the regression intercept and slope for school j. Suppose now that we wanted to test a composite null hypothesis that Catholic and public schools are similar both in their intercepts and slopes. This is a simultaneous test of two hypotheses. The level-2 model might be written as

$$\beta_{0j} = \gamma_{00} + \gamma_{01}(\text{SECTOR})_j + u_{0j}, \qquad [3.85a]$$

$$\beta_{1j} = \gamma_{10} + \gamma_{11}(\text{SECTOR})_j + u_{1j}, \qquad [3.85b]$$

where $(\text{SECTOR})_j$ is an indicator variable ($1 = $ Catholic, $0 = $ public). The hypothesis to be tested is that both γ_{01} and γ_{11} are null. If this composite hypothesis were retained, $(\text{SECTOR})_j$ might be dropped entirely from this model.

TABLE 3.2 Common Hypothesis Tests for Hierarchical Models

Type of Hypothesis	Fixed Effect	Random Level-1 Coefficient	Variance Component
Single parameter	t ratio	t ratio	univariate χ^2 or z ratio
Multiparameter	general linear hypothesis test[a]	general linear hypothesis test	likelihood-ratio test (χ^2)

a. A likelihood-ratio test also may be used in the case of the MLF model.

To understand our approach to such multiparameter tests requires a reformulation of Equation 3.85 in matrix notation:

$$
\begin{pmatrix} \beta_{0j} \\ \beta_{1j} \end{pmatrix} = \begin{pmatrix} 1 & (\text{SECTOR})_j & 0 & 0 \\ 0 & 0 & 1 & (\text{SECTOR})_j \end{pmatrix} \begin{pmatrix} \gamma_{00} \\ \gamma_{01} \\ \gamma_{10} \\ \gamma_{11} \end{pmatrix}
$$

$$
+ \begin{pmatrix} u_{0j} \\ u_{1j} \end{pmatrix}. \tag{3.86}
$$

That is,

$$
\boldsymbol{\beta}_j = \mathbf{W}_j \boldsymbol{\gamma} + \mathbf{u}_j.
$$

The composite hypothesis could be written as

$$
H_0: \mathbf{C}^T \boldsymbol{\gamma} = \mathbf{0}, \tag{3.87}
$$

where

$$
\mathbf{C}^T = \begin{pmatrix} 0 & 1 & 0 & 0 \\ 0 & 0 & 0 & 1 \end{pmatrix},
$$

so that, according to the null hypothesis,

$$
\mathbf{C}^T \boldsymbol{\gamma} = \begin{pmatrix} \gamma_{01} \\ \gamma_{11} \end{pmatrix} = \begin{pmatrix} 0 \\ 0 \end{pmatrix}. \tag{3.88}
$$

Given that $\mathrm{Var}(\hat{\boldsymbol{\beta}}_j) = \boldsymbol{\Delta}_j$ is known, the sampling variance of $\hat{\boldsymbol{\gamma}}$ is

$$
\mathrm{Var}(\hat{\boldsymbol{\gamma}}) = \left(\sum \mathbf{W}_j^T \boldsymbol{\Delta}_j^{-1} \mathbf{W}_j \right)^{-1} = \mathbf{V}_{\hat{\gamma}}. \tag{3.89}
$$

Thus, the *contrast vector*, $\mathbf{C}'\hat{\boldsymbol{\gamma}}$, has variance

$$
\mathrm{Var}(\mathbf{C}^T \hat{\boldsymbol{\gamma}}) = \mathbf{C}^T \mathbf{V}_{\hat{\gamma}} \mathbf{C} = (\text{say}) \mathbf{V}_c. \tag{3.90}
$$

When $\mathbf{V}_{\hat{\gamma}}$ is not known but is estimated by

$$
\widehat{\mathbf{V}}_{\hat{\gamma}} = \left(\sum \mathbf{W}_j^T \widehat{\boldsymbol{\Delta}}_j^{-1} \mathbf{W}_j \right)^{-1},
$$

an approximate test statistic for the null hypothesis $H_0 : \mathbf{C}^T \boldsymbol{\gamma} = \mathbf{0}$ is given by

$$
H = \hat{\boldsymbol{\gamma}}^T \mathbf{C} \widehat{\mathbf{V}}_c^{-1} \mathbf{C}^T \hat{\boldsymbol{\gamma}}, \tag{3.91}
$$

which has a large-sample χ^2 distribution under H_0 with degrees of freedom equal to the number of contrasts to be tested (i.e., the number of rows in $\mathbf{C}^T$). In the present example, $\mathbf{C}^T$ has two rows so that the degrees of freedom are two.

Multiparameter tests regarding γ are useful for

omnibus tests of the relationship between a categorical level-2 predictor and a β_{qj} parameter. (Example: Is school mean achievement related to region of the country, where five regions [Northeast, Southeast, Midwest, Southwest, and Pacific Coast] are represented by four dummy variables?)

contrasts between categories of a level-2 predictor. (Example: Do students in the South achieve significantly more or less than students in the Midwest?)

examining whether a level-2 characteristic interacts with any of several level-1 predictors. (Example: Do the effects on achievement of student SES, minority group status, or academic background depend on sector?)

examining whether some subset of level-2 predictors is needed in a particular β_{qj} model. (Example: Does overall school climate—academic, disciplinary, and social—predict school mean achievement?)

There are many possible uses for multiparameter tests, some of which are illustrated in later chapters. One benefit of multiparameter hypothesis tests is protection against the heightened probability of type I errors that arises from performing many univariate tests. One might employ the strategy of using post-hoc univariate tests only when the relevant omnibus (multiparameter) hypothesis has been rejected.

Another approach to multiparameter testing is a likelihood-ratio test. In the case of fixed effects, this testing approach is available under MLF estimation only. It is based on estimating and comparing results from two models. The first or "null" model excludes the fixed effects hypothesized to be null. The second or "alternative" model estimates all effects—those hypothesized to be null along with any other effects in the model. For each model, a deviance statistic is computed and the difference between the deviance statistics is used to test the multivariate hypothesis. Intuitively, the deviance is a measure of model fit: the higher the deviance, the poorer the fit.

Procedurally, for the null model, we compute the deviance D_0, which is twice the negative log-likelihood or

$$D_0 = -2\log(L_0), \qquad\qquad [3.92]$$

where L_0 is the value of the likelihood associated with the maximum likelihood estimates under the null hypothesis. Similarly, D_1 is the deviance associated with the maximum likelihood estimates computed under the alternative model:

$$D_1 = -2\log(L_1). \qquad\qquad [3.93]$$

Under the null hypothesis, the difference between deviances,

$$D_0 - D_1, \qquad\qquad [3.94]$$

has a large-sample χ^2 distribution with degrees of freedom equal to the difference in the number of parameters estimated. Large values of the statistic are taken as evidence that the null hypothesis is implausible and that the null model is therefore "too simple" a description of the data.

The likelihood-ratio test will produce results that are nearly identical to those of the general linear hypothesis test of Equation 3.87. There are three advantages of the latter, however. First, using the general linear hypothesis approach, any set of linear hypotheses can be tested after computing estimates for just one model (the alternative model). In contrast, the likelihood-ratio approach requires recomputation of the estimates for any null hypothesis to be tested. Second, the general linear hypothesis approach allows for arbitrary linear contrasts among the parameters. For example, one might want to test the difference between two fixed effects or a linear contrast in the fixed effects. To test such hypotheses using the likelihood-ratio approach would actually require reprogramming the estimation algorithm in order to introduce the needed constraints among the parameters. Third, the likelihood-ratio approach is unavailable under MLR, and as mentioned above, there are circumstances where MLR is advantageous.

We note that when using the likelihood-ratio approach to test hypotheses about fixed effects, the variance-covariance components specification must be identical for both the null and the alternative models. As we discuss below, the likelihood-ratio approach can also be used to test hypotheses about the structure of the variance-covariance component in the model, and joint hypotheses about both fixed effects and variance-covariance components.

Hypothesis Tests for Random Level-1 Coefficients

Continuing with our example of research on high schools, a researcher may be interested in testing a hypothesis that a regression coefficient in a particular school is null or that a regression coefficient in one school is larger than the comparable coefficient in a second school. The first question is an example of a single-parameter hypothesis, and the second may be viewed as a multiparameter test, in that it is a comparison among two or more components of the random-coefficients vector.

Single-Parameter Tests. The hypothesis that a particular regression coefficient for an individual school is null may be formulated as

$$H_0: \beta_{qj} = 0. \qquad [3.95]$$

The appropriate test is directly analogous to the fixed-effects case; that is, we compute the ratio of the estimated coefficient to its estimated standard error. However, the researcher has a choice of using the empirical Bayes or OLS estimates.

In the empirical Bayes approach, the ratio may be denoted

$$z = \beta^*_{qj}/V^{*1/2}_{qqj}, \tag{3.96}$$

where

β^*_{qj} is the empirical Bayes estimate;

V^*_{qqj} is the qth diagonal element of the posterior dispersion of the β_{qj} coefficients; and

z is distributed approximately as a unit normal variate when the null hypothesis is true.

General expressions for the posterior means and variances under MLF and MLR are derived in Chapter 14. We note, however, that the posterior variances will be larger—and more realistic—under MLR than under MLF. This will especially be true when the number of level-2 units (e.g., schools) is small. Under MLF, the fixed effects are assumed known so that the posterior variance of β_{qj} does not reflect uncertainty about them. This assumption is realistic only when the number of level-2 units, J, is large.

We strongly caution the reader that regardless of whether we use MLF or MLR, these tests will be too liberal, with actual significance levels substantially exceeding the nominal values, unless J is large. Further, little is known about how large J must be or how liberal the tests are.

A much more conservative t test, but one that has an exact t distribution under the null hypothesis, is available when β estimates can be computed by means of ordinary least squares. One simply computes the regression for a particular level-2 unit and tests the hypotheses in the standard manner. In many applications, where level-1 sample sizes are small, this test will be too conservative to be of much use.

Multiparameter Tests. If we consider $\boldsymbol{\beta}$ to be the entire vector of random parameters—with dimension $J(Q+1)$ by 1 where the parameter vector for each level-2 unit is stacked one on top of the other—then the general linear hypothesis associated with $\boldsymbol{\beta}$ is

$$H_0: \mathbf{C}^T\boldsymbol{\beta} = \mathbf{0}. \tag{3.97}$$

If the empirical Bayes estimates $\boldsymbol{\beta}^*$ are used as the basis of the test, the test statistic will be

$$H_{EB} = \boldsymbol{\beta}^{*T}\mathbf{C}(\mathbf{C}^T\mathbf{V}^*\mathbf{C})^{-1}\mathbf{C}^T\boldsymbol{\beta}^*, \tag{3.98}$$

where $\mathbf{V}^*$ is the entire $J(Q + 1)$ by $J(Q + 1)$ variance-covariance matrix of the coefficients. Under MLR, $\mathbf{V}^*$ is a *full* matrix. That is, under MLR, the empirical Bayes estimates for different level-2 units are mutually dependent because they all rely on the same estimates of the fixed effects. Under MLF, on the other hand, the empirical Bayes estimates for different level-2 units are independent, but this independence is based on the unrealistic assumption that the fixed effects are known.

For a single level-2 unit, it is straightforward to test hypotheses about components of $\boldsymbol{\beta}_j$ using either MLR or MLF empirical Bayes estimates. It is also relatively easy to compare coefficients from a small number of level-2 units (i.e., when only a small submatrix of Equation 3.98 is needed). In general, both the MLR and MLF approaches will be too liberal unless J is large.

An alternative to the empirical Bayes approach provides exact but very conservative multivariate tests. If the entire vector of OLS estimates, say $\hat{\boldsymbol{\beta}}$, can be computed, then the general linear hypothesis given by Equation 3.97 can be tested by means of the statistic

$$H_{\text{OLS}} = \hat{\boldsymbol{\beta}}^T \mathbf{C} (\mathbf{C}^T \widehat{\mathbf{V}} \mathbf{C})^{-1} \mathbf{C}^T \hat{\boldsymbol{\beta}}, \qquad [3.99]$$

where $\widehat{\mathbf{V}}$ is a block diagonal matrix with each $(Q + 1)$ by $(Q + 1)$ block equal to

$$\widehat{\mathbf{V}}_j = \hat{\sigma}^2 (\mathbf{X}_j^T \mathbf{X}_j)^{-1}. \qquad [3.100]$$

Hypothesis Testing for Variance and Covariance Components

Single-Parameter Tests. In nearly all applications of hierarchical analysis, investigators will need to decide whether level-1 coefficients should be specified as fixed, random, or nonrandomly varying (see Chapter 2).

To ask whether random variation exists, we may test a null hypothesis

$$\text{H}_0 \text{: } \tau_{qq} = 0, \qquad [3.101]$$

where $\tau_{qq} = \text{Var}(\beta_{qj})$. If this hypothesis is rejected, the investigator may conclude that there is random variation in β_q.

A simple and useful test of H_0: $\tau_{qq} = 0$ is possible if all (or at least most) groups have sufficient data to compute the OLS estimates. Let $\widehat{V}_{qqj}$ represent the qth diagonal element of $\widehat{V}_j = \hat{\sigma}^2 (\mathbf{X}_j^T \mathbf{X}_j)^{-1}$. Then, under the model

$$\beta_{qj} = \gamma_{q0} + \sum_{s=1}^{S_q} \gamma_{qs} W_{sj}, \qquad [3.102]$$

the statistic

$$\sum_{j}\left(\hat{\beta}_{qj} - \hat{\gamma}_{q0} - \sum_{s=1}^{S_q}\hat{\gamma}_{qs}W_{sj}\right)^2 \Big/ \hat{V}_{qqj} \qquad [3.103]$$

will be distributed approximately χ^2 with $J - S_q - 1$ degrees of freedom.

A second test of the hypothesis H_0: $\tau_{qq} = 0$ is based on the estimated standard error of $\hat{\tau}_{qq}$ computed from the inverse of the information matrix. The ratio

$$z = \hat{\tau}_{qq} / [\mathrm{Var}(\hat{\tau}_{qq})]^{1/2} \qquad [3.104]$$

is approximately normally distributed under the large-sample theory of maximum likelihood estimates. In many cases, however, especially when τ_{qq} is near zero, the normality approximation will be extremely poor. Technically, the likelihood is unlikely to be symmetric about the mode (i.e., asymptotic normality has not yet been achieved), and a test based on a symmetric confidence interval for τ_{qq} may be highly misleading.

Multiparameter Tests. The most general form of hypothesis testing for variances and covariances is based on a likelihood-ratio test. This test is available under both MLF and MLR estimation. A common use of this test is to examine the null hypothesis that

$$H_0: \mathbf{T} = \mathbf{T}_0 \qquad [3.105]$$

versus the alternative

$$H_1: \mathbf{T} = \mathbf{T}_1, \qquad [3.106]$$

where $\mathbf{T}_0$ is a reduced form of $\mathbf{T}_1$. For example, the qth row and column (or some set of rows and columns) in $\mathbf{T}_1$ may be null. For any model, the *deviance* is -2 times the value of the log-likelihood function evaluated at the maximum (see Chapter 4 for details). To test a composite hypothesis, one estimates the two models, computes deviances D_0 and D_1 associated with each model, and then computes the test statistic

$$H = D_0 - D_1. \qquad [3.107]$$

This statistic has an approximate χ^2 distribution with m degrees of freedom, where m is the difference in the number of unique variance and covariance components estimated in the two models. In using a likelihood-ratio test for variances or covariances, the models compared must be identical with respect to the specification of the fixed effects. The likelihood ratio test will tend to be somewhat conservative in this setting (Pinheiro and Bates, 2000).

Finally, we note that under MLF estimation of the variance and covariance components, it is possible to simultaneously test hypotheses about both fixed effects and variance-covariance components. The procedure is identical to that already described above. A restricted model is posed and D_0 is computed. This is tested against the deviance statistic, D_1, from the more general model using Equation 3.107. The goodness of fit of a whole set of alternative nested models can be examined sequentially in this fashion. An application of this procedure is illustrated in Chapter 6.

Summary of Terms Introduced in This Chapter

General two-level model:

$$Y_{ij} = \beta_{0j} + \beta_{1j}X_{1ij} + \beta_{2j}X_{2ij} + \cdots + \beta_{Qj}X_{Qij} + r_{ij}$$

$$= \beta_{0j} + \sum_{q=1}^{Q} \beta_{qj}X_{qij} + r_{ij} \quad \text{where } r_{ij} \sim N(0, \sigma^2),$$

$$\beta_{qj} = \gamma_{q0} + \gamma_{q1}W_{1j} + \gamma_{q2}W_{2j} + \cdots + \gamma_{qS_q}W_{S_qj} + u_{qj}$$

$$= \gamma_{q0} + \sum_{s=1}^{S_q} \gamma_{qs}W_{sj} + u_{qj} \quad \text{for each } q = 0, \ldots, Q.$$

We assume that the random components, $u_{qj}, q = 0, \ldots, Q$, are multivariate normal, each with a mean of 0, and some variance, $\text{Var}(u_{qj}) = \tau_{qq}$. For any pair of random effects q and q', $\text{Cov}(u_{qj}, u_{q'j}) = \tau_{qq'}$. These variance and covariance components can be collected into a $(Q + 1)$ by $(Q + 1)$ dispersion matrix, **T**.

Precision: Reciprocal of the error variance of a statistic.

Precision-weighted average: A weighted average of a set of statistics in which each statistic is weighted proportional to its precision (Equation 3.9).

Ordinary least squares (OLS) estimator: An estimator that minimizes a sum of squared residuals. In the case of a single predictor, the OLS slope estimate is a sum of cross-products divided by a sum of squares (Equation 3.15).

Weighted least squares (WLS) estimator: An estimator that minimizes a weighted sum of squared residuals. In the case of a single predictor, the WLS slope estimate is a weighted sum of cross-products divided by a weighted sum of squares (Equation 3.17).

Generalized least squares (GLS) estimator: An estimator that minimizes a weighted sum of squares and cross-products (Equation 3.31).

Error variance: The variance of a statistic (e.g., $\hat{\beta}_{qj}$) used to estimate an unknown level-1 coefficient (e.g., β_{qj}). This variance includes several sources: sampling error, measurement error, and *model error* (e.g., incomplete specification of the level-1 model).

Parameter variance: The variance of an unknown level-1 coefficient (e.g., β_{qj}) across the population of level-2 units.

Empirical Bayes estimate of a random level-1 coefficient: An estimate of the unknown level-1 coefficient for a particular unit, which utilizes not only the data from that unit but also the data from all other similar units (e.g., Equations 3.41, 3.48, and 3.56).

Reliability: In the case of a two-level hierarchical linear model, we refer to the reliability of $\hat{\beta}_{qj}$ as the reliability of the ordinary least squares estimator as a measure of an unknown level-1 coefficient β_{qj}. Reliability indices can be computed for each level-2 unit (see Equation 3.58) and an overall or average reliability for the set of J level-2 units (see Equation 3.59).

Unconditional shrinkage: The principle of shrinking a least squares estimator of a random level-1 coefficient toward the grand mean by a factor proportional to its unreliability.

Conditional shrinkage: The principle of shrinking a least squares estimator of a random level-1 coefficient toward a predicted value rather than toward the grand mean.

Least squares residual at level 2 ($\hat{u}_{qj}$): The deviation of a least squares estimate, $\hat{\beta}_{qj}$, from its predicted value based on the level-2 model (see Equations 3.50 and 3.60).

Empirical Bayes residual at level 2 (u_{qj}^*): The deviation of an empirical Bayes estimate, β_{qj}^* from its predicted value based on the level-2 model (see Equations 3.51 and 3.61).

Least squares residual at level 1 ($\hat{r}_{ij}$): The deviation of the level-1 outcome, Y_{ij}, from its predicted value based on the level-2 model fixed-effects estimates and least squares residuals, $\hat{u}_j$ (see Equation 3.62).

Empirical Bayes residual at level 1 (r_{ij}^*): The deviation of the level-1 outcome, Y_{ij}, from its predicted value based on the level-2 model fixed-effects estimates and the empirical Bayes residuals, u_j^* (see Equation 3.63).

Single-parameter test: A test of the null hypothesis regarding a single parameter.

Multiparameter test: A test of a combined null hypothesis involving multiple parameters.

Notes

1. This section requires some basic knowledge of matrix algebra and is optional.

2. Technically, the estimate β_{0j}^* is the conditional posterior mean of the random parameter β_{0j} given the data and the variances σ^2 and τ_{00}.

3. To be precise, this estimator is optimal in the specific sense that no other point estimator of β_{0j} has smaller expected-mean squared error, where the expectation is taken over the conditional distribution of β_{0j} given the data, σ^2, and τ_{00}.

4. Formally, V_j^* is the posterior variance of β_{0j} given the data and the variances σ^2 and τ_{00}.

5. The problem of spuriously short confidence intervals is exacerbated in the MLF case in which γ_{00} is also assumed known and therefore $V_j^* = (V_j^{-1} + \tau_{00}^{-1})^{-1}$ fails to adjust for uncertainty in $\hat{\gamma}_{00}$ as an estimator of γ_{00}.

6. This section requires some knowledge of matrix algebra and is optional.

7. A better correction for minimizing mean squared error is $n - Q + 1$ rather than $n - Q - 1$.

8. The restricted likelihood requires integration of the full likelihood with respect to γ. This notion of "integrating the likelihood" is a Bayesian idea that makes sense if we view the likelihood as the joint posterior density of γ, σ^2, and $\mathbf{T}$. The restricted likelihood can also be viewed in classical terms as the conditional density of Y given $\hat{\gamma}$.

9. This posterior distribution is calculated by "integrating out" σ^2 and $\mathbf{T}$ from the joint posterior distribution of γ, σ^2, and $\mathbf{T}$. For any specific set of values of $(\sigma^2, \mathbf{T})$, there is an estimate of γ and its standard error. The Bayesian approach essentially takes a weighted average of all possible estimates of this kind where the weight accorded any single estimate is proportional to the posterior density of $(\sigma^2, \mathbf{T})$.

4 An Illustration

Introduction

The purpose of this chapter is to illustrate the use of the techniques of estimation and hypothesis testing presented in Chapter 3. We present a series of analyses based on the models introduced in Chapter 2. For each model, we illustrate the estimation of the fixed effects and variance-covariance components, and demonstrate the use of appropriate hypothesis testing procedures for these various parameters. We also introduce through these examples some useful auxiliary description statistics that can be computed based on the maximum likelihood variance-covariance component estimates. Applications of estimation and hypothesis testing procedures for random level-1 coefficients are demonstrated in the last section of this chapter.

The examples presented below use data from a nationally representative sample of U.S. public and Catholic high schools. These data are a subsample from the 1982 High School and Beyond (HS&B) Survey,[1] and include information on 7,185 students nested within 160 schools: 90 public and 70 Catholic. Sample sizes averaged about 45 students per school.

Attention is restricted to two student-level variables: (a) the outcome, Y_{ij}, a standardized measure of math achievement; and (b) one predictor, $(SES)_{ij}$,

TABLE 4.1 Descriptive Statistics from American High School Data

	Variable Name	Mean	sd
Student-level variables			
Math achievement	Y_{ij}	12.75	6.88
Socioeconomic status	$(SES)_{ij}$	0.00	0.78
School-level variables			
Sector	$(SECTOR)_j$	0.44	0.50
School average SES	$(MEAN\ SES)_j$	0.00	0.41

student socioeconomic status, which is a composite of parental education, parental occupation, and parental income. School-level variables include $(SECTOR)_j$, an indicator variable taking on a value of one for Catholic schools and zero for public schools, and $(MEAN\ SES)_j$, the average of the student SES values within each school. In the language introduced in Chapter 2, the level-1 units are students and the level-2 units are schools. $(SES)_{ij}$ is a level-1 predictor; $(SECTOR)_j$ and $(MEAN\ SES)_j$ are level-2 predictors. Means and standard deviations of these variables are supplied in Table 4.1.

Questions motivating these analyses include the following:

1. How much do U.S. high schools vary in their mean mathematics achievement?
2. Do schools with high MEAN SES also have high math achievement?
3. Is the strength of association between student SES and math achievement similar across schools? Or is SES a more important predictor of achievement in some schools than in others?
4. How do public and Catholic schools compare in terms of mean math achievement and in terms of the strength of the SES-math achievement relationship, after we control for MEAN SES?

The One-Way ANOVA

The one-way ANOVA with random effects, described in Chapter 2, provides useful preliminary information about how much variation in the outcome lies within and between schools and about the reliability of each school's sample mean as an estimate of its true population mean.

The Model

The level-1 or student-level model is

$$Y_{ij} = \beta_{0j} + r_{ij}, \qquad [4.1]$$

where we assume $r_{ij} \sim$ independently $N(0, \sigma^2)$ for $i = 1, \ldots, n_j$ students in school j, and $j = 1, \ldots, 160$ schools. We refer to σ^2 as the student-level variance. Notice that this model characterizes achievement in each school with just an intercept, β_{0j}, which in this case is the mean.

At level 2 or the school level, each school's mean math achievement, β_{0j}, is represented as a function of the grand mean, γ_{00}, plus a random error, u_{0j}:

$$\beta_{0j} = \gamma_{00} + u_{0j}, \qquad [4.2]$$

where we assume $u_{0j} \sim$ independently $N(0, \tau_{00})$. We refer to τ_{00} as the school-level variance.

This yields a combined model, also often referred to as a mixed model, with fixed effect γ_{00} and random effects u_{0j} and r_{ij}:

$$Y_{ij} = \gamma_{00} + u_{0j} + r_{ij}. \qquad [4.3]$$

Results

Fixed Effects. From Table 4.2, the weighted least squares estimate for the grand-mean math achievement (using the estimator from Equation 3.9) is

$$\hat{\gamma}_{00} = 12.64.$$

This has a standard error of 0.24 and yields a 95% confidence interval (see Equation 3.12) of

$$12.64 \pm 1.96 \, (0.24) = (12.17, 13.11).$$

Variance Components. Table 4.2 also lists restricted maximum likelihood estimates of the variance components. At the student level,

$$\widehat{Var}(r_{ij}) = \hat{\sigma}^2 = 39.15.$$

TABLE 4.2 Results from the One-Way ANOVA Model

Fixed Effect	Coefficient	se		
Average school mean, γ_{00}	12.64	0.24		

Random Effect	Variance Component	df	χ^2	p Value
School mean, u_{0j}	8.61	159	1,660.2	.000
Level-1 effect, r_{ij}	39.15			

At the school level, τ_{00} is the variance of the true school means, β_{0j}, around the grand mean, γ_{00}. The estimated variability in these school means is

$$\widehat{\text{Var}}(\beta_{0j}) = \widehat{\text{Var}}(u_{0j}) = \hat{\tau}_{00} = 8.61.$$

To gauge the magnitude of the variation among schools in their mean achievement levels, it is useful to calculate the *plausible values range* for these means. Under the normality assumption of Equation 4.2, we would expect 95% of the school means to fall within the range:

$$\hat{\gamma}_{00} \pm 1.96(\hat{\tau}_{00})^{1/2}, \qquad [4.4]$$

which yields

$$12.64 \pm 1.96(8.61)^{1/2} = (6.89, 18.39).$$

This indicates a substantial range in average achievement levels among schools in this sample of data.

We may wish to test formally whether the estimated value of τ_{00} is significantly greater than zero. If not, it may be sensible to assume that all schools have the same mean. Formally, this hypothesis is

$$H_0: \tau_{00} = 0,$$

which may be tested using Equation 3.103. This test statistic reduces in a one-way random ANOVA model to

$$H = \sum n_j (\overline{Y}_{\cdot j} - \hat{\gamma}_{00})^2 / \hat{\sigma}^2, \qquad [4.5]$$

which has a large-sample χ^2 distribution with $J - 1$ degrees of freedom under the null hypothesis. In our case, the test statistic takes on a value of 1,660.2 with 159 degrees of freedom ($J = 160$ schools). The null hypothesis is highly implausible ($p < .001$), indicating significant variation does exist among schools in their achievement.

Auxiliary Statistics. The *intraclass correlation*, which represents in this case the proportion of variance in Y between schools, is estimated by substituting the estimated variance components for their respective parameters in Equation 2.10:

$$\hat{\rho} = \hat{\tau}_{00} / (\hat{\tau}_{00} + \hat{\sigma}^2) = 8.61/(8.61 + 39.15) = 0.18, \qquad [4.6]$$

indicating that about 18% of the variance in math achievement is between schools.

Similarly, an estimator of the *reliability of the sample mean* in any school for the true school mean, β_{0j}, can also be derived by substituting the estimated variance components into Equation 3.42. That is,

$$\hat{\lambda}_j = \text{reliability}(\overline{Y}._j) = \hat{\tau}_{00}/[\hat{\tau}_{00} + (\hat{\sigma}^2/n_j)].   \quad [4.7]$$

In general, the reliability of the sample mean $\overline{Y}._j$ will vary from school to school because the sample size, n_j, varies. However, an overall measure of the reliability can be obtained by averaging the individual school estimates:

$$\hat{\lambda} = \sum \hat{\lambda}_j/J.   \quad [4.8]$$

For the HS&B data, $\hat{\lambda} = .90$, indicating that the sample means tend to be quite reliable as indicators of the true school means.

In summary, this one-way ANOVA produces useful preliminary information in our study of math achievement in U.S. high schools. It provides an estimate of the grand mean; a partitioning of the total variation in math achievement into variation between and within schools; a *range of plausible values* for the school means and a test of the hypothesis that the variability is null; information on the degree of dependence of the observations within each school (the intraclass correlation); and a measure of the reliability of each school's sample average math achievement as an estimate of its true mean.

Regression with Means-as-Outcomes

The Model

The student-level model of Equation 4.1 remains unchanged: Student math achievement scores are viewed as varying around their school means. The school-level model of Equation 4.2 is now elaborated, however, so that each school's mean is now predicted by the MEAN SES of the school:

$$\beta_{0j} = \gamma_{00} + \gamma_{01}(\text{MEAN SES})_j + u_{0j},   \quad [4.9]$$

where γ_{00} is the intercept, γ_{01} is the effect of MEAN SES on β_{0j}, and we assume $u_{0j} \sim$ independently $N(0, \tau_{00})$.

Notice that the symbols u_{0j} and τ_{00} have different meanings than they had in Equation 4.2. Whereas the random variable u_{0j} had been the deviation of school j's mean from the grand mean, it now represents the residual $\beta_{0j} - \gamma_{00} - \gamma_{01}(\text{MEAN SES})_j$. Correspondingly, the variance τ_{00} is now a residual or conditional variance, that is, $\text{Var}(\beta_{0j}|\text{MEANSES})$, the school-level variance in β_{0j} after controlling for school MEAN SES.

Substituting Equation 4.9 into Equation 4.1 yields the combined model (or "mixed model")

$$Y_{ij} = \gamma_{00} + \gamma_{01}(\text{MEAN SES})_j + u_{0j} + r_{ij} \qquad [4.10]$$

having fixed effects γ_{00}, γ_{01}, and random effects u_{0j}, r_{ij}.

Results

Table 4.3 provides estimates and hypothesis tests for the fixed effects and the variances of the random effects.

Fixed Effects. We see a highly significant association between school MEAN SES and mean achievement ($\hat{\gamma}_{01} = 5.68, t = 16.22$). The t ratio employed for hypothesis testing of an individual fixed effect is simply the ratio of the estimated coefficient to its standard error (see Equation 3.83):

$$t = \hat{\gamma}_{01}/[\text{Var}(\hat{\gamma}_{01})]^{1/2} = 5.86/0.36 = 16.22.$$

It is also possible to test the hypothesis that the grand mean is null, that is, $H_0 = \gamma_{00} = 0$, but that hypothesis is of no interest in this case.

Variance Component. The residual variance between schools, $\hat{\tau}_{00} = 2.64$, is substantially smaller than the original, $\hat{\tau}_{00} = 8.61$, estimated in the context of the random ANOVA model (see Table 4.2). A range of plausible values for school means, given that all schools have a MEAN SES of zero, is

$$\hat{\gamma}_{00} \pm 1.96(\hat{\tau}_{00})^{1/2} = 12.65 \pm 1.96(2.64)^{1/2} = (9.47, 15.83).$$

TABLE 4.3 Results from the Means-as-Outcomes Model

Fixed Effect	Coefficient	se	t Ratio	
Model for school means				
INTERCEPT, γ_{00}	12.65	0.15	—	
MEAN SES, γ_{01}	5.86	0.36	16.22	
Random Effect	*Variance Component*	df	χ^2	p Value
School mean, u_{0j}	2.64	158	633.52	0.000
Level-1 effect, r_{ij}	39.16			

Though this is a fairly wide range of plausible values, it is considerably smaller than the range of plausible values when MEAN SES is not held constant (Equation 4.4), which was (6.89, 18.39).

Do school achievement means vary significantly once MEAN SES is controlled? Here the null hypothesis that $\tau_{00} = 0$, where τ_{00} is now a residual variance, is tested by means of the statistic

$$\sum n_j \left[\overline{Y}_{\cdot j} - \hat{\gamma}_{00} - \hat{\gamma}_{01} (\text{MEAN SES})_j \right]^2 / \hat{\sigma}^2, \qquad [4.11]$$

which, under the null hypothesis, has a χ^2 distribution with $J - 2 = 158$ degrees of freedom. In our case, the statistic has a value of 633.52, $p < .001$, indicating that the null hypothesis is easily rejected; after controlling for MEAN SES, significant variation among school mean math achievement remains to be explained.

Auxiliary Statistics. By comparing the τ_{00} estimates across the two models, we can develop an index of the *proportion reduction in variance or "variance explained"* at level 2. In this application,

Proportion of variance explained in β_{0j}

$$= \frac{\hat{\tau}_{00}(\text{random ANOVA}) - \hat{\tau}_{00}(\text{MEAN SES})}{\hat{\tau}_{00}(\text{random ANOVA})}, \qquad [4.12]$$

where $\hat{\tau}_{00}(\text{random ANOVA}) = \text{Var}(\beta_{0j})$ and $\hat{\tau}_{00}(\text{MEAN SES}) = \text{Var}(\beta_{0j} \mid \text{MEAN SES})$ refer to the estimates of τ_{00} under the alternative level-2 models specified by Equations 4.2 and 4.9, respectively. Note the $\hat{\tau}_{00}(\text{random ANOVA})$ provides the base in this application, because it represents the total parameter variance in the school means that is potentially explainable by alternative level-2 models for β_{0j}. The estimated proportion of variance between schools explained by the model with MEAN SES is

$$(8.61 - 2.64)/8.61 = 0.69.$$

That is, 69% of the true between-school variance in math achievement is accounted for by MEAN SES.

After removing the effect of school MEAN SES, the correlation between pairs of scores in the same school, which had been .18, is now reduced:

$$\hat{\rho} = \hat{\tau}_{00}/(\hat{\tau}_{00} + \hat{\sigma}^2)$$

$$= 2.64/(2.64 + 39.16) = .06.$$

The estimated ρ is now a *conditional intraclass correlation* and measures the degree of dependence among observations within schools that are of the same MEAN SES.

Similarly, we can calculate the reliability of the least squares residuals, $\hat{u}_{0j}$,

$$\hat{u}_{0j} = \overline{Y}_{\cdot j} - \hat{\gamma}_{00} - \hat{\gamma}_{01}(\text{MEAN SES})_j. \qquad [4.13]$$

This reliability is a *conditional reliability*, that is, the reliability with which one can discriminate among schools that are identical on MEAN SES. Substituting our new estimates of $\hat{\tau}_{00}$ and $\hat{\sigma}^2$ into Equations 4.7 and 4.8 yields an average reliability of .74. As one might expect, the reliability of the residuals is less than the reliability of the sample means.

In summary, we have learned from the means-as-outcomes model that MEAN SES is significantly positively related to mean achievement. Nonetheless, even after we hold constant, or control for, MEAN SES, schools still vary significantly in their average achievement levels.

The Random-Coefficient Model

We now consider an analysis of the SES-math achievement relationship within the 160 schools. We conceive of each school as having "its own" regression equation with an intercept and a slope, and we shall ask the following:

1. What is the average of the 160 regression equations (i.e., what are the average intercept and slope)?
2. How much do the regression equations vary from school to school? Specifically, how much do the intercepts vary and how much do the slopes vary?
3. What is the correlation between the intercepts and the slopes? (Do schools with large intercepts [e.g., high mean achievement] also have large slopes [strong relationships between SES and achievement]?)

The Model

To answer these questions, we use the random-coefficient regression model introduced in Chapter 2. Specifically, we formulate at level 1 the student-level model

$$Y_{ij} = \beta_{0j} + \beta_{1j}(X_{ij} - \overline{X}_{\cdot j}) + r_{ij}. \qquad [4.14]$$

Each school's distribution of math achievement is characterized by two parameters: the intercept, β_{0j}, and the slope, β_{1j}. Because the student-level predictor is centered around its school mean, the intercept, β_{0j}, is the school-mean outcome (see Equation 2.29). Again, we assume $r_{ij} \sim$ independently $N(0, \sigma^2)$, where now σ^2 is the residual variance at level 1 after controlling for student SES.

These parameters, β_{0j} and β_{1j}, vary across schools in the level-2 model as a function of a grand mean and a random error:

$$\beta_{0j} = \gamma_{00} + u_{0j}, \qquad [4.15a]$$

$$\beta_{1j} = \gamma_{10} + u_{1j}, \qquad [4.15b]$$

where

γ_{00} is the average of the school means on math achievement across the population of schools;

γ_{10} is the average SES-math regression slope across those schools;

u_{0j} is the unique increment to the intercept associated with school j; and

u_{1j} is the unique increment to the slope associated with school j.

Substituting Equation 4.15 into Equation 4.14 yields a mixed model:

$$Y_{ij} = \gamma_{00} + \gamma_{10}(X_{ij} - \overline{X}_{\cdot j}) + u_{0j} + u_{1j}(X_{ij} - \overline{X}_{\cdot j}) + r_{ij}. \qquad [4.16]$$

We assume that u_{0j} and u_{1j} are multivariate normally distributed, both with expected values of 0. We label the variances in these school effects as

$$\text{Var}(u_{0j}) = \tau_{00},$$

$$\text{Var}(u_{1j}) = \tau_{11}$$

and the covariance between them as

$$\text{Cov}(u_{0j}, u_{1j}) = \tau_{01}.$$

Collecting these terms into a variance-covariance matrix,

$$\text{Var}\begin{bmatrix} u_{0j} \\ u_{1j} \end{bmatrix} = \begin{bmatrix} \tau_{00} & \tau_{01} \\ \tau_{10} & \tau_{11} \end{bmatrix} = \mathbf{T}. \qquad [4.17]$$

Because the level-2 model is unconditional for both β_{0j} and β_{1j} (i.e., no predictors are included in Equations 4.15a and 4.15b),

$$\text{Var}(u_{0j}) = \text{Var}(\beta_{0j} - \gamma_{00}) = \text{Var}(\beta_{0j}),$$
$$\text{Var}(u_{1j}) = \text{Var}(\beta_{1j} - \gamma_{10}) = \text{Var}(\beta_{1j}). \qquad [4.18]$$

Thus, the random-coefficient regression model provides estimates for the unconditional parameter variability in the random intercepts and slopes.

TABLE 4.4 Results from the Random-Coefficient Model

Fixed Effect		Coefficient	se	t Ratio
Overall mean achievement, γ_{00}		12.64	0.24	—
Mean SES-achievement slope, $\gamma_{10}{}^a$		2.19	0.13	17.16
Random Effect	*Variance*	*df*	χ^2	*p Value*
School mean, u_{0j}	8.68	159	1,770.9	0.000
SES-achievement				
slope, u_{1j}	0.68	159	213.4	0.003
Level-1 effect, r_{ij}	36.70			

Results

Fixed Effects. Table 4.4 provides the estimates for the average regression equation within schools. Using the generalized least squares estimator of Equation 3.31 (or, equivalently, Equation 3.37), we find the average school mean

$$\hat{\gamma}_{00} = 12.64$$

and the average SES-achievement slope

$$\hat{\gamma}_{10} = 2.19.$$

The corresponding standard errors, based on Equation 3.32 (or Equation 3.38), are 0.24 and 0.13, respectively. We can use this information to formally test the null hypothesis that, *on average*, student SES is not related to math achievement within schools, that is,

$$H_0: \gamma_{10} = 0.$$

Based on the test statistic of Equation 3.83:

$$t = \hat{\gamma}_{10}/(\widehat{V}_{\hat{\gamma}_{10}})^{1/2} = 2.19/0.13 = 17.16,$$

we find that, on average, student SES is significantly related ($p < .001$) to math achievement within schools.

Variance-Covariance Components. Using the general procedures for maximum likelihood estimation discussed in Chapter 3, we estimate the variance and covariance components of Equation 4.17:

$$\widehat{\text{Var}}\begin{bmatrix} u_{0j} \\ u_{1j} \end{bmatrix} = \begin{bmatrix} \hat{\tau}_{00} & \hat{\tau}_{01} \\ \hat{\tau}_{10} & \hat{\tau}_{11} \end{bmatrix} = \begin{bmatrix} 8.68 & 0.04 \\ 0.04 & 0.68 \end{bmatrix} = \widehat{\mathbf{T}}.$$

Table 4.4 also provides the test statistics (see Equation 3.101) for the hypotheses that each of the variance components along the diagonal of T are null, that is,

$$H_0: \tau_{qq} = 0 \quad \text{for } q = 0, 1.$$

Specifically, the estimated variance among the means is $\hat{\tau}_{00} = 8.68$, with a χ^2 statistic of 1,770.5, to be compared to the critical value of χ^2 with $J - 1 = 159$ degrees of freedom. We infer that highly significant differences exist among the 160 school means, a result quite similar to that encountered in the one-way ANOVA with random effects.

The estimated variance of the slopes is $\hat{\tau}_{11} = 0.68$ with a χ^2 statistic of 213.4 and 159 degrees of freedom, $p < .003$. Again, we reject the null hypothesis, in this case that $\tau_{11} = 0$, and infer that the relationship between SES and math achievement within schools does indeed vary significantly across the population of schools.

We can also now calculate a range of plausible values for both the school means and the school-specific SES-achievement slopes. Generalizing from Equation 4.4, the 95% plausible value range is

$$\hat{\gamma}_{qo} \pm 1.96(\hat{\tau}_{qq})^{1/2} \qquad [4.19]$$

for the $q = 0, \ldots, Q$ random coefficients in the level-1 model. (In this example, $Q = 1$.) The 95% plausible value range for the school means is

$$12.64 \pm 1.96(8.68)^{1/2} = (6.87, 18.41),$$

and for the SES-achievement slopes is

$$2.19 \pm 1.96(0.68)^{1/2} = (0.57, 3.81).$$

The results for the school means are similar to those previously reported for the one-way ANOVA model. In terms of the school-specific SES-achievement slopes, here, too, we find considerable variability among schools. This relationship is over seven times stronger in the most socially differentiating schools as compared to the least differentiating schools.

Auxiliary Statistics. Associated with β_{0j} and β_{1j} is also a reliability estimate (see Equation 3.59). The results are

$$\text{reliability}(\hat{\beta}_0) = 0.91$$

and

$$\text{reliability}(\hat{\beta}_1) = 0.23.$$

These indices provide answers to the question "How reliable, on average, are estimates of each school's intercept and slope based on computing the OLS regression separately for each school?" These reliabilities depend on two factors: the degree to which the true underlying parameters vary from school to school and the precision with which each school's regression equation is estimated.

The precision of estimation of the intercept (which in this application is a school mean) depends on the sample size within each school. The precision of estimation of the slope for school j depends both on the sample size and on the variability of SES within that school. Schools that are homogeneous with respect to SES will exhibit slope estimates with poor precision.

The results indicate that the intercepts are quite reliable (.91) based on an average of 50 students per school. The slope estimates are far less reliable (.23). The primary reason for the lack of reliability of the slopes is that the true slope variance across schools is much smaller than the variance of the true means. Also, the slopes are estimated with less precision than are the means because many schools are relatively homogeneous on SES.

Analogous to Equation 4.12, we can develop an index of the *proportion reduction in variance or "variance explained"* at level 1 by comparing the σ^2 estimates from these two alternative models. Notice that the estimate of the student-level variance $\hat{\sigma}^2$ is now 36.70. By comparison, the estimated variance in the one-way random ANOVA model, which did not include SES as a level-1 predictor, was 39.15. Thus,

$$\text{Proportion variance explained at level 1}$$

$$= \frac{\hat{\sigma}^2(\text{random ANOVA}) - \hat{\sigma}^2(\text{SES})}{\hat{\sigma}^2(\text{random ANOVA})}$$

$$= \frac{39.15 - 36.70}{39.15} = .063, \qquad [4.20]$$

where $\hat{\sigma}^2(\text{random ANOVA})$ and $\hat{\sigma}^2(\text{SES})$ refer to estimates of σ^2 based on the level-1 models specified by Equations 4.1 and 4.14, respectively. Note that $\sigma^2(\text{random ANOVA})$ provides the appropriate base in this application because it represents the total within-school variance that can be explained by any level-1 model.

We see that adding SES as a predictor of math achievement reduced the within-school variance by 6.3%. Hence, we can conclude that SES accounts for about 6% of the student-level variance in the outcome. When we recall that MEAN SES accounted for better than 60% of the between-school variance in the outcome, it is clear that the association between these two variables is far stronger at the school level than at the student level.

Finally, the model also produces a maximum likelihood estimate of the covariance between the intercept and the slope. When combined with the estimates of the intercept and slope variances, we can estimate the *correlation between the intercept and slope* using Equation 2.3. In this case, the correlation of slope and intercept is .02, indicating that there is little association between school means and school SES effects.

An Intercepts- and Slopes-as-Outcomes Model

Having estimated the variability of the regression equations across schools, we now seek to build an explanatory model to account for this variability. That is, we seek to understand *why* some schools have higher means than others and why in some schools the association between SES and achievement is stronger than in others.

The Model

The student-level model remains the same as in Equation 4.14. However, we now expand the school-level model to incorporate two predictors: SECTOR and MEAN SES. The resulting school-level model can be written as

$$\beta_{0j} = \gamma_{00} + \gamma_{01}(\text{MEAN SES})_j + \gamma_{02}(\text{SECTOR})_j + u_{0j}, \qquad [4.21a]$$

$$\beta_{1j} = \gamma_{10} + \gamma_{11}(\text{MEAN SES})_j + \gamma_{12}(\text{SECTOR})_j + u_{1j}, \qquad [4.21b]$$

where u_{0j} and u_{1j} are again multivariate normally distributed with means of zero and variance-covariance matrix $\mathbf{T}$. The elements of $\mathbf{T}$ are now residual or conditional variance-covariance components. That is, they represent residual dispersion in β_{0j} and β_{1j} after controlling for MEAN SES and SECTOR.

Combining the school-level model (Equation 4.21) and the student-level model (Equation 4.14) yields

$$\begin{aligned}
Y_{ij} = {} & \gamma_{00} + \gamma_{01}(\text{MEAN SES})_j + \gamma_{02}(\text{SECTOR})_j \\
& + \gamma_{10}(X_{ij} - \overline{X}_{\cdot j}) + \gamma_{11}(\text{MEAN SES})_j(X_{ij} - \overline{X}_{\cdot j}) \\
& + \gamma_{12}(\text{SECTOR})_j(X_{ij} - \overline{X}_{\cdot j}) + u_{0j} + u_{1j}(X_{ij} - \overline{X}_{\cdot j}) + r_{ij}, \qquad [4.22]
\end{aligned}$$

which illustrates that the outcome may be viewed as a function of the overall intercept (γ_{00}), the main effect of MEAN SES (γ_{01}), the main effect of SECTOR (γ_{02}), the main effect of SES (γ_{10}), and two cross-level interactions involving SECTOR with student SES (γ_{12}) and MEAN SES with student SES (γ_{11}), plus a random error

$$u_{0j} + u_{1j}(X_{ij} - \overline{X}_{\cdot j}) + r_{ij}.$$

Three kinds of questions motivate the analysis:

1. Do MEAN SES and SECTOR significantly predict the intercept? We estimate γ_{01} to study whether high-SES schools differ from low-SES schools in mean achievement (controlling for SECTOR). Similarly, we estimate γ_{02} to learn whether Catholic schools differ from public schools in terms of the mean achievement once MEAN SES is controlled.

2. Do MEAN SES and SECTOR significantly predict the within-school slopes? We estimate γ_{11} to discover whether high-SES schools differ from low-SES schools in terms of the strength of association between student SES and achievement within them (controlling for SECTOR). We estimate γ_{12} to examine whether Catholic schools differ from public schools in terms of the strength of association between student SES and achievement (controlling for MEAN SES).

3. How much variation in the intercepts and the slopes is explained by using SECTOR and MEAN SES as predictors? To answer these questions, we estimate $\mathrm{Var}(u_{0j}) = \tau_{00}$ and $\mathrm{Var}(u_{1j}) = \tau_{11}$ and compare these with the estimates presented above from the random-coefficient regression model.

Results

Fixed Effects. Table 4.5 displays the results. We see, first, that MEAN SES is positively related to school mean math achievement, $\hat{\gamma}_{01} = 5.33$, $t = 14.45$. Also, Catholic schools have significantly higher mean achievement than do public schools, controlling for the effect of MEAN SES, $\hat{\gamma}_{02} = 1.23$, $t = 4.00$.

With regard to the slopes, there is a tendency for schools of high MEAN SES to have larger slopes than do schools with low MEAN SES, $\hat{\gamma}_{11} = 1.03$, $t = 3.42$. Catholic schools have significantly weaker SES slopes, on average, than do public schools, $\hat{\gamma}_{12} = -1.64$, $t = -6.76$.

These results are depicted graphically in Figure 4.1. The fitted relationship between SES and math achievement is displayed for the Catholic and public sectors. Within each sector, results are displayed for (1) a high-SES school (one standard deviation above the mean), (2) a medium-SES school, and (3) a low-SES school (one standard deviation below the mean). Perhaps the most notable feature of the figure is that the within-school math-SES slopes are substantially less steep in the Catholic sector than in the public sector. This sector effect holds for schools at each level of MEAN SES. There is also

TABLE 4.5 Results from the Intercepts- and Slopes-as-Outcomes Model

Fixed Effects	Coefficient	se	t Ratio	
Model for school means				
INTERCEPT, γ_{00}	12.10	0.20	—	
MEAN SES, γ_{01}	5.33	0.37	14.45	
SECTOR, γ_{02}	1.23	0.31	4.00	
Model for SES-achievement slopes				
INTERCEPT, γ_{10}	2.94	0.16	—	
MEAN SES, γ_{11}	1.03	0.30	3.42	
SECTOR, γ_{12}	−1.64	0.24	−6.76	
Random Effects	Variance Component	df	χ^2	p Value
School mean, u_{0j}	2.38	157	605.30	0.000
SES-achievement				
slope, u_{1j}	0.15	157	162.31	0.369
Level-1 effect, r_{1j}	36.68			

a tendency for high-SES schools to have steeper slopes than do low-SES schools. This tendency is evident in both sectors. Main effects of MEAN SES and SECTOR are also evident. The MEAN SES effect is manifest by the solid lines that in both plots have positive slopes.

Chapter 3 discusses a procedure for testing multiparameter hypotheses regarding the fixed effects. One may wonder, for example, whether the variable SECTOR is needed in the model. Perhaps no distinction is justified between Catholic and public schools in terms of effectiveness or equity. The null hypothesis may be written as

$$H_0: \gamma_{02} = 0$$

$$\gamma_{12} = 0.$$

If $\gamma_{02} = 0$, Catholic and public schools do not differ in mean achievement after controlling for MEAN SES. Similarly, if $\gamma_{12} = 0$, Catholic and public schools do not differ with respect to their average SES-math achievement relationships with schools. If both null hypotheses are true, the variable SECTOR may be dropped from the model. Using Equation 3.91, we obtain a χ^2 statistic of 64.38, df $= 2$, $p < .001$, indicating that one or both of the null hypotheses is false.

Variance-Covariance Components. Recall that the results of fitting the random-coefficient model provided information about the variation and

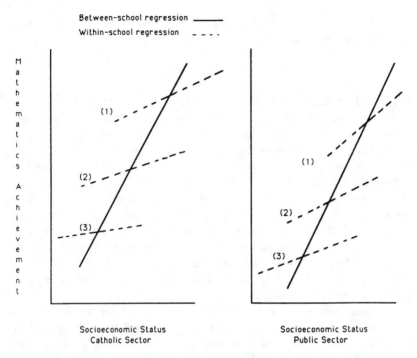

Figure 4.1. Regressions of Mathematics Achievement as a Function of Student and School SES Within Catholic and Public Sectors

NOTE: Schools 1, 2, and 3 are of high, medium, and low SES, respectively.

covariation of the intercepts and SES slopes across schools. Our interest now focuses on the residual variation and covariation of the intercepts and slopes, that is, the variation left unexplained by SECTOR and MEAN SES. The maximum likelihood point estimates are

$$\widehat{\text{Var}}\begin{pmatrix} u_{0j} \\ u_{1j} \end{pmatrix} = \begin{pmatrix} \hat{\tau}_{00} & \hat{\tau}_{01} \\ \hat{\tau}_{10} & \hat{\tau}_{11} \end{pmatrix} = \begin{pmatrix} 2.38 & 0.19 \\ 0.19 & 0.15 \end{pmatrix}. \qquad [4.23]$$

We note that both $\hat{\tau}_{00}$ and $\hat{\tau}_{11}$, the estimated variances of the intercepts and the slopes, are considerably smaller than they had been without control for SECTOR and MEAN SES. Perhaps there remains no significant residual variation in the intercepts and slopes after control for SECTOR and MEAN SES. Regarding the intercepts, the null hypothesis

$$H_0: \tau_{00} = 0$$

is rejected, as indicated by the χ^2 statistic of 605.30, df $= J - S_q - 1 = 157, p < .001$. Thus, significant variation in the intercepts remains unexplained even after controlling for SECTOR and MEAN SES. Regarding the slopes, the null hypothesis

$$H_0: \tau_{11} = 0$$

is retained, as indicated by the χ^2 statistic of 162.31, df $= J - S_q - 1 = 157$, $p = .369$. This test suggests that no significant variation in the slopes remains unexplained after controlling for SECTOR and MEAN SES.

Another way to examine the significance of variance and covariance components is to compare two models, one model including the variance components of interest and a second, simpler model that constrains certain components to zero. If the fit of the simpler model to the data is significantly worse than the fit of the more complex model, the simpler model is rejected as inadequately representing the variation in the data. However, if there is no significant difference in the fit of the two models, the simpler model will typically be preferred. Applying this logic to the current data, we compare a model with random intercepts and slopes to a model with only a random intercept.

Our "intercepts- and slopes-as-outcomes" model included four unique variance and covariance parameters: (a) the student-level variance, σ^2; (b) the residual variance of the school means, τ_{00}; (c) the residual variance of the SES-math slopes, τ_{11}; and (d) the residual covariance between the means and the slopes, τ_{01}. In general, the number of variance-covariance parameters estimated in a two-level model is $m(m+1)/2 + 1$, where m is the number of random effects in the level-2 model. In our case, $m = 2$. Chapter 3 (see Equations 3.105 through 3.107) described a likelihood-ratio test that can be used to test the composite null hypothesis

$$H_0: \begin{pmatrix} \tau_{11} = 0 \\ \tau_{01} = 0 \end{pmatrix}.$$

One first estimates the full model with four variance-covariance parameters, and then one estimates a reduced model with just two parameters (σ^2 and τ_{00})—that is, where τ_{11} and τ_{01} have been constrained to zero. One then compares the deviance associated with the two models and asks whether the reduction in deviance associated with the more complex model is justified.

In our case, the results are as follows:

Model	Number of Parameters	Deviance
Restricted, D_0	2	46,514.0
Unrestricted, D_1	4	46,513.1

The reduction in deviance is 0.9, which is not significant when compared against the χ^2 distribution with 2 df. Hence, the simpler model seems justified. We infer that explanatory power is not significantly enhanced by specifying the residual SES-achievement slopes as random. The reduced model with β_{1j} specified as nonrandomly varying appears sufficient.

Auxiliary Statistics. Analogous to Equation 4.12, we can develop a *proportion reduction in variance or variance-explained statistic for each of the random coefficients (intercepts and slopes) from the level-1 model*. The variance estimates from the random-coefficient regression model estimated earlier provide the base for these statistics:

Proportion variance explained in β_{qj}

$$= \frac{\hat{\tau}_{qq}(\text{random regression}) - \hat{\tau}_{qq}(\text{fitted model})}{\hat{\tau}_{qq}(\text{random regression})}, \qquad [4.24]$$

where $\hat{\tau}_{qq}$(random regression) denotes the qth diagonal element of **T** estimated under the random-regression model (Equations 4.14 and 4.15) and $\hat{\tau}_{qq}$(fitted model) denotes the corresponding element in the T matrix estimated under an intercepts- and slopes-as-outcomes model (in this case Equations 4.14 and 4.21).

In this application, we see a substantial reduction in variance of the school means once MEAN SES and SECTOR are controlled. Specifically, whereas the unconditional variance of intercepts had been 8.68, the residual variance is now $\hat{\tau}_{00} = 2.38$. This means that 73% of the parameter variation in mean achievement, $\text{Var}(\beta_{0j})$, has been explained by MEAN SES and SECTOR [i.e., $(8.68 - 2.38)/8.68 = 0.73$]. Similarly, the residual variance of the slopes is $\hat{\tau}_{11} = 0.15$, which, when compared to the unconditional variance of .68, implies a reduction of 78%. Clearly, most of the slope variability is associated with MEAN SES and SECTOR. Once this is controlled, only a small residual portion of variation remains unexplained. Chapter 5 provides a more detailed discussion, with some caveats, of strategies for monitoring explained variance (see "Use of Proportion Reduction in Variance Statistics").

Estimating the Level-1 Coefficients for a Particular Unit

In this chapter, we have characterized the distribution of achievement in each high school in terms of two school-specific parameters: a school's mean math achievement and a regression coefficient describing the relationship between SES and math achievement. We have viewed these level-1 coefficients as "random parameters" varying over the population of schools with some of that random variation a function of measured predictors. As mentioned in Chapter 3, we can obtain both point and interval estimates for each random level-1 coefficient. Formally, these are empirical Bayes estimators, also known as shrinkage estimators. These shrinkage estimators may be subdivided into two categories: *unconditional* and *conditional* shrinkage estimators. We illustrate each approach and compare these with the OLS estimates.

Ordinary Least Squares

The most obvious strategy for estimating the regression equation for a particular school is simply to fit a separate model to each school's data by ordinary least squares (OLS). The model for each school might simply be Equation 4.14. Recall that with SES centered around the school mean, the intercept β_{0j} is the mean outcome for that school, and the regression coefficient β_{1j} represents the expected difference in achievement per unit difference in SES within that school. OLS will produce unbiased estimates of these parameters for any school that has at least two cases. Indeed, if the errors of the model are independently normally distributed, the OLS estimates are the unique, minimum-variance, unbiased estimators of these parameters. Nonetheless, the OLS estimates for any given school may not be very accurate as we illustrate below.

Columns 1 and 2 in Table 4.6 present separate OLS estimates for 12 selected schools out of the 160 cases in the HS&B data set. These estimates were calculated for each school using Equation 3.54. Based on these estimates, we might identify case 4 as an especially good school where there is a high average level of achievement, $\hat{\beta}_{04} = 16.26$, that is distributed in an equitable social fashion, $\hat{\beta}_{14} = 0.13$.

Figure 4.2a shows the OLS estimates for all 160 schools. The intercept estimates (vertical axis) are plotted against the slope estimates (horizontal axis). Quite a few schools yield negative estimates of the SES-achievement relationship. Moreover, the apparent dispersion of the OLS estimates greatly exceeds the maximum likelihood estimate of the variance of the true slopes. Earlier, we estimated the variance of the true slope parameters to be 0.68. Yet the sample variance of the OLS slope estimates depicted in Figure 4.2a is 2.66. If we were to define effective and equitable schools as those with large means and small SES-math achievement slopes, we might identify many schools like case 4.

TABLE 4.6 Comparison of Estimated Level-1 Coefficients for a Sample of HS&B Cases

Case	OLS Estimates $\hat{\beta}_{0j}$	$\hat{\beta}_{1j}$	Empirical Bayes Estimates Unconditional Model β_{0j}^*	β_{1j}^*	Empirical Bayes Estimates Conditional Model β_{0j}^*	β_{1j}^*	n_j	MEAN SES	SECTOR
4	16.26	0.13	15.62	2.05	16.20	1.82	20	0.53	1
15	15.98	2.15	15.74	2.19	16.01	1.85	53	0.52	1
17	18.11	0.09	17.41	1.95	17.25	3.67	29	0.69	0
22	11.14	−0.78	11.22	1.16	10.89	0.58	67	−0.62	1
27	13.40	4.10	13.32	2.53	12.95	3.02	38	−0.06	0
53	9.52	3.74	9.76	2.74	9.37	2.47	51	−0.64	0
69	11.47	6.18	11.64	2.71	11.92	3.06	25	0.08	0
75	9.06	1.65	9.28	2.01	9.30	0.70	63	−0.59	1
81	15.42	5.26	15.25	3.12	15.52	2.01	66	0.43	1
90	12.14	1.97	12.18	2.14	12.34	3.01	50	0.19	0
135	4.55	0.25	6.42	1.93	8.55	2.61	14	0.03	0
153	10.28	0.76	10.71	2.07	9.67	2.36	19	−0.59	0

Unconditional Shrinkage

In general, the accuracy of OLS regression estimates for any school depends on the sample size within the school, n_j, and the range represented in the level-1 predictor variable, X_{ij}. If n_j is small, the mean estimate, $\hat{\beta}_{0j}$, will be imprecise. If a school has a small sample or a restricted range on SES, the slope estimate, $\hat{\beta}_{1j}$, will also tend to be imprecise. The empirical Bayes (EB) estimates of each school's regression line takes into account this imprecision in the OLS estimates.

Columns 3 and 4 in Table 4.6 present the EB estimates for the 12 selected schools from HS&B. These estimates, β_{0j}^* and β_{1j}^*, are based on the unconditional level-2 model (Equations 4.14 and 4.15) and calculated using Equation 3.56 (or, equivalently, Equation 3.66). Notice that the EB estimates for case 4 differ substantially from the OLS estimates. The estimated average achievement level has dropped by 0.64 (from 16.26 to 15.62) and the SES-achievement slope has risen from 0.13 to 2.05. While the estimate of the overall achievement level for the school remains relatively high, the equity effect has disappeared. While case 4 looked superior to case 15 in terms of the OLS estimates, these two schools appear indistinguishable in terms of the empirical Bayes estimates (15.62 versus 15.74 for β_{0j}^* and 2.05 versus 2.19 for β_{1j}^*). The key factor here is the relatively small sample size of only 20 students in case 4. As a result, the OLS estimates for this unit are not very precise, and the EB estimates are shrunk toward the overall mean achievement, $\hat{\gamma}_{00} = 12.64$, and the overall mean SES-achievement slope, $\hat{\gamma}_{10} = 2.19$. Notice that this occurs for all of the cases with relatively small sample sizes (cases 17, 69, 135, and 153), with sample sizes 29, 25, 14, and 19, respectively.

Figure 4.2b displays the empirical Bayes estimates of the intercepts (vertical axis) and the math-SES slopes (horizontal axis) for all 160 schools. Notice that the empirical Bayes slope estimates are much more concentrated around the sample average than are the OLS estimates in Figure 4.2a. Unlike the collection of OLS slope estimates, none of the empirical Bayes estimates is negative. Also, the sample variance of the empirical Bayes slope estimates is only .14, much smaller than the sample variance of the OLS slope estimates (2.66). In fact, the sample variance of the empirical Bayes slope estimates is smaller than the maximum likelihood estimate of the variance of the true slopes (0.68).

We note that these results generalize:

$$\text{Var}(\hat{\beta}_j) \qquad > \qquad \widehat{\text{Var}}(\beta_j) \qquad > \qquad \text{Var}(\beta_j^*)$$

observed	maximum	observed variability
variability in >	likelihood estimates >	in the empirical
OLS estimates	of variance in level-	Bayes estimates
	1 coefficients, i.e.	
	$\hat{\tau}_{00}, \hat{\tau}_{11}$ under	
	Equation 4.15	

The fact that the empirical Bayes estimates have less variance than the estimated true variance is an expected result. In general, the shrinkage is slightly exaggerated; empirical Bayes tends to pull the estimates "too far" toward the sample average.

It is also interesting to contrast the slope shrinkage in Figure 4.2, with the results for the achievement intercepts. Recall that the intercepts are just the mean achievement in each school and are much more reliably estimated than are the slopes (.91 versus .23). Given the greater precision of the intercept estimates, we would expect that the empirical Bayes estimator would rely more heavily on this component, and less shrinkage should occur. This result is displayed in Figure 4.2 (compare the vertical axes of Figures 4.2a and 4.2b). Unlike the slopes, where the shrinkage is substantial, the difference between the OLS and the empirical Bayes estimates for the intercepts is only modest. This same pattern can be observed in the results for the 12-school subsample presented in Table 4.6.

In general, the behavior of the empirical Bayes estimator is simpler in the case of random-intercept models than in models that also have random slopes.

(a) Ordinary Least Squares

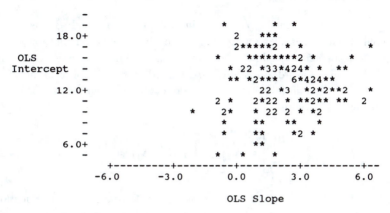

OLS Slope

(b) Empirical Bayes[a]

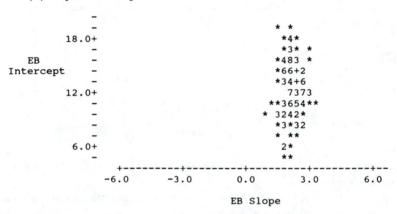

EB Slope

Figure 4.2. Ordinary Least Squares and Empirical Bayes Intercept and Slope Estimates for 160 High Schools

NOTE: Intercept estimates are plotted on the vertical axis, slope estimates on the horizontal axis.
a. A "+" indicates the presence of more than nine observations.

For example, consider the present case, in which we focus on each school's SES-achievement slope and its intercept. The empirical Bayes estimate of each component will depend on the other component. This dependence will be strong when the maximum likelihood estimate of the correlation between the two components is large.

Conditional Shrinkage

A tool for increasing accuracy in estimating β_{0j} and β_{1j} is conditional shrinkage. Rather than pulling each OLS regression line toward the grand-mean regression line of $\hat{\gamma}_{00}$ and $\hat{\gamma}_{10}$, the OLS regression lines will now be pulled toward a *predicted value* based on the school-level model.

Unconditional shrinkage of the random-coefficient regression model (i.e., Equation 4.15) yields

$$\begin{bmatrix} \beta_{0j}^* \\ \beta_{1j}^* \end{bmatrix} = \Lambda_j \begin{bmatrix} \hat{\beta}_{0j} \\ \hat{\beta}_{1j} \end{bmatrix} + (\mathbf{I} - \Lambda_j) \begin{bmatrix} \hat{\gamma}_{00} \\ \hat{\gamma}_{10} \end{bmatrix}, \tag{4.25}$$

where Λ_j is based on the estimation of σ^2 and $\mathbf{T}$ for the model in Equations 4.14 and 4.15. In contrast, the intercepts- and slopes-as-outcomes model (see Equation 3.56 or, equivalently, Equation 3.66) yields conditional shrinkage toward predicted values of β_{0j} and β_{1j}. That is,

$$\begin{bmatrix} \beta_{0j}^* \\ \beta_{1j}^* \end{bmatrix} = \Lambda_j \begin{bmatrix} \hat{\beta}_{0j} \\ \hat{\beta}_{1j} \end{bmatrix}$$

$$+ (\mathbf{I} - \Lambda_j) \begin{bmatrix} \hat{\gamma}_{00} + \hat{\gamma}_{01} \ (\text{MEAN SES})_j \ + \hat{\gamma}_{02} \ (\text{SECTOR}); \\ \hat{\gamma}_{10} + \hat{\gamma}_{11} \ (\text{MEAN SES})_j \quad \hat{\gamma}_{12} \ (\text{SECTOR}); \end{bmatrix}, \tag{4.26}$$

where Λ_j is now based on the estimation of σ^2 and $\mathbf{T}$ for the model in Equations 4.14 and 4.21.

As with unconditional shrinkage, the effects of conditional shrinkage can be quite extreme when the within-group sample size, n_j, is small. (See results in columns 5 and 6 in Table 4.6.) Notice for case 135 that the OLS estimates for β_{0j} and β_{1j} were $(4.55, 0.25)$ respectively; with unconditional shrinkage, they moved to $(6.42, 1.93)$, respectively; and for conditional shrinkage they ended up at $(8.55, 2.61)$. Under conditional shrinkage, the OLS regression line for case 135 is being pulled toward a predicted value for β_{0j} and β_{1j} based on the information from this school about its social class (MEAN SES $= .03$) and sector (SECTOR $= 0 =$ public). Substituting these values into the estimated equations in Table 4.5 yields predictions of

$$\hat{E}(\beta_{0j}) = 12.10 + 5.33(0.03) + 1.23(0) = 12.26,$$

$$\hat{E}(\beta_{1j}) = 2.94 + 1.03(0.03) - 1.64(0) = 2.97.$$

Notice that the empirical Bayes estimate for β_{1j}, $\beta_{1j}^* = 2.61$, entails virtual complete shrinkage from the original OLS value of 0.25 toward the predicted value of 2.97. In addition to the fact that the sample size is small for this unit ($n_{135} = 14$) and that regression slopes are less reliable, the amount of change under conditional shrinkage also depends on the precision of the prediction equations, which, in turn, are a function of the residual variances in **T**. Since $\hat{\tau}_{11} = 0.15$, the prediction equation is relatively precise in this application and the shrinkage more extensive. We note that the same factors are at work in the conditional shrinkage of $\hat{\beta}_{0j}$ toward β_{0j}^*. The proportional amount of shrinkage $\hat{\beta}_{0j}$ versus $\hat{\beta}_{1j}$ is less, however, because school means are considerably more reliable than slopes, for any fixed value of n_j. Since the original sample mean is relatively more precise, empirical Bayes gives relatively more weight to $\hat{\beta}_{0j}$ in the estimation of β_{0j}^*.

Results in Table 4.6 also illustrate the differential effect that conditional shrinkage can have on various units. Compare, for example, case 22 (a low-SES Catholic school) with case 27 (an average-SES public school). The OLS estimates suggest substantial differences between these two schools in both average achievement level (11.14 versus 13.40) and SES-achievement slopes (-0.78 versus 4.10). With unconditional shrinkage, much of the observed differences are "shrunk out." We know, however, from the results in Table 4.6 that school MEAN SES and SECTOR predict both the mean achievement level and the SES-achievement slope for a school. When we take this into account through conditional shrinkage, most of the original differences reappear: 10.89 versus 12.95 for β_{0j} and 0.58 versus 3.02 for β_{1j}.

Another interesting set of comparisons are schools 17 and 81. Both are relatively high SES schools, with case 17 being public and case 81 being Catholic. Both schools have relatively high average achievement levels ($\hat{\beta}_{0,17} = 18.11$; $\hat{\beta}_{0,81} = 15.42$), but the Catholic school has a very steep SES-achievement slope ($\hat{\beta}_{1,81} = 5.26$) as compared to the public school ($\hat{\beta}_{1,17} = 0.09$). Both of the schools are multivariate outliers in that their OLS slope estimates appear inconsistent with all the other information we have in the data set. That is, from Table 4.5 we expect high-SES public schools to have steep slopes, not their Catholic counterparts. In this instance, conditional shrinkage literally reorders the two equations. While β_{0j}^* remains higher for the public school (17.25 versus 15.52), the conditional shrinkage estimate for the SES-achievement slopes is now lower in the Catholic school than in the public (2.01 versus 3.67)!

The effects of conditional shrinkage can also be discerned through the use of OLS and empirical Bayes residuals (see Equations 3.50, 3.60; and

3.49, 3.61 respectively). The OLS residuals for the intercepts and slopes in Equation 4.21 are

$$\hat{u}_{0j} = \hat{\beta}_{0j} - \left[\hat{\gamma}_{00} + \hat{\gamma}_{01}(\text{MEAN SES})_j + \hat{\gamma}_{02}(\text{SECTOR})_j\right], \qquad [4.27a]$$

$$\hat{u}_{1j} = \hat{\beta}_{1j} - \left[\hat{\gamma}_{10} + \hat{\gamma}_{11}(\text{MEAN SES})_j + \hat{\gamma}_{12}(\text{SECTOR})_j\right]. \qquad [4.27b]$$

The corresponding empirical Bayes residuals are

$$u_{0j}^* = \beta_{0j}^* - \left[\hat{\gamma}_{00} + \hat{\gamma}_{01}(\text{MEAN SES})_j + \hat{\gamma}_{02}(\text{SECTOR})_j\right], \qquad [4.28a]$$

$$u_{1j}^* = \beta_{1j}^* - \left[\hat{\gamma}_{10} + \hat{\gamma}_{11}(\text{MEAN SES})_j + \hat{\gamma}_{12}(\text{SECTOR})_j\right]. \qquad [4.28b]$$

Figure 4.3 displays the results. The intercept residuals are plotted on the vertical axis and the slope residuals on the horizontal axis. The OLS slope residuals are highly misleading. They suggest considerable unexplained variability in the SES-achievement relationships. In contrast, the empirical Bayes residuals are tightly clumped around zero with even less dispersion than in Figure 4.2. This result is consistent with the results in Table 4.5, where 78% of the variability in β_{1j} was accounted for by MEAN SES and SECTOR.

In contrast, the empirical Bayes and OLS residuals for the intercept are much more similar. These residuals, however, are less dispersed than for the unconditional model (Figure 4.2), which is consistent with the fact that Equation 4.21a accounts for about 73% of the variance in β_{0j}.

Comparison of Interval Estimates

In addition to point estimates for the level-1 coefficients, we can also compute empirical Bayes interval estimates using Equation 3.65. We illustrate here the use of these procedures for two selected schools, cases 22 and 135 from the HS&B data, and compare results to confidence interval estimates from separate OLS regressions on each school's individual data set. The 95% confidence intervals for β_{0j} and β_{1j} under ordinary least squares, unconditional and conditional shrinkage appear in Table 4.7.

Notice that for case 22, where $n_j = 67$, the widths of the confidence intervals for school mean achievement, β_{0j}, are quite similar across all three analyses. This results from the large within-school sample size coupled with the overall high reliability for school means. In contrast, case 135, where $n_j = 14$, experiences some reduction in the width of the confidence intervals as we move from OLS to unconditional shrinkage to conditional shrinkage. The 95% confidence interval under the conditional model of Equation 4.21 is about a third smaller than obtained from ordinary least squares estimates

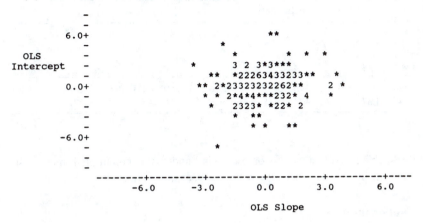

(a) Ordinary Least Squares Residuals

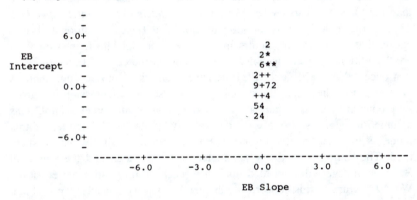

(b) Empirical Bayes Residuals[a]

Figure 4.3. Ordinary Least Squares and Empirical Bayes Intercept and Slope Residuals for 160 High Schools

NOTE: Intercept residuals are plotted on the vertical axis, slope residuals on the horizontal axis.
a. A "+" indicates the presence of more than nine observations.

using only this school's data. A gain in precision has been effected by bringing to bear on this estimation problem all of the information in the data set.

These improvements in precision are even more substantial when we compare the confidence interval estimates for the SES-achievement slopes. For case 22, the empirical Bayes 95% confidence interval, based on the conditional model, is about 75% smaller than OLS; for case 135, it is about 85% smaller. Notice that in both cases the likelihood of a negative

TABLE 4.7 Comparison of 95% Confidence Interval Estimates for Random
Level-1 Coefficients

	OLS		Unconditional Shrinkage		Conditional Shrinkage	
Case	β_{0j}	β_{1j}	β_{0j}	β_{1j}	β_{0j}	β_{1j}
22	(9.69, 12.59)	(−3.01, 1.45)	(9.81, 12.63)	(−0.15, 2.43)	(9.64, 12.24)	(0.24, 1.10)
135	(1.37, 7.73)	(−4.11, 4.61)	(3.65, 9.21)	(0.41, 3.45)	(6.43, 10.77)	(2.19, 3.11)

SES-achievement slope becomes trivial under the conditional model; in
contrast, under OLS, negative results appear quite plausible.

Cautionary Note

The conditional shrinkage estimators will be substantially more accurate
than the OLS estimators *when the level-2 model is appropriately specified.*
That is, the underlying assumption of empirical Bayes conditional shrinkage is that, given the predictors in the level-2 model, the regression lines
are "conditionally exchangeable." This means, in the case of Equation 4.21,
that once MEAN SES and SECTOR have been taken into account, there is
no reason to believe that the deviation of any school's regression line from
its predicted value is larger or smaller than that of any other school. This
assumption depends strongly on the validity of the level-2 model. If that
model is misspecified, the empirical Bayes estimates will also be misspecified: The estimates of the γ parameters will be biased and the empirical
Bayes shrinkage will lead to distortion in each group's estimated equation.
We shall return to this concern in Chapter 5 when we consider the problem
of estimating the effectiveness of individual organizations.

Summary of Terms Introduced in This Chapter

Plausible value range for β_q: We can compute a range of plausible values
for any random level-1 coefficient, β_q. The 95% plausible value range for
β_q is $\gamma_{q0} \pm 1.96(\tau_{qq})^{1/2}$. Based on the assumption that the random effects at
level 2 are normally distributed, we would expect to find values of β_{qj} within
range for 95% of the level-2 units.

Proportion of variance explained at level 1: An index of the proportion
reduction in variance or "variance explained" at level 1 as X predictors are

entered into the level-1 model. This is computed by comparing the residual σ^2 estimate from a fitted model with the σ^2 estimate from some "base" or reference model. The reference model chosen for computing these statistics at level 1 is often the one-way random-effects ANOVA model. (See Equation 4.20.)

Proportion of variance explained at level 2 in each β_q: An index of the proportion reduction in variance or "variance explained" in each random level-1 coefficient (intercepts and slopes) as W predictors are added to the level-2 model for any β_{qj}. This is computed by comparing the residual τ_{qq} estimate from a fitted model with the τ_{qq} estimate from some "base" or reference model. The reference model chosen for computing these statistics at level 2 is often the random-coefficient regression model. (See Equation 4.24.)

Note

1. Data files and a user's manual are available from the Office of Educational Research and Improvement, U.S. Department of Education, 55 New Jersey Avenue, Washington, DC 20208-1327.

Section II
Basic Applications

Applications in Organizational Research

Background Issues in Research on Organizational Effects

A number of conceptual and technical difficulties have plagued past analyses of multilevel data in organizational research. Among the most commonly
encountered difficulties have been aggregation bias, misestimated standard
errors, and heterogeneity of regression.

In brief, aggregation bias can occur when a variable takes on different
meanings and therefore may have different effects at different organizational
levels. In educational research, for example, the average social class of a
school may have an effect on student achievement above and beyond the
effect of the individual child's social class. At the student level, social class
provides a measure of the intellectual and tangible resources in a child's
home environment. At the school level, it is a proxy measure of a school's

resources and normative environment. Hierarchical linear models help resolve this confounding by facilitating a decomposition of any observed relationship between variables, such as achievement and social class, into separate level-1 and level-2 components.

Misestimated standard errors occur with multilevel data when we fail to take into account the dependence among individual responses within the same organization. This dependence may arise because of shared experiences within the organization or because of the ways in which individuals were initially drawn into the organization. Hierarchical linear models resolve this problem by incorporating into the statistical model a unique random effect for each organizational unit. The variability in these random effects is taken into account in estimating standard errors. In the terminology of survey research, these standard error estimates adjust for the intraclass correlation (or related to it, the design effect) that occurs as a result of cluster sampling.

Heterogeneity of regression occurs when the relationships between individual characteristics and outcomes vary across organizations. Although this phenomenon has often been viewed as a methodological nuisance, the causes of heterogeneity of regression are often of substantive interest. Hierarchical linear models enable the investigator to estimate a separate set of regression coefficients for each organizational unit, and then to model variation among the organizations in their sets of coefficients as multivariate outcomes to be explained by organizational factors. Burstein (1980) provided an early review of this idea of slopes-as-outcomes.

Formulating Models

Many questions about how organizations affect the individuals within them can be formulated as two-level hierarchical linear models. At level 1, the units are persons and each person's outcome is represented as a function of a set of individual characteristics. At level 2, the units are organizations. The regression coefficients in the level-1 model for each organization are conceived as outcome variables that are hypothesized to depend on specific organizational characteristics.

Person-Level Model (Level 1)

We denote the outcome for person i in organization j as Y_{ij}. This outcome is represented as a function of individual characteristics, X_{qij}, and a model error r_{ij}:

$$Y_{ij} = \beta_{0j} + \beta_{1j}X_{1ij} + \beta_{2j}X_{2ij} + \cdots + \beta_{Qj}X_{Qij} + r_{ij}, \qquad [5.1]$$

where we will initially assume that $r_{ij} \sim N(0, \sigma^2)$. (Extensions to models with heterogeneous level-1 variances are introduced in a later section of this chapter.)

The regression coefficients β_{qj}, $q = 0, \ldots, Q$, indicate how the outcome is distributed in organization j as a function of the measured person characteristics. We therefore term these coefficients *distributive effects*.

Organization-Level Model (Level 2)

The effects for each organization, captured in the set of β_{qj}s in Equation 5.1, are presumed to vary across units. This variation is in turn modeled in a set of $Q + 1$ level-2 equations—one for each of the regression coefficients from the level-1 model. Each β_{qj} is conceived as an outcome variable that depends on a set of organization-level variables, W_{sj}, and a unique organization effect, u_{qj}. Each β_{qj} has a model of the form

$$\beta_{qj} = \gamma_{q0} + \gamma_{q1}W_{1j} + \gamma_{q2}W_{2j} + \cdots + \gamma_{qS_q}W_{S_qj} + u_{qj}. \qquad [5.2]$$

$$
\begin{array}{ccc}
\begin{array}{c}\text{distributive}\\ \text{effects in}\\ \text{organization } j\end{array} & = & \begin{array}{c}\text{effects of organizational}\\ \text{characteristics on the}\\ \text{distribution of outcomes}\\ \text{within organization } j\end{array} + \begin{array}{c}\text{unique effect}\\ \text{associated with}\\ \text{organization } j\end{array}
\end{array}
$$

where a unique set of predictors W_s ($s = 1, \ldots, S_q$) may be specified for each β_q.

The γ_{qs} coefficients capture the influence of organizational variables, W_{sj}, on the within-organization relationships represented by β_{qj}. We assume that the set of $Q + 1$ level-2 random effects is multivariate normally distributed. Each u_{qj} has a mean of 0, some variance, τ_{qq}, and with covariances, $\tau_{qq'}$, between any two random effects q and q'. These are the standard level-2 model assumptions introduced in Chapter 3 and discussed in more detail in Chapter 9.

The next two sections of this chapter demonstrate how this model can be applied to investigate two broad classes of organizational effects. In "Case 1," some aspect of the organization such as its technology, structure, or climate exerts a common influence on each person within it. Such organization effects modify only the mean level of the outcome for the organization. They leave unchanged the distribution of effects among persons within the organization. In statistical terms, only the intercept, β_{0j}, varies across organizations; all other level-1 coefficients remain constant. As discussed in this section, such problems involve the use of random-intercept models.

In "Case 2," organization effects may modify not only the mean level of outcomes but also how effects are distributed among individuals. In statistical terms, the intercept and regression slopes vary among the units. This section details this application of the full hierarchical linear model with both intercepts- and slopes-as-outcomes.

The remainder of the chapter consists of a series of "special topics" concerning the design and use of hierarchical models in organizational applications. Much of the material presented here is new to the second edition. We demonstrate how the basic hierarchical model can be generalized to model heterogeneous variances at level 1. Following this, we detail how the choice of centering for level-1 variables affects the estimation of random level-1 coefficients, β_j, fixed effects, γ, and the variance-covariance components $\tau_{qq}, \tau_{qq'}, \sigma^2$. We then discuss some complications that can arise in interpreting proportion in variance-explained statistics in more complex organizational effects models. Following this, we describe how to use the empirical Bayes estimates of level-1 coefficients as performance indicators for specific organizational units and discuss validity concerns that may arise in such applications. The chapter concludes with an introduction to power considerations in designing new data collections for two-level organizational effects studies.

Case 1: Modeling the Common Effects
of Organizations via Random-Intercept Models

The basic problem in this case is that the key predictors are measured at the organization level, but the outcome variable is measured at the person level. Historically, such data have raised questions about the appropriate unit of analysis (organization or person) and the problems associated with either choice. If the data are analyzed at the person level, thereby ignoring the nesting of individuals within organizational units, the estimated standard errors will be too small, and the risk of type I errors inflated. Alternatively, if the data are analyzed at the organization level, using the means of the person responses as the outcome, it becomes problematic to incorporate other level-1 predictors into the analysis. In addition, inefficient and biased estimates of organizational effects can result. The key fact is that random variation and structural effects may exist at both levels, and a multilevel modeling framework is required to explicitly represent these features.

A Simple Random-Intercept Model

The basic idea of the random-intercept model was previously introduced in Chapter 2. The key feature of such models is that only the intercept parameter in the level-1 model, β_{0j}, in Equation 5.1, is assumed to vary at level 2. Specifically, the organization model at level 2 consists of

$$\beta_{0j} = \gamma_{00} + \gamma_{01}W_{1j} + \gamma_{02}W_{2j} + \cdots + \gamma_{0S}W_{Sj} + u_{0j}$$

$$\beta_{1j} = \gamma_{10}$$

$$\beta_{2j} = \gamma_{20}$$

. .

. . [5.3]

. .

$$\beta_{QJ} = \gamma_{Q0}.$$

Example: Examining School Effects on Teacher Efficacy

Bryk and Driscoll (1988) used the Administrator and Teacher Supplement of the High School and Beyond Survey to investigate how characteristics of school organization were related to teachers' sense of efficacy in their work. Specifically, they hypothesized that teachers' efficacy would be higher in schools with a communal, rather than a bureaucratic, organizational form. The data consisted of responses from over 8,000 teachers nested within 357 schools. The average school sample size was 22 teachers.

The teacher-level model specified that the sense of efficacy varied among teachers within a school. Because no teacher variables were considered as level-1 predictors, Equation 5.1 reduced to

$$Y_{ij} = \beta_{0j} + r_{ij}, \qquad [5.4]$$

where Y_{ij} was the reported efficacy for teacher i in school j, and β_{0j} was the true mean level of efficacy in school j.

Three school-level models were estimated. The first was an unconditional model for β_{0j}. This results in a one-way random-effects ANOVA model, which partitions the total variance in Y_{ij} into its within- and between-school components. These estimates of σ^2 and τ_{00}, respectively, prove helpful in evaluating the results of subsequent models. The second model examined the effects of several measures of school composition and size on teacher efficacy (see Table 5.1 for description of variables). Formally,

$$\beta_{0j} = \gamma_{00} + \gamma_{01}(\text{MEAN BACKGROUND})_j + \gamma_{02}(\text{MEAN SES})_j$$

$$+ \gamma_{03}(\text{HI MINORITY})_j + \gamma_{04}(\text{SIZE})_j + \gamma_{05}(\text{ETHNIC MIX})_j$$

$$+ \gamma_{06}(\text{SES MIX})_j + u_{0j}. \qquad [5.5]$$

TABLE 5.1 Description of Variables Used in the Study of the Effects of School Organization on Teacher Efficacy

Variable Name	Description
TEACHERS EFFICACY	A factor composite of five teacher responses about their sense of satisfaction in their work. It is a standardized measure (i.e., mean = 0; sd = 1.0).
MEAN BACKGROUND	A factor composite of four items about students' academic experiences prior to high school (e.g., retained in grade) and initial placement (e.g., remedial English or math). It is a standardized variable (mean = 0; sd = 1.0) with positive scores indicating a stronger background
MEAN SES	Average social class of students in the school. It is a standardized variable with positive values indicating more affluent schools.
HI MINORITY	A dummy variable indicating schools with minority enrollment in excess of 40%.
SIZE	The natural log of number of students enrolled in the school.
ETHNIC MIX	A standardized measure of the diversity in students ethnicity within the school. Low values imply a single ethnic group. High positive values indicate significant student representation in several ethnic groups.
SES MIX	Like ethnic mix, this is a standardized measure of the social class diversity within the school. Positive values indicate a socially heterogeneous school.
COMMUNAL	A composite measure based on 23 separate indices of the extent to which a school has a communal organization. It is a standardized measure with positive values indicating a greater frequency of shared activities, consensuson common beliefs, teacher collegiality, and a broader teacher role. Low values indicate a more segmented, specialized, bureaucratic organization.

NOTE: For a further discussion of the measures, see Bryk and Driscoll (1988).

The third model added a measure of the degree of communal organization in the school, COMMUNAL, to Equation 5.5. In both models, the residual school-specific effects, u_{0j}, were assumed normally distributed with mean 0 and variance τ_{00}.

One-Way Random-Effects ANOVA Model. The analysis began with fitting an unconditional model for β_{0j} at level 2. The estimate for the within-school or level-1 variance [i.e., $\text{Var}(r_{ij}) = \sigma^2$] was 0.915. This estimate remains the same for the three analyses discussed here, because the level-1 model

(Equation 5.4) is identical for all three. The overall variability among the true school means on teacher efficacy [i.e., $\text{Var}(\beta_{0j}) = \tau_{00}$] was 0.084. This resulted in an intraclass correlation of 0.084 (see Equation 4.6), and an estimated reliability for the school means on teacher efficacy of 0.669 (see Equations 4.7 and 4.8).

Two Explanatory Models at Level 2. The first two columns in Table 5.2 present the results of the hierarchical linear model analyses. In the top panel are the estimates for the compositional model and in the bottom panel are the results after the COMMUNAL variable was added. In the compositional model (top panel) students' MEAN BACKGROUND ($\hat{\gamma}_{01} = 0.044$, se $= 0.020$) and the school's MEAN SES ($\hat{\gamma}_{02} = 0.133$, se $= 0.023$) were positively related to teachers' sense of efficacy. School SIZE had a significant

TABLE 5.2 Effects of School Organization on Teacher Efficacy

	Hierarchical Analysis		Teacher-Level Analysis		School-Level Analysis	
	Coefficient	*se*	*Coefficient*	*se*	*Coefficient*	*se*
Compositional model						
MEAN						
BACKGROUND, γ_{01}	0.044	0.020	0.046	0.014	0.040	0.021
MEAN SES, γ_{02}	0.133	0.023	0.132	0.015	0.137	0.023
HI MINORITY, γ_{03}	0.031	0.046	0.028	0.031	0.035	0.047
SIZE, γ_{04}	−0.066	0.027	−0.066	0.019	−0.068	0.026
ETHNIC MIX, γ_{05}	−0.014	0.019	−0.014	0.013	−0.013	0.019
SES MIX, γ_{06}	−0.028	0.023	−0.029	0.016	−0.025	0.023
Proportion of variance accounted for	0.345		0.029		0.234	
Communal model						
MEAN						
BACKGROUND, γ_{01}	0.038	0.017	0.040	0.013	0.033	0.018
MEAN SES, γ_{02}	0.015	0.022	0.015	0.017	0.019	0.023
HI MINORITY, γ_{03}	−0.055	0.040	−0.056	0.031	−0.051	0.041
SIZE, γ_{04}	0.061	0.026	0.062	0.021	0.060	0.025
ETHNIC MIX, γ_{05}	−0.014	0.016	−0.014	0.013	−0.014	0.017
SES MIX, γ_{06}	0.001	0.020	0.002	0.016	−0.000	0.020
COMMUNAL, γ_{07}	0.504	0.045	0.507	0.035	0.493	0.045
Proportion of variance accounted for	0.631		0.054		0.426	
Incremental variance	0.286		0.025		0.192	

NOTE: Residual variance estimates for hierarchical analyses: τ_{00} (compositional model) $= 0.055$; τ_{00} (communal model) $= 0.031$.

negative effect ($\hat{\gamma}_{04} = -0.066$, se $= 0.027$). The effects of the other three level-2 predictors were small both in absolute terms and in comparison to their estimated standard errors.

The results for the communal organization model were quite startling. The estimated effect of COMMUNAL ($\hat{\gamma}_{07} = 0.504$, se $= 0.045$) was by far the largest—almost an order of magnitude bigger than all the others. (Note: This interpretation depends on the fact that all of the level-2 predictors, except the dummy variable HI MINORITY, were standardized to mean $= 0$, sd $= 1.0$.) This means that teacher efficacy was substantially higher in schools with a communal organization, even after controlling for compositional differences among schools. We also note that the effects of MEAN SES found in the composition model have largely disappeared (0.015 versus 0.133). This suggests that the positive levels of teacher efficacy found in high social-class schools may reflect the greater prevalence of communal organizational features in these schools. Notice also that the school-size effect has become positive, implying somewhat higher levels of teacher efficacy in larger schools *after* controlling for communal organization. As Bryk and Driscoll (1988) explain, teacher efficacy tends to be lower in large schools because these schools are less likely to be communal. Once this effect is controlled for, however, large schools appear to promote somewhat greater efficacy presumably by virtue of the greater resources and expanded professional opportunities typically found there.

After controlling for composition effects, as specified in Equation 5.5, the residual variability at level 2, $\hat{\tau}_{00}$, was 0.055. We refer to this as $\hat{\tau}_{00}$(compositional model). The model accounted for 34.5% of the total parameter variance among schools in mean levels of teacher efficacy. This proportion reduction in variance statistic was computed using the procedure introduced in Chapter 4. Specifically,

$$\begin{aligned}
\text{Proportion variance explained} &= \frac{\hat{\tau}_{00}(\text{unconditional}) - \hat{\tau}_{00}(\text{compositional model})}{\hat{\tau}_{00}(\text{unconditional})} \\[2mm]
&= \frac{0.084 - 0.055}{0.084} = 0.345,
\end{aligned} \qquad [5.6]$$

where $\hat{\tau}_{00}$(unconditional) is the overall variability in the true school means as estimated from the one-way random-effects ANOVA model.

The percentage of variance explained jumped to 63.1% after COMMUNAL was entered into the model. That is, the residual variance in β_{0j}, $\hat{\tau}_{00}$ (communal model), was 0.031. Replacing $\hat{\tau}_{00}$(compositional model) in

Equation 5.6 with $\hat{\tau}_{00}$(communal model) yields a proportion of variance explained as

$$\frac{0.084 - 0.031}{0.084} = 0.631. \qquad [5.7]$$

The incremental variance explained by adding COMMUNAL to the model was 28.6%. This statistic is just the difference between the proportion reduction-in-variance statistics calculated in Equations 5.6 and 5.7.

Comparison of Results with Conventional Teacher-Level and School-Level Analyses

Table 5.2 also presents results from teacher (level-1) and school (level-2) analyses. A comparison of these conventional alternatives to the multilevel results helps to clarify some of the basic features of estimates in random-intercept models. We compare below the fixed-effect estimates, the standard errors of these estimates, and the variance-explained statistics typically reported with such analyses.

Fixed Effects. Notice in Table 5.2 that the estimates for the regression coefficients are quite similar across the three analyses. The hierarchical estimates, however, are somewhat closer to the results from the teacher analysis, which will generally be the case.

As presented in Chapter 3, the estimators for the level-2 coefficients in a hierarchical linear model can be viewed as weighted least squares estimators where the weights are of the form

$$\Delta_j^{-1} = (V_j + \tau_{00})^{-1}. \qquad [5.8]$$

Assuming a homogeneous level-1 variance (i.e., $\sigma_j^2 = \sigma^2$ for all J), then $V_j = \sigma^2/n_j$ and the variation in the weights depends strictly on n_j.

In comparison, the typical OLS level-1 analysis of these data is also weighted, but the weights are just n_j. Specifically, suppose we estimate a simple univariate model where the teacher outcome, Y_{ij}, depends on one school characteristic, W_j:

$$Y_{ij} = \gamma_0 + \gamma_1 W_j + e_{ij}. \qquad [5.9]$$

The estimator for γ_1 based on an OLS level-1 analysis is simply

$$\hat{\gamma}_1 = \frac{\sum_j n_j (W_j - \overline{W}.)(\overline{Y}._j - \overline{Y}..)}{\sum_j n_j (W_j - \overline{W}.)^2}. \qquad [5.10]$$

Notice that the numerator and denominator are sums of squares and cross-products, weighted by n_j instead of Δ_j^{-1}.

In contrast, the level-2 analysis is unweighted. The comparable univariate model would be

$$\overline{Y}_{\cdot j} = \gamma_0 + \gamma_1 W_j + \bar{r}_{\cdot j} \qquad [5.11]$$

and the corresponding estimator for γ_1 is

$$\hat{\gamma}_1 = \frac{\sum_j (W_j - \overline{W}.)(\overline{Y}_{\cdot j} - \widetilde{Y}..)}{\sum_j (W_j - \overline{W}.)^2}, \qquad [5.12]$$

where

$$\widetilde{Y}.. = \sum \overline{Y}_{\cdot j}/J \quad \text{and} \quad \overline{W}. = \sum W_j/J.$$

All three estimators are unbiased, but the hierarchical estimator is the most efficient. Variations in results among the three analyses will depend on the degree of imbalance in the n_j. (If the sample sizes n_j are identical for each of the J organizations, the three estimators are the same.) In the Bryk and Driscoll (1988) application, the n_j were not grossly different. Most schools had between 20 and 30 cases. Thus, the level-2 results were quite similar in this application.

In general, a robustness concern arises when estimating fixed effects with a level-2 analysis in the presence of unbalanced data. A unit with a very small sample size can easily become an outlier or leverage point because of the instability associated with the limited amount of information about that unit. The weighting employed in the hierarchical and level-1 analyses protect against this.

Standard Errors of the Fixed Effects. As noted in the introduction to this chapter, the standard errors produced by a level-1 analysis will generally be too small, because this analysis fails to take into account the fact that level-1 units are not independent but rather are actually clustered within level-2 units. In the compositional analysis, for example, the level-1 standard-error estimates are about a third smaller than those provided by the hierarchical and level-2 analyses.

A direct comparison of the formulas for the three different standard errors is difficult when sample sizes are unequal. Some basic features can be ascertained, however, if we consider the balanced data case with a single W_j predictor. It can readily be shown that the expected values of the estimators for the sampling variance for γ_1 from the hierarchical linear model and level-2 analyses are identical:

$$E[\text{Var}(\hat{\gamma}_1)]_{\text{hierarchical}} = \frac{V + \tau_{00}}{\sum_j (W_j - \overline{W}.)^2}. \qquad [5.13]$$

As for the level-1 analysis, the expected value of the sampling variance estimator is

$$E[Var(\hat{\gamma}_1)]_{level\ 1} = \frac{J(n-1)\sigma^2 + (J-2)n(V + \tau_{00})}{(Jn-2)n \sum_j (W_j - \overline{W}.)^2}. \qquad [5.14]$$

When the level-1 and level-2 samples (n and J, respectively) are large, the ratio of the expected sampling variance from a level-1 analysis, Equation 5.14, to that from a hierarchical analysis (or, equivalently, a level-2 analysis), Equation 5.13, is approximately

$$\frac{E[Var(\hat{\gamma}_1)]_{level\ 1}}{E[Var(\hat{\gamma}_1)]_{hierarchical}} \approx 1 - \lambda, \qquad [5.15]$$

where $\lambda = \tau_{00}/[(\sigma^2/n) + \tau_{00}]$, and is the reliability of the OLS estimated school means, $\hat{\beta}_{0j}$.

Equation 5.15 closely approximates the empirical results reported in Table 5.2. With an average level-1 sample size of 22 teachers per school, a level-1 variance estimate, $\hat{\sigma}^2 = 0.915$, and an estimate of τ_{00} for the compositional model of 0.055,

$$1 - \lambda = 1 - \frac{0.055}{(0.915/22) + (0.055)} = 0.431.$$

As for the relative size of the standard errors, their ratio is simply $(1 - \lambda)^{1/2}$, which, for the compositional model, yields a value of 0.657. This ratio closely corresponds to the results reported in the top panel of Table 5.2. Visual inspection indicates that the level-1 standard errors are approximately two thirds of the more appropriate values reported by the hierarchical and level-2 analyses.

In sum, the hierarchical analysis captures the best features of both the level-1 and level-2 analyses. It provides unbiased and efficient estimates of the fixed effects, which are more closely approximated by the level-1 analysis, and provides proper standard error estimates, regardless of the degree of within-unit clustering, that are more closely approximated by the level-2 analysis.

The results obtained above are typical of what one might routinely encounter in this type of analysis. The fixed-effects estimates will often be similar across the three analyses; however, the estimated standard errors will not.

Variance-Explained Statistics. The estimates of the proportion of variance explained from a hierarchical analysis may be quite different from those generated in conventional level-1 or level-2 analyses and may lead to different conclusions. In the Bryk and Driscoll (1988) study, for example, a judgment about the importance of communal organization depended considerably on the analysis considered (bottom panel in Table 5.2). The incremental reduction in variance associated with COMMUNAL was 28.6% in the hierarchical linear model analysis. The comparable statistics from the teacher and school-level analyses were 2.5% and 19.2% respectively. Although most analysts would probably judge 28.6% sufficiently substantial to merit further consideration of the construct under study, the 2.5% statistic could easily lead to the opposite inference.

To understand why the proportion of variance accounted for by COMMUNAL is so different requires a closer consideration of how the total outcome variability is partitioned in the three analyses. In a random-intercept problem, level-2 variables such as COMMUNAL can only account for variation among the true school means, β_{0j}. That is, only the parameter variation, τ_{00}, is explainable. (This is why we use τ_{00} from the unconditional model as the denominator in the proportion reduction in variance statistic.) The 28.6% variance explained by COMMUNAL implies that a substantial portion of the variation among the true school means is associated with variation in school organization. Relative to all other school-level sources of variation, communal organization is indeed important.

In comparison, the level-1 analysis employs the total outcome variability in Y_{ij}, $\tau_{00} + \sigma^2$, as the denominator for the variance-explained statistics. The within-unit variation, σ^2, however, reflects individual effects and errors of measurement in the outcome variable, both of which are unexplainable by organizational features. Judged against this standard, some researchers might erroneously conclude that the COMMUNAL is trivially small.

In general, the relative variance explained by a hierarchical versus a level-1 analysis depends on the ratio

$$\frac{\text{Variance explained (level 1)}}{\text{Variance explained (hierarchical)}} \approx \frac{\tau_{00}}{\tau_{00} + \sigma^2} = \rho, \qquad [5.16]$$

where ρ is the intraclass correlation coefficient (see Equation 2.10). Note that the intraclass correlation represents the theoretically maximal amount of the total variance in the outcome Y_{ij} that is explainable by all school factors. As noted earlier, the estimated intraclass correlation was 0.084 for the teacher-efficacy data. We can use $\hat{\rho}$ to relate the variance-explained statistics from the level-1 and hierarchical analyses. For example,

$$\hat{\rho} \times \begin{bmatrix} \text{Incremental variance} \\ \text{explained (hierarchical)} \end{bmatrix} \approx \begin{bmatrix} \text{Incremental variance} \\ \text{explained (level 1)} \end{bmatrix}$$

$$0.084 \times [0.286] \approx 0.024.$$

A similar formula can be derived for comparing the variance-explained statistics from the hierachical and level-2 analyses. The denominator for the variance-explained statistic in a level-2 analyses is $\tau_{00} + \sigma^2/n_j$, which is just the total variance of the *sample* means. Thus, the relative variance explained by a hierarchical versus level-2 analysis is approximately

$$\frac{\text{Variance explained (level 2)}}{\text{Variance explained (hierarchical)}} \approx \frac{\tau_{00}}{\tau_{00} + (\sigma^2/\bar{n}.)} = \bar{\lambda}, \qquad [5.17]$$

where $\bar{\lambda}$ is the average reliability of the $\bar{Y}_{.j}$ as estimates of μ_{Y_j} (see Equation 4.8) based on an average level-1 sample size of $\bar{n}..$. For the teacher-ef-ficacy data, $\hat{\lambda}$ was 0.669, and the variances explained by the level-2 analyses were approximately two thirds of those represented in the corresponding hierarchical analyses.

In sum, the variance-explained statistic from the hierarchical analysis provides the clearest evidence for making judgments about the importance of level-2 predictors. They are not affected by the degree of clustering as the level-1 statistics are (i.e., the dependence on ρ), nor are they affected by the unreliability of $\bar{Y}_{.j}$ as the level-2 statistics are. Further, because good estimates of λ and ρ are not generally available with conventional analyses, the analyst has no way to assess the explanatory power of a set of level-2 predictors relative to the maximum amount explainable by *any* model. Intuitively, this is what variance-explained statistics should tell us.

A Random-Intercept Model with Level-1 Covariates

In the previous example, we estimated the relationship between organizational characteristics and mean outcomes. We made no attempt to adjust the level-2 effect estimates for the different characteristics of the individuals in the various organizations.

In general, statistical adjustments for individual background are important for two reasons. First, because persons are not usually assigned at random to organizations, failure to control for background may bias the estimates of organization effects. Second, if these level-1 predictors (or covariates) are strongly related to the outcome of interest, controlling for them will increase the precision of any estimates of organizational effects and the power of hypothesis tests by reducing unexplained level-1 error variance, σ^2.

The formal model for this type of analysis was introduced in Chapter 2. At level 1,

$$Y_{ij} = \beta_{0j} + \beta_{1j}(X_{1ij} - \bar{X}_1..) + \beta_{2j}(X_{2ij} - \bar{X}_2..)$$
$$+ \cdots + \beta_{Qj}(X_{Qij} - \bar{X}_Q..) + r_{ij}. \qquad [5.18]$$

The level-2 model is Equation 5.3. Because each covariate is centered around its respective grand mean, the random intercept, β_{0j}, is now the adjusted mean rather than the raw mean. As in ANCOVA models, Equation 5.18 assumes homogeneous level-1 coefficients for $\beta_{1j}, \ldots, \beta_{Qj}$. The validity of this assumption can be easily tested using the methods described in Chapter 3. If needed, any level-1 coefficient can be specified as either non-randomly varying or as a random effect.

Example: Evaluating Program Effects on Writing

This example uses data from the Cognitive Strategies in Writing Project (Englert et al., 1988). The project sought to improve childrens' writing and to enhance childrens' self-perceptions of academic competence through a variety of strategies. The outcome variable was a measure of perceived academic self-competence (mean = 2.918; sd = 0.580) for which a pretest, denoted X_{ij}, served as the covariate. The study involved 256 children in 22 classrooms in a standard two-group design, with 15 experimental classrooms and 7 control classrooms. Because classroom teachers implemented the treatments to intact classrooms, we have, in classical terms, a nested or hierarchical design: Students are nested within classrooms with the treatment administered at the classroom level. As in the previous example, we first present the results of a hierarchical analysis. We then compare these results to conventional alternatives: an ANCOVA at the student level ignoring classes and an ANCOVA based on class means.

For the hierarchical analysis, the level-1 model was

$$Y_{ij} = \beta_{0j} + \beta_{1j}(X_{ij} - \overline{X}..) + r_{ij}, \qquad [5.19]$$

where

Y_{ij} is the self-perceived competence of child i in class j ($j = 1, \ldots, 22$ classrooms);

β_{0j} is the *adjusted* mean outcome in class j after controlling for differences in pretest status; and

β_{1j} is the fixed level-1 covariate effect.

A preliminary analysis specified a model where both β_{0j} and β_{1j} were random and tested the homogeneity hypothesis for the covariate effect [H_0: Var(β_{1j}) = 0]. Because the null hypothesis was retained for β_{1j}, it was appropriate to assume a fixed effect for the pretest covariate. The final level-2 model was

$$\beta_{0j} = \gamma_{00} + \gamma_{01} W_j + u_{0j},$$
$$\beta_{1j} = \gamma_{10}, \qquad [5.20]$$

where

W_j is a treatment-indicator variable (1 = experimental; 0 = control);

γ_{00} is the adjusted mean achievement in the control-group classrooms;

γ_{01} is the treatment effect; and

γ_{10} is the pooled within-classroom regression coefficient for the level-1 covariate.

The results of this analysis appear in Table 5.3. The estimated difference between experimental and control means adjusted for the pretest was .188 ($t = 1.87$, df = 20, p [one tail] < .04). The estimated pooled within-classroom regression slope for the posttest on the pretest was 0.396 ($t = 7.02$, $p < .001$).

Comparison of Results with Conventional Student- and Classroom-Level Analyses

The model for the student-level analyses was

$$Y_i = \gamma_{00} + \gamma_{01} W_i + \gamma_{10}(X_i - \overline{X}.) + r_i, \qquad [5.21]$$

where the parameters γ_{00}, γ_{01}, and γ_{10} represent the intercept, the treatment effect, and the covariate effect, respectively, and $\overline{X}.$ is the mean pretest score (i.e., $\sum_{i=1}^{N} X_i/N$). Notice that the j subscript has disappeared because class membership is ignored as is the effect associated with classrooms (i.e., u_{0j}) in Equation 5.20.

The results for this analysis appear in the second column of Table 5.3. They indicate that experimental children developed a significantly higher perceived self-competence than did the control children ($\hat{\gamma}_{01} = .160$, $t = 2.17$, p [one-tail] < .02). The estimated pooled within-treatment groups regression slope for the posttest on the pretest was 0.406 ($t = 7.25$, $p < .001$).

TABLE 5.3 Effects of Experimental Instruction on Self-Perceived Competence in Writing

	Hierarchical Analysis[a]		Student-Level Analysis[b]		Classroom-Level Analysis[c]	
	Coefficient	se	Coefficient	se	Coefficient	se
Intercept, γ_{00}	2.774	0.084	2.802	0.063	2.763	0.112
Treatment indicator, γ_{01}	0.188	0.100	0.160	0.074	0.209	0.135
Pretest, γ_{10}	0.396	0.056	0.406	0.056	0.649	0.223

a. Residual Variance estimates: $\hat{\sigma}^2 = 0.258$; $\hat{\tau}_{00} = 0.019$.
b. Estimated residual variance = 0.273.
c. Estimated residual variance = 0.087.

As for the classroom-level analyses, the model was

$$\overline{Y}_{\cdot j} = \gamma_{00} + \gamma_{01}W_j + \gamma_{10}(\overline{X}_{\cdot j} - \widetilde{X}_{\cdot\cdot}) + u_{0j}, \qquad [5.22]$$

where $j = 1, \ldots, 22$ classrooms. Here $\overline{X}_{\cdot j}$ is the pretest mean for class j; $\overline{Y}_{\cdot j}$ is the posttest class mean. The grand mean for the pretest, $\widetilde{X}_{\cdot\cdot}$, is the mean of the classroom means (i.e., $\widetilde{X}_{\cdot\cdot} = \sum \overline{X}_{\cdot j}/J$). These results appear in the third column of Table 5.3. Although the estimated treatment-effect size ($\hat{\gamma}_{01} = 0.209$) is actually larger than the hierarchical and classroom-level estimates, it is not statistically significant due to the substantially larger standard error [$se(\hat{\gamma}_{01}) = 0.135$]. The estimated covariate effect, $\hat{\gamma}_{10} = 0.649$, is also substantially larger, as is its standard error of .223.

It may seem surprising that the hierarchical analysis produced inferences similar to those of the student-level analysis and different from the class-level analysis. In each case, the test statistic for the effect of innovative instruction depends on a ratio of two quantities: the fixed-effect size estimate and the standard error of this estimate. A comparison of each is offered below.

Fixed Effects. The estimate for the treatment effect is reasonably similar in all three analyses, with the student-level analysis producing the smallest effect (.160), the classroom-level analysis the largest (.209), and the hierarchical estimate falling in between (.188). In all three analyses, the treatment-effect estimator is of the general form

$$\hat{\gamma}_{10} = \hat{\mu}_{Y_T} - \hat{\mu}_{Y_C} - \hat{\beta}_{Y\cdot X}(\hat{\mu}_{X_T} - \hat{\mu}_{X_C}). \qquad [5.23]$$

where $\hat{\mu}_{Y_T}$ and $\hat{\mu}_{Y_C}$ are estimates of the posttest means for experimentals and controls, respectively. The key differences among the analyses are in the way $\beta_{Y\cdot X}$ and the pre- and posttest means are estimated. Table 5.4 presents the relevant statistics from each analysis.

TABLE 5.4 Treatment Effect Estimates: Hierarchical, Student-Level, and Classroom-Level Analyses

	Hierarchical Analysis	Student-Level Analysis	Class-Level Analysis
$\overline{Y}_E$	2.968	2.980	2.964
$\overline{Y}_C$	2.742	2.754	2.980
$\overline{X}_E$	2.895	2.921	2.855
$\overline{X}_C$	2.797	2.759	2.893
$\hat{\beta}_{Y\cdot X}$	0.396	0.406	0.649
$\overline{Y}_E - \overline{Y}_C - \hat{\beta}_{Y\cdot X}(\overline{X}_E - \overline{X}_C)$	0.188	0.160	0.209

For the student-level analysis, $\beta_{Y \cdot X}$ is the regression of the posttest on the pretest, pooled within the treatment and control groups. The hierarchical analysis is similar, except $\beta_{Y \cdot X}$ is pooled within each of the 22 classrooms. In contrast, the class-level analysis regresses the posttest means for the 22 classes on their corresponding pretest means. As Table 5.4 shows, the $\beta_{Y \cdot X}$ are quite similar in the hierarchical ($\hat{\beta}_{Y \cdot X} = .396$) and the student-level analyses ($\hat{\beta}_{Y \cdot X} = .406$). The classroom-level estimate, however, is quite discrepant ($\hat{\beta}_{Y \cdot X} = .649$).

The three alternative methods also employ different estimators of the pre- and posttest means for each treatment group. Consider, for example, the experimental posttest mean. The hierarchical-analysis estimator is a weighted average,

$$\overline{Y}_{E(hierarchical)} = \sum_j^{J_E} \Delta_{jE}^{-1} \overline{Y}_{\cdot jE} / \sum_j \Delta_{jE}, \qquad [5.24]$$

where $\overline{Y}_{\cdot jE}$ is the mean of the jth classroom in the experimental group. The weight, Δ_{jE}^{-1}, is the precision of the corresponding sample mean. Thus, the hierarchical estimates are precision-weighted averages.

The student-level estimators weight by sample sizes:

$$\overline{Y}_{Ej}(\text{student level}) = \sum_j^{J_E} n_{jE} \overline{Y}_{\cdot jE} / \sum_j n_{jE}, \qquad [5.25]$$

where n_{jE} is the sample size of the jth classroom in the experimental group. In contrast, the classroom-level analysis uses an unweighted average:

$$\overline{Y}_{Ej}(\text{classroom level}) = \sum_j \overline{Y}_{\cdot jE} / J_E, \qquad [5.26]$$

where J_E is the number of classrooms in the experimental group.

When the reliability of individual classroom means varies significantly, the classroom-level estimate is likely to be inaccurate because it will be strongly influenced by extreme classroom means, which may result from unreliability. This is not true of the student-level or hierarchical estimators. In fact, when the precisions Δ_j^{-1} are known or estimated accurately, the hierarchical weighting scheme is optimal. The classroom-level estimate is defensible only if the sample means are equally reliable.

Standard Errors. The standard errors of the treatment effect estimates are also different across the three analyses. The value of 0.074 for the student-level analysis is clearly misleading because, as noted earlier, this analysis fails to take into account the dependence among the observations within class-rooms. In essence, the student-level analysis assumes more information is present than is actually the case (i.e., it assumes that each individual response within a classroom provides an additional independent piece of information). But why is the standard error estimated under the hierarchical model (0.100) smaller than the estimate based on the class-level analysis (0.135)?

Apart from sample size, the standard error of the difference between two treatment groups in an ANCOVA depends on three factors: (a) the unexplained variance in the outcome, (b) the precision of the estimated regression coefficient for the covariate, and (c) the magnitude of the difference between the groups on the covariate. The hierarchical analysis is generally more powerful than the class-level analysis because factors (a) and (b) work in its favor.

In terms of factor (a), the unexplained variance in the outcome is smaller in the hierarchical analysis. The variance of $\overline{Y}_{.j}$, classroom j's sample mean, is $\Delta_j = \tau_{00} + \sigma^2/n_j$. In a class-level analysis, only τ_{00} is potentially explainable by the covariate. In the hierarchical analysis, both τ_{00} and σ^2 may be explained. The reduction in σ^2 can be substantial if the level-1 covariate is strongly related to the outcome within classrooms, yielding a potentially substantial advantage in power over the class-level analysis.

In terms of factor (b), the precision of the estimated covariate effect in the hierarchical analysis is greater than in the class-level analysis, because the hierarchical analysis uses all of the data to estimate the covariate effect. In contrast, the class-level analysis uses only information about the covariation between the class means on the pre- and posttest.

Specifically, the $se(\hat{\beta}_{Y \cdot X})$ for the hierarchical analysis will generally be smaller than $se(\hat{\beta}_{Y \cdot X})$ from the class-level analysis, as is demonstrated in Table 5.3. This is significant because the standard error of the treatment effect, $se(\hat{\gamma}_{10})$, depends on the $se(\hat{\beta}_{Y \cdot X})$, which is obvious from an inspection of Equation 5.23.

In sum, the hierarchical analysis offers several advantages in this application. First, it is an *honest* model. Rather than erroneously assuming independent responses within classes, the hierarchical model takes into account the dependence among responses within classrooms.

Second, it provides efficient estimates of treatment effects in unbalanced, nested designs. Traditionally, the class-level analysis has been recommended as the preferred alternative to the student-level analysis because of the untenability of the assumption of independent errors. Researchers have lamented, however, that such analyses, although perhaps more appropriate, have low power to detect effects, and for this reason, researchers have tended to ignore this advice. The key point is that researchers no longer have to make a choice between a clearly untenable model (i.e., student-level analysis) and an honest but low-power alternative (class-level analysis). The hierarchical linear model properly represents the sources of variation in nested designs and provides efficient parameter estimates.

Finally, the hierarchical model enables a test for homogeneity of regression and provides a sensible way to proceed, regardless of the outcome. In this application, the regression of posttest on pretest was homogeneous with regard to classrooms, so we treated the covariate as a fixed effect. However, if the regression coefficients had been found to vary across classrooms, we could have built a model to predict such variation. Any unexplained variation in this level-1 coefficient would then be incorporated into inference about treatments.

Case 2: Explaining the Differentiating Effects of Organizations via Intercepts- and Slopes-as-Outcomes Models

In the applications discussed above, organizational characteristics exercised a common influence on all individuals within the organization. The sole effect of the organizational variable under study was to shift the mean level of the outcomes, leaving the distribution of outcomes otherwise unaffected. In this section we consider situations where organizational features affect level-1 relationships, either amplifying or attenuating them. The corresponding statistical model for such phenomena is the full hierarchical model represented in Equations 5.1 and 5.2. The within-organization relations are represented by the regression coefficients in the level-1 model. The effects of organization variables on each of these relationships is represented in the corresponding level-2 model.

Difficulties Encountered in Past Efforts at Modeling Regression Slopes-as-Outcomes

The use of regression coefficients or slopes-as-outcomes is appealing because it extends substantially the kinds of questions that organizational research can examine. Unfortunately, a number of technical difficulties inhibited past use of models that incorporate slopes-as-outcomes.

First, as a general rule, regression coefficients have considerably greater sampling variability than do sample means. If the sample within a unit is small, the regression coefficients will be estimated with large error. The resultant unreliability in slopes weakens our power to detect relationships in the level-2 model. This imprecision is exacerbated when the dispersion in the level-1 predictors is constrained. For example, students tend to be more homogeneous in social class within schools than they are in a true random sample. As a result, the sampling variability of the estimated within-schools SES-achievement slope is increased. The analysis can produce negative slope estimates for individual schools even when the structural parameter is clearly positive (see Figure 4.2). This is particularly problematic because such outliers can exert undue influence on the level-2 results.

Second, the sampling precision of the estimated slopes varies across units depending on the data-collection design used within each unit. But ordinary least squares, the estimation method typically used for the level-2 analysis, assumes equal variances across units on the dependent variable. Ignoring the variation in sampling precision across units results in a weakened efficiency in parameter estimation that further limits our ability to detect relationships between slopes and the level-2 variables hypothesized to account for them.

Third, the total variability in the estimated slopes consists of two components. First, there may be real differences across organizations in the slope parameters. It is essential, however, to distinguish between this parameter variance and the error variance in the slope estimates. This distinction becomes especially important when we attempt to interpret the results from the level-2 model. As noted earlier in this chapter, only parameter variance in the level-1 coefficients is potentially explainable by level-2 predictors. In many applications, much of the observed variance in the slopes is error variance for the reasons noted above. A level-2 model that explains only a small percentage of the observed variance in a regression slope might be discounted, when in fact it is explaining a very large portion of what can, in principle, be explained. Unfortunately, the simple slopes-as-outcomes model provides little guidance in this regard.

Fourth, to include multiple slopes-as-outcomes in the level-2 model requires us to take into account the special covariance structure that exists among the multiple-regression coefficients estimated for each level-2 unit. In the absence of such a model, further weakened precision is a likely result.

Fifth, in many applications, the sample of organization members will not support an ordinary least squares regression for every organization. If the sample size for a particular organization is very small, or if that sample does not vary for a particular X, it will not be possible to compute the regression. Using the slopes-as-outcomes approach, such organizations must be discarded, possibly biasing the sample as well as reducing precision. Such organizations need not be discarded when using a hierarchical model with maximum likelihood estimation.

Example: The Social Distribution of Achievement in Public and Catholic High Schools

Lee and Bryk (1989) used hierarchical analyses on a subset data from the High School and Beyond Survey, similar to that used in Chapter 4, to examine whether academic achievement had a more equitable social distribution in the Catholic than in the public sector. Specifically, they drew a sample of 74 Catholic high schools and a random subsample of 86 public high schools. Data were combined from two cohorts of students to increase the level-1 sample sizes, n_j, to yield a total sample size, N, of 10,999 students. Table 5.5 describes selected variables used in their analyses. We discuss below some of their analyses and comment on the logic involved in using an intercepts- and slopes-as-outcomes model to explain the social distribution of achievement in Catholic and public high schools.

TABLE 5.5 Description of Variables from a Study of the Social Distribution of Math Achievement in Public and Catholic High Schools (Lee & Bryk, 1989)

Variable Name	Description
Student-level	
MATH ACHIEVEMENT	A mathematics test in senior year (mean = 12.92, sd = 6.70).
SES	A composite measure of social class provided by High School and Beyond. For the analytic sample it had a mean of approximately zero and standard deviation of 0.8.
MINORITY	A dummy variable (1 = black or Hispanic; 0 = other).
BACKGROUND	A composite measure of students' academic background up to high school entry. It includes information on retention in elementary school, assignment to remedial classes in 9th grade, and educational expectation at high school entry. It is a standardized measure (mean = 0; sd = 1.0).
School-level	
SECTOR	An effects-coded variable (1 = Catholic; -1 = public).
AVSES	Average social class of students within a school (i.e., school mean for SES).
HIMNRTY	An effects-coded variable (1 = school enrollment exceeds 40% minority; -1 = otherwise).
AVBACKGRD	Average academic background of students within a school (i.e., school mean for BACKGROUND).

NOTE: AVSES and AVBACKGRD were constructed from a larger sample of students than those in this analytic sample.

A Random-Effects ANOVA Model. The analysis began with fitting a one-way random-effects ANOVA model in order to determine the total amount of variability in the outcome (senior-year mathematics achievement) within and between schools. The average school mean, γ_{00}, was estimated as 12.125. The pooled within-school or level-1 variance, $\hat{\sigma}^2$, was 39.927, and the variance among the J school means, $\hat{\tau}_{00}$, was 9.335. Using these results and Equation 4.6, we can estimate the proportion of variance between schools (i.e., the intraclass correlation) as 0.189. We note that the estimate of σ^2 from the random-effects ANOVA model represents the total level-1 variance. As we will see below, some of this variance is explained as predictors are introduced into the level-1 model.

A Random-Coefficient Regression Model. The next step in the analysis involved posing a model to represent the social distribution of achievement in each of the J schools. Specifically, at level 1 (the student model), the mathematics achievement for student i in school j (Y_{ij}) was regressed on minority status (MINORITY), social class (SES), and academic background (BACKGROUND):

$$Y_{ij} = \beta_{0j} + \beta_{1j}(\text{MINORITY})_{ij} + \beta_{2j}(\text{SES})_{ij}$$
$$+ \beta_{3j}(\text{BACKGROUND})_{ij} + r_{ij}. \qquad [5.27]$$

Note that the variance of r_{ij}, σ^2, now represents the residual variance at level 1 that remains unexplained after taking into account students' minority status, social status, and academic background.

Each school's distribution of achievement is characterized in terms of four parameters: an intercept and three regression coefficients. The MINORITY, SES, and BACKGROUND variables were all group-mean centered (see Chapter 2). As a result, the four parameters can be interpreted as follows:

β_{0j} is the mean achievement in school j;

β_{1j} is the "minority" gap in school j (i.e., the mean difference between the achievement of white and minority students);

β_{2j} is the differentiating effect of social class in school j (i.e., the degree to which SES differences among students relate to senior-year achievement); and

β_{3j} is the differentiating effect of academic background in school j (i.e., the degree to which differences in students' academic BACKGROUND eventuate in senior-year achievement differences).

Each of the distributive effects, $\beta_{0j}, \beta_{1j}, \beta_{2j}$, and β_{3j}, are net of the others. For example, the minority gap in school j, β_{1j}, is the adjusted mean achievement difference between white and minority students in school j after controlling for the effects of individual student's SES and BACKGROUND.

In terms of this model, an effective and equitable school would be characterized by a high level of mean achievement (i.e., a large positive value for β_{0j}), a small minority gap (i.e., a near-zero value for β_{1j}), and weak differentiating effects for social class and academic background (i.e., small positive values for β_{2j} and β_{3j}, respectively).

Each of the four coefficients in Equation 5.27 was specified as random in the level-2 model. Specifically,

$$\beta_{qj} = \gamma_{q0} + u_{qj} \quad \text{for } q = 0, 1, 2, 3, \qquad [5.28]$$

where γ_{q0} is the mean value for each school effect. Because there are four level-2 random effects, the variances and covariances among them now form a 4 by 4 matrix:

$$\mathbf{T} = \begin{bmatrix} \text{Var}(u_{0j}) & & \text{Symmetric} & \\ \text{Cov}(u_{1j}, u_{0j}) & \text{Var}(u_{1j}) & & \\ \text{Cov}(u_{2j}, u_{0j}) & \text{Cov}(u_{2j}, u_{1j}) & \text{Var}(u_{2j}) & \\ \text{Cov}(u_{3j}, u_{0j}) & \text{Cov}(u_{3j}, u_{1j}) & \text{Cov}(u_{3j}, u_{2j}) & \text{Var}(u_{3j}) \end{bmatrix}$$

$$= \begin{bmatrix} \tau_{00} & & \text{Symmetric} & \\ \tau_{10} & \tau_{11} & & \\ \tau_{20} & \tau_{21} & \tau_{22} & \\ \tau_{30} & \tau_{31} & \tau_{32} & \tau_{33} \end{bmatrix}.$$

The random-coefficient regression model specified by Equations 5.27 and 5.28 formally represents the hypothesis that the social distribution of achievement, as defined here, varies across the J schools. As shown below, the diagonal elements of the $\mathbf{T}$ matrix provide empirical evidence for examining this hypothesis.

In general, estimation of a random-coefficient regression model is an important early step in a hierarchical analysis. The results from this model guide the final specification of the level-1 equation and provide a range of useful statistics for subsequent model building at level 2.

Table 5.6 presents the results reported by Lee and Bryk (1989). As in the random-effects ANOVA, the average school achievement was estimated as 12.125. The average minority gap, $\hat{\gamma}_{10}$, was −2.78 points. This means that in a typical school, minority students were scoring 2.78 points behind white schoolmates with academic and social backgrounds like their own. Similarly, student SES and BACKGROUND ($\hat{\gamma}_{20}$ and $\hat{\gamma}_{30}$, respectively) were positively related to achievement. This means that in the average high school, more affluent students and those who enter better prepared had higher math achievement in their senior year. The reported t ratios are quite large, indicating that each of the level-1 predictors was statistically significant.

TABLE 5.6 Random-Coefficient Regression Model of the Social Distribution of Mathematics Achievement

Fixed Effect	Coefficient	se	t Ratio	
School mean achievement, γ_{00}	12.125	0.252	48.207	
Minority gap, γ_{10}	−2.780	0.242	−11.515	
SES differentiation, γ_{20}	1.135	0.104	10.882	
Academic differentiation, γ_{30}	2.582	0.093	27.631	
Random Effect	Variance Component	df	χ^2	p Value
Mean achievement, u_{0j}	9.325	137	1,770.70	0.000
Minority gap, u_{1j}	1.367	137	161.01	0.079
SES differentiation, u_{2j}	0.360	137	173.39	0.019
Academic differentiation, u_{3j}	0.496	137	219.02	0.000
Level-1 effect, r_{ij}	31.771			

Correlation Among School Effects	Mean Achievement	Minority Gap	SES Differentiation
Minority gap	0.397		
SES differentiation	0.182	−0.109	
Academic differentiation	0.327	0.085	0.652

Reliability of OLS Regression-Coefficient Estimates

Mean achievement	0.922
Minority gap	0.098
SES differentiation	0.167
Academic differentiation	0.330

The estimated variances of the random effects at levels 1 and 2 (σ^2 and τ_{qq}, respectively) are reported in the second panel of Table 5.6. Note that the level-1 variance has been reduced from 39.927 in the random-effects ANOVA model to 31.771 after taking into account students' minority status, social class, and academic background. The proportion of variance explained by this level-1 model is

$$(39.927 - 31.771)/39.927 = 0.204.$$

The estimated level-2 variances for the random-coefficient regression model provide empirical evidence about the variability in the social distribution of achievement across schools. The homogeneity of variance tests for these level-2 random effects (see Equation 3.103) can be used to test whether the structure of the social distribution achievement differs across schools. That is, rejecting the hypotheses that

$$H_0: \text{Var}(u_{qj}) = \text{Var}(\beta_{qj}) = 0 \quad \text{for } q = 0, 1, 2, 3 \qquad [5.29]$$

implies variation among schools in their social distribution of achievement.

In terms of the univariate χ^2 tests, the probability of the estimated variability in the β_{qj} coefficients, under a homogeneity hypothesis, is less than .001 for average achievement and academic differentiation, and less than .02 for the SES differentiation. The p value associated with the hypothesis of slope homogeneity for the minority gap coefficients is marginal (.079). Because substantial differences between sectors in minority achievement had been previously reported, however, this effect was maintained as random by Lee and Bryk.

We note that these χ^2 tests provide only approximate probability values for two reasons. First, they are simple univariate tests that do not take into account the other random effects in the model. Second, they are estimated on the basis of only those schools that have sufficient data to compute a separate OLS regressions. In this particular application, only 138 of the total of 160 schools could be used, because the remaining 22 schools had no variation on minority status, which is why $df = 137$ in the second panel of Table 5.6.

When in doubt, the results of these univariate homogeneity tests can be cross-checked through the use of a multivariate likelihood-ratio test (see Equations 3.105 to 3.107), which uses all of the data available. Specifically, the deviance statistic from the full random-coefficient regression model can be compared with the corresponding statistic from a restricted model, say for example, a model with only a random intercept:

$$\beta_{0j} = \gamma_{00} + u_{0j},$$
$$\beta_{qj} = \gamma_{qj} \quad \text{for } q = 1, 2, 3. \qquad [5.30]$$

In the Lee and Bryk (1989) data, the deviance statistic for the full random-coefficient regression model was 58,248.4 with 11 df. For the restricted model (which specified all regression slopes as fixed), it was 58,283.6 with 2 df. As a result, the likelihood-ratio test statistic was 35.2 with 9 df ($p < .001$), which offers confirming evidence that schools do vary in their distributive effects.

Plausible value estimates (see Equation 4.19) from the random-coefficient regression model provide useful descriptive statistics of how much schools really vary in terms of mean achievement, size of the minority gaps, and social- and academic-differentiation effects. Under the normality assumption, we would expect the effects for 95% of the schools to fall within the range

$$\hat{\gamma}_{q0} \pm 1.96(\hat{\tau}_{qq})^{1/2}. \qquad [5.31]$$

Thus, in this High School and Beyond Survey data, school means (β_{0j}) would be expected in the range of $(6.140, 18.110)$. Minority gaps (β_{1j}) of $(-5.072, -0.488)$ are quite plausible, as are social- and academic-differentiation effects of $(-0.041, 2.311)$ and $(1.202, 3.962)$, respectively. Clearly, these results suggest considerable variation among schools on each effect. Interestingly, we could expect to find some schools where minority performance approximates white achievement and where social-class differences are inconsequential because values near zero are plausible for both β_{1j} and β_{2j}. However, all schools appear to engage in some degree of academic differentiation in that values of zero for β_{3j} do not appear plausible. We note that the plausible values are for the true school parameters, β_{qj}, and not the separate OLS estimates of these parameters, $\hat{\beta}_{qj}$. The OLS estimates, especially of the regression slopes, would be far more variable because of the unreliability of sample estimates of these individual school parameters.

Another useful set of descriptive statistics that can be computed from the level-2 variance-covariance components are the correlations among the school effects. For any two random effects u_{qj} and $u_{q'j}$ (or, equivalently, in the random-coefficient regression model β_{qj} and $\beta_{q'j}$, respectively),

$$\hat{\rho}(u_{qj}, u_{q'j}) = \hat{\tau}_{qq'}/(\hat{\tau}_{qq}\hat{\tau}_{q'q'})^{1/2}. \qquad [5.32]$$

These results are reported in the third panel of Table 5.6. Schools displaying high levels of achievement tended to have small minority gaps $(\hat{\rho}_{01} = 0.397)$ but were somewhat more differentiating with regard to social class $(\hat{\rho}_{02} = 0.182)$ and academic background $(\hat{\rho}_{03} = 0.327)$ than schools with lower achievement levels. Interestingly, the social- and academic-differentiation effects were correlated 0.652, suggesting that these two school effects may share some common causes.

In general, it is important to inspect the correlations estimated from the random-coefficient regression model. Although social and academic differentiation were moderately to strongly correlated in this application, there was still sufficient independent variation to treat each of them as separate school effects. In applications discussed later in this book, correlations of .90 and higher were found. In such cases, the two random effects are carrying essentially the same variation across the level-2 units. A reduction of the model to specify one of these level-1 effects as fixed or nonrandomly varying would be warranted. Theory and research purposes should dictate which of the two is more important to treat as a random effect.

Table 5.6 also reports the reliabilities for each of the level-2 random effects. In the random-coefficient regression model, these are equivalent to the reliabilities of the OLS estimates, $\hat{\beta}_{qj}$, as measures of the true parameters,

β_{qj}. These reliabilities were computed by substituting the estimated values for the level-1 and level-2 variance components into Equation 3.59. We note that these statistics, like the χ^2 homogeneity statistics, use the separate OLS estimates for each level-2 unit. Thus, they are based on 138 schools in this application.

The reliability estimates from the random-coefficient regression model are helpful in that they provide additional guidance on appropriate specification of the level-1 coefficients (i.e., as fixed, random, or nonrandomly varying). Because the metric of τ_{qq} depends on the metric of the corresponding X_q and Y_{ij}, interpreting the absolute values of τ_{qq} takes some care. The reliability provides an alternative indicator of amount of signal present in these data. That is, it tells us how much of the observed variation in the $\hat{\beta}_{qj}$ is potentially explainable. Past experiences working with these methods suggest that whenever the reliability of a random level-1 coefficient drops below 0.05, that coefficient is a candidate for treatment either as fixed or nonrandomly varying.

These statistics also offer insight into the power of a particular data set to detect hypothesized structural effects. We have considerable power in the High School and Beyond data for examining hypotheses about effects of school characteristics on school mean achievement since the intercept estimates are highly reliable. In contrast, the data set is only marginally useful for studying how school characteristics influence the relative achievement of majority and minority children. As noted above, 22 schools have no information on this effect and some of the others have only limited information. This suggests caution in inferring that "school characteristics don't seem to matter" in terms of influencing the relative achievement levels of majority and minority group children. The reliability coefficients tell us that these data provide little evidence for making such assertions. In short, they caution us against overzealous interpretation of a null hypothesis affirmed.

An Intercepts- and Slopes-as-Outcomes Model: The Effects of Sector and Context. The results from the random-coefficient regression model indicated that each of the level-1 predictors had, on average, a significant relationship with math achievement. (This judgment is based on the fixed-effect estimates, their standard errors, and t ratios.) Thus, each of these predictors should remain at least as a fixed effect in the student-level model. Further, the statistical evidence provided by the τ_{qq} point estimates, the χ^2 homogeneity tests, the likelihood-ratio test, and the reliability statistics indicated that there was sufficient variability among schools in each of the level-1 regression coefficients to treat these coefficients, at least initially, as random.

Lee and Bryk (1989) next sought to develop explanatory models to illuminate how differences among schools in their organizational characteristics might influence the social distribution of achievement within schools.

One model hypothesized differential effects of sector and composition. The investigators noted that the student composition in both Catholic and public schools varied considerably and that these contextual differences might affect outcomes, even after adjusting for the individual student characteristics already included in the level-1 model. (This idea of compositional effects in organizational research is discussed more fully later.) Thus, they modeled the joint effects of SECTOR and context (as measured by AVSES, HIMN-RTY, AVBACKGRD from Table 5.5) on mean achievement, minority gap, social differentiation, and academic differentiation. They also hypothesized that these context effects might be different in the two sectors. Therefore, they included the interactions between SECTOR and each of the context measures as predictors in the level-2 models.

The investigators allowed the level-1 model to remain as in Equation 5.27. They posed the following level-2 model:

$$\beta_{0j} = \gamma_{00} + \gamma_{01}(\text{AVSES})_j + \gamma_{02}(\text{HIMNRTY})_j + \gamma_{03}(\text{AVBACKGRD})_j$$
$$+ \gamma_{04}(\text{SECTOR})_j + \gamma_{05}(\text{SECTOR} \times \text{AVSES})_j$$
$$+ \gamma_{06}(\text{SECTOR} \times \text{HIMNRTY})_j$$
$$+ \gamma_{07}(\text{SECTOR} \times \text{AVBACKGRD})_j + u_{0j},$$
$$\beta_{1j} = \gamma_{10} + \gamma_{11}(\text{HIMNRTY})_j + \gamma_{12}(\text{SECTOR})_j \qquad\qquad [5.33]$$
$$+ \gamma_{13}(\text{SECTOR} \times \text{HIMNRTY})_j + u_{1j},$$
$$\beta_{2j} = \gamma_{20} + \gamma_{21}(\text{AVSES})_j + \gamma_{22}(\text{SECTOR})_j$$
$$+ \gamma_{23}(\text{SECTOR} \times \text{AVSES})_j + u_{2j},$$
$$\beta_{3j} = \gamma_{30} + \gamma_{31}(\text{AVBACKGRD})_j + \gamma_{32}(\text{SECTOR})_j$$
$$+ \gamma_{33}(\text{SECTOR} \times \text{AVBACKGRD})_j + u_{3j}.$$

In their first analysis using this model, several of the estimated coefficients were trivially small ($\gamma_{06}, \gamma_{07}, \gamma_{11}, \gamma_{13}, \gamma_{31}, \gamma_{33}$). Each of the corresponding level-2 predictors were deleted and a reduced model estimated. The results for this are presented in Table 5.7 and discussed below.

School Mean Achievement. The average academic background of students (AVBACKGRD) was positively related to school mean achievement ($\hat{\gamma}_{03} = 1.301, t = 2.514$). Mean achievement was lower in schools with high minority concentrations ($\hat{\gamma}_{02} = -1.488, t = -2.699$). The effect of average social class (AVSES) on school mean achievement varied across the two sectors. That is, a significant interaction effect was detected ($\hat{\gamma}_{05} = -1.572, t = -3.642$). In the Catholic sector, the relationship of AVSES with school mean achievement was 2.534 [i.e., $\hat{\gamma}_{01} + (1)\hat{\gamma}_{05} = 4.106 - 1.572$]. In the public sector, the relationship was much stronger, at 5.678 [i.e., $\hat{\gamma}_{01} + (-1)\hat{\gamma}_{05} = 4.106 + 1.572$].

TABLE 5.7 Estimated Effects of Sector and Control on the Social Distribution of Achievement

Fixed Effect	Coefficient	se	t Ratio
School mean achievement			
BASE, γ_{00}	13.678	0.186	73.393
AVSES, γ_{01}	4.106	0.493	8.327
HIMNRTY, γ_{02}	−1.488	0.551	−2.699
AVBACKGRD, γ_{03}	1.301	0.517	2.514
SECTOR, γ_{04}	0.716	0.194	3.700
SECTOR × AVSES, γ_{05}	−1.572	0.432	−3.642
Minority gap			
BASE, γ_{10}	−2.894	0.256	−11.300
SECTOR, γ_{12}	0.721	0.256	2.816
Social class differentiation			
BASE, γ_{20}	1.381	0.141	9.819
AVSES, γ_{21}	0.131	0.325	0.402
SECTOR, γ_{22}	−0.362	0.141	−2.571
SECTOR × AVSES, γ_{23}	−0.869	0.325	−2.671
Academic differentiation			
BASE, γ_{30}	2.482	0.093	26.650
SECTOR, γ_{32}	0.072	0.093	0.778

Random Effect	Variance Component	df	χ^2	p Value
Mean achievement	2.681	132	631.19	0.000
Minority gap	0.624	136	151.04	0.179
SES differentiation	0.218	134	159.94	0.063
Academic differentiation	0.475	136	221.70	0.000
Level-1 effect, r_{ij}	31.778			

The presence of such an interaction effect means that the magnitude of the sector effect depends on the social class of the schools compared. In general, the sector effect on mean achievement was

Catholic prediction − public prediction

$$= (1)\hat{\gamma}_{04} + (1)(\text{AVSES})(\hat{\gamma}_{05}) - [(-1)\hat{\gamma}_{04} + (-1)(\text{AVSES})(\hat{\gamma}_{05})]$$
$$= 2[\hat{\gamma}_{04} + (\text{AVSES})_j(\hat{\gamma}_{05})].$$

For schools of average social class (AVSES = 0), the sector effect was 1.432 points, or $2[\hat{\gamma}_{04} + (0)\hat{\gamma}_{05}]$. The Catholic advantage was greater for low social-class schools. For example, if AVSES = −1.0, the sector effect was 4.576 points, or $2[\hat{\gamma}_{04} + (-1)\hat{\gamma}_{05}]$. For affluent schools, however (AVSES > 1), average mathematic achievement was actually higher in public schools.

Minority Gap. The minority gap was also different in the two sectors ($\hat{\gamma}_{12} = 0.721$, $t = 2.816$). In the average Catholic school, minority students scored 2.173 points behind their white classmates [$\hat{\gamma}_{10} + (1)\hat{\gamma}_{12}$]. (This is a net effect after controlling for students' SES and BACKGROUND.) In the average public school, the minority gap was 3.615 points [$\hat{\gamma}_{10} + (-1)\hat{\gamma}_{12}$].

Social Class Differentiation. The differentiating effect of social class within a school depended jointly on the AVSES and SECTOR. The estimated interaction effect, $\hat{\gamma}_{23}$, was larger in magnitude than either of the main effects, $\hat{\gamma}_{21}$ and $\hat{\gamma}_{22}$. In the public sector, high social-class schools were more differentiating with regard to student social class than were low social-class schools. In the Catholic sector, the opposite was true: High social-class schools were *less* socially differentiating than were low social-class schools. This can be seen by computing the effect of AVSES on social-class differentiation separately for the Catholic and public schools based on $\hat{\gamma}_{21} + (\text{SECTOR})\hat{\gamma}_{23}$. For public schools, the effect of AVSES is $.131 + (-1)(-.869) = 1.000$. For Catholic schools, the effect of AVSES is $.131 + (1)(-.869) = -.738$.

Academic Differentiation. With regard to academic differentiation, there was no evidence of context, sector, or sector-by-context effects.

Auxillary Statistics. The bottom panel of Table 5.6 reports the estimated-variance components at level 1 and level 2 for the sector-context effects model. The level-1 variance estimate, $\hat{\sigma}^2$, was virtually identical to that reported for the random-coefficient regression model, an expected result because the level-1 models are the same. In general, some slight variation in the estimation of $\hat{\sigma}^2$ may occur, becasue all fixed and random effects are estimated jointly and each parameter estimate depends on all of the others.

At level 2, each $\hat{\tau}_{qq}$ estimate is now a conditional or residual variance. That is, u_{qj} is a residual school effect unexplained by the level-2 predictors included in the model. In contrast, each $\hat{\tau}_{qq}$ associated with the random-coefficient model was an unconditional variance. Comparison of these conditional variances (Table 5.7) with the unconditional variances (Table 5.6) indicates a substantial reduction in variation once sector and context are taken into account. The proportion variance explained by the sector-context model at level 2, using Equation 4.24, was

$$
\begin{matrix} \text{Proportion} \\ \text{variation} \\ \text{explained} \\ \text{in } \beta_q \end{matrix} = \frac{\hat{\tau}_{qq}(\text{unconditional}) - \hat{\tau}_{qq}(\text{conditional})}{\hat{\tau}_{qq}(\text{unconditional})}.
$$

TABLE 5.8 Proportion of Variance Explained Final Model

Model	Average Achievement Var(β_{0j})	Minority Status Var(β_{1j})	Social Class Var(β_{2j})	Academic Background Var(β_{3j})
Unconditional model	9.325	1.367	0.360	0.496
Conditional model	2.681	0.624	0.218	0.475
Proportion of variance explained (in percentage)	71.2	54.4	39.4	4.2

These statistics are reported in Table 5.8. Substantial proportions of the variance in average achievement, minority gap, and social differentiation have been explained. Variation among schools in academic differentiation remains virtually unexplained. Because the reliability of the academic-differentiation effects was relatively high (0.330 in Table 5.6), we can be reasonably confident that the substantial differences observed in academic differentiation were probably not related to sector or context, but rather to other factors. In fact, subsequent analysis reported by Lee and Bryk (1989) explained a substantial variation in β_{3j} as a function of differences in the academic organization and normative environments of schools.

Returning to Table 5.7, we note that χ^2 statistics for both the minority gap and SES differentiation effect were consistent with the hypothesis that the residual variation in these two school effects is zero. These results, of course, do not mean that this null hypothesis is actually true. Because the researchers had theoretical reasons to investigate whether these distributive effects also varied as a function of school organization and normative environments, they proceeded to estimate additional models with an expanded set of level-2 predictors for each of the four random school effects. Many hypothesized organizational relations were detected. The point is that the homogeneity tests for intercepts and slopes are only a guide and should *not* substitute for informed judgement.

Applications with Both Random and Fixed Level-1 Slopes

In the interest of clarity of exposition, we have organized this chapter around two distinct classes of applications. In Case 1, only the intercept parameter varied across organizations, with the effects of level-1 predictors, if included, treated as fixed coefficients. In Case 2 just discussed, all level-1 coefficients were treated as random. In fact, many applications are well suited for a model with both random and fixed level-1 coefficients. For example, suppose we had one randomly varying level-1 slope, β_{1j}, and a series of other level-1 predictors that we sought to introduce as covariates:

$$Y_{ij} = \beta_{0j} + \beta_{1j}(X_{1ij} - \overline{X}_{1 \cdot j}) + \sum_{q=2}^{Q} \beta_{qj}(\overline{X}_{q \cdot j} - \overline{X}_{q} \cdot \cdot) + r_{ij}. \qquad [5.34]$$

At level 2,

$$\beta_{qj} = \gamma_{q0} + \sum_{s=1}^{S_q} \gamma_{qs} W_{sj} + u_{qj} \quad \text{for } q = 0, 1 \qquad [5.35a]$$

and

$$\beta_{qj} = \gamma_{q0} \quad \text{for } q = 2, \ldots, Q, \qquad [5.35b]$$

where u_{q0} and u_{q1} are assumed bivariate normal with means of 0, variances τ_{00} and τ_{11}, respectively, and covariances τ_{01}.

In this model, two random effects, an intercept and one slope, are hypothesized for each organization. The intercept, β_{0j}, is an adjusted mean taking into account differences among the individuals in these organizations with regard to $X_2, \ldots, X_Q$. Similarly, the slope β_{1j} is net of any fixed effects associated with $X_2, \ldots, X_Q$. At level 2, β_{0j} and β_{1j} are hypothesized to vary as a function of measured organizational features, W_{sj}.

In general, any combination of random, nonrandomly varying, and fixed coefficients can be employed in the level-1 model. Theoretical considerations are primary in deciding whether a level-1 coefficient should be conceived as random.

Special Topics

The remainder of the chapter consists of a series of "special topics" concerning the design and use of hierarchical models in organizational applications. Much of the material presented here is new to the second edition. We demonstrate how the basic hierarchical model can be generalized to represent and model heterogeneous variances at level 1. Following this, we detail how the choice of centering for level-2 variables affects the estimation of random level-1 coefficients, β_j, fixed effects, γ, and the variance-covariance components in T. We then discuss some complications that can arise in interpreting proportion in variance-explained statistics in more complex organizational effects models. Following this, we describe how to use the empirical Bayes estimates of level-1 coefficients as performance indicators for specific organizational units and discuss validity concerns that may arise in such applications. The chapter concludes with an introduction to power considerations in designing new data collection for two-level organizational effects studies.

Applications with Heterogeneous Level-1 Variance

All of the applications considered so far in this chapter have assumed a homogeneous residual error at level 1, that is, $\text{Var}(r_{ij}) = \sigma^2$. There is some statistical evidence which suggests that the estimation of the fixed effects, γ, and their standard errors will be robust to violations of this assumption (Kasim & Raudenbush, 1998). Nonetheless, situations can arise where notable heterogeneity occurs at level 1, which may be substantively significant. In such cases, the analyst may wish to model this heterogeneity as a function of measured variables. These predictors may be defined at either level 1 or level 2.

For example, the High School and Beyond (HS&B) data on students' mathematics achievement, used in Chapter 4, displays heterogeneous residual variance at level 1. (Procedures for detecting heterogeneity of level-1 variance are described in Chapter 9 and illustrated with the HS&B data.) We might hypothesize that the residual variance at level 1 in these data is different for public and Catholic schools. Alternatively, the residual variance might depend on some level-1 characteristic such as gender. (There is some research evidence, for example, that the academic achievement is more variable among boys than girls [Hedges & Nowell, 1995].)

Formally, since the level-1 variance, σ^2, is constrained to be positive, it is more sensible to model the $\ln(\sigma^2)$ as a linear function of some measured level-1 or level-2 variables, X or W, rather than to model σ^2 itself. This assures that estimates are consistent with only positive values of σ^2. Therefore, we now add an additional structural specification to the basic hierarchical linear model:

$$\ln(\sigma^2) = \alpha_0 + \sum \alpha_j C_j, \qquad [5.36]$$

where C_j may be either a level-1 or a level-2 predictor, X or W, respectively. Since the α coefficients in Equation 5.36 will be estimated through maximum likelihood, the coefficients relative to their standard errors form z statistics under large-sample theory. This test statistic can be used, as illustrated below, for purposes of testing hypotheses about the sources of level-1 heterogeneity.

Example: Modeling Sector Effects on the Level-1 Residual Variance in Mathematics Achievement

To illustrate this extension of hierarchical linear models using the HS&B data, we consider whether the level-1 residual variance might be different in Catholic and public schools. We pose a simple model with student social class, X_{ij}, group mean centered at level 1, and SECTOR as a level-2 predictor for both school mean achievement, β_{0j}, and the SES differentiation effect, β_{1j}. That is,

$$Y_{ij} = \beta_{0j} + \beta_{1j}(X_{ij} - \overline{X}._j) + r_{ij}$$

and

$$\beta_{0j} = \gamma_{00} + \gamma_{01}(\text{SECTOR}) + u_{0j},$$
$$\beta_{1j} = \gamma_{10} + \gamma_{11}(\text{SECTOR}) + u_{1j},$$

where now r_{ij} is assumed to be distributed $N(0, \sigma_{ij}^2)$. In this particular example, we specify that

$$\ln(\sigma_{ij}^2) = \alpha_0 + \alpha_1(\text{SECTOR})_j.$$

Table 5.9 presents the results for this model estimated both with and without the heterogeneous variance specification at level 1. There is clear evidence that the residual level-1 variability, after controlling for student social class, is different within public and Catholic high schools ($\alpha_1 = -.182$, with $z = 5.409$). By exponentiating the results from the model for $\ln(\sigma^2)$, we can compute separate level-1 residual variance estimates for Catholic and public schools. The homogeneous model produced an overall level-1 residual variance estimate of 36.705. We see that the residual level-1 variance in Catholic schools is 33.31 while in public schools it is considerably higher, 39.96.

In general, the heterogeneous model appears to fit these data better than the simple homogeneous level-1 specification. In addition to the highly significant z test statistic for α_1, this inference is also confirmed in the results from the likelihood-ratio test that compares the deviances from the two models, $\chi^2 = 29.139$, with 1 df, and $p < .000$. Even so, we note that the parameter estimates from the two models for γ, the se(γ) and **T**, remain quite similar.

Data-Analytic Advice About the Presence of Heterogeneity at Level 1

The potential to model level-1 residual variances represents a useful extension to the basic model for some substantive applications. As discussed in Chapter 9 (see also Raudenbush & Bryk, 1987), the presence of heterogeneity of variance at level 1 can be viewed as an omnibus indicator of level-1 model misspecification. That is, heterogeneity will result at level 1 when an important level-1 predictor has been omitted from the model or the effect of a level-1 predictor has been erroneously specified as fixed, when it should

TABLE 5.9 Comparison of Homogeneous and Heterogeneous Level-1 Variance Models for Mathematics Achievement from High School and Beyond

(i) Results for Homogeneous Variance Model, $\mathrm{Var}(r_{ij}) = \sigma^2$

Fixed Effect	Coefficient	se	t Ratio	df	p Value
School mean achievement					
BASE, γ_{00}	11.394	0.291	39.166	158	0.000
SECTOR, γ_{01}	2.807	0.436	6.434	158	0.000
Social class differentiation					
BASE, γ_{10}	2.803	0.154	18.215	158	0.000
SECTOR, γ_{11}	−1.341	0.232	−5.777	158	0.000

Random Effect	Standard Deviation	Variance Component	df	χ^2	p Value
Mean achievement, u_{0j}	2.577	6.641	158	1,383.31	0.000
SES differentiation, u_{1j}	0.489	0.239	158	175.24	0.165
Level-1 effect, r_{ij}	6.058	36.705			

Deviance = 46632.04
Number of estimated parameters = 8

(ii) Results for Heterogeneous Variance Model, $\ln[\mathrm{Var}(r_{ij})] = \alpha_0 + \alpha_1(\mathrm{SECTOR})$

Fixed Effect	Coefficient	se	t Ratio	df	p Value
School mean achievement					
BASE, γ_{00}	11.393	0.292	38.982	158	0.000
SECTOR, γ_{01}	2.807	0.436	6.441	158	0.000
Social class differentiation					
BASE, γ_{10}	2.802	0.160	17.472	158	0.000
SECTOR, γ_{11}	−1.341	0.232	−5.789	158	0.000

Random Effect	Standard Deviation	Variance Component	df	χ^2	p Value
Mean achievement, u_{0j}	2.574	6.626	158	1,392.58	0.000
SES differentiation, u_{1j}	0.499	0.249	158	173.52	0.189

Model for Level-1 Variance

Parameter	Coefficient	se	z Ratio	p Value
Intercept, α_0	3.688	0.024	154.533	0.000
SECTOR, α_1	−0.182	0.033	−5.409	0.000

For public schools, $\hat{\sigma}^2 = \exp[3.688 - 0.182(0)] = 39.96$
For Catholic schools, $\hat{\sigma}^2 = \exp[3.688 - 0.182(1)] = 33.31$

Summary of Model Fit

Model	Number of Parameters	Deviance
1. Homogeneous level-1 variance	8	4,6632.04
2. Heterogeneous level-1 variance	9	4,6602.90

	χ^2	df	p Value
Model 1 versus Model 2	29.139	1	0.000

be treated as either random or nonrandomly varying. Thus, the sector differences for σ^2 found in the application above suggest that we pursue further the specification of the level-1 model. What could cause these differences in residual variances between Catholic and public schools? Two immediate explanations arise: (1) The student intake into Catholic and public high schools might differ on other factors, in addition to social class, and these student-level background controls need to be added to the model; and/or (2) students might have different academic experiences within Catholic and public high schools that contribute to a different final distribution of achievement in these two sectors. For example, students pursue more differentiated course taking patterns in public schools, which could result in the greater heterogeneity found there (Bryk, Lee, & Holland, 1993). This explanation suggests adding a student-level measure of course taking to the model. In either instance, as we fill out the level-1 model, we would expect the residual heterogeneity to decline.

In short, the presence of heterogeneity at level 1 suggests a need for further modeling efforts at this level. The possibility exists that the model is misspecified in ways that might bias the estimates of γ and **T**. Moreover, while a heterogeneous specification for σ^2 at level 1 can help provide clues about the sources of this heterogeneity, it does not per se protect against model misspecification bias. Only a more elaborated level-1 model can help in this regard.

Centering Level-1 Predictors
in Organizational Effects Applications

As discussed in Chapter 2 (see "Location of Xs"), choice of location for level-1 predictors affects the definition of the level-1 intercept in two-level models. In some applications, centering around a constant such as the grand mean of X is advisable, while in other settings, centering around a level-2 mean (i.e., "group-mean centering") will be preferable. We now consider how these choices affect inferences for five purposes:

- estimating fixed level-1 coefficients;
- disentangling person-level and compositional effects;
- estimating level-2 effects while adjusting for level-1 covariates;
- estimating the variances of level-1 coefficients; and
- estimating random level-1 coefficients.

Estimating Fixed Level-1 Coefficients

In addition to estimating how organizational factors influence person-level outcomes, multilevel data are often also used to estimate person-level effects. For example, in the High School and Beyond data, a primary analytic concern was the relationship between student social class and math achievement. The fact that students were nested within schools represented a nuisance consideration in an effort to obtain an appropriate estimate of this level-1 relationship. Burstein (1980) provided an extensive review of the modeling issues that arise in such applications. We offer below a brief account of these concerns and show how they can be resolved through the formulation of hierarchical models that explictly represent the nesting structure. These methods are illustrated using the High School and Beyond data. We assume for now that the level-1 relationship of interest is fixed across level-2 units.

We begin by considering the most commonly employed technique for analyzing multilevel data—an OLS regression analysis at level 1, which simply ignores the nesting of persons within groups. The first column of Table 5.10 presents the model for this analysis, and the results from a regression of math achievement on student SES. The estimated regression coefficient for SES was 3.184, with a standard error of 0.097. For reasons that will become clear below, we refer to the regression coefficient in this model as β_t.

For comparison, we present in the second column of Table 5.10 the corresponding model for a level-2 or between-group analysis. When person-level data are not available, this regression coefficient, referred to as β_b, has often been used as an estimator of the person-level relationship. (Robinson [1950] Burstein [1980] and Aitkin and Longford [1986] discuss the conditions under which such use is appropriate.) In this particular application, however, the estimated β_b of 5.909 is almost twice as large as $\hat{\beta}_t$. Clearly, these two analyses provide very different answers about the magnitude of the relationship between individual social class and math achievement. Notice also that the standard error is considerably larger in this case (0.371 versus 0.097), primarily reflecting the fact that the degrees of freedom in the level-2 analysis are 158, compared with 7,183 in the level-1 analysis. Even when it is appropriate to use $\hat{\beta}_b$ as an estimator of the person-level relationship (which does not appear to be the case here), the estimate will generally be less precise than an estimate based on a level-1 analysis. Typically, there is just less information available in the unit means than in the full individual data.

It is frequently argued (see, e.g., Firebaugh, 1978) that the person-level coefficient really of interest is the pooled-within-organization relationship between math achievement and student SES. That is, we want to estimate the level-1 relationship net of any group-membership effects. This coefficient

TABLE 5.10 Comparison of Alternative Estimators of Level-1 Regression Coefficient

		Alternative Statistical Models	
OLS Regression at Level 1 (an ungrouped analysis)	OLS Regression at Level 2 (a between-group analysis)	Hierarchical Linear Model (group-mean centering)	Hierarchical Linear Model (grand-mean centering)
$Y_i = \beta_0 + \beta_1 X_i + r_i$, $i = 1, \ldots, N$ persons (note nesting of persons within organizations is ignored)	$\overline{Y}_{\cdot j} = \beta_0 + \beta_1 \overline{X}_{\cdot j} + u_{\cdot j}$, $j = 1, \ldots, J$ organizations	$Y_{ij} = \beta_{0j} + \beta_{1j}(X_{ij} - \overline{X}_{\cdot j}) + r_{ij}$ $\beta_{0j} = \gamma_{00} + u_{0j}$ $\beta_{1j} = \gamma_{10}$	$Y_{ij} = \beta_{0j} + \beta_{1j}(X_{ij} - \overline{X}_{\cdot \cdot}) + r_{ij}$ $\beta_{0j} = \gamma_{00} + u_{0j}$ $\beta_{1j} = \gamma_{10}$
$\beta_1 = \beta_t$	$\beta_1 = \beta_b$	$\gamma_{10} = \beta_w$	$\gamma_{10} = \dfrac{w_1 \beta_w + w_2 \beta_b}{w_1 + w_2}$

Estimates Using High School and Beyond Data

$\hat{\beta}_t = 3.184$	$\hat{\beta}_b = 5.909$	$\hat{\beta}_w = 2.191$	$\hat{\gamma}_{10} = 2.391$
$\text{se}(\hat{\beta}_t) = 0.097$	$\text{se}(\hat{\beta}_b) = 0.371$	$\text{se}(\hat{\beta}_w) = 0.109$	$\text{se}(\hat{\gamma}_{10}) = 0.106$

NOTE: For the illustrative purposes of this section, we have specified the SES coefficient as fixed. Results presented in Chapter 4, however, indicate that there is considerable variability among schools in β_{1j}. Estimation of this model with β_{1j} specified as a random coefficient did not substantially change the γ_{10} estimates (2.193 vs. 2.191). The standard error, however, increased from 0.109 to 0.125. By assuming a fixed level-1 coefficient for SES, we constrained the $\text{Var}(\beta_{1j}) = \tau_{11} = 0$. Because τ_{11} is a component of the standard error of γ_{10} (see Chapter 3), setting it to zero when it is not at least close to zero will result in an underestimate of the standard error.

is typically referred to as β_w and can be obtained with OLS methods by estimating the equation

$$Y_{ij} - \overline{Y}._j = \beta_w(X_{ij} - \overline{X}._j) + r_{ij}. \qquad [5.37]$$

Column 3 of Table 5.10 presents the equivalent hierarchical linear model. For the High School and Beyond data, $\hat{\beta}_w$ was 2.191 with a standard error of 0.109. Although the estimated standard error for $\hat{\beta}_w$ was quite similar to the standard error for $\hat{\beta}_t$ (which will typically be the case), $\hat{\beta}_t$ was actually partway between $\hat{\beta}_w$ and $\hat{\beta}_b$. It can readily be shown that $\hat{\beta}_t$ is formally a weighted combination of β_w and β_b:

$$\hat{\beta}_t = \eta^2\hat{\beta}_b + (1 - \eta^2)\hat{\beta}_w, \qquad [5.38]$$

where η^2 is the ratio of the between-schools sum of squares on SES to the total sum of squares on SES.

The relationships among β_w, β_b, and β_t are depicted in Figure 5.1. The figure shows a hypothetical data set with three schools: a school with low mean SES, a school with medium SES, and a school with high mean SES. Within each school is a regression line with slope β_w that describes the association between student SES and Y within that school. These within-school slopes are assumed equal. There is also a regression line (the bold line) that describes the association between mean SES and mean Y. This is the line one would estimate using only three data points, that is, the mean

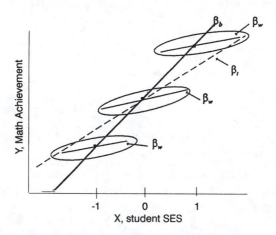

Figure 5.1. Within-Group Regression Lines (Inside the Elipses) have Slope β_w, Between Group Regression Lines (Bold Lines) has Slope β_b, and Total Regression (Dashed Line) Has Slope β_t.

SES and mean Y for each school. This line has slope β_b. A final dashed line describes the association between student SES and Y, ignoring the clustering of students within schools. The slope β_t of this line is neither as flat as β_w nor as steep as β_b.

Thus, ignoring the nested structure of the data can lead to misleading results when person-level effect estimates are desired. As Cronbach (1976) noted, $\hat{\beta}_t$ is generally an uninterpretable blend of $\hat{\beta}_w$ and $\hat{\beta}_b$. In most research applications, the person-level effect estimate of interest is $\hat{\beta}_w$ and not $\hat{\beta}_t$.

In estimating β_w based on a hierarchical analysis, the group-mean centering of X_{ij} plays a critical role. By contrast, if the data are grand-mean centered, as in the fourth column of Table 5.10, the resulting estimator is a mix of β_w and β_b. The weights, W_1 and W_2, are quite complex for the general case. Note that the coefficient estimate for the High School and Beyond data with grand-mean centering was 2.391.

This result derives from the fact that the model with grand-mean centering actually involves both X_{ij} and $\overline{X}._j$, but the analysis is constrained to estimate only one parameter rather than separate estimates for β_w and β_b (a hierarchical model for the joint estimator of β_w and β_b is presented in the next section).

It is important to note that if in a given application β_b and β_w were in fact identical then the estimated model with grand-mean centering would be most efficient. Under the hypothesis that $\beta_b = \beta_w = \beta$, $\hat{\beta}_b$ and $\hat{\beta}_w$ are independent, unbiased estimators of β. In a balanced design, the sampling variances of each of these OLS estimates, respectively, is

$$\mathrm{Var}(\hat{\beta}_b) = \Delta / \sum_j (\overline{X}._j - \overline{X}..)^2,$$

with

$$\Delta = \tau_{00} + \sigma^2/n,$$

and

$$\mathrm{Var}(\hat{\beta}_w) = \sigma^2 / \sum_j \sum_i (X_{ij} - \overline{X}._j)^2.$$

In this specific case, the estimator of β provided in column 4 of Table 5.10,

$$\hat{\gamma}_{10} = \hat{\beta} = \frac{W_1\hat{\beta}_b + W_2\hat{\beta}_w}{W_1 + W_2} \qquad [5.39]$$

simplifies in that

$$W_1 = [\widehat{\mathrm{Var}}(\hat{\beta}_b)]^{-1} = \sum(\overline{X}._j - \overline{X}..)^2/\widehat{\Delta}$$

and

$$W_2 = [\widehat{\mathrm{Var}}(\hat{\beta}_w)]^{-1} = \sum\sum(X_{ij} - \overline{X}._j)^2/\hat{\sigma}^2.$$

In this specific case, $\hat{\gamma}_{10}$ is a weighted average of $\hat{\beta}_b$ and $\hat{\beta}_w$ where the weights are the precisions of each estimator. Because both $\hat{\beta}_b$ and $\hat{\beta}_w$ contain information about β, the hierarchical estimator optimally combines the information to yield a single estimator with greater precision than either of the two component estimators. Formally,

$$[\text{Var}(\hat{\beta}_{\text{hierarchical}})]^{-1} = W_1 + W_2, \qquad [5.40]$$

that is, the precision of the hierarchical estimate is the sum of the precisions of $\hat{\beta}_b$ and $\hat{\beta}_w$. It is of interest that W_1 is approximately proportional to J and W_2 to Jn.

In unbalanced designs, the formulas become more complicated. The same principle still applies, however. Assuming $\beta_w = \beta_b$, the hierarchical estimator with grand-mean centering will be most efficient.

When $\beta_b \neq \beta_w$, as appears true in this application, the hierarchical estimator under grand-mean centering is an inappropriate estimator of the person-level effect. It too is an uninterpretable blend: neither β_w nor β_b, nor β_t. Thus, when an unbiased estimate of β_w is desired, group-mean centering will produce it. Two alternative hierarchical models that allow joint estimation of β_w and β_b are presented below.

Disentangling Person-Level and Compositional Effects

Compositional or contextual effects are of enduring interest in organizational sociology (see, e.g., Erbring & Young, 1979; Firebaugh, 1978). Such effects are said to occur when the aggregate of a person-level characteristic, $\overline{X}_{\cdot j}$, is related to the outcome, Y_{ij}, even after controlling for the effect of the individual characteristic, X_{ij}. In an OLS level-1 regression analysis, these effects are represented through the inclusion of both $(X_{ij} - \overline{X}_{\cdot j})$ and $\overline{X}_{\cdot j}$ as predictors:

$$Y_{ij} = \beta_0 + \beta_1(X_{ij} - \overline{X}_{\cdot j}) + \beta_2\overline{X}_{\cdot j} + r_{ij}. \qquad [5.41]$$

The compositional effect is the extent to which the magnitude of the organization-level relationship, β_b, differs from the person-level effect, β_w. Formally, the compositional effect is

$$\beta_c = \beta_2 - \beta_1 = \beta_b - \beta_w. \qquad [5.42]$$

The compositional effect is graphed in Figure 5.2. We note that a nonzero estimate for β_2 does note necessarily imply a compositional effect. If β_1 and β_2 are equal, no compositional effect is present.

Compositional effects are open to widely varying interpretations. Such effects may occur because of normative effects associated with an organization or because $\overline{X}_{\cdot j}$ acts as a proxy for other important organizational

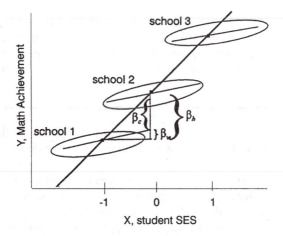

Figure 5.2. Illustration of the Contextual Effect, β_c, Associated with Attending School 2 versus School 1

variables omitted from the model. They may also signal a statistical artifact where $\overline{X}_{\cdot j}$ carries part of the effect of a poorly measured X_{ij}. Whatever their source, past empirical research indicates that compositional effects occur with considerable regularity (see Willms' [1986] review).

TABLE 5.11 Illustration of Person-Level and Compositional (or Contextual) Effects

	Statistical Model		
Group-Mean Centering		*Grand-Mean Centering*	

$Y_{ij} = \beta_{0j} + \beta_{1j}(X_{ij} - \overline{X}_{\cdot j}) + r_{ij}$ $Y_{ij} = \beta_{0j} + \beta_{1j}(X_{ij} - \overline{X}_{\cdot \cdot}) + r_{ij}$

$\beta_{0j} = \gamma_{00} + \gamma_{01}\overline{X}_{\cdot j} + u_{0j}$ $\beta_{0j} = \gamma_{00} + \gamma_{01}\overline{X}_{\cdot j} + u_{0j}$

$\beta_{1j} = \gamma_{10}$ $\beta_{1j} = \gamma_{10}$

$\gamma_{01} = \beta_b$ $\gamma_{01} = \beta_c$

$\gamma_{10} = \beta_w$ $\gamma_{10} = \beta_w$

$\beta_c = \gamma_{01} - \gamma_{10}$ $\beta_b = \gamma_{01} + \gamma_{10}$

	Estimates Using High School and Beyond Data		
	Coefficient	*se*	*Coefficient*	*se*

	Coefficient	se		Coefficient	se
$\hat{\gamma}_{00}$	12.648	0.149	$\hat{\gamma}_{00}$	12.661	0.149
$\hat{\gamma}_{01} = \hat{\beta}_b$	5.866	0.362	$\hat{\gamma}_{01} = \hat{\beta}_c$	3.675	0.378
$\hat{\gamma}_{10} = \hat{\beta}_w$	2.191	0.109	$\hat{\gamma}_{10} = \hat{\beta}_w$	2.191	0.109
$\hat{\beta}_c$	3.675	0.378*	$\hat{\beta}_b$	5.866	0.362[a]

a. Not directly estimated but can be determined from the sampling variance-covariance matrix for the γ coefficients.

Within a hierarchical modeling framework, these effects can be estimated in two different ways. In both cases, the person-level X_{ij} is included in the level-1 model and its aggregate, $\overline{X}_{.j}$, is included in the level-2 model for the intercept. The difference between the two approaches, as displayed in columns 1 and 2 of Table 5.11, is in the choice of centering for X_{ij}. When group-mean centering is chosen as in column 1, the relationship between X_{ij} and Y_{ij} is directly decomposed into its within- and between-group components. Specifically, γ_{01} is β_b and γ_{10} is β_w. The compositional effect can be derived by simple subtraction. Alternatively, if X_{ij} is centered around the grand mean, as in column 2, the compositional effect is estimated directly and β_b is derived by simple addition.

The presence of a context effect is graphically illustrated in Figure 5.2. As before, we present results from three schools, each differing respectively from the other by one unit on mean SES. Also, as before, the within-school relationship, β_w, is graphed for each school, as is the between-school relationship among the schools, β_b. β_w represents the expected difference in Y between two students in the same school who differ by one unit on SES. (This is illustrated within School 1.) In contrast, β_b is the expected difference between the means of two schools, which differ by one unit in mean SES. (This is illustrated for School 1 versus School 2). The contextual effect, $\beta_c = \beta_b - \beta_w$, is the expected difference in the outcomes between two students who have the same individual SES, but who attend schools differing by one unit in mean SES. As illustrated in Figure 5.2, the contextual effect, β_c, is the increment to learning that accrues to a student by virtue of being education in School 2 versus School 1.

In terms of the High School and Beyond data, the student-level effect was 2.191 (the same as in column 3 of Table 5.10), the school-level effect was 5.866, and the difference between these two, the compositional effect, was 3.675. Identical estimates result from the two alternative formulations. Clearly, the social-class composition of the school has a substantial association with math achievement, even larger than the individual student-level association.

We should note that similar point estimates for β_b, β_w, and β_c can be obtained through use of a level-1 OLS regression based on Equation 5.41. In general, the OLS estimates are unbiased but not as efficient as the hierarchical linear model estimators (see Chapter 3). Also, the OLS standard errors for $\hat{\beta}_c$ and $\hat{\beta}_b$ are negatively biased because Equation 5.41 fails to represent explicitly the random variation among schools captured in the u_{0j}.

Estimating Level-2 Effects While Adjusting for Level-1 Covariates

One of the most common applications of HLM in organizational research is simply to estimate the association between a level-2 predictor and the mean of Y, adjusting for one or more level-1 covariates. It is assumed (or established through empirical analysis) that there is no compositional effect. We saw an example of this earlier (see "Evaluating Program Effects on Writing"). In this setting, group-mean centering would be inappropriate. Under the group-mean-centered model, the level-1 intercept is the unadjusted mean of the outcome, denoted here as μ_j for emphasis,

$$Y_{ij} = \mu_j + \beta_{1j}(X_{ij} - \overline{X}_{\cdot j}) + r_{ij}. \qquad [5.43]$$

Note the influence of the level-1 predictor X disappears when we compute the sample mean for each school:

$$\overline{Y}_j = \mu_j + \bar{r}_{\cdot j}. \qquad [5.44]$$

A simple level-2 model represents the contribution of a level-2 predictor W_j:

$$\mu_j = \gamma_{00} + \gamma_{01} W_j + u_{0j}. \qquad [5.45]$$

In short, under group-mean centering, the effect of W_j is not adjusted for X in this analysis.

In contrast, when we grand-mean-center X, the level-1 model becomes

$$
\begin{aligned}
Y_{ij} &= \beta_{0j} + \beta_{1j}(X_{ij} - \overline{X}_{..}) + r_{ij} \\
&= \beta_{0j} + \beta_{1j}(X_{ij} - \overline{X}_{\cdot j} + \overline{X}_{\cdot j} - \overline{X}_{..}) + r_{ij} \\
&= \beta_{0j} + \beta_{1j}(\overline{X}_{\cdot j} - \overline{X}_{..}) + \beta_{1j}(X_{ij} - \overline{X}_{\cdot j}) + r_{ij}. \qquad [5.46]
\end{aligned}
$$

A comparison of Equations 5.43 and 5.46 reveals that

$$\beta_{0j} = \mu_j - \beta_{1j}(\overline{X}_{\cdot j} - \overline{X}_{..}). \qquad [5.47]$$

Thus, in the grand-mean-centered model, the intercept, β_{0j}, is the mean μ_j minus an adjustment. Now, viewing this adjusted mean as the outcome, we have, at level 2,

$$\beta_{0j} = \mu_j - \beta_{1j}(\overline{X}_{\cdot j} - \overline{X}_{..}) = \gamma_{00} + \gamma_{01} W_j + u_{0j}. \qquad [5.48]$$

In Equation 5.48, the estimate of the effect of W_j will be adjusted for differences between organizations in the mean of X, the level-1 explanatory variable.

Estimating the Variances of Level-1 Coefficients

Let us again consider a level-1 model with a single level-1 covariate, X. The key goal of the analysis now is to estimate the variance, τ_{11}, of the level-1 coefficient, β_{1j}. If every organization has the same mean of X, apart from sampling variation and randomly missing data, choice of centering would have no important effect on inference about τ_{11}. In this case, the analyst can choose the location for X that gives the most sensible definition of the intercept without concern about the effect of centering on the estimation of the variance of the level-1 slopes.

Estimation of τ_{11} becomes considerably more complex, however, when the group mean of X varies systematically across schools. Such variation will typically arise in organizational research for two reasons. First, persons are often selected or assigned to organizations in ways that segregate those organizations, to some degree, on X. Schools, for example, will be somewhat segregated on the basis of social class, firms will be somewhat segregated on the basis of workers' educational background, neighborhoods will be segregated to some degree on the basis of income and ethnicity. Second, organizations may capitalize on their compositions to create effects. Schools with high average social class may have more positive peer influences on student learning than will schools with lower mean social class. Firms with highly educated workers may introduce new technology more quickly than other firms.

In general, if the mean of X systematically varies across schools, choice of centering (i.e., group-mean centering versus centering around a constant) will make a difference in estimating τ_{11}. In such situations, we recommend group-mean centering to detect and estimate properly the slope heterogeneity. To develop the rationale for this recommendation, we turn again to the data from High School and Beyond (HS&B).

Recall that in our analysis of math achievement in U.S. high schools, MEAN SES is related to both the intercept and the SES-achievement slope. In this context, let us see how choice of centering affects estimation of the level-2 variances. We begin with an unconditional level-2 model, then turn to a model that includes MEAN SES. In each case, the model uses either group-mean centering, that is,

$$Y_{ij} = \mu_j + \beta_{1j}(X_{ij} - \overline{X}._{j}) + r_{ij}, \qquad [5.49]$$

or grand-mean centering, that is,

$$Y_{ij} = \beta_{0j} + \beta_{1j}(X_{ij} - \overline{X}..) + r_{ij}. \qquad [5.50]$$

TABLE 5.12 Effect of Centering on Estimation of Level-1 Slope Variation

Model	
Level 1	$Y_{ij} = \beta_{0j} + \beta_{1j}X_{ij} + r_{ij}$ $\qquad r_{ij} \sim N(0, \sigma^2)$
Level 2	Unconditional
	$\beta_{0j} = \gamma_{00} + u_{0j}$
	$\beta_{1j} = \gamma_{10} + u_{1j}$
Level 2	Conditional
	$\beta_{0j} = \gamma_{00} + \gamma_{01}(\text{SECTOR})_j + \gamma_{02}(\text{MEANSES})_j + u_{0j}$
	$\beta_{1j} = \gamma_{10} + \gamma_{11}(\text{SECTOR})_j + \gamma_{12}(\text{MEANSES})_j + u_{1j}$
	$\text{Var}\begin{pmatrix} u_{0j} \\ u_{1j} \end{pmatrix} = \begin{pmatrix} \tau_{00} & \tau_{01} \\ \tau_{10} & \tau_{11} \end{pmatrix}$

Unconditional Results	*Conditional Results*
Group-mean centering	
$\widehat{\mathbf{T}} = \begin{bmatrix} 8.68 & 0.05 \\ 0.05 & 0.68 \end{bmatrix}$	$\widehat{\mathbf{T}} = \begin{bmatrix} 2.38 & 0.19 \\ 0.19 & 0.15 \end{bmatrix}$
$\hat{\sigma}^2 = 36.70$	$\hat{\sigma}^2 = 36.70$
Grand-mean centering	
$\widehat{\mathbf{T}} = \begin{bmatrix} 4.83 & -0.15 \\ -0.15 & 0.42 \end{bmatrix}$	$\widehat{\mathbf{T}} = \begin{bmatrix} 2.41 & 0.19 \\ 0.19 & 0.06 \end{bmatrix}$
$\hat{\sigma}^2 = 36.83$	$\hat{\sigma}^2 = 36.74$

Unconditional Model. Based on the unconditional level-2 model, we obtain the variance-covariance estimates given in Table 5.12 (column 1). The variance of the intercept, τ_{00}, is much larger at 8.68 in the group-mean-centered model than 4.83 in the grand-mean-centered model. This can be explained by the fact that the intercept in the group-mean-centered model is the unadjusted mean, while the intercept in the grand-mean-centered model is the adjusted mean (see previous section). However, we also note that the τ_{11} estimates are also quite different, at .68 in the group-mean-centered model and .42 in the grand-mean-centered model. Why should this slope variance differ as a function of centering? Given that MEAN SES and SECTOR are related to both the intercept and the slope, we might speculate that adding these predictors at level 2 will eliminate the discrepancy in the τ_{11} estimates as a function of centering.

Conditional Model. The results with SECTOR and MEAN SES as predictors at level 2 of both β_{0j} and β_{1j} are given in Table 5.12, column 2. Note that the two estimates of τ_{00}, the variance of the intercepts, now essentially converge at 2.38 (group-mean-centered model) and 2.41 (grand-mean-centered model). This occurs because both models now incorporate a compositional effect, β_c, on the intercept. However, the τ_{11} estimates remain quite different, at 0.15 in the group-mean-centered model and 0.06 in the grand-mean-centered model. This occurs even though MEAN SES and SECTOR are incorporated into the model for the slope. Clearly, the choice of centering for X in this application affects our estimates for the $\tau_{11} = \text{Var}(\beta_{1j})$.

How Centering Affects Estimation of τ_{11}. To understand how group- and grand-mean centering affect the estimation of the variance of a random coefficient requires some understanding of how the method of maximum likelihood (ML) works in this setting. Formally, the new ML estimate at each iteration of the EM algorithm (see Equation 3.76) is the sum of two components:

$$\hat{\tau} = J^{-1} \left[\sum_{j=1}^{J} \left(u_{1j}^{*2} + V_{11j}^* \right) \right].$$

The first component, u_{1j}^{*2}, is the square of the empirical Bayes (EB) residual associated with the regression coefficient β_{1j}. This EB residual is also known as the expected value of u_{1j} given the data Y and current estimates of the model parameters. The second component, V_{11j}^*, is the posterior variance of u_{1j} given the data Y and the current estimates of the model parameters. Similarly, the estimate of τ_{00} is based on the squared empirical Bayes residual for the intercept plus the posterior variance of u_{0j}. These formulas indicate that the estimation of the variances of the slope and intercept depend directly on the empirical Bayes residuals. Group-mean and grand-mean centering, however, create different definitions for these residuals.

This difference can be made vivid by considering Figure 5.3, an idealized version of the HS&B data. The figure shows three types of schools: low-mean-SES schools, average-mean-SES schools, and high-mean-SES schools. Within each type of school, the OLS estimates of the achievement-SES slopes vary somewhat. Under group-mean-centering (not shown in Figure 5.3), the OLS estimates of the intercept will experience some shrinkage. The shrinkage will be large when the estimated intercept has low reliability. However, this shrinkage will not have much influence on the slope, unless the two are highly correlated, which is not the case in the HS&B data. While unreliable OLS slope estimates will certainly experience shrinkage, the direction of the shrinkage will be relatively unaffected by the shrinkage of the intercept.

In contrast, the intercept in a grand-mean-centered model estimates an adjusted mean. A heuristic illustration of the OLS estimates for the adjusted means, β_{0j}, for six schools appear in Figure 5.3a. The key point here is that for schools that are either very low or very high on mean SES, the

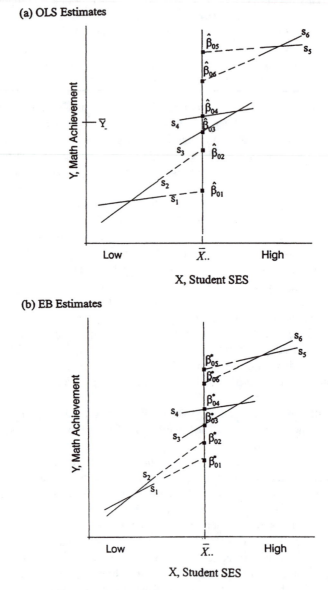

Figure 5.3. Illustration of Slope Homogenization Under Grand-Mean Centering

NOTE: Solid lines represents the range of actual data collected in each school; dashed lines are extrapolations based on fitted models.

adjusted means can entail an extrapolation (represented by the dashed lines) well beyond the data actually collected in these schools (represented by the solid lines). That is, the adjusted mean for school j represents the expected outcome for a child at that school who is at the grand mean on SES. As the figure illustrates, however Schools 1, 2, 5, and 6 do not enroll any children like this. As a result, their adjusted grand means are less reliably measured than for Schools 3 and 4 (assuming similar sample sizes in all six schools.) Consequently, the empirical Bayes estimates for β_{0j} in Schools 1, 2, 5, and 6 will be shrunk extensively toward the grand mean of Y. (Compare the OLS estimated β_{0j} in Figure 5.3a with those in Figure 5.3b). A key consequence of the shrinkage in the adjusted means is a corollary shrinkage in the slopes, β_{1j}, as well. Specifically, schools with relatively flat OLS slopes and extreme values on school SES (either high or low) record substantially increased empirical Bayes slope estimates. (Notice the substantial impact on the slope estimate for School 1 for example.) The overall result is a homogenization of the slope variability and underestimation of τ_{11}.

We now apply these ideas to analyze the effects on estimating τ_{11} under grand-mean centering with the HS&B data. We have shown previously that there is considerable variability among schools on mean SES. As a result, the "extrapolation problem" under grand-mean centering identified above should plague both very low and very high SES schools. One additional complication enters in the HS&B data. We also showed previously that the magnitude of the achievement-SES slopes depends on school SES. Specifically, we found that high-SES schools tend to have steeper achievement-SES slopes and low-SES schools have flatter slopes (see Table 4.5). Based on the heuristic example discussed above, we expect the empirical Bayes estimates of the slopes in low-SES schools to experience substantial positive shrinkage under grand-mean centering toward steeper slopes. As for the high-SES schools, because their OLS slopes tend to be steeper here, somewhat less shrinkage is likely to occur for the empirical Bayes slopes in these schools under grand-mean centering. That is, with steeper OLS slopes in high-SES schools, the OLS adjusted means for these schools are already projected down toward $\overline{Y}\ldots$ Although these OLS adjusted means may be just as unreliable for low-SES schools, since they are not as deviant from $\overline{Y}..$, less absolute shrinkage should occur under grand-mean centering. This is exactly what we observe in Figure 5.4.

The vertical axis in Figure 5.4 plots the difference between the EB slope residuals under group- versus grand-mean centering, that is,

$$Y = u^*_{1j(\text{group})} - u^*_{1j(\text{grand})},$$

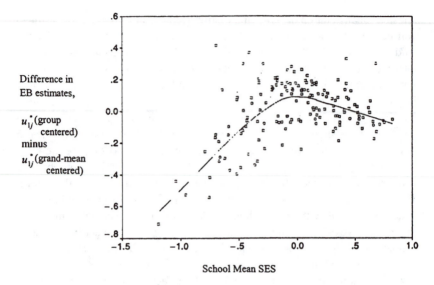

Figure 5.4. Difference between Group-Mean Centered and Grand-Mean-Centered Empirical Bayes Estimates of Achievement-SES Slopes, β_{1j}, as a Function of School Mean SES

while the horizontal axis gives the school mean SES. As predicted, in low SES schools, the empirical Bayes residuals are more negative under group-mean centering than under grand-mean centering. This happens because the grand-mean centering has artificially steepened the slopes for these schools (see Figure 5.3). If the achievement-SES slopes had not been related to school SES, we would have expected the exact same phenomenon to occur in high-SES schools and an overall symmetric curvilinear relationship should have appeared. That is, we would have expected to find more negative residuals in high-SES schools under group-mean centering as compared to grand-mean centering. Negative residuals do occur for high SES schools but not as frequently as with low-SES schools.

In general, the empirical Bayes slope estimates based on grand-mean centering are less credible because they can be significantly perturbed by the extrapolations necessary to compute an adjusted mean for each school. The empirical Bayes intercept estimates can experience significant shrinkage toward the center of the distribution. In the process, the regression slopes are artificially homogenized and the end result is negatively biased estimates of the slope variability. Such perturbation does not occur under group-mean centering. Moreover, as noted previously, incorporating mean SES as a predictor variable for both β_{0j} and β_{1j} does not solve this problem.

We note that this problem with grand-mean centering is not unique to organizational effects studies. It can arise in any hierarchical modeling context where variation exists among units on the mean of a level-1 predictor and where substantial slope variability exists for that predictor. We consider, for example in Chapter 6, how choice of centering can affect estimation of the variance of growth rates in a longitudinal context.

Estimating Random Level-1 Coefficients

We saw in the previous section how centering affects the estimation of the variance of level-1 regression coefficients. The distortions that arose in estimating this variance arose from the empirical Bayes estimates of the intercept and slope. The same issues are clearly present, therefore, in the estimation of the unit-specific regression equations. The following conclusions appear justified:

1. If the level-1 sample size is large for a given level-2 unit, OLS and EB estimates of that unit's regression function will converge. This convergence does not depend on the method of centering chosen for X.

2. When the level-1 sample size is small or moderate, EB estimates will tend to be more stable and have smaller mean-squared error of estimation than will the OLS estimates. In this case, there are two possibilities:
   a. If the group mean of X is invariant across level-2 units, or if its variation is ignorable (representing only sampling fluctuations or randomly missing data), group-mean versus grand-mean centering should produce similar results, though grand-mean centering may add a modicum of precision.
   b. If the group mean of X varies substantially, group-mean centering is likely to produce more robust estimates of unit-specific regression equations than is grand-mean centering.

Use of Proportion Reduction in Variance Statistics

We have detailed throughout this chapter how the introduction of predictors in a hierarchical linear model can explain variance at both levels 1 and 2. We have also illustrated how to compute this proportion reduction in variance relative to some base model. In general, the principles introduced in this chapter for two-level organizational effects models extend directly to two-level growth models (see Chapter 6) and three-level models (see Chapter 8) as well. The use of these techniques, however, can become confusing and estimation anomalies can arise as the models grow more complex, especially at level 2 (or levels 2 and 3 in a three-level application.) For this reason, we summarize below some key data analysis advice that has worked well on most problems that we have encountered.

Random-Intercept-Only Models. In these applications, we have two statistics to track, the proportion reduction in variance at level 1 and the proportion reduction in variance in the level-2 intercepts. Typically, the introduction of level-1 predictors will reduce the level-1 residual variance and may also change the level-2 variance, τ_{00}, as well. This occurs, in part, because as each new level-1 predictor is entered into the model, the meaning of the intercept, β_{0j}, may change. (Recall that β_{0j} is the predicted outcome for an individual in unit j with values of 0 on all of the level-1 predictors.) As a result, τ_{00} represents the variability for a different parameter. The only exception is when all level-1 predictors are group mean centered, in which case β_{0j} remains constant as the group mean. Formally, the introduction of predictors at level 1 need not reduce the level-2 variance. Indeed, the residual variance at level 2 can be smaller or larger than the unconditional variance.

This observation gives rise to a key principle in using the proportion reduction in variance statistics at level-2 in hierarchical models. Technically speaking, the variance explained in a level-2 parameter, such as β_{0j}, is conditional on a fixed level-1 specification. As a result, proportion reduction in variance statistics at level 2 are interpretable only for the same level-1 model. Consequently, we recommend that researchers develop their level-1 model first, and then proceed to enter level-2 predictors into the analysis. Assuming the level-1 model remains fixed, no anomalies should arise in the computation of proportion reduction in variance as new level-2 predictors are entered into the equation for β_{0j}. The proportion reduction in variance, or the "variance explained," will increase as significant predictors enter the model. The introduction of nonsignificant predictors should have little or no impact on these "R^2" statistics. We note that it is mathematically possible under maximum likelihood estimation for the residual variance to increase slightly if a truly nonsignificant predictor is entered into the equation. Such cases result in the computation of slightly negative-variance-explained statistics for the variable just entered. The negative differences here, however, will typically be quite small.

Snijders and Bosker (1999) offer an alternative approach to monitoring the proportion of variation explained. This approach, which applies to random intercept models, considers the "proportion reduction in prediction error" at each level; that is, the proportion reduction in error of prediction of Y_{ij} at level 1, and the proportion reduction in error of prediction of $\overline{Y}_{.j}$ at level 2. This approach ensures that the proportion of variance explained is positive. Note that the variation explained is the variation in the observed outcome (which typically includes measurement error).

Random-Slopes and -Intercepts Models. Variance-explained statistics at level 2 can become more complicated when there are multiple random effects at level 2 as in the intercepts- and slopes-as-outcomes model for the social distribution of achievement illustrated above. These complications arise because the level-2 random effects may be correlated with one another. As a result, predictors entered into one level-2 equation can affect variance estimates in another equation.

The social distribution of achievement example was a relatively straight-forward case because all of the level-1 predictors were group-mean centered and all of the coefficients were treated as random. (See the discussion below for the further complexities that can arise when some level-1 predictors are grand-mean centered and/or their coefficients are fixed.) In cases like this, the only "anomaly" that may arise is that the introduction of a level-2 predictor in one equation can seemingly explain variance in another level-2 equation. This will occur when the errors in the random effects from the two equations are correlated and the predictor in question really belongs in both equations but is absent from one. For example, the introduction of a predictor for say the SES differentiation effect might result in a reduced residual variance estimate for the intercept term (i.e., the variability in school mean achievement) even though it had not yet been entered into the intercept equation. Such a phe-nomenon is evidence of a model misspecification, which can be corrected by entering the predictor in both equations. (A procedure to test for such model misspecification is detailed in Chapter 9.) We note that in extreme cases a predictor may appear to have a significant effect in one level-2 equation that totally disappears when the model misspecification is addressed in the other equation.

This gives rise to another model building principle for data analysis. Although it is possible to enter a different set of level-2 predictors for each outcome in the level-2 model, this flexibility should be used judiciously and with caution. The safest way to proceed is to introduce a common set of level-2 predictors in all of the level-2 equations. Unfortunately, following this advice is not always feasible as it can result in the estimation of an excessive number of fixed-effects parameters. In addition, in many applica-tions a different variable set may be hypothesized to predict mean differences as compared to modeling differentiating effects. In these circumstances, we generally recommend specification of the intercept model, β_{0j}, first. If additional predictors are considered for one or more of the slope equations, they should also be entered into the intercept model. Only if they are truly nonsignificant in the intercept model should they be deleted. Similarly, when two or more random slopes are moderately to highly correlated, any level-2 predictor entered into one of the equations should also be entered into the other. Only if the effect is truly insignificant in one of the equations should it be dropped.

Complex Models with Fixed and Random Level-1 Coefficients and Mixed Forms of Centering. Anomalies in variance-explained statistics are most likely in these complex hierarchical models, and the reasons for this are not fully understood in all cases. In addition to following the advice already detailed above, we have generally found the following to work well. For each level-1 predictor, whether group- or grand-mean centered (or no centering), the aggregate of that level-1 predictor, $\overline{X}_{.j}$, should also be entered in the intercept model. This allows representation for each level-1 predictor of the two separate relationships, β_w and β_b, that might exist. If β_w and β_b are different, as is often the case in organizational applications, the failure to represent both relations introduces a model misspecification. As noted above, the presence of model misspecifications can result in anomalous "explained-variance statistics" because of the correlated error terms at level 2. The safest procedure is to assume the coefficients are different and only restrict the model when evidence to the contrary has been assembled.

Estimating the Effects of Individual Organizations

Conceptualization of Organization Specific Effects

An important practical use of multilevel data is to monitor the performance of individual organizations—firms, schools, or classrooms, for example. One might use such data to hold organizational leaders accountable, to rank units for purposes of evaluation, or to identify for further study organizations that are unusually effective or ineffective.

We discuss below the uses of hierarchical models in this context. Our discussion is built around the problem of developing good individual school accountability indicators. The issues raised here, however, apply more generally.

Commonly Used Estimates of School Performance

The most common estimator of school performance uses the predicted mean outcome for each school based on the background and prior ability of students in that school. Schools that score higher than predicted are viewed as effective. Typically, the effectiveness score or performance indicator is just the actual mean achievement minus the predicted mean score for each school. Specifically, in the case of one background variable, the performance indicator or school effect is

$$\overline{Y}._j - \overline{Y}.. - \beta(\overline{X}._j - \overline{X}..), \qquad [5.51]$$

where

$\overline{Y}._j$ is the mean outcome for school j;

$\overline{Y}..$ is the grand-mean outcome across all schools;

$\overline{X}._j$ is the school mean on the background variable X_{ij};

$\overline{X}..$ is the grand mean of X; and

β is a coefficient of adjustment.

A focus of the methodological controversy has been the choice of method for estimating β. Aitkin and Longford (1986) summarize common alternatives. One of their key conclusions is that estimates of β based on OLS regression (ignoring students' membership in schools) can be quite misleading. An alternative method is to use an ANCOVA model in which school membership is included as a series of dummy variables. However, this approach quickly becomes impractical as the number of schools increases. Both OLS regression (ignoring group membership) and the ANCOVA can produce unstable estimates of school effects when sample sizes per school are small. Raudenbush and Willms (1995) discuss threats to valid inference in using these indicators.

Use of Empirical Bayes Estimators

The empirical Bayes residuals estimated under a hierarchical linear model provide a stable indicator for judging individual school performance. These empirical Bayes estimates have distinct advantages over previous methods. They (a) take into account group membership even when the number of groups is large and (b) produce relatively stable estimates even when sample sizes per school are modest.

The random-intercepts model discussed earlier is a common choice for those applications. At the student level,

$$Y_{ij} = \beta_{0j} + \sum_q \beta_{qj}(X_{qij} - \overline{X}_q..) + r_{ij}. \qquad [5.52]$$

At the school level,

$$\beta_{0j} = \gamma_{00} + u_{0j} \qquad [5.53]$$

and

$$\beta_{qj} = \gamma_{q0} \quad \text{for } q = 1, \ldots, Q, \qquad [5.54]$$

where the γ_{00} is the overall intercept. Notice that all level-1 regression coefficients except the intercept are constrained to be constant across schools, and the unique individual-school effect is just u_{0j}.

In the combined form, the model is

$$Y_{ij} = \gamma_{00} + \sum_q \gamma_{q0}(X_{qij} - \overline{X}_q..) + u_{0j} + r_{ij}. \qquad [5.55]$$

This model hypothesizes that all students within school j have an effect, u_{0j}, added to their expected score as a result of attending that school. Formally, this is an ANCOVA model where the Xs are covariates and the set of J schools constitute independent groups in a one-way random-effects ANCOVA. A key difference from a traditional random-effects ANCOVA, however, is that our goal here is literally to estimate the effects for each level-2 unit and not just their variance.

Estimation. An OLS estimator of the effect for each school J is

$$\hat{u}_{0j} = \overline{Y}._j - \hat{\gamma}_{00} - \sum_q \hat{\gamma}_{qs}(\overline{X}_q._j - \overline{X}_q..). \qquad [5.56]$$

Note that $\hat{u}_{0j}$ in Equation 5.56 is just the school mean residual for the ANCOVA. Schools with the small samples, n_j, will tend to yield unstable estimates for $\hat{u}_{0j}$. As a result, these schools are more likely to appear extreme purely as a result of chance. Thus, to select out the largest or smallest values of $\hat{u}_{0j}$ as indicators of the most or least effective organizations is likely to capitalize on extreme chance occurrences.

As noted in Chapter 4, the estimator for u_{0j} in the hierarchical analysis, u_{0j}^*, is an empirical Bayes or shrinkage estimator. The u_{0j}^* shrinks the OLS school-effect estimate proportional to the unreliability of $\hat{u}_{0j}$. The more reliable the OLS estimate from a school is, the less shrinkage occurs. Hence, values that are extreme because they are unstable will be pulled toward zero.

Specifically, the estimated school effect under a hierarchical analysis is

$$u_{0j}^* = \lambda_j \hat{u}_{0j}, \qquad [5.57]$$

where

$$\lambda_j = \tau_{00}/[\tau_{00} + \sigma^2/n_j]$$

is a measure of the reliability of $\hat{u}_{0j}$ as an estimate of u_{0j}.

Threats to Valid Inference Regarding Performance Indicators

Despite the technical advantages of empirical Bayes estimators, major validity issues remain in using such statistics as performance indicators. We consider some of these below. See Raudenbush and Willms (1995) for a more detailed discussion.

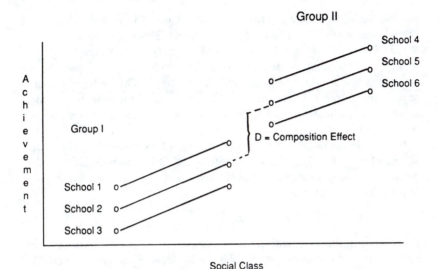

Figure 5.5. A Hypothetical Example of the Relationship between Achievement and Student Social Class in Two Groups of Schools: Low-Social-Class Schools (Group 1) and High-Social-Class Schools (Group2)

Bias. Studies of performance indicators may profitably be viewed as quasi-experiments in which each unit is a treatment group. The problem of valid causal inference in such settings has been extensively studied (Cook & Campbell, 1979). When random assignment of subjects to treatments is impossible, an attempt must be made to identify and control for individual background differences that are related to group membership and also to the outcome. This poses two problems: First, one can never be confident that all of the relevant background variables have been identified and controlled. Second, reasonable people can disagree about proper models for computing adjustment coefficients, and this choice of adjustments can have a substantial impact on inferences about the individual school effects. One general principle does emerge, however, in considering adjustments: The more dramatically different the groups are on background characteristics, the more sensitive inferences are likely to be to different methods of adjustment and the less credible the resulting inferences.

This principle can be illustrated by a deliberately exaggerated and hypothetical example. Consider Figure 5.5. Student achievement (vertical axis) is plotted against student SES (horizontal axis). Associated with each school is a regression line describing the relationship between social class and achievement. The length of each line represents the range of social class within each school. Notice that there are two types of schools: The students in Group 1 schools are of low SES, and in Group 2 schools, SES is considerably higher. Within Groups 1 and 2, schools vary only slightly in their effectiveness, as indicated by the small distances between the parallel regression lines. Notice also that there is a compositional effect, D. That is, Group 1 and Group 2 schools differ by more than one would predict given the regression of student achievement on individual SES, and this appears related to the average SES of the schools.

Now we shall consider two alternative models for estimating the individual school effects. The first is a fixed-effects ANCOVA controlling for student social class but ignoring the compositional effect. Formally, using the model implied by Equation 5.51,

$$Y_{ij} = \beta_{0j} + \beta_1(X_{ij} - \overline{X}..) + r_{ij}, \qquad [5.58]$$

β_1 is the adjustment coefficient associated with student SES and β_{0j} represents the fixed school effect in this case. Because the achievement-SES relationship is homogeneous across the six schools, the difference in effects between any two schools is the distance between their regression lines. For example, the difference between School 2 and School 5 is very large. Notice that under this model every Group 2 school will appear more effective than any Group 1 school.

The second model explicitly controls for school SES when estimating the school effects. This involves extending Equation 5.58 to include mean school SES, $\overline{X}._j$, as a second covariate. For example,

$$Y_{ij} = \beta_{0j} + \beta_1(X_{ij} - \overline{X}._j) + \beta_2(\overline{X}._j - \overline{X}..) + r_{ij}. \qquad [5.59]$$

In practice, Equation 5.59 implies comparing "like with like." Now Group 1 schools are compared to each other, and Group 2 schools are compared to each other. From Figure 5.5, we see that Schools 2 and 5 are now viewed as equally effective: Each is about average compared with schools in its group (schools having similar social composition).

This strategy may seem fairer than the first, but is it? Suppose that the Group 2 schools have more effective staff and that staff quality, not student composition, causes the elevated test scores. The results in Figure 5.5 could occur, for example, if the school district assigned its best principals and teachers to the more affluent schools. If so, the second strategy would give no credit to these leaders for their effective practices.

The key concern is that without having formulated an explicit model of school quality, we can never be sure that we have disentangled the effect of school composition from other school factors with which composition is often correlated.

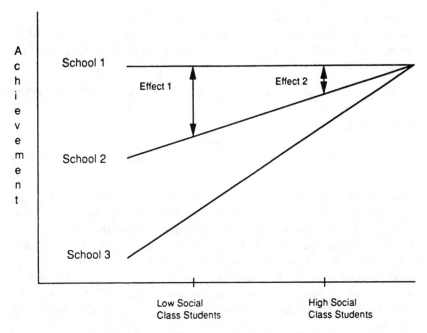

Figure 5.6. Identifying School Effects when the Relationship between Achievement and Student Background is Heterogenous

Heterogeneity of Regression. Problematic as this may seem, the example above is far simpler than reality is likely to be. Our example assumes that the SES-achievement regression lines are identical in all schools. In many cases, the regressions may be heterogeneous, as indicated in Figure 5.6. Now, regardless of the method of adjustment, the estimate of a school's effectiveness will depend on the social class of the child in question. For example, School 1 appears very effective relative to School 2 for low-SES students (i.e., effect 1 in Figure 5.6). However, for high-SES students, the differences between two schools are negligible (i.e., effect 2).

Shrinkage as a Self-Fulfilling Prophecy. As discussed in Chapter 3, the shrinkage estimator, u_{0j}^*, has a smaller expected mean-squared error than does the least squares estimator, $\hat{u}_{0j}$, and protects us against capitalizing on chance. However, shrinkage estimators are conditionally biased. From Equation 5.56, we can see that the expected value of $\hat{u}_{0j}$ given the true value of u_{0j} is

$$E(\hat{u}_{0j} \mid u_{0j}) = u_{0j} = \mu_{Y_j} - \sum_q \gamma_{qs}(\overline{X}_{q \cdot j} - \overline{X}_{q \cdot \cdot}), \qquad [5.60]$$

where μ_{Y_j} is the unadjusted mean outcome in group j. Notice that u_{0j} is the deviation of group j's unadjusted mean, μ_{Y_j}, from a value predicted on the basis of student-background variables. The conditional expectation of the empirical Bayes estimator, u_{0j}^*, is

$$E(u_{0j}^* \mid u_{0j}) = \lambda_j u_{0j}, \qquad [5.61]$$

so the bias is

$$\text{bias}(u_{0j}^* \mid u_{0j}) = -(1 - \lambda_j)\left[\mu_{Y_j} - \sum_q \gamma_{qs}(\overline{X}_{q\cdot j} - \overline{X}_{q\cdot\cdot})\right]. \qquad [5.62]$$

This formula indicates that to the extent $\hat{u}_{0j}$ is unreliable, the estimate u_{0j}^* will be biased *toward* the value predicted on the basis of student background. For example, unusually effective schools that have children of disadvantaged backgrounds will have their high mean effect estimates biased downward toward the value typically displayed by other, similarly disadvantaged schools. This procedure then operates as a kind of statistical self-fulfilling prophecy in which, to the extent the data are unreliable, schools effects are made to conform more to expectations than they do in actuality.

Power Considerations in Designing
Two-Level Organization Effects Studies

A key consideration in designing two-level studies of organization effects is choosing the sample size, n, per organization as well as the number of organizations, J. The best choice of n and J depends strongly on the aims of the study. We briefly consider three cases: where the key explanatory variable of interest is at level 2; where the key explanatory variable is at level 1; and where primary interest focuses on a cross-level interaction (i.e., the effect of a level-2 predictor on a level-1 slope coefficient).

Key Explanatory Variables at Level 2. An optimal n per organization depends on the cost of sampling units at each level and the variability at each level. A large n is helpful when (a) it is comparatively expensive to sample organizations (as compared to sampling organization members once an organization has been selected) and (b) variation within organizations is comparatively large (Raudenbush, 1997; Snijders & Bosker, 1999). In the simple case of a balanced design with one level-1 predictor and a single level-2 predictor, a well-known result from sampling research (cf. Cochran, 1975) is that the optimal n per cluster is

$$n_{\text{opt}} = \left(\frac{C_2}{C_1} * \frac{1-\rho}{\rho} \right)^{1/2}, \qquad \rho > 0, \qquad [5.63]$$

where C_2/C_1 is the relative cost of sampling at level 2 versus level 1 and $\rho = \tau_{00}/(\tau_{00} + \sigma^2)$ is the intra-organization correlation. Raudenbush (1997) discusses how adding covariates at level 1 can increase power by reducing τ_{00} and σ^2.

Key Explanatory Variable at Level 1. When the key explanatory variable is at level 1, interest may focus on the average effect of the level-1 variable, that is, γ_{10}. Suppose, for example, the level-1 variable is an indicator for a treatment ($X_{ij} = 1$ if experimental, 0 if control) and there are no other predictors at any level. Then the optimal n per organization

$$n_{\text{opt}} = \sqrt{\frac{C_2}{C_1} * \frac{\sigma^2}{\tau_{11}}}, \qquad \tau_{11} > 0, \qquad [5.64]$$

where τ_{11} is the variance of the level-1 slope and σ^2 is the level-1 or "within-cluster" variance. We note that if the primary aim is to estimate τ_{11} with precision the required n will typically be larger than n_{opt} (Raudenbush & Liu, 2000).

Cross-level Interactions. Suppose the aim is to make inferences about a cross-level interaction; for example, a treatment indicator at level 2, W, affects a within-unit slope associated with some level-1 predictor, X_1. Assuming $\tau_{11} > 0$ (where τ_{11} is the residual variance in the level-1 slope after controlling for W_j), Equation 5.64 will apply. However, if $\tau_{11} = 0$, precision will depend on the total sample size nJ.

A Windows-based computer program to calculate optimal sample designs and power for a variety of organizational effect and growth study designs has been developed by Raudenbush and Liu and is available at www.ssicentral.com.

Applications in the Study of Individual Change

- Background Issues in Research on Individual Change
- Formulating Models
- A Linear Growth Model
- A Quadratic Growth Model
- Some Other Growth Models
- Centering of Level-1 Predictors in Studies of Individual Change
- Comparison of Hierarchical, Multivariate Repeated-Measures, and Structural Equation Models
- Effects of Missing Observations at Level 1
- Using a Hierarchical Model to Predict Future Status
- Power Considerations in Designing Studies of Growth and Change

Background Issues in Research on Individual Change

Valid techniques for research on change have long perplexed behavioral scientists. Many concerns catalogued by Harris (1963) troubled quantitative studies of growth for many years. These methodological problems led to a bewildering array of well-intentioned but misdirected suggestions about design and analysis. Rogosa, Brand, and Zimowski (1982), Rogosa and Willett (1985), and Willett (1988), however, dispelled many of these misconceptions. Raudenbush (2001) reviews these problems and recent developments.

In brief, research on change has been plagued by inadequacies in conceptualization, measurement, and design. The conceptual concern is that a model is needed to guide inquiry into the phenomenon under study. Yet, until

160

recently, research on individual change rarely identified an explicit model of individual growth. Regarding measurement, studies of change typically use instruments that were developed to discriminate among individuals at a fixed point in time. The adequacy of such measures for distinguishing differences in rates of change among individuals is rarely considered. In addition, the practice of scaling instruments to have a constant variance over time can be fatal to studying change and the determinants of change (Rogosa et al., 1982). Finally, and perhaps most important, is the problem of design. Many studies of change collect data at only two time points. Such designs are often inadequate for studying individual growth (Bryk & Weisberg, 1977; Rogosa et al., 1982; Bryk & Raudenbush, 1987). The frequency and duration of longitudinal studies strongly affect statistical precision (Raudenbush & Liu, 2001).

The development of hierarchical linear models has created a powerful set of techniques for research on individual change. When applied with valid measurements from a multiple-time-point design, these models afford an integrated approach for studying the structure and predictors of individual growth.

Like Chapter 5, this chapter has also been substantially expanded in the second edition. A new section on the effects of centering level-1 predictors has been added. The section on comparing hierarchical models to multivariate repeated-measures and structural equation models has been substantially revised and extended to include a discussion of the major developments that have occurred in this field since the first edition. We also demonstrate how heterogeneous errors at level 1 can now be incorporated into hierarchical growth models, and consider the effects of missing time-series observations at level 1 on inferences. The final section of this chapter on power considerations in designing growth curve studies is also new to this edition.

Formulating Models

Many individual change phenomena can be represented through a two-level hierarchical model. At level 1, each person's development is represented by an individual growth trajectory that depends on a unique set of parameters. These individual growth parameters become the outcome variables in a level-2 model, where they may depend on some person-level characteristics. Formally, we view the multiple observations on each individual as nested within the person. This treatment of multiple observations as nested allows the investigator to proceed without difficulty when the number and spacing of time points vary across cases.

We introduce a new notation in this chapter for representing the two-level hierarchical model. The level-1 coefficients are now denoted by π and the level-2 coefficients by β. The level-1 and level-2 predictors are a_{ti} and X_{pq}, and the random effects are now e_{ti} and r_{pi}, respectively. This new notation facilitates our presentation in Chapter 8 where we bring together the study of individual growth and organizational effects in a three-level model.

Repeated-Observations Model (Level 1)

We assume that Y_{ti}, the observed status at time t for individual i, is a function of a systematic growth trajectory or growth curve plus random error. It is especially convenient when systematic growth over time can be represented as a polynomial of degree P. Then, the level-1 model is

$$Y_{ti} = \pi_{0i} + \pi_{1i}a_{ti} + \pi_{2i}a_{ti}^2 + \cdots + \pi_{Pi}a_{ti}^P + e_{ti} \qquad [6.1]$$

for $i = 1, \ldots, n$ subjects, where a_{ti} is the age at time t for person i and π_{pi} is the growth trajectory parameter p for subject i associated with the polynomial of degree P (i.e., $p = 0, \ldots, P$).[1] Each person is observed on T_i occasions. Note that the number and spacing of measurement occasions may vary across persons.

It is most common to assume a simple error structure for e_{ti}, namely, that each e_{ti} is independently and normally distributed with a mean of 0 and constant variance, σ^2. The error structure, however, can take on a variety of more complex forms as discussed later in this chapter. We first consider the case of independent level-1 errors with constant variance, before turning attention to more complex assumptions.

Person-Level Model (Level 2)

An important feature of Equation 6.1 is the assumption that the growth parameters vary across individuals. We formulate a level-2 model to represent this variation. Specifically, for each of the $P + 1$ individual growth parameters,

$$\pi_{pi} = \beta_{p0} + \sum_{q=1}^{Q_p} \beta_{pq}X_{qi} + r_{pi}, \qquad [6.2]$$

where

X_{qi} is either a measured characteristic of the individual's background (e.g., sex or social class) or of an experimental treatment (e.g., type of curriculum employed or amount of instruction);

β_{pq} represents the effect of X_q on the pth growth parameter; and

r_{pi} is a random effect with mean of 0. The set of $P + 1$ random effects for person i are assumed multivariate normally distributed with full covariance matrix, **T**, dimensioned $(P + 1) \times (P + 1)$.

We assume this multivariate normality for all applications discussed in this chapter.

A Linear Growth Model

In many situations, particularly when the number of observations per individual are few (e.g., three or four occasions), it is convenient to employ a linear individual growth model for Equation 6.1. When the time period is relatively short, this model can provide a good approximation for more complex processes that cannot be fully modeled because of the sparse number of observations.

Under a linear model at level 1, Equation 6.1 simplifies to

$$Y_{ti} = \pi_{0i} + \pi_{1i}a_{ti} + e_{ti},$$ [6.3]

where we assume that the errors e_{ti} are independent and normally distributed with common variance σ^2.

Here, π_{1i} is the growth rate for person i over the data-collection period and represents the expected change during a fixed unit of time. The intercept parameter, π_{0i}, is the true ability of person i at $a_{ti} = 0$. Thus, the specific meaning of π_{0i} depends on the scaling of the age metric.

Both the intercept and growth-rate parameters are allowed to vary at level 2 as a function of measured person characteristics. Thus, Equation 6.2 becomes

$$\pi_{0i} = \beta_{00} + \sum_{q=1}^{Q_0} \beta_{0q}X_{qi} + r_{0i},$$

$$\pi_{1i} = \beta_{10} + \sum_{q=1}^{Q_1} \beta_{1q}X_{qi} + r_{1i}.$$ [6.4]

Note there are two level-2 random effects, r_{0i} and r_{1i}, with variances τ_{00} and τ_{11}, respectively, and with covariance τ_{01}.

In this section, we illustrate how the linear individual growth model can be applied to (a) estimate a mean growth curve and the extent of individual variation around it; (b) asses the reliability of measures for studying both status and change; (c) estimate the correlation between initial status and rate of change; and (d) model relations of person-level predictors to both status and change.

Example: The Effect of Instruction on Cognitive Growth

The data consist of test results on a measure of natural science knowledge from 143 children enrolled in the Head Start program. They were collected as part of a large effort to develop measures of children's growth (rather than just status) during the preschool and early elementary years. The measures were generated through an item-response-theory scaling of a set of test items and are represented in "a logit metric." This metric references a person's ability to the log of the odds of a correct response to items of selected difficulty.

The original design called for each child to be tested on four occasions approximately equally spaced throughout the year. In practice, the testing dates varied across children and not every child was assessed at each time point. The age variable, a_{ti}, was defined as the amount of time in months that had elapsed from the first data-collection point. Under this specification, π_{0i} in Equation 6.3 represents the true ability level of person i at the onset of data collection, or what we call the *initial status*. In addition to the test data, information was collected on students' home language (Spanish or English) and amount of direct instruction (hours per academic year).

A Random-Coefficient Regression Model

Equation 6.3 specifies the level-1 model. At level 2, we begin with the simplest person-level model:

$$\pi_{0i} = \beta_{00} + r_{0i},$$
$$\pi_{1i} = \beta_{10} + r_{1i}. \qquad [6.5]$$

We note that Equation 6.5 is an unconditional model in that no level-2 predictors for either π_{0i} or π_{1i} have been introduced. As in the organizational research application discussed in the previous chapter, a hierarchical analysis typically begins with the fitting of an unconditional model. This model provides useful empirical evidence for determining a proper specification of the individual growth equation and baseline statistics for evaluating subsequent level-2 models. Table 6.1 presents the results for this analysis.

Mean Growth Trajectory. The estimated mean intercept, $\hat{\beta}_{00}$, and mean growth rate, $\hat{\beta}_{10}$, for the natural science data were -0.135 and 0.182, respectively. This means that the average natural science score at the first testing was estimated to be -0.135 logits and children were gaining an average 0.182 logits per month during the study.

TABLE 6.1 Linear Model of Growth in Natural Science Knowledge (Unconditional Model)

Fixed Effect	Coefficient	se	t Ratio	
Mean initial status, β_{00}	−0.135	0.005	−27.00	
Mean growth rate, β_{10}	0.182	0.025	7.27	

Random Effect	Variance Compenent	df	χ^2	p Value
Initial status, r_{0i}	1.689	139	356.90	<0.001
Growth rate, r_{1i}	0.041	139	724.91	<0.001
Level-1 error, e_{ti}	0.419			

Reliability of OLS Regression Coefficient Estimate

Initial status, π_{0i}	0.854
Growth rate, π_{1i}	0.799

As discussed in Chapter 3, hypothesis tests for fixed effects, now denoted β, use the ratio of the estimated effects to their standard error. Both the mean intercept and growth rate have large t statistics indicating that both parameters are necessary for describing the mean growth trajectory.

Individual Variation in Growth Trajectories. Next, we consider the nature of the deviations of the individual growth trajectories from the mean curve. The estimates for the variances of individual growth parameters π_{0i} and π_{1i} were 1.689 and 0.041, respectively. As discussed in Chapter 3, the simplest test of homogeneity, that there is no true variation in individual growth parameters, involves use of a χ^2 statistic. Application of Equation 3.103 resulted in a test statistic for the intercept term of 356.90 (df = 139, $p <$ .001). This leads us to reject the null hypotheses and conclude that children vary significantly in their knowledge of natural science at entry into Head Start. The corresponding χ^2 test statistic for the hypothesis that there are no individual differences among children's growth rates (i.e., H_0: $\tau_{11} = 0$) was 724.91 (df = 139, $p <$ .001), which leads us to conclude that there is also significant variation in their learning rates.

The variance estimate $\hat{\tau}_{11} = .041$ implies an estimated standard deviation of 0.202. Thus, a child whose growth is one standard deviation above average is expected to grow at the rate of .182 + .202 = .384 logits per month.

Reliability of Initial Status and Change. Estimation of the unconditional model also allows us to investigate the psychometric characteristics of the estimated individual growth parameters. If most of the variability in the OLS estimate, $\hat{\pi}_{pi}$, of a person's growth parameters, π_{pi}, were due to model error, we would be unlikely to find any systematic relations between these estimates and person-level variables. Without knowledge of the reliability of the estimated growth parameters, we might falsely conclude that there are no relations, when in fact the data may simply be incapable of detecting such relations.

Recall from Equation 3.28 that the total variability in the OLS estimated level-1 coefficients consists of error variance and parameter variance. In the notation of this chapter,

$$\mathrm{Var}(\hat{\pi}_{pi}) = \mathrm{Var}(\hat{\pi}_{pi} \mid \pi_{pi}) + \mathrm{Var}(\pi_{pi})$$

$$= v_{ppi} + \tau_{pp}. \qquad [6.6]$$

Following classical measurement theory, the ratio of the "true" parameter variance, $\mathrm{Var}(\pi_{pi})$, to the "total" observed variance, $\mathrm{Var}(\hat{\pi}_{pi})$, is the reliability of the OLS estimate, $\hat{\pi}_{pi}$, as a measure of the "true" growth parameters, π_{pi}. Analogous to Equation 3.58, for any person i,

$$\text{reliability of } (\hat{\pi}_{pi}) = \mathrm{Var}(\pi_{pi}) / \mathrm{Var}(\hat{\pi}_{pi})$$

$$= \tau_{pp} / (v_{ppi} + \tau_{pp}) \qquad [6.7]$$

for the $p = 0, \ldots, P$ growth parameter estimates.[2] Averaging across the n persons (as in Equation 3.59) provides a summary index of the reliability of each growth parameter estimate for this population of persons. For the natural science data, the estimated reliabilities for initial status and growth rates were .854 and .799, respectively (see Table 6.1). These results indicate that there is a substantial signal in these data in terms of individual differences in both initial status and growth rates. Modeling each parameter as a function of person-level variables is certainly warranted.[3]

Correlation of Change with Initial Status. The correlation between individual change and initial status is an important characteristic of interest in much research on change. It is impossible, however, to obtain a consistent estimate of this relationship in a simple pretest-posttest design. Researchers have typically found spurious negative correlations between initial status and rate of growth in pre-post studies, correlations that occur because the measurement errors in the pretest and the observed change score are negatively correlated.

With multiwave data, however, a consistent estimate of the correlation of true initial status and true change can be obtained. Under a linear individual growth model, this correlation is just the correlation between π_{0i} and π_{1i}. Analogous to Equation 2.3,

$$\hat{\rho}(\pi_{0i},\ \pi_{1i}) = \hat{\tau}_{01}/(\hat{\tau}_{00} + \hat{\tau}_{11})^{1/2}. \tag{6.8}$$

For the natural science data, the estimated correlation between true change and true initial status was $-.278$. This means that students who had limited natural science knowledge at entry into Head Start tended to gain at a somewhat faster rate. We can infer this is a true negative relationship and not a spurious result of the measurement process. Note that the correlation between initial status and rate of growth will vary depending on the specific time point selected for initial status. As noted earlier, the meaning of π_{0i} depends on the scaling of the age or time variable, a_{ti}.

An Intercepts- and Slopes-as-Outcomes Model

The level-1 model remains as in Equation 6.3. We now introduce two predictors into the level-2 model: LANGUAGE (a dummy variable indicating home language: $1 =$ non-English, $0 =$ English); and HOURS (a continuous measure of the number of hours of direct classroom instruction received by the child in that program year). The person-level model is now

$$\pi_{0i} = \beta_{00} + \beta_{01}(\text{LANGUAGE})_i$$
$$+ \beta_{02}(\text{HOURS})_i + r_{0i} \tag{6.9}$$

and

$$\pi_{1i} = \beta_{10} + \beta_{11}(\text{LANGUAGE})_i$$
$$+ \beta_{12}(\text{HOURS})_i + r_{1i}. \tag{6.10}$$

Table 6.2 presents the estimated fixed-effects results for this analysis.

Neither home language nor hours of instruction was strongly related to entry ability. The t ratios were less than 2.0 in both cases. The estimated effects were plausible, however. On average, Spanish speakers started behind English-speaking children by .463 logits, that is, $\hat{\beta}_{01} = -.463$. It is commonly encountered in Head Start that children from non-English-speaking families tend to score lower initially but are also likely to show rapid progress.

The positive relation between total hours of instruction and initial status was also reasonable because the first testing occasion, t_1, occurred between

TABLE 6.2 Linear Model of Growth in Natural Science Knowledge (Effects of Home Language and Hours of Instruction)

Fixed Effect	Coefficient	se	t Ratio
Model for initial status, π_{0i}			
BASE, β_{00}	0.895	0.267	3.35
LANGUAGE, β_{01}	−0.463	0.304	−1.52
HOURS, β_{02}	1.523×10^{-3}	0.853×10^{-3}	1.79
Model for growth rate, π_{1i}			
BASE, β_{10}	0.029	0.039	0.74
LANGUAGE, β_{11}	0.187	0.045	4.20
HOURS, β_{12}	4.735×10^{-4}	1.252×10^{-4}	3.78

6 and 14 weeks into the program year. Because a substantial amount of instruction had already been given, the observed effect was not surprising.

Both home language and hours of instruction related significantly to individual growth rates. The test scores for children whose home language was Spanish increased, on average, at a rate of .187 logits per month faster than the scores of their English-speaking companions (i.e., $\hat{\beta}_{11} = .187$). Similarly, each additional hour of instruction per year was associated with a .000474 logit increment to the growth rate (i.e., $\hat{\beta}_{12} = .000474$). To understand the latter result, consider the expected growth rates for two children who had the same home language but received varying amounts of instruction. Specifically, suppose the first child received 40 hours per month of instruction and the second 80 hours. (These numbers approximate the minimum and maximum hours of instruction in the Head Start sample.) The model predicts that over a 9-month period, the extra 40 hours per month of instruction received by the second child will yield an increment to that child's growth rate of $9 \times 40 \times .0004735 = .170$ logits per month. That is, the child in the 80-hour-per-month program will be expected to grow at a rate of .170 logits per month faster than his counterpart in the 40-hour-per-month program.

Table 6.3 displays the estimated variances for the random effects in this model and compares these results with those from the unconditional model (Equation 6.5). As in Equation 4.24, the proportion of variance explained is the difference between the total parameter variance (estimated from the unconditional model) and the residual parameter variance (based on the fitted model) relative to the total parameter variance. In the Head Start application, home language and hours of instruction account for 54.9% of the parameter variance in the initial status and 75.6% of the parameter variance in growth rates on the natural science test.

TABLE 6.3 Variance Explained in Initial Status and Growth Rate as a Result of Home Language and Hours of Instruction

Model	Initial Status Var(π_{0i})	Growth Rate Var(π_{1i})
Unconditional[a]	1.689	0.041
Conditional on LANGUAGE and HOURS[b]	0.761	0.010
Proportion of variance explained	54.9	75.0

a. From Table 6.1.
b. These are residual variances based on the model estimated in Table 6.2.

A Quadratic Growth Model

We illustrate in this section the use of a quadratic growth model and demonstrate how various hypothesis testing procedures can be used during the process of developing a model. The model at level 1 is now of the form

$$Y_{ti} = \pi_{0i} + \pi_{1i}(a_{ti} - L) + \pi_{2i}(a_{ti} - L)^2 + e_{ti}. \qquad [6.11]$$

Note that we have introduced a specific or *a priori* centering constant, L, for the level-1 predictors that are powers of a_{ti}. Each of the growth parameters in Equation 6.11 has a substantive meaning. The intercept, π_{0i}, represents the status of person i at time L. The linear component, π_{1i}, is the instantaneous growth rate for person i at time L, and π_{2i} captures the curvature or acceleration in each growth trajectory. Although acceleration is a characteristic of the entire trajectory, the initial status and instantaneous rate parameters depend on the particular choice of value for L.

At, level 2, we have a separate equation for each level-1 coefficient, π_{pi}, where $p = 0, 1, 2$. That is,

$$\pi_{pi} = \beta_{p0} + \sum_{q=1}^{Q_p} \beta_{pq} X_{qi} + r_{pi}. \qquad [6.12]$$

The variances and covariances for the level-2 random effects, r_{pi}, now form a 3×3 matrix:

$$\mathbf{T} = \begin{bmatrix} \tau_{00} & \text{Symmetric} & \\ \tau_{10} & \tau_{11} & \\ \tau_{20} & \tau_{21} & \tau_{22} \end{bmatrix}$$

$$= \begin{bmatrix} \text{Var}(\pi_{0i}) & & \text{Symmetric} \\ \text{Cov}(\pi_{1i}, \pi_{0i}) & \text{Var}(\pi_{1i}) & \\ \text{Cov}(\pi_{2i}, \pi_{0i}) & \text{Cov}(\pi_{2i}, \pi_{1i}) & \text{Var}(\pi_{2i}) \end{bmatrix}.$$

Example: The Effects of Maternal Speech on Children's Vocabulary

We illustrate use of a quadratic growth model with data on children's vocabulary development during the second year of life (Huttenlocher et al., 1991). The Huttenlocher et al. study hypothesized that maternal use of language in the home affects a child's early vocabulary acquisition. Sex differences in vocabulary growth were also expected.

The data actually consist of results from two closely related studies. In the first study, 11 children were observed in the home on six or seven occasions at 2-month intervals during the period from 14 to 26 months of age. (For some cases, the 14-month data point is missing.) A measure of the child's vocabulary size at each measurement occasion, Y_{ti}, was derived from these observations. In the second study, another 11 children were observed at 16, 20, and 24 months. In both studies, the amount of maternal speech was also recorded when the child was 16 months.

One of the strengths of a hierarchical analysis of individual change is that diverse repeated measure data patterns such as the above can be combined into a single analysis. Because of slight differences in research procedures employed in two studies, however, the investigators worried about combining the data. Yet to treat the two studies separately ran the risk of failing to detect substantively important relations because of possible low power in each of the individual studies. The analysis described here illustrates how to combine data from two studies while still permitting a rigorous test of study effects and study-person interaction effects.

A Random-Coefficient Regression Model

A visual examination of the individual child vocabulary growth trajectories, displayed in Figure 6.1, clearly indicated a nonlinear growth pattern. In fact, all 22 trajectories displayed upward curvature, indicating that the rate of new word acquisition was increasing over time. These observations suggested fitting a quadratic individual growth model as in Equation 6.11.

The centering parameter, L, was deliberately set at 12 months, because this is about the time that most children begin to express their first words. Thus, π_{0i} represents the child's vocabulary size at 12 months, which should be close to 0; and π_{1i} is the instantaneous growth rate at 12 months, which also should be close to zero because prior research has demonstrated that initial vocabulary acquisition occurs very slowly.

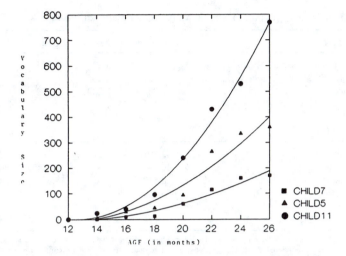

Figure 6.1. A Sample of Individual Vocabulary Growth Trajectories

SOURCE: Huttenlocher, Haight, Bryk, & Seltzer (1991).
NOTE: ■, ●, ▲ represent the actual observations. The smooth curves result from fitting a separate quadratic polynomial to each child's vocabulary data.

As is customary, the researchers began with an unconditional level-2 model. That is,

$$\pi_{0i} = \beta_{00} + r_{0i}, \qquad [6.13a]$$

$$\pi_{1i} = \beta_{10} + r_{1i}, \qquad [6.13b]$$

$$\pi_{2i} = \beta_{20} + r_{2i}. \qquad [6.13c]$$

Table 6.4 presents the results. Both the mean vocabulary size at 12 months and the mean growth rate were very close to zero. (Note that the estimated coefficients for both of these parameters were considerably smaller than their respective standard errors.) The mean acceleration was positive ($\hat{\beta}_{20} = 2.035$) and highly significant. This indicates that, on average, children were acquiring new words at an increasing rate over time.

In general, the growth rate at any particular age is the first derivative of the growth model evaluated at that age. For quadratic growth,

$$\text{growth rate at age } t = \pi_{1i} + 2\pi_{2i}(a_{ti} - L). \qquad [6.14]$$

At 14 months of age, for example, the average growth rate was 7.81 new words per month $[-.327 + 2(2.035)(14 - 12)]$. By 16 months, the average growth rate had grown to 15.91 new words per month.

TABLE 6.4 Model 1: Full Quadratic Model of Vocabulary Growth

Fixed Effect	Coefficient	se	t Ratio
Mean vocabulary size at 12 months, β_{00}	−3.879	5.427	−0.715
Mean growth rate at 12 months, β_{10}	−0.327	2.295	−0.143
Mean acceleration, β_{20}	2.035	0.200	10.172

Random Effect	Variance Component	df	χ^2	p Value[a]
12-month status, r_{0i}	62.307	10	0.790	>0.500
Growth rate, r_{1i}	46.949	10	6.211	>0.500
Acceleration, r_{2i}	0.510	10	17.434	0.065
Level-1 error, e_{ti}	676.882			

Deviance = 1,277.03 with 7 df

a. These results are based on only the 11 cases for whom sufficient data exist to compute separate OLS estimates for each individual child. The χ^2 statistics and p values are rough approximation given the small number of persons.

The standard deviation of the individual observations around any individual growth trajectory was 26.02 words (i.e., $\hat{\sigma} = 676.88^{1/2}$).[4] The χ^2 statistics associated with π_{0i} and π_{1i} suggest that the observed variability in both vocabulary size and instantaneous growth rates at 12 months reflects mostly error variability in the OLS estimates. In reality, there probably are significant differences among children in these parameters, but we have relatively little information in this study to detect these effects, because no direct observations were made before 14 months. We also note that reliability statistics were not reported in this application because half of the cases had only three observations. As a result, the OLS estimates fit these data perfectly and the reliability statistics would be quite misleading.

These results suggest that some simplification of the level-1 model is in order. The estimates for the mean initial status and growth rate at 12 months were not significantly different from zero (and are in fact small in absolute terms). The homogeneity hypothesis was also sustained for both of these random parameters. Further evidence for a model simplification is provided by the estimated correlations among the random effects (see Table 6.5). The intercept coefficient, π_{0i}, is nearly colinear with both the growth rate, π_{1i}, and acceleration, π_{2i}. At a minimum, this suggests that a "no-intercept" model be fitted. That is, the level-1 model reduces to

$$Y_{ti} = \pi_{1i}(a_{ti} - L) + \pi_{2i}(a_{ti} - L)^2 + e_{ti}. \qquad [6.15]$$

The results for this model are presented in Table 6.6.

TABLE 6.5 Correlations Among Random Coefficients in the Full Quadratic Model

	π_{0i}	π_{1i}	π_{2i}
12-month status, π_{0i}	1.000		
Growth rate at 12 months, π_{1i}	−0.982	1.000	
Acceleration, π_{2i}	−0.895	0.842	1.000

The basic findings of the first model are sustained in the reduced model. The average growth rate at 12 months is still close to zero and the average acceleration is virtually unchanged. The standard deviation around the individual growth trajectories has risen only slightly ($\hat{\sigma} = \text{Var}(e_{ti})^{1/2} = 26.63$), which indicates that a no-intercept level-1 model fits the data about as well as the initial model. The χ^2 statistics associated with the random growth rate and acceleration parameters indicate that there is substantial individual variation in both of these parameters.

The correlation between these two random coefficients remains very high at .904. The latter suggests that the χ^2 tests for parameter homogeniety might be misleading, because these are independent univariate tests that do not take into account the relations among the random effects.

As a check, a likelihood-ratio test was computed (see Chapter 3). Specifically, the deviance statistic from the second model (1,285.02 with 4 df) was compared with the corresponding statistic from a model where the instantaneous growth rate, π_{1i}, was specified as a fixed effect. As a result, the variance in the growth rates and the covariance between growth rate and acceleration were constrained to 0. That is, the level-1 model remained as in

TABLE 6.6 Model 2: Quadratic Model of Vocabulary Growth (No Intercept)

Fixed Effect	Coefficient	se	t Ratio	
Mean growth rate at 12 months, β_{10}	−1.294	1.557	−0.831	
Mean acceleration, β_{20}	2.087	0.205	10.201	

Random Effect	Variance Component	df	χ^2	p Value
Growth rate, r_{1i}	21.908	21	37.532	0.015
Acceleration, r_{2i}	0.663	21	89.359	0.000
Level-1 error, e_{it}	709.231			

Deviance = 1,285.02 with 4 df

Equation 6.15, but at level 2

$$\pi_{1i} = \beta_{10},$$
$$\pi_{2i} = \beta_{20} + r_{2i}.$$
[6.16]

The deviance statistic for the alternative model was 1,292.03 with 2 df. The difference between these two deviance statistics is 7.01, which is distributed as approximately χ^2 with 2 df. The test result is highly significant ($p < .001$) and implies that the model reduction is not warranted. This result confirms the univariate homogenity test. A random growth rate component should remain in the model.

We can, however, make one further simplification by constraining the average growth rate coefficient to 0. That is, the level-1 model remains as is in Equation 6.15, but the level-2 model is reduced to

$$\pi_{1i} = r_{1i},$$
$$\pi_{2i} = \beta_{20} + r_{2i}.$$
[6.17]

The results for this "best" specification are presented in Table 6.7.

An Intercepts- and Slopes-as-Outcomes Model of the Effects of Maternal Speech, Sex, and Study Group

Having identified an appropriate level-1 model, the researchers proceeded to test the formal hypotheses of the study. Specifically, they posed the

TABLE 6.7 Model 3: Quadratic Model of Vocabulary Growth (No Intercept Term and No Fixed Effect for the Linear Rate)

Fixed Effect	Coefficient	se	t Ratio	
Mean acceleration, β_{20}	2.098	0.206	10.172	
Random Effect	*Variance Component*	*df*	χ^2	*p Value*
Growth rate, r_{1i}	20.158	22	40.947	0.006
Acceleration, r_{2i}	0.685	21	88.528	0.000
Level-1 error, e_{ti}	708.085			

Deviance = 1,286.57 with 4 df

following person-level model:

$$\pi_{1i} = r_{1i}, \quad [6.18a]$$

$$\pi_{2i} = \beta_{20} + \beta_{21}(\text{STUDY})_i + \beta_{22}(\text{SEX})_i$$
$$+ \beta_{23}(\text{MOMSPEECH})_i + \beta_{24}(\text{STUDY} \times \text{SEX})_i$$
$$+ \beta_{25}(\text{STUDY} \times \text{MOMSPEECH})_i + r_{2i}. \quad [6.18b]$$

Equation 6.18a specifies a pure random-effects model for π_{1i}. No intercept term appears in this level-2 equation because, as in the previous model, the mean rate was constrained to 0. Variation in the individual acceleration parameters was modeled as a function of STUDY ($-1 =$ study 1 and $1 =$ study 2), child's SEX ($-1 =$ male, $1 =$ female), MOMSPEECH (count of words spoken, in natural log metric, and centered around the grand mean), and interaction terms of STUDY with SEX and MOMSPEECH. (Note, the $-1, 1$ coding scheme for STUDY and SEX was adopted in order to test these interaction effects.) The results for this model appear in Table 6.8.

There was a significant difference in the average acceleration rates between the two studies of .866 words/month^2 [i.e., effect of study 1 $-$ effect of study 2 $= (-1)(-.433) - (1)(-.433)$]. This difference resulted from the somewhat different procedures employed in the two studies to estimate total vocabulary size at each age. As hypothesized, the average acceleration was

TABLE 6.8 Final Quadratic Growth Model

Fixed Effect	Coefficient	se	t Ratio
Mean acceleration, π_{2i}			
Base, β_{20}	2.031	0.157	12.887
Study effect, β_{21}	−0.433	0.157	−2.747
Sex effect, β_{22}	0.312	0.165	1.891
Mom-speech effect, β_{23}	0.793	0.334	2.370
Study × sex, β_{24}	0.144	0.165	0.876
Study × speech, β_{25}	−0.158	0.334	−0.473

Random Effect	Variance Component	df	χ^2	p Value
Growth rate, r_{1i}	18.778	22	39.547	0.010
Acceleration, r_{2i}	0.282	16	39.864	0.001
Level-1 error, e_{ti}	707.156			

Deviance $= 1,284.3$ with 4 df[a]

a. The deviance statistics in Tables 6.6 through 6.8 cannot be compared because the fixed effects vary across these three models and MLR estimation was employed (see Chapter 3).

significantly higher for girls than boys by .624 words/month^2. Similarly, the amount of mother's speech was positively related to vocabulary acquisition ($\hat{\beta}_{23} = 0.793$, t ratio $= 2.370$). There was no evidence that the child-sex and mother-speech effects vary across the two studies; that is, both the interaction terms were small and insignificant (t ratios < 1.0 for both $\hat{\beta}_{24}$ and $\hat{\beta}_{25}$). Thus, we have some confidence in interpreting the results from the pooling of data across the two studies. The residual variance in the acceleration parameters, π_{2i}, was reduced to .282 from the total parameter variance of .685 estimated in the unconditional model (Table 6.7). Almost 59% of the total variability in individual acceleration, $[(.685 - .282)/.685)]$, was associated with study-group, child-sex, and maternal-speech effects.

In general, the hierarchical analysis provided strong evidence of effects for maternal speech and child's sex on early vocabulary acquisition. The residual variability in vocabulary acceleration after controlling only for study group (i.e., a reduced version of Equation 6.18b where only the STUDY variable was included) was .551. When the nonsignificant interaction terms were deleted from Equation 6.18b and the final model reestimated, the residual variability in π_{2i} was .257. Comparing these results indicates that an estimated 53.4% of the remaining variability in acceleration parameters after controlling for study group was associated with child's sex and maternal speech.

Some Other Growth Models

The procedures illustrated in the previous two sections generalize directly to more complex growth models. In principle, a polynomial of any degree can be fitted and tested as long as the time series is sufficiently long. For at least some level-2 units (e.g., children in the above application), the number of observations, T_i, must exceed the number of random parameters, $P + 1$, specified in the individual growth model (Equation 6.1). So long as this is true, however, other units that fail to meet this criterion can be still be included in the analysis. (See discussion in Chapter 3 on "Deficient Rank Data" for details of estimation when some units have insufficient data for separate OLS estimation.)

Alternative age metrics can also be easily accommodated by transforming either the outcome or the age variable first, and then proceeding as above. For example, $(Y_{ti})^{1/2}$ could have been used as the outcome variable in the vocabulary study and a linear growth model posed for this square-root metric. In general, we suggest visual examination of the individual time series and mean trajectories to identify possible models that might be fitted to the data. We note that the mean growth curve and the individual growth curves can have different forms. For example, in fitting a quadratic model to the data, we might find that some individual trajectories with positive curvatures cancel out others with negative curvatures. In this case, a line might be a fine description for the mean curve but an inadequate representation for individual growth. It is for this reason that we examined in the random-coefficient regression model both the mean growth parameters and the amount of individual variation around them.

We also note that it is possible to represent individual growth phenomena where the outcome of interest may be a discrete variable. In such situations, we may wish to model the changing probability of some event occurring over time or the changing rate of some behavior such as the propensity to commit crime through the adolescent years. Growth models for discrete outcome variables are taken up in Chapter 10.

More Complex Level-1 Error Structures

Up to this point, we have assumed a simple level-1 error structure where each e_{ti} is independently and normally distributed with a mean of 0 and constant variance, σ^2. Several generalizations are possible:

1. The e_{ti} may depend on measured characteristics at either level 1 or level 2. For example in the vocabulary growth data we might specify σ_t^2 as a function of age since greater heteroscedasticity at level 1 was observed for the later time points. Similarly, heteroscedasticity differences in heterogeneity at level 1 might be represented as a function of gender or study design.

2. If the data are time patterned, as in the vocabulary growth example when t corresponds to 12, 14, 16, . . . , 26 months, then another alternative is to estimate a separate level-1 variance for each time point.

Both of these options can be accomplished by specifying a log-linear model for σ_t^2 as a function of measured characteristics (e.g., age, gender, or a set of dummy variables for time point). We illustrated this extension of hierarchical models in Chapter 5 (see "Applications with Heterogeneous Level-1 Variance").

3. Autocorrelations may exist among e_{ti} for each person. For example, we might posit a first-order autoregression "AR(1)" model. This results in a structure where the error at any time point, t, depends on the previous time point, $t - 1$.

An application of this alternative appears below in a later section on "Comparison of Hierarchical, Multivariate Repeated-Measures, and Structural Equation Models."

Piecewise Linear Growth Models

When an exploratory examination of the data suggests nonlinearity, one option is to break up the curvilinear growth trajectories into separate linear components. This approach is particularly attractive where, for substantive reasons, we wish to compare growth rates during two different periods. Possible research questions include "Is growth more variable in period 1 than period 2?" and "Are the correlates of growth different in the two periods?"

For example, Frank and Seltzer (1990) analyzed data on the acquisition of reading ability for students in the Chicago public schools in Grades 1 through 6. Each student was scheduled to be tested at the end of each academic year, but for a variety of logistical reasons some children missed one or more testing occasions. Exploratory analysis of growth trajectories for a sample of individual students and selected subgroups by gender, race, and school membership indicated that the acquisition of reading ability in Grades 1 through 3 followed a different pattern than in Grades 4 and beyond. Growth rates appeared faster and more variable in the early grades than later. These results suggested the possibility of a two-piece linear growth model: one individual growth rate for period 1, and a second, different growth rate for period 2. Specifically, the level-1 model was of the form

$$Y_{ti} = \pi_{0i} + \pi_{1i} a_{1ti} + \pi_{2i} a_{2ti} + e_{ti}, \qquad [6.19]$$

where a_{1ti} and a_{2ti} are coded variables, as defined in Table 6.9a, to represent the piecewise regression.

Although the coding schemes of Table 6.9 may seem a bit odd at first glance, their operation can be easily seen through a simple substitution of values for a_{1t} and a_{2t} into Equation 6.19 to generate predicted outcomes. For example, using the first coding scheme in Table 6.9a, the predicted status at each grade level would be π_0, $\pi_0 + \pi_1$, $\pi_0 + 2\pi_1$, $\pi_0 + 2\pi_1 + \pi_2$, $\pi_0 + 2\pi_1 + 2\pi_2$, and $\pi_0 + 2\pi_1 + 3\pi_2$, respectively. Thus, the growth rate is π_1 per grade during Grades 2 and 3, and π_2 per grade during Grades 4, 5, and 6.

Figure 6.2 presents a sample of 50 fitted growth trajectories reported by Frank and Seltzer (1990), based on Equation 6.19 and an unconditional level-2 model with π_{0i}, π_{1i}, and π_{2i} random. The trajectories displayed are empirical Bayes or shrunken estimates based on the formula

$$\pi_i^* = \Lambda_i \hat{\pi}_i + (\mathbf{I} - \Lambda_i)\beta^*, \qquad [6.20]$$

where

$\hat{\pi}_i$ is a 3 by 1 vector of OLS estimates $(\hat{\pi}_{0i}, \hat{\pi}_{1i}, \hat{\pi}_{2i})^T$ for each individual's growth parameter based only on that person's data;

TABLE 6.9 Some Possible Coding Schemes for a Two-Piece Linear Model (Reading Achievement Example)

(a) Two-Rate Model

	1	2	3	4	5	6	Interpretation of πs:
			Grades				
a_{1t}	0	1	2	2	2	2	π_1 growth rate period 1
a_{2t}	0	0	0	1	2	3	π_2 growth rate period 2
							π_0 status Grade 1
a_{1t}	−2	−1	0	0	0	0	π_1 growth rate period 1
a_{2t}	0	0	0	1	2	3	π_2 growth rate period 2
							π_0 status Grade 3

(b) Increment (Decrement) Model

	1	2	3	4	5	6	Interpretation of πs:
			Grades				
a_{1t}	0	1	2	3	4	5	π_1 base growth rate
a_{2t}	0	0	0	1	2	3	π_2 increment (decrement) to growth in period 2
							π_0 status Grade 1
a_{1t}	−2	−1	0	1	2	3	π_1 base growth rate
a_{2t}	0	0	0	1	2	3	π_2 increment (decrement) to growth in period 2
							π_0 status Grade 3

β^* is a 3 by 1 vector containing estimates of the three parameters describing the mean growth trajectory; and

Λ_i is a 3 by 3 multivariate reliability matrix for subject i (see Equation 3.57).

We note that the two-piece linear growth model in Equation 6.19 could have been parameterized as the base rate for the entire period (Grades 1 through 6) and increment (or decrement) to the base rate in either period 1 or 2. This would have been accomplished by using an alternative coding scheme for a_{1t} and a_{2t} as detailed in Table 6.9b.

Time-Varying Covariates

In some applications, we may have other level-1 predictors, besides age or time, that explain variation in Y_{ti}. We term these *time-varying covariates*. For example, suppose in the reading achievement research that we had a measure of student absenteeism in each grade. Presumably, if a child is absent a good deal during a particular academic year, then the achievement for

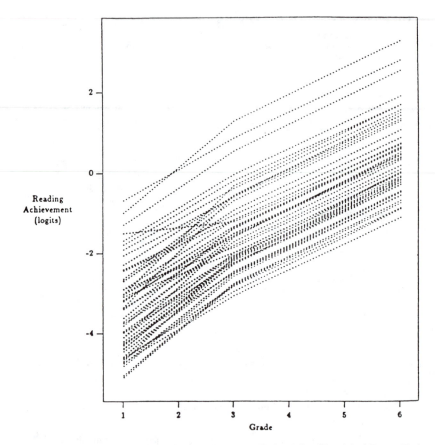

Figure 6.2. A Sample of Reading Achievement Trajectories (Empirical Bayes Estimates, Chicago Public Schools Data)

that child at year end might be somewhat below the value predicted by that individual's growth trajectory. This temporal variation can be captured by adding a measure of student's absenteeism at each grade to the level-1 model of Equation 6.19. Specifically, if we define a_{3ti} as the student's absenteeism in a particular period, the level-1 model would be

$$Y_{ti} = \pi_{0i} + \pi_{1i}a_{1ti} + \pi_{2i}a_{2ti} + \pi_{3i}a_{3ti} + e_{ti}. \qquad [6.21]$$

Because student absenteeism was intended as a covariate, it would normally be specified at level 2 as fixed (i.e., $\pi_{3i} = \gamma_{30}$). However, it also could be specified as nonrandomly varying, allowing, for example, for different effects in Grades 1 through 3 versus Grades 4 and above. It could even be specified as random. We illustrate use of a time-varying covariate in Chapter 8 in a three-level analysis of student learning and summer-drop-off effects.

Centering of Level-1 Predictors in Studies of Individual Change

We discussed in earlier chapters how the choice of location for level-1 predictors has important implications in the formulation and parameter estimation of hierarchical linear models. (See "Location of the Xs" in Chapter 2 and "Centering Level-1 Predictors in Organizational Effects Applications" in Chapter 5.) We now consider how the location for the level-1 predictors in studies of individual change affects:

- definition of the intercept in linear growth models;
- definitions of other growth parameters in higher-order polynomial models;
- possible biases in studying time-varying covariates; and
- estimation of the variance of growth parameters.

Definition of the Intercept in Linear Growth Models

Consider a level-1 model in which each child's growth with respect to an outcome Y is represented by a straight line:

$$Y_{ti} = \pi_{0i} + \pi_{1i} a_{ti} + e_{ti},$$

where the intercept, π_{0i}, is the expected outcome when $a_{ti} = 0$. Suppose children are assessed annually at ages 2, 3, 4, 5, and 6. If we define a_{ti} to be zero at age 2, then π_{0i} is the status of child i at age 2, and might be described as the "initial status" of that child, given that data collection began at that time. (We used a similar definition in the first example in this chapter, involving the growth of science knowledge of children in Head Start.) The validity of this definition of π_{0i} as "initial status" depends on the accuracy of the straight line as a representation of individual change. Indeed, π_{0i} is a predicted value of Y at age 2 based on all of the data collected between ages 2 and 6. If the growth curves were actually curvilinear, the predicted initial status under a straight-line model might be quite inaccurate.

Other choices for a location of a_{ti} might be (age$_{ti}$-4), defining π_{0i} as child i's status at age 4, the midpoint of the study; or (age$_{ti}$-6), so that the intercept would be the status at age 6, the end of the study. Because the choice of centering will affect the definition of the intercept, it will also affect interpretation of the level-2 variance of the intercept and the covariance between the intercept and the slope. Thus, for example, the correlation between "initial status" and the growth rate will be different from the correlation between status at age 4 and the growth rate. Moreover, interpretations of level-2 coefficients in the model for π_{0i} will depend crucially on the definition of π_{0i} generated by the choice of location of a_{ti}.

Definitions of Other Growth Parameters in Higher-Order Polynomial Models

Consider now a quadratic model

$$Y_{ti} = \pi_{0i} + \pi_{1i}a_{ti} + \pi_{2i}a_{ti}^2 + e_{ti}.$$

Once again, the intercept π_{0i} will be the status of child i when $a_{ti} = 0$. Now, however, the definition of the linear coefficient, π_{1i}, will also be contingent on choice of location for a_{ti}. In such a model, the rate of increase of Y with respect to age will change with age, and π_{1i} will be the rate of growth for participant i at $a_{ti} = 0$. Returning to our hypothetical example with students assessed at ages 2–6, defining a_{ti} as $(age_{ti} - 2)$ would define π_{1i} as the "initial rate of growth," that is, the instantaneous growth rate of the child at age 2. A problem with this choice is that the data really supply very little information about the growth rate of a child at the onset of a study. Moreover, such a definition will induce a high correlation between the two predictors a_{ti} and a_{ti}^2. This collinearity may destabilize the estimation procedure, especially in studies with large numbers of time points.

In contrast, centering "in the middle," that is, around $a_{ti} = 4$, will have two desirable effects. First, this centering will define π_{1i} not only as the rate of growth at age 4 but also as the average rate of growth during the data collection period, or "average velocity." This quantity will be conceptually important in some studies. Second, centering around the midpoint will minimize the correlation between a_{ti} and a_{ti}^2, with the effect of stabilizing the estimation procedure.[5]

We note that the interpretation of the quadratic coefficient π_{2i} does not depend on choice of centering for a_{ti}. It represents the rate of acceleration regardless of centering. Suppose, however, that we had specified a cubic model. In that case, the meaning of the intercept, linear, and quadratic coefficients would depend on choice of location for a_{ti}; only the interpretation of the cubic coefficient would be invariant. In general, for any polynomial, the highest-order coefficient has an invariant interpretation while all lower-order coefficients take on meanings that depend on the choice of centering.

Possible Biases in Studying Time-Varying Covariates

Recall that, in the context of organizational studies, the effect of a level-1 predictor can be biased if the aggregate of the level-1 predictor has a separate and distinct relationship with the intercept (see the discussion about β_w and β_b in Chapter 5 on "Estimating Fixed Level-1 Coefficients"). We pointed out that group-mean centering would eliminate this bias. An alternative was to incorporate the mean of the level-1 predictor in the level-2 model for the intercept, which also eliminates this bias. The same problem arises in the context of studies of repeated measures.

Horney, Osgood, and Marshall (1995) studied the association between changes in life circumstances (employment and marital status) and propensity for criminal behavior. The data consisted of repeated monthly observations of criminal behavior, Y_{ti}, among high-rate offenders over a three-year period. The time-varying covariates at level 1 (employment and marital status) were also measured monthly. Horney et al. found that change in employment status and change in marital status were associated with changes in offending rates. In particular, becoming employed and moving in with a spouse were associated with lower rates. One threat to validity in this kind of study is that persons will vary on the mean of the time-varying covariates: Some will be employed most of the time, others seldom; some will be living with a spouse-most (or all) of the time, others seldom (or never). These differences between people on the aggregate values of the level-1 predictors might be associated with person-level effects on offending rate, and these effects would bias the estimation of the level-1 coefficients unless care is taken. Horney et al. centered the time-varying covariates within persons, thus assuring unbiased estimates of the associations between these level-1 predictors and outcomes. They also modeled variation between persons in mean offending rates as a function of mean differences in percentage time employed and percentage time living with a spouse.

Estimation of the Variance of Growth Parameters

In Chapter 5, we discussed how centering can affect estimation of the variance of random coefficients (see "Estimating the Variances of Level-1 Coefficients"). The same considerations apply in the study of growth models for individual change. If the time-series design is invariant across all participants (apart from randomly missing data), there will be no variation in the mean of a level-1 predictor such as age or time. In this case, choice of centering will not affect the estimation of the variance of the growth rate. In some studies, however, the time-series design will vary systematically across participants. In particular, if participants vary in terms of mean age, person-mean centering may be useful to avoid bias.

Consider data from seven birth cohorts from the National Youth Survey (Miyazaki & Raudenbush, 2000). Participants were sampled at ages 11, ..., 17 in 1976 and interviewed annually on five occasions until 1980 when they were 15, ..., 21, respectively. The outcome was a measure of antisocial attitudes. Figure 6.3 displays fitted quadratic change curves.[6] Our interest focuses on the average rate of change in antisocial attitudes per year for each participant and the variation in those rates across participants. Although the curves in Figure 6.3 are quadratic, we consider only the linear rate. Table 6.10 provides estimates based on (a) centering around the overall median age of 16 versus (b) centering around cohort-specific median ages (these are 13, ..., 19 for cohorts 1–7, respectively). (Apart from missing data, cohort-median centering is equivalent to person-mean centering and provides a convenient interpretation in this case.) Note that the variance of the linear rates is estimated to be nearly twice as large under cohort-median centering as compared to under grand-median centering.[7] Which is more accurate?

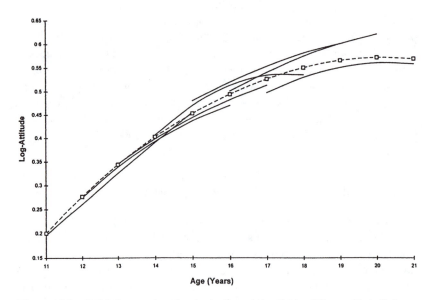

Figure 6.3. Solid Curves Are Quadratic Curves for Each of Seven Birth Cohorts; the Dashed Curve Is the Average Curve

TABLE 6.10 Effect of Centering on Estimation of Variance of Linear Rates of
            Change

Approach	Estimate	se
(a) Grand-median centering	.00122	.00015
(b) Cohort-median centering	.00269	.00022
(c) Robust, consistent estimator	.00269	.00022

To assess the validity of these estimates, we compare them to a robust consistent estimate that does not use information about the intercept as occurs when using maximum likelihood. The estimate is based on a weighted average of the unbiased estimates of τ_{11} across the 576 participants in the study:

$$\hat{\tau}_{11} = \frac{\sum_{i=1}^{n} \lambda_i^2 \left[(\hat{\pi}_{1i} - \hat{\beta}_{10})^2 - v_{11i} \right]}{\sum_{i=1}^{n} \lambda_i^2},$$

where $\hat{\pi}_{1i}$ is the OLS slope estimate for participant i, v_{11i} is the sampling variance of that estimate, λ_i is the reliability of the estimate, and $\hat{\beta}_{10}$ is the estimated grand-mean slope. The results show that this robust estimate and the cohort-median-centered estimate coincide to three significant digits. Cohort-median centering, as opposed a to grand-median centering, has protected the estimate from bias that arises from systematic variation in mean age across the seven cohorts. The reasons are identical to those discussed in Chapter 5 (see "Estimating the Variances of Level-1 Coefficients").

Comparison of Hierarchical, Multivariate Repeated-Measures, and Structural Equation Models

The hierarchical approach to growth models discussed in this chapter has appeared in the literature under a variety of terms, including random-effects models (Laird & Ware, 1982), mixed linear models (Diggle, Liang, & Zeger, 1994; Goldstein, 1995), random-coefficients models (Longford, 1993), as well as hierarchical linear models (Strenio et al., 1983; Bryk & Raudenbush, 1987) or "HLM." We discuss below how this approach relates to other common approaches, including multivariate repeated-measures (MRM) analysis of variance and structural equation modeling (SEM).

Multivariate Repeated-Measures (MRM) Model

A key difference between HLM and MRM is the conceptual orientation to modeling individual change. The level-1 model of HLM explicitly represents each individual's trajectory of change as a function of person-specific parameters plus random error. The level-2 model describes the variation in these growth parameters across a population of persons. In contrast, the MRM approach requires (a) specification of main effects and interactions that describe the expected trajectory for different subgroups or kinds of persons and (b) specification of the variation and covariation of the repeated measures over time.

A second difference involves the kind of data for which the models are appropriate. Conventional MRM requires that every person have a fixed time-series design; that is, the number and spacing of time points must be invariant across people. In contrast, the hierarchical model is generally more flexible in terms of its data requirements because the repeated observations are viewed as nested within the person rather than as the same fixed set for all persons as in MRM. Both the number of observations and the timing of the observations may vary randomly over participants. Level-1 predictors, including time or age, may be continuous, taking on a different distribution for each member of the sample.

Third, the formulation of models for individual change in a hierarchical approach leads naturally to the study of how external environments such as communities or organizations affect individual development over time. A third level of the model can be introduced to represent this contextual variation (see Chapter 8). This extension is difficult or impossible to estimate efficiently in the standard framework for MRM.

Structural Equation Models (SEM)

An alternative approach that has gained considerable popularity is based on structural equation models (SEM) using software such as LISREL (Joreskog & Sorbom, 1989), M-plus (Muthén and Muthén, 1998), or EQS (Bentler, 1995).[8] Building on the work of McArdle (1986) and Meridith and Tisak (1990), Willett and Sayer (1994) showed that some two-level growth models can also be estimated within the framework of SEM. The measurement model of SEM corresponds to the level-1 model of HLM. The latent variables of SEM are the individual growth parameters of HLM. The structural model in SEM then corresponds to HLM's level-2 or "between-person" model. An advantage of the reformulation proposed by Willett and Sayer (1994) is that, once the model is translated into the framework of SEM, the full range of covariance structures associated with software for SEM becomes available. These include autocorrelated level-1 random effects and heterogeneous level-1 random effects. Using SEM, one can test a wide range of covariance structures. A disadvantage of the approach is that it requires balanced "time-structured" data within subpopulations. That is, as with MRM, each participant is required to have the same number and spacing of time points, and level-1 predictors having random effects must have the same distribution across all participants in each subpopulation.[9] In contrast, HLM allows unequal numbers and spacing of time points, and level-1 predictors having random effects can have different distributions across participants.

Thus, it appears that analysts face a forced choice between the HLM approach, which allows a wide variety of data structures and level-1 models but a limited choice of covariance structures, and the SEM approach, which allows a wide array of covariance structures but is inflexible in handling unbalanced designs. Under further scrutiny, however, this forced choice reflects limitations in current software capabilities rather than limitations in modeling possibilities.

Often overlooked in psychological research is important work by Jennrich and Schlucter (1986),[10] who developed a flexible approach to studying time-series data having multivariate normal distributions. Their approach is like SEM in that it allows estimation of several alternative covariance structures: "random-effects" covariance structures identical to those specified in HLM as well as autocorrelation models, models for heteroscedastic level-1 variances, and models having a factor-analytic structure. Like the SEM approach, they assume that the design is "time structured" (that is, spacing between intended time points will not vary from person to person), but it does allow randomly missing time-series data. This approach, popular in biomedical applications, thus combines advantages of allowing missing data while also allowing a broad range of covariance structures. Thum (1997) extended this approach to three levels (see Chapter 8). The approach developed by Jennrich and Schlucter can be implemented both within the framework of hierarchical models and SEM.

To understand the similarities and differences between MRM, SEM, and HLM, it is important to consider three different kinds of data: (1) The observed data are balanced; (2) the "complete data" are balanced, but time points are missing at random so that the number of time points per person varies; and (3) the "complete data" are unbalanced, as when level-1 predictors have different distributions across people.

Suppose we have outcome Y_{ti} at time t, for person i, with T_i time points ($t = 1, \ldots, T_i$) observed for person i. We might formulate a simple linear model at level 1:

$$Y_{ti} = \pi_{0i} + \pi_{1i}a_{ti} + e_{ti}, \qquad e_{ti} \sim \mathrm{N}(0, \sigma^2), \qquad [6.22]$$

where a_{ti} is the age of person i at time t. For simplicity, we adopt an unconditional model at level 2:

$$\pi_{0i} = \beta_{00} + u_{0i},$$

$$\pi_{1i} = \beta_{10} + u_{1i}, \qquad\qquad\qquad [6.23]$$

$$\begin{pmatrix} u_{0i} \\ u_{1i} \end{pmatrix} \sim N\left[\begin{pmatrix} 0 \\ 0 \end{pmatrix}, \begin{pmatrix} \tau_{00} & \tau_{01} \\ \tau_{10} & \tau_{11} \end{pmatrix}\right].$$

The combined model may then be written as

$$Y_{ti} = \beta_{00} + \beta_{10}a_{ti} + \varepsilon_{ti}, \qquad\qquad\qquad [6.24]$$

where

$$\varepsilon_{ti} = u_{0i} + u_{1i}a_{ti} + e_{ti},$$

$$\mathrm{Var}(\varepsilon_{ti}) = \delta_{ti}^2 = \tau_{00} + 2a_{ti}\tau_{01} + a_{ti}^2\tau_{11} + \sigma^2, \qquad [6.25]$$

$$\mathrm{Cov}(\varepsilon_{ti}, \varepsilon_{t'i}) = \delta_{tt'i} = \tau_{00} + (a_{ti} + a_{t'i})\tau_{01} + a_{ti}a_{t'i}\tau_{11}.$$

Case 1: Observed Data are Balanced

Suppose every person has T observations ($T_i = T$ for all i). Then the data Y_{ti} for person i will follow a T-variate multivariate normal distribution with variances δ_{ti}^2 at time t and covariance $\delta_{tt'i}$ between observations at time t and time t'. Suppose further that the age of person i at time t is the same for all persons (e.g., every person is observed annually on his or her birthday and all persons are the same age at the start of the study).[11] Thus, $a_{ti} = a_t$ for all i. In this case, the data will follow the assumption of homogeneity of dispersion, that is, $\delta_{ti}^2 = \delta_t^2$ and $\delta_{tt'i} = \delta_{tt'}$ for all i (substitute a_t for a_{ti} in Equation 6.25). In sum, every person's data will follow a T-variate normal distribution with a common covariance matrix having variances δ_t^2 and covariances $\delta_{tt'}$. In principle, the common covariance matrix will have $T(T+1)/2$ parameters: T variances (one for each time point) and $T(T-1)/2$ covariances (one for each pair of time points). For, example, if $T = 5$, in the example below, there will be 5 variances and 10 covariances. However, under the two-level model of Equations 6.22 and 6.23, these variances and covariances will be functions of only four underlying parameters ($\tau_{00}, \tau_{01}, \tau_{11}, \sigma^2$). Thus, in this case, the hierarchical model of Equations 6.22 and 6.23 is a special case of a more general T-variate normal model with restrictions imposed upon the $T(T+1)/2$ covariance parameters as specified in Equation 6.25. The HLM of Equations 6.22 and 6.23 can thus be viewed as a specific "covariance structure" model. Standard software for SEM can estimate this model and allow for a variety of other covariance structures (e.g., autocorrelated level-1 residuals and level-1 residuals having different variances at different times).

Case 2: Complete Data are Balanced

Suppose now that, while the aim of the study was to collect T observations for each person, data are missing at random. Thus, person i will have T_i observations with $T_i \leq T$. Now the data for person i will be T_i-variate normal, that is, the distribution will be person specific. Standard approaches to multivariate analysis for repeated measures no longer apply, because these require a common covariance matrix for all persons in a given subpopulation. Thus, the HLM of Equations 6.22 and 6.23 can no longer be viewed as a special case of a T-variate normal distribution.

We can solve this problem, however, by conceiving the $Y_{ti}^*, t = 1, \ldots, T,$ as the "complete data," that is, the data we aimed to collect, while $Y_{ri}, r = 1, \ldots, R_i,$ are the observed data, the subset of the Y values that we actually observe. Thus, Equations 6.22 and 6.23 constitute a hierarchical model that is a special case of a T-variate normal model. Following Joreskog and Sorbom (1996) and Goldstein (1995), we create a new level-1 model that describes the pattern of missing data:

$$Y_{ri} = \sum_{t=1}^{T} m_{tri} Y_{ti}^*, \qquad [6.26]$$

where m_{tri} takes on a value of 1 if Y_{ti}^* is observed at time t and 0 otherwise. For example, consider a participant in NYS who was observed at times 2 and 4, but was unavailable at times 1, 3, and 5. Thus, person i's first observation came at $t = 2$ and his second came at $t = 4$ or

$$
\begin{aligned}
Y_{1i} &= m_{11i} Y_{1i}^* + m_{21i} Y_{2i}^* + m_{31i} Y_{3i}^* + m_{41i} Y_{4i}^* + m_{51i} Y_{5i}^* \\
&= (0) * Y_{1i}^* + (1) * Y_{2i}^* + (0) * Y_{3i}^* + (0) * Y_{4i}^* + (0) * (Y_{5i}^*) \\
&= Y_{2i}^*. \qquad [6.27]
\end{aligned}
$$

In the same vein, person i's second observation occurred at time $t = 4$:

$$
\begin{aligned}
Y_{2i} &= (0) * Y_{1i}^* + (0) * Y_{2i}^* + (0) * Y_{3i}^* = (1) * Y_{4i}^* + (0) * Y_{5i}^* \\
&= Y_{4i}^*.
\end{aligned}
$$

In the language of HLM, the m_{tri} values are level-1 predictors and the complete data $Y_{1i}^*, Y_{2i}^*, Y_{3i}^*, Y_{4i}^*, Y_{5i}^*$ are the level-1 coefficients. There is no level-1 random effect.

The level-2 model then conceives the latent Y_{ti}^* as the outcome, equivalent to Equation 6.24. Chapter 14 considers estimation theory for this special case of a hierarchical linear model.

Modeling Alternative Covariance Structures. We present below several alternative growth model analyses using the first cohort of the National Youth Survey (NYS). For a description of NYS, see Elliott, Huizinga, and Menard (1989). The intent was to interview all 239 members of cohort 1 at ages 11, 12, 13, 14, and 15. Thus, $T = 5$. In fact, 168 members have a full complement of five data points, while 45 have four data points, 14 had three, 5 have two, and 7 had only one.

A key aim of NYS was to assess antisocial attitudes and behavior of youth. We focus here on attitudes toward deviant behavior, an approximately continuous scale score obtained through annual interviews. The general theory of crime of Gottfredson and Hirschi (1990) predicts a near-linear increase in antisocial behavior during the early adolescent (11–15) years. It is reasonable to also hypothesize that for the outcome of interest in this example, tolerance of deviant thinking, a linear relationship might also hold. Thus, we might formulate as a model for the complete data, Y_{ti}^*:

$$Y_{ti}^* = \pi_{0i} + \pi_{1i}a_t + e_{ti}, \qquad [6.28]$$

where

Y_{ti}^* is the tolerance score for person i at occasion t;

a_t is the age minus 13 for that person at occasion t; so that

π_{0i} represents the expected tolerance level for person i at age 13,

π_{1i} represents the annual rate of increase in tolerance between the ages of 11 and 15; and

e_{ti} is the within-person residual.

We present below the results from a series of models of increasing complexity.

(i) Compound Symmetry. A covariance structure commonly assumed in univariate repeated-measures analysis of variance requires the variances to be the same at every time point and also that all covariances are the same. This is equivalent to assuming (a) that level-1 random effects, e_{ti}, are independent with homogeneous level-1 variance, σ^2, and (b) that all participants have the same linear slope. Under compound symmetry, the level-2 model of Equation 6.23 reduces to

$$\pi_{0i} = \beta_{00} + u_{0i},$$
$$\pi_{1i} = \beta_{10}. \qquad [6.29]$$

The combined model is then a special case of Equations 6.24 and 6.25 with τ_{11} and τ_{01} set to zero:

$$\varepsilon_{ti} = u_{0i} + e_{ti},$$
$$\text{Var}(\varepsilon_{ti}) = \delta_t^2 = \tau_{00} + \sigma^2, \qquad [6.30]$$
$$\text{Cov}(\varepsilon_{ti}, \varepsilon_{t'i}) = \delta_{tt'} = \tau_{00}.$$

Thus, the compound symmetry model would represent the 15 variance-covariance parameters for $T = 5$ in the NYS data as functions of just two underlying parameters (τ_{00} and σ^2).

(ii) First-Order-Autoregressive or "AR(1)" Model. This adds an autocorrelation term to the compound symmetry of Equation 6.30, yielding

$$\delta_t^2 = \tau_{00} + \sigma^2,$$
$$\delta_{tt'} = \tau_{00} + \sigma^2 \rho^{|t-t'|}. \qquad [6.31]$$

Thus, the model represents 15 possible variances and covariances in the NYS data as functions of three underlying parameters ($\tau_{00}, \rho, \sigma^2$).

(iii) Random Slopes, Homogeneous Level-1 Variance. This is the widely used HLM of Equations 6.22 and 6.23. It represents the 15 variance-covariance parameters as a function of four underlying parameters ($\tau_{00}, \tau_{01}, \tau_{11}, \sigma^2$).

(iv) Random Slopes, Heterogeneous Level-1 Variance. This elaborates the model of Equations 6.22 and 6.23 to allow a different variance at each time point. It therefore represents the 15 variance-covariance parameters as a function of eight underlying parameters ($\tau_{00}, \tau_{01}, \tau_{11}, \sigma_1^2, \sigma_2^2, \sigma_3^2, \sigma_4^2, \sigma_5^2$). An alternative and more parsimonious specification for heterogeneity at level 1 models the log variance as a function of age, for example,

$$\ln(\sigma_t^2) = \alpha_0 + \alpha_1 a_t. \qquad [6.32]$$

(The rationale for a linear model as the log of the variance was previously discussed in Chapter 5, "Applications with Heterogeneous Level-1 Variance.")

(v) An Unrestricted Model. In this model, there is a $T \times 1$ vector of errors having a common T-variate normal distribution with means of 0 and a general variance-covariance matrix, Σ. In the NYS application, the unrestricted model includes 15 unique variance-covariance parameters to be estimated. Note that, as T increases, this model becomes inordinately complex. For example, an unrestricted model with 20 time points would have 210 variance-covariance parameters. Nevertheless, with small T, this model can serve as a standard to test the fit of more parsimonious submodels.

Results: Level-2 Coefficients. Table 6.11 displays model estimates and fit statistics for five models. Looking across the five sets of estimates, the overall intercept, β_{00} (expected outcome at age 13), is very similar (ranging from 0.321 to 0.328) in each case with each analysis producing a similar standard error (rounded to 0.013 in each case). Estimates of the average growth rate, β_{10}, are also similar. However, the standard error estimate is smaller for the compound symmetry model than for the others. In general, inferences for the fixed level-2 coefficients in this example are insensitive to choice of model for the covariance structure with the exception that the compound symmetry model underestimates the uncertainty about the average growth rate in pro-deviant thinking. (Table 6.11 does not show the results of the log-linear model as age was found unrelated to the level-1 variances.)

Results: Model Fit. Generally, we seek the most parsimonious model that adequately describes our data (see Table 6.12). Not surprisingly, the unrestricted model, which allows separate estimation of 17 parameters (five variances, 10 covariances, and 2 fixed level-2 coefficients), provides a better fit than does any of the simpler models. Note the model deviance of -378.26. The most complex of the remaining models allows random slopes and time-specific level-1 variances (10 parameters in all), yielding a model deviance of -348.57. The difference between deviances of $-348.57 - (-378.26) = 29.68$, when compared to the percentiles of the χ^2 distribution with $17 - 10 = 7$ degrees of freedom, yields $p < .001$, suggesting that the simpler model must be rejected. It is possible that a more complex growth model, for example, with randomly varying linear and quadratic slopes, would produce an adequate fit.

The worst fitting model is the compound symmetry model, yielding a deviance of -229.00 with 4 degrees of freedom. Adding a single parameter, the autocorrelation parameter, reduces the deviance by $-294.32 - (-229.00) = 65.32$. The estimated autocorrelation is .40. Allowing random slopes substantially improves the fit (note the deviance of -338.07) by adding just two parameters to the compound symmetry model. The model fits substantially better than AR(1). Allowing separate level-1 variance for each time point in the random-slopes model marginally reduces the deviance to -348.57. We note that we found it impossible to simultaneously estimate the autocorrelation parameter while also allowing randomly varying slopes in this data set.[12] We suspect that more time points are needed to estimate these two parameters simultaneously.

Results: Fitted Variances and Correlations. Comparing deviance statistics offers an empirical method for model comparison. An alternative, more substantive gauge of various models is to assess their capacity to reproduce the

TABLE 6.11 A Comparison of Five Models for the NYS Data

Level-2 Coefficients	Compound Symmetry Coeff.	se	AR(1) Coeff.	se	Random Slopes, σ^2 Coeff.	se	Random Slopes, σ_t^2 Coeff.	se	Unrestricted Model Coeff.	se
Average intercept, β_{00}	0.328	0.013	0.328	0.013	0.328	0.013	0.328	0.013	0.321	0.013
Average growth rate, β_{10}	0.064	0.004	0.061	0.005	0.065	0.005	0.063	0.005	0.059	0.005

Variance-Covariance Component

Level 2:

Compound Symmetry: $\hat{\tau}_{00} = 0.034$

AR(1): $\hat{\tau}_{00} = 0.034$

Random Slopes, σ^2:
$$\hat{\tau} = \begin{bmatrix} 0.034 & 0.008 \\ & 2.5 \times 10^{-3} \end{bmatrix}$$

Random Slopes, σ_t^2:
$$\hat{\tau} = \begin{bmatrix} 0.034 & 0.008 \\ & 2.9 \times 10^{-3} \end{bmatrix}$$

Unrestricted Model:
$$\hat{\Sigma} = \begin{bmatrix} 0.035 & & & & & \\ 0.017 & 0.019 & 0.022 & 0.025 & & \\ 0.045 & 0.028 & 0.025 & 0.027 & & \\ & 0.073 & 0.053 & 0.048 & & \\ & & 0.086 & 0.066 & & \\ & & & 0.090 & & \end{bmatrix}$$

Level 1:

Compound Symmetry: $\hat{\sigma}^2 = 0.032$

AR(1): $\hat{\sigma}^2 = 0.042$, $\hat{\rho} = 0.397$

Random Slopes, σ^2: $\hat{\sigma}^2 = 0.026$

Random Slopes, σ_t^2: $\hat{\sigma}_1^2 = 0.020$, $\hat{\sigma}_2^2 = 0.028$, $\hat{\sigma}_3^2 = 0.034$, $\hat{\sigma}_4^2 = 0.025$, $\hat{\sigma}_5^2 = 0.019$

Model Fit

	Compound Symmetry	AR(1)	Random Slopes, σ^2	Random Slopes, σ_t^2	Unrestricted Model
Deviance	−229.00	−294.32	−338.07	−348.57	−378.26
df	4	5	6	10	17

TABLE 6.12 Comparison of Deviance Statistics Across Alternative Models

(a) Models Summary	Deviance	df
(1) Random intercept—"compound symmetry"—model (homogeneous level-1 variances)	−229.00	4
(2) Random intercept model [AR(1) level-1 variances]	−294.32	5
(3) Random slope model (homogeneous level-1 variances)	−338.07	6
(4) Random slope model (separate level-1 variance for each time point)	−348.57	10
(5) Random slope model (log-linear model on level-1 variances)	−347.71	8
(6) Unrestricted model	−378.26	17

(b) Selected Model Comparison	Differences in Deviances	df	p
Model 1 versus Model 3	109.07	2	.000
Model 3 versus Model 4	10.51	4	.032
Model 5 versus Model 4	0.87	2	n.s.
Model 4 versus Model 6	29.68	7	.000

basic structure reflected in the variances and correlations estimated under the unrestricted model. This is possible only when the number of time points is sufficiently small to allow stable estimation of the unrestricted model. Such is the case in our example with $T = 5$ and 239 participants. Table 6.13 provides the fitted variance and covariances associated with the five time points.

The variance-covariance structure in the unrestricted model has three key features. First, the variance increases with age: Note estimates of 0.035, 0.045, 0.073, 0.086, 0.090 as we move from age = 11 to age = 15. Second, the correlations between adjacent time points also increase with age, suggesting a "crystallization of attitudes" (see correlations of .42, .49, .67, .76 just above the diagonal in the bottom panel of Table 6.13). Third, there is a tendency for correlations between adjacent time points to be higher than correlations between more distance time points: Note, for example, correlations between time 5 (outcome at age 15) and earlier time points of .76, .59, .43, .44. Assuming these are core covariance structure features of the data set, we might now ask: How well do simpler models capture these three elements?

The compound symmetry model does a poor job. Under that model, variances do not increase with age but are rather constrained to be constant at .066. Nor do the correlations increase with age or decay with distance, as these are constrained to be constant at .51.

The autoregressive model does a somewhat better job in that the correlations do decay with distance (note correlations between the residuals at age 15 and the residuals at earlier ages of .62, .47, .41, .38). However, the

TABLE 6.13 Fitted Covariance and Correlation Matrices

(a) Covariance Matrix

Compound Symmetry

.066	.034	.034	.034	.034
	.066	.034	.034	.034
		.066	.034	.034
			.066	.034
				.066

AR(1)

0.066	.041	.031	.027	.025
	0.066	.041	.031	.027
		.066	.041	.031
			.066	.041
				.066

Random Linear Slope, Homogeneous σ²

.040	.016	.019	.021	.024
	.048	.026	.032	.037
		.061	.042	.050
			.079	.062
				.102

Unrestricted Model

.035	.017	.019	.022	.025
	.045	.028	.025	.027
		.073	.053	.048
			.086	.066
				.090

(b) Correlation Matrix

Compound Symmetry

1.00	**.51**	**.51**	**.51**	**.51**
	1.00	**.51**	**.51**	**.51**
		1.00	**.51**	**.51**
			1.00	**.51**
				1.00

AR(1)

1.00	**.62**	.47	.41	**.38**
	1.00	**.62**	.47	**.41**
		1.00	**.62**	.47
			1.00	**.62**
				1.00

Random Linear Slope, Homogeneous σ²

1.00	**.37**	.38	.38	**.38**
	1.00	**.49**	.52	**.53**
		1.00	**.61**	**.63**
			1.00	**.70**
				1.00

Unrestricted Model

1.00	**.42**	.37	.39	**.44**
	1.00	**.49**	.40	**.43**
		1.00	.67	**.59**
			1.00	**.76**
				1.00

estimated model required the variances to remain constant with age and the correlation between adjacent time points to also remain constant.

The model having random slopes (with homogeneous level-1 variance) does a much better job of reproducing the key features of the covariance structure. Note that the estimated variances increase with age (0.040, 0.048, 0.061, 0.079, 0.102); the correlations between adjacent time points increase with age (.37, .49, .61, .70) and decay with the distance between time points (correlations between residuals at age 15 and earlier ages are .70, .63, .53, .38, respectively).

Representing the Unrestricted Model as a Polynomial Model for Individual Change. For time-structured data, there is always a "standard" HLM (i.e., a polynomial model for individual change) that will duplicate the results of the unrestricted model. Specifically, if the level-1 model is a polynomial of degree $T - 2$ with all coefficients random, and if the level-1 variance is allowed to vary with time (one variance per time point), the two-level HLM will include $T(T + 1)/2$ covariance parameters, exactly reproducing the marginal variance and covariance estimates of the unrestricted model. In our example, with $T = 5$, a random cubic model with heterogeneous variances will reproduce the results of the unrestricted model.

At level 1, the model is

$$Y_{ti}^* = \pi_{0i} + \pi_{1i}a_t + \pi_{2i}a_t^2 + \pi_{3i}c_t + e_{ti},$$
$$e_{ti} \sim N(0, \sigma_t^2).$$

[6.33]

Here c_t is a cubic contrast, literally, a residual computed from a regression of a_t^3 on a_t and a_t^2. Given that a_t is centered, this approach assures that the three polynomial terms (a_t, a_t^2, and c_t) will be orthogonal. At level 2, the four change parameters (π_{0i}, π_{1i}, π_{2i}, π_{3i}) vary and covary around their means. Thus, the level-2 variance-covariance matrix is 4 by 4 and has 10 parameters. Finally, there are five level-1 variances, σ_t^2, $t = 1, \ldots, 5$, which yields 15 variance-covariance parameters overall.

Case 3: Complete Data are Unbalanced

Suppose now that the model includes a level-1 predictor such as a_{ti} having a random effect π_{1i} and that a_{ti} takes on a different set of values for each participant. In a large-scale field study, it is often impossible to control tightly the time interval between observations for a variety of reasons. For example, many participants will be hard to find or will ask to reschedule appointments, and cost constraints require a flexible deployment of data collectors. In this case, the age distribution will be essentially unique to each participant. In fact, no two participants may have the same a_{ti} at time t. Moreover, even if the ages are nearly the same for all level-2 units, other level-1 predictors may have different values across participants. As illustrated below using the NYS, the antisocial attitudes of one's peers is a time-varying covariate having a random effect in the model; the set of values of this covariate will tend to be different for each participant. In such cases, not even the complete data can be viewed as balanced, even if the number of time points per person is held constant at T. Thus, the variance δ_{ti}^2 will vary continuously across participants as will each covariance $\delta_{tt'i}$. Such heteroscedastic models cannot be estimated within the framework of MRM or SEM. In such cases, the standard HLM approach cannot be viewed as a simplified version of an "unrestricted model." The HLM is, in fact, more encompassing in this regard.

Example. In the NYS data, we have at each occasion a measure of the exposure of the participant to peers who tolerate deviant behavior (see Raudenbush & Chan, 1993, for details). This "EXPO" variable differs over time for different participants. Suppose we specify "EXPO" as a predictor (a "time-varying covariate") in the level-1 model of HLM. Then the marginal variance-covariance matrix will be heterogeneous if either of two conditions hold:

1. exposure has a random coefficient; or
2. σ_{ti}^2 is a function of EXPO.

To illustrate, we estimate a "standard" two-level model, where at level 1 we have

$$Y_{ti} = \pi_{0i} + \pi_{1i}a_{ti} + \pi_{2i}a_{ti}^2 + \pi_{3i}(\text{EXPO})_{ti} + e_{ti} \qquad [6.34]$$

and the level-1 variance is allowed to remain homogeneous, σ^2. At level 2, all coefficients are random:

$$\pi_{pi} = \beta_{p0} + u_{pi}, \qquad p = 0, 1, 2, 3. \qquad [6.35]$$

Since T is now a 4×4 matrix, the level-2 model has 10 variance-covariance parameters, and the overall model has 11. We compare this to the "unrestricted model"

$$Y_{ti}^* = \beta_{00} + \beta_{10}a_t + \beta_{20}a_t^2 + \beta_{30}(\text{EXPO})_{ti} + \varepsilon_{ti}, \qquad [6.36]$$

which involves 15 variance-covariance parameters. Results are displayed in Table 6.14. Note that inferences about the fixed effects are essentially iden-

TABLE 6.14 A Comparison Between an Unrestricted MRM Model and an HLM Model with a Time-Varying Covariate Having a Random-Effect

Fixed Effects	Unrestricted MRM			HLM Model		
	Coeff.	se	t ratio	Coeff.	se	t ratio
Intercept, β_{00}	0.3252	0.0127	25.56	0.3251	0.0125	25.86
Linear, β_{10}	0.0487	0.0045	10.74	0.0466	0.0047	10.00
Quadratic, β_{10}	−0.0006	0.0030	−0.21	0.0006	0.0030	0.21
Exposure, β_{30}	0.3186	0.0244	13.07	0.3430	0.0295	11.62

Variance-Covariance Component

$$\hat{\Sigma} = \begin{bmatrix} 0.035 & 0.011 & 0.014 & 0.015 & 0.014 \\ & 0.035 & 0.018 & 0.016 & 0.016 \\ & & 0.035 & 0.034 & 0.028 \\ & & & 0.054 & 0.042 \\ & & & & 0.062 \end{bmatrix}$$

$$\hat{\tau} = \begin{bmatrix} 0.0236 & 0.0034 & -0.0016 & 0.0072 \\ & 0.0021 & 0.0000 & -0.0029 \\ & & 0.0038 & 0.0000 \\ & & & 0.0457 \end{bmatrix}$$

$$\hat{\sigma}^2 = 0.0210$$

Model Fit

Deviance	−517.26			−522.47		
df	19			15		

tical for the two models. However, the deviance associated with the HLM model based on only 11 variance-covariance parameters is actually *smaller* than the deviance associated with the unrestricted model, which has 15 variance-covariance parameters (and 19 total parameters including the fixed effects). The HLM model estimated here, which has fewer parameters, is not a submodel of the unrestricted MRM model. This HLM model allows heterogeneous variance-covariance matrices across participants as a function of participant variation in exposure, while the unrestricted model is general only with respect to the class of models assuming homogeneous variance-covariance matrices. In this instance, the unrestricted MRM model cannot represent a key feature present in the NYS data.

Effects of Missing Observations at Level 1

An important advantage of using the HLM to study growth in conjunction with maximum likelihood estimation is the flexibility of the approach in handling missing data. Unlike conventional methods, the approach can readily incorporate all participants who have been observed at least once. Results of the analysis can be interpreted as if no missing data were present under the assumption that the data are missing at random. This assumption is not as severe as it might seem. To see this, let us consider the three types of missing data that might arise by attrition according to Little and Rubin (1987); also see Schafer (1997).

1. The attrition may lead to data *missing completely at random* (MCAR). Data that are MCAR result when the missing time points are a random sample of all time points or the drop-outs are a random sample of all participants. In this case, unbiased estimation follows easily using conventional methods, for example, analyzing only those cases with complete data. However, to assume that data are MCAR is generally implausible, impossible to verify, and risky. Moreover, discarding cases with incomplete data entails a loss of precision that will be substantial in some applications.

2. The data may be *missing at random* (MAR). MAR occurs when the probability of missing a time point is independent of the missing data given the observed data. This assumption is reasonable when the observed data capture key confounding influences, for example, variables related to both attrition and the outcome of interest. In the MAR case, estimation of the treatment effect will be unbiased if (a) all of the data are used in the analysis and (b) a fully efficient estimation procedure is used. For example, maximum likelihood estimation of hierarchical models will efficiently use all of the available time points to estimate the model, ensuring asymptotically unbiased estimation of treatment

effects under the MAR case. Under these conditions, the mechanism that produces the missingness is *ignorable*. Use of multiple, *model-based imputation* (Little & Rubin, 1987; Schafer, 1997) will also ensure ignorable missingness when data are MAR. (See further discussion in Chapter 11.)

3. *Nonignorable missingness* arises when the data are neither MCAR nor MAR. In this case, the probability of attrition does depend on the missing value, even after controlling for all observed data. Results will be robust to nonignorable missingness to the extent that (a) all of the data are efficiently used and (b) the fraction of missing information is small.[13]

Little (1995) and Hedeker and Gibbons (1997) describe methods for nonignorably missing longitudinal data under the rubric of pattern-mixture models. Using this approach, participants are grouped according to their data patterns and key relationships are estimated within these groups. This enables the analyst to assess sensitivity of inferences to attrition.

Using a Hierarchical Model to Predict Future Status

Our primary purpose in this chapter has been to demonstrate how studies of change can be constructively pursued by means of hierarchical linear models. We have illustrated the formulation and interpretation of some commonly employed level-1 models and the testing of growth hypotheses.

Another advantage of hierarchical models, as noted in Chapters 1 and 3, is that the empirical Bayes estimates of the level-1 coefficients, such as the growth parameters in Equation 6.20, have smaller mean-squared error than do the OLS estimates that use only the separate time trend data from each individual. This feature can prove advantageous in many applications. We illustrated in Chapter 4, for example, how the empirical Bayes estimates of level-1 coefficients can be used to identify organizations with unusual patterns of effectiveness. They can also be useful in growth studies where individual growth curve estimates may be needed (e.g., to predict future status). We now illustrate this feature with a subset of the vocabulary data analyzed earlier.

For purposes of this comparison, we used the Huttenlocher data through 22 months as a basis for predicting vocabulary size at 24 months. We then compared these predicted values with the actual observed values. Specifically, we posed a level-1 model as in Equation 6.15 and an unconditional level-2 model as in Equation 6.17. We compared the predictions at 24 months based on the empirical Bayes estimates of π_{pi} (see Equation 6.20) with those based on OLS estimation of a no-intercept quadratic regression for each child. The results are presented in Table 6.15. The first column presents the measured vocabulary size for the 22 children at 24 months. The second and third

TABLE 6.15 Comparison of Hierarchical Model Predictions with Ordinary Least Squares at 24 Months

Case	Actual Vocabulary Size	OLS Prediction	Empirical Bayes Prediction	OLS Error	Empirical Bayes Error
1	139.00	126.649	127.898	12.351	11.102
2	449.00	505.802	512.202	−56.802	−63.202
3	142.00	111.458	111.028	30.542	30.972
4	579.00	723.594	702.335	−144.594	−123.335
5	317.00	326.472	311.864	−9.472	5.136
6	78.00	56.648	55.519	21.352	22.481
7	577.00	703.864	690.083	−126.864	−113.083
8	491.00	489.922	492.341	1.078	−1.341
9	595.00	634.180	656.442	−39.180	−61.442
10	604.00	727.508	715.186	−123.508	−111.186
11	137.00	145.040	138.352	−8.040	−1.352
12	350.00	366.000	346.939	−16.000	3.061
13	149.00	126.007	134.250	22.993	14.750
14	56.00	6.007	28.904	49.993	27.096
15	188.00	186.000	239.329	2.000	−51.329
16	172.00	228.007	240.512	−56.007	−68.512
17	240.00	174.007	190.903	65.993	49.097
18	292.00	153.007	167.123	138.993	124.877
19	99.00	111.007	127.636	−12.007	−28.636
20	142.00	174.000	176.779	−32.000	−34.779
21	265.00	120.000	163.448	145.000	101.552
22	329.00	432.007	432.892	−103.007	−103.892
Root mean square error of prediction				75.30	66.51

columns are the OLS and empirical Bayes predictions. The corresponding prediction errors appear in columns 4 and 5.

Notice that, as expected, the standard deviation of the prediction errors based on the empirical Bayes estimates is smaller than for OLS (66.51 versus 75.30). This is achieved mainly because empirical Bayes provides somewhat better predictions for the extreme cases, such as 4, 7, 10, 18, and especially 21. The empirical Bayes advantage in this particular application is modest because the OLS estimates are fairly reliable, given the careful measurement procedures employed in this study. For the model employed in this prediction application, the hierarchical analysis estimated the reliability of the linear rate component at .51 and the quadratic term at .88. This can also be seen in Figure 6.1, where the individual OLS quadratic trajectories provide a close fit to the data.

In general, the empirical Bayes advantage over OLS would be greater in applications where the time trend data have more random noise. Even so, the conventional caution still applies. Polynomial growth models can provide reliable predictions only for time points that are relatively near to the time points represented in the data. In our example, prediction to age 24 months seemed reasonable. Predictors much beyond 24 months, however, might not be trustworthy.

Power Considerations in Designing Studies of Growth and Change

In Chapter 5, we considered power issues in the design of organizational research studies. We asked how choice of sample size n, the number of persons per organization, and J, the number of organizations, affect the power to detect various effects. We saw that the effects of n and J on power depend on the magnitude of variances within and between organizations, on the cost of sampling at each level, and on the research question.

In repeated-measures studies, the analogous sample sizes are T, the number of time points per person, and n, the number of people. One might reason that adding more time points would be most helpful when the within-person variance, σ^2, is large, while increasing the sample size, n, would help most when variation between people in their growth rates is large. While there is some truth in this intuition, the design problem is a bit more complicated.

One can increase the number of time points, T, in a repeated-measures study by increasing the frequency of observation per unit time (holding constant the duration of the study) or increasing the duration (holding constant the frequency). The costs and benefits of these two ways of increasing T may be quite different.

Let D denote the duration of a study in some meaningful metric (e.g., years), and let T denote the number of time-series observations. For example, the National Youth Survey, analyzed previously in this chapter, began in 1976 and stopped in 1980, so $D = 4$ years and $T = 5$ time points (the first time point occurred at the outset in 1976 and then participants were observed annually until 1980). Similarly, in the vocabulary growth study, $D = 14$ months (i.e., Huttenlocher et al. observed vocabulary growth between 12 and 26 months) and the complete data consisted of $T = 8$ time points (i.e., 12, 14, 16, 18, 20, 22, 24, and 26 months). Assuming equally spaced time points starting at time 0, the frequency of observation will be $f = (T - 1)/D$. For the NYS, f equals 1 per year and for the vocabulary growth f equals 0.5 per month.

Assuming a linear growth model

$$Y_{ti} = \pi_{0i} + \pi_{1i}a_{ti} + e_{ti}, \qquad e_{ti} \sim N(0, \sigma^2), \qquad [6.37]$$

where $a_{ti} = Dt/(T-1)$ at time points $t = 0, 1, \ldots, T-1$, Raudenbush and Liu (2001) show that the least squares estimator of the person-specific growth rates is then

$$\text{Var}(\hat{\pi}_{1i}|\pi_{1i}) \equiv V_1 = \frac{\sigma^2}{\sum_{t=0}^{T-1} a_{ti}^2} = \frac{\sigma^2}{T} \bigg/ \frac{D^2(T+1)}{12(T-1)}. \qquad [6.38]$$

Now suppose our aim is to compare two treatment groups (an experimental group versus a control group) with respect to their average growth rates. The part of the level-2 model that is relevant is

$$\pi_{1i} = \beta_{10} + \beta_{11}X_i + u_{1i}, \qquad u_{1i} \sim N(0, \tau_{11}), \qquad [6.39]$$

where $X_i = 1$ if experimental, 0 if control. The power to detect this treatment effect would depend on the noncentrality parameter

$$\varphi = n\lambda\delta^2/4 \qquad [6.40]$$

of the F distribution with df $= (1, n - 2)$, where $\delta = \beta_{11}/(\tau_{11})^{1/2}$ is a standardized effect size and λ is the reliability

$$\lambda = \tau_{11}/(\tau_{11} + V_1). \qquad [6.41]$$

Changing the duration or frequency changes the noncentrality parameter *only by changing the reliability*, λ. Suppose, for example, we choose $T = 5$ time points with a frequency of one observation per year, so that $D = 4$. Then, using Equations 6.38 and 6.41, the reliability will be $\tau_{11}/(\tau_{11} + \sigma^2/10)$. On the other hand, with the same number of time points but with frequency of observation twice per year, the duration would be $D = 2$. Now the reliability is $\tau_{11}/(\tau_{11} + \sigma^2/2.50)$, possibly considerably less, especially if σ^2 is large relative to τ_{11}. Despite holding constant the number of time points, the second study produces a smaller reliability because the duration of the study has shortened, thereby reducing the study's leverage in estimating person-specific growth rates.

When σ^2 is small relative to τ_{11} and persons vary a lot on their growth rates, the reliability will converge toward 1.0. In this case, the total sample size becomes much more important in determining power than either the frequency of observation or the duration of the study. The formulas presented above apply only for linear growth models. Raudenbush and Liu (2001) provide analogous results for assessing power in applications of higher-order polynomial (e.g., acceleration rates) growth models.

Notes

1. It is generally important to center the predictors a_{ti} to reduce collinearity among a_{ti}, a_{ti}^2, and a_{ti}^3. For higher-order polynominals, orthogonal transformations may be helpful or essential (see Krik, 1982, pp. 151–154).

2. The notion that each person has a unique set of reliabilities may seem strange in the light of classical measurement theory, which defines reliability as a characteristic of a measurement instrument applied to population. The classical definition assumes, however, that a standard instrument has been applied to all persons sampled. In more modern applications, such as tailored testing, each person may receive a somewhat different set of test items.

3. The precision with which we can estimate the association between a person-level variable and a growth parameter depends on the total number of persons, n, and the reliability of the growth curve estimate. Thus, if reliability is low, a larger sample of persons is required to obtain adequate precision.

4. Note that there was some evidence of heterogeneity of level-1 errors as a function of Y_{ti}. Not surprisingly, the level-1 residual variability is smaller when vocabulary size is small. Because the heterogeneity does not materially affect the key results reported here, we have chosen to ignore it in this introductory illustration. Models with more complex error structures at level 1 are discussed later in this chapter.

5. Our example involving vocabulary growth during the second year of life violates this advice in that we centered age around the initial age of 12 months. In that case, however, we had strong theoretical reasons to believe that both π_{0i} and π_{1i} would be zero. This enabled us to specify a parsimonious model that fit the data quite well; and given the small sample size, parsimony was a key consideration.

6. We thank *Psychological Methods* for permission to reproduce Figure 6.3, which appeared in Miyazaki and Raudenbush (2000).

7. Median rather than mean centering was employed here in order to retain a level-1 metric in whole years, which is easier to interpret. The same basic effects as unit-mean centering were obtained with these data.

8. Perhaps a more accurate descriptor than "structural equation models" for these approaches is "covariance structure models" because such models are derived by imposing certain constraints on the covariance matrix of the multivariate normal distribution. However, we adopt the more widely used term "structural equation models" here.

9. Some SEM software packages require a time-structured design but allow randomly missing data.

10. This work has been embodied in BMDP's Program 5v, which has strongly influenced more recent software development by SPSS and SAS.

11. Of course, it would never be true that every person would be observed at exactly the same ages, but this may be approximately true.

12. The attempt produced a negative estimate of the variance of the slopes using the Fisher scoring algorithm.

13. The fraction of missing information is not the fraction of missing data points. It is, rather, related to the amount of variation in the missing data that is not explained or accounted for by the observed data. If the associations between the observed and missing data are strong, the fraction of missing data will be small, even if the fraction of missing cases appears quite large.

7

Applications in Meta-Analysis and Other Cases where Level-1 Variances are Known

- Introduction
- Formulating Models for Meta-Analysis
- Example: The Effect of Teacher Expectancy on Pupil IQ
- Other Level-1 Variance-Known Problems
- The Multivariate *V*-Known Model
- Meta-Analysis of Incomplete Multivariate Data

Introduction

Researchers in many fields are interested in quantitative methods summarizing results from a series of related studies. In this form of inquiry, called "meta-analysis" (Glass, 1976), or "research synthesis" (Cooper & Hedges, 1994), individual studies conducting tests of the same hypothesis become cases in a "study of the studies."

A key question in meta-analysis is the consistency of study results. If each implementation of a new experimental treatment produces the same effect, it is sensible to summarize the entire stream of studies by a single common-effect size estimate. However, if the study results are inconsistent, so that the magnitude of the treatment effect varies from study to study, the meta-analyst's task requires formulating and testing possible explanations for *why* study results vary. What characteristics of treatment implementation, subject background, study context, or study methodology might predict differences in study results?

The central difficulty in assessing consistency of study results and in accounting for inconsistency is that even when every study produces a common "true" effect, the estimates of that effect will vary from study to study as a result of sampling error. For example, in a true experiment, the estimated treatment effect is influenced both by the treatment's effectiveness and by random differences between the experimental and control group. Therefore, variations will appear in a set of estimated effects from a series of studies, even if the studies are identically designed and implemented, and even if the studies draw random samples from the same population. The task facing the meta-analyst is to distinguish between components of variation in the estimated effects, where one component arises from sampling error, and a second component represents inconsistency in the effect-size parameters.

If inconsistency is discovered, one may formulate a model to account for it. The question of components of variation again arises: Of the residual variation in the estimated study effects, how much reflects sampling error, and how much represents true inconsistency that the model fails to explain?

The hierarchial model provides a useful framework for addressing the problem of components of variation in meta-analysis (Raudenbush & Bryk, 1985). This model enables the meta-analyst (a) to estimate the average effect size across a set of studies; (b) to estimate the variance of the effect-size parameters; (c) to estimate the residual variance of the effect-size parameters for each linear model; and (d) to use information from all studies to derive empirical Bayes estimates of each study's effect.

This last goal is important when research interest focuses on the true effect sizes for particular studies. We illustrate such a case later (see "Unconditional Analysis"). Chapter 13 extends this approach to derive the posterior distribution of effect sizes using fully Bayesian methods.

New to the second edition, we also consider multivariate applications in which not every study reports a full set of effect sizes. We illustrate how multivariate models for missing data can be applied to such problems.

The Hierarchical Structure of Meta-Analytic Data

It is natural to apply hierarchical linear models to meta-analytic data because such data are hierarchically structured: Subjects are "nested" within studies. Models are needed that take into account variation at the subject and the study level. Indeed, each study's investigator seeks to learn about sources of variation among subjects. It is the task of the meta-analyst to sort out variation across studies.

Applications discussed previously in this book may themselves be viewed as meta-analyses. In Chapter 5, for example, we conceived of each school as characterized by a relationship between student background and student mathematics achievement. The level-2 model enabled us to compare differences in this relationship across schools. In a sense, each school yielded a study of the relationship between social background and achievement. The level-2 model enabled us to combine results from these "studies," to assess consistency in that relationship, and to account for inconsistency. Similarly, the growth examples presented in Chapter 6 may be viewed as meta-analytic. Each child's data provides a "study" of the relationship between age and an outcome. By combining data across children, we are able to study variation in that relationship.

Two features, however, distinguish meta-analysis from the kinds of application described in previous chapters. First, in meta-analysis, the raw data from each study are rarely available. Instead, only summary statistics published in research reports are accessible to the meta-analyst. Second, different studies typically use different outcome measures, even though these are viewed as measures of the same construct. For example, in the series of studies of teacher expectancy on pupil IQ reported below, investigators used different IQ tests, each measured on a different scale.

To cope with these problems, meta-analysts have employed a variety of standardized measures of effect, the most common being standardized mean differences and correlation coefficients (see Cooper & Hedges, 1994, for a comprehensive review). Using standardized measures of effect translates each study's results to a common scale so that they may be compared.

Extensions to Other Level-1 "Variance-Known" Problems

If standardized effect measures are based on moderately large sample, say 30 or more cases per study, the sampling distribution of the statistics will be approximately normally distributed with a sampling variance that can be assumed known (see below). Thus, from a statistical point of view, meta-analysis presents the analyst with a series of independent effect estimates, each normally distributed with known variance at level 1.

Interestingly, a variety of other research problems, in addition to meta-analysis, have this same structure. A single statistic (say a standard deviation, proportion, or correlation) is available from each of many contexts and the goal is to compare these statistics. Often, a transformation of the statistic justifies the assumptions of normality and known variance. We label such cases *level-1 variance-known (or V-known)* applications. Meta-analysis thus represents a particular and important instance of this type.

Organization of This Chapter

We first consider applications of the hierarchical linear model to meta-analyses in which a single standardized effect is available for each of a series of studies. The next section presents the formulation of the model, and the one following illustrates its application in research on the effect of teacher expectancy on pupil IQ. The following section generalizes the meta-analytic methods to the broader class of "level-1 variance-known" problems, and the last two sections consider the case of multiple-outcome variables at level 1.

Formulating Models for Meta-Analysis

Standardized Mean Differences

As mentioned, a meta-analyst rarely has access to the raw data from each study. Instead, data on subjects from each study are summarized by a statistic. This statistic characterizes the magnitude of an effect or the strength of association between variables. We denote this statistic d_j as the "effect-size estimate" for study j.

In many applications, d_j is the standardized mean difference between an experimental group and a control:

$$d_j = (\overline{Y}_{Ej} - \overline{Y}_{Cj})/S_j, \qquad [7.1]$$

where

$\overline{Y}_{Ej}$ is the mean outcome for the experimental group;

$\overline{Y}_{Cj}$ is the mean outcome for the control group; and

S_j is the pooled, within-group standard deviation.

Each d_j estimates the population mean difference between the experimental and control groups in standard deviation units. For example, $d_j = .50$ indicates that experimental subjects in study j were estimated to score half a standard deviation higher, on average, than controls.

The statistic d_j may be viewed as estimating the corresponding population parameter, δ_j, where

$$\delta_j = (\mu_{Ej} - \mu_{Cj})/\sigma_j. \qquad [7.2]$$

Of course, the accuracy of d_j as an estimate of δ_j depends on the experimental- and control-group sample sizes, n_{Ej} and n_{Cj}, respectively. Hedges (1981) showed that for a fixed value of δ_j, the statistic d_j is approximately unbiased and normally distributed with variance V_j, that is,

$$d_j \mid \delta_j \sim N(\delta_j, V_j) \qquad [7.3]$$

with

$$V_j = (n_{Ej} + n_{Cj})/(n_{Ej}n_{Cj}) + \delta_j^2/[2(n_{Ej} + n_{Ej})]. \qquad [7.4]$$

Actually, d_j is not exactly unbiased. Hedges (1981) also presents a correction for bias that is especially helpful when n_{Ej} or n_{Cj} is very small. It is common to substitute d_j for δ_j in Equation 7.4 and then to assume V_j is "known".[1]

Level-1 (Within-Studies) Model

The level-1 model is simply

$$d_j = \delta_j + e_j \tag{7.5}$$

for studies $j = 1, \ldots, J$, where e_j is the sampling error associated with d_j as an estimate of δ_j and for which we assume $e_j \sim N(0, V_j)$.

We note that Equation 7.5 generalizes to meta-analyses using effect-size measures other than standardized mean differences. That is, d_j is any standardized effect measure from study j; δ_j is the corresponding parameter; and V_j is the sampling variance of d_j as an estimate of δ_j. For example, suppose a correlation, r_j, is reported for a series of studies. The standardized effect measure, d_j, is

$$d_j = \frac{1}{2} \log[(1 + r_j)/(1 - r_j)], \tag{7.6}$$

and the corresponding parameter is

$$\delta_j = \frac{1}{2} \log[(1 + \rho_j)/(1 - \rho_j)]. \tag{7.7}$$

The sampling variance of d_j is approximately

$$V_j = 1/(n_j - 3), \tag{7.8}$$

where

r_j is the sample correlation between two variables observed in study j;

ρ_j is the corresponding population correlation; and

n_j is the sample size in study j.

In this case, d_j is "Fisher's r to Z" transformation. Note that V_j is independent of the unknown ρ_j, which is an advantage.

Level-2 (Between-Studies) Model

In the level-2 model, the true unknown-effect size, δ_j, depends on study characteristics and a level-2 random error:

$$\begin{aligned} \delta_j &= \gamma_0 + \gamma_1 W_{1j} + \gamma_2 W_{2j} + \cdots + \gamma_S W_{Sj} + u_j \\ &= \gamma_0 + \sum_s \gamma_s W_{sj} + u_j, \end{aligned} \tag{7.9}$$

where

$W_{1j}, \ldots, W_{Sj}$ are study characteristics predicting these effect sizes;
$\gamma_0, \ldots, \gamma_S$ are regression coefficients; and
u_j is a level-2 random error for which we assume $u_j \sim N(0, \tau)$.

Combined Model

Substituting Equation 7.9 into Equation 7.5 yields the single model for the observed d_j:

$$d_j = \gamma_0 + \sum_s \gamma_s W_{sj} + u_j + e_j, \qquad [7.10]$$

from which it is clear that d_j is normally distributed,

$$d_j \sim N\left(\gamma_0 + \sum_s \gamma_s W_{sj}, \ \tau + V_j \right),$$

and for simplicity we denote

$$\text{Var}(d_j) = \tau + V_j = \Delta_j. \qquad [7.11]$$

Estimation

Estimation follows the basic procedure outlined in Chapter 3, except that it simplifies because each V_j is assumed known. Now there is only one variance component to estimate, τ. Given a maximum likelihood estimate of τ, the level-2 coefficients (the γs) are estimated by means of weighted least squares where the weights are the precisions, Δ_j^{-1}, as previously seen in Equation 3.17.

The empirical Bayes estimator, δ_j^*, of each study's effect, δ_j, is

$$\delta_j^* = \lambda_j d_j + (1 - \lambda_j)\left(\hat{\gamma}_0 + \sum_s \hat{\gamma}_s W_{sj} \right), \qquad [7.12]$$

where $\lambda_j = \tau/(\tau + V_j)$.

Example: The Effect of Teacher Expectancy on Pupil IQ

The hypothesis that teachers' expectations influence pupils' intellectual development as measured by IQ (intelligence quotient) scores has been the

TABLE 7.1 Experimental Studies of Teacher Expectancy Effects on Pupil IQ

Study	Weeks of Prior Contact	Effect Size Estimate, d_j	Standard Error of d_j	Empirical Bayes Estimates, δ_j^* Unconditional Model	Conditional Model
1. Rosenthal et al. (1974)	2	0.03	0.125	0.05	0.09
2. Conn et al. (1968)	3	0.12	0.147	0.10	−0.06
3. Jose & Cody (1971)	3	−0.14	0.167	−0.00	−0.06
4. Pellegrini & Hicks (1972)	0	1.18	0.373	0.22	0.41
5. Pellegrini & Hicks (1972)	0	0.26	0.369	0.11	0.41
6. Evans & Rosenthal (1969)	3	−0.06	0.103	−0.01	−0.06
7. Fielder et al. (1971)	3	−0.02	0.103	0.02	−0.06
8. Claiborn (1969)	3	−0.32	0.220	−0.03	−0.06
9. Kester & Letchworth (1972)	0	0.27	0.164	0.16	0.41
10. Maxwell (1970)	1	0.80	0.251	0.25	0.25
11. Carter (1970)	0	0.54	0.302	0.16	0.41
12. Flowers (1966)	0	0.18	0.223	0.11	0.41
13. Keshock (1970)	1	−0.02	0.289	0.06	0.25
14. Henrickson (1970)	2	0.23	0.290	0.11	0.09
15. Fine (1972)	3	−0.18	0.159	−0.03	−0.06
16. Greiger (1970)	3	−0.06	0.167	0.03	−0.06
17. Rosenthal & Jacobson (1968)	1	0.30	0.139	0.19	0.25
18. Fleming & Anttonen (1971)	2	0.07	0.094	0.07	0.09
19. Ginsburg (1970)	3	−0.07	0.174	0.02	−0.06

source of sustained and acrimonious controversy for over 20 years. (See, for example, Wineburg's [1987] review and Rosenthal's [1987] response.) Raudenbush (1984) was able to find 19 reports of experiments testing this hypothesis. In these studies, the experimental group consisted of children for whom teachers were encouraged to have "high" expectations. The controls were children for whom no particular expectations were encouraged. The studies, their sample sizes, and the reported standardized mean differences are presented in Table 7.1.

The reported effect sizes seem to vary a great deal, from −0.32 to 1.18. However, some of the most extreme results (e.g., Study 4) are based on studies with small samples and large standard errors (i.e., $V_j^{1/2}$). Because the estimated effects in Table 7.1 vary, in part because of sampling errors in each d_j, the total variation among the d_js is probably substantially greater than the variability among the unknown-effect parameters, the δ_js.

We perform two analyses below. The goal of the first analysis is to assess the variability in the true-effect parameters. The goal of the second is to account for that variation. Specifically, in the first analysis we estimate the mean and variance of the true effects and the empirical Bayes estimates of each study's effect size. In the second analysis, we formulate a model to predict the effect sizes, to estimate the residual variance in the true effects, and to compute new empirical Bayes estimates for each study.

Unconditional Analysis

Using Equation 7.5, the level-1 model is

$$d_j = \delta_j + e_j, \qquad [7.13]$$

where d_j (as reported in column 3 of Table 7.1) is the estimated standardized mean difference in study j between experimental children (those assigned to a "high expectancy" condition) and control children, and δ_j is the corresponding parameter value. Hence, each d_j estimates δ_j with a known sampling variance, V_j (given by Equation 7.4 with d_j substituted for δ_j).

In an unconditional analysis, no predictors are involved in the level-2 model. We view the true-effect sizes, δ_j, as simply varying around a grand mean, γ_0, plus a level-2 error, u_j. Thus, at level 2,

$$\delta_j = \gamma_0 + u_j. \qquad [7.14]$$

Substituting Equation 7.14 into Equation 7.13 yields the combined model

$$d_j = \gamma_0 + u_j + e_j, \qquad [7.15]$$

implying $d_j \sim N(\gamma_0, \Delta_j)$ with $\Delta_j = \tau + V_j$.

Results. Table 7.2 presents estimates of the grand mean, γ_0, and Level-2 variance, τ. The estimated grand-mean effect size is small, $\hat{\gamma}_0 = .083$, implying that, on average, experimental students scored about .083 standard deviation units above the controls. However, the estimated variance of the

TABLE 7.2 Unconditional Model for the Meta-Analysis of Teacher Expectancy Effects

Fixed Effect	Coefficient	se	t Ratio	
Grand mean, γ_0	0.083	0.052	1.62	
Random Effect	Variance Component	df	χ^2	p Value
True effect size, δ_j	0.019	18	35.85	.009

effect parameters is $\hat{\tau} = .019$. This corresponds to a standard deviation of .138, which implies that important variability exists in the true-effect sizes. For example, an effect one standard deviation above the average would be $\delta_j = .22$, which is of nontrivial magnitude.

One might wonder whether the estimate $\hat{\tau} = .019$ is a chance result. Using the procedure introduced in Chapter 3, we test this null hypothesis, $H_0: \tau = 0$, with the statistic

$$H = \sum V_j^{-1}(d_j - \bar{d}.)^2, \quad\quad [7.16]$$

where $\bar{d}. = \sum V_j^{-1} d_j / \sum V_j^{-1}$. This statistic has a χ^2 distribution with $J - 1$ degrees of freedom, and is the "H statistic" discussed by Hedges (1982) and Rosenthal and Rubin (1982). Here $H = 35.85$, df $= 18$, $p < .01$, implying that studies do vary significantly in their effects.

Table 7.1 (column 5) lists the empirical Bayes estimates, $\delta_j^* = \lambda_j d_j + (1 - \lambda_j)\hat{\gamma}_0$, for each study. A comparison between these estimates and the original estimates, d_j, is displayed in Figure 7.1. Lines connect the two estimates from each study. Notice that the empirical Bayes estimates are substantially more concentrated about $\hat{\gamma}_0 = .083$ than are the d_j values. Some values of d_j, especially those with small samples and those far from .083, have experienced substantial shrinkage. For example, in Study 4 the d_4 of 1.18 is "shrunk" to 0.22.

Conditional Analysis

The "expectancy" treatment depended on deception for its effectiveness. In some cases, experimenters presented teachers with a list of pupils who allegedly displayed potential for dramatic intellectual growth. In fact, these "high expectancy" pupils had been assigned at random to the experimental condition. In other cases, researchers presented teachers with inflated IQs for pupils assigned at random to the high expectancy condition. In either case, if the deception failed and teachers refused to believe the experimenter's information, no treatment effect could have been observed, simply because no treatment had been implemented. Such an implementation failure does not refute expectancy theory, which can be tested only if the experimenters had successfully modified the teachers' expectations for their students.

Raudenbush (1984) hypothesized that the variability in teacher expectancy effects might be related to how well the teachers knew their pupils at the time they encountered the deceptive information, as indicated by the number of weeks of pupil-teacher contact prior to the experiment. This hypothesis was based on past research suggesting that when teachers know their pupils

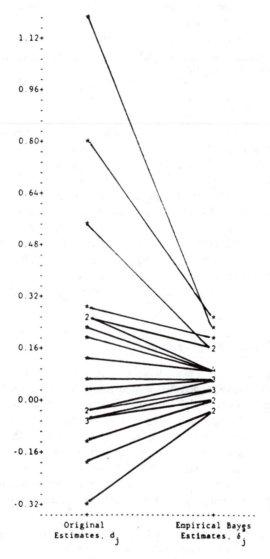

Figure 7.1. Comparison Between Original Standardized Mean Difference Estimates, d_j, and Empirical Bayes Estimates, δ_j^*, Based on the Unconditional Model

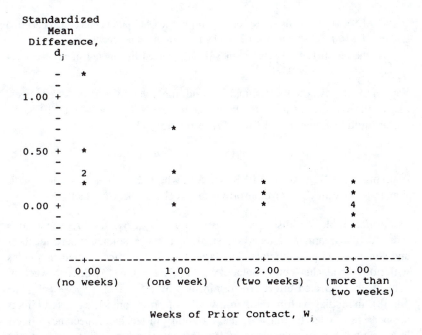

Figure 7.2. Plot of Observed Standardized Mean Difference, d_j (vertical axis), as a Function of Weeks of Prior Teacher-Pupil Contact, W_j (horizontal axis)

well, they are likely to ignore new information that is discrepant from their established views.

The effect sizes from the 19 studies are plotted against weeks of pupil-teacher contact prior to experiment in Figure 7.2. This graphical display is consistent with Raudenbush's (1984) hypothesis. Estimation of a conditional model provides an explicit test of this hypothesis.

The level-1 model remains unchanged (Equation 7.5). At level 2, we now use the information about prior contact between teachers and children to predict the effect sizes. The model is

$$\delta_j = \gamma_0 + \gamma_1 (\text{WEEKS})_j + u_j, \qquad [7.17]$$

where

γ_0 is the expected effect size for a study with no prior teacher-pupil contact;

γ_1 is the expected difference in effect size between two studies differing by one week in prior contact;

(WEEKS)$_j$ is 0, 1, 2, or 3, respectively, if prior teacher-pupil contact had occurred for 0, 1, 2, or more than 2 weeks prior to the experiment; and

u_j is the residual effect size in study j unexplained by amount of prior contact where $u_j \sim N(0, \tau)$.

We note that τ is now the residual or conditional variance of the effect sizes, that is, the variance of the true-effect-size residuals, $\delta_j - \gamma_0 - \gamma_1(\text{WEEKS})_j$. Substituting Equation 7.17 into Equation 7.5 yields

$$d_j = \gamma_0 + \gamma_1(\text{WEEKS})_j + u_j + e_j, \qquad [7.18]$$

implying $d_j \sim N[\gamma_0 + \gamma_1(\text{WEEKS})_j, \Delta_j]$, where $\Delta_j = \tau + V_j$ is the conditional variance in d_j after controlling for weeks of prior contact.

Results. Table 7.3 displays the estimates of γ_0, γ_1, and τ. The results indicate that treatment effects are smaller in those studies where teachers and students had prior contact. The largest predicted effects occur in studies with no prior teacher-pupil contact, $\hat{\gamma}_0 = .407$, $t = 4.67$. With each week of contact, the expected effect size diminishes by .157 (i.e., $\hat{\gamma}_1 = -.157$, $t = -4.38$). In studies with more than 2 weeks of prior contact, expected effects are near zero. Clearly, much of the variability in teacher expectancy effects is accounted for by knowledge of the amount of prior contact. In fact, the maximum likelihood point estimate for the residual variation in δ_j after controlling for (Weeks)$_j$ was virtually zero.

The empirical Bayes estimates of δ_j^* under the model specified by Equation 7.18 are

$$\delta_j^* = \lambda_j d_j + (1 - \lambda_j)[\hat{\gamma}_0 + \hat{\gamma}_1(\text{WEEKS})_j]. \qquad [7.19]$$

However, if $\hat{\tau} = 0$, then $\lambda_j = \tau/(\tau + V_j) = 0$ for all j, so that, in this case,

$$\delta_j^* = \hat{\gamma}_0 + \hat{\gamma}_1(\text{WEEKS})_j.$$

TABLE 7.3 Conditional Model for the Meta-Analysis of Teacher Expectancy Effects

Fixed Effect	Coefficient	se	t Ratio	
INTERCEPT, γ_0	0.407	0.087	4.67	
WEEKS, γ_1	−0.157	0.036	−4.38	
Random Effect	Variance Component	df	χ^2	p Value
True effect size, δ_j	0.000	17	16.57	>0.500

Figure 7.3 displays the shrinkage for each d_j toward δ_j^* under this model. (The empirical Bayes estimates of δ_j^* yielded by Equation 7.19 are located in Table 7.1, column 6.) This is another instance of *conditional* shrinkage (as introduced in Chapter 3 and previously illustrated in Chapter 4). In contrast with Figure 7.1, where each d_j was shrunk in the direction of the estimated grand mean of .083, now each d_j is shrunk toward a value that is conditional on the amount of prior contact. Because $(\text{WEEKS})_j$ can take on four values, the shrinkage is toward four points. Shrinkage toward these points is complete because τ is estimated to be essentially zero.

Bayesian Meta-Analysis

The estimates of the fixed level-2 coefficients (the γs) in the teacher expectancy example are weighted least squares estimates where the weights are the precisions, Δ_j^{-1}. These weights are assumed known when, in fact, they are estimated from the data. The estimated weights are

$$\widehat{\Delta}_j^{-1} = \left(\hat{\tau} + V_j\right)^{-1}, \qquad [7.20]$$

where $\hat{\tau}$ is the estimate of the between-study variance. If the sample size, J, of studies is large, this variance estimate will be precise and the assumption that the weights in Equation 7.20 are known, though technically false, will have negligible practical effect. However, if J is small, the sampling error in this variance estimate may be appreciable, leading to extra uncertainty about the γs. This extra uncertainty will not be reflected in the standard error of the γ estimates derived from maximum likelihood. The effects of this extra uncertainty will be most pronounced when the weights are highly variable, which occurs when the sample sizes per study are widely discrepant. When the data are nearly balanced, this extra uncertainty will be negligible.

Bayesian methods provide an alternative approach that allows the analyst to fully account for the uncertainty in the variance estimates when making inferences about other unknowns. The benefits of this approach extend to inferences about study-specific effect sizes, δ_j, as well. We consider this Bayesian approach in detail in Chapter 13, where we reanalyze the teacher expectancy data.

Other Level-1 Variance-Known Problems

The essential statistical features of meta-analysis applications that distinguish them from the others discussed in this book are two: Only summary data are available at level 1; and the sampling variance, V_j, of the

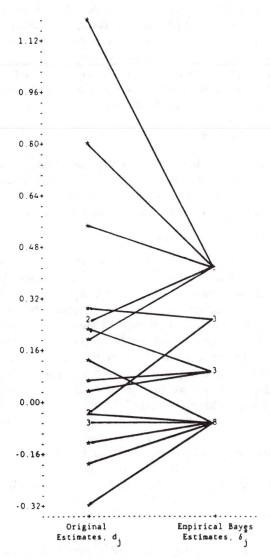

Figure 7.3. Comparison Between Original Standardized Mean Difference Estimates, d_j, and Empirical Bayes Estimates, δ_j^*, Based on a Conditional Model

TABLE 7.4 Some Univariate *V*-Known Cases

	Level-1 Parameter, δ_j	Sample Estimator, d_j	Approximate Variance, V_j
Standardized mean difference[a]	$(\mu_E - \mu_C)/\sigma$	$(\overline{Y}_E - \overline{Y}_C)/S$	$(n_E + n_C)/(n_E n_C)$ $+ d^2/[2(n_E + n_C)]$
Correlation	$\frac{1}{2}\log[(1+\rho)/(1-\rho)]$	$\frac{1}{2}\log[(1+r)/(1-r)]$	$1/(n-3)$
Logit[b]	$\log[p/(1-p)]$	$\log[\hat{p}/(1-\hat{p})]$	$n^{-1}\hat{p}^{-1}(1-\hat{p})^{-1}$
Log(sd)[c]	$\log(\sigma)$	$\log(S) + [1/(2f)]$	$1/(2f)$

a. Typically, σ is the pooled, within-treatment standard deviation, μ_E, μ_C are the experimental and control population means, and $\overline{Y}_E$ and $\overline{Y}_C$ the corresponding sample estimates.
b. We denote p as the proportion of subjects in the population with a given characteristic; $\hat{p}$ is the sample proportion.
c. We denote σ as a standard deviation, S as the sample estimate, and f as the degrees of freedom associated with S. Thus, $f = n - 1$ when σ is a standard deviation, but $f = n - p$ when σ is the residual standard deviation estimated in a regression model with p parameters.

level-1 parameter estimate, d_j, can be assumed known. A variety of non-meta-analysis research problems have a similar structure. We refer to this class of problems, which includes meta-analysis as a specific case, as level-1 *V*-known problems.

In a *V*-known analysis, some statistic or set of statistics is computed separately for each study, organization, or other level-2 unit. In addition to standardized mean differences, these statistics might be correlations, proportions, or standard deviations. Often a transformation of these statistics will improve the tenability of the normality and *V*-known assumptions. For example, the sample correlation, r, has a sampling distribution that is approximately normal, but this approximation is poor, especially when the parameter value is near -1.0 or 1.0. Fisher's transformation (Equation 7.6) has a sampling distribution that is much more nearly normal for nonzero values of ρ. Also, the sampling variance of r depends on the unknown value of ρ, whereas the sampling variance of Fisher's transformed r does not.

Table 7.4 lists some parameters that might be studied in a *V*-known analysis (column 1). For each parameter, its sample estimator (column 2) and approximate sampling variance (column 3) are provided. The hierarchical linear model of Equations 7.5 and 7.9 can be applied to any of these statistics.

Example: Correlates of Diversity

Most studies of school effects focus on *mean* differences. However, Raudenbush and Bryk (1987) sought to study school differences in the *dispersion* of mathematics achievement using a sample of data from the High School and Beyond survey, similar to that employed in Chapter 4. Of special interest was the question of whether school differences in organization, policy, and practice affect dispersion in achievement. Do large schools produce greater inequality than smaller schools? If students within a school differ widely in course taking, do wide differences in achievement result?

Choice of the Outcome. Such questions suggest using the standard deviation in mathematics achievement, computed separately for each school, as the outcome to be explained by differences in school-level predictors. To be credible, an analysis must also take into account that schools differ in their student composition. Therefore, the investigators first computed a *residual* standard deviation (i.e., the standard deviation for each school) after controlling for SES, minority status, sex, and a measure of prior academic background (see Raudenbush & Bryk, 1987, for details).

The sampling distribution of a standard deviation (or a residual standard deviation) is approximately normal when samples are large, but positively skewed otherwise. Moreover, the sample variance of the sample standard deviation, S_j, is approximately $\sigma_j^2/(2n)$, which depends on the unknown population standard deviation, σ_j. A logarithmic transformation of S_j helps on both counts. The sampling distribution of $\log(S_j)$ is more nearly normal than that of S_j, and its sampling variance does not depend upon σ_j. Specifically, the investigators used the following:

$$\delta_j = \log(\sigma_j),$$
$$d_j = \log(S_j) + 1/(2f_j),$$
$$V_j = 1/(2f_j), \qquad\qquad [7.21]$$

where

S_j is the estimated residual standard deviation in school j;

σ_j is the population residual standard deviation for school j;

δ_j is the natural logarithm of σ_j;

f_j is the degrees of freedom associated with S_j;

d_j is an estimate of δ_j where $1/(2 f_j)$ is a small-sample correction for a negative bias; and

V_j is the sampling variance of d_j.

As in the meta-analysis case, the level-1 model (Equation 7.5) simply describes the sampling distribution of the estimate, d_j, where now d_j, δ_j, and V_j are defined as above.

At the school level, the dispersions, δ_j, were presumed to vary as a function of certain school characteristics. Specifically, small schools and schools where students were similar in math course taking were expected to have smaller variation in math achievement. Other school-level predictors included the heterogeneity of each school's student membership in terms of SES and academic background and public versus Catholic sector:

$$\delta_j = \gamma_0 + \gamma_1 (\text{SD SES})_j + \gamma_2 (\text{SD BACKGROUND})_j + \gamma_3 (\text{SECTOR})_j$$
$$+ \gamma_4 (\text{SIZE})_j + \gamma_5 (\text{SD MATH COURSES})_j + u_j, \qquad [7.22]$$

where

SD SES is the standard deviation of the socioeconomic status of students in the school;

SD BACKGROUND is the standard deviation of a measure of academic background of students in the school;

SECTOR is an indicator variable (0 = public, 1 = Catholic);

SIZE is the number of pupils enrolled in the school;

SD MATH COURSES is the standard deviation of the number of math courses taking by students in the school; and

u_j is a residual for which we assume $u_j \sim N(0, \tau)$.

The results in Table 7.5 indicate that schools that were heterogeneous in student SES (i.e., large positive values on SD SES) tended to display greater diversity in math achievement ($\hat{\gamma}_1 = .231$, $t = 4.64$). Similarly, heterogeneity in students' academic background also predicted diversity in math achievement ($\hat{\gamma}_2 = .525$, $t = 5.78$). Catholic schools tended to have less dispersion in math achievement than did public schools ($\hat{\gamma}_3 = -.048$, $t = -2.05$). Larger schools were more diverse in math achievement than were smaller schools ($\hat{\gamma}_4 = 4.15 \times 10^{-5}$, $t = 2.47$). And schools characterized by substantial dispersion in math course taking were also more diverse in math achievement ($\hat{\gamma}_5 = .139$, $t = 4.06$).

The investigators noted that an earlier analysis, without SIZE and SD MATH COURSES included as predictors, had shown a substantial SECTOR effect with Catholic schools displaying much less variation in math achievement than public schools. In their final analysis (see Table 7.5), the estimate of the effect of SECTOR is much smaller. The investigators concluded that the smaller variation in achievement within Catholic schools was largely explainable by the small average size of those schools and by their more restrictive course-taking requirements.

It is useful at this point to test the hypothesis that all of the variability among δ_j has been accounted for in the model (i.e., H_0: $\tau = 0$). If this

TABLE 7.5 Effects of School Characteristics on Mathematics Dispersion

Fixed Effect	Coefficient	se	t Ratio	
INTERCEPT, γ_0	1.324	0.1007	—	
SD SES, γ_1	0.231	0.0498	4.64	
SD BACKGROUND, γ_2	0.525	0.0909	5.78	
SECTOR, γ_3	−0.048	0.0235	−2.05	
SIZE, γ_4	4.15×10^{-5}	1.68×10^{-5}	2.47	
SD MATH, γ_5	0.139	0.0342	4.06	
Random Effect	Variance Component	df	χ^2	p Value
True school dispersion, δ_j	0.0019	154	179.81	0.075

hypothesis were true, the only unexplained variation in the estimates, d_j, would have resulted from "estimation error" (i.e., imprecise estimation of the true dispersion, δ_j, by its sample estimate, d_j). The test statistic (see Equation 3.103) under such a null hypothesis is distributed as a χ^2 variate with $J - S - 1$ degrees of freedom. In this case, the statistic was 179.81 with $160 - 6 = 154$ df and $p = .075$. These results suggest that little if any variability in δ_j remains to be explained. Our model has, in fact, accounted for over 85% of the total variability in δ_j. (This variance-explained statistic is computed by comparing the τ estimates from the unconditional and conditional models using the procedures previously illustrated, as in Equation 5.6.)

The Multivariate V-Known Model

Level-1 Model

The multivariate model is a straightforward extension of the univariate case. Within each unit, Q parameters $\delta_{1j}, \delta_{2j}, \ldots, \delta_{Qj}$ are estimated by means of statistics $d_{1j}, d_{2j}, \ldots, d_{Qj}$. Conditional on the true parameters, the statistics are assumed to have a multivariate normal sampling distribution with variances V_{qqj} and covariances $V_{qq'j}$ for each pair of statistics q and q'. These variances and covariances are assumed known. The level-1 model is then

$$d_{qj} = \delta_{qj} + e_{qj} \qquad [7.23]$$

for each of the $q = 1, \ldots, Q$ separate statistics.

Level-2 Model

The true parameter, δ_{qj}, varies as a function of predictor variables measured at level 2, plus error:

$$\delta_{qj} = \gamma_{q0} + \sum_{s=1}^{S_q} \gamma_{qs} W_{sj} + u_{qj}, \qquad [7.24]$$

where

W_{sj} is a predictor variable;

γ_{qs} is the corresponding regression coefficient; and

u_{qj} is the unique effect for each unit j.

These effects are assumed multivariate normally distributed, each with a mean of 0, variance τ_{qq}, and with covariances of $\tau_{qq'}$ between u_{qj} and $u_{q'j}$. We note that a different set of level-2 predictors can be specified for each δ_{qj}.

Like the univariate V-known model, the multivariate model can be applied to a variety of parameters. Table 7.6 presents some of these possibilities. Again, transformations can improve the tenability of the assumptions of multivariate normality for d_{qj} and of the assumption of known variances and covariances.

TABLE 7.6 Some Multivariate V-Known Cases[a]

Level-1 Parameters, δ_q	Sample Estimators, d_q	Variances, V_{qq}	Covariances, $V_{qq'}$
Standardized mean difference[b, c] $(\mu_{Eq} - \mu_{Cq})/\sigma_q$	$(\overline{Y}_{Eq} - \overline{Y}_{Cq})/S_q$	$\sigma^2(d_q)$	$\dfrac{\rho_{qq'}(n_E + n_C)}{n_E \, n_C}$ $+ \dfrac{\rho_{qq'}^2 \, d_q d_{q'}}{2(n_E + n_C)}$
Multinomial proportion[d] $\log[p_q/(1 - p_q)]$	$\log[\hat{p}_q/(1 - \hat{p}_q)]$	$n^{-1}\hat{p}_q^{-1}(1 - \hat{p}_q)^{-1}$	$-n^{-1}(1 - \hat{p}_q)^{-1}$ $\times (1 - \hat{p}_{q'})^{-1}$
Standard deviation[e] $\log(\sigma_q)$	$\log(S_q) + [1/(2f)]$	$1/(2f)$	$\rho_{qq'}^2/(2f)$

a. Each sample is said to produce Q statistics $q = 1, \ldots, Q$, where d_q and $d_{q'}$ are estimates of any pair of parameters δ_q and $\delta_{q'}$, respectively.
b. Here $\sigma^2(d_q) = (n_E + n_C)/(n_E \, n_C) + d_q^2/[2(n_E + n_C)]$.
c. Here $\rho_{qq'}$ is the correlation between the variates Y_q and $Y_{q'}$ used in estimated effect sizes d_q and $d_{q'}$ (Hedges & Olkin, 1985).
d. We assume that objects have fallen into category q with probability p_q where $\sum p_q = 1$.
e. Here $p_{qq'}$ is the correlation between variates Y_q and $Y_{q'}$ used in estimating σ_q and $\sigma_{q'}$.

Meta-Analysis of Incomplete Multivariate Data

The multivariate V-known model described in the previous section requires every study to have measured the same Q outcome variables. However, the meta-analyst will rarely encounter a stream of research in which every study reports results for exactly the same set of dependent variables. Rather, different studies will typically report effect sizes for different dependent variables. In research on teacher expectancy effects, for example, outcomes might include teacher behavior, student IQ, and student attitudes. However, not all studies will measure all three of these outcomes. In the illustrative example below, each study assesses the effect of test coaching on students' Scholastic Aptitude Test (SAT) scores. However, some studies administered the verbal subtest (SAT-V), some administered the math subtest (SAT-M), and others administered both.

Following Kalaian and Raudenbush (1996), we regard these examples as involving "incomplete multivariate data" (cf. Jennrich & Schlucter, 1996; Little & Rubin, 1987; Schafer, 1997). In the SAT example, we conceive of the true SAT-V and SAT-M effect sizes as the "complete data" for each study. In studies that administered both of these tests, the observed data consist of the pair of estimated effect sizes. In studies that estimated only one of the two effect sizes, the observed data include that estimate, but we nonetheless conceive of the complete data as the pair of true effect sizes, both SAT-V and SAT-M.

To handle such incomplete multivariate data, we formulate a level-1 model that specifies the association between the observed and the complete data. The level-2 model describes how the true effect sizes ("the complete data") vary over a population of studies.

Level-1 Model

Associated with each study j are Q "true" effect sizes, $\delta_{1j}, \ldots, \delta_{Qj}$. However, study j produces P_j effect-size estimates, $d_{1j}, \ldots, d_{P_j j}$, with $P_j \leq Q$. The level-1 model regards the observed effect sizes as the outcomes, the true effect sizes as the coefficients, and uses indicators as "level-1 predictors" that associate each observed effect size with its corresponding true effect size:

$$d_{pj} = \sum_{q=1}^{Q} \delta_{qj} X_{qpj} + e_{pj}, \qquad [7.25]$$

where $X_{qpj} = 1$ if d_{pj} estimates δ_{qj}, and 0 if not. The errors of estimate e_{pj} for study j are assumed multivariate normal in distribution with a mean vector of zero and variance-covariance matrix V_j, assumed known. The exact structure of V_j depends on the type of effect size (e.g., standardized mean difference, correlation, etc., as displayed in Table 7.6).

Level-2 Model

The level-2 model is the same as before (Equation 7.24). It regards the true effect sizes as outcomes that may depend on study characteristics plus random effects assumed multivariate normal in distribution.

Illustrative Example

SAT scores can be influential in college admissions decisions. Test preparation programs claim they can boost students' SAT scores by means of a comparatively short-term program of instruction known as "test coaching." To evaluate these claims, a number of investigators have conducted studies that compare an experimental group (those who receive coaching) with a control group (those who do not). Studies vary in terms of the duration of the coaching received by the experimental group. It is interesting to assess the impact of coaching and to discover how this impact varies with duration.

Kalaian and Raudenbush (1996) combined data from 47 studies of the effect of coaching on SAT performance.[2] Only 17 of these studies reported results for both SAT-V and SAT-M. Of the remaining studies, 18 assessed SAT-V only and 12 assessed SAT-M only. The authors were interested in two questions that require a multivariate analysis:

- Are test coaching effects similar for the SAT-V and the SAT-M?
- Does the association between hours of coaching and effect size differ for the two outcomes?

Level-1 Model. In this example, we have $Q = 2$ possible outcomes, so the level-1 model is

$$d_{pj} = \delta_{1j}X_{1pj} + \delta_{2j}X_{2pj} + e_j, \qquad [7.26]$$

where $X_{1pj} = 1$ if d_{pj} is the SAT-V effect size, and 0 otherwise; and $X_{2pj} = 1$ if d_{pj} is the SAT-M effect size, 0 otherwise.

Each outcome is a standardized effect size. Therefore, the level-1 random effects are assumed to have variances given by Equation 7.4 and covariances between them, as specified in Table 7.6:

$$\text{Cov}(e_{1j}, e_{2j}) = \frac{\rho_{12j}(n_{Ej} + n_{Qj})}{n_{Ej}n_{Cj}} + \frac{\delta_{1j}\delta_{2j}\rho_{12j}^2/2}{n_{Ej} + n_{Cj}}. \qquad [7.27]$$

TABLE 7.7 Fitted Model for SAT Coaching Data

Predictor	Coefficient	se	t Ratio	p
For SAT-verbal				
Intercept, γ_{10}	0.103	0.025	4.18	.000
log(hours), γ_{11}	0.058	0.033	1.74	.088
For SAT-math				
Intercept, γ_{20}	0.099	0.042	2.33	.029
log(hours), γ_{21}	0.149	0.061	2.42	.024

$$\begin{bmatrix} \hat{\tau}_{11} & \hat{\tau}_{12} \\ & \hat{\tau}_{22} \end{bmatrix} = \begin{bmatrix} 7.68 * 10^{-3} & -8.35 * 10^{-3} \\ & 28.48 * 10^{-3} \end{bmatrix}$$

Here ρ_{12} is the correlation between SAT-V and SAT-M in study j. It is generally estimated from that study's data or estimated from previous large-scale data on the SAT. Sample estimates for δ_{1j} and δ_{2j} are substituted into Equation 7.27. The variances and covariance from a study with both outcomes are assembled into a 2 by 2 covariance matrix V_j, assumed known. For studies having only one effect size, V_j is the variance associated with that effect size.

Level-2 Model. Regardless of whether only one or both effect sizes are actually estimated in a given study, we conceive of each study as having two latent "true" effect sizes, one for each of the two outcomes. Thus, we have, at level 2,

$$\delta_{1j} = \gamma_{10} + \gamma_{11} * (\text{LOG HOURS})_j + u_{1j},$$
$$\delta_{2j} = \gamma_{20} + \gamma_{21} * (\text{LOG HOURS})_j + u_{2j}. \qquad [7.28]$$

Here LOG HOURS is the natural logarithm of the hours of coaching supplied to the experimental group, expressed as a deviation from the grand mean across the ensemble of studies. Thus, γ_{10} and γ_{20} are expected effect sizes for SAT-V and SAT-M, respectively, for a study with mean LOG HOURS of coaching. The level-2 random effects have the usual variance structure, where **T** is a 2 by 2 covariance matrix.

Results. Table 7.7 provides estimates and standard errors for this model. We see, first, that the average coaching effects are significantly positive for SAT-V ($\hat{\gamma}_{10} = 0.103$, $t = 4.18$) and for SAT-M ($\hat{\gamma}_{20} = 0.099$, $t = 2.33$). The association between LOG HOURS and the effect size appears larger for SAT-M ($\hat{\gamma}_{21} = 0.149$, $t = 2.42$) than for SAT-V ($\hat{\gamma}_{11} = 0.058$, $t = 1.74$).

However, a multivariate hypothesis test (see Equation 3.91) failed to reject the null hypothesis

$$H_0: \gamma_{11} = \gamma_{21},$$

based on a χ^2 statistic of 1.61, df $= 1$, $p = .20$. Kalaian and Raudenbush (1996) also compared the fit of the estimated model (Table 7.7) and a model that constrained the SAT-M effect-size variance τ_{11} and the covariance τ_{12} to zero. A χ^2 statistic of 9.30, df $= 2$, led to a rejection of the null hypothesis, supporting the model that includes the 2 by 2 variance-covariance matrix, **T**.

Notes

1. Hedges and Olkin (1983) present a transformation of d_j that eliminates the dependence of the sampling variance on δ_j. This transformation is especially useful when n_{Ej} or n_{Cj} is small.

2. The data are listed in Kalaian and Raudenbush (1996).

Three-Level Models

- Formulating and Testing Three-Level Models
- Studying Individual Change Within Organizations
- Measurement Models at Level 1
- Estimating Random Coefficients in Three-Level Models

We have demonstrated in the last three chapters how two-level models can be used to represent a wide range of psychological, sociological, and educational phenomena. This chapter introduces the three-level model and provides several illustrations from recent research.

Formulating and Testing Three-Level Models

In the interests of clarity, we introduce the three-level model in the context of a specific problem: a single cross-section of data with a three-level structure consisting of students (level 1) nested within classrooms (level 2) nested within schools (level 3). Other common examples of three-level cross-sections involve individuals within households within geographic areas or workers within firms within different industries. Longitudinal applications involving three-level models are considered in the next section, and the following section considers an application to the study of latent variables.

A Fully Unconditional Model

The simplest three-level model is fully unconditional; that is, no predictor variables are specified at any level. Such a model represents how variation in an outcome measure is allocated across the three different levels (child, classroom, and school).

Child-Level Model. We model academic achievement for each child as a function of a classroom mean plus a random error:

$$Y_{ijk} = \pi_{0jk} + e_{ijk}, \qquad [8.1]$$

where

Y_{ijk} is the achievement of child i in classroom j and school k;

π_{0jk} is the mean achievement of classroom j in school k; and

e_{ijk} is a random "child effect," that is, the deviation of child ijk's score from the classroom mean. These effects are assumed normally distributed with a mean of 0 and variance σ^2.

The indices i, j, and k denote children, classrooms, and schools where there are

$i = 1, 2, \ldots, n_{jk}$ children within classroom j in school k;

$j = 1, 2, \ldots, J_k$ classrooms within school k; and

$k = 1, 2, \ldots, K$ schools.

Classroom-Level Model. We view each classroom mean, π_{0jk}, as an outcome varying randomly around some school mean:

$$\pi_{0jk} = \beta_{00k} + r_{0jk}, \qquad [8.2]$$

where

β_{00k} is the mean achievement in school k;

r_{0jk} is a random "classroom effect," that is, the deviation of classroom jk's mean from the school mean. These effects are assumed normally distributed with a mean of 0 and variance τ_π. Within each of the K schools, the variability among classrooms is assumed the same.

School-Level Model. The level-3 model represents the variability among schools. We view the school means, β_{00k}, as varying randomly around a grand mean:

$$\beta_{00k} = \gamma_{000} + u_{00k}, \qquad [8.3]$$

where

γ_{000} is the grand mean;

u_{00k} is a random "school effect," that is, the deviation of school k's mean from the grand mean. These effects are assumed normally distributed with a mean of 0 and variance τ_β.

Variance Partitioning and Reliabilities

This simple three-level model partitions the total variability in the outcome Y_{ijk} into its three components: (level 1) among children within classrooms, σ^2; (level 2) among classrooms within schools, τ_π; and (level 3) among schools, τ_β. It also allows us to estimate the proportion of variation that is within classrooms, among classrooms within schools, and among schools. That is,

$$\sigma^2/(\sigma^2 + \tau_\pi + \tau_\beta) \text{ is the proportion of variance within}$$
$$\text{classrooms;} \qquad\qquad [8.4]$$

$$\tau_\pi/(\sigma^2 + \tau_\pi + \tau_\beta) \text{ is the proportion of variance among}$$
$$\text{classrooms within schools; and} \qquad [8.5]$$

$$\tau_\beta/(\sigma^2 + \tau_\pi + \tau_\beta) \text{ is the proportion of variance among}$$
$$\text{schools.} \qquad\qquad [8.6]$$

As in the two-level model, we can also examine the reliability of the least squares estimated coefficients. Now, however, reliabilities are estimated at two levels: classrooms, $\hat{\pi}_{0jk}$, and schools, $\hat{\beta}_{00k}$. For each classroom jk at level 2,

$$\text{reliability}(\hat{\pi}_{0jk}) = \tau_\pi/[\tau_\pi + \sigma^2/n_{jk}] \qquad [8.7]$$

is the reliability of a classroom sample mean for use in discrimination among classrooms within the same school. For any school k at level 3,

$$\text{reliability}(\hat{\beta}_{00k}) = \frac{\tau_\beta}{\tau_\beta + \left\{\sum[\tau_\pi + \sigma^2/n_{jk}]^{-1}\right\}^{-1}} \qquad [8.8]$$

is the reliability of the school's sample mean as an estimate of its true mean.

The averages of these reliabilities across classrooms (Equation 8.7) and schools (Equation 8.8) may be viewed as summary measures of the reliability of the class and school means, respectively.

Conditional Models

The fully unconditional model, Equations 8.1 to 8.3, allows estimation of variability associated with the three levels—students, classes, and schools. Presumably, part of the variability at each level can be explained or accounted for by measured variables at each level. That is, child background characteristics, classroom characteristics, and school characteristics could be used as predictors. Further, some of the relationships at the class and school levels may vary randomly among these units. For example, suppose that within classrooms child's sex was related to academic achievement. The magnitude of this sex difference might depend perhaps on certain teacher characteristics (e.g., teacher expectations or methods of classroom organization). In such a situation, the regression coefficient representing the sex effect might vary depending on characteristics of teachers and classrooms.

Similarly, regression coefficients can vary randomly at the school level. School intercepts would typically be random; regression slopes could also differ across schools. For example, the effect of student social class on achievement might vary from school to school. These possibilities encourage us to formulate a general structural model at each level.

General Level-1 Model. Within each classroom, we model student achievement as a function of student-level predictors plus a random student-level error:

$$Y_{ijk} = \pi_{0jk} + \pi_{1jk} a_{1ijk} + \pi_{2jk} a_{2ijk} + \cdots + \pi_{Pjk} a_{Pijk} + e_{ijk}, \qquad [8.9]$$

where

Y_{ijk} is the achievement of child i in classroom j and school k;

π_{0jk} is the intercept for classroom j in school k;

a_{pijk} are $p = 1, \ldots, P$ child characteristics that predict achievement;

π_{pjk} are the corresponding level-1 coefficients that indicate the direction and strength of association between each child characteristic, a_p, and the outcome in classroom jk; and

e_{ijk} is a level-1 random effect that represents the deviation of child ijk's score from the predicted score based on the student-level model. These residual child effects are assumed normally distributed with a mean of 0 and variance σ^2.

General Level-2 Model. Each of the regression coefficients in the child-level model (including the intercept) can be viewed as either fixed, nonrandomly varying, or random. These possibilities lead to the following general formulation of the model for variation among classrooms within schools. For each classroom effect, π_{pjk},

$$\pi_{pjk} = \beta_{p0k} + \sum_{q=1}^{Q_p} \beta_{pqk} X_{qjk} + r_{pjk},\qquad\qquad [8.10]$$

where

β_{p0k} is the intercept for school k in modeling the classroom effect π_{pjk};

X_{qjk} is a classroom characteristic used as a predictor of the classroom effect π_{pjk} (note that each π_p may have a unique set of these level-2 predictors $X_{qjk}, q = 1, \ldots, Q_p$);

β_{pqk} is the corresponding coefficient that represents the direction and strength of association between classroom characteristic X_{qjk} and π_{pjk}; and

r_{pjk} is a level-2 random effect that represents the deviation of classroom jk's level-1 coefficient, π_{pjk}, from its predicted value based on the classroom-level model.

Note that there are $P + 1$ equations in the level-2 model: one for each of the level-1 coefficients. The random effects in these equations are assumed to be correlated. Formally, we assume that the set of r_{pjk} are multivariate normally distributed each with a mean of 0, some variance τ_{pp}, and some covariance between elements r_{pjk} and $r_{p'jk}$ of $\tau_{pp'}$. We collect these variances and covariances in a matrix labeled $\mathbf{T}_\pi$ whose dimensionality depends on the number of level-1 coefficients specified as random. For example, if a classroom effect, π_{pjk}, is specified as fixed, no level-2 predictors would be included in Equation 8.10 for that effect and the corresponding r_{pjk} would be set to zero. If π_{pjk} is specified as nonrandomly varying, X variables would appear, but r_{pjk} would still be zero.

General Level-3 Model. A similar modeling process is replicated at the school level. Each level-3 "outcome" (i.e., each β_{pq} coefficient) may be predicted by some school-level characteristic. That is,

$$\beta_{pqk} = \gamma_{pq0} + \sum_{s=1}^{S_{pq}} \gamma_{pqs} W_{sk} + u_{pqk},\qquad\qquad [8.11]$$

where

> γ_{pq0} is the intercept term in the school-level model for β_{pqk};
>
> W_{sk} is a school characteristic used as a predictor for the school effect, β_{pqk} (note that each β_{pq} may have a unique set of the level-3 predictors, W_{sk}, $s = 1, \ldots, S_{pq}$);
>
> γ_{pqs} is the corresponding level-3 coefficient that represents the direction and strength of association between school characteristic W_{sk} and β_{pqk}; and
>
> u_{pqk} is a level-3 random effect that represents the deviation of school k's coefficient, β_{pqk}, from its predicted value based on the school-level model.

Note that for each school there are $\sum_{p=0}^{P}(Q_p + 1)$ equations in the level-3 model. The residuals from these equations are assumed multivariate normally distributed. Each is assumed to have a mean of zero, some variance, and covariance among all pairs of elements. Here, too, the variances and covariances are collected in a matrix, $\mathbf{T}_\beta$. The dimensionality of $\mathbf{T}_\beta$ depends on the number of level-2 coefficients that are specified as random. As was true for the π coefficients in the level-2 model, each of the β coefficients (including the intercept) can be viewed as either fixed, nonrandomly varying, or random in the level-3 model. If β_{pq} is specified as either fixed or nonrandomly varying, the corresponding u_{pqk} is assumed zero.

Many Alternative Modeling Possibilities

Between the fully unconditional model of Equations 8.1 to 8.3 and the full three-level model of Equations 8.9 through 8.11, many alternative formulations are possible. If we introduce predictors into the level-1 model, specify all corresponding π parameters as random at levels 2 and 3, and pose unconditional models at both levels, we would have a random-coefficient model with two sources of variation in the π coefficients: classrooms and schools.

Alternatively, perhaps only the intercept in the child-level model might be random with the child-level predictors having fixed effects at both levels 2 and 3. If the child-level predictors were grand-mean centered (i.e., $a_{pijk} - \bar{a}_{p}...$), then π_{0jk} would be the mean outcome in classroom jk adjusted for mean differences among classrooms on the child-level predictors. A variety of classroom and school variables may be introduced in the level-2 and level-3 models, respectively, to explain variability in these adjusted classroom means.

A different application might not have any predictors in the level-1 model. That is, the level-1 model might simply represent the variation of individuals around their classroom means. Variations in these classroom means may be fully modeled at levels 2 and 3. In addition, some of the predictors introduced at level 2 might be specified as random or nonrandomly varying to be subsequently modeled at level 3. This application is illustrated later.

There are far more possibilities than we are able to illustrate or even fully describe here. In most general terms, the analyst using a three-level model may choose to (a) introduce predictors at each level (i.e., specify a structural model at each level); (b) specify whether the structural effects in each model (i.e., intercepts and slopes) are considered fixed, nonrandomly varying, or random at that level; and (c) specify alternative models for the variance-covariance components other than those assumed in Equations 8.9 to 8.11.

On the latter point, many options are possible for σ^2, $\mathbf{T}_\pi$, and $\mathbf{T}_\beta$ depending on the substantive hypotheses under study and the availability of sufficient data for estimating model parameters implied by these hypotheses. For example, the covariances among the classroom-level effects might have a different structure in each of the K schools—that is, a set of $\mathbf{T}_{\pi k}$, $k = 1, \ldots, K$, might be estimated. Alternatively, the level-1 variation could be heteroscedastic among classrooms or schools—for example, a set of $k = 1, \ldots, K$ variances, σ_k^2, might be estimated. In general, the more complex the model specified, the greater the amount of data needed for estimation and inference.

Hypothesis Testing in the Three-Level Model

Testing hypotheses in three-level models is directly analogous to the procedures introduced in Chapter 3 for two-level models. In brief, we can pose and test hypotheses about fixed effects, random coefficients, and variance-covariance components at any of the three levels. For each of these types of hypotheses, both single and multiparameter tests are available.

Univariate tests for the fixed effects help the analyst decide which specific coefficients are needed. Multiparameter tests for the fixed effects enable both *omnibus tests* and a priori comparisons among fixed effects. Suppose, for example, that schools are classified according to sector (public, Catholic, or other private) and that two dummy variables are used to represent this. An omnibus test would be that the effects of both dummy variables were null. If this hypothesis were retained, school sector could be dropped from the model. Alternatively, single degree-of-freedom comparisons might be considered, such as the difference between private schools and public schools or between Catholic schools and other private schools.

Single-parameter tests for variance components may be posed at either level 2 or level 3. That is, any diagonal element of either $\mathbf{T}_\pi$ or $\mathbf{T}_\beta$ could be hypothesized as zero. Multiparameter tests for variance components can be used to examine hypotheses about more than one variance component, including elements at both levels 2 and 3. For example, suppose that a model were fitted in which the effects of sex and social class were allowed to vary randomly at level 2 (among classes in the schools). Perhaps the investigator wonders whether a simpler model—in which both of these effects were presumed constant among classes in the same school—would be adequate. To test this hypothesis, the investigator reestimates the model, now fixing the effects of sex and social class. A comparison of the deviance statistics from the restricted model (with fixed slopes for sex and social class within schools) and the more general alternative (i.e., the random slopes model) is a likelihood-ratio test, as previously discussed in Chapter 3.

Example: Research on Teaching

This illustration is based on data from 57 high school math teachers working in 14 schools in the United States (Raudenbush, Rowan, & Cheong, 1991).[1] These teachers were assigned to teach four math classes, on average, per day. The teachers' objectives tended to vary across classes. Raudenbush et al. focused on the extent to which each teacher emphasized higher order thinking (HOT). For each class, each teacher was asked to respond to a four-item scale indicating the degree of emphasis on construction of proofs, the formulation of mathematical arguments, and the articulation of reasoning underlying mathematical algorithms. The HOT index was constructed as the mean of these four items. Here the level-1 units are classes, the level-2 units are teachers, and the level-3 units are schools.

We consider the fully unconditional model given by Equations 8.1, 8.2, and 8.3, where

Y_{ijk} is the HOT score for class i of teacher j in school k;

π_{0jk} is teacher jk's mean on HOT;

β_{00k} is school k's mean on HOT; and

γ_{000} is the grand mean.

Results. In a fully unconditional model, there is only one fixed effect, γ_{000}, which in this case is the average classroom mean. For the HOT data, $\hat{\gamma}_{000} = -0.252, t = -0.959$ (see Table 8.1). The average HOT classroom mean was not significantly different from zero, an expected result because the scale was standardized to a mean of zero.

In terms of the variance partitioning, $\sigma^2 = \text{Var}(e_{ijk})$ is the variance within teachers over classes, $\tau_\pi = \text{Var}(r_{0jk})$ is the variance between teachers within schools, and $\tau_\beta = \text{Var}(u_{00k})$ is the variance between schools. Substituting the estimates for each of these variance components into Equations 8.4, 8.5,

TABLE 8.1 Three-Level Analysis of HOT Data (Fully Unconditional Model)

Fixed Effect		Coefficient	se	t Ratio
Average classroom mean, γ_{000}		−0.252	0.262	−0.959

Random Effect	Variance Component	df	χ^2	p Value
Classes (level 1), e_{ijk}	5.85			
Teachers (level 2), r_{0jk}	3.11	56	195.2	0.000
Schools (level 3), u_{00k}	0.01	13	11.7	>0.500

Variance Decomposition (Percentage by Level)

Level 1	65.2
Level 2	34.7
Level 3	0.1

and 8.6 yields estimates of the percentage of variance in Y_{ijk} at each level (see third panel of Table 8.1). The largest percentage (65.2%) lies between classes within teachers (i.e., at level 1); a substantial, though smaller, percentage (34.7%) lies between teachers within schools (i.e., at level 2); and only a trivial portion (0.1%) lies between schools (i.e., at level 3). The variation between teachers is statistically significant, $\chi^2 = 195.2$ with 56 df ($p < .001$), but the variance between schools is not, $\chi^2 = 11.7$ with 13 df ($p > .500$).

These results imply that teachers tend to tailor their objectives differently for different math classes. Raudenbush et al. (1991) therefore formulated a level-1 model to predict HOT:

$$Y_{ijk} = \pi_{0jk} + \pi_{1jk}(\text{TRACK})_{ijk} + e_{ijk}, \qquad [8.12]$$

where $(\text{TRACK})_{ijk}$ measures the track or level of each class and was coded −1 for vocational and general classes, 0 for academic classes, and 1 for academic honors classes. (This contrast seemed to adequately capture the variation among the three tracks.) The coefficients π_{0jk} and π_{1jk} were allowed to vary randomly over teachers and schools but were not predicted by teacher- or school-level variables. Thus, the level-2 model was

$$\pi_{0jk} = \beta_{00k} + r_{0jk}, \qquad [8.13a]$$

$$\pi_{1jk} = \beta_{10k} + r_{1jk}. \qquad [8.13b]$$

Note, there were two random effects at level 2 and, as a result, $\mathbf{T}_\pi$ was a 2 by 2 matrix. At level 3,

$$\beta_{00k} = \gamma_{000} + u_{00k}, \qquad\qquad [8.14a]$$

$$\beta_{10k} = \gamma_{100} + u_{10k}, \qquad\qquad [8.14b]$$

where there were also two random effects and $\mathbf{T}_\beta$ was a 2 by 2 matrix. The results (not reproduced here) indicated that HOT was strongly related to track. That is, $\hat{\gamma}_{100}$ was a large, significant positive effect. This means that teachers were more likely to emphasize higher order thinking in high track classes. The magnitude of this track effect, π_{1jk}, however, varied across teachers. That is, $\hat{\tau}_{\pi 11} = \widehat{\mathrm{Var}}(r_{1jk})$ was significantly greater than zero. In contrast, there was no evidence that the track effect varied among schools. That is, the hypothesis that $\tau_{\beta 11} = \mathrm{Var}(u_{10k}) = 0$ was sustained.

The next step in the analysis was to introduce additional class-level predictors (for example, grade level, type of math taught) in the level-1 model and additional teacher-level predictors (amount of education, preparation in math, and professional experience) in the level-2 model. The teacher-level predictors were hypothesized to explain both variation in teacher means on HOT, π_{0jk}, and variation among teachers in their tendency to emphasize HOT in high-track classes, π_{1jk}.

Because the number of schools was small and because there was little evidence of school-to-school variation, no level-3 predictors were specified. In fact, the apparent absence of any school-level variation in either β_{0jk} or β_{1jk} provides an argument for considering a simpler, two-level analysis of classes at level 1 and teachers at level 2, ignoring schools.

Studying Individual Change Within Organizations

A fundamental phenomenon of interest in educational research is the growth of the individual learner within the organizational context of classrooms and schools. To study the growth of children who are nested within schools, we combine the approaches developed in Chapter 5 for modeling individuals nested within organizations, and that of Chapter 6 for modeling individual change over time. Individual growth trajectories comprise the level-1 model; the variation in growth parameters among children within a school is captured in the level-2 model; and the variation among schools is represented in the level-3 model.

Bryk and Raudenbush (1988) illustrated this approach with a small subsample of the longitudinal data from the Sustaining Effects Study (Carter, 1984).[2]

The data from 618 students in 86 schools, each measured at five occasions between the spring of first grade and the spring of third grade.

Unconditional Model

We begin at level 1 with an individual growth model of the academic achievement at time t of student i in school j:

$$Y_{tij} = \pi_{0ij} + \pi_{1ij}(\text{ACADEMIC YEAR})_{tij}$$
$$+ \pi_{2ij}(\text{SUMMER PERIOD})_{tij} + e_{tij}, \qquad [8.15]$$

where

Y_{tij} is the outcome at time t for child i in school j;

(ACADEMIC YEAR)$_{tij}$ is 0 at spring of Grade 1 and fall of Grade 2, 1 at spring of Grade 2 and fall of Grade 3, and 2 at spring of Grade 3;

(SUMMER PERIOD)$_{tij}$ takes on a value of 0 in the spring of Grade 1, a value of 1 in fall and spring of Grade 2, and a value of 2 in fall and spring of Grade 3;

π_{0ij} is the initial status of child ij, that is, the expected outcome for that child in the spring of first grade (when ACADEMIC YEAR = 0 and SUMMER PERIOD = 0);

π_{1ij} is the learning rate for child ij during the academic year; and

π_{2ij} is the summer period mathematics learning rate for child ij.

The results of a preliminary analysis suggested considerable random variation in π_0 and π_1 at both levels 2 and 3. The student-level reliability for π_{2ij}, however, was less than .02, and the null hypothesis that $\tau_{\pi22} = 0$ was retained. (Note also that the model took over 1000 iterations to converge!) At the school level, the reliability of π_{2ij} was about .20, and the corresponding null hypothesis that $\tau_{\beta22} = 0$ was borderline significant. In addition, there was a strong negative correlation between π_{0ij} and π_{2ij} (greater than $-.90$). Given the relatively modest sample of schools ($J = 86$), these results suggested that we retain π_{2ij} in the level-1 model but treat it as fixed at level 2 and at level 3. Formally, the SUMMER PERIOD is a time-varying covariate in the level-1 model with fixed effects at levels 2 and 3.

Specifically, at level 2,

$$\pi_{0ij} = \beta_{00j} + r_{0ij}, \qquad [8.16a]$$

$$\pi_{1ij} = \beta_{10j} + r_{1ij}, \qquad [8.16b]$$

$$\pi_{2ij} = \beta_{20j}, \qquad [8.16c]$$

and, at level 3,

$$\beta_{00j} = \gamma_{000} + u_{00j}, \qquad [8.17a]$$

$$\beta_{10j} = \gamma_{100} + u_{10j}, \qquad [8.17b]$$

$$\beta_{20j} = \gamma_{200}. \qquad [8.17c]$$

Note that β_{00j} represents the mean initial status within school j, while γ_{000} is the overall mean initial status; β_{10j} is the mean academic year learning rate within school j, while γ_{100} is the overall mean academic year learning rate; and β_{20j} is the SUMMER PERIOD effect in school j, which we assume is constant for all schools at γ_{200}, a fixed SUMMER PERIOD effect.

Results. The results presented in Table 8.2 indicate, as expected, a strong positive overall growth trajectory averaged across all children and schools. The estimated initial status, $\hat{\gamma}_{000}$, was 403.685. The average learning rate per academic year was estimated at 56.537 (i.e., $\hat{\gamma}_{100}$). During the SUMMER PERIOD, however, student learning on average was virtually zero (i.e., $\hat{\gamma}_{200} = 0.272$, n.s.).

Of substantive interest in this application was the decomposition of the variance in π_{0jk} and π_{1jk} into their within- and between-schools components. The estimates for these variance components appear in the second panel of Table 8.2. The χ^2 statistics accompanying these variance components indicate significant variation among children within schools for initial status and academic year learning rates (i.e., π_{0ij} and π_{1ij}) and significant variation between schools for mean initial status and mean academic year learning rates (i.e., β_{00j} and β_{10j}).

Based on these variance component estimates, we can also compute the percentage of variation that lies between schools for both initial status and learning rates. Formally,

$$\% \text{ variance between schools on } \pi_{pjk} = \frac{\tau_{\beta pp}}{\tau_{\beta pp} + \tau_{\pi pp}} \qquad [8.18]$$

for $p = 0, \ldots, P$. In this case, $p = 0, 1$. Substituting the corresponding estimates for the variance components into Equation 8.18 yields the results presented in the third panel of Table 8.2. We find that about 8.0% of the variance in initial status lies between schools. This result is slightly less than typically encountered in cross-sectional studies of school effects where 10% to 30% of the achievement variability is between schools. The results for learning rates, however, are startling: Almost 60% of the variance is between schools.

TABLE 8.2 Three-Level Analysis of Sustaining-Effects Study Data (Unconditional Model at Levels 2 and 3)

Fixed Effect	Coefficient	se	t Ratio
Average initial status, γ_{000}	403.685	2.054	196.516
Average academic year learning rate, γ_{100}	56.537	1.411	40.095
Average summer period learning rate, γ_{200}	0.272	0.096	0.283

Random Effect	Variance Component	df	χ^2	p Value
Level 1				
Temporal variation, e_{tij}	600.112			
Level 2 (students within schools)				
Individual initial status, r_{0ij}	1,127.633	532	2,536.8	.000
Individual academic year learning rate, r_{1ij}	48.970	532	695.9	.000
Level 3 (between schools)				
School mean status, u_{00j}	98.546	85	126.7	.002
School mean learning rate, u_{10j}	68.568	85	221.7	.000

Level-1 Coefficient	Percentage of Variance Between Schools
Initial status, π_{0ij}	8.0
Learning rate, π_{1ij}	58.3

Variance-Covariance Components and Correlations Among the Level-2 and Level-3 Random Effects

Level 2 $\begin{pmatrix} 1{,}127.633 & 0.236 \\ 55.478 & 48.970 \end{pmatrix} = \widehat{\mathbf{T}}_\pi = \begin{pmatrix} \hat{\tau}_{\pi 11} & \\ \tau_{\pi 12} & \hat{\tau}_{\pi 22} \end{pmatrix}$

Level 3 $\begin{pmatrix} 98.546 & 0.361 \\ 29.697 & 68.568 \end{pmatrix} = \widehat{\mathbf{T}}_\beta = \begin{pmatrix} \hat{\tau}_{\beta 11} & \\ \hat{\tau}_{\beta 12} & \hat{\tau}_{\beta 22} \end{pmatrix}$

NOTE: The lower triangles contain the covariances; the upper triangles contain the correlations.

Also of potential interest is the decomposition of the correlation between initial status and academic year learning rate into its within-(level-2) and between-school (level-3) components. (See the last panel of Table 8.2). Within a typical SES school, the estimated correlation is 0.236. This relationship is somewhat stronger, 0.361, at the school level. We note that in other applications the decomposition of a relationship can result in very different estimates of associations, including the possibility of a positive relation at one level and a negative association at the other.

In general, unconditional level-2 and level-3 models should be fit prior to consideration of any explanatory models at either level. The unconditional model provides important statistics for studying individual growth, including the partitioning of variability in the individual growth parameters into level-2 and level-3 components; the correlations among the growth parameters; and the reliability of effects at each level (as in Equations 8.7 and 8.8).

In this particular application, the variance component decomposition highlighted an important feature of the data: the high percentage of variation in learning rates lying between schools. The reliability estimates also help us to discern whether certain random effects in the level-2 and level-3 models might be constrained to zero.

Conditional Model

We now consider an explanatory model that allows estimation of the separate effects of child poverty and school poverty concentration on individual mathematics learning. The level-1 model remains as in Equation 8.15. The level-2 model represents the variability in each of the growth parameters, π_{pij}, among students within schools. The effects of CHILD POVERTY are represented here. Specifically, we formulated the following level-2 model:

$$\pi_{0ij} = \beta_{00j} + \beta_{01j}(\text{CHILD POVERTY})_{ij} + r_{0ij}, \qquad [8.19a]$$

$$\pi_{1ij} = \beta_{10j} + \beta_{11j}(\text{CHILD POVERTY})_{ij} + r_{1ij}, \qquad [8.19b]$$

$$\pi_{2ij} = \beta_{20j}. \qquad [8.19c]$$

We hypothesize in Equations 8.19a and 8.19b that CHILD POVERTY (a dummy variable indicating whether the child comes from a poor family) is related to initial status and academic year learning rate. Equation 8.19c specifies that the summer period effect is the same for all students within each school j. Because CHILD POVERTY is a dummy variable, the corresponding regression coefficients can be interpreted as poverty-gap effects. That is, β_{01j} is the poverty gap on initial status (i.e., the extent to which a poor child starts behind his or her more advantaged counterparts within school j), and β_{11j} is the poverty gap on academic year learning rates in school j (i.e., the difference between the two groups in subsequent rates of learning).

The level-3 model represents the variability among schools in the five β coefficients. We hypothesize in this illustration that school poverty predicts school mean initial status and learning rate and that the effect of child poverty on initial status is constant across all schools, but that the poverty gap on learning rates varies across schools as a function of school poverty. We also hypothesize, for reasons discussed below, that school poverty is related to the size of the summer-drop-off effect. Thus, we pose the following level-3 model:

β_{00j} = mean status in school j for an "advantaged" child

$$= \gamma_{000} + \gamma_{001}(\text{SCHOOL POVERTY})_j + u_{00j} \qquad [8.20a]$$

β_{01j} = poverty gap on initial status

$$= \gamma_{010} \qquad [8.20b]$$

β_{10j} = academic year learning rate for an advantaged child in school j

$$= \gamma_{100} + \gamma_{101}(\text{SCHOOL POVERTY})_j + u_{10j} \qquad [8.20c]$$

β_{11j} = child poverty gap on the academic year learning rate in school j

$$= \gamma_{110} + \gamma_{111}(\text{SCHOOL POVERTY})_j \qquad [8.20d]$$

β_{20j} = summer period effect in school j

$$= \gamma_{200} + \gamma_{201}(\text{SCHOOL POVERTY})_j \qquad [8.20e]$$

Note that there are two random effects per school: u_{00j} and u_{10j}. The estimated fixed effects for this model are presented in Table 8.3.

The γ_{000} coefficient represents in this application the predicted initial status for an "advantaged child" (CHILD POVERTY = 0) in an "affluent school" (SCHOOL POVERTY = 0). For such a student, the predicted math achievement is 414.958. For each 10% increment in SCHOOL POVERTY, the expected initial status is reduced by 4.574 points (i.e., $10 \times \hat{\gamma}_{001}$). At the initial data collection point, the child poverty gap, $\hat{\gamma}_{010}$, is 12.032 points. This means that children from poor families (CHILD POVERTY = 1) start out 12.032 points behind their more advantaged schoolmates.

The predicted academic year learning rate for an advantaged child in an affluent school, $\hat{\gamma}_{100}$, is 60.491. On average, such children gain about 60 points per academic year. The learning rate for advantaged children, however, declines slightly as a function of school poverty concentration ($\hat{\gamma}_{101} = -0.179$).

For a poor child in an affluent school, the academic year learning rate is 8.215 points lower than that for an advantaged child (i.e., $\hat{\gamma}_{110}$). The average gain for such a child from one academic year of instruction is $\hat{\gamma}_{100} + \hat{\gamma}_{110} = 60.499 - 8.215 = 52.284$ points. SCHOOL POVERTY may have a small positive effect on academic year learning for the poor child. After adjusting for CHILD POVERTY, a 10% increase in school poverty concentration pre-

TABLE 8.3 Effects of Child and School Poverty on Student Learning (a Three-Level Analysis of Sustaining-Effects Study Data)

Fixed Effect	Coefficient	se	t Ratio
Model for initial status, π_{0ij}			
Model for mean status of advantaged			
child, β_{00j}			
INTERCEPT, γ_{000}	414.958	2.310	179.599
SCHOOL POVERTY, γ_{001}	−0.457	0.095	−4.818
Model for child poverty gap on initial			
status, β_{01j}			
INTERCEPT, γ_{010}	−12.032	4.845	−2.484
Model for academic year learning rate, π_{1ij}			
Model for learning rate of			
advantaged child, β_{10j}			
INTERCEPT, γ_{100}	60.491	2.123	28.489
SCHOOL POVERTY, γ_{101}	−0.179	0.080	−2.220
Model for child poverty gap on			
learning rate, β_{11j}			
INTERCEPT, γ_{110}	−8.215	4.134	−1.988
SCHOOL POVERTY, γ_{111}	0.164	0.099	1.655
Model for summer period learning rate, π_{2ij}			
Model for school effect, β_{20j}			
INTERCEPT, γ_{200}	−2.309	1.369	−1.687
SCHOOL POVERTY, γ_{201}	0.132	0.050	2.652

dicts an *increment* to learning of 1.64 points (i.e., $10 \times \hat{\gamma}_{111}$). Presumably, the SCHOOL POVERTY measure is acting in this analysis as a proxy for the amount of compensatory education resources available in the school, which depends directly on the poverty level of the school.

This pattern of effects for SCHOOL POVERTY also appears in modeling the summer period effects. In schools with higher levels of poverty concentration, positive summer learning appears to occur. For example, in a school with all poor children (SCHOOL POVERTY = 100), the expected summer period effect would be $\hat{\gamma}_{200} + 100 * \hat{\gamma}_{201} = -2.309 + (.132)100 = 10.89$. Although we do not have data on the specific summer programs available in schools, we know that, in general, compensatory funds were used for this purpose. Thus, these results suggest possible compensatory education effects on student learning during the summer.

Table 8.4 presents estimated variances and related χ^2 statistics from the three-level decomposition. These results suggest that residual parameter variance still remains to be explained in π_{0ij}, π_{1ij}, and β_{10j}. In contrast, little residual variance remains in β_{00j} to be explained (note n.s. χ^2 statistic).

TABLE 8.4 Variance Decomposition from a Three-Level Analysis of the Effects of Child and School Poverty on Student Learning

Random Effect	Variance Component	df	χ^2	p Value
Level-1 variance				
Temporal variation, e_{tij}	597.67			
Level 2 (student within schools)				
Individual initial status, r_{0ij}	1,116.30	531	3,231.9	0.000
Individual learning rate, r_{1ij}	47.92	531	694.50	0.000
Level 3 (between schools)				
School mean status, u_{00j}	2.72	84	87.01	0.389
School mean learning rate, u_{10j}	68.72	84	223.18	0.000
Deviance = 29,932.31				
Number of estimated parameters = 16				

An Alternative Coding Scheme for the Level-1 Model. The original Bryk and Raudenbush (1988) analysis of the SES data posed a different individual growth model of the academic achievement at time t of student i in school j:

$$Y_{tij} = \pi_{0ij} + \pi_{1ij}(\text{TIME POINT})_{tij}$$
$$+\pi_{2ij}(\text{SUMMER DROP})_{tij} + e_{tij}, \qquad [8.21]$$

where

   Y_{tij} is the outcome at time t for child i in school j;

   (TIME POINT)$_{tij}$ is 0 at spring of Grade 1, 1 at fall of Grade 2, 2 at spring of Grade 2, 3 at fall of Grade 3, and 4 at spring of Grade 3;

   (SUMMER DROP)$_{tij}$ takes on a value of 1 in the fall (time points 1 and 3) and 0 at the spring time points;

   π_{0ij} is the initial status of child ij, that is, the expected outcome for that child in the spring of first grade (when TIME POINT = 0 and SUMMER DROP = 0);

   π_{1ij} is the learning rate per time period for child ij; and

   π_{2ij} is the summer drop off from π_{1ij} in mathematics learning for child ij during the summer period.

According to this model, the expected learning rate for child ij over the course of a full year is $2 * \pi_{1ij}$. The coefficient π_{2ij} captures the summer drop-off in student learning. As a result, $\pi_{1ij} + \pi_{2ij}$ would now be the expected learning rate during the summer period. While it is possible to translate results from the model of Equation 8.21 with those from Equation 8.15, in retrospect Equation 8.15 represents a more straightforward model for this problem in that the learning over the course of a year is directly decomposed into an academic year and summer period effect. As a result, these can be subsequently modeled as outcome variables at both level 2 and level 3, respectively. This affords another illustration of how a different formulation of the level-1 model can result in a more informative overall analysis.

Measurement Models at Level 1

As noted earlier, level 1 in a hierarchical linear model can always be thought of as a measurement model. We have shown how in organizational effects applications level-1 coefficients measure properties of the organization based on the responses from multiple individuals within it. Similarly, in growth applications, we have shown how level-1 coefficients measure individual growth parameters based on time series data. We now illustrate how a level-1 model can be formulated as an explicit measurement model that combines results from multiple survey items into an overall scale. We also demonstrate how externally provided psychometric information can be incorporated into a multilevel modeling framework.

Example: Research on School Climate

Studies of organizational climate are often based on individuals' perceptions. Typically, climate measures are constructed from several survey items that are combined to create an overall measure as reported by, say, a teacher or student. These individual measures are then aggregated at the organizational level to create an overall measure of the climate. The problem is that the climate measures at the person or organizational level may have different meanings and different measurement properties. Correlations will be attenuated by measurement error to different degrees at each level, potentially rendering the research uninterpretable. The three-level model can be formulated to address this problem. We illustrate this in a case with five climate measures based on teacher survey reports: principal leadership, staff cooperation, teacher control, teacher efficacy, and teacher satisfaction.

Raudenbush, Rowan, and Kang (1991) analyzed data from questionnaires administered to 1,867 teachers nested within 110 schools. The data consisted of 35 Likert-scaled items measuring five latent constructs: principal leadership, staff cooperation, teacher control, teacher efficacy, and teacher satisfaction. The analyses sought to examine the psychometric properties of the measures and to investigate structural relations between school characteristics and the latent constructs.

We reproduce the results of their unconditional analysis below. Level 1 of the model represents variation among the item scores within each teacher. Level 2 represents variation among teachers within schools, and level 3 represents variation across schools.

Level-1 Model. For simplicity, we assume that each item measuring a given construct will be equally weighted. Further, items at level 1 were rescaled to have approximately equal error variances.[3] The level-1 model is

$$Y_{ijk} = \sum_p \pi_{pjk} a_{pijk} + e_{ijk}, \qquad [8.22]$$

where

a_{pijk} takes on a value of 1 if item i measures construct p and 0 otherwise, for constructs $p = 1, \ldots, 5$;

π_{pjk} is the latent true score for person j in school k on construct p; and

e_{ijk} is an error assumed to be normally distributed with a mean of 0 and a variance σ^2.

The assumption that e_{ijk} is normal will have little effect in cases where the item is, for example, a Likert scale with a reasonably symmetric distribution. (See Chapter 10 for more refined methods for ordinal data.)

Level-2 Model. The level-2 model describes the distribution of the true scores, π_p, across teachers within schools:

$$\pi_{pjk} = \beta_{pk0} + r_{pjk}, \qquad [8.23]$$

where β_{pk0} is the true score mean on construct p for school k, and r_{pjk} is a person-specific effect. For each person, the five random effects $r_{1jk}, \ldots, r_{5jk}$ are assumed multivariate normal with means of 0 and a 5 by 5 covariance matrix $\mathbf{T}_\pi$.

Level-3 Model. At level 3, the school means scores vary around their respective grand means:

$$\beta_{pk0} = \gamma_{p00} + u_{pk0}. \qquad [8.24]$$

For each school, the random effects $u_{1k}, \ldots, u_{5k}$ are assumed multivariate normal with means of 0 and a 5 by 5 covariance matrix, $\mathbf{T}_\beta$.

TABLE 8.5 Psychometric Analysis

Fixed Effect	Coefficient	se	t Ratio
Mean principal leadership, γ_{100}	3.76	5.36	0.70
Mean staff cooperation, γ_{200}	9.63	4.42	2.18
Mean teacher control, γ_{300}	14.24	3.66	3.89
Mean teacher efficacy, γ_{400}	9.65	3.04	3.17
Mean teacher satisfaction, γ_{500}	10.79	4.05	2.66

Variance-Covariance Components for Random Effects at Levels 1, 2, and 3 and Correlations Among the Level-2 and Level-3 Random Effects

Level 1, $\hat{\sigma}^2 = 9979$

$$\text{Level 2, } \widehat{\mathbf{T}}_\pi = \begin{pmatrix} 6052 & .615 & .579 & .578 & .561 \\ 3436 & 5156 & .382 & .527 & .531 \\ 2324 & 1413 & 2660 & .561 & .468 \\ 2964 & 2498 & 1909 & 4351 & .980 \\ 4241 & 3709 & 2347 & 6285 & 9447 \end{pmatrix}$$

$$\text{Level 3, } \widehat{\mathbf{T}}_\beta = \begin{pmatrix} 2957 & .746 & .560 & .633 & .690 \\ 1584 & 1694 & .605 & .709 & .734 \\ 1000 & 862 & 1198 & .648 & .579 \\ 694 & 621 & 478 & 453 & .898 \\ 1077 & 915 & 607 & 579 & 916 \end{pmatrix}$$

NOTE: The lower triangles contain the covariances; the upper triangles contain the correlations.

Results. The results appear in Table 8.5. The fixed effects are the five grand means. The table also presents maximum likelihood estimates of the two covariance matrices, $\mathbf{T}_\pi$ and $\mathbf{T}_\beta$, and the level-1 variance σ^2. (Note that variance-covariances appear in the lower triangle and the corresponding correlations are located in the upper triangle of the two matrices.)

Perhaps the most interesting feature of the results is the insight they provide about the correlations among the latent constructs. For example, we see that the estimated correlation between the teacher efficacy and teacher satisfaction (constructs 4 and 5) at the teacher level is .98. The implication is that these two constructs are virtually indistinguishable at the teacher level. This inference, however, contrasts markedly with what might have been concluded by examining the correlations among the observed scores. These comparisons are provided in Table 8.6. Note that the correlation among the observed scores is .56. The explanation for the difference is that only two items are used to measure each of these constructs. As a result, the observed score correlation is actually remarkably high given the paucity of items used in each case. Not surprisingly, the hierarchical estimates of the correlations among the true constructs are larger than the observed correlations at the teacher and school levels.

TABLE 8.6 Correlations at Each Level

	Teacher Level		School Level	
	Ordinary[a]	Hierarchical	Ordinary[b]	Hierarchical
Principal leadership with:				
Staff cooperation	.57	.62	.68	.75
Teacher control	.48	.58	.55	.56
Teacher efficacy	.38	.58	.46	.63
Teacher satisfaction	.44	.56	.56	.69
Staff cooperation with:				
Teacher control	.35	.38	.52	.61
Teacher efficacy	.35	.53	.53	.71
Teacher satisfaction	.41	.53	.61	.73
Teacher control with:				
Teacher efficacy	.35	.56	.51	.65
Teacher satisfaction	.34	.47	.51	.58
Teacher efficacy with:				
Teacher satisfaction	.56	.98	.74	.90

[a] Based on teacher-level observations, ignoring school membership.
[b] Based on school means.

The results also show that the correlation structure is not the same at the two levels. Essentially, the three-level analysis corrects the correlations for measurement error, which yields different corrections at each level because the measurement error structure at each level is quite different. At the teacher level, the reliability depends on the number of items in the scale and the interitem agreement. At the school level, although affected somewhat by these factors, the reliability depends more heavily on the number of teachers sampled per school and the level of teacher agreement within schools.

Raudenbush, Rowan, and Kang (1991) extended this analysis by employing characteristics of teachers (e.g., education and social background) and of schools (e.g., sector, size, social composition) to explain variation in the latent-climate variables. In essence, their analyses involved a multivariate two-level model (i.e., multiple latent-climate constructs defined on teacher within schools). This explanatory model enabled the investigators to assess the relative strength of school- and teacher-level predictors for each of the five different latent-climate constructs.

Example: Research on School-Based Professional Community and the Factors That Facilitate It

Bryk, Camburn, and Louis (1999) analyzed data collected by the Consortium on Chicago School Research from 5,690 teachers in 248 Chicago elementary schools to assess the impact of a variety of structural, human, and social factors on the workplace organization of schools. Their key outcome variable of interest, school-based professional community, was a composite of six separate measures (reflective dialogue, deprivatization of practice, staff collaboration, new teacher socialization, focus on student learning, and collective responsibility for school improvement) derived from individual teacher survey responses. Each of the six scales was developed through a separate Rasch rating scale analysis (Wright & Masters, 1982) that yielded both a measure and a standard error of measurement on each scale for each teacher. Since not all teachers answered all survey items, it was especially important to take the differences in the standard errors of measurement into account in the analysis. Also, like the previous example, the composite measure of professional community has components of variation and predictors at both the teacher and the school level. The basic formulation of the hierarchical linear model for this research is presented below. For further details on this study and findings, see Bryk, Camburn, and Louis (1999).

At level 1, the six component measures $i = 1, \ldots, 6$ for teacher j in school k were used to predict a "true score" on a professional community composite:

$$Y_{ijk} = \pi_{jk} + e_{ijk}, \qquad e_{ijk} \sim \mathrm{N}\,(0, \sigma_{ijk}^2), \qquad [8.25]$$

where

   Y_{ijk} is a rating scale measure for one of the six component measures of professional community for teacher j in school k;

   π_{jk} is the "true" value of the professional community composite for that teacher; and

   e_{ijk} is the error of measurement associated with teacher $j\,k$'s responses on the ith component of professional community.

Note that a key function of this level-1 model is to aggregate the six separate component measures into an overall composite index, π_{jk}.

Up to this point in our various examples, we have typically assumed that the measurement error, e_{ijk}, at level 1 was unknown and normally distributed with mean 0 and some constant variance. However, the standard errors estimated for each Rasch rating scale measure, s_{ijk}, permit us to explicitly represent measurement error in our model. Specifically, we adjusted the component measures for their unreliability by multiplying both sides of Equation 8.25 by the inverse of the standard error estimates for each component, $a_{ijk} = s_{ijk}^{-1}$, so that

$$Y_{ijk}^* = a_{ijk}\,\pi_{jk} + e_{ijk}^*, \qquad e_{ijk}^* \sim \mathrm{N}(0, 1), \qquad [8.26]$$

where $Y_{ijk}^* = a_{ijk} Y_{ijk}$ and $e_{ijk}^* = a_{ijk} e_{ijk}$. Note that when we adjust for measurement error, σ^2 is now fixed at 1.

At level 2, teachers' "true scores" were modeled as a function of a set of teacher-level characteristics, X_{pjk}. Individual teacher variation in the "true scores" was captured in r_{jk}, which was assumed to be normally distributed with mean 0 and variance τ_π:

$$\pi_{jk} = \beta_{0k} + \sum_{p=1}^{P} \beta_{pk}(X_{pjk} - \overline{X}_{p..}) + r_{jk}, \qquad r_{jk} \sim N(0, \tau_\pi). \quad [8.27]$$

By centering the teacher-level predictors about their grand means, β_{0k} became the predicted mean for school k if it had an "average" faculty composition as measured by the predictor variables. The relationship between these $p = 1, \ldots, P$ predictors and the outcome was captured in β_{pk}.

At level 3, the adjusted school means, β_{0k}, were modeled as a function of school characteristics:

$$\beta_{0k} = \gamma_{00} + \sum_{q=1}^{Q} \gamma_{0q} W_{qk} + u_{0k}, \qquad u_{0k} \sim N(0, \tau_\beta),$$

$$\beta_{pk} = \gamma_{p0} \qquad\qquad [8.28]$$

for $p = 1, \ldots, P$, where γ_{00} was the estimated grand mean of the professional community composite adjusted for measurement error and faculty composition. The γ_{0q} are $q = 1, \ldots, Q$ coefficients that express the relationship between school characteristics and professional community, and u_{0k} represents individual variation attributable to school k.

Estimating Random Coefficients in Three-Level Models

This chapter has focused on the use of three-level models for estimating multilevel fixed effects and variance-covariance components. The three-level model can also provide empirical Bayes estimates of the random coefficients at both level 2 and level 3. We return to the simple model introduced earlier (see "A Fully Unconditional Model") of academic achievement of students nested within classrooms that are in turn nested within schools. For this unconditional three-level model, the hierarchical analysis provide the following composite estimates (empirical Bayes) for each classroom (level-2) and school (level-3) mean:

$$\pi_{0jk}^* = \hat{\lambda}_{\pi_{jk}} \overline{Y}_{\cdot jk} + (1 - \hat{\lambda}_{\pi_{jk}})\beta_{00k}^*, \qquad [8.29]$$

$$\beta_{00k}^* = \hat{\lambda}_{\beta_k} \hat{\beta}_{00k} + (1 - \hat{\lambda}_{\beta_k})\hat{\gamma}_{000}, \qquad [8.30]$$

where $\lambda_{\pi_{jk}}$ and λ_{β_k} are the reliabilities of the class- and school-level means defined in Equations 8.7 and 8.8; $\hat{\gamma}_{000}$ is the estimate of the grand mean; and $\hat{\beta}_{00k}$ is the weighted least squares estimator of β_{00k}:

$$\hat{\beta}_{00k} = \frac{\sum_j [\hat{\tau}_\pi + \hat{\sigma}^2/n_{jk}]^{-1} \overline{Y}_{.jk}}{\sum_j [\hat{\tau}_\pi + \hat{\sigma}^2/n_{jk}]^{-1}}.$$ [8.31]

Note that β_{00k}^* shrinks the classical weighted least squares estimator $\hat{\beta}_{00k}$ toward the grand mean, $\hat{\gamma}_{000}$, by an amount proportional to $1 - \hat{\lambda}_{\beta_k}$, the unreliability of $\hat{\beta}_{00k}$. Similarly, π_{0jk}^* shrinks the sample mean $\overline{Y}_{.jk}$ toward β_{00k}^* by an amount proportional to $1 - \hat{\lambda}_{\pi_{jk}}$, the unreliability of $\overline{Y}_{.jk}$ computed within school k.

Notes

1. We wish to thank the Center for Research on the Context of Secondary School Teaching at Stanford University (funded by the Office of Educational Research and Improvement, U.S. Department of Education, Cooperative Agreement No. OERI-G0089C235) for use of these data.

2. The results presented here differ from those previously published in the first edition, which closely followed Bryk and Raudenbush (1988). A new coding scheme for the level-1 predictors is used here, which more directly represents the intent of the initial study.

3. The error variances for each construct were estimated in a separate analysis as described by Raudenbush, Rowan, and Kang (1991). Let σ_p^2 denote the error variance for construct p. The items were then weighted by $100/\sigma_p$, yielding a level-1 variance of 10,000 in the reweighted data.

Assessing the Adequacy of Hierarchical Models

Introduction

A good data analysis begins with a careful examination of the univariate frequency distribution of each variable that may be employed in a subsequent multivariate analysis. Examination of the shape and scale of each variable provides a check on the quality of the data, identifies outlying observations, and may suggest a need for a variable transformation. The next step in model building involves exploration of the bivariate relationships. Plots of two continuous variables can identify possible nonlinear relationships and identify discrepant cases that could arise from some erroneous observations. Prior to fitting a hierarchical model, such analyses are needed at each level.

In addition, cross-level exploratory analyses are needed. For example, prior to a school effects study, it is useful to examine the OLS regressions for each school. This enables the analyst to look for *outlier* schools, that is, schools with implausible regression intercepts or slopes. One may then investigate the possible causes of these odd results, which could arise because of small samples, unusual characteristics of the school in question, or even coding errors. Implausible results arising from units with small sample size are not a problem because the estimation methods detailed in Chapter 3 are robust in this regard. Distorted regressions from bad data, however, are more serious because discrepant schools may exert undue influence on estimation.

Thinking about Model Assumptions

Inferences based on standard linear models depend for their validity on the tenability of assumptions about both the structural and random parts of the model. In terms of the structural part, OLS requires a properly specified model where the outcome is a linear function of the regression coefficients. Misspecification occurs when some component included in the error term is associated with one or more of the predictors in the model.

In hierarchical linear models, specification assumptions apply at each level. Moreover, misspecification at one level can affect results at other levels. Further, because level-2 equations may have correlated errors, the misspecification of one equation can bias the estimates in another. For example, in Chapter 4 we modeled each school's intercept and slope as a bivariate outcome in the level-2 model. It is important to know how misspecification of the model for the intercept might affect estimates of the level-2 coefficients in the slope model.

In terms of the random part of the model, OLS regression assumes independent errors with equal variances. Standard hypothesis tests also require that the errors be normally distributed. In a hierarchical analysis, assumptions about normally distributed error forms are made at both level 1 and level 2. Although a violation of these assumptions will not bias the level-2 coefficient estimates, it can adversely influence their estimated standard errors and inferential statistics. Similarly, estimation of random level-1 coefficients and variance-covariance components can be distorted.

Skillful data analysts pay close attention to the assumptions required by their models. They investigate the tenability of assumptions in light of the available data; they consider how sensitive their conclusions are likely to be to violations of these assumptions; and they seek ameliorative strategies when significant violations are discovered. Our remarks in this chapter focus on the estimated fixed effects, their standard errors, and inferential statistics because these are of primary interest in most applications and because most is known about their properties. Some implications for inference regarding the random coefficients and variance-covariance components are also sketched.

Organization of the Chapter

Chapters 5 through 7 sought to illustrate the logic of hierarchical modeling through a range of applications of two-level models. In this chapter, we focus on key decisions involved in formulating such models, the assumptions on which we rely, and empirical procedures that can assist us in the model-building process. Although a hierarchical linear model involves an interrelated set of specifications and assumptions at both level 1 and level 2, for purposes of clarity of presentation we proceed by first discussing the level-1 model and then the level-2 model. This discussion actually follows the general flow of the model-building process. The analyst settles on a tentative level-1 model, then considers the level-2 model, which may eventuate in some changes at level 1. We assume throughout most of this chapter that the conditions for large-sample theory of maximum likelihood estimation hold. The final section, however, discusses the properties of estimates when the samples sizes at levels 1 and 2 are modest.

The illustrations presented in this chapter use data on high school mathematics achievement similar to those discussed in Chapter 4. We consider a level-1 model

$$Y_{ij} = \beta_{0j} + \beta_{1j}(\text{SES})_{ij} + r_{ij}, \qquad [9.1]$$

where Y_{ij} is the mathematics achievement of student i in school j, which depends on the student's social class. At level 2,

$$\beta_{0j} = \gamma_{00} + \gamma_{01}(\text{MEAN SES})_j + \gamma_{02}(\text{SECTOR})_j + u_{0j}$$

and

$$\beta_{1j} = \gamma_{10} + \gamma_{11}(\text{MEAN SES})_j + \gamma_{12}(\text{SECTOR})_j + u_{1j}. \qquad [9.2]$$

Key Assumptions of a Two-Level Hierarchical Linear Model

Equations 9.1 and 9.2 are a specific case from the general two-level model, where, at level 1,

$$Y_{ij} = \beta_{0j} + \sum_{q=1}^{Q} \beta_{qj} X_{qij} + r_{ij} \qquad [9.3]$$

and at level 2, for each β_{qj},

$$\beta_{qj} = \gamma_{q0} + \sum_{s=1}^{S_q} \gamma_{qs} W_{sj} + u_{qj}. \qquad [9.4]$$

Formally, we assumed the following:

1. Each r_{ij} is independent and normally distributed with a mean of 0 and variance σ^2 for every level-1 unit i within each level-2 unit j [i.e., $r_{ij} \sim$ iid $N(0, \sigma^2)$].

2. The level-1 predictors, X_{qij}, are independent of r_{ij} [i.e., $\text{Cov}(X_{qij}, r_{ij}) = 0$ for all q].

3. The vectors of $Q + 1$ random errors at level 2 are multivariate normal, each with a mean of 0, some variance, τ_{qq}, and covariance among the random elements, q and q', of $\tau_{qq'}$. The random-error vectors are independent among the J level-2 units [i.e., $u_j = (u_{0j}, \dots, u_{Qj})' \sim$ iid $N(0, \mathbf{T})$].

4. The set of level-2 predictors (i.e., all the unique elements in W_{sj} across the $Q + 1$ equations) are independent of every u_{qj} [i.e., for every W_{sj} and u_{qj}, $\text{Cov}(W_{sj}, u_{qj}) = 0$].

5. The errors at level 1 and level 2 are also independent [i.e., $\text{Cov}(r_{ij}, u_{qj}) = 0$ for all q].

6. The predictors at each level are not correlated with the random effects at the other level. That is, $\text{Cov}(X_{qij}, u_{q'j}) = 0$ for all q, q'; and $\text{Cov}(W_{sj}, r_{ij}) = 0$.

Assumptions 2, 4, and 6 focus on the relationship between the variables included in the structural portion of the model—the Xs and Ws—and those factors relegated to the error terms, r_{ij} and u_{qj}. They pertain to the adequacy of model specification. Their tenability affects the bias in estimating γ_{qs}, that is, whether $E(\hat{\gamma}_{qs}) = \gamma_{qs}$. Assumptions 1, 3, and 5 focus only on the random portion of the model (i.e., r_{ij} and u_{qj}). Their tenability affects the consistency of the estimates of $\text{se}(\hat{\gamma}_{qs})$, the accuracy of β_{qj}^*, $\hat{\sigma}^2$, and $\widehat{\mathbf{T}}$, and the accuracy of hypothesis tests and confidence intervals.

In terms of the simple two-level model of Equations 9.1 and 9.2, we are assuming the following:

1. Conditional on a student's social class, the within-school errors are normal and independent with a mean of 0 in each school and equal variances across schools (assumption 1).

2. Whatever student-level predictors of math achievement are excluded from the model and thereby relegated to the error term r_{ij} are independent of student social class (assumption 2). We emphasize that the excluded variables to worry about are truly predictors rather than correlated outcomes.

3. The residual school effects, u_{0j} and u_{1j}, are assumed bivariate normal with variances τ_{00} and τ_{11}, respectively, and covariance τ_{01} (assumption 3).

4. The effects of whatever school predictors are excluded from the model for the intercept and SES slope are independent of MEAN SES and SECTOR (assumption 4).

5. The error at level 1, r_{ij}, is independent of the residual school effects, u_{0j} and u_{1j}.
6. Whatever student-level predictors are excluded from the level-1 model and thereby relegated to the error term, r_{ij}, are independent of the level-2 predictors in the model, that is, MEAN SES and SECTOR. Also, whatever school-level predictors are excluded from the model and thereby relegated to the level-2 random effects, u_{qj}, are uncorrelated with the student-level predictor, that is, SES.

We describe the assumptions in this way to facilitate systematic inquiry into their validity. Assumptions 1 and 2 are internal to the level-1 model and can be explored to some degree by examining the level-1 data and residuals; assumptions 3 and 4 are internal to the level-2 model and can, to some degree, be examined by exploring level-2 data and residuals. In contrast, assumptions 5 and 6 concern cross-level associations and require some extra discussion.

We now proceed to consider each of these assumptions in the process of building the level-1 and level-2 models.

Building the Level-1 Model

The early phases of model building involve an interplay of theoretical and empirical considerations. The substantive theory under study should suggest a relatively small number of predictors for possible consideration in the level-1 model. There are two questions here: (a) Should a candidate X_q be included in the model? If yes, (b) how should its coefficient be specified: random, fixed, or nonrandomly varying?

Initially, the level-2 predictors are held aside and the analysis focuses on comparing some alternative hierarchical models, each of which is unconditional at level 2. A natural temptation is to estimate a "saturated" level-1 model—that is, where all potential predictors are included with random slopes—and then to work backward deleting nonsignificant effects from the model. Unfortunately, such a strategy is generally not useful unless the level-1 sample sizes are very large (e.g., sufficient to sustain stable OLS estimation of the specified level-1 model in each separate unit). Even here, such a saturated model might require hundreds of iterations to converge and often will produce a large array of nonsignificant findings that offer little direction as to next steps. Intuitively, there is only a fixed amount of variation to be explained. If one overfits the model by specifying too many random level-1 coefficients, the variation is partitioned into many little pieces, none of which is of much significance. The problem here is analogous to focusing a projector. If one moves beyond the proper range, the image loses focus.

In general, we have found it more productive to use a "step-up" strategy. Assuming some external theoretical guidance that has defined a relatively small set of level-1 predictors, we build up from univariate to bivariate to trivariate (and so on) models based on promising submodels. Often the best subset level-1 predictors can be identified through preliminary modeling using OLS level-1 analyses.

Empirical Methods to Guide Model Building at Level 1

In terms of a hierarchical analysis, two questions need to be addressed: (a) Is the fixed effect of X_{qij} significant? and (b) Is there any evidence of slope heterogeneity [i.e., $\text{Var}(\beta_q) > 0$]? Statistical evidence of slope heterogeneity includes the point estimates, $\hat{\tau}_{qq}$, and the corresponding homogeneity test statistics (χ^2 and likelihood-ratio tests introduced in Chapter 3). Also useful in this regard are the estimated reliabilities for the OLS intercepts and slopes.

When the reliabilities become small (e.g., <0.05), the variances we wish to estimate are likely to be close to zero (or what is technically referred to as near the boundary of the parameter space). Such cases cause a variety of numerical difficulties depending on the particular iterative computing routines employed in the variance-covariance component estimation. Although some algorithms abnormally terminate (or require a fix-up to override such a termination), the EM algorithm simply slows down. In extreme cases, it becomes tediously slow to converge. Inspection of the reliabilities may suggest that a random level-1 coefficient be respecified as either fixed or nonrandomly varying. This respecified model may now converge very quickly.

Interestingly, the rate of convergence for the EM, as indicated by the number of iterations, is itself diagnostic. If the data are highly informative, the EM algorithm will converge rapidly (e.g., in less than 10 iterations). In contrast, if the model has an extensive number of random effects and the data are relatively sparse, hundreds of iterations may be needed.

Inspection of the correlations among the level-1 coefficients is also diagnostic (see the vocabulary growth analysis in Chapter 6). If a high degree of collinearity or multicollinearity is found, the model must be simplified. One option is to constrain one or more random effects to be zero, thus eliminating the collinearity. This works well if the random effect set to zero has little or no variability. If the variability of each random effect is nonnegligible, a better option is to impose linear constraints on the random effects. For example, two random effects can be constrained to have a correlation of 1.0 or -1.0 while being allowed to have nonzero variances. This approach can be viewed as a special case of imposing a factor model on the level-2 random effects (Miyazaki, 2000).

In general, analysts must use some caution in specifying level-1 coefficients as random. The number of variance-covariance components to be estimated in a two-level model (with homogeneous variance and independent errors at level 1) is $m(m + 1)/2 + 1$, where m is the number of random level-1 predictors in the model. Clearly, this number rapidly increases with m. As the number of random effects grows, significantly more information is required to obtain reasonable estimates of the variance-covariance components. For example, using the High School and Beyond data with about 45 students per school and 160 schools, we have found that three random coefficients plus a random intercept is about as rich a model as the data can sustain. (This number would increase if more observations per school were available or if the level-1 model fit was very good, i.e., σ^2 was small.) One cannot be definitive about how many random effects can be specified because the maximum will depend on several factors: the magnitude of the variance components, the degree of intercorrelation among the random effects, the magnitude of σ^2, and other characteristics of the data.

One additional caution is in order, however. Although the inferential and descriptive statistics may indicate that some τ_{qq} is zero or close to zero, this does not preclude the possibility of a nonrandomly varying specification for the corresponding β_{qj}. If theoretical arguments suggest that such effects might be present, the analyst should proceed with posing level-2 models for β_{qj}. This occurred, for example, in the Lee and Bryk (1989) study on minority-gap effects discussed in Chapter 5. Prior research had indicated sector differences, and an effort to explain such differences as a function of school factors was certainly warranted. Again, evidence consistent with a null hypothesis does not mean it is true.

Finally, there is the question of whether a particular level-1 predictor belongs in the model at all. To delete a variable, two conditions must apply: first, no evidence of slope heterogeneity, as discussed above; and second, no evidence of an "average" or fixed effect. In the latter case, the corresponding γ_{q0} would be small in magnitude and the t ratio would be nonsignificant.

To check for the possibility that a level-1 predictor has, on average, a nonzero fixed effect, one can simply add that predictor to the model and test the significance of the associated coefficient. This method assumes that the association between the predictor of interest and the outcome is linear. The linearity assumption can be examined graphically by plotting the level-1 empirical Bayes residuals (see Equation 3.63) against the predictor of interest. Fitting a nonparametric nonlinear curve (such as a "lowess" line) will generally reveal nonlinearities in the association. Such nonparametric curves are now routinely computed by standard statistical software.

Specification Issues at Level 1

The specification assumption implies that no level-1 predictor can be omitted from the model if that predictor is both related to Y_{ij} and related to one of the Xs in the model. If such a predictor is omitted, estimation of one or more of the βs will be biased. As a consequence, the level-2 model for this β may also be biased. However, as we discuss below, there are conditions under which such bias will not occur.

We note that this assumption may be violated even if an omitted level-1 predictor has, on average, no effect within units. That is, its fixed effect may be null, but failure to include it will still misspecify the level-1 model if the predictor's effect varies from group to group and is related to other random level-1 coefficients. For example, in Raudenbush, Kidchanapanish, and Kang's (1991) study of primary schools in Thailand, the fixed effect of student gender on mathematics achievement across Thai primary schools was null. However, the magnitude and direction of the effect varied from school to school. In some schools, boys significantly outscored girls, whereas in other schools, girls scored higher.

Consequences of Level-1 Misspecification for Level-2 Estimates

Intercept Model. It is well known that failure to specify a level-1 covariate can lead to a serious bias in the estimation of level-2 predictors of the intercept. For example, there is available in the High School and Beyond data a measure of student's prior academic background (ACADEMIC BACKGROUND) that we have ignored so far in our analyses. If ACADEMIC BACKGROUND is related to math achievement, and if Catholic and public school students differ significantly on ACADEMIC BACKGROUND, then our previous estimates of the effect of SECTOR on β_{0j} will be biased.

This bias can be removed in one of two ways, depending on the centering option selected for ACADEMIC BACKGROUND. If ACADEMIC BACKGROUND is entered at level 1 and centered around its grand mean, each unit's intercept, β_{0j}, is adjusted for mean differences among schools on this variable, and this source of bias is thereby eliminated, assuming ACADEMIC BACKGROUND is measured without error and is linearly related to the outcome. Alternatively, ACADEMIC BACKGROUND could be added at level 1 with group-mean centering. In this case, the bias is eliminated by including the school mean of ACADEMIC BACKGROUND as a level-2 predictor of the intercept. The latter option is preferable if a compositional effect of ACADEMIC BACKGROUND exists (see Chapter 5) or if the ACADEMIC BACKGROUND slopes were treated as random.

TABLE 9.1 Confounding Effects of Academic Background[a]

Fixed Effect	Original Model Estimates		With Fixed Effect of ACADEMIC BACKGROUND Added	
	Coefficient	se	Coefficient	se
Model for school means, β_{0j}				
INTERCEPT, γ_{00}	13.73	0.20	13.74	0.20
MEAN SES, γ_{01}	4.54	0.48	4.55	0.48
SECTOR, γ_{02}	0.83	0.20	0.83	0.20
Model for SES slopes, β_{1j}				
INTERCEPT, γ_{10}	1.78	0.16	1.13	0.16
MEAN SES, γ_{11}	0.68	0.38	0.29	0.36
SECTOR, γ_{12}	−0.58	0.16	−0.39	0.15
Model for ACADEMIC BACKGROUND slopes, β_{2j}				
INTERCEPT, γ_{20}			2.14	0.09

a. The data employed in this chapter are similar but not identical to those analyzed in Chapters 4 and 5. Because of missing information on the new level-1 predictor, ACADEMIC BACKGROUND, the analytic sample is somewhat different here. Also MEAN SES is a school measure of social class and not the simple average of the individual student's information used at level 1. Finally, SECTOR is coded as −1 for PUBLIC SCHOOLS and 1 for CATHOLIC SCHOOLS. These differences have no effect on the illustrations of this chapter, but they do mean that results are not strictly comparable to those of earlier chapters.

Slope Model. Consequences of misspecification at level 1 on the modeling of slopes at level 2 are a bit more complex than for the intercept. These consequences are most easily understood in the context of a specific example. (For a formal derivation, see the appendix to this chapter.) Suppose that in the level-1 model of Equation 9.1 a confounding variable, ACADEMIC BACKGROUND, should have been included. To illustrate the effects on the estimated γ coefficients in the slope model, we reanalyzed the data, adding ACADEMIC BACKGROUND as a predictor at level 1. Table 9.1 provides the results. Formally, ACADEMIC BACKGROUND is a confounding variable at level 1: It both predicts the outcome and is related to SES.

In order to restrict our attention at this point to consequences for the SES slope model, we centered ACADEMIC BACKGROUND about its school mean. As Table 9.1 indicates, the addition of ACADEMIC BACKGROUND under these conditions has no effect on the model for the intercept. (Note that $\hat{\gamma}_{01}$ and $\hat{\gamma}_{02}$ are virtually identical with and without ACADEMIC BACKGROUND.)

On the other hand, the estimated effects in the slope model have changed quite substantially. It is logical that the estimate of γ_{10} should be affected by the omission of ACADEMIC BACKGROUND. Because ACADEMIC BACKGROUND and SES are both positively related to achievement and positively related to each other, γ_{10}, which is the average SES slope within schools, ought to be smaller when ACADEMIC BACKGROUND is controlled. The results in Table 9.1 confirm this reasoning: The γ_{01} estimate diminishes from 1.78 to 1.13 when ACADEMIC BACKGROUND is added.

The sources of bias in estimating γ_{11} and γ_{12} are more complicated. These two coefficients are termed *cross-level interaction effects* because they involve the interaction between level-2 variables (MEAN SES and SECTOR) and a level-1 variable (SES). For an omitted level-1 predictor to confound inferences about cross-level interactions, three conditions must hold (these are proved in the appendix to this chapter):

1. The omitted variable must be related to Y, controlling for other predictors in the model.
2. The omitted variable must be related to an X already included in the model.
3. The association between the omitted variable and X must itself vary from unit to unit; and the strength of this association between the omitted variable and X must be related to a level-2 predictor.

It is clear from Table 9.1 that the failure to include ACADEMIC BACKGROUND biases estimates of γ_{11} and γ_{12}. In both cases, the magnitudes of their effects are substantially diminished after ACADEMIC BACKGROUND is added: The effect of MEAN SES on the SES slope drops from .68 to .29; the magnitude of the SECTOR effect goes from $-.58$ to $-.39$.

Each of the three conditions stated above applies in this case. Condition 1 can be examined through a simple regression analysis of math achievement on SES and ACADEMIC BACKGROUND. Not suprisingly, ACADEMIC BACKGROUND is related to math achievement even after controlling for SES. Conditions 2 and 3 can be investigated using a random-coefficient model that regresses ACADEMIC BACKGROUND on SES (see Table 9.2). Clearly, the mean ACADEMIC BACKGROUND-SES slope, γ_{01}, is highly significant, $t = 11.56$ (condition 2). Further, there is evidence that these relationships vary across schools [$\mathrm{Var}(\beta_{1j}) = .016, p = .017$], and that these slopes are significantly related to other school variables considered in the analysis, MEAN SES and SECTOR (condition 3; see t-to-enter statistics in the last panel of Table 9.2).

Consequences of Level-2 Misspecification for Level-1 Estimates

If an omitted level-2 predictor is associated with a level-1 predictor, the coefficient for that level-1 predictor will be estimated with bias. In this case, we have $\mathrm{Cov}(u_{qj}, X_{q'ij}) \neq 0$. This problem can be solved, however, without

TABLE 9.2 Random-Coefficient Regression of ACADEMIC BACKGROUND on SES

Model

$$Y_{ij} = \beta_{0j} + \beta_{1j}(SES)_{ij} + r_{ij}$$

where Y_{ij} = academic background of student i in school j

$$\beta_{0j} = \gamma_{00} + u_{0j}$$
$$\beta_{1j} = \gamma_{01} + u_{1j}$$

Fixed Effect	Coefficient	se	t Ratio
Mean intercept, γ_{00}	0.052	0.027	1.939
MEAN SES slope, γ_{01}	0.262	0.023	11.560

Random Effect	Variance Component	df	χ^2	p Value
INTERCEPT, u_{0j}	0.081	159	597.5	0.000
SES slope, u_{1j}	0.016	159	198.9	0.017

Exploratory Regressions of β_{1j}^* on MEAN SES and SECTOR[a]

	Coefficient	se	Approximate t-to-Enter
MEAN SES	−0.038	0.014	−2.750
SECTOR	−0.030	0.005	−5.591

a. Based on use of empirical Bayes residuals as described in this chapter.

elaborating the level-2 model. Any covariance between a level-1 predictor, X_{qij}, and a level-2 random effect must operate through the covariance between the group mean $\overline{X}_{qj}$ and that random effect. Such a covariance can be eliminated by group-mean centering of the level-1 predictor.[1] Alternatively, inclusion of $\overline{X}_{qj}$ as a covariate in each level-2 equation will eliminate any confounding between X_{qij} and omitted variables at level 2.

These two approaches suggest a specification test for the effect of omitted level-2 predictors on a fixed level-1 coefficient. One runs the model with and without group-mean centering of the level-1 coefficient. If the fixed level-1 coefficient associated with that level-1 predictor remains essentially unchanged, the model is not vulnerable to this type of bias.

Errors of Measurement in Level-1 Predictors

If SES were measured with error, the β_{1j} estimates would be biased, and the mean slope, γ_{10}, would also be biased. In terms of the cross-level interactions, γ_{11} and γ_{12}, it is shown in the appendix to this chapter that bias results only if (a) the reliability of the SES measure varies from school to school; and (b) this variation in reliability is related to one or more level-2 predictors included in the model.

Examining Assumptions about Level-1 Random Effects

Homogeneity of Variance

In most multilevel applications, the errors in the level-1 model are assumed to have equal variance, σ^2. Because of limits on the amount of data available within each unit, investigators generally will wish to begin with this homogeneity assumption. (Some alternative specifications for the level-1 variance were discussed in Chapters 5 and 6.) If the level-1 variance varies randomly over level-2 units but these variances are assumed equal, consequences for inference about the level-2 coefficients will be mild. No bias will arise, and even the standard errors have been found to be quite robust (Kasim & Raudenbush, 1998). On the other hand, if the variances depend systematically as a function of level-1 or level-2 predictors, consequences may be more serious.

Once a tentative model has been specified, the investigator may test the homogeneity of level-1 variances. Heterogeneity may have several causes:

1. One or more important level-1 predictor variables may have been omitted from the model. If such a variable were distributed with unequal variance across groups, failure to include it would cause heterogeneity of variance at level 1.

2. The effects of a level-1 predictor that is random or nonrandomly varying may have been erroneously treated as fixed or omitted entirely from the model.

3. One or more units may have bad data. For example, a simple coding error could cause inflated variance in one or a few groups, yielding significant heterogeneity of variance overall.

4. Nonnormal data with heavy tails (i.e., more extreme observations than normally expected) can cause a significant test statistic for heterogeneity of variance. Parametric tests are sensitive to such nonnormality, and kurtosis (heavy tails) can masquerade as variance heterogeneity.

Because these causes are quite different in their implications, we advise investigation of the possible sources of heterogeneity before concluding that a more complex variance assumption is needed. For this purpose, it is useful to compute the standardized measure of dispersion for each group j introduced in Chapter 7:

$$d_j = \frac{\ln(S_j^2) - [\sum f_j \ln(S_j^2)/ \sum f_j]}{(2/f_j)^{1/2}}.$$ [9.5]

A simple and commonly used test statistic for homogeneity is

$$H = \sum d_j^2,$$ [9.6]

which has a large sample χ^2 distribution with $J - 1$ degrees of freedom under the homogeneity hypothesis. This test is appropriate when the data are normal and sample sizes per unit are 10 or more (Bartlett & Kendall, 1946; see also Raudenbush & Bryk, 1987).

A likelihood-ratio test can also be used to assess heterogeneity at level 1. The model with homogeneous variance becomes the restricted model to be compared with a more general alternative (e.g., a different level-1 variance, σ_j^2, for each of the J level-2 units). The deviance statistics from these alternative models are compared using the standard procedure introduced in Chapter 3.

To illustrate, we tested the homogeneity of variance assumption after fitting the model specified by Equations 9.1 and 9.2. The H statistic was 312.13 with 159 df, which is significant beyond the .001 level. This result indicates that heterogeneity of level-1 variance exists among the 160 schools, and encourages closer scrutiny of the level-1 model before proceeding further.

One possibility is that a few unusual schools account for most of the observed heterogeneity. In fact, a probability plot of the standardized dispersion measures suggests an unusually large number of schools with smaller than expected residual dispersion (see Figure 9.1). These cases are readily apparent in a stem and leaf of the d_j (see Figure 9.2). Next, we visually inspected data from the five most extreme cases identified in Figure 9.2. The recorded information seemed accurate, and the problem appears to be an unusually homogeneous intake of students. This suggests that we consider including additional variables in Equation 9.1 in an attempt to remove at least some of the residual heterogeneity.

In general, a violation of the homogeneity assumption is not per se a serious problem for estimating either the level-2 coefficients or their standard errors. We are principally concerned about it because such heterogeneity may indicate a possible misspecification of the level-1 model. In particular, unidentified slope heterogeneity at level 1 would appear as heterogeneity of level-1 error variance. As noted earlier, such slope heterogeneity can bias estimates of the level-2 coefficients.

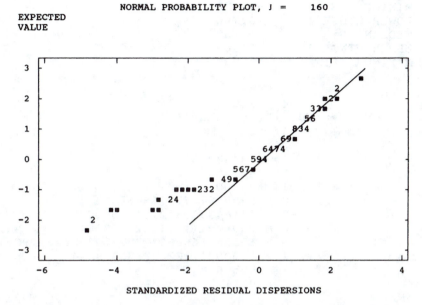

Figure 9.1. Probability Plot of Residual Dispersions for 160 High Schools[a]

a. The standardized residual dispersion is given by Equation 9.5.

A word of caution is in order about the standardized residuals and heterogeneity statistics illustrated above. Although these statistics can be informative, they are quite sensitive to violation of normality in the observed data. We also note that extreme individual values of d_j contribute most to the magnitude of the heterogeneity statistic, H. Hence, examining these, as we did above, can inform investigators about which types of units may have unusual variances. Some further investigation of the quality of data within certain units may be needed. In other cases, a transformation of Y may reduce the effect of heavy-tailed data. In other instances, we may identify a regular pattern where d_j is related to a particular unit characteristic such as sector. Such variables are candidates for inclusion in the level-2 models as predictors for random level-1 slope coefficients. (For a further discussion, see Raudenbush and Bryk, 1987.)

When level-1 variances are suspected to depend on measured predictors, one option is to fit log-linear models that incorporate these predictors (see "Applications with Heterogeneous level-1 Variance" in Chapter 5). In some cases, heterogeneous level-1 variances signal the need to specify certain level-1 coefficients as randomly varying at level 2.

```
MINIMUM IS:          -4.878
LOWER HINGE IS:      -0.706
MEDIAN IS:            0.159
UPPER HINGE IS:       0.962
MAXIMUM IS:           2.789
```

```
        -4    86510
    ***OUTSIDE VALUES***
        -3    0
        -2    995
        -2    43333210
        -1    866555
        -1    33300
        -0  H 9998887777776666555
        -0    44444333332211111000000
         0  M 000000111111222233344
         0  H 5555556666667777777788888889999
         1    000000111222223334444444
         1    555567889
         2    0111
         2    7
```

Figure 9.2. Stem-and-Leaf Plot of Residual Dispersions for 160 High Schools

Normality Assumption

Chapter 10 discusses application of hierarchical models for several types of outcomes for which normality at level 1 is clearly implausible. These include binary outcomes, count data, ordinal outcomes, and multinomial outcomes. In these cases, probability models other than the normal are clearly preferable. Moreover, nonlinear link functions are also sensible and lead to natural and interpretable effect sizes for coefficients at each level.

Suppose, however, that the outcome is continuous and a linear model at level 1 seems natural. The normality assumption may nonetheless fail. In this case, nonnormality of the errors at level 1 will not bias estimation of the level-2 effects, but it will introduce bias into standard errors at both levels and therefore into the computation of confidence intervals and hypothesis tests. Little is currently known about the direction and severity of such effects.

Data normality can be checked by computing separate probability plots for each unit or, if the number of units J is large, by looking at a normal probability plot for the residuals pooled across units. (These pooled plots will be misleading in the presence of heterogeneity of variance, however.) A transformation of the outcome or one or more of the predictors may improve the normality of the error distribution.

Building the Level-2 Model

Much of what we have said about model building at level 1 also applies at level 2. Ideally, the task should be theory-driven, where specific hypotheses are posed about expected relationships in each of the $Q + 1$ level-2 equations. Again, a backward solution of entering all possible level-2 predictors and removing the nonsignificant ones is generally not workable because of limits imposed by the number of level-2 units and likely multicollinearity problems.

A common rule of thumb for a regression analysis is that one needs at least 10 observations for each predictor. The analogous rules for hierarchical models are a bit more complex. For predicting a single level-2 outcome, for example, β_{0j}, the number of observations is the number of level-2 units, J, and the conventional 10-observations rule can be applied against this count.

With multiple βs as level-2 outcomes the total number of predictors that may be included in all level-2 equations is not clear. If the βs were mutually independent, then the 10-observations rule would apply separately to each of the $Q + 1$ equations. We suspect that this rule is too liberal, however, with correlated outcomes and the possibility of multicollinearity both within and between equations. Therefore, we urge a cautious approach examining possible collinearity among the level-2 predictors and monitoring the standard errors of the estimates as new predictors are entered.

When adding fixed level-1 predictors to the model, the intraclass correlation for each predictor is crucial. If this is null (for example when predictors are group-mean centered), the total number of observations for applying the 10-observations rule is the total number of level-1 units. In contrast, as the intraclass correlation approaches 1.0, the number of level-1 predictors that can be added is constrained by the number of level-2 units, J.

If hierarchical analyses are to be used in an exploratory mode, we suggest dividing the level-2 predictors into conceptually distinct subsets and fitting a submodel for each. The strongest predictors from these submodels might then be combined in an overall model. This exploratory approach was used by Bryk and Thum (1989) in an examination of school correlates of student absenteeism and dropping out.

Whenever hierarchical models involve both random intercepts and random or nonrandomly varying slopes, the analyst will usually want to develop a tentative model for the intercept, β_{0j}, before proceeding to fit models for the random slopes. This is akin in a general linear model analysis to fitting the main effects first before considering interaction effects. In a hierarchical analysis, the interactions of primary interest are cross-level. (Of course, interactions at just level 1 or level 2 are also possible.)

Empirical Methods to Guide Model Building at Level 2

The most direct evidence of whether a level-2 predictor should be included is the magnitude of its estimated effect and related t ratio. Predictors with t ratios near or less than 1 are obvious candidates for exclusion from the model.

Analysis of Empirical Bayes Residuals

On the more exploratory side, an examination of the empirical Bayes residuals at level 2 is often helpful. These empirical Bayes residuals exist for each group (even those with deficient rank data) and tend to be less influenced by estimation error than do the OLS residuals (although these too can be used).

Table 9.3 presents simple Pearson correlations between both empirical Bayes and OLS residuals and school-level variables considered as potential candidates for entry into the level-2 model. (The residuals are based on the level-1 model of Equation 9.1 and an unconditional level-2 model.) Note that the correlations with the intercept, β_{0j}, are quite similar for both empirical Bayes and OLS. Given the high reliability of $\hat{\beta}_{0j}$ (reported as .91 in Chapter 4), this is not surprising. The correlations involving the empirical Bayes residuals for the SES slope, however, are much stronger than those

TABLE 9.3 Correlations of Empirical Bayes and OLS residuals[a] (Level 2) with Other Potential School-Level Variables

School-Level Variables to Enter	Empirical Bayes INTERCEPT	SES Slope	Ordinary Least Squares INTERCEPT	SES Slope
Average # math courses	0.644	−0.348	0.643	−0.099
School size	−0.109	0.187	−0.095	0.109
High minority	−0.343	0.057	−0.340	−0.005
sd math courses	−0.289	0.336	−0.277	0.199
% academic program	0.634	−0.334	0.630	−0.093
Academic climate	0.595	−0.289	0.597	−0.060
Disciplinary climate	−0.469	0.327	−0.472	0.123

a. The OLS and empirical Bayes residuals are computed using the procedure illustrated by Equations 3.49 and 3.50.

EB RESIDUALS
FOR SES SLOPES

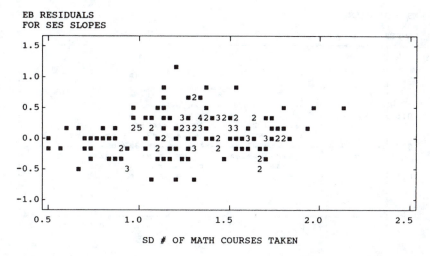

Figure 9.3. Plots of SES Slope Residuals Versus Excluded Variable (SD # OF MATH COURSES)

based on the OLS residuals. The larger sampling variability associated with $\hat{\beta}_{1j}$ (the estimated reliability of $\hat{\beta}_{1j}$ was .23 in Chapter 4) accounts for the much smaller correlations when using OLS residuals.

Plots of residuals against potential level-2 predictor variables can also help to identify the functional form of these additional relations. Figure 9.3 plots the empirical Bayes residuals for the SES slopes against the standard deviation of the number of math courses taken in each school. SES slopes have a positive linear relationship with this school variable ($r = .336$ from Table 9.3). This suggests that the SES differentiation effects (i.e., SES slopes) are somewhat greater in schools where there is more diversity in math course taking.

Similarly, plotting the residuals against the predictors in the tentative model provides a graphical check on the adequacy of the structural portion for each level-2 equation. In Figure 9.4, the empirical Bayes residuals for the SES slope from the fitted model of column 1 in Table 9.1 are plotted against MEAN SES. Because MEAN SES was included as a predictor of the SES slope, we expect homoscedastic residuals randomly dispersed around zero. With the exception perhaps of one case, circled in the plot, the assumption of a linear relationship between MEAN SES and the SES slope seems quite reasonable.

EB RESIDUALS
FOR SES
SLOPES

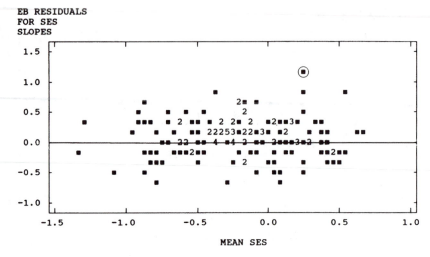

Figure 9.4. Plot of Empirical Bayes Residuals for SES Slopes Versus Included Variable (MEAN SES)

Approximate t-to-Enter Statistics

Another approach to investigating potential variables to be included in the level-2 model involves a simple univariate regression of the empirical Bayes residuals from each of the $Q + 1$ equations on W variables that might be added to the model. One can compute an approximate "t-to-enter" statistic in this way. An example of these statistics was reported in the last panel of Table 9.2. These t statistics are often the best indicators for selecting W variables.

Although regression coefficients based on empirical Bayes residuals are preferable to those based on the OLS residuals, they still underestimate the effects of the W variables when actually included in the model. Fortunately, the standard errors for the regression coefficients are also underestimated by approximately the same proportion, and thus the t-to-enter statistics will often provide a good indication of the likely consequences. These statistics are, however, only approximate because the model is doubly multivariate with errors correlated across equations and multiple predictors for each equation. They will usually provide a good indication of the next *single* variable to enter *one* of the level-2 equations. If several variables are entered simultaneously (e.g., one on each of several equations), the actual results may not follow the pattern suggested by these statistics.

Specification Issues at Level 2

A proper specification is assumed for each of the $Q + 1$ level-2 equations. That is, the error term, u_{qj}, for each equation is assumed uncorrelated with predictors in that equation. This means that any omitted predictors are unrelated to those already included in the model. A corollary of this assumption is that all predictors (i.e., the W_js) are measured without error.

If a confounding variable (i.e., a significant predictor correlated with one or more of the level-2 predictors already included in the equation) is ignored in one of these equations, estimation of one or more level-2 coefficients in that equation will be biased. The degree of bias depends on the predictive power of the omitted variable and its strength of association with other variables in the model.

Further, misspecification of one equation can cause biased estimates in another equation. That is, an individual level-2 equation could be properly specified and yet its estimated coefficient be biased. This bias is induced through the correlation among the errors in the properly and improperly specified equations. A specification test and ameliorative procedures for such cross-equation bias are described below.

Consequences of Level-2 Misspecification

Again, we revert to a specific example to illuminate the problem. For this purpose, we assume Equations 9.1 and 9.2 are properly specified. Thus, the "correct" estimates appear in the first column of Table 9.4.

Assume that MEAN SES were incorrectly dropped from the intercept model. Results for this incorrect specification are reported in the second

TABLE 9.4 Illustration of Misspecification Effects

	Original Model		MEAN SES Missing		Specification Test (Fixed SES Slopes)	
	Coefficient	se	Coefficient	se	Coefficient	se
Model for school means, β_{0j}						
INTERCEPT, γ_{00}	13.73	0.20	12.90	0.23	12.90	0.23
MEAN SES, γ_{01}	4.53	0.48	—	—	—	—
SECTOR, γ_{02}	0.83	0.20	1.56	0.23	1.56	0.23
Model for SES slopes, β_{1j}						
INTERCEPT, γ_{10}	1.78	0.16	1.82	0.16	1.80	0.15
MEAN SES, γ_{11}	0.68	0.38	0.93	0.38	0.73	0.34
SECTOR, γ_{12}	−0.58	0.16	−0.62	0.16	−0.61	0.14

set of columns in Table 9.4. Because MEAN SES and SECTOR are positively correlated, deleting MEAN SES results in an overestimation of the SECTOR effect in the intercept equation by a factor of almost two from 0.83 to 1.56. Further, as noted above, the estimates in the SES slope model are also affected. The coefficient for MEAN SES, γ_{11}, is now inflated by a factor of 40% from 0.68 to 0.93. The misspecification of the intercept model has led to a distortion in the slope model as well. This has occurred because the errors of the two models are correlated.

A Specification Test

The coefficient estimates for the intercept and slope equations are independent (and thus not influenced by a specification error in the other) if the sum of the sampling covariance between $\hat{\beta}_{0j}$ and $\hat{\beta}_{1j}$ and the covariance of the true β_{0j} and β_{1j} are zero. Although this condition will rarely arise in practice, the analyst can use this as the basis for a specification test. Specifically, centering the level-1 predictors around their unit means guarantees that the sampling covariances with the intercept will be null; and constraining that slope to have a zero error term sets the parameter covariance of the slope and intercept to zero. This leads to a specification check to examine whether the estimates in each level-2 equation have been distorted by misspecification in another equation.

The last set of columns in Table 9.4 demonstrates the specification check where the residual variance for the SES slope model has been set to zero. Even though the BASE model is seriously misspecified due to the omission of MEAN SES, notice that the γ estimates in the SES slope model are not nearly as distorted as in column 3. The fact that the results in columns 3 and 5 differ indicate a likely misspecification for the model in column 3. We caution, however, that a model with a level-2 variance constrained to zero should be used only as a specification test (assuming that the corresponding variance component is really not zero). By setting the residual variance to zero, we have overestimated the precision of the γ coefficients. Note that the standard errors for the γs in the slope model in column 6 are artificially smaller than the corresponding estimates in column 2.

An Ameliorative Strategy

The biased estimates in a properly specified level-2 equation that result from a misspecification in another level-2 equation and correlated errors between these two equations can be avoided if the same predictor set is used for all $Q + 1$ equations. Formally, if the same predictor set is used in each equation *and* if the data are perfectly balanced (i.e., each school had the same sample size and the same set of SES values), the estimates of the level-2 coefficients in the slope model would be independent of the estimated coefficients in the intercept model. Even when the data are unbalanced, the estimates in the slope model will be *asymptotically* independent of the estimates in the intercept model and they will be asymptotically unbiased.

In many applications, the analyst will not want to force every W in any of the $Q + 1$ equations into all of the $Q + 1$ equations. (Parsimony objects and so may your computer.) At a minimum, the investigator should check that any predictor included in one of the level-2 equations but excluded from others is in fact nonsignificant. The exploratory analyses using empirical Bayes residuals described above can provide a useful check in this regard.

Errors of Measurement in Level-2 Predictors

Errors of measurement can be viewed as a specific form of a misspecification problem (see the chapter appendix). Thus, all of the concerns described above also apply to fallible level-2 predictors. In general, if a level-2 predictor is measured with error, its coefficient and possibly other level-2 coefficients will be biased. The degree of bias depends on the explanatory power of the true predictor, the degree of unreliability of measurement, and the intercorrelations among the predictors.

Chapter 11 provides methods for incorporating knowledge about the measurement error of level-2 predictors through the use of latent variable models. Explicit measurement models for these predictors can enable the analyst to control bias in the estimation of level-2 coefficients.

Examining Assumptions about Level-2 Random Effects

Homogeneity

We typically assume that the dispersion of the level-2 random effects is homogeneous across the J units. A failure of this assumption could occur in the High School and Beyond data, for example, if schools in the Catholic sector had less variable random effects than did schools in the public sector. (Parenthetically, such sector differences might be of substantive interest.)

In terms of the fixed effects, the consequences of inappropriately assuming homogeneity would be a somewhat less than optimal weighting in estimating these effects, resulting in some loss of efficiency. The level-2 coefficients estimates would, however, remain unbiased. In terms of the random effects, the shrinkage in β_j^* would be incorrect and result in an increased mean squared error for estimation of β_j.

Equality of dispersion in $\mathbf{T}$ can formally be tested against alternative hypotheses. For example, one might estimate separate $\mathbf{T}$ matrices for the Catholic and public sectors. This would add $m(m+1)/2$ variance-covariance components to be estimated and a likelihood-ratio test could be employed to test the equality of the $\mathbf{T}$ matrices. Discovering the sources of such inequalities would be very much like the process described above for studying heterogeneity of σ^2.

Normality

Estimation of the fixed effects will not be biased by a failure of the normality assumption at level 2. However, if the level-2 random effects have heavy tails, hypothesis tests and confidence intervals based on normality may be sensitive to outliers. A failure of the normality assumption will affect the validity of the confidence intervals and hypothesis tests for the fixed effects. The nature of these effects depends on the true shape of the distribution of the random effects. Seltzer (1993) discusses the types of distortion that can occur.

Checking for normality at level 2 is complicated by the fact that the level-2 outcomes, β_{qj}, are not directly observed. The empirical Bayes residuals can be plotted and the plots inspected for outlier values. Moreover, their marginal variances can be estimated so that they can be standardized and compared to the expected values of normal order statistics from the unit normal distribution. However, when the sample size per group, n_j, is small, these variance estimates will be quite uncertain, so that the true variance of the standardized residuals may be somewhat greater than unity.

Complicating the checking of the normality assumption is that the $Q+1$ correlated random effects may be estimated per unit. A *Mahalanobis distance measure* for each unit can help in assessing the degree of departure of the random effects from normality and allows detection of outliers. This statistic measures the distance between the residual estimates for each group relative to the expected distance based on the model.[2] Given sufficiently large samples at level 1, this statistic will have a χ^2 distribution with $Q+1$ degrees of freedom when the data are normal. Plotting the observed distance statistics against the expected order statistics allows graphical inspection of possible departures from normality. In addition, one can identify outlier units for further examination.

Figure 9.5 displays Mahalanobis distance plots for two different models. The first plot is from a level-1 model with a random intercept and SES slope.

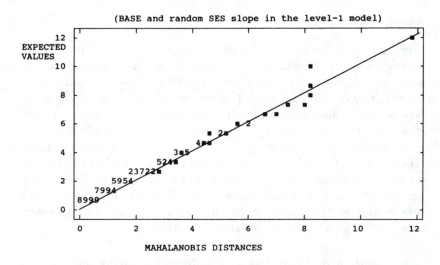

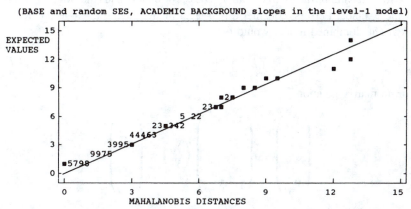

Figure 9.5. Mahalanobis Plots for Examining Normality Assumption

The second plot is based on a model where a random ACADEMIC BACK-GROUND slope has been added. Neither model appears grossly nonnormal.

If serious nonnormality is encountered at level 2, procedures developed by Seltzer (1993) can be helpful. In particular, if the random effects at level 2 have heavy tails, Seltzer has demonstrated that the *data augmentation* method of Tanner and Wong (1987) can be used to estimate the hierarchical linear model. In addition, his results show that a "*t* prior" for the level-2 random effects provides robust estimates of the fixed effects. These estimates are less sensitive to outlier values at level 2.

Robust Standard Errors

In many applications, the primary interest is in the fixed coefficients, denoted by γ. In standard applications of hierarchical models, inferences about these depend to some degree on assumptions about the distribution of the random effects at each level. It would be unfortunate if false assumptions about the random effects seriously distorted inferences about the fixed effects. To check the sensitivity of inferences about the fixed effects to these assumptions about the random effects, it is often useful to compute robust or "Huber-corrected" standard errors. Liang and Zeger (1986) discussed these in the case of longitudinal analysis using nonlinear models. Use of these robust standard errors is most appropriate when the number of highest-level units is large. Such standard errors can be computed in conjunction with ordinary least squares (OLS) or HLM estimates of the fixed effects.

Robust Standard Errors Under OLS. To understand the logic behind robust standard errors, consider a two-level model having a single predictor, X_{ij}. The combined model would be

$$Y_{ij} = \gamma_0 + \gamma_1 X_{ij} + e_{ij} \qquad [9.7]$$

or, in matrix notation,

$$\begin{pmatrix} Y_{1j} \\ \cdot \\ \cdot \\ \cdot \\ Y_{n_j j} \end{pmatrix} = \begin{pmatrix} 1 & X_{1j} \\ & \cdot \\ & \cdot \\ & \cdot \\ 1 & X_{n_j j} \end{pmatrix} \begin{pmatrix} \gamma_0 \\ \gamma_1 \end{pmatrix} + \begin{pmatrix} e_{1j} \\ \cdot \\ \cdot \\ \cdot \\ e_{n_j j} \end{pmatrix} \qquad [9.8]$$

or, more compactly,

$$\mathbf{Y}_j = \mathbf{X}_j \boldsymbol{\gamma} + \mathbf{e}_j. \qquad [9.9]$$

Under OLS assumptions and normality, we have

$$\mathbf{e}_j \sim \mathrm{N}(\mathbf{0}, \sigma^2 \mathbf{I}_{n_j}), \qquad [9.10]$$

justifying the OLS estimator

$$\hat{\boldsymbol{\gamma}} = \left(\sum_{j=1}^{J} \mathbf{X}_j^T \mathbf{X}_j \right)^{-1} \sum_{j=1}^{J} \mathbf{X}_j^T \mathbf{Y}_j. \qquad [9.11]$$

To derive the variance of this estimator, we recall that, if C is a constant matrix and Z is a random vector, $\text{Var}(CZ) = C\text{Var}(Z)C^T$. Applying this identity to Equation 9.11 yields

$$\text{Var}(\hat{\boldsymbol{\gamma}}) = \left(\sum_{j=1}^{J} \mathbf{X}_j^T \mathbf{X}_j\right)^{-1} \sum_{j=1}^{J} \mathbf{X}_j^T [\text{Var}(\mathbf{Y}_j)] \mathbf{X}_j \left(\sum_{j=1}^{J} \mathbf{X}_j^T \mathbf{X}_j\right)^{-1} . \quad [9.12]$$

Under the OLS assumptions, $\text{Var}(\mathbf{Y}_j) = \sigma^2 \mathbf{I}$, and Equation 9.12 simplifies to

$$\text{Var}(\hat{\boldsymbol{\gamma}}) = \sigma^2 \left(\sum_{j=1}^{J} \mathbf{X}_j^T \mathbf{X}_j\right)^{-1} . \quad [9.13]$$

Suppose, however, that the OLS assumptions were false and that the variance of Y had some unknown structure. We can exploit the fact that each level-2 unit j provides an approximately unbiased estimator

$$\widehat{\text{Var}}(Y_j) = (\mathbf{Y}_j - \mathbf{X}_j\hat{\boldsymbol{\gamma}})(\mathbf{Y}_j - \mathbf{X}_j\hat{\boldsymbol{\gamma}})^T \quad [9.14]$$

to derive a robust variance estimator

$$\widehat{\text{Var}}(\hat{\boldsymbol{\gamma}}) = \left(\sum_{j=1}^{J} \mathbf{X}_j^T \mathbf{X}_j\right)^{-1} \sum_{j=1}^{J} \mathbf{X}_j^T (\mathbf{Y}_j - \mathbf{X}_j\hat{\boldsymbol{\gamma}})$$

$$\times (\mathbf{Y}_j - \mathbf{X}_j\hat{\boldsymbol{\gamma}})^T \mathbf{X}_j \left(\sum_{j=1}^{J} \mathbf{X}_j^T \mathbf{X}_j\right)^{-1} . \quad [9.15]$$

This estimator is J-consistent, meaning that as J increases without bound, the estimator converges to the true standard error even if the OLS assumptions about e_j are false. Moreover,

$$(\hat{\gamma}_{qs} - \gamma_{qs})/[\widehat{\text{Var}}(\hat{\gamma}_{qs})]^{1/2} \quad [9.16]$$

is approximately normally distributed with zero mean and unit variance for large J. This enables computation of sensible confidence intervals and tests even when the underlying residuals e_{ij} are not normally distributed.

Robust Standard Errors Under GLS. The estimators of the γs under HLM are estimated generalized least squares estimators. Suppose that the residual under the model (Equation 9.7) is actually

$$e_{ij} = u_{0j} + u_{1j}X_{ij} + \varepsilon_{ij} \quad [9.17]$$

or, in matrix notation,

$$\mathbf{e}_j = \mathbf{X}_j\mathbf{u}_j + \boldsymbol{\varepsilon}_j. \quad [9.18]$$

Here $\mathbf{u}_j$ is the vector of level-2 random effects. The standard HLM assumptions would be

$$\mathbf{u}_j \sim N(0, \mathbf{T}), \qquad \boldsymbol{\varepsilon}_j \sim N(0, \sigma^2 \mathbf{I}_{n_j}), \qquad [9.19]$$

so that

$$\text{Var}(\mathbf{Y}_j) = \text{Var}(\mathbf{X}_j \mathbf{u}_j + \boldsymbol{\varepsilon}_j) \equiv \mathbf{V}_j = \mathbf{X}_j \mathbf{T} \mathbf{X}_j^T + \sigma^2 \mathbf{I}_{n_j}. \qquad [9.20]$$

Under these assumptions and normality, we have the GLS estimator

$$\hat{\boldsymbol{\gamma}} = \left(\sum_{j=1}^{J} \mathbf{X}_j^T \mathbf{V}_j^{-1} \mathbf{X}_j \right)^{-1} \sum_{j=1}^{J} \mathbf{X}_j^T \mathbf{V}_j^{-1} \mathbf{Y}_j. \qquad [9.21]$$

The computed GLS estimator substitutes estimates of T and σ^2 into Equation 9.21. The approximate variance of this estimator is

$$\text{Var}(\hat{\boldsymbol{\gamma}}) = \left(\sum_{j=1}^{J} \mathbf{X}_j^T \mathbf{V}_j^{-1} \mathbf{X}_j \right)^{-1}$$

$$\times \sum_{j=1}^{J} \mathbf{X}_j^T \mathbf{V}_j^{-1} [\text{Var}(\mathbf{Y}_j)] \mathbf{X}_j \mathbf{V}_j^{-1} \left(\sum_{j=1}^{J} \mathbf{X}_j^T \mathbf{V}_j^{-1} \mathbf{X}_j \right)^{-1}. \qquad [9.22]$$

Under the GLS assumptions, $\text{Var}(\mathbf{Y}_j) = \mathbf{V}_j$, and Equation 9.22 simplifies to

$$\text{Var}(\hat{\gamma}) = \left(\sum_{j=1}^{J} \mathbf{X}_j^T \mathbf{V}_j^{-1} \mathbf{X}_j \right)^{-1}. \qquad [9.23]$$

Suppose, however, that the GLS assumptions were false and that the variance of Y had some unknown structure. We can derive a robust variance estimator

$$\widehat{\text{Var}}(\hat{\boldsymbol{\gamma}}) = \left(\sum_{j=1}^{J} \mathbf{X}_j^T \mathbf{V}_j^{-1} \mathbf{X}_j \right)^{-1}$$

$$\times \sum_{j=1}^{J} \mathbf{X}_j^T \mathbf{V}_j^{-1} (\mathbf{Y}_j - \mathbf{X}_j \hat{\boldsymbol{\gamma}})(\mathbf{Y}_j - \mathbf{X}_j \hat{\boldsymbol{\gamma}})^T \mathbf{X}_j \mathbf{V}_j^{-1} \left(\sum_{j=1}^{J} \mathbf{X}_j^T \mathbf{V}_j^{-1} \mathbf{X}_j \right)^{-1}. \quad [9.24]$$

This robust variance estimator for the GLS case is J-consistent and supplies a basis for large-J confidence intervals and hypothesis tests even if the HLM assumptions about the distribution and covariance structure of the random effects are incorrect.

The robust variance estimates can be highly diagnostic. The analyst can examine discrepancies between model-based and robust standard errors. Large discrepancies typically signal model misspecification. For example, when slope heterogeneity exists but is not modeled, we typically find discrepancies between the model-based and robust standard errors. Incorporating the slope heterogeneity will, in this case, eliminate the discrepancy.

Illustration

We return to the model specified in Equations 9.1 and 9.2 for the High School and Beyond data. The combined model is

$$Y_{ij} = \gamma_{00} + \gamma_{01}(\text{MEAN SES})_j + \gamma_{02}(\text{SECTOR})_j + \gamma_{10}(\text{SES})_{ij}$$
$$+ \gamma_{11}(\text{MEAN SES})_j * (\text{SES})_{ij} + \gamma_{12}(\text{SECTOR})_j * (\text{SES})_{ij}$$
$$+ u_{0j} + u_{1j}(\text{SES})_{ij} + \varepsilon_{ij}. \qquad [9.25]$$

Table 9.5 provides estimates and standard errors of four types: (a) OLS estimates with OLS model-based standard errors; (b) OLS estimates with robust standard errors; (c) HLM estimates with model-based standard errors; and (d) HLM estimates with robust standard errors. A comparison of the four sets of results yields the following insights:

1. OLS and HLM point estimates of the γ coefficients are quite similar. Given the reasonably large J of 160, this is not surprising.

TABLE 9.5 Model-Based and Robust Variance Estimators for Fixed Effects[a]

Coefficient	OLS Coefficient	(a) OLS Model-Based se	(b) OLS Robust se
For β_{0j}			
INTERCEPT, γ_{00}	12.08	0.107	0.170
MEAN SES, γ_{01}	5.16	0.191	0.334
SECTOR, γ_{02}	1.28	0.158	0.299
For β_{1j}			
INTERCEPT, γ_{10}	2.94	0.155	0.148
MEAN SES, γ_{11}	1.04	0.300	0.333
SECTOR, γ_{12}	−1.64	0.240	0.237

Coefficient	HLM Coefficient	(c) HLM Model-Based se	(d) HLM Robust se
For β_{0j}			
INTERCEPT, γ_{00}	12.10	0.199	0.174
MEAN SES, γ_{02}	5.33	0.369	0.335
SECTOR, γ_{01}	1.23	0.306	0.308
For β_{1j}			
INTERCEPT, γ_{10}	2.94	0.157	0.148
MEAN SES, γ_{12}	1.03	0.303	0.333
SECTOR, γ_{11}	−1.64	0.243	0.237

a. Note that the sample and coding scheme for SECTOR used here are the same as in Chapter 4 (Table 4.5) but different from Table 9.1. This difference has no effect on the illustration.

2. The OLS model-based standard error estimates for predictors of the intercept are much smaller than the robust standard errors. In particular, for the association between SECTOR and the school intercept (see γ_{02}), the model-based estimate of 0.158 is just a little more than half of the robust standard error of 0.299. This makes sense: The OLS model is based on the false assumption of no variation between schools in the random effects u_{0j}. Given the large and highly statistically significant estimate of $\mathrm{Var}(u_{0j}) = \tau_{00}$, this OLS assumption leads to a severely negatively biased estimate of the standard error. In contrast, the robust standard error is not based on this assumption and does incorporate this source of between-school variation into the estimate.

3. The OLS model-based standard error estimates for predictors of the SES slope are not much different from the robust standard errors. In particular, for the association between SECTOR and the SES slope (see γ_{12}), the model-based estimate of 0.240 is nearly identical to the robust standard error of 0.237. This makes sense: The OLS model is based on the assumption of no variation between schools in the random effects u_{1j}. The HLM results give evidence in favor of this assumption; recall that the null hypothesis $\mathrm{Var}(u_{1j}) = \tau_{11} = 0$ was retained. Thus, for the SES slope, the OLS assumption finds support in the data and the OLS model-based standard errors and the robust standard errors agree.

4. The HLM model-based and robust standard errors are in quite close agreement with each other and with the robust standard errors based on OLS. Thus, the robust standard errors give no signal that the HLM is misspecified. This does not mean that the HLM assumptions are correct. It simply implies that the standard errors are insensitive to any error in the HLM assumptions regarding the covariance structure of the residuals.

Validity of Inferences when Samples are Small

In the special case of completely balanced data,[3] small-sample theory for inferences about the fixed effects holds. For example, the estimated value of a fixed effect divided by its standard error will be distributed exactly as a t variate. Exact inference about fixed effects is possible in the balanced case because the point estimates of the fixed effects do not depend on the variance components.[4]

In unbalanced cases, we rely on large-sample theory. Estimates of the fixed effects and their standard errors depend on point estimates of each of the variance and covariance components in the model. Because of the mutual dependence of the point estimates of the fixed effects and the point estimates of the variance-covariance components, the exact sampling distributions of the resulting estimators are unknown. However, when maximum likelihood estimation is used, the large-sample properties of the maximum likelihood estimators are known. The question in this section is: How well does the large-sample-distribution theory work?

For any particular application, the answer depends on the inferences sought. We consider below estimation of fixed effects γ, the variance-covariance components (σ^2 and $\mathbf{T}$), and the random effects, $\mathbf{u}$. To explicate basic principles and clarify the logic, we illustrate with a one-way random-effects ANOVA model.

Inferences about the Fixed Effects

For any sample size, fixed-effects estimates are unbiased. However, in the unbalanced case, the standard error estimates for the fixed effects are generally too small, and hypothesis tests based on the unit normal reference distribution will be too liberal.

The point estimate of γ_{00} in the one-way random-effects ANOVA model is from Equation 3.9:

$$\hat{\gamma}_{00} = \sum (\widehat{V}_j + \hat{\tau}_{00})^{-1} \overline{Y}_{\cdot j} / \sum (\widehat{V}_j + \hat{\tau}_{00})^{-1}, \qquad [9.26]$$

where

$$\widehat{V}_j = \hat{\sigma}^2 / n_j$$

and

$$\overline{Y}_{\cdot j} = \sum Y_{ij} / n_j.$$

The estimated standard error of $\hat{\gamma}_{00}$ is

$$[\widehat{V}(\hat{\gamma}_{00})]^{1/2} = \left[\sum (\widehat{V}_j + \hat{\tau}_{00})^{-1} \right]^{-1/2}. \qquad [9.27]$$

Note that, in general, the point estimate of γ_{00} and its estimated standard error are a function of estimates of σ^2 and τ_{00}. However, in the balanced case, this is not true:

$$\hat{\gamma}_{00} = \sum \overline{Y}_{\cdot\cdot} / J. \qquad [9.28]$$

Clearly, in the balanced case, $\hat{\gamma}_{00}$ does not depend on σ^2 or τ_{00}. Further, $V(\hat{\gamma}_{00})$ requires only an estimate of $V + \tau_{00}$ and not the separate components. (The usual estimate of $V + \tau_{00}$ is just the mean square between groups divided by n.)

Thus, in the balanced case,

$$(\hat{\gamma} - \gamma_0) / (\text{MS between} / nJ)^{1/2} \qquad [9.29]$$

will have a t distribution with $J - 1$ degrees of freedom under the null hypothesis $H_0: \gamma = \gamma_0$.

However, in the unbalanced case, no such exact test exists. We can say, however, that if σ^2 and τ_{00} are estimated by maximum likelihood, the large-sample distribution of

$$Z = (\hat{\gamma} - \gamma_0)/[V(\hat{\gamma})]^{1/2} \qquad [9.30]$$

is unit normal. In practice, however, use of a t reference distribution may be more appropriate. Fotiu (1989) simulated unbalanced data from hypothetical small-sample studies of classrooms in which both the intercept and the slope from each classroom depended on the assignment of that class to an experimental or control condition. His results showed that using the t distribution rather than the unit normal as the reference distribution produced substantially more accurate hypothesis tests for the fixed effects.

Second, the estimate $V(\hat{\gamma}_{00})$ is negatively biased. The true variance of $\hat{\gamma}_{00}$ will be

$$\mathrm{Var}(\hat{\gamma}_{00}) = \mathrm{E_m}\big[\mathrm{Var_c}(\hat{\gamma}_{00} \mid \hat{\tau}_{00}, \hat{\sigma}^2)\big] + \mathrm{Var_m}\big[\mathrm{E_c}(\hat{\gamma}_{00} \mid \hat{\tau}_{00}, \hat{\sigma}^2)\big], \qquad [9.31]$$

where the expectation and variance $\mathrm{E_m}$ and $\mathrm{Var_m}$ are taken over the joint distribution of $\hat{\tau}_{00}$ and $\hat{\sigma}^2$ and $\mathrm{E_c}$ and $\mathrm{Var_c}$ are taken over the conditional distribution of $\hat{\gamma}_{00}$ given $\hat{\tau}_{00}$ and $\hat{\sigma}^2$. The second term, which is the bias under maximum likelihood estimation, is zero in the balanced case and will converge to zero as J increases in the unbalanced case. Even in many small-sample cases (which are not too badly unbalanced), this term will be very small.

Given small to moderate sample size J at level 2, the key determinant of the size of the bias for $\widehat{V}(\hat{\gamma}_{00})$ will be the sensitivity of the $\hat{\gamma}_{00}$ estimates to differential weighting. Recall from Equation 9.26 that the estimate for $\hat{\gamma}_{00}$ is a weighted average based on $(V_j + \tau_{00})^{-1}$. As τ_{00} approaches zero, these weights approach n_j/σ^2 and $\hat{\gamma}_{00}$ approaches the weighted mean $\sum n_j \overline{Y}_{\cdot j}/ \sum n_j$. In contrast, for nonzero τ_{00}, $\hat{\gamma}_{00} = \sum \lambda_j \overline{Y}_{\cdot j}/ \sum \lambda_j$ with $\lambda_j = \tau_{00}/[\tau_{00} + (\sigma^2/n_j)]$. Hence, as τ_{00} increases, λ_j approaches 1 and $\hat{\gamma}_{00}$ approximates the arithmetic mean $\sum \overline{Y}_{\cdot j}/J$. If the weighted mean $\sum n_j \overline{Y}_{\cdot j}/ \sum n_j$ is highly discrepant from the arithmetic mean, the bias term in Equation 9.31 will be large and the hierarchical estimate of $V(\hat{\gamma}_{00})$ will be too small. If these weighted and unweighted averages are similar, the hierarchical estimate of $V(\hat{\gamma}_{00})$ will be nearly unbiased.

This analysis leads to the following general recommendations:

1. Use the t rather than the normal distribution to test hypotheses about γ.
2. Examine the sensitivily of the $\hat{\gamma}$ estimates to the choice of the weighting scheme. If the estimates are insensitive to the weighting scheme, use $V(\hat{\gamma})$ as the standard error estimate.

3. If the results are sensitive to the weighting scheme, t tests based on $V(\hat{\gamma})$ should be viewed as liberal. An exact solution is available through a Bayes approach. The Bayes estimates, which require substantial computation, take full account of the uncertainty about σ^2 and $\mathbf{T}$ in estimating the γs and their standard errors (Seltzer, 1993). See Chapter 13 for a detailed discussion.

Inferences about the Variance Components

Inferences about the variance components, σ^2 and $\mathbf{T}$, depend on the large-sample properties of maximum likelihood estimates. Technically, standard errors and hypothesis tests are based on the "information matrix" (see Chapter 10). Point estimates of σ^2 will generally be quite accurate in most applications. If σ^2 is assumed equal in every unit, then the precision of its estimation will depend on the total sample size ($N = \sum n_j$), which will typically be large. Similarly, likelihood-ratio tests and standard errors for σ^2 will tend to be accurate.

Problems may arise, however, if σ^2 is assumed to vary across level-2 units. The key issue is the number of observations n_j upon which each σ_j^2 is estimated. In these applications, the sample size in each unit, n_j, should be large. On the other hand, if σ_1^2 and σ_2^2 are estimated for each of two school sectors (e.g., Catholic versus public), the accuracy of estimation of these σ^2s and the credibility of inferences about them will depend on the total sample size in each sector.

In terms of $\mathbf{T}$, the accuracy of estimation depends on the number of level-2 units, J. Standard errors for the variances in $\mathbf{T}$ based on the information matrix require large J for credibility, especially if the estimate of the variance is near zero.

MLR Versus MLF. In Chapter 2, we introduced the distinction between the full and restricted likelihood. We noted that when J is small, MLF estimates for the $\mathbf{T}$ matrix are negatively biased and this problem will be exacerbated as the number of fixed effects in the model increases. However, MLF estimates, though biased, are not necessarily less accurate than MLR estimates as judged by expected mean squared error.

Type of Test. Chapter 2 introduced three types of tests for elements of $\mathbf{T}$: a univariate χ^2 test, a univariate test based on the ratio of an estimate to its standard error, and a likelihood-ratio test that is generally multivariate (because it simultaneously tests two or more elements of $\mathbf{T}$). Each of these tests is based on large-sample theory. However, our experience suggests that the test using the estimated standard errors of the $\mathbf{T}$ elements are especially untrustworthy when sample sizes are small. These tests are based on the notion of constructing a confidence interval with the estimate at its center. Such a test is informative only if the likelihood is symmetric about the mode. In many cases, however, the likelihood will be highly skewed. This will be especially true when the true variance is small, which is when the test is most needed. In general, the smaller the variance component, the more data are needed to justify the large-sample normality approximation on which the test is based.

A caution is in order in using the likelihood ratio statistic to test the null hypothesis that one or more variance components is null, i.e., $H_0 : \tau_{qq} = 0$. In this case, the value of the variance under H_o is on the boundary value of the parameter space, and the likelihood ratio statistic will tend to be conservative (Pinheiro and Bates, 2000), decreasing the chances of rejecting a false null hypothesis.[5] This problem is not shared by the univariate χ^2 test described in Chapter 3 (see Equation 3.103). Our experience suggests that the results of the two tests tend to be convergent in most applications.

All of the tests for $\mathbf{T}$ elements depend asymptotically on J. That is, even if the sample size within units, n_j, were infinite, the tests would be accurate only if the number of units, J, were large. More investigation is needed, however, to discern the effects of small-sample sizes on the accuracy of these tests. We suspect that the likelihood for $\mathbf{T}$ can be quite skewed if each n_j is small, even if J is large, thus rendering test results inaccurate. One possibility is to graph the likelihood as suggested by Raudenbush and Bryk (1985). This procedure, however, becomes difficult when $\mathbf{T}$ is of high dimension.

Inferences about Random Level-1 Coefficients

Chapter 3 discussed procedures for constructing confidence intervals and tests for the random coefficients, β_j. We mentioned that exact tests and intervals are possible using separate OLS estimation for each unit. However, these intervals will be very large and the tests very conservative unless sample sizes per unit are quite large.

The alternative is to base intervals and tests on the empirical Bayes estimates, β_j^*. However, these tests and intervals do not reflect uncertainty about the variance components. Thus, the intervals will be too short and the tests too liberal unless $\mathbf{T}$ and σ^2 are precisely determined.

MLR Versus MLF. The accuracy of inferences about the random coefficients using the empirical Bayes approach also depends on choice of likelihood: MLF versus MLR. Inferences based on MLF require the assumption that the fixed effects in the model are equal to their ML estimate. Thus, the MLF-based intervals will be shorter than those based on MLR. The intervals will converge as J becomes large.

Appendix

Misspecification of the Level-1 Structural Model

Earlier we discussed the consequences of misspecification of the level-1 model for estimation of the level-2 coefficients. Restricting our attention to predictors of level-1 slopes, we asserted that if three conditions were met, estimated effects would be biased. These conditions are (a) an omitted level-1 variable must be related to Y; (b) it must be related to a level-1 predictor already in the model; and (c) the statistical association between the omitted variable and this predictor must vary from unit to unit, and the degree of this statistical association must be related to one of the level-2 predictors in the model. We prove these assertions below. We emphasize that the conditions do not apply to level-2 predictors of the intercept.

Suppose that the true level-1 model were

$$\mathbf{Y} = \mathbf{X}_1\beta_1 + \mathbf{X}_2\beta_2 + \mathbf{r}, \qquad \mathbf{r} \sim N(\mathbf{0}, \sigma^2\mathbf{I}), \qquad [9.32]$$

where $\mathbf{Y}$ is a vector of outcomes, $\mathbf{X}_1$ and $\mathbf{X}_2$ are matrices of known predictors (with full column rank), β_1 and β_2 are vectors of unknown effects, and $\mathbf{r}$ is the vector of errors, where vectors and matrices are conformable. The variable $\mathbf{Y}$ is assumed to have a mean of zero with each group (i.e., the level-1 model has no intercept).

Suppose, however, that the model actually estimated is

$$\mathbf{Y} = \mathbf{X}_1\beta_1 + \mathbf{e}, \qquad [9.33]$$

where $\mathbf{e} = \mathbf{X}_2\beta_2 + \mathbf{r}$. Then, using OLS regression within units,

$$\hat{\beta}_1 = (\mathbf{X}_1^T\mathbf{X}_1)^{-1}\mathbf{X}_1^T\mathbf{Y},$$

which has expectation

$$E(\hat{\beta}_1) = \beta_1 + (\mathbf{X}_1^T\mathbf{X}_1)^{-1}\mathbf{X}_1^T\mathbf{X}_2\beta_2. \qquad [9.34]$$

This reveals that $\hat{\beta}_1$ is a biased estimator of β_1 if two conditions hold: β_2 is nonnull; and the matrix of regression coefficients

$$\beta_{2\cdot 1} = (\mathbf{X}_1^T\mathbf{X}_1)^{-1}\mathbf{X}_1^T\mathbf{X}_2$$

is nonnull.

At level 2, the true model is

$$\beta_1 = \mathbf{W}_1\gamma_1 + \mathbf{u}_1, \qquad [9.35]$$

$$\beta_2 = \mathbf{W}_2\gamma_2 + \mathbf{u}_2, \qquad [9.36]$$

where $\mathbf{W}_1$ and $\mathbf{W}_2$ are matrices of predictors, γ_1 and γ_2 are fixed-effect vectors, and $\mathbf{u}_1$ and $\mathbf{u}_2$ are random-error vectors. Hence, the true combined model may be written as

$$\mathbf{Y} = \mathbf{X}_1\mathbf{W}_1\gamma_1 + \mathbf{X}_2\mathbf{W}_2\gamma_2 + \varepsilon, \tag{9.37}$$

where $\varepsilon = \mathbf{X}_1\mathbf{u}_1 + \mathbf{X}_2\mathbf{u}_2 + \mathbf{r}$. The model estimated, however, is

$$\mathbf{Y} = \mathbf{X}_1\mathbf{W}_1\gamma_1 + \varepsilon^*,$$

where $\varepsilon^* = \mathbf{X}_1\mathbf{u}_1 + \mathbf{X}_2\beta_2 + \mathbf{r}$. Then the generalized least squares estimator of γ_1 will be

$$\hat{\gamma}_1 = (\mathbf{W}_1^T\mathbf{V}^{*-1}\mathbf{W}_1)^{-1}\mathbf{W}_1^T\mathbf{V}^{*-1}\hat{\beta}_1, \tag{9.38}$$

where $\mathbf{V}^*$ is the dispersion matrix of ε^*. The expectation of $\hat{\gamma}_1$ will be

$$E(\hat{\gamma}_1) = \gamma_1 + (\mathbf{W}_1^T\mathbf{V}^{*-1}\mathbf{W}_1)^{-1}\mathbf{W}_1^T\mathbf{V}^{*-1}\beta_{2\cdot1}\mathbf{W}_2\gamma_2. \tag{9.39}$$

The bias term will be null if any of the following conditions hold:

1. $E(\beta_2) = \mathbf{W}_2\gamma_2 = 0$ (no association between $\mathbf{W}_2$ and β_2).
2. $\beta_{2\cdot1} = 0$ (no association between $\mathbf{X}_1$ and $\mathbf{X}_2$).
3. $\beta_{2\cdot1}$ is unrelated to $\mathbf{W}_1$. [Note that $(\mathbf{W}_1^T\mathbf{V}^{*-1}\mathbf{W}_1)^{-1}\mathbf{W}_1^T\mathbf{V}^{*-1}\beta_{2\cdot1}$ is the matrix of regression coefficients in which $\beta_{2\cdot1}$ is the outcome and $\mathbf{W}_1$ is the predictor.]

Hence the three conditions listed earlier must be satisfied for bias to occur.

Level-1 Predictors Measured with Error

Suppose that the true level-1 model is

$$\mathbf{Y} = \mathbf{X}\beta + \mathbf{r}, \tag{9.40}$$

but the estimated model is

$$\mathbf{Y} = \mathbf{X}_o\beta + \mathbf{r}^*,$$

where $\mathbf{X}_o = \mathbf{X} + \mathbf{E}$ is a fallible measure of $\mathbf{X}$ with error $\mathbf{E}$ having a null expectation. Then the true model may be written as

$$\mathbf{Y} = \mathbf{X}_o\beta - \mathbf{E}\beta + \mathbf{r}, \tag{9.41}$$

and we have a special case of misspecification (Equations 9.32 and 9.33) with $\mathbf{X}_1 = \mathbf{X}_o$, $\mathbf{X}_2 = -\mathbf{E}$, and $\beta_1 = \beta_2 = \beta$. Hence, the results of part one apply. Condition 1, that $E(\beta_2) = \mathbf{0}$, clearly does not apply. Now, however,

$$\beta_{2\cdot1} = -(\mathbf{X}_o^T\mathbf{X}_o)^{-1}\mathbf{X}_o^T\mathbf{E}$$

measures the degree of unreliability of $\mathbf{X}_o$ as a measure of $\mathbf{X}$. Our previous results imply that errors of measurement $\mathbf{E}$ will bias estimation of γ_1 if and only if (a) the measurement reliability varies from unit to unit; and (b) that reliability is related to elements of the level-2 predictor matrix, $\mathbf{W}$.

Notes

1. Economists refer to such an approach as a "fixed effects" analysis because group-mean centering has the same effect as including $J - 1$ dummy variables as predictors, thus removing the fixed effect of every level-2 unit from the level-1 analysis.

2. Specifically, the Mahalanobis distance is

$$\mathbf{u}_j^{*T} \mathbf{V}_j^{-1} \mathbf{u}_j^*,$$

where u_j^* is the empirical Bayes estimate of the vector $\mathbf{u}_j$ of random effects for unit j, and V_j is the error dispersion of that vector. Specifically,

$$\mathbf{V}_j = \sigma^2 (\mathbf{X}_j^T \mathbf{X}_j)^{-1} + \mathbf{T} - \text{Var}(\mathbf{W}_j \hat{\boldsymbol{\gamma}}),$$

where $\text{Var}(\mathbf{W}_j \hat{\boldsymbol{\gamma}})$ is the dispersion matrix of the $P + 1$ elements of $\mathbf{W}_j \hat{\boldsymbol{\gamma}}$.

3. Completely balanced cases are an extremely restricted set. In a two-level hierarchy, the following conditions must hold for the data to be completely balanced:

a. Sample sizes within units must be equal.

b. The same set of level-1 predictor values must be present within each unit.

c. For each of the $Q + 1$ level-2 equations, the same set of predictor variables must be used.

d. Level-1 and level-2 variance components must be constant for every unit.

4. In the balanced case, the level-2 model is a classical multivariate linear model in which the OLS regression coefficients from each unit may be viewed as the outcome vectors distributed independently and identically as multivariate normal:

$$\hat{\boldsymbol{\beta}}_j = \mathbf{W}_j \boldsymbol{\gamma} + \mathbf{u}_j + \mathbf{e}_j, \qquad \mathbf{u}_j + \mathbf{e}_j \sim \text{N}(\mathbf{0}, \boldsymbol{\Sigma}),$$

where $\boldsymbol{\Sigma} = \sigma^2 (\mathbf{X}^T \mathbf{X})^{-1} + \mathbf{T}$. Point estimates of σ^2 and $\mathbf{T}$ are not needed to estimate $\boldsymbol{\gamma}$. Rather, the OLS estimator $\hat{\boldsymbol{\gamma}} = (\Sigma \mathbf{W}_j^T \mathbf{W}_j)^{-1} \Sigma \mathbf{W}_j^T \hat{\boldsymbol{\beta}}_j$ is also the maximum likelihood estimator of $\boldsymbol{\gamma}$. The independence of $\hat{\boldsymbol{\gamma}}$ and $\boldsymbol{\Sigma}$ lays the basic for exact F tests of linear hypotheses concerning γ.

5. In this case, the large-sample distribution of the likelihood ratio statistic will not be χ^2_{k1-k2}, where $k1$ is the number of parameters in the null model and $k2$ is the number of parameters in the alternative, simpler model. Rather, the statistic will be distributed as a mixture of χ^2 distributions (Stram and Lee, 1994). Pinheiro and Bates (2000) have conducted simulations that compare the likelihood ratio test to alternative approaches that attempt to approximate the correct large-sample distribution of the statistic. They find that it is difficult to construct the correct mixture and recommend use of the standard likelihood ratio statistic, which is easy to use, keeping in mind that it is somewhat conservative.

Section III
Advanced Applications

10   Hierarchical Generalized
        Linear Models

The hierarchical linear model (HLM) as described in the previous chapters is appropriate for two- and three-level nested data where (a) the expected outcome at each level may be represented as a linear function of the regression coefficients and (b) the random effects at each level can reasonably be assumed normally distributed. The linearity assumption can be checked using standard graphical procedures (see Chapter 9). The assumption of normality at level 1 is quite widely applicable when the outcome variable is continuous. Even when a continuous outcome is highly skewed, a transformation can often be found that will make the distribution of level-1 random effects (residuals) at least roughly normal. Methods for assessing the normality of random effects at levels 2 and 3 are discussed in Chapter 9.

There are important cases, however, for which the assumptions of linearity and normality are clearly not realistic and no transformation can make them so. An example is a binary outcome, Y, indicating the presence of a disease ($Y = 1$ if the disease is present; $Y = 0$ if the disease is absent), graduation from high school ($Y = 1$ if a student graduates on time; $Y = 0$ if not), or the commission of a crime ($Y = 1$ if a person commits a crime during a given time interval; $Y = 0$ if not). The use of the standard level-1 model in these cases would be inappropriate for three reasons:

1. There are no restrictions on the predicted values of the level-1 outcome in the standard HLM. They can legitimately take on any real value. In contrast, the predicted value of a binary outcome Y, if viewed as the probability that $Y = 1$, must lie in the interval $(0, 1)$. This constraint gives meaning to the effect sizes defined by the model. A nonlinear transformation of the predicted value, such as a logit or probit transformation, will satisfy this constraint.

2. Given the predicted value of the outcome, the level-1 random effect can take on only one of two values and, therefore, cannot be normally distributed.

3. The level-1 random effect cannot have homogeneous variance. Instead, the variance of this random effect depends on the predicted value as specified below.

A second example of data not appropriately analyzed using the standard HLM involves count data, for example, where Y is the number of crimes a person commits during a year or Y is the number of questions a child asks during the course of a one-hour class period. In these cases, the possible values of Y are nonnegative integers $0, 1, 2 \ldots$. Such data will typically be positively skewed. If there are few zeros in the data, a transformation, such as $Y^* = \log(1 + Y)$ or $Y^* = \sqrt{Y}$, may solve this problem and allow sensible use of a linear model. However, in some applications event rates are low and there are many zeros (e.g., many persons will not commit a crime during a given year and many children will not raise a question during a one-hour class). In these cases, the normality assumption cannot be approximated by a transformation. Predicted values based on a linear model might be negative, a sure sign that the coefficients of the model are not interpretable. Also, as in the case of the binary outcome, the variance of the level-1 random effects will depend on the predicted value (i.e., higher predicted values will be associated with larger residual variance).

Hierarchical generalized linear models (HGLMs), also known as generalized linear mixed models (cf. Breslow & Clayton, 1993) or generalized linear models with random effects (Schall, 1991), offer a coherent modeling framework for multilevel data with nonlinear structural models and nonnormally distributed errors. The comparison between HLM and HGLM parallels a comparison in "single-level" models between the standard linear regression model and the generalized linear model of McCullagh and Nelder (1989). However, some new issues arise in moving to the multilevel setting.

In this chapter, we consider how the generalized linear model can be extended to include repeated measures and multilevel data. The chapter has several aims. Using a variety of examples, we consider:

- HLM as a special case of HGLM with a normal sampling model and identity link function at level 1;
- models for binary outcomes with a Bernoulli sampling model and logit link;
- models of two types for counted data; a binomial sampling model with logit link and Poisson sampling model with log link;
- ordered categorical data with multinomial sampling model and cumulative logit link; and
- nominal-scale categorical data with multinomial sampling model and multinomial logit link.

We also consider special issues that arise in HGLMs:

- unit-specific versus population-average models; and
- overdispersion (or underdispersion).

The Two-Level HLM as a Special Case of HGLM

The level-1 model in HGLM consists of three parts: a sampling model, a link function, and a structural model. In fact, HLM can be viewed as a special case of HGLM where the sampling model is normal, the link function is the identity link, and the structural model is linear.

Level-1 Sampling Model

The sampling model for a two-level HLM might be written as

$$Y_{ij}|\mu_{ij} \sim \text{NID}(\mu_{ij}, \sigma^2), \qquad [10.1]$$

meaning that the level-1 outcome Y_{ij}, given the predicted value, μ_{ij}, is normally and independently distributed with an expected value of μ_{ij} and a constant variance, σ^2. The level-1 expected value and variance may alternatively be written as

$$\text{E}(Y_{ij}|\mu_{ij}) = \mu_{ij}, \qquad \text{Var}(Y_{ij}|\mu_{ij}) = \sigma^2. \qquad [10.2]$$

Level-1 Link Function

In general, it is possible to transform the level-1 predicted value, μ_{ij}, to ensure that the predictions are constrained to lie within a given interval.

We shall denote this transformed predicted value η_{ij}. This transformation is called a link function. In the normal case, no transformation is necessary. However, this decision *not* to transform may be explicitly noted by writing

$$\eta_{ij} = \mu_{ij}. \qquad [10.3]$$

The link function in this case is viewed as the "identity link function."

Level-1 Structural Model

The transformed predicted value η_{ij} is now related to the predictors of the model through the linear structural model

$$\eta_{ij} = \beta_{0j} + \beta_{1j}X_{1ij} + \beta_{2j}X_{2ij} + \cdots + \beta_{pj}X_{pij}. \qquad [10.4]$$

It is clear that combining the level-1 sampling model (Equation 10.1), the level-1 link function (Equation 10.3), and the level-1 structural model (Equation 10.4) reproduces the usual level-1 model of HLM. In the context of HLM, it seems silly to write three equations where only one is needed, but the value of the extra equations becomes apparent as we move to more complex nonlinear cases.

Two- and Three-Level Models for Binary Outcomes

While the standard HLM uses a normal sampling model and an identity link function, the binary outcome model uses a binomial sampling model and a logit link.

Level-1 Sampling Model

Let Y_{ij} be the number of "successes" in m_{ij} trials and let φ_{ij} be the probability of success on each trial. Then we write

$$Y_{ij}|\varphi_{ij} \sim B(m_{ij}, \varphi_{ij}) \qquad [10.5]$$

to denote that Y_{ij} has a binomial distribution with m_{ij} trials and probability of success per trial as φ_{ij}. According to the binomial distribution, the expected value and variance of Y_{ij} are then

$$E(Y_{ij}|\varphi_{ij}) = m_{ij}\varphi_{ij}, \qquad \text{Var}(Y_{ij}|\varphi_{ij}) = m_{ij}\varphi_{ij}(1 - \varphi_{ij}). \qquad [10.6]$$

When $m_{ij} = 1$, Y_{ij} is a binary variable taking on a value of either zero or unity. This is a special case known as the Bernoulli distribution. We note that in some applications the data may not follow this model precisely. The actual level-1 variance may be larger than that assumed (overdispersion) or smaller than that assumed (underdispersion). For example, if undetected clustering exists within level-1 units or if the level-1 model is underspecified, overdispersion may arise. It is possible in these cases to generalize the model to estimate a scalar variance component, σ^2, so that the level-1 variance will be $\sigma^2 m_{ij}\varphi_{ij}(1 - \varphi_{ij})$. Our analyses of high school course failures (see below) provides an example of this.

Level-1 Link Function

Several link functions are possible when the level-1 sampling model is binomial (cf. Hedeker & Gibbons, 1994), though perhaps the most common and convenient is the logit link, that is,

$$\eta_{ij} = \log\left(\frac{\varphi_{ij}}{1 - \varphi_{ij}}\right), \qquad [10.7]$$

where η_{ij} is the log of the odds of success. If the probability of success, φ_{ij}, is .5, the odds of success $\varphi_{ij}/(1 - \varphi_{ij}) = .5/.5 = 1.0$ and the log-odds or "logit" is $\log(1) = 0$. When the probability of success is less than .5, the odds are less than 1.0 and the logit is negative. When the probability is greater than .5, the odds are greater than 1.0 and the logit is positive. Note that while φ_{ij} is constrained to be in the interval (0, 1), η_{ij} can take on any real value.

Level-1 Structural Model

This has exactly the same form as Equation 10.4. Note that estimates of the βs in Equation 10.4 make it possible to generate a predicted log-odds (η_{ij}) for any case. Such a predicted log-odds can be converted to an odds by taking the $\exp(\eta_{ij})$. A predicted log-odds can also be converted to a predicted probability by computing

$$\varphi_{ij} = \frac{1}{1 + \exp\{-\eta_{ij}\}}. \qquad [10.8]$$

Clearly, whatever the value of η_{ij}, applying Equation 10.8 will produce a value of φ_{ij} between zero and one.

Level-2 and Level-3 Models

In the case of a two-level analysis, the level-2 model has the same form as the level-2 model in previous chapters:

$$\beta_{qj} = \gamma_{q0} + \sum_{s=1}^{S_q} \gamma_{qs} W_{sj} + u_{qj}, \qquad [10.9]$$

where the random effects u_{qj}, $q = 0, \ldots, Q$, constitute a vector u_j having a multivariate normal distribution with component means of zero and variance-covariance matrix $\mathbf{T}$. In the case of a three-level analysis, the level-2 and level-3 models are the same as those described in Chapter 8 for the three-level HLM.

A Bernoulli Example: Grade Retention in Thailand

A national survey of primary education in Thailand, conducted in 1988, provides information on 7,516 sixth graders nested within 356 primary schools.[1] Of interest is the probability that a child will repeat a grade during the primary years (REPETITION = 1 if yes; 0 if no). Descriptive statistics are found in Table 10.1.

There are six level-1 variables. Note that about 14% of the sample repeated at least one grade during primary schools. The table also indicates that 51% of the sample was male (MALE = 1 if male; 0 if female), 48% spoke Central

TABLE 10.1 Descriptive Statistics for Thailand Data

Level-1 Descriptive Statistics					
Variable Name	N	Mean	sd	Minimum	Maximum
SES	7,516	0.00	0.68	−1.76	3.48
MALE	7,516	0.51	0.50	0	1
DIALECT	7,516	0.48	0.50	0	1
BREAKFAST	7,516	0.84	0.36	0	1
PREPRIM	7,516	0.50	0.50	0	1
REPETITION	7,516	0.14	0.35	0	1
Level-2 Descriptive Statistics					
Variable Name	J	Mean	sd	Minimum	Maximum
MEANSES	356	−0.01	0.44	−0.93	2
SIZE	356	0.00	0.85	−1.77	1.61
TEXTS	356	0.01	1.85	−5.95	2.59

Thai dialect (DIALECT = 1), 84% had breakfast daily (BREAKFAST = 1), and 50% had some preprimary experience (PREPRIM = 1). Socioeconomic status (SES) is a composite of parents' occupational prestige, education, and income. School-level variables include the school mean SES (MEANSES), the size of the school's enrollment (SIZE), and a measure of the availability of textbooks in the school (TEXTS).

Unconditional Model. To gauge the magnitude of variation between schools in grade repetition, we estimate a model with no predictors at either level. Given a Bernoulli sampling model and a logit link function, the level-1 model is simply

$$\eta_{ij} = \beta_{0j}, \qquad [10.10]$$

where the level-2 model is

$$\beta_{0j} = \gamma_{00} + u_{0j}, \qquad u_{0j} \sim N(0, \tau_{00}). \qquad [10.11]$$

Here γ_{00} is the average log-odds of repetition across Thai primary schools, while τ_{00} is the variance between schools in school-average log-odds of repetition. The estimated results are $\hat{\gamma}_{00} = -2.22$ (se = 0.084), $\hat{\tau}_{00} = 1.70$ (se = 0.16). Thus, for a school with a "typical" repetition rate, that is, for a school with a random effect $u_{0j} = 0$, the expected log-odds of repetition is -2.22, corresponding to an odds of $\exp\{-2.22\} = .109$, or about 1 to 9. This corresponds to a probability of $1/(1 + \exp\{2.22\}) = .097$.

Note that this "typical" probability, associated with a school-level random effect of 0, is considerably less than the population-wide repetition rate estimate of .14 (see Table 10.1). This difference is attributable to the nonlinear relationship between η_{ij}, the log-odds of repetition, and φ_{ij}, the probability of repetition. As Figure 10.1 shows, the upper and lower limits of the 95% prediction interval for η_{ij} is symmetric about the mean of -2.22. However, the corresponding interval for φ_{ij} is not symmetric around the corresponding value of $\varphi = .097$. The normal distribution for η_{ij} implies that the mean and median will be equal at -2.22. In contrast, the positively skewed distribution for φ_{ij} implies that the population-average probability will be higher than the median of .097. (See "Population-Average Models" for further discussion.)

Assuming the schools' log-odds of grade repetition, β_{0j}, to be approximately normally distributed with mean -2.22 and variance $\hat{\tau}_{00} = 1.70$, we would expect about 95% of the primary schools to have values of β_{0j} between $-2.22 \pm 1.96 * \sqrt{1.70} = (-4.78, 0.34)$. Converting these log-odds to probabilities, Figure 10.1 shows that 95% of the schools lie between (.008, .59) with respect to the probability of grade repetition. It appears that some

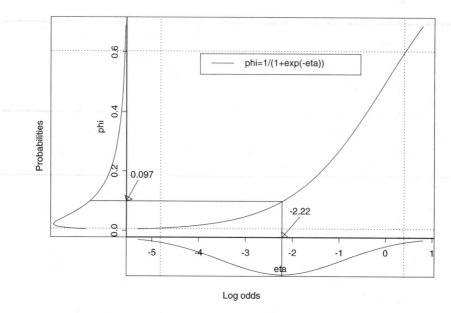

Log odds

Figure 10.1. School-Specific Probability of Retention as a Function of School-Specific Log-Odds of Retention

NOTE: The vertical dotted lines mark the limits of the 95% prediction interval for the school-specific log-odds of retention, while the dotted horizontal lines mark the limits of the 95% prediction interval for school-specific probabilities of retention.

schools have repetition rates near zero, while in others, more than half the students will have repeated a grade during the primary year.

Within the framework of a standard two-level hierarchical linear model, the intraclass correlation, that is, the ratio of level-2 variance to the total variation, is a useful index. Unfortunately, this measure is less informative in the case of nonlinear link functions, because the level-1 variance is now heteroscedastic. For example, in the Bernoulli case the level-1 variance will equal $\varphi_{ij}(1 - \varphi_{ij})$ where φ_{ij} is the predicted probability according to the level-1 model. A more useful way to gauge the magnitude of level-2 variation in the case of binomial data is to inspect graphs such as Figure 10.1.[2]

Conditional Model. We hypothesize that lower repetition rates will be associated at level 1 with having some preprimary experience; having high socioeconomic status; being female; speaking the regular language of instruction, Central Thai dialect; and having breakfast daily. We hypothesize a "contextual effect" (see Chapter 5) at level 2 such that the higher school-mean

SES (MEANSES) will predict lower rates of repetition. We also expect larger schools will have lower retention rates, and schools with textbooks for each student will have lower retention rates.[3]

Specifically, the level-1 structured model is

$$\eta_{ij} = \beta_{0j} + \beta_{1j}(\text{SES})_{ij} + \beta_{2j}(\text{MALE})_{ij} + \beta_{3j}(\text{DIALECT})_{ij}$$
$$+ \beta_{4j}(\text{BREAKFAST})_{ij} + \beta_{5j}(\text{PREPRIM})_{ij}, \qquad [10.12]$$

where SES is grand-mean centered and all other level-1 predictors remain in their dummy variable metric.

At level 2, we model β_{0j} as a function of the level-2 predictors. We view the other level-1 coefficients, β_{pj}, $p > 0$, as fixed:

$$\beta_{0j} = \gamma_{00} + \gamma_{01}(\text{MEANSES})_j + \gamma_{02}(\text{SIZE})_j + \gamma_{03}(\text{TEXTS})_j + u_{0j},$$
$$\beta_{pj} = \gamma_{p0} \quad \text{for } p > 0. \qquad [10.13]$$

Consider first the results in column (*a*) of Table 10.2. These are obtained when we assume normality at level 1 and an identity link function (i.e., a standard two-level model). On their face, the results look plausible. For example, we see an intercept of 0.161. This is the predicted probability of repetition for a participant with $(\text{SES})_{ij} = (\text{MALE})_{ij} = (\text{DIALECT})_{ij} = (\text{BREAKFAST})_{ij} = (\text{PREPRIM})_{ij} = 0$, that is, for a noncentral Thai-speaking female of average SES who did not attend preprimary school, does

TABLE 10.2 Estimates of Level-2 Coefficients Based on (a) Identity Link Function, (b) School-Specific Model with Logit Link, and (c) Population-Average Model with Logit Link

	Fixed Effect	*(a) Identity Link*	*(b) Logit Link:* *Unit-Specific* *Model*	*(c) Logit Link:* *Population-* *Average Model*
INTERCEPT, β_{0j}	INTERCEPT, γ_{00}	0.161***	−2.175***	−1.734***
	MEANSES, γ_{01}	−0.064*	−0.691*	−0.018*
	SIZE, γ_{02}	−0.017	−0.232	−0.193
	TEXTS, γ_{03}	0.000	0.016	−0.001
SES slope, β_{1j}	INTERCEPT, γ_{10}	−0.0234**	−0.363***	−0.319***
MALE slope, β_{2j}	INTERCEPT, γ_{20}	0.056***	0.562***	0.476***
DIALECT slope, β_{3j}	INTERCEPT, γ_{30}	0.025	0.309*	0.2
BREAKFAST slope, β_{4j}	INTERCEPT, γ_{40}	−0.030*	−0.347***	−0.295**
PREPRIM slope, β_{5j}	INTERCEPT, γ_{50}	−0.050***	−0.492***	−0.431***

* Indicates |coeff/se| > 2.00.
** Indicates |coeff/se| > 2.50.
*** Indicates |coeff/se| > 3.00.

not eat breakfast daily, and who attends a "typical school" (i.e., $u_{0j} = 0$). The model suggests that attending preprimary school is associated with a reduction of 0.050 in the probability of repetition to $.161 - .050 = .111$. Access to daily breakfast is associated with a further reduction of .030 to $.111 - .030 = .081$. Now suppose, in addition, that MEANSES is one unit above average. The expected probability of repetition rate then declines by another .064 to .017. Herein lies the rub: One more unit increase in MEANSES would lead to an expected negative probability of repetition!

This result illustrates the difficulty in conceiving of probability as a linear function of covariates. As the predicted probability moves toward zero, one would expect the benefit of additional units of a favorable covariate to *diminish*. Suppose, for example, that an intervention costing T dollars per person reduces the repetition rate from .10 to .05. It makes little sense to believe that spending $2T$ dollars would further reduce the rate to zero and no sense to think that more spending would render the rate negative. Thus, logic demands a nonlinear model on the probability scale.

Column (b) of Table 10.2 presents the results for the logit link function. We see here that preprimary experience is associated with a lower log-odds of retention, $\hat{\gamma}_{10} = -0.492$, $t = -4.78$, holding constant the other predictors in the model and the random effect, u_{0j}. The expected odds of retention of students who experienced preprimary education are $\exp\{-0.492\} = 0.611$ times the odds of retention of an otherwise-similar student who did not experience preprimary education. SES is associated with lower repetition, $\hat{\gamma}_{20} = -.363$, *ceteris paribus*. Thus, a unit increase in SES reduces the log-odds of retention by .363. Associated with this is a relative odds ratio of $\exp\{-.363\} = 0.696$. That is, if we compare two students who are similar in other ways but differ by one unit in SES, we can expect the odds of retention of the higher-SES student to be 0.696 times the odds of retention of the lower-SES student. But what is the meaning of "one unit SES"? We see from Table 10.1 that SES has a standard deviation of 0.68. We can therefore say that one standard deviation difference in SES is associated with a difference in the log-odds of repetition of $0.68 * (-0.363) = -0.247$ or a relative odds of $\exp\{-0.247\} = 0.781$. In a similar vein, Table 10.2 indicates that being male is associated with a higher relative odds of $\exp\{0.562\} = 1.754$. Having breakfast daily is associated with a lower log-odds of repetition, with an odds ratio of $\exp\{-.347\} = 0.707$. Perhaps surprisingly, speaking Central Thai was associated with a *higher* odds of repetition, relative odds of 1.362. At level 2, the log-odds of repetition was unrelated to textbook availability and school size, but was negatively related to school MEANSES, holding other predictors constant, $\hat{\gamma}_{03} = -0.691$, $t = -2.09$. Two otherwise similar schools that differ by one standard deviation in MEANSES (see Table 10.1) could be expected to be $(0.44) * (-0.691) = -0.304$ units apart in log-odds of repetition, a relative odds of $\exp\{-0.311\} = 0.738$.

How do these results translate into predicted probabilities? As a comparison to the results based on the identity link function (column a) described above, let us again consider a noncentral Thai female without daily breakfast and preprimary education. If that student was of average SES and attended a typical school, his predicted log-odds of repetition would be -2.175, corresponding to a probability of $1/(1 + \exp\{2.175\}) = .102$. Adding one unit to MEANSES would lead to a predicted log-odds of $-2.175 - .691 = -2.866$, associated with a predicted probability of .054. An additional unit increase in MEANSES would lead to a predicted log-odds of $-2.175 + (2) * (-0.691)$, corresponding to a predicted probability of .029. As demanded by logic, successive increments to MEANSES lead to smaller decrements in the expected probability, a virtue not shared by the linear model.

Population-Average Models

Before proceeding on to consider other HGLM applications, we need to make a brief detour to consider a distinction—between *population-average* and *unit-specific* results—that arises in models with nonlinear link functions. Though inferences based on these two models often appear quite similar, the models are oriented toward somewhat different research aims.

Unconditional Model. In the unconditional model, we noted that the probability of repetition for a median school (i.e., a school with $u_{0j} = 0$) was not the population-average probability. A school with a random effect of zero is found at the center of the distribution of random effects. Because the level-2 random effects are assumed to be normally distributed, the mean and median random effect are identical. However, the corresponding distribution of probability is positively skewed, with a mean that therefore exceeds the median.

This idea is depicted in detail in Figure 10.1. The figure displays the probability, φ_{ij} (vertical axis), as a function of the log-odds, η_{ij} (horizontal axis). The estimated distribution of β_{0j} is graphed below the horizontal axis. It is a unimodal symmetric distribution centered at $\hat{\gamma}_{00} = -2.22$ with a standard deviation of $\sqrt{\hat{\tau}_{00}} = 1.30$. The corresponding distribution of probabilities is graphed to the left of the vertical axis. The median log-odds corresponds to the median probability of $1/(1 + \exp\{2.22\}) = .097$. However, the mean probability must exceed the median. The mean will be the average of $1/(1 + \exp\{-(\gamma_{00} + u_{0j})\}) \simeq 1/(1 + \exp\{(-2.22 - u_{0j})\})$ taken over all schools j.

We can approximate the population-average probability using the second-order Maclaurin series expansion

$$\varphi_{ij} = \varphi_{ij}(u_{0j}) = \frac{1}{1 + e^{-(\gamma_{00}+u_{0j})}}$$

$$\simeq \varphi_{ij}(0) + u_{0j}\varphi'_{ij}(0) + \frac{1}{2}u_{0j}^2\varphi''(0), \qquad [10.14]$$

where

$$\varphi_{ij}(0) = \frac{1}{1 + e^{-\gamma_{00}}},$$

$$\varphi'_{ij}(0) = \varphi_{ij}(0)[1 - \varphi_{ij}(0)],$$

$$\varphi''_{ij}(0) = \varphi'_{ij}(0)[1 - 2\varphi_{ij}(0)].$$

We now take the expectation over $u_{0j} \sim N(0, \tau_{00})$ to obtain

$$E(\varphi_{ij}) \simeq \varphi_{ij}(0) + \tau_{00}\varphi'_{ij}(0)[.5 - \varphi_{ij}(0)]. \qquad [10.15]$$

This comparison reveals that the average probability, that is, $E(\varphi_{ij})$, will be equal to $\varphi_{ij}(0)$ if $\varphi_{ij}(0) = .50$ or $\tau_{00} = 0$. For $\varphi_{ij}(0) < .50$, the population average, $E(\varphi_{ij})$, will be "pulled" upward toward .50; for $\varphi_{ij}(0) > .50$, $E(\varphi_{ij})$ will be "pulled" downward toward .50. In each case, the magnitude of the difference will be greatest when τ_{00} is large and $\varphi_{ij}(0)$ is far from .50.

In our case, based on Equation 10.14, we expect the population-average φ_{ij} to be greater than .097. Specifically,

$$E(\varphi_{ij}) \simeq \hat{\varphi}_{ij}(0) + \hat{\tau}_{00}\hat{\varphi}''_{ij}(0)(.5 - \hat{\varphi}_{ij}(0))$$

$$= .097 + 1.70 * (.097) * (1 - .097) * (.50 - .097) \quad [10.16]$$

$$= .157.$$

As an alternative, we can directly estimate a population-average model, which, in the unconditional case, is

$$Y_{ij} = \frac{1}{1 + e^{-\gamma_{00}^*}} + e_{ij}. \qquad [10.17]$$

In this model, the level-2 random effects are absorbed into e_{ij} rather than represented in the exponentiated denominator.

We add an asterisk in our notation for γ_{00}^* to distinguish this population-average intercept from the unit-specific estimate of γ_{00} based on Equation 10.11. Correspondingly,

$$E(Y_{ij}) = E\left(\frac{1}{1 + e^{-(\gamma_{00}+u_{0j})}}\right) = \frac{1}{1 + e^{-\gamma_{00}^*}}. \qquad [10.18]$$

The model residuals, e_{ij}, are assumed correlated among individuals within schools. The covariance structure for the residuals can be derived from our previous results (Zeger, Liang, & Albert, 1988). For the Thailand data, we estimate $\hat{\gamma}_{00}^* = 1.73$, se = .069. Based on this, the estimated population-average probability is

$$E(Y_{ij}) \simeq 1/(1 + \exp\{1.73\}) = .151, \qquad [10.19]$$

which is reasonably close to our Maclaurin series approximation of .157. However, the estimate based on Equation 10.19 is more accurate.

Conditional Model. The coefficients in column (*b*) in Table 10.2 are interpreted as the expected difference in the log-odds of repetition associated with (*a*) unit increase in the predictor, holding constant the other predictors *and* holding constant the value of the random effect, u_{0j}. We refer to these as "unit-specific" estimates or, in this case, "school-specific" estimates (see Zeger, Liang, & Albert, 1988, for the origin of this terminology). In contrast, column c displays the "population-average estimates." This column gives the expected difference in the log-odds of repetition associated with a unit increase in the predictors, holding constant the other predictors, but averaging over the distribution of level-2 random effects. We note that the directions of all findings are identical, and the statistical significance nearly identical in the two models. However, the population-average coefficients are uniformly "shrunk" toward zero, as we would expect from our approximation formula, in comparison to the unit-specific coefficients.

Robust Standard Errors. Robust standard errors can be computed for unit-specific and population-average models and for linear as well as nonlinear link functions (see Chapter 9). We recommend comparing the model-based and robust standard errors. Their similarity does not ensure that assumptions about the distribution of the random effects is correct, but their similarity does imply that inferences about the precision of the regression coefficient estimates are not sensitive to departures of the data from those assumptions. Finding important differences in model-based and robust standard errors gives evidence of a misspecification of the distribution of random effects, a misspecification that does make a difference for inferences about the regression coefficients. The inferences in this example about the regression coefficients (the γ^*s) were similar for both model-based and robust standard errors.

Choosing Population-Average Versus Unit-Specific Models. The unit-specific model (i.e., the hierarchically structured model) describes a process that is occurring in each level-2 unit. This process is captured by the level-1 model and, particularly, by the level-1 coefficients (the βs). Of central interest is the question of how these processes differ over a population of level-2 units. In some cases, as in the Thailand example, the only difference is the intercept, but in other cases described in this book, the processes differ in multiple ways. The level-2 model describes how differences in explanatory variables at level 2 relate to differences in the level-1 processes in each level-1 unit. Such questions are intrinsically "unit-specific" questions (see Raudenbush, 2000).

Population-average models, in contrast, give answers to population-average questions. If we use a regression model to simulate how differences in prepri-mary experiences relate to the risk of repetition (holding constant school attended), we are asking a unit-specific question. If we want to know how the risk of repetition differs between those who do and do not have prepri-mary experience nationwide (not holding constant school attended), we need a population-average estimate.

If the unit-specific model is correct, it provides an entire distribution of out-comes over all level-2 units. The population-average results can be deduced as one characteristic of the distribution of the unit-specific results. In con-trast, the population-average estimates cannot inform about the distribution of outcomes across level-2 units other than by specifying the mean. However, population-average inferences are based on fewer assumptions and will be quite robust to erroneous assumptions about the random effects in the model (Heagarty & Zeger, 2000). Unit-specific inferences, in contrast, are likely to be more dependent on assumptions about the distribution of random effects. Thus, unit-specific models are richer, but the price is greater sensitivity to model assumptions.[4]

The distinction between unit-specific and population-average inference arises in all models considered in the chapter that use nonlinear link functions.

A Binomial Example: Course Failures During First Semester of Ninth Grade

The data for this example describe 19,569 ninth graders in 66 Chicago public high schools during the 1997–1998 academic year. The outcome vari-able of interest is the number of courses that students fail during their first semester of high school. Descriptive statistics for these data can be found in Table 10.3. The typical ninth grader is enrolled in four courses (CRSTAKEN) during the fall semester and, on average, fails about one of these (i.e., the overall mean for number of courses failed, CRSFAIL, is 0.94). Some students

TABLE 10.3 Descriptive Statistics for Course Failure Data

		Level-1 Descriptive Statistics			
Variable Name	*N*	*Mean*	*sd*	*Minimum*	*Maximum*
CRSTAKEN	19,569	4.06	0.64	1.00	10.00
CRSFAIL	19,569	0.94	1.34	0.00	6.00
READ97	19,569	1.17	0.98	−3.28	5.98
FEMALE	19,569	0.51	0.50	0.00	1.00
BLACK	19,569	0.56	0.50	0.00	1.00
HISPANIC	19,569	0.30	0.46	0.00	1.00
		Level-2 Descriptive Statistics			
Variable Name	*J*	*Mean*	*sd*	*Minimum*	*Maximum*
INTEGRT	66	0.18	0.39	0.00	1.00
PRBLACK	66	0.47	0.50	0.00	1.00
PRHISP	66	0.09	0.29	0.00	1.00
AVEACH	66	168.55	40.43	101.50	329.00

can be enrolled in as many as 10 courses and fail up to a maximum of 6. In the context of a binomial model, the outcome variable, Y_{ij}, is now the number of courses failed and the number of trials, m_{ij}, is the number of courses taken. We assume that each student i in school j has some probability of failing any given course, denoted by φ_{ij}.

The level-1 predictors consist of a standardized measure of reading achievement from the end of eighth grade (READ97, which is in a metric defined by an item response model) and three dummy variables indicating gender (FEMALE) and race/ethnicity (BLACK, HISPANIC). The sample consists of 51% females, 56% African-Americans, and 30% Hispanics. Four predictors are of interest at level 2: an indicator of the prior average achievement level of the high school (AVEACH, which is in a test-specific metric) and three dummy variables capturing the racial/ethnic composition of the school (INTEGRT, more that 30% white students; PRBLACK, over 85% African-American students; and PRHISP, over 85% Hispanic students). In the 1997–1998 school year, 18% of Chicago's high schools were integrated, 47% were predominately African-American, and 9% were predominately Hispanic. The remaining 26% were of mixed ethnicities, but with relatively few white students.

Unconditional Model. The link function remains the logit link. To gauge the magnitude of variation among high schools in course failing, we estimate a fully unconditional model (Equations 10.10 and 10.11). As in the Bernoulli case, γ_{00} is the average log-odds of failing a course in a Chicago public high school. We see in Table 10.4 that the unit-specific estimate $\hat{\gamma}_{00} = -1.200$. This means that for a school with a random effect, $u_{0j} = 0$, the expected odds of failing any randomly selected course is $\exp\{-1.200\} = 0.30$. System wide, the odds of failing a course, based on the population-average model, is just slightly higher, $\exp\{-1.140\} = 0.32$. In general, in applications like this where event probabilities are neither rare nor very common, that is, $0.80 > \varphi_{ij} > 0.20$, the population-average and unit-specific models will produce similar results, especially if τ_{00} is small..

The unconditional model also provides valuable information about the between-school variability in course failure rates. Given the estimate of $\hat{\tau}_{00} = 0.255$, we expect 95% of the high schools to have log-odds of failure between -2.190 and -0.210. This is equivalent to odds ratios of 0.11 and 0.81, respectively. Converting the log-odds to probabilities, $\hat{\varphi}_{ij}$ yields school failure rates in Chicago that range from a low of 0.10 to a high of 0.45. Finally, to predict the actual number of courses failed by any student i in school j, we would multiply the number of courses taken, m_{ij}, by $\hat{\varphi}_{ij}$.

This model also provides evidence of overdispersion at level 1. The estimated overdispersion scalar variance component is $\hat{\sigma}^2 = 2.294$. If the binomial level-1 sampling model were correct, we should have obtained a value close to 1.0. This difference is highly unlikely by chance alone since the estimated standard error for σ^2 in this analysis is 0.02.

Models with Level-1 Predictors. The next step in our analysis is to consider the effects of various student-level characteristics on the log-odds of course failure. Specifically, at level 1, we have

$$\eta_{ij} = \beta_{0j} + \beta_{1j}(\text{READ})_{ij} + \beta_{2j}(\text{FEMALE})_{ij} + \beta_{3j}(\text{BLACK})_{ij}$$
$$+ \beta_{4j}(\text{HISPANIC})_{ij}.$$

At level 2, we initially treat the intercept as random and the remaining β coefficients as fixed, that is,

$$\beta_{0j} = \gamma_{00} + u_{0j},$$
$$\beta_{pj} = \gamma_{p0} \quad \text{for } p > 0.$$

The second panel of Table 10.4 displays these results. High reading achievement in eight grade is associated with a lower log-odds of course failure, $\hat{\gamma}_{10} = -0.255$, holding constant the other predictors in the model and the random school effect, u_{0j}. The log-odds of course failure is also lower for female students, $\hat{\gamma}_{20} = -0.450$, but it is higher for both black

TABLE 10.4 Binomial Example: Results for Number of Courses Failed in First Semester of High School[a]

	Unconditional Model				Level-1 Model with Fixed Effects				Level-1 Model with Random Effects				Final Model			
	Unit-Specific Coeff.	Pop. Ave. Coeff.	Model se	Robust se	Unit-Specific Coeff.	Pop. Ave. Coeff.	Model se	Robust se	Unit-Specific Coeff.	Pop. Ave. Coeff.	Model se	Robust se	Unit-Specific Coeff.	Pop. Ave. Coeff.	Model se	Robust se
Fixed effects																
INTERCEPT, γ_{00}	−1.200	−1.140	0.064	0.055	−1.217	−1.155	0.066	0.058	−1.225	−1.249	0.067	0.054	−1.232	−1.192	0.047	0.044
AVEACH, γ_{01}													−0.009	−0.009	0.001	0.001
READ slope, γ_{10}					−0.255	−0.245	0.015	0.029	−0.246	−0.216	0.028	0.024	−0.246	−0.227	0.028	0.025
FEMALE slope, γ_{20}					−0.450	−0.432	0.025	0.028	−0.450	−0.425	0.025	0.026	−0.447	−0.436	0.026	0.029
BLACK slope, γ_{30}					0.317	0.298	0.048	0.076	0.251	0.201	0.070	0.061	0.269	0.254	0.073	0.072
HISPANIC slope, γ_{40}					0.167	0.156	0.045	0.044	0.130	0.110	0.045	0.038	0.132	0.125	0.047	0.046
Variance Components																
σ^2	2.294				2.247				2.223				2.223			
T	0.255				0.266				2.223	$\begin{bmatrix} 0.279 & & \\ 0.031 & 0.032 & \\ -0.042 & -0.002 & 0.102 \end{bmatrix}$				$\begin{bmatrix} 0.129 & & \\ 0.019 & 0.032 & \\ -0.090 & -0.003 & 0.106 \end{bmatrix}$		
95% plausible values																
School-average log-odds of failure, β_{0j}	−2.190	−0.210							−2.260	−0.190						
Prior achievement differentiating effects, β_{ij}									−0.597	0.105						
Black effects, β_{3j}									−0.375	0.877						

a. Model se is based on the population-average model.

and Hispanic students, $\hat{\gamma}_{30} = 0.317$ and $\hat{\gamma}_{40} = 0.167$, respectively. A one standard deviation increase in prior reading achievement reduces the odds of failing any course by $\exp\{-0.255 * 0.98\} = 0.78$ times. In a similar vein, being female reduces the odds by $\exp\{-0.450\} = 0.64$ times. Being black or Hispanic increases the relative odds of course failure, even after controlling for prior achievement, gender, and the high-school-specific effect, u_{0j}, by factors of 1.37 and 1.18, respectively.

Also significant in this application is that the estimated model-based and robust standard errors diverge quite substantially for both $\hat{\gamma}_{10}$ and $\hat{\gamma}_{30}$. This indicates that the random-intercept model underrepresents the actual variability in our data. Given that these effects appear for only two of the fixed-effect estimates, this suggests treating both of these level-1 coefficients as random rather than fixed; that is, the level-2 model is now specified as

$$\beta_{pj} = \gamma_{p0} + u_{pj} \quad \text{for } p = 0, 1, 3,$$
$$\beta_{pj} = \gamma_{p0} \quad \text{for } p = 2, 4.$$

The third panel of Table 10.4 presents the results for this model. The variability among high schools in prior achievement effects and black effects is indeed substantial. Both of these estimated variance components, $\hat{\tau}_{11}$ and $\hat{\tau}_{22}$, had highly significant χ^2 test statistics. Moreover, the 95% plausible value ranges for each are quite wide. For prior achievement, the log-odds of course failure can range from almost -0.6 to 0.1; for the black gap in course failure, the range is from almost -0.4 to 0.9. In most high schools, being black and having low prior achievement increase the log-odds of failing a course. In at least a few high schools, however, the reverse appears true (i.e., the log-odds turn positive for prior achievement and negative for the black effect). Also notice that the robust and model-based standard errors are more similar, providing further confirmation that this model better fits these data.

Adding Level-2 Predictors. The next step in the analysis was to consider evidence of possible school context effects on course failure rates as a function of racial/ethnic school composition variables (INTEGRT, PRBLACK, PRHISP) and the high school's average achievement level (AVEACH). We explored possible effects both on the adjusted school log-odds of course failure, β_{0j}, and on the differentiating effects of prior achievement and student race/ethnicity, that is, β_{pj} for $p = 1, \ldots, 4$. We found no evidence of racial composition effects on any of the level-2 outcomes and found only an academic achievement context effect on β_{0j}. The last panel of Table 10.4 presents the results from the best fitting final model. Not surprisingly, the prior average achievement level of a high school has a strong effect on the log-odds of course failures, $\hat{\gamma}_{01} = -0.009$. This means that a one standard deviation increase in AVEACH (i.e., 40.43 points) reduces the log-odds of failure by 0.36, which corresponds to a decrease in the relative odds by a factor of 0.70, all other predictors and the school random effects, u_{pj} for $p = 0, 1, 3$, being held constant.

Also notice that the intercept variance, $\hat{\tau}_{00}$, was reduced from 0.279 to 0.129 after AVEACH was introduced into the model. Not surprisingly, over 50% of the variance in adjusted school log-odds of course failing is accounted for by the prior average achievement level of the high school. Even so, substantial between-school variability in both school average failure rates and differentiating effects of prior achievement and race/ethnicity still remain unexplained. This suggests considering possible differences among high schools in their internal structures and policies, for example, the presence of tracking, the strength of their counseling programs, and so on, which might account for some of these effects.

Similarly, substantial overdispersion at level 1 remains. The binomial model assumes that the responses for any student i in school j are independent across trials (i.e., the different courses that a student takes) conditional only on φ_{ij}. Since course failures are related to student absenteeism, however, this could introduce a clustering effect in the data. That is, students who are absent a lot from school are more likely to fail multiple courses. Thus, we might consider introducing a measure of absenteeism into the level-1 model in subsequent analyses. If our reasoning is correct, the overdispersion at level 1 should be reduced.

Hierarchical Models for Count Data

A standard generalized linear model for count data uses a Poisson sampling model and a log link function. These extend directly to hierarchical models.

Level-1 Sampling Model

Let Y_{ij} be the number of events occurring during an interval of time having length m_{ij}. For example, Y_{ij} could be the number of crimes a person i in neighborhood j commits during five years, so that $m_{ij} = 5$. The time interval m_{ij} may be termed the "exposure." Then we write

$$Y_{ij}|\lambda_{ij} \sim P(m_{ij}, \lambda_{ij}) \qquad [10.20]$$

to denote that Y_{ij} has a Poisson distribution with exposure m_{ij} and event rate per time period of λ_{ij}. According to the Poisson distribution, the expected value and variance of Y_{ij}, given the event rate, λ_{ij}, are then

$$E(Y_{ij}|\lambda_{ij}) = m_{ij}\lambda_{ij}, \qquad Var(Y_{ij}|\lambda_{ij}) = m_{ij}\lambda_{ij}. \qquad [10.21]$$

In words, the expected number of events, Y_{ij}, for unit i in group j is its event rate, λ_{ij}, times its exposure, m_{ij}; and the variance equals this mean. The exposure m_{ij} need not be a measure of time. For example, in a classic application of a Poisson model, Y_{ij} was the number of bombs dropped on neighborhood i of city j during a war, and m_{ij} was the area of that neighborhood. A common case arises when for every i and j the exposure is the same (e.g., Y_{ij} is the number of crimes committed during one year for each person i within each neighborhood j). In this case, we set $m_{ij} = 1$ for simplicity. According to our level-1 model, the predicted value of Y_{ij} when $m_{ij} = 1$ will be the event rate λ_{ij}.

Level-1 Link Function

The standard link function when the level-1 sampling model is Poisson is the log link, that is,

$$\eta_{ij} = \log(\lambda_{ij}). \qquad [10.22]$$

In words, η_{ij} is the log of the event rate. Thus, if the event rate, λ_{ij}, is 1, the log is 0. When the event rate is less than 1, the log is negative; when the event rate is greater than 1, the log is positive. Thus, while λ_{ij} is constrained to be nonnegative, $\log(\lambda_{ij})$ can take on any real value.

Level-1 Structural Model

This has exactly the same form as Equation 10.4. Note that estimates of the βs in Equation 10.4 make it possible to generate a predicted log event rate, $\hat{\eta}_{ij}$, for any case. Such a predicted log event rate can be converted to an event rate, $\hat{\lambda}_{ij}$, by computing $\hat{\lambda}_{ij} = \exp\{\hat{\eta}_{ij}\}$. Clearly, whatever the value of $\hat{\eta}_{ij}$, $\hat{\lambda}_{ij}$, will be nonnegative.

Level-2 Model

The level-2 model has the same form as the level-2 model in the binomial and normal cases (e.g., Equation 10.9).

Example: Homicide Rates in Chicago Neighborhoods

Sampson, Raudenbush, and Earls (1997) studied the association between community characteristics and homicide rates in Chicago neighborhoods. They first divided the city into 342 neighborhood clusters (NCs), which are geographically contiguous areas that approximate local neighborhoods. Past research had indicated that neighborhoods characterized by concentrated disadvantage[5] have high homicide rates. The authors were interested in the extent to which this association could be explained by the quality of relationships among neighbors. Using citywide survey data of over 8,000 residents, they constructed for each of the 342 NCs a measure of "collective efficacy," which indicates the extent to which neighbors know each other, share common values, and can count on each other to intervene to maintain public order. We refer the reader to that 1997 article for details and provide a simplified version of the analysis here.

Figure 10.2a displays a histogram of the observed homicide rates per 100,000 residents in each neighborhood in 1995. The modal value is zero, and the rates are highly skewed. Clearly, no transformation can normalize these data. The scatterplot in Figure 10.2b displays the association between concentrated disadvantage and the observed homicide rate per 100,000 residents. There is a great concentration of cases in the lower left corner of the graph and severe heteroscedasticity with the variance in homicide rates increasing as a function of increased concentrated disadvantage. Moreover, the association between concentrated disadvantage and homicide rate appears to be nonlinear. Nonetheless, for simplicity, we begin by considering a linear regression model. The estimated equation is

$$\widehat{Y}_j = 30.96 + 21.0 * (CONDIS)_j, \qquad [10.23]$$

where Y_j is the number of homicides per 100,000 population in neighborhood j and CONDIS is standardized with a mean of 0 and a standard deviation of 1. This equation will produce negative expected homicide rates for six neighborhoods. All of these features—the semicontinuous nature of the outcome (with a high frequency at zero), the nonlinearity of the association between predictor and outcome, the heteroscedasticity of the residuals, and the production of negative predicted values—suggest nonlinear regression methods. While a transformation to $Y_j^* = \log(1 + Y_j)$ in the homicide rate eliminates the out-of-bounds predictors, the other problems remain. In addition, effect sizes for predictors are hard to interpret in the metric of $\log\{1 + Y_j\}$. These problems can be addressed more productively by using a nonlinear model with variance of the residuals proportional to the mean.

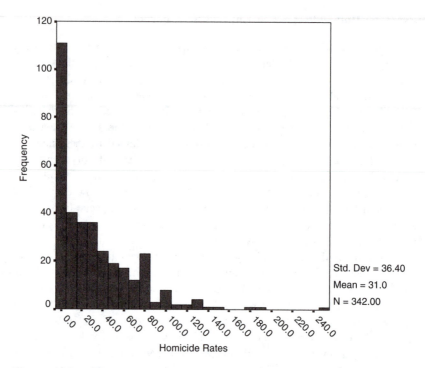

Figure 10.2a. Histogram of Homicide Rates per 100,000 Population in Chicago Neighborhoods

Level-1 Model. The outcome Y_j is the number of homicides occurring in NC_j in 1995, and the exposure, m_j, is the population of the NC_j, in 100,000s, according to the 1990 Census. A natural model for the number of homicides in NC_j is then $E(Y_j | \lambda_j) = m_j \lambda_j$. Under a Poisson model, the variance and mean are equal, that is, $\text{Var}(Y_j | \lambda_j) = m_j \lambda_j$. Using the log link $\eta_j = \log(\lambda_j)$, we have the level-1 model

$$\eta_j = \beta_{0j}. \qquad [10.24]$$

It may seem counterintuitive that our level-1 outcome has only one subscript, j. In what sense is this a two-level model? The key point is that there are two sources of variation: the sampling variance of Y_j, given λ_j, and the variance among neighborhoods in λ_j itself. Under the Poisson model, the sampling variance of Y_j, given λ_j, depends only on λ_j. Thus, under a Poisson model, no degrees of freedom are needed to estimate the level-1 variance. This problem is similar to the cases of research synthesis in Chapter 7. We might view

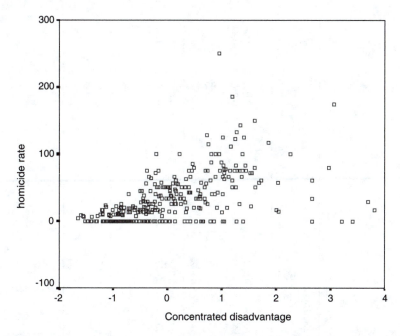

Figure 10.2b. Plot of Homicide Rate by Concentrated Disadvantage

each neighborhood as a "study" producing an effect size λ_j that is estimated with known variance.

Level-2 Model. At level 2, we model the variation between neighborhoods in their log homicide rates as a function of explanatory variables plus a normally distributed random error:

$$\beta_{0j} = \gamma_{00} + \gamma_{01}(\text{CONDIS})_j + \gamma_{02}(\text{COLLEFF})_j + u_{0j},$$
$$u_{0j} \sim N(0, \tau_{00}). \qquad [10.25]$$

Table 10.5 gives neighborhood-specific and population-average estimates for (a) the unconditional model, (b) a model with concentrated disadvantage as a predictor, and (c) a model with concentrated disadvantage and collective efficacy as predictors.

Unconditional Results. The unconditional level-2 model is

$$\beta_{0j} = \gamma_{00} + u_{0j}. \qquad [10.26]$$

TABLE 10.5 Log-Linear Models for Log Homicide Rates in Chicago

| | Unit-Specific Models for Log Homicide Rate, β_{0j} | | | | | | | | |
| | (a) | | | (b) | | | (c) | | |
Fixed Effect	Coefficient	se	exp(coeff)	Coefficient	se	exp(coeff)	Coefficient	se	exp(coeff)
INTERCEPT, γ_{00}	3.164	0.063	23.69	3.124	0.054	22.74	3.098	0.055	22.5
CONDIS, γ_{01}				0.678	0.049	1.97	0.523	0.061	1.69
COLLEFF, γ_{11}							-1.068	0.261	0.34
Level-2 variance, τ_{00}		0.775			0.353			0.323	

Population-Average Models for Log Homicide Rate, β_{0j}

Fixed Effect	Coefficient	se	exp(coeff)	Coefficient	se	exp(coeff)	Coefficient	se	exp(coeff)
INTERCEPT, γ_{00}	3.419	0.058	30.54	3.195	0.051	24.41	3.168	0.052	23.76
CONDIS, γ_{01}				0.738	0.045	2.09	0.589	0.057	1.80
COLLEFF, γ_{11}							-0.978	0.248	0.38

Descriptive Statistics

	Mean	sd
CONDIS	0.003	0.993
COLEFF	0.000	0.263
HOMICIDE	2.325	2.678

	J
CONDIS	342
COLEFF	342
HOMICIDE	342

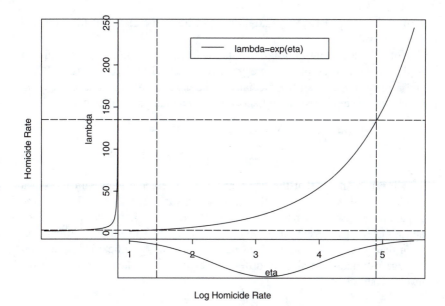

Figure 10.3. Neighborhood-Specific Homicide Rates as a Function of Neighborhood-Specific Log of Homicide Rate

NOTE: The vertical dotted lines mark the limits of the 95% prediction interval for the neighborhood-specific log-homicide rates, while the horizontal dotted lines mark the limits of the 95% prediction interval for neighborhood-specific homicide rates.

Under this model, the event rate for neighborhood j, given its random effect, u_{0j}, is

$$\lambda_j = \exp\{\gamma_{00} + u_{0j}\}. \qquad [10.27]$$

Our estimates from Table 10.5 are $\hat{\gamma}_{00} = 3.165$, $\hat{\tau}_{00} = .775$. Figure 10.3 displays, on the horizontal axis, the 95% plausible value interval for neighborhood log event rates based on these estimates. This interval is symmetric with a mean of $\hat{\gamma}_{00} = 3.165$ and a standard deviation of $\sqrt{\hat{\tau}_{00}} = \sqrt{.775} = .880$. Thus, under normality, we would expect 95% of the neighborhood log event rates to be found in the interval $3.165 \pm 1.96 * 0.880 = (1.44, 4.89)$. The translation to event rates, λ_{ij}, is given on the vertical axis, where the 95% plausible value interval is $(\exp\{1.44\}, \exp\{4.89\}) = (4.22, 132.95)$. Thus, under normality of the log event rate, most homicide rates are expected to be between 4.22 and 132.95 per 100,000, an indicator of large variation among neighborhoods. Notice that the event rate associated with a random effect of zero, that is, $\exp\{3.165\} = 23.69$, does not lie in the center of the expected 95% interval.

While the log event rates are symmetric about 3.165 under the assumption of the model, the event rates are positively skewed with a median of 23.69 and a mean larger than the median. In the case of the log link, there is an exact relationship between unit-specific and population-average expectations:

$$E(\exp\{\gamma_{00} + u_{0j}\}) = \exp\{\gamma_{00} + \tau_{00}/2\}$$

$$\simeq \exp\{3.165 + .775/2\} = 34.90. \qquad [10.28]$$

This formula shows that the mean and median diverge approximately by a factor of $\exp\{\frac{1}{2}\tau_{00}\}$. For small τ_{00}, these will be very similar. In fact, the population-average estimate of $\gamma_{00} = 3.419$ (Table 10.5, middle panel) yields an estimated mean event rate of $\exp\{3.419\} = 30.5$. This number differs a bit from that given in Equation 10.28 because the unit-specific and population-average estimates use slightly different weighting schemes in estimating the level-2 coefficients.

Conditional Models. Column (*b*) of Table 10.5 shows a strong positive association between neighborhood concentrated disadvantage and log homicide rates in the unit-specific model $\hat{\gamma}_{01} = .678$, se = .049. A one standard deviation increase in concentrated disadvantage ($sd_{CONDIS} = 0.993$) multiplies the event rate by $\exp\{(.993) * (.678)\} = 1.96$, or a 96% increase in the homicide rate per 100,000. The residual between neighborhood variance is estimated to be 0.353, less than half the unconditional variance of 0.775.

According to column c of Table 10.5, collective efficacy is significantly negatively related to log homicide rates, $\hat{\gamma}_{11} = -1.068$, se = 0.26. If two neighborhoods differ by one standard deviation in collective efficacy ($sd_{COLLEFF} = 0.263$), one would expect that the homicide rate of the neighborhood with higher collective efficacy would be $100 * \exp\{(0.263) * (-1.068)\} = 76\%$ times that of neighborhood with lower collective efficacy, a reduction of .24, or 24%, holding constant concentrated disadvantage.

Poisson Dispersion at Level 1. As mentioned earlier, if the data follow the assumed level-1 sampling model, the level-1 Poisson variance of the Y_{ij} will be w_{ij}, where

$$w_{ij} = n_{ij}\lambda_{ij}. \qquad [10.29]$$

However, if the level-1 data do not follow this model, the actual level-1 variance may be larger than that assumed (overdispersion) or smaller than that assumed (underdispersion). As in the binomial case, it is possible to generalize our model to include a scalar variance component, σ^2, so that the level-1 variance will be $\sigma^2 w_{ij}$. We note, however, that we could not estimate σ^2 in the case of our neighborhood data. With only one estimate of λ_{ij} per neighborhood, no degrees of freedom remain to estimate σ^2. This can be solved by including multiple counts for each neighborhood, for example, one for each age group.

Hierarchical Models for Ordinal Data

Ordered categorical outcomes are common in many social science and medical research applications. For example, attitude surveys assess how strongly people agree with a given statement, with responses recorded as "strongly agree," "agree," "neutral," "disagree," or "strongly disagree." Child development researchers ask how often children display a certain symptom such as shyness or aggression, with responses "never," "sometimes," or "often." In some studies, the outcome of interest is continuous, for example, annual income, but the available data have been grouped into categories (e.g., "high," "middle," and "low"). In all of these applications, the outcome data tell us about how cases are ordered but they do not establish a distance between cases on the outcome. Ordinal regression models specify associations between explanatory variables and such ordinal outcomes. Such models are well established for single-level data (cf. Agresti, 1996, chap. 8; Long, 1997, chap. 5; McCullagh & Nelder, 1989, chap. 5). Hedeker and Gibbons (1994) extend this logic to the multilevel setting; see also Goldstein (1995, p. 108).

The Cumulative Probability Model for Single-Level Data

A standard model for ordinal regression is the cumulative probability model. Its logic is easily conveyed in the context of a simple example. Suppose we have data about teachers' commitment to their profession. In particular, we have asked the following hypothetical question: "If you could go back to college and start all over again, would you again choose teaching as a profession?" Possible responses were: 1 = yes; 2 = not sure; 3 = no. Of interest are characteristics of the teachers that predict their responses to the question.

We can motivate the ordinal regression model by conceiving a latent continuous variable, z, labeled "degree of commitment to the profession." The relationship between this latent variable and the response data is displayed

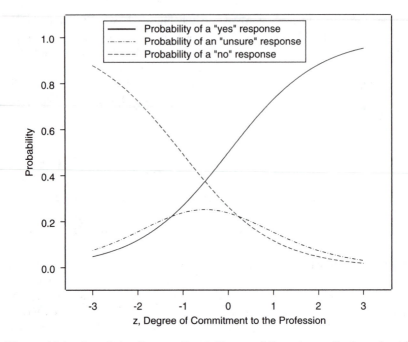

Figure 10.4. Association Between Latent Degree of Commitment (horizontal axis) and Probabilities of Responding "Yes," "Unsure", or "No" (vertical axis)

in Figure 10.4. Teachers with very low commitment to the profession have a very high probability of choosing "no" as a response. Thus, for low values of z, Prob("no"), the probability of saying "no," is high. This means, of course, that Prob("not sure") and Prob("yes") are small. However, as z becomes somewhat larger, indicating a modest commitment to teaching, Prob("no") diminishes and Prob("not sure") and Prob("yes") begin to increase. As z achieves very high values, Prob("no") becomes very small; and the Prob("not sure") becomes small as well. These teachers are not at all ambivalent about teaching, so they are very likely to say "$1 =$ yes," they would indeed choose teaching again. Thus, for very high values of z, P("yes") is high, and, correspondingly, the other probabilities are small.

To formalize this idea, we may, in general, have M possible ordered categories, $m = 1, \ldots, M$. Our response variable is denoted R, and R takes on the value of m with probability

$$\varphi_m = \text{Prob}(R = m).$$

In the above example, $M = 3$, and

$$\varphi_1 = \text{Prob}(R = 1) = \text{Prob}(\text{"yes"}),$$

$$\varphi_2 = \text{Prob}(R = 2) = \text{Prob}(\text{"not sure"}),$$

$$\varphi_3 = \text{Prob}(R = 3) = \text{Prob}(\text{"no"}).$$

To develop a single regression equation that captures the ordered nature of the data, it is convenient to work with *cumulative* probabilities rather than the probabilities themselves. We denote these cumulative probabilities as

$$\varphi_m^* = \text{Prob}(R \le m) = \varphi_1 + \varphi_2 + \cdots + \varphi_m. \qquad [10.30]$$

In our illustrative example, we have

$$\varphi_1^* = \varphi_1,$$

$$\varphi_2^* = \varphi_1 + \varphi_2, \qquad [10.31]$$

$$\varphi_3^* = \varphi_1 + \varphi_2 + \varphi_3 = 1.$$

Note that $\varphi_3^* = 1$ is redundant. In general, only $M - 1$ cumulative probabilities are of interest as $\varphi_M^* = 1$ in all studies.

Figure 10.5 graphs the cumulative probabilities associated with z for our example. Note that the solid line, representing φ_1^*, is the same as φ_1 in Figure 10.4 and that the dotted line in Figure 10.4 is the sum $\varphi_1 + \varphi_2$. The idea of cumulative probabilities leads naturally to the cumulative logit

$$\eta_m = \log\left(\frac{\varphi_m^*}{1 - \varphi_m^*}\right) = \log\left(\frac{\text{Prob}(R \le m)}{\text{Prob}(R > m)}\right) \qquad [10.32]$$

for $m = 1, \ldots, M - 1$. We can now formulate a simple logistic regression model

$$\eta_{mi} = \theta_m + \beta X_i. \qquad [10.33]$$

The model has an intercept, θ_m, for each category m, called a "threshold," and a common slope β. Formally, Equation 10.33 is called a "proportional odds" model. Suppose we compare the expected log-odds for two cases, one with $X = X_1$ and the second with $X = X_2$. The expected difference in log-odds between these two cases will be

$$\eta_{m1} - \eta_{m2} = \beta(X_1 - X_2), \qquad [10.34]$$

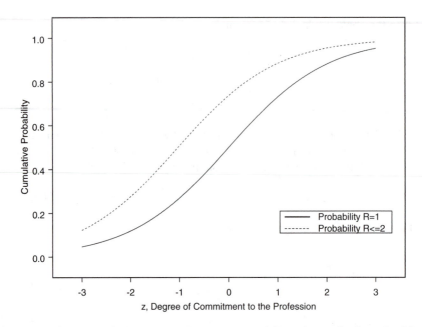

Figure 10.5. Association Between Latent Degree of Commitment (horizontal axis) and Cumulative Probability (vertical axis)

which does not depend on m. Thus, expected differences in log-odds between cases differing on X does not depend on a particular category. The relative odds for these two cases will be

$$\frac{\text{Odds}_{m1}}{\text{Odds}_{m2}} = \exp\{\beta(X_1 - X_2)\}. \tag{10.35}$$

Thus, the proportional-odds model makes a key assumption that X affects the odds ratio in the same way for every category m. This assumption must generally be checked; we provide an example in which the assumption fails in the next section. Note that the model also assumes that, for any X, the difference in log-odds between any two cumulative logits, say η_1 and η_2, for categories $m = 1$ and $m = 2$, depends only on the respective intercepts, that is,

$$\eta_1 - \eta_2 = \theta_1 - \theta_2. \tag{10.36}$$

It does not depend on X.

Extension to Two Levels

In terms of our example, suppose teachers are nested within schools and that we have one level-1 predictor, X_{ij}, that assesses the task variety in teaching for teacher i in school j. Based on organizational theory, we hypothesize that task variety increases teacher commitment. Then our level-1 model would be

$$\eta_{1ij} = \theta_{1j} + \beta_{1j}X_{1ij},$$
$$\eta_{2ij} = \theta_{2j} + \beta_{1j}X_{1ij}. \qquad [10.37]$$

The problem that arises in Equation 10.37 is that there are three potentially random coefficients: the slope for X, β_{1j}, and the two thresholds, θ_{1j} and θ_{2j}. To allow both thresholds to randomly vary, however, would make interpretation of the results very difficult. It would imply that the underlying teacher commitment, z_{ij}, translates into response categories in different ways in different schools. Moreover, such a strategy would require at least two random effects per school, and these would likely be highly correlated. These problems of interpretation and estimability would increase as more response categories are added.

A more coherent approach is to work with the difference,

$$\delta = \theta_1 - \theta_2 \qquad [10.38]$$

and to add a common intercept, β_0. The level-1 model for our data would become

$$\eta_{1ij} = \beta_{0j} + \beta_{1j}X_{1ij},$$
$$\eta_{2ij} = \beta_{0j} + \beta_{1j}X_{1ij} + \delta. \qquad [10.39]$$

This model allows the overall level of teacher commitment, β_{0j}, to vary randomly over schools; the slope for X, that is, β_{1j}, may also vary randomly, as in many examples of this book. The threshold, δ, however, would typically be held constant, though it could, in principle, vary as well.

Level-1 Structural Model. Generalizing to M categories, the level-1 model becomes

$$\eta_{mij} = \beta_{0j} + \sum_{q=1}^{Q} \beta_{qj}X_{qij} + \sum_{m=2}^{M-1} D_{mij}\delta_m, \qquad [10.40]$$

where D_{mij} is an indicator for category m.

Level-1 Sampling Model. As in the other cases of a generalized linear model, it is also useful to keep in mind the level-1 sampling model. Given the ordered nature of the data, we derive the $M - 1$ dummy variables $Y_{1ij}, \ldots, Y_{m-1ij}$ for case i in unit j as

$$Y_{mij} = 1 \quad \text{if } R_{ij} \leq m, \qquad 0 \text{ otherwise.} \qquad [10.41]$$

For example, in our example, with $M = 3$, we have

$$Y_{1ij} = 1 \quad \text{if } R_{ij} = 1,$$
$$Y_{2ij} = 1 \quad \text{if } R_{ij} \leq 2. \qquad (10.42)$$

The probabilities $\varphi^*_{mij} = \text{Prob}(Y_{mij} = 1)$ are thus cumulative probabilities. It can then readily be shown that

$$E(Y_{mij}|\varphi^*_{mij}) = \varphi^*_{mij},$$
$$\text{Var}(Y_{mij}|\varphi^*_{mij}) = \varphi^*_{mij}(1 - \varphi^*_{mij}), \qquad [10.43]$$
$$\text{Cov}(Y_{mij}, Y_{m'ij}|\varphi_{mij}, \varphi_{m'ij}) = \varphi^*_{mij}(1 - \varphi^*_{m'ij}).$$

Level-2 Model. The level-2 model has the usual form

$$\beta_{qj} = \gamma_{q0} + \sum_{s=1}^{S_q} \gamma_{qs} W_{sj} + u_{qj}, \qquad [10.44]$$

where the random effect, u_{qj}, can be estimated or constrained to be zero for all j. We typically assume multivariate normality for these random effects.

An Example: Teacher Control and Teacher Commitment

Data are from a 1990 survey of 650 teachers working in 16 public schools in California and Michigan. The schools were purposively selected to vary in terms of size, organizational structure, and urban versus suburban location. The outcome variable is the three-category measure of teacher commitment already described.

Unconditional Model. To assess the magnitude of variation among schools in the absence of covariates, we specified the level-1 model

$$\eta_{mj} = \beta_{0j} + D_{2ij}\delta_{2j}, \qquad [10.45]$$

where D_{2ij} is a dummy variable indicating whether $m = 2$ (i.e., $D_{2ij} = 1$ if $m = 2$, $D_{2ij} = 0$ if $m = 1$). This formulation thus summarizes the two equations

$$\eta_{1ij} = \beta_{0j},$$
$$\eta_{2ij} = \beta_{0j} + \delta_{2j}. \tag{10.46}$$

At level 2, the model is standard:

$$\beta_{0j} = \gamma_{00} + u_{0j}, \qquad u_{0j} \sim N(0, \tau_{00}),$$
$$\delta_{2j} = \delta_2. \tag{10.47}$$

The results (see Table 10.6) indicate $\hat{\gamma}_{00} = 0.222$, $\hat{\delta} = 1.027$, $\hat{\tau}_{00} = 0.126$.

Conditional Model. Next, we consider the introduction of predictors into this model. Rowan, Raudenbush, and Cheong (1993) hypothesized that teachers would express high levels of commitment if they had a job with a high degree of task variety and also experienced a high degree of control over school policies and teaching conditions. Conceptually, task variety varies at the teacher level, while teacher control varies at the school level (see Rowan et al., 1993, for details). The level-1 model is

$$\eta_{mij} = \beta_{0j} + \beta_{1j} * (\text{TASK VARIETY})_{ij} + D_{2ij}\delta_{2j}, \tag{10.48}$$

while the level-2 model is

$$\beta_{0j} = \gamma_{00} + \gamma_{01}(\text{TEACHER CONTROL})_j + u_{0j},$$
$$\beta_{1j} = \gamma_{10}, \tag{10.49}$$
$$\delta_{2j} = \delta_2.$$

The results (see Table 10.6) indicate that, within schools, TASK VARIETY is significantly related to commitment, $\hat{\gamma}_{10} = 0.349$, $t = 4.00$; between schools, TEACHER CONTROL is also strongly related to commitment, $\hat{\gamma}_{01} = 1.541$, $t = 4.22$. Inclusion of TEACHER CONTROL reduced the point estimate of the between-school variance to 0.00. Figures 10.6 and 10.7 display the predicted cumulative logits and the predicted cumulative probabilities as a function of TEACHER CONTROL (holding TASK VARIETY constant at the grand mean). The predicted probability of "yes" increases with TEACHER CONTROL as does the probability of either "yes" or "not sure." As TEACHER CONTROL becomes very high, the two probabilities converge: In schools with very high TEACHER CONTROL, there is little ambivalence about the appeal of teaching.

TABLE 10.6 Cumulative Logit Models for Teacher Commitment Data[a]

Parameter	(a) Unconditional Model			(b) Conditional Model		
	Coefficient	se	t Ratio	Coefficient	se	t Ratio
INTERCEPT, γ_{00}	0.222	0.123	1.795	0.334	0.090	3.27
TEACHER CONTROL, γ_{01}				1.541	0.366	4.22
TASK VARIETY slope, γ_{10}				0.349	0.087	4.00
THRESHOLD DIFFERENCE, δ_2	1.027	0.078	13.100	1.055	0.081	13.05
Level-2 variance, τ_{00}	0.126			0.00		

Descriptive Statistics

Variable	Sample Size	Mean	sd
TASK VARIETY	650	0.000	0.884
TEACHER CONTROL	16	0.009	0.324

Teacher Commitment

Value	Frequency	Percentage	Cumulative Percentage
1 = yes	354	54.5	54.5
2 = not sure	144	22.2	76.6
3 = no	152	23.4	100

a. All estimates are based on the unit-specific model.

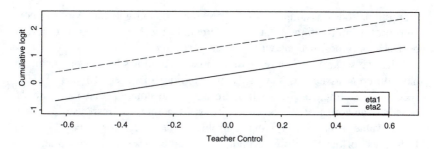

Figure 10.6. Predicted Cumulative Logits (vertical axis) as a Function of Teacher Control (Horizontal axis)

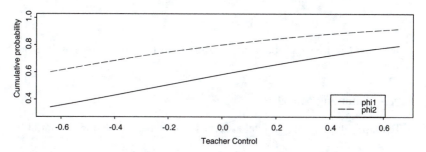

Figure 10.7. Predicted Cumulative Probabilities (vertical axis) as a Function of Teacher Control (horizontal axis)

Hierarchical Models for Multinomial Data

The previous section considered ordered multicategorical outcomes. Often, however, the multiple categories will not be clearly ordered. In other cases, the ordinal nature of the data may be debatable, and the key assumption of proportional odds may be questionable. In these instances, multinomial regression models are useful.

Again, a practical example helps introduce key ideas. The National Educational Longitudinal Study (NELS) enables us to use family background and secondary school experience to predict destinations in young adulthood. In particular, we are interested in whether a 20-year-old (a) is attending a four-year college, (b) is attending (or has attended) a two-year college (or community college), or (c) has not attended a postsecondary school. While these three categories may possibly be viewed as ordered, our inclination is to suspect that the backgrounds and experiences that predict four-year college are somewhat different from those that predict two-year college. If so, the proportional-odds assumption of the previous section will fail. More important, useful information about the differential processes leading to different postsecondary destinations will be lost.

What we seek, then, is a regression model that allows level-1 predictors to have different associations with the probabilities of different types of postsecondary experience. We shall again adopt the notation that there are M possible categories of the outcome. Thus, as before, the response, R, takes on the value of m with probability $\text{Prob}(R = m) = \varphi_m$, for $m = 1, \ldots, M$. In the case of our three postsecondary destinations, we have $M = 3$ and

$$\text{Prob}(R_{ij} = 1) = \varphi_{1ij},$$

$$\text{Prob}(R_{ij} = 2) = \varphi_{2ij}, \qquad\qquad [10.50]$$

$$\text{Prob}(R_{ij} = 3) = \varphi_{3ij} = 1 - \varphi_{1ij} - \varphi_{2ij}.$$

Note that $M - 1 = 2$ probabilities are required to specify the possible outcomes.

Level-1 Sampling Model

To clarify the sampling model at level 1, we construct the dummy variables

$$Y_{mij} = 1 \quad \text{if } R_{ij} = m, \qquad Y_{mij} = 0 \text{ otherwise.}$$

According to the multinomial distribution, the expected value and variance of Y_{mij}, given φ_{mij}, are then

$$\text{E}(Y_{mij}|\varphi_{mij}) = \varphi_{mij}, \qquad \text{Var}(Y_{mij}|\varphi_{mij}) = \varphi_{mij}(1 - \varphi_{mij}). \quad [10.51]$$

The covariance between outcomes Y_{mi} and $Y_{m'ij}$ is

$$\text{Cov}(Y_{mij}, Y_{m'ij}|\varphi_{mij}, \varphi_{m'ij}) = -\varphi_{mij}\varphi_{m'ij}. \qquad\qquad [10.52]$$

Level-1 Link Function

A common and convenient link function for multinomial regression models is the multinomial logit link. For each category $m = 1, \ldots, M - 1$, we have

$$\eta_{mij} = \log\left(\frac{\varphi_{mij}}{\varphi_{Mij}}\right) = \log\left(\frac{\text{Prob}(R_{ij} = m)}{\text{Prob}(R_{ij} = M)}\right). \qquad [10.53]$$

The outcome at level 1 is thus the log-odds of falling into category m relative to category M. We shall refer to category M as the "reference category."

Level-1 Structural Model

At level 1, we have

$$\eta_{mij} = \beta_{0j(m)} + \sum_{q=1}^{Q_m} \beta_{qj(m)} X_{qij} \qquad [10.54]$$

for $m = 1, \ldots, M - 1$. For example, with $M = 3$, there would be two level-1 equations, for η_{1ij} and η_{2ij}, respectively,

$$\eta_{1ij} = \beta_{0j(1)} + \sum_{q=1}^{Q_1} \beta_{qj(1)} X_{qij},$$

$$\qquad [10.55]$$

$$\eta_{2ij} = \beta_{0j(2)} + \sum_{q=1}^{Q_2} \beta_{qj(2)} X_{qij}.$$

Level-2 Model

The level-2 model has a parallel form

$$\beta_{qj(m)} = \gamma_{q0(m)} + \sum_{s=1}^{S_q} \gamma_{qs(m)} W_{sj} + u_{qj(m)}, \qquad [10.56]$$

for

$$q = 0, \ldots, Q_m.$$

Thus, for $M = 3$, there would be two sets of level-2 equations, as illustrated below.

Illustrative Example: Postsecondary Destinations

Unconditional Model. Returning to our example of postsecondary destinations, we first estimate an unconditional model simply to gauge the extent of between-school variation on the two outcomes: η_{1ij}, the log-odds of attending a four-year school (relative to no school), and η_{2ij}, the log-odds of attending a two-year school (relative to no school).

We thus have the pair of equations at level 1:

$$\eta_{1ij} = \beta_{0j(1)},$$

$$\qquad [10.57]$$

$$\eta_{2ij} = \beta_{0j(2)}.$$

According to this model, each student's pair of log-odds is equal to a school-specific intercept.

At level 2, the school-specific intercepts vary randomly over schools:

$$\beta_{0j(1)} = \gamma_{00(1)} + u_{0j(1)},$$

$$\beta_{0j(2)} = \gamma_{00(2)} + u_{0j(2)},$$

$$\begin{pmatrix} u_{0j(1)} \\ u_{0j(2)} \end{pmatrix} \sim N \left[\begin{pmatrix} 0 \\ 0 \end{pmatrix}, \begin{pmatrix} \tau_{00(1)00(1)} & \tau_{00(1)00(2)} \\ \tau_{00(2)00(1)} & \tau_{00(2)00(2)} \end{pmatrix} \right].$$

[10.58]

We see from Table 10.7 that, for students in the "typical school," the log-odds of attending a four-year college are greater than the log-odds of no school, $\hat{\gamma}_{00(1)} = 0.306$, $t = 2.75$, while the log-odds of attending a two-year school are less than the log-odds of no school, $\hat{\gamma}_{00(2)} = -0.605$, $t = -6.32$. There is statistically significant variation between schools in the log-odds of a four-year school (relative to no school), $\hat{\tau}_{00(1)00(1)} = 1.135$, $\chi^2 = 379$, df = 175, $p = .000$. However, there is less evidence of variation across schools in the log-odds of attending a two-year school (relative to no school), $\hat{\tau}_{00(2)00(2)} = 0.304$, $\chi^2 = 189$, df = 175, $p = .21$. An option for future analyses is to constrain the random effect $u_{0j(2)}$ to zero in the interest of parsimony. Such constraints are likely to be especially useful in multinomial models as the number of categories of the outcome increases.

Conditional Model. We now examine whether attendance at a private school is associated with increased access to postsecondary education, after taking into account math achievement at grade 8 as well as sex, ethnicity, socioeconomic status, and family structure.

The pair of logits at level 1 is now modeled as a function of sex (FEMALE, an indicator for females), ethnicity (indicators for ASIAN, BLACK, and HISPANIC ethnic background), socioeconomic status (SES, a composite of family income, parental education, and parental occupation), family structure (TWO-PARENT, indicator for two-parent household), and eighth-grade math achievement (PRE-MATH). Thus, for $m = 1, 2$,

$$\eta_{mij} = \beta_{0j(m)} + \beta_{1j(m)} * (\text{FEMALE})_{ij} + \beta_{2j(m)} * (\text{ASIAN})_{ij}$$

$$+ \beta_{3j(m)} * (\text{HISPANIC})_{ij} + \beta_{4j(m)} * (\text{BLACK})_{ij}$$

$$+ \beta_{5j(m)} * (\text{PRE-MATH})_{ij} + \beta_{6j(m)} * (\text{TWO-PARENT})_{ij}$$

$$+ \beta_{7j(m)} * (\text{SES})_{ij}.$$

[10.59]

At level 2, we model each intercept as a function of school sector (indicators for CATHOLIC and OTHER PRIVATE, with public schools as the reference group). We allow these intercepts to continue to vary randomly, even after controlling for sector. For simplicity, we constrain all other level-1 regression coefficients to be fixed in this preliminary analysis. Thus, we have

$$\beta_{0j(m)} = \gamma_{00(m)} + \gamma_{01(m)} * (\text{CATHOLIC})_j$$
$$+ \gamma_{02(m)} * (\text{OTHER PRIVATE})_j + u_{0j(m)}, \qquad [10.60]$$
$$\beta_{qj(m)} = \gamma_{q0(m)}, \qquad q = 1, \dots, 7.$$

The results in Table 10.7 indicate generally larger associations between the covariates and the log-odds of attending a four-year school ("Category 1") relative to no school than between the covariates and the log-odds of attending a two-year school ("Category 2") relative to no school. Level-1 effects associated with a heightened odds of attending a four-year college include high eighth-grade math achievement, high socioeconomic status, having both parents at home, being female, as well as Asian ethnicity and black ethnicity (relative to whites). In predicting the odds of attending a two-year school (relative to no school), each of the corresponding coefficients is smaller and only eighth-grade math achievement and socioeconomic status have coefficients that are significantly different from zero. These results, of course, are net the effects of all other covariates, including school sector.

Switching to level 2, controlling for the student background variables, those attending Catholic schools or other private schools have higher log-odds of attending a four-year school than do public school students. The same is not true in the case of predicting attendance at a two-year school. In this case, the point estimates associated with Catholic and other private schools are actually negative, though they fail to achieve statistical significance.

The tendency of school sector to relate to the odds of a four-year college differently than to the odds of a two-year college undermines the notion of using an ordinal regression model based on the proportional-odds assumption. Recall that this assumption implies that an explanatory variable should have a similar association with each successive cumulative odds. In contrast, our multinomial results suggest that while private school students are more likely to attend four-year colleges than are public school students, they are not more likely than public school students to attend a two-year college. They may, in fact, be less likely to attend a two-year school, though the estimated negative coefficients do not achieve statistical significance.

Comparison of Coefficients Across Equations. It is often useful to compare corresponding coefficients in the separate equations. Consider, for example,

TABLE 10.7 Multinomial Logit Models for Postsecondary Outcome Data[a]

Fixed Effect		(a) Unconditional Model			(b) Conditional Model		
		Coefficient	se	t Ratio	Coefficient	se	t Ratio
For category 1							
INTERCEPT, $\beta_{0j(1)}$	INTERCEPT, $\gamma_{00(1)}$	0.306	0.111	2.75	0.181	0.112	1.61
	CATHOLIC, $\gamma_{01(1)}$				1.194	0.314	3.80
	PRIVATE, $\gamma_{02(1)}$				0.606	0.296	2.05
FEMALE slope, $\beta_{1j(1)}$	$\gamma_{10(1)}$				0.567	0.161	3.52
ASIAN slope, $\beta_{2j(1)}$	$\gamma_{20(1)}$				0.832	0.260	3.20
HISPANIC slope, $\beta_{3j(1)}$	$\gamma_{30(1)}$				0.392	0.248	1.58
BLACK slope, $\beta_{4j(1)}$	$\gamma_{40(1)}$				0.697	0.263	2.65
PRE-MATH slope, $\beta_{5j(1)}$	$\gamma_{50(1)}$				0.087	0.008	10.88
TWO-PARENT slope, $\beta_{6j(1)}$	$\gamma_{60(1)}$				0.317	0.169	1.87
SES slope, $\beta_{7j(1)}$	$\gamma_{70(1)}$				0.792	0.129	6.16
For category 2							
INTERCEPT, $\beta_{0j(2)}$	INTERCEPT, $\gamma_{00(2)}$	−0.605	0.096	−6.32	−0.296	0.112	−2.65
	CATHOLIC, $\gamma_{01(2)}$				−0.520	0.413	−1.26
	PRIVATE, $\gamma_{02(2)}$				−0.504	0.343	−1.47
FEMALE slope, $\beta_{1j(2)}$	$\gamma_{10(2)}$				0.098	0.168	0.56
ASIAN slope, $\beta_{2j(2)}$	$\gamma_{20(2)}$				0.372	0.272	1.37
HISPANIC slope, $\beta_{3j(2)}$	$\gamma_{30(2)}$				0.423	0.233	1.81
BLACK slope, $\beta_{4j(2)}$	$\gamma_{40(2)}$				−0.490	0.315	−1.56
PRE-MATH slope, $\beta_{5j(2)}$	$\gamma_{50(2)}$				0.021	0.008	2.45
TWO-PARENT slope, $\beta_{6j(2)}$	$\gamma_{60(2)}$				0.129	0.174	0.74
SES slope, $\beta_{7j(2)}$	$\gamma_{70(2)}$				0.532	0.134	3.97
		Variance-Covariance Components					
Variances	$\tau_{00(1)00(1)}$	1.135			0.333		
	$\tau_{00(2)00(2)}$	0.039			0.171		
Covariance	$\tau_{00(1)00(2)}$	−0.523			−0.209		

Student Level	N	Mean	sd	Minimum	Maximum
Descriptive Statistics for Postsecondary Data					
FEMALE	1,259	0.48	0.50	0.00	1.00
ASIAN	1,259	0.15	0.36	0.00	1.00
HISPANIC	1,259	0.17	0.37	0.00	1.00
BLACK	1,259	0.12	0.32	0.00	1.00
PRE-MATH ACH.	1,259	38.81	12.51	16.58	66.81
TWO PARENT	1,259	0.65	0.48	0.00	1.00
BYSES	1,259	0.10	0.81	-2.23	1.85
School Level					
PUBLIC	176	0.73	0.45	0.00	1.00
CATHOLIC	176	0.13	0.33	0.00	1.00
PRIVATE	176	0.15	0.36	0.00	1.00

Outcome = Postsecondary Status

	N	Percentage
1. Four-year school	735	48.4
2. Community college	296	19.5
3. Not in school	489	32.2

the odds ratio between Catholic and public students of attending a four-year school (relative to no school). This is given by

$$e^{\gamma_{01(1)}} = \frac{\text{Prob}(R = 1|\text{Catholic})/\text{Prob}(R = 3|\text{Catholic})}{\text{Prob}(R = 1|\text{public})/\text{Prob}(R = 3|\text{public})}. \qquad [10.61]$$

Similarly, the odds ratio between Catholic and public students of attending a two-year school is given by

$$e^{\gamma_{01(2)}} = \frac{\text{Prob}(R = 2|\text{Catholic})/\text{Prob}(R = 3|\text{Catholic})}{\text{Prob}(R = 2|\text{public})/\text{Prob}(R = 3|\text{public})}. \qquad [10.62]$$

It therefore follows that the odds ratio between Catholic and public students of attending a four-year school, as compared to attending a two-year school, are given by

$$e^{\gamma_{01(1)} - \gamma_{01(2)}} = \frac{\text{Prob}(R = 1|\text{Catholic})/\text{Prob}(R = 2|\text{Catholic})}{\text{Prob}(R = 1|\text{public})/\text{Prob}(R = 2|\text{public})}. \qquad [10.63]$$

Using the multivariate hypothesis testing features of software for hierarchical models, we can therefore test whether Catholic school students are more likely than public school students to attend a four-year college (relative to a two-year school). The result is $\hat{\gamma}_{01(1)} - \hat{\gamma}_{01(2)} = 1.714$, yielding a χ^2 statistic of 11.78, $p = .001$. The odds of attending a four-year school, relative to attending a two-year school, are higher for Catholic than for public school students. The relative odds ratio, $\exp\{1.714\} = 5.55$, is a large effect.

Estimation Considerations in Hierarchical Generalized Linear Models

Our primary aim in this chapter has been to offer an intuitive, conceptual introduction to multilevel models with discrete level-1 outcomes. Because the models themselves become considerably more complex than in the continuous outcome cases previously considered, we have deferred until the end of the chapter any discussion of estimation considerations.

The fact that the level-1 sampling model for discrete outcomes is not normal while the higher-level models involve multivariate normal assumptions poses a problem for conventional estimation theory. The methods described in Chapter 3 are no longer appropriate. Parameter estimation in hierarchical generalized linear models is more complicated, involving approximations to maximum likelihood. The most frequently used methods are based on a first- or second-order Taylor series expansion around an estimate of the fixed and random portions of the model. This is referred to as penalized quasi-likelihood estimation (PQL), as described by Breslow and Clayton (1993) and Goldstein (1991). More precise methods, based on Gauss-Hermite quadrature (Hedeker & Gibbons, 1994; Pinheiro & Bates, 1995) or a Laplace approximation (Raudenbush, Yang, & Yosef, 2000), have also been developed. Strategies for estimation and computation for hierarchical generalized line models are detailed in Chapter 14.

Summary of Terms Introduced in This Chapter

Generalized linear model: A regression model in which the expected outcome is transformed and this transformation is equated to a linear function of regression coefficients. The latter is called the *structural model*. The transformation of the expected outcomes is called the *link function*. A *sampling model* is selected based on the type of outcome variable under study. This approach can be tailored to various types of data, including continuous outcomes, categorical outcomes, and counted data. (See Table 10.8.)

TABLE 10.8 Examples of Two-Level Generalized Linear Models

Type of Outcome	Level-1 Sampling Model	Expected Level-1 Outcome	Level-1 Link Function
Continuous $-\infty < Y_{ij} < \infty$	Normal	μ_{ij}	$\eta_{ij} = \mu_{ij}$ (identity)
Binary $Y_{ij} \in \{0, 1\}$	Bernoulli	φ_{ij}	$\eta_{ij} = \log\left[\varphi_{ij}/(1 - \varphi_{ij})\right]$ (logit)
Counts $Y_{ij} \in \{0, 1, \ldots, m_{ij}\}$	Binomial	$m_{ij}\varphi_{ij}$	$\eta_{ij} = \log\left[\varphi_{ij}/(1 - \varphi_{ij})\right]$ (logit)
Counts $Y_{ij} \in \{0, 1, \ldots\}$	Poisson	λ_{ij}	$\eta_{ij} = \log(\lambda_{ij})$ (log)
Ordered categories $R_{ij} \in \{1, 2, \ldots, M\}$	Multinomial	φ^*_{mij}	$\eta^*_{mij} = [\varphi^*_{mij}/(1 - \varphi^*_{mij})]$ (cumulative logit)
Nominal categories $R_{ij} \in \{1, 2, \ldots, M\}$	Multinomial	φ_{mij}	$\eta_{mij} = [\varphi_{mij}/(\varphi_{Mij})]$ (multinomial logit)

Hierarchical generalized linear model: The generalized linear model can be extended to include multiple levels of nesting. The standard generalized linear model then becomes the level-1 model.

Level-1 expected value: The expected value of the level-1 outcome, holding constant all random coefficients in the level-1 model.

Level-1 sampling model: The level-1 outcome is assumed to arise from a specific probability distribution, holding constant the level-1 expected value. This level-1 probability distribution is called the *level-1 sampling model*.

Level-1 link function: The expected value of the level-1 outcome is transformed and this transformation, η_{ij}, is equated to a linear function of the regression coefficients. The transformation is called the *Level-1 link function* (see η_{ij} in Table 10.8).

Level-1 structural model: The level-1 link function, η_{ij}, is equated to a linear model having level-1 coefficients. This linear model is the level-1 *structural model*.

Overdispersion and underdispersion: The variability in the level-1 outcome may be greater than expected under the level-1 sampling model. This is *overdispersion. Underdispersion* occurs when the variability in the level-1 outcome is less than expected under the level-1 sampling model.

Unit-specific model: A *unit-specific model* defines fixed regression coefficients that can be interpreted as the expected change in the outcome associated with a one-unit increase in the relevant predictor, holding constant other predictors and all random effects in the model.

Population-average model: In contrast to the unit-specific model, a *population-average model* defines regression coefficients that can be interpreted as the expected change in the outcome associated with a one-unit increase in the relevant predictor holding constant other predictors but without controlling any random effects.

Notes

1. The survey was a collaborative project involving researchers from Michigan State University and the Thai Office of the National Primary Education Commission with support form the U.S. Agency for International Development. See Raudenbush and Bhumirat (1992) for details.

2. An alternative conception of the intraclass correlation for binomial models derives from reconceiving the level-1 model in terms of a latent variable $Z_{ij} = \eta_{ij} + r_{ij}$ (Snijders & Bosker, 1999, chap. 14). Here η_{ij} remains the linear predictor of Equation 10.4, and the level-1 random effect is assumed to have a standard logistic distribution with a mean of 0 and variance $\pi^2/3$. Under this model, the intraclass correlation can be computed as $\rho = \tau_{00}/(\tau_{00} + \pi^2/3)$. This conception of ρ depends on the choice of η_{ij} as the logit link and the assumption that a latent r_{ij} follows the logistic distribution. The intracluster correlation would have a different value if r_{ij} were assumed unit normal and η_{ij} were the probit link function (Long, 1997, chap. 3).

3. Large schools in Thailand tend to have more resources than small schools and to be located in comparatively advantaged urban areas.

4. Heagarty and Zeger (2000) have developed maximum likelihood estimates for population-average regression coefficients. Their model also supplies unit-specific estimates.

5. Concentrated disadvantage, based on data from the 1990 Census, is a composite of a neighborhood's poverty rate, percentage receiving public assistance, percentage female-headed households, percentage unemployed, percentage less than 18, and percentage African American. The last two items were included because the data showed that children and African Americans are disproportionately exposed to high poverty, unemployment, public assistance, and female-headed households.

11

Hierarchical Models for Latent Variables

- Regression with Missing Data
- Regression when Predictors are Measured with Error
- Regression with Missing Data and Measurement Errors
- Estimating Direct and Indirect Effects of Latent Variables
- Nonlinear Item Response Models
- Summary of Terms Introduced in This Chapter

Conventional statistical models represent associations among a set of observable variables. These relationships are indexed by certain unknown population parameters (e.g., regression coefficients, correlations, odds ratios, mean differences). Often, however, interest focuses on *latent variables*: variables that are not directly observed. For example, a child's level of aggression may not be directly observable but, rather, inferred from a set of item responses from an interview of that child's teacher. An experimental treatment designed to reduce aggression is not aimed primarily at the specific interview items or laboratory checklists used to measure aggression but, rather, at the underlying level of aggression that gives rise to these indicators. The aim of the experimental study, then, is to assess associations between an experimental treatment and a latent variable, but these associations must be inferred from the observed, fallible data. This logic suggests a two-stage inferential problem: To make inferences about the population parameters that generate the latent data, one must first consider how the latent variables generate the fallible data (Bock, 1989). This chapter considers how this two-stage inferential problem can be addressed within the framework of a hierarchical model.

Associations among latent variables are obscured not only by measurement error in the indicators, but also by missing data. Suppose, for example, that n respondents are sampled at random from a population and then data on P

variables are to be collected from each respondent. However, data are missing on one or more variables for one or more persons. The fact that data are missing does not change the purpose of the investigation—to make inferences about the target population based on the *n* cases sampled to represent that population. The variables having some missing values may be viewed as latent variables.

In a way, latent variable analysis may always be regarded as a missing data problem. We may regard the observed data as the incomplete data. The incomplete data augmented by the missing data are viewed as the complete data (Little & Rubin, 1987). The analytic aim is to use the incomplete data to draw valid inferences about the parameters that generate the complete data.

In reality, this entire book may be viewed as dealing with latent variables. For example, in Chapter 4, we considered the SES-achievement slope in each of many high schools. This slope was a latent, or unobservable, variable. Our object was to make inferences about the distribution of these slopes in a population of schools. We therefore formulated a level-1 model that described the observed math outcome for each child as a function of latent variables (school means and slopes). The level-2 model described the distribution of these two latent variables in a population of schools. Similarly, in Chapter 6, we considered models for children's growth in vocabulary during the second year of life (Huttenlocher et al., 1991). The level-1 model represented each child's observed vocabulary count at each of several occasions as a function of several latent growth parameters. The key growth parameter turned out to be the rate of acceleration. The level-2 model represented the distribution of latent acceleration across a population of children. We used the observed data (vocabulary counts and ages) to make inferences about the population distribution of latent variables (acceleration rates).

Readers familiar with structural equation models (SEMs) will immediately see the parallel between these two-level models and those estimated using software such as LISREL (Joreskog & Sorbom, 1996), EQS (Bentler, 1983) AMOS (Arbuckle, 1994), or M-Plus (Muthén & Muthén, 1998). SEM analysis involves, first, a measurement model describing the distribution of the observed data given the latent data and, second, a structural model describing the associations among the latent variables. Willett and Sayer (1994) clarify the connections between HLM and SEM in the context of models for individual change.

In light of the fact that hierarchical models may be regarded explicitly as latent variable models, it is not surprising that HLM may be tailored to solve a number of problems arising from missing data and measurement error. This chapter focuses on both of these two issues.

Regression with Missing Data

Suppose the aim is to explain variation in an outcome variable, Z, by explanatory variables, $X_1, X_2, \ldots, X_{P-1}$ using multiple linear regression. Assuming independent and normally distributed model errors, standard estimation via ordinary least squares (OLS) will yield efficient estimates of P regression coefficients (an intercept and $P - 1$ slopes) and the residual variance, plus standard t or F tests. However, if any unit is missing a value on Y or on one of the Xs, the OLS formulas cannot be evaluated. To use OLS, one must then either drop from the analysis the cases that contain the missing values, impute the missing values for those cases, or use some other device such as a pairwise missing data procedure. Each of these options poses certain risks to statistical inference (Little, 1992).

Dropping incomplete cases will bias the analytic sample unless the data are missing completely at random. Discarding data in this way will also weaken precision. Imputing missing values is better if the method of imputation is thoughtful. However, standard error estimates will be negatively biased. Pairwise deletion can lead to serious problems of estimation and computation. These issues are reviewed in detail by Little (1992) and Schafer (1997).

Multiple Model-Based Imputation

A satisfactory solution to the missing data problem involves multiple, model-based imputation (Little & Rubin, 1987; Schafer, 1997). A multiple imputation procedure produces M "complete" data sets. Each data set is analyzed via OLS and the results are averaged to arrive at a point estimate of each regression coefficient. Appropriate sampling variances are computed as the average of the M sampling variances plus an inflation factor that represents the variation among the M point estimates. The formulas for computing these standard errors were published by Little and Rubin (1987), Little and Schenker (1995), and Schafer (1997).

In addition to producing realistic standard errors, multiple model-based imputation will produce unbiased inferences about the parameters generating the complete data as long as the model assumptions hold and the data are "missing at random" (MAR). MAR is a mild condition, much less stringent than "missing completely at random" (MCAR). MCAR assumes that the missing data are a simple random sample of the complete data. In contrast, MAR assumes only that the probability of missingness is independent of the values of the complete data after controlling for all the observed data. This assumption will often be realistic because the variables contained in the observed data set will often carry considerable information about both the missing data themselves and the probability that a data point will be missing. Moreover, even if MAR fails, the multiple imputation results will be robust as long as the fraction of missing information is small. We note that the fraction of missing information is not the fraction of missing data points. Rather, it is related to the unexplained variation in the missing data given the observed data. If the relationships among the variables of interest are strong, the fraction of missing information may be small even if the fraction of missing cases is large. Other methods mentioned above (dropping missing cases, imputing single missing values, pairwise deletion) do not produce results that are unbiased under MAR or that are generally robust to violations of MAR.

Applying HLM to the Missing Data Problem

The crucial step in producing multiple model-based imputations is the efficient estimation of the P-variate distribution of the complete data given only the observed data. In their seminal paper, Dempster, Laird, and Rubin (1977) showed how to use the EM algorithm to compute maximum likelihood estimates of a P-variate normal distribution based on incomplete data.[1] (See also Orchard & Woodbury, 1972; Goldstein, 1995, chap. 4, for closely related approaches.)

Unfortunately, the process of multiple imputation can be somewhat cumbersome in that it entails multiple analysis and synthesis of results. The advantages of valid inference under MAR can also be obtained through a somewhat simpler approach based on maximum likelihood estimates of the P-variate distribution of the complete data given the incomplete data. This is the same as the first step in programs that produce multiple imputations (Little, 1992). However, instead of creating imputations, the next step is simply to transform these estimates into the needed regression coefficient estimates and standard errors. Given the invariance properties of maximum likelihood, the resulting estimates will also be maximum likelihood.

The approach is best illustrated with a simple example.[2] Consider the artificial data in Table 11.1. We have an outcome, Z, and two predictors, X_1 and X_2. Thus, $P = 3$. There are $J = 15$ participants. There are no missing data. Using OLS regression, estimates and standard errors for the three regression coefficients are given at the bottom of Table 11.1.

Suppose, however, that some of the values in Table 11.1 were not available to the researcher. The available or "incomplete" data are given in Table 11.2. We see, for example, that case 4 has data on Z and X_2 but not on X_1. Case 3 has data only on Z.

TABLE 11.1 Hypothetical Data for Regression Analysis:
Z = Outcome, Predictors Are X_1 and X_2

Complete Data

Case	Z	X_1	X_2
1	48.92	41.86	60.41
2	55.54	56.06	52.99
3	59.49	39.65	53.38
4	46.52	37.31	55.25
5	56.20	57.59	52.54
6	50.40	58.75	47.94
7	51.55	42.34	51.42
8	75.41	58.95	69.87
9	36.13	45.74	44.62
10	43.88	51.54	44.04
11	68.01	62.26	48.52
12	56.65	62.11	48.90
13	40.49	47.21	55.69
14	35.52	39.75	39.45
15	60.48	64.43	66.00

Regression Results

Predictor	Coefficient	se
Intercept	−13.093	15.542
X_1	0.562	0.220
X_2	0.697	0.259

Reorganization of the Data. We first reconceive the variables for each case j as "occasions of measurement." If the data are complete, each case has $P = 3$ occasions. If case j is missing one value, there will be only two occasions for that case, and if case j is missing two values, there will be only one occasion for that case. The outcome is then reconceived as Y_{ij}, that is, the value of the datum collected at occasion i for case j, with $i = 1, \ldots, n_j$, and with $n_j < P = 3$. If the data are complete for case j, then $Y_{1j} = Z_j$, $Y_{2j} = X_{1j}$, $Y_{3j} = X_{2j}$. The reorganized complete data are presented in Table 11.3 and the corresponding incomplete data in Table 11.4. Note that we have created dummy variables D_{zij}, D_{1ij}, and D_{2ij} to indicate whether Y_{ij} is Z_j, X_{1j}, or X_{2j}. Consider, for example, case 4 (Table 11.4, case 4). Recall that X_{14} was missing. Thus, we have $Y_{14} = Z_4 = 46.52$, $Y_{24} = X_{24} = 55.25$. This is indicated by D_z taking on a value of 1 for the first record, and D_2 taking on a value of 1 in the second record for this case.

TABLE 11.2 Hypothetical Data for Regression Analysis:
Z = Outcome, Predictors Are X_1 and X_2

	Incomplete Data		
Case	Z	X_1	X_2
1	48.92	41.86	60.41
2	????	56.06	52.99
3	59.49	????	????
4	46.52	????	55.25
5	56.20	57.59	????
6	50.40	58.75	47.94
7	51.55	????	51.42
8	75.41	58.95	69.87
9	36.13	45.74	44.62
10	43.88	51.54	44.04
11	68.01	62.26	48.52
12	56.65	62.11	48.90
13	40.49	47.21	55.69
14	35.52	39.75	39.45
15	60.48	64.43	66.00

Level-1 Model. The first-level units are measurement occasions and the second-level units are persons. The level-1 model simply indicates which elements of the complete data have been observed:

$$Y_{ij} = D_{zij}Z_j + D_{1ij}X_{1j} + D_{2ij}X_{2j}. \qquad [11.1]$$

Thus, for case 1, we have

$$Y_{11} = (1) * Z_1 + (0) * X_{11} + (0) * X_{21} = Y_1 = 48.92,$$
$$Y_{21} = (0) * Z_1 + (1) * X_{11} + (0) * X_{21} = X_{11} = 41.86, \qquad [11.2]$$
$$Y_{31} = (0) * Z_1 + (0) * X_{11} + (1) * X_{21} = X_{21} = 60.41,$$

or, in matrix notation,

$$\begin{pmatrix} Y_{11} \\ Y_{21} \\ Y_{31} \end{pmatrix} = \begin{pmatrix} 1 & 0 & 0 \\ 0 & 1 & 0 \\ 0 & 0 & 1 \end{pmatrix} \begin{pmatrix} Z_1 \\ X_{11} \\ X_{21} \end{pmatrix} = \begin{pmatrix} 48.92 \\ 41.86 \\ 60.41 \end{pmatrix}. \qquad [11.3]$$

However, consider the incomplete data for case 4 (Table 11.4). Here we have

$$Y_{14} = (1) * Z_4 + (0) * X_{14} + (0) * X_{24} = Z_4 = 46.52,$$
$$Y_{24} = (0) * Z_4 + (0) * X_{14} + (1) * X_{24} = X_{24} = 55.25, \qquad [11.4]$$

TABLE 11.3 Complete Data, Transformed

Case	Y	D_z	D_1	D_2
1	48.92	1	0	0
1	41.86	0	1	0
1	60.41	0	0	1
2	55.54	1	0	0
2	56.06	0	1	0
2	52.99	0	0	1
3	59.49	1	0	0
3	39.65	0	1	0
3	53.38	0	0	1
4	46.52	1	0	0
4	37.31	0	1	0
4	55.25	0	0	1
5	56.20	1	0	0
5	57.59	0	1	0
5	52.54	0	0	1
6	50.40	1	0	0
6	58.75	0	1	0
6	47.94	0	0	1
7	51.55	1	0	0
7	42.34	0	1	0
7	51.42	0	0	1
8	75.41	1	0	0
8	58.95	0	1	0
8	69.87	0	0	1
9	36.13	1	0	0
9	45.74	0	1	0
9	44.62	0	0	1
10	43.88	1	0	0
10	51.54	0	1	0
10	44.04	0	0	1
11	68.01	1	0	0
11	62.26	0	1	0
11	48.52	0	0	1
12	56.65	1	0	0
12	62.11	0	1	0
12	48.90	0	0	1
13	40.49	1	0	0
13	47.21	0	1	0
13	55.69	0	0	1
14	35.52	1	0	0
14	39.75	0	1	0
14	39.45	0	0	1
15	60.48	1	0	0
15	64.43	0	1	0
15	66.00	0	0	1

Continued

TABLE 11.3 (continued)

| | | | Maximum Likelihood Estimates | | | | | |
Parameter			Coefficient			se		
γ_z			52.346			2.786		
γ_1			51.037			2.372		
γ_2			52.734			2.021		
τ_{zz}	τ_{z1}	τ_{z2}	116.433	59.673	52.558	42.515	29.880	25.687
	τ_{11}	τ_{12}		84.435	17.525		30.831	19.116
		τ_{22}			61.280			22.376

or, in matrix notation,

$$\begin{pmatrix} Y_{14} \\ Y_{24} \end{pmatrix} = \begin{pmatrix} 1 & 0 & 0 \\ 0 & 0 & 1 \end{pmatrix} \begin{pmatrix} Z_4 \\ X_{14} \\ X_{24} \end{pmatrix} = \begin{pmatrix} 46.52 \\ 55.25 \end{pmatrix}. \qquad [11.5]$$

In general, we can write the matrix equation as

$$\mathbf{Y}_j = \mathbf{D}_j \mathbf{Y}_j^*, \qquad [11.6]$$

where Y_j is the n_j by 1 vector of observed values, Y_j^* is the vector of complete values, and D_j is the matrix of dummy variables indicating which elements of the complete data have been observed. Notice that the complete data Y_j^* exist, in principle, for every case j. These complete data become outcomes at level 2.

Level-2 Model. While the level-1 model represents the incomplete data as a function of the complete latent data, the level-2 model describes the distribution of the compete data:

$$Z_j = \gamma_z + u_{zj},$$

$$X_{1j} = \gamma_1 + u_{1j},$$

$$X_{2j} = \gamma_2 + u_{2j}, \qquad [11.7]$$

$$\begin{pmatrix} u_{zj} \\ u_{1j} \\ u_{2j} \end{pmatrix} \sim N \left[\begin{pmatrix} 0 \\ 0 \\ 0 \end{pmatrix}, \begin{pmatrix} \tau_{zz} & \tau_{z1} & \tau_{z2} \\ \tau_{1z} & \tau_{11} & \tau_{12} \\ \tau_{2z} & \tau_{21} & \tau_{22} \end{pmatrix} \right],$$

where Z_j, X_{1j}, and X_{2j} are now the complete data in Y_j^*. Thus, γ_z, γ_1, and γ_2 are, respectively, the mean values of the complete Z, X_1, and X_2. The level-2

TABLE 11.4 Incomplete Data, Transformed

Case	Y	D_z	D_1	D_2
1	48.92	1	0	0
1	41.86	0	1	0
1	60.41	0	0	1
2	56.06	0	1	0
2	52.99	0	0	1
3	59.49	1	0	0
4	46.52	1	0	0
4	55.25	0	0	1
5	56.20	1	0	0
5	57.59	0	1	0
6	50.40	1	0	0
6	58.75	0	1	0
6	47.94	0	0	1
7	51.55	1	0	0
7	51.42	0	0	1
8	75.41	1	0	0
8	58.95	0	1	0
8	69.87	0	0	1
9	36.13	1	0	0
9	45.74	0	1	0
9	44.62	0	0	1
10	43.88	1	0	0
10	51.54	0	1	0
10	44.04	0	0	1
11	68.01	1	0	0
11	62.26	0	1	0
11	48.52	0	0	1
12	56.65	1	0	0
12	62.11	0	1	0
12	48.90	0	0	1
13	40.49	1	0	0
13	47.21	0	1	0
13	55.69	0	0	1
14	35.52	1	0	0
14	39.75	0	1	0
14	39.45	0	0	1
15	60.48	1	0	0
15	64.43	0	1	0
15	66.00	0	0	1

Continued

TABLE 11.4 (Continued)

Parameter			Maximum Likelihood Estimates					
			Coefficient			se		
γ_z			52.256			2.836		
γ_1			53.828			2.081		
γ_2			53.052			2.221		
τ_{zz}	τ_{z1}	τ_{z2}	118.204	62.598	54.445	43.913	27.952	28.143
	τ_{11}	τ_{12}		58.789	20.014		23.171	18.425
		τ_{22}			67.676			26.269

model may be written in matrix notation as

$$Y_j^* = \gamma + u_j, \qquad u_j \sim N(0, \mathbf{T}). \qquad [11.8]$$

The level-2 model thus represents the multivariate normal distribution of the complete data.

Combined Model. The combined model, in matrix notation, is found by substituting the level-2 model (Equation 11.8) into the level-1 model (Equation 11.6) to yield

$$\mathbf{Y}_j = \mathbf{D}_j\gamma + \mathbf{D}_j\mathbf{u}_j, \qquad \mathbf{D}_j\mathbf{u}_j \sim N(0, \mathbf{D}_j\mathbf{T}\mathbf{D}_j^T). \qquad [11.9]$$

It is not difficult to estimate this model using the EM algorithm or Fisher scoring, as described in the Chapter 14.

Results: Complete Data. The HLM analysis begins with maximum likelihood estimates of the means (γ_z, γ_1, γ_2) and the variance-covariance elements in $\mathbf{T}$ (Table 11.3, bottom). These estimates contain all of the needed information for computing the needed regression parameters. Under standard theory for multivariate normal distributions, we have

$$E(Z_j | X_{1j}, X_{2j}) = \gamma_z + \begin{bmatrix} \tau_{z1} & \tau_{z2} \end{bmatrix} \begin{bmatrix} \tau_{11} & \tau_{12} \\ \tau_{21} & \tau_{22} \end{bmatrix}^{-1} \begin{bmatrix} X_{1j} - \gamma_1 \\ X_{2j} - \gamma_2 \end{bmatrix}. \qquad [11.10]$$

Substituting the maximum likelihood estimates from the bottom of Table 11.3, we have

$$\widehat{E}(Z_j | X_{1j}, X_{2j}) = 52.346 + \begin{bmatrix} 59.673 & 52.558 \end{bmatrix} \begin{bmatrix} 84.435 & 17.525 \\ 17.525 & 61.280 \end{bmatrix}^{-1}$$

$$\times \begin{bmatrix} X_{1j} - 51.037 \\ X_{2j} - 52.735 \end{bmatrix}$$

$$= -13.093 + 0.562 * X_{1j} + 0.697 * X_{2j}. \qquad [11.11]$$

Thus, the two-step HLM analysis duplicates the OLS analysis (Table 11.1, bottom).

Results: Incomplete Data. By reorganizing the incomplete data in the form of Table 11.4 and employing the HLM analysis described above, we can obtain maximum likelihood estimates for the regression coefficients. Again, the HLM analysis begins with maximum likelihood estimates of the means (γ_z, γ_1, γ_2) and the variance-covariance elements in T (see Table 11.4, bottom). Again substituting the maximum likelihood estimates into Equation 11.10, we now have

$$
\begin{aligned}
\widehat{E}(Z_j|X_{1j}, X_{2j}) &= 52.256 + \begin{bmatrix} 62.598 & 54.445 \end{bmatrix} \begin{bmatrix} 58.789 & 20.014 \\ 20.014 & 67.676 \end{bmatrix}^{-1} \\
&\quad \times \begin{bmatrix} X_{1j} - 53.828 \\ X_{2j} - 53.052 \end{bmatrix} \\
&= -23.950 + 0.879 * X_{1j} + 0.544 * X_{2j}.
\end{aligned}
\qquad [11.12]
$$

Standard errors are derived from the large-sample covariance matrix of the ML estimates of γ_j, γ_1, γ_2, and T (see Raudenbush & Sampson, 1999a, for details).

Regression when Predictors are Measured with Error

The consequences of measurement error for inference in multiple regression are well known (cf. Fuller, 1987). If the outcome is measured with error, no bias occurs in estimating the regression coefficients, but precision and statistical power are weakened, and estimates of the explanatory power of the predictors (e.g., R-squared) are attenuated.[3] In contrast, measurement error in one or more predictors will bias estimation of the regression coefficients. For example, if a single predictor is measured with error, the coefficient estimate for that predictor will be biased toward zero, and there will be an underadjustment for that predictor in estimating other coefficients in the equation.

The standard SEM handles measurement error in outcomes and explanatory variables by incorporating a measurement model to supplement the structural model. The SEM can be viewed as a hierarchical model: the level-1 model describes the association between the latent and fallible data, while the level-2 model describes the structural relations among the latent data. This fits with the reality that measurement errors vary across items within a given case, while a latent variable for that case varies over cases. The level-1 units are, then, items, while the level-2 units are the cases. In the context of a standard regression problem, the level-1 model becomes the measurement model and the level-2 model represents the distribution of the latent variables. The advantages are as follows: (a) As in SEM, the analysis provides efficient estimates of the regression model for the latent data; (b) it is easy to incorporate a missing data model (as described in the previous section); (c) we can add levels that reflect nested data structures such as students within schools (see next section); and (d) we can incorporate measurement models for items that are binary or involve count or ordinal data. We now illustrate the features by continuing our example of a standard multiple regression problem.

Incorporating Information about Measurement Error in Hierarchical Models

This can be accomplished in several ways. One thoughtful approach is to study the item responses in a scale or test by means of item response theory (IRT) (Lord, 1980; Wright & Masters, 1982; van der Linden & Hambleton, 1996). Assuming an appropriate scale can be constructed, the IRT analysis will produce a scale score and standard error of measurement for each case (See Chapter 8 for an example). In other applications, the reliability of a measure may be known from external study or may be estimated from the sample. Alternatively, one may directly model the item responses within HLM, an approach we consider at the end of this chapter.

In the current example, we assume for simplicity that the reliability of measurement for each variable is, at least approximately, known. In particular, we assume that Z is measured with reliability .85, X_1 with reliability .90, and X_2 with reliability .70. To simulate this setting, we added measurement error to the complete data (Table 11.2), and the resulting fallible data are listed in Table 11.5.

Level-1 Model. We represent the observable data, Y_{ij}, as a function of the "true" or latent data plus a measurement error:

$$Y_{ij} = D_{zij}(Z_j + e_{zj}) + D_{1ij}(X_{1j} + e_{1j}) + D_{2ij}(X_{2j} + e_{2j}). \quad [11.13]$$

Here the variance of the errors of measurement is treated as known from a prior item analysis. These measurement errors conform to reliabilities of .85, .90, and .70, respectively, for the three variables:

$$\begin{aligned}
e_{zj} &\sim N(0, 4.50^2), \\
e_{1j} &\sim N(0, 2.60^2), \\
e_{2j} &\sim N(0, 4.90^2).
\end{aligned} \quad [11.14]$$

TABLE 11.5 Complete Data with Measurement Error Added

Case	Y	D_z	D_1	D_2
1	48.13	1	0	0
1	44.29	0	1	0
1	60.50	0	0	1
2	52.91	1	0	0
2	57.22	0	1	0
2	55.49	0	0	1
3	58.57	1	0	0
3	36.93	0	1	0
3	45.67	0	0	1
4	43.41	1	0	0
4	35.96	0	1	0
4	50.99	0	0	1
5	56.95	1	0	0
5	56.63	0	1	0
5	56.66	0	0	1
6	56.40	1	0	0
6	57.28	0	1	0
6	42.54	0	0	1
7	54.31	1	0	0
7	43.51	0	1	0
7	51.61	0	0	1
8	71.42	1	0	0
8	57.87	0	1	0
8	77.13	0	0	1
9	40.66	1	0	0
9	46.53	0	1	0
9	51.89	0	0	1
10	43.40	1	0	0
10	50.57	0	1	0
10	39.23	0	0	1
11	64.29	1	0	0
11	57.19	0	1	0
11	43.94	0	0	1
12	65.64	1	0	0
12	64.61	0	1	0
12	51.57	0	0	1
13	35.45	1	0	0
13	48.14	0	1	0
13	56.61	0	0	1
14	29.70	1	0	0
14	40.62	0	1	0
14	45.20	0	0	1
15	63.96	1	0	0
15	68.20	0	1	0
15	61.99	0	0	1

Continued

TABLE 11.5 (continued)

Parameter			Maximum Likelihood Estimates Coefficient			se		
γ_z			52.346			2.990		
γ_1			51.037			2.439		
γ_2			52.735			2.363		
τ_{zz}	τ_{z1}	τ_{z2}	113.840	69.370	40.208	48.963	33.439	29.262
	τ_{11}	τ_{12}		82.439	26.023		32.571	23.304
		τ_{22}			59.746			30.575

We write the matrix equation, in general, as

$$\mathbf{Y}_j = \mathbf{D}_j(\mathbf{Y}_j^* + \mathbf{e}_j), \qquad \mathbf{e}_j \sim N(\mathbf{0}, \mathbf{V}_j), \qquad [11.15]$$

where $\mathbf{Y}_j$ is the n_j by 1 vector of observed variables, $\mathbf{D}_j$ is an n_j by 3 matrix of indicators, $\mathbf{Y}_j^*$ is the 3 by 1 vector of latent or "true" values, and $\mathbf{e}_j$ is a 3 by 1 vector of measurement errors. Here $\mathbf{V}_j$ is a diagonal 3 by 3 matrix with diagonal elements 4.50^2, 2.60^2, and 4.90^2 equal to the measurement error variances for each latent variable. Note that the model is flexible in allowing the precision of measurement to vary across cases, $j = 1, \ldots, J$, though, in the current case, we assume for simplicity that the variances are constant across cases for a given latent variable. As before, $\mathbf{D}_j$ is a matrix of dummy variables indicating which latent variable is observed at each occasion.

Level-2 Model. While the level-1 model represents the observed data as a function of the latent data plus a measurement error, the level-2 model describes the distribution of the latent data:

$$Z_j = \gamma_z + u_{zj},$$

$$X_{1j} = \gamma_1 + u_{1j},$$

$$X_{2j} = \gamma_2 + u_{2j}, \qquad [11.16]$$

$$\begin{pmatrix} u_{zj} \\ u_{1j} \\ u_{2j} \end{pmatrix} \sim N \begin{pmatrix} 0 \\ 0 \\ 0 \end{pmatrix}, \begin{pmatrix} \tau_{zz} & \tau_{z1} & \tau_{z2} \\ \tau_{1z} & \tau_{11} & \tau_{12} \\ \tau_{2z} & \tau_{21} & \tau_{22} \end{pmatrix}.$$

Thus, γ_z, γ_1, and γ_2 are the mean values of Z, X_1, and X_2, respectively. The level-2 model may be written in matrix notation as

$$\mathbf{Y}_j^* = \boldsymbol{\gamma} + \mathbf{u}_j, \qquad \mathbf{u}_j \sim N(\mathbf{0}, \mathbf{T}). \qquad [11.17]$$

The level-2 model thus represents the multivariate normal distribution of the latent data.

Combined Model. The combined model, in matrix notation, is found by substituting the level-2 model (Equation 11.17) into the level-1 model (Equation 11.15) to yield

$$\mathbf{Y}_j = \mathbf{D}_j(\mathbf{\gamma} + \mathbf{u}_j + \mathbf{e}_j),$$
$$\mathbf{D}_j(\mathbf{u}_j + \mathbf{e}_j) \sim N[\mathbf{0}, \mathbf{D}_j(\mathbf{T} + \mathbf{V}_j)\mathbf{D}_j^T].$$

[11.18]

Again, it is not difficult to estimate this model using the EM algorithm or Fisher scoring (Chapter 14). It is also straightforward to include other explanatory variables measured without error or to reconceive the outcome variable to be multivariate.[4]

Results. The HLM analysis proceeds exactly as in the case of missing data, except that now the analysis takes into account measurement errors in the level-1 model. Thus, the maximum likelihood estimates of the marginal means and variance-covariances are transformed to produce regression coefficient estimates. It is instructive to compare these results to those that would have been obtained by applying OLS to the fallible variables (see Table 11.6). We see that OLS gives a substantially different result for the contribution of X_2 (i.e., note the OLS estimate of 0.262 as opposed to 0.355 from the HLM analysis). Other estimates are similar in this case, because X_1 and Z are measured fairly accurately and because X_1 and X_2 are weakly correlated. Notice the increase in all standard errors in the HLM analysis, especially for the coefficient for X_2, the less reliable predictor. These larger standard errors reflect the extra uncertainty that arises from the measurement errors.

TABLE 11.6 Regression Model Estimates, With and Without Accounting for Measurement Error

Predictor	HLM, Accounting for Measurement Error	OLS, Not Accounting for Measurement Error
	Coefficient (se)	Coefficient (se)
Constant	−3.61	2.73
	(19.16)	(17.49)
X_1	0.729	0.701
	(0.287)	(0.277)
X_2	0.355	0.262
	(0.382)	(0.286)

NOTE: Maximum likelihood of the HLM model controls for measurement error; OLS does not.

Regression with Missing Data and Measurement Errors

Suppose that the predictors are measured with error and that there are also missing data. The modeling approach described in the previous section can be applied without any changes. The rows of Table 11.5 containing missing values would simply be deleted; the marginal means and variance-covariance elements would be estimated via maximum likelihood; those estimates would be transformed to compute the needed regression estimates and standard errors.

Estimating Direct and Indirect Effects of Latent Variables

It is common in social science research to ask questions about mediators of well-known relationships. Researchers ask whether cognitive skills mediate the link between education and occupational status (Rivera-Batiz, 1992; Bowles & Gintis, 1996), whether disciplinary climate mediates the link between school social composition and student achievement (Lee & Bryk, 1989), whether birth control practices mediate the link between maternal education and fertility (Mason, Wong, & Entwisle, 1984). Structural equation modeling is widely used in such studies. These models allow predictors and outcomes to be measured with error and enable study of associations among latent variables viewed as exogenous predictors, mediators, and outcomes.

The study of mediated effects often entails multilevel data. In Lee and Bryk's (1989) study, social composition and disciplinary climate varied at the school level, whereas the outcome varied at the student level. Sampson, Raudenbush, and Earls (1997) asked whether the association between neighborhood social composition and violent crime is mediated by "collective efficacy," a social process involving cohesion, trust, and the capacity of residents to intervene to protect public order. Here the key constructs varied at the neighborhood level, but multiple informants within neighborhoods provided the observed data. In these cases, key mediators (e.g., disciplinary climate, collective efficacy) are assessed from survey data and are likely to be measured with a nonnegligible error. Such measurement errors, if ignored, will lead to biased estimates of the effects of key explanatory variables.

Methodologists have approached the problem of latent variables in the multilevel setting in two broadly different ways. The first adapts standard methods for structural equation models to incorporate multilevel data (Lee, 1990; Muthén, 1994; McDonald, 1994). The second begins with a hierarchical model and then incorporates models for measurement error (Raudenbush, Rowan, & Kang, 1991; Longford, 1993; Goldstein, 1995). Following this second approach (see Raudenbush & Sampson, 1999a), we extend the ideas previously introduced in this chapter to the case of multilevel designs. Once again, the first level of the model relates the observed data to the latent variables. However, the latent variables themselves now vary at two levels. By estimating the joint distribution of these latent variables, we are able to estimate direct and indirect effects involving such variables.

A Three-Level Illustrative Example with Measurement Error and Missing Data

The question motivating this illustrative analysis is whether the relationship between the social composition of urban neighborhoods and levels of violence in those neighborhoods is explained (mediated) by measurable characteristics of neighborhood social organization. Data for the analysis were collected during 1995 under the auspices of the Project on Human Development in Chicago Neighborhoods (PHDCN). The results reported here are intended to illustrate the methodology rather than to provide conclusive substantive evidence. A more fine-grained analysis making stronger claims about the importance of neighborhood social organization appears in Sampson, Raudenbush, and Earls (1997).

Our current interest focuses on "social control," a five-item scale. Residents were asked about the likelihood that their neighbors could be counted on to intervene in various ways if (a) children were skipping school and hanging out on a street corner, (b) children were spray-painting graffiti on a local building, (c) children were showing disrespect to an adult, (d) a fight broke out in front of their house, and (e) the fire station closest to home was threatened with budget cuts. Responses were on a five-point Likert scale coded 1 to 5. Most respondents answered all five questions, and for those respondents, the scale score was the average of the five responses. However, anyone responding to at least one item provided data for the analysis. A person-specific standard error of measurement was calculated based on a simple linear item response model that took into account the number and "difficulty" of the items to which each resident responded (see Raudenbush & Sampson, 1999a, for details).

Respondents were also asked five questions regarding the occurrence of incidents of violence in the neighborhood. Specifically, they were asked how often each of the following occurred in the neighborhood during the past six months: (a) a fight in which a weapon was used, (b) a violent argument between neighbors, (c) gang fights, (d) a sexual assault or rape, and (e) a robbery or mugging. Scale construction for perceived violence mirrored that

TABLE 11.7 Description of the Sample

(a) Person-Level Data Variable	N	Mean	se	Minimum	Maximum
GENDER[a]	7,729	0.59	0.49	0.00	1.00
AGE	7,729	42.59	16.73	17.00	100.00
SES[b]	7,729	0.00	1.32	−4.08	4.33
(b) Neighborhood Cluster-Level Data Variable	N	Mean	se	Minimum	Maximum
POVERTY CONCENTRATION	342	20.43	17.31	0.23	88.18
ETHNIC ISOLATION	342	41.21	43.67	0.00	99.81
% FOREIGN BORN	342	16.54	15.63	0.00	64.62
VIOLENCE[c]	342	1.88	0.41	1.13	3.17
SOCIAL CONTROL	342	3.49	0.40	2.38	4.63

a. Gender is coded 1 = female, 0 = male.
b. SES is the first principal component of household income, respondent education, and respondent occupation.
c. Violence and social control here are the neighborhood cluster means of the observed scores for persons in that cluster.

for social control. Reasonably complete data are available from 7,729 persons residing in 342 neighborhood clusters (NCs).

NC social composition was measured independently from the 1990 Census. This includes POVERTY CONCENTRATION (percentage below the poverty line), ETHNIC ISOLATION (percentage African American), and percentage FOREIGN BORN, each of which is believed positively associated with perceived violence within NCs. We hypothesized that the links between social composition and violence will be at least partially mediated by neighborhood SOCIAL CONTROL.

Table 11.7 describes the sample. We see that the mean percentage African American across the 342 neighborhood clusters is 41.2% with a large standard deviation. The mean percentage below the poverty line (about 20%) and percentage foreign born (about 16.5%) reflect Chicago's diverse population.

It was also important in this study to control for social selection effects. Within a neighborhood, survey responses may be shaped by the socioeconomic status, age, gender, and so forth of the respondents. Any link between social-demographic background and responses that occurs *within* neighborhoods should be statistically controlled in an analysis that seeks to understand variation and covariation in outcomes *between* neighborhoods. Otherwise, the composition of the sample with respect to AGE, SES, GENDER, and so on would bias the measure of NC characteristics. Table 11.7 describes the person-level covariates used in the illustrative analysis: AGE,

GENDER (coded 1 for females; 0 for males), and SES (the first principal component of the respondent's years of education, occupation status, and income).

The Model

An analytic model is needed that (a) controls for the varying measurement error of survey-based measures of social control and perceived violence, (b) controls for personal characteristics related to responses within neighborhoods, and (c) appropriately accounts for the clustered nature of the sample, in which item responses are nested within persons who are themselves nested within NCs.

Level-1 Model. At level 1, we model the measurement error associated with perceived violence, Y_{jk}, and social control, Z_{jk}:

$$R_{ijk} = D_{1ijk}(Y_{jk} + \varepsilon_{1jk}) + D_{2ijk}(Z_{jk} + \varepsilon_{2jk}) \qquad [11.19]$$

with

$$\varepsilon_{1jk} \sim N(0, \sigma_{1jk}^2)$$

and

$$\varepsilon_{2jk} \sim N(0, \sigma_{2jk}^2).$$

Equation 11.19 may be viewed as a classical measurement model in which R_{ijk} is a fallible measure of latent variable i for person j living in neighborhood k. In this example, there are two latent variables: Y_{jk}, the "true" value of perceived violence in neighborhood k as perceived by person j, and Z_{jk}, the "true" level of neighborhood social control in neighborhood k as perceived by person j. The predictor D_{1ijk} is an indicator variable taking on a value of 1 if R_{ijk} is a measure of perceived violence and 0 if not; similarly, D_{2ijk} takes on a value of 1 if R_{ijk} measures social control, 0 if not ($i = 1, 2$; $j = 1, \ldots, J_k$; $k = 1, \ldots, K$). Unlike a conventional HLM model, however, the level-1 variances are now heteroscedastic; that is, σ_{1jk}^2 and σ_{2jk}^2 will generally not be the same. Since the item scaling for the observed measures of perceived violence and social control produces good estimates for the standard errors of measurement of R_{ijk} (i.e., $\hat{\sigma}_{1jk}$ and $\hat{\sigma}_{2jk}$, respectively), we can use them to reweight Equation 11.19 and thereby remove the heteroscedasticity. That is,

$$(1/\hat{\sigma}_{1jk})R_{ijk} = (1/\hat{\sigma}_{1jk})Y_{jk} + \varepsilon_{1jk}/\hat{\sigma}_{1jk} \qquad [11.20]$$

if $D_{1ijk} = 1$, or

$$(1/\hat{\sigma}_{2jk})R_{ijk} = (1/\hat{\sigma}_{2jk})Z_{jk} + \varepsilon_{2jk}/\hat{\sigma}_{2jk}$$

if $D_{2ijk} = 1$, where now

$$\varepsilon_{1jk}/\hat{\sigma}_{1jk} \sim N(0, 1)$$

and

$$\varepsilon_{2jk}/\hat{\sigma}_{2jk} \sim N(0, 1).$$

Here we assume $\hat{\sigma}_{1jk}$ and $\hat{\sigma}_{2jk}$ equal to σ_{1jk} and σ_{2jk}.

Note also, as in earlier examples in this chapter, this formulation allows utilization of all available data in the analysis, avoiding, for example, the listwise deletion of persons giving data on social control but not perceived violence.

Level-2 Model. The second level model describes variation in the two latent variables among respondents within neighborhoods:

$$Y_{jk} = Y_k + \beta_{y1k}(\text{AGE})_{jk} + \beta_{y2k}(\text{GENDER})_{jk} + \beta_{y3k}(\text{SES})_{jk} + r_{yjk},$$

$$Z_{jk} = Z_k + \beta_{z1k}(\text{AGE})_{jk} + \beta_{z2k}(\text{GENDER})_{jk} + \pi_{z3k}(\text{SES})_{jk} + r_{zjk},$$

$$\begin{pmatrix} r_{yjk} \\ r_{zjk} \end{pmatrix} \sim N\left[\begin{pmatrix} 0 \\ 0 \end{pmatrix}, \begin{pmatrix} \Omega_{yy} & \Omega_{yz} \\ \Omega_{zy} & \Omega_{zz} \end{pmatrix} \right]. \qquad [11.21]$$

Thus, within neighborhoods, latent responses are viewed as possibly depending on AGE (in years), GENDER (1 = female; 0 = male), and SES. AGE, GENDER, and SES are grand-mean centered. Of central interest in this analysis are Y_k and Z_k, the "true" neighborhood means on perceived violence and social control, adjusted for the possible within-neighborhood response biases linked to AGE, GENDER, and SES. The random effects r_{yjk} and r_{zjk}, having covariance Ω_{yz}, capture the dependence among multiple latent variables within neighborhoods, conditional on Y_k, Z_k, and the βs in Equation 11.21.

Level-3 Model. The third and final level of the model describes the variation across neighborhoods in the adjusted mean perceived violence and social control:

$$Y_k = \gamma_{y0} + \gamma_{y1}(\text{POV CON})_k + \gamma_{y2}(\text{ETHNIC ISO})_k$$
$$+ \gamma_{y3}(\% \text{ FOR BORN})_k + u_{yk},$$

$$Z_k = \gamma_{z0} + \gamma_{z1}(\text{POV CON})_k + \gamma_{z2}(\text{ETHNIC ISO})_k \qquad [11.22]$$
$$+ \gamma_{z3}(\% \text{ FOR BORN})_k + u_{zk},$$

$$\begin{pmatrix} u_{yk} \\ u_{zk} \end{pmatrix} \sim N\left[\begin{pmatrix} 0 \\ 0 \end{pmatrix}, \begin{pmatrix} \tau_{yy} & \tau_{yz} \\ \tau_{zy} & \tau_{zz} \end{pmatrix} \right].$$

Thus, the adjusted mean perceived violence, Y_k, and social control, Z_k, vary across NCs as a function of poverty concentration, ethnic isolation, and percentage foreign born plus a pair of random effects (u_{yk}, u_{zk}) assumed bivariate normal in distribution. These random effects capture the dependence between persons living in the same neighborhood.

For parsimony, all within-neighborhood regression coefficients other than the adjusted mean, that is, all β_{yfk} and β_{zfk} for $f = 1, 2, 3$, are constrained to be fixed. Formally, we have

$$\beta_{yfk} = \gamma_{yf0}, \qquad \beta_{zfk} = \gamma_{zf0}, \qquad f = 1, 2, 3. \qquad [11.23]$$

We note that the model and estimation procedure can incorporate random variation in these coefficients. Suppose, for example, that the association between age and perceived violence varies randomly over neighborhoods. The model for respondents' age effects on perceived violence might then be

$$\beta_{y1k} = \gamma_{y10} + u_{y1k}, \qquad\qquad [11.24]$$

where u_{y1k} is the random effect of neighborhood k. Since the function of the level-2 model in this application is primarily to control for individual response bias, we choose to fix these coefficients to a constant value for all NCs.

Results. The three-level model was estimated via ML as described in Chapter 14. Results are provided in Table 11.8.

(i) Controlling Response Bias. As Table 11.8 indicates, AGE (but not GENDER or SES) is linked to resident responses to questions about violence. Older residents report lower levels of violence than do younger residents within the same NC, $\hat{\gamma}_{y10} = -0.521$, $t = -9.80$. AGE and SES (but not GENDER) are associated with responses to questions about social control. Older and higher-SES respondents more readily perceived their neighbors as willing to exercise social control ($\hat{\gamma}_{z10} = 0.306$, $t = 4.95$; $\hat{\gamma}_{z30} = 2.86$, $t = 3.73$). Thus, there is some evidence that demographic differences between persons living in the same neighborhood are associated with their perceptions about that neighborhood. This source of bias is controlled in examining between-neighborhood associations.

(ii) Total Effect of neighborhood social composition on Y. As hypothesized, neighborhood POVERTY CONCENTRATION ($\gamma_{y1} = 1.285$, $t = 12.21$), ETHNIC ISOLATION ($\gamma_{y2} = 0.352$, $t = 5.87$), and % FOREIGN BORN ($\gamma_{y3} = 0.636$, $t = 4.34$) are positively related to perceived violence.

TABLE 11.8 Perceived Violence and Social Control as a Function of Neighborhood Social Composition[a]

Fixed Effect	Perceived Violence		
	Coefficient	*se*	*t ratio*
INTERCEPT, γ_{y0}			
Level-2 predictors			
AGE, γ_{y10}	−0.521	0.053	−9.80
GENDER, γ_{y20}	0.880	1.734	0.51
SES, γ_{y30}	1.024	0.725	1.41
Level-3 predictors			
POVERTY CON, γ_{y1}	1.285	0.105	12.21
ETHNIC ISO, γ_{y2}	0.352	0.060	5.87
% FOREIGN BORN, γ_{y3}	0.636	0.147	4.34

Fixed effect	Social Control		
	Coefficient	*se*	*t ratio*
INTERCEPT, γ_{z0}			
Level-2 predictors			
AGE, γ_{z10}	0.306	0.062	4.95
GENDER, γ_{z20}	0.481	2.051	0.23
SES, γ_{z30}	2.863	0.849	3.73
Level-3 predictors			
POVERTY CON, γ_{z1}	−0.912	0.108	−8.47
ETHNIC ISO, γ_{z2}	−0.462	0.062	−7.49
% FOREIGN BORN, γ_{z3}	−1.246	0.151	−8.24

Variance-Covariance Components

Within-NC components	
Perceived violence	$\begin{bmatrix} 3,925 & \\ -1,601 & 5,829 \end{bmatrix}$
Social control	
Between-NC components	
Perceived Violence	$\begin{bmatrix} 443 & \\ -205 & 375 \end{bmatrix}$
Social Control	

a. In this and other tables, variances were multiplied by 10,000 to ensure printing of a reasonable number of significant digits without resort to scientific notation.

(iii) Association Between Neighborhood Social Composition and Z. In contrast, neighborhood POVERTY CONCENTRATION, ETHNIC ISOLATION, and % FOREIGN BORN are negatively linked to social control ($\hat{\gamma}_{z1} = -0.912, t = -8.47$; $\hat{\gamma}_{z2} = -0.462, t = -7.49$; and $\hat{\gamma}_{z3} = -1.246, t = -8.24$).

(iv) Transformation of Hierarchical Model Estimates to Estimate Direct and Indirect Effects. We now transform Equation 11.22, which specifies the

distribution of Y_k, $Z_k | X_{sk}$ to estimate the distribution of $Y_k | Z_k, X_{sk}$ (where X_{sk} for $s = 1, 2, 3$ are POV CON, ETHNIC ISO, and % FOR BORN, respectively). The new model is

$$Y_k = \gamma_{y0.z} + \gamma_{y1.z}(\text{POV CON})_k + \gamma_{y2.z}(\text{ETHNIC ISO})_k$$
$$+ \gamma_{y3.z}(\% \text{ FOR BORN})_k + \gamma_{yz.x}Z_k + u_k,$$
$$u_k \sim N(0, \tau^2). \tag{11.25}$$

Notice that the latent social control measure, Z_k, which had been one of the two outcome variables (Equation 11.22), has now become a latent predictor variable on the right-hand side of Equation 11.25. Of interest are not only the association between that variable and perceived violence, but also the direct effects of neighborhood social composition (the Xs) on Y and the indirect effects of neighborhood social composition on Y as mediated by Z, social control.

(v) *Association Between Z and Y given X.* As Table 11.9 indicates, there is strong evidence of a negative association between social control and perceived violence, $\gamma_{yz.x} = -0.546$, $t = -5.55$, net the contributions of social composition (poverty concentration, ethnic isolation, and percentage foreign born).

(vi) *Direct Effect of X on Y.* The results of this analysis can also be represented in a path diagram form (see Figure 11.1). Adjustment for social control reduces the contributions of ethnic isolation and percentage for-

TABLE 11.9 Perceived Violence as a Function of Social Control and Neighborhood Social Composition

Fixed Effect	Coefficient	se	t Ratio
INTERCEPT, $\gamma_{y0.z}$	375.00	39.07	9.60
Level-3 Predictors			
POVERTY CON, $\gamma_{y1.z}$	0.787	0.133	5.90
ETHNIC ISO, $\gamma_{y2.z}$	0.100	0.072	1.39
% FOREIGN BORN, $\gamma_{y3.z}$	−0.044	0.184	−0.24
SOCIAL CONTROL, $\gamma_{yz.x}$	−0.546	0.098	−5.55
Variance-Covariance Components			
Between NC variance, τ^2	311		

NOTE: Results for level-1 predictors remain the same as in Table 11.8. This will generally be the case in these models as the estimates of fixed effects are independent across levels. For further detail see Chapter 14.

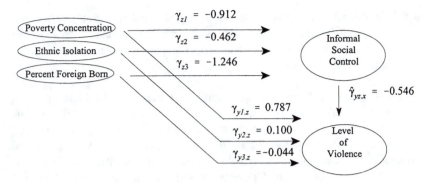

Figure 11.1. Direct and Indirect Effects of Exogenous Predictors on Level of Violence with Informal Social Control as a Mediator

eign born to nonsignificance ($\hat{\gamma}_{y2.z} = 0.100$, $t = 1.39$; $\hat{\gamma}_{y3.z} = -0.044$, $t = -0.24$). Poverty concentration remains positively related to perceived violence, $\gamma_{y1.z} = 0.787$, $t = 5.90$, but its coefficient appears considerably smaller than prior to the adjustment for social control (compare the $\hat{\gamma}_{y1.z}$ coefficients for poverty concentration here to $\hat{\gamma}_{y1}$ in Table 11.8 ($\hat{\gamma}_{y1} = 1.285$).

(vii) Indirect effects. Table 11.10 lists the total effects, the direct effects, and the indirect effects. It also tabulates the relevant standard errors. We see substantial indirect effects for each aspect of social composition. Thus, in each case, social composition is linked to violence through its association with social control.[5] The magnitude of each indirect effect is far larger than its standard error, giving evidence of statistically significant mediating effects of social control. We note that the indirect effects are the differences between the total effects (associations between X and Y) and the direct effects (associations between X and Y, controlling for Z). The large size

TABLE 11.10 Decomposition of Total Effects into Direct and Indirect Components

	Total (se)	Direct (se)	Indirect (se)
POVERTY CON	1.285	0.787	0.498
	(0.105)	(0.133)	(0.107)
ETHNIC ISO	0.352	0.100	0.252
	(0.060)	(0.072)	(0.056)
% FOREIGN BORN	0.636	−0.044	0.680
	(0.147)	(0.184)	(0.148)

of these differences relative to these estimated standard errors implies that the differences between the relevant coefficients is significantly greater than zero. The standard errors can be used to compute confidence intervals for such differences.

(viii) Summary. Based on the results of Tables 11.8 to 11.10, we can conclude that (a) the three social composition indicators are associated positively as hypothesized with perceived violence (total effects); (b) given social composition, neighborhood social control is negatively related to perceived violence; (c) adjusting for social control, we find a statistically significant direct effect of concentrated poverty on violence but no significant direct effects between either ethnic isolation or percentage foreign born and violence; (d) links between the Xs (poverty concentration, ethnic isolation, and percentage foreign born) and perceived violence are partially "explained" or "mediated" by neighborhood social control (as indicated by statistically significant indirect effects).

Importance of Controlling for Errors of Measurement of Neighborhood Social Control. To illustrate the impact of the latent variable model on statistical inference, we computed a second multilevel analysis of perceived violence with exactly the same predictors but now where manifest social control rather than latent social control was included. This reduces the three-level model of Equations 11.20 to 11.23 to a two-level model where the former level-2 and level-3 predictors are now, respectively, level-1 and level-2 predictors. Manifest social control enters in this case as just another level-2 predictor of social control.

The manifest version of social control was computed as the neighborhood cluster mean response of sample responses within each NC (descriptive statistics in Table 11.7). We note that the reliability of manifest social control at the NC level depends heavily on the sample size of informants per NC. As sample sizes range from 20 to 50, the reliability ranges from .70 to .86. While the latent variable analysis takes this varying reliability into account, the analysis based on the manifest variable does not.

The results (Table 11.11) show, as might be expected, that the estimate of the social control coefficient is smaller when the manifest social control is used than when the latent variable model is estimated ($-.412$ as compared to $-.546$). Note also that the estimated standard error of the coefficient is substantially larger in the case of the latent variable analysis, reflecting the additional uncertainty regarding the error of measurement of social control. Also, the adjustments to the contributions of ethnic isolation and percentage foreign born are less severe when manifest social control rather than latent

TABLE 11.11 Consequences of Modeling Measurement Error in Social Control

	Latent Social Control as Predictor			Manifest Social Control as Predictor		
	Coefficient	se	t Ratio	Coefficient	se	t Ratio
Level-2 predictors						
POVERTY CON	0.787	0.133	5.90	0.877	0.108	8.13
ETHNIC ISO	0.100	0.072	1.39	0.157	0.059	2.64
% FOREIGN BORN	−0.044	0.184	−0.24	0.097	0.148	0.66
SOCIAL CONTROL	−0.546	0.098	−5.55	−0.412	0.048	−8.63
Between-NC variance	331			327		

social control is included in the model. In fact, ethnic isolation retains a significant direct effect on violence in the full model when the manifest indicator of social control is used.

In sum, if one ignores measurement error of social control, (a) one's belief about the importance of social control is diminished, (b) the confidence interval for the social control coefficient is shortened, and (c) social control appears less important as a mediator of the association between social composition and perceived violence. Stated somewhat differently, the direct effects of social composition on violence are exaggerated.

A Two-Level Latent Variable Example for Individual Growth

Latent variable models can also be used in the context of growth studies. The individual growth model, introduced in Chapter 6, can easily be extended to applications where one latent growth parameter, say, for example, a person's growth rate, may be a function of another latent growth parameter, say, for example, the person's latent initial status. We now illustrate such an application.

In this example, we are interested in gender differences in the growth of mathematics achievement during the high school years. The widening gender gap in math during these years is a matter of some concern to policy makers, educators, and parents. A crucial question is whether high school experience contributes to the widening gap or whether this widening gap reflects a process already in motion prior to high school. As we shall show, boys score significantly higher on standardized math tests than girls do in eighth grade. Moreover, boys display faster growth rates than girls during the high school years. There is, in general, a positive association between eighth-grade status and growth rate, and, as a result, the gender gap in growth rates may be attributable to this positive association. We thus pose a model in which gender predicts both eighth-grade status and high school rate of growth. We wonder whether the association between gender and high school rate of growth can be explained away by gender differences in eighth-grade status. If so, then this implies that the widening gender gap during high school results from a process set in motion prior to high school. On the other hand, if there is a direct association between gender and high school growth rate, after taking into account eighth-grade status, one might argue that high school experience actively contributes to the widening gender gap during high school.[6]

Data for this example are from the National Educational Longitudinal Study (NELS). Students were sampled in eighth grade in 1988 and followed through high school. The subset of data used here include information from 2,081 students.[7] Most students have a full complement of three time points.

Level-1 Model. We pose a simple linear model for growth in mathematics:

$$Y_{ti} = \pi_{0i} + \pi_{1i} * (\text{grade} - 8)_{ti} + e_{ti}, \qquad [11.26]$$

where Y_{ti} is the math achievement of student i at time t, and $(\text{grade} - 8)_{ti}$ is the grade during which math achievement was assessed (grade $= 8, 10, 12$ for a student with a full complement of data). Thus, π_{0i} is the "initial status," that is, the math achievement of student i in eighth grade and π_{1i} is that student's annual growth rate over the high school years. The level-1 residuals, $e_{ti}, t = 1, \ldots, T_i$, are assumed normally distributed with mean 0 and constant variance σ^2.

Level-2 Model. Initial status and rate of growth vary across the population of students as a function of gender and person-specific random effects:

$$\pi_{0i} = \beta_{00} + \beta_{01} * (\text{FEMALE})_i + u_{0i},$$
$$\pi_{1i} = \beta_{10} + \beta_{11} * (\text{FEMALE})_i + u_{1i}, \qquad [11.27]$$

where $(\text{FEMALE})_i$ is an indicator for female gender ($1 = $ female, $0 = $ male) and we assume the random effects are bivariate normally distributed with variances τ_{00}, τ_{11} and covariance τ_{01}.

Results (Table 11.12) indicate that math achievement for males is, on average, $\hat{\gamma}_{00} = 41.33$ at eighth grade. There is a significant gender gap of $\hat{\gamma}_{01} = -1.84, t = -3.27$. This is a small difference, about one eighth of a standard deviation (see descriptive statistics in Table 11.12). The annual growth rate for boys is $\hat{\gamma}_{10} = 3.27, t = 49.83$. For girls, the growth rate is smaller by $\hat{\gamma}_{11} = -0.20, t = -2.11$. Although a seemingly small effect, a

TABLE 11.12

(a) Descriptive Statistics for Math Growth Data

	n	Mean	sd
Level 1			
MATH ACHIEVEMENT	5,645	46.30	14.84
Grade 8	5,645	1.82	1.60
Level 2			
FEMALE	2,081	0.50	0.50

(b) Initial Status and Growth Rates as Outcomes

Outcome	Predictor	Coefficient	se	t Ratio
Initial status, π_{0i}	INTERCEPT, β_{00}	41.328	0.398	103.93
	FEMALE, β_{01}	−1.837	0.562	−3.27
Growth rate, π_{1i}	INTERCEPT, β_{10}	3.266	0.065	49.83
	FEMALE, β_{11}	−0.196	0.093	−2.11

(c) Growth Rate as Outcome, Initial Status and Female as Predictors

Predictor	Coefficient	se	t ratio
INTERCEPT, α_{10}	1.897	0.181	10.16
FEMALE, α_{11}	−0.135	0.095	−1.43
INITIAL STATUS, α_{12}	0.033	0.004	7.85

(d) Comparison of Original and Adjusted Coefficient

Predictor	Original Coefficient	Adjusted Coefficient	Difference	se of Difference
INTERCEPT	$\hat{\beta}_{10} = $ 3.266	$\hat{\alpha}_{10} = $ 1.897	1.369	0.187
FEMALE	$\hat{\beta}_{11} = $ −0.196	$\hat{\alpha}_{11} = $ −0.135	−0.061	0.020

relative loss of 0.20 points would leave girls $4 * (0.20)$ or 0.80 points farther behind than their male counterparts by 12th grade, leaving them about $1.84 + (0.80) = 2.64$ points behind at that time, a little less than one fifth of a standard deviation.

To test the hypothesis that the divergence in math achievement during high school is a function of initial differences at entry, we formulate a model for latent growth rate as a function of gender and now also the latent initial status:

$$\pi_{1i} = \alpha_{10} + \alpha_{11} * (\text{FEMALE})_i + \alpha_{12} * \pi_{0i} + u_{1i}^*. \qquad [11.28]$$

Of interest here are the direct effect of gender on the growth rate, that is, α_{11}, which is the mean difference in growth rates between boys and girls, holding constant their initial status, and the indirect effect of gender on growth rate as it operates through the gender gap in initial status. We note that

$$\beta_{11} - \alpha_{11} = \alpha_{12}\beta_{01}, \tag{11.29}$$

where

$$\alpha_{12} = \tau_{01}/\tau_{00},$$

$$\alpha_{10} = \beta_{10} - \alpha_{12}\beta_{00}.$$

The residual u_{1i}^* is the part of the growth rate not explained by the combination of gender and initial status, and has variance

$$\text{Var}(u_{1i}^*) = \tau_{11} - \frac{\tau_{01}^2}{\tau_{00}} = \tau_{11}(1 - \rho_{u_0,u_1}^2). \tag{11.30}$$

The results (Table 11.12) indicate (a) as expected, there is a significantly positive association between initial status and growth rate within gender, $\hat{\alpha}_{12} = 0.03, t = 7.85$; (b) there is no significant effect of gender, $\hat{\alpha}_{11} = -0.14, t = -1.43$; but (c) there is a significant indirect effect of gender, $\hat{\beta}_{11} - \hat{\alpha}_{11} = -0.06$, se $= 0.02$. One might interpret this analysis as indicating that the growing gender gap in math achievement during high school is largely attributable to the gender gap in status that exists upon entry into high school. That is, conditional on the initial status at entry, high schools do not increase the gender gap in math achievement. Rather, the expanding gender gap during high school is just part of a larger high school organization effect. Students' initial status influences how much all students gain in math learning while in high school. Because girls tend to enter somewhat behind, they also tend to gain somewhat less. This same pattern of results would be expected for any student who also enters high school somewhat behind, regardless of gender.

Several criticisms can be made of this model and the interpretations that flow from its estimation. First, seniors are a select group because of dropouts that occur between 8th and 12th grade. If drop-out rates are higher for boys than for girls, the estimated gender gap in growth rates would be biased, presumably in favor of boys. This assumption can be partially checked by comparing drop-out rates. Second, the assumption that π_{0i} measures initial status is contingent on the validity of the straight-line growth model. This assumption can be checked by estimating models that include quadratic effects. Third, the analysis assumes bivariate normality of the random effects. This assumption is more difficult to check, though methods described in Chapter 9 are applicable.

Nonlinear Item Response Models

Item response models are commonly used within educational testing to estimate the abilities of the examinees (see van der Linden & Hambleton's 1996 review). Defining a meaningful interval scale for an ability is essential to important research goals, including the study of growth (see Chapter 6) and assessing the effects of interventions. Item response models also enable test constructors to evaluate the functioning of a test, to inspect the properties of specific items, and to identify examinees whose response patterns are anomalous. Applications of these models have recently broadened to include the assessment of attitudes, social behaviors, and mental health.

An item response model can be conceived as a hierarchical model, and there are benefits in doing so (Adams, Wilson, & Wu, 1997; Bock, 1989; Cheong & Raudenbush, 2001; Kamata, 1998; Raudenbush & Sampson, 1999b). The hierarchical formulation provides a natural framework for achieving several analytic goals:

1. It facilitates the study of multidimensional assessment, that is, the assessment of multiple abilities or traits.

2. It naturally incorporates variation between social settings such as schools or firms when the persons being assessed are nested in those social settings.

3. It allows specification of explanatory variables measured at several levels in the context of the item response model.

4. It provides a natural framework for studying measurement error in the assessment of the social settings themselves.

5. Latent variables defined by the item response model may be studied as explanatory variables as described in the previous sections of this chapter.

6. The hierarchical framework provides a natural way to manage item nonresponse.

We first show how a simple one-parameter item response model may be represented as a two-level hierarchical model that defines the "difficulty" of each item and the "ability" of each examinee on a single trait. Next, we extend this model to define multiple traits per examinee. We then consider extensions to multiple levels of nesting and to latent variable analysis more generally.

A Simple Item Response Model

To clarify the basic ideas, let us consider a test with P items designed to measure a single ability or trait (e.g., "word recognition" in reading). The test is administered to J examinees. Each item is scored as "correct response $= 1$"

and "incorrect response $= 0$." A one-parameter item response model, also known as a Rasch model (cf. Wright & Masters, 1982), represents the log-odds of a correct response as depending on the ability of the examinee and the difficulty of the item, that is,

$$\eta_{jp} = \alpha_j - \delta_p, \qquad\qquad [11.31]$$

where η_{pj} is the log-odds of a correct response, α_j is the ability of examinee j, and δ_p is the difficulty of item p. Either the abilities or the difficulties are assumed to have a mean of zero. Accordingly, the probability that examinee j responds correctly to item p is

$$\text{Prob}(Y_{ij} = 1) = \varphi_{ij} = \frac{1}{1 + \exp\{-\eta_{ij}\}}. \qquad\qquad [11.32]$$

In the classic Rasch model, the abilities and difficulties are fixed unknown parameters. In our reformulation as a hierarchical model, the abilities vary randomly over a population of examinees. The benefits of viewing the abilities as random are considered by Bock and Aitkin (1981) and Thissen (1982).

We reformulate the Rasch model with random abilities as a two-level model. The first level describes how the item effects and the person abilities shape the log-odds of a correct response. The second level defines how the abilities vary over the population of examinees.

Level-1 Model. Our sampling model is Bernoulli. We thus assume that, given the item effects and the person abilities, Y_{ij} takes on a value of 1 with probability φ_{ij}. Our link function is the logit link, such that $\eta_{ij} = \log[\varphi_{ij}/(1 - \varphi_{ij})]$. Our level-1 model is thus

$$\eta_{ij} = \pi_{0j} + \sum_{p=1}^{P-1} \pi_{pj} X_{pij}, \qquad\qquad [11.33]$$

where

    π_{0j} is the ability of examinee j;

    X_{pij} is a dummy variable that takes on a value of unity if response i for person j is to item p, 0 otherwise; and

    π_{pj} is thus the difference in log-odds of a correct response between item p and a "reference item" for examinee j.

Note that while there are P items, only $P - 1$ dummy variables are included. The item not represented by a dummy variable is the reference item, whose difficulty is arbitrarily set to zero.

It may seem odd to have two subscripts, i and p, to represent the response occasions. Indeed, if all examinees respond to all items, only one subscript is needed. However, some examinees may not respond to some items. While such nonresponses are commonly regarded as incorrect and thus coded zero in educational achievement tests, there are many important cases in which nonresponse is by design. Such sampling occurs in the U.S. National Assessment of Educational Progress, the International Adult Literacy Survey, and the Third International Mathematics and Science Study. The hierarchical model provides a natural framework for such missing data designs. Moreover, omitted answers will be viewed differently when an attitude or aspect of mental health is being assessed rather than when the achievement is being tested. To accommodate missing responses in a flexible way, we therefore do not assume that response i is to any specific item, and two subscripts are needed.

Level-2 Model. The level-1 model defines abilities (π_{0j}) and item effects (π_{pj}) that can, presumably, vary over a population of persons as a function of measured covariates and/or random effects. However, to conform to the Rasch model, we formulate an unconditional model for the abilities and we fix all the item effects:

$$\pi_{0j} = \beta_{00} + u_{0j}, \qquad u_{0j} \sim N(0, \tau_{00}),$$
$$\pi_{pj} = \beta_{p0} \quad \text{for } p > 0. \tag{11.34}$$

Here τ_{00} represents the variance of the abilities in the population. Item effects are constrained to be invariant across examinees. This constraint reflects the belief that, for a "good" test, an item should have the same difficulty for subsets of examinees who have the same ability. Otherwise, the item may be regarded as biased against the subset of examinees for whom it is more difficult.

Under this model, the log-odds that person j will respond correctly to item p is

$$\beta_{00} + u_{0j} \tag{11.35}$$

for the reference item and

$$\beta_{00} + \beta_{p0} + u_{0j} \tag{11.36}$$

for any other item p. Substituting into the Rasch model (Equation 11.31), we therefore define the ability of person j as

$$\alpha_j = \pi_{0j} = \beta_{00} + u_{0j} \tag{11.37}$$

while the item difficulties are

$$\delta_p = 0 \tag{11.38}$$

for the reference item and

$$\delta_p = -\beta_{0p} \qquad [11.39]$$

for any other item p. Thus, in terms of our hierarchical model, differences between item difficulties are represented as differences between regression coefficients. Differences between abilities of different examinees are represented as differences between random intercepts. The item difficulties and person abilities lie on an interval scale defined in a logit metric.

When examinees respond to different subsets of items, the ability π_{0j} is adjusted for the difficulty of the items to which the examinee responded. When those being assessed are nested within social settings such as schools, a third level can be added to the two-level item response model to represent this social membership. Explanatory variables may then be entered at the second or third level to account for variation in latent ability, π_{0j}. Modeling possibilities expand further when we consider the case of multiple traits or abilities.

An Item Response Model for Multiple Traits

Our aim now is to measure M traits using P_m items to measure trait m, for $m = 1, \ldots, M$. Parallel to our discussion of univariate assessment, there will be a reference item and $P_m - 1$ dummy variables for each trait. The outcome is again scored in a binary fashion: a "correct response = 1" and an "incorrect response = 0."

The first level of our model describes how the item effects and multiple person abilities shape the log-odds of a correct response. The second level defines how the traits vary and covary over the population of examinees.

Level-1 Model. Our sampling model for each item is Bernoulli, given the ability of the person on each trait and given the item effects. We again use a logit link. Our level-1 structural model is

$$\eta_{ij} = \sum_{m=1}^{M} D_{mij} \left(\pi_{m0j} + \sum_{p=1}^{P_m - 1} \pi_{mpj} X_{mpij} \right), \qquad [11.40]$$

where

D_{mij} is a dummy variable that takes on a value of 1 if the response of person j at occasion i is to an item measuring trait m, 0 otherwise;

π_{m0j} is the ability of examinee j on trait m;

X_{mpij} is a dummy variable that takes on a value of unity if the response is to the pth item that measures trait m, 0 otherwise; and

π_{mpj} is thus the difference in log-odds of a correct response between item mp and a "reference item" for examinee j on trait m.

Level-2 Model. We formulate a multivariate unconditional model for the traits and we fix all the item effects:

$$\pi_{m0j} = \beta_{m00} + u_{m0j},$$

$$\pi_{mpj} = \beta_{mp0} \quad \text{for } m = 1, \ldots, M, p > 0. \tag{11.41}$$

Here the random effects $u_{10j}, \ldots, u_{M0j}$ are M-variate normal in distribution with zero means and $\text{Var}(u_{m0j}) = \tau_{m00}$ and $\text{Cov}(u_{m0j}, u_{m'0j}) = \tau_{m00, m'00}$. As before, item effects are constrained to be invariant across examinees.

The multivariate item response model allows one to assess the extent to which traits are correlated (controlling for measurement error) and to examine whether covariates have different or similar associations with different traits. In addition, one or more traits can be viewed as latent covariates in a model to account for variation in one or more of the remaining traits.

Example 1: Aggression and Delinquency During Adolescence. Cheong and Raudenbush (2000) studied correlates of aggression and delinquency based on 33 items of the Child Behavior Checklist (CBCL) of Achenbach (1991). Each item response was coded dichotomously (1 indicated that the child did manifest the behavior of interest; 0 indicated that the child did not manifest the behavior). According to the CBCL manual, 20 of the items assess aggression, while the remaining 13 items assess delinquency.

(i) Level-1 Model. Cheong and Raudenbush used a logit link function at level 1 with

$$\eta_{ij} = D_{\text{agg } ij} \left(\pi_{\text{agg } 0j} + \sum_{p=1}^{19} \pi_{\text{agg } pj} X_{\text{agg } pij} \right)$$

$$+ D_{\text{del } ij} \left(\pi_{\text{del } 0j} + \sum_{p=1}^{12} \pi_{\text{del } pj} X_{\text{del } pij} \right). \tag{11.42}$$

where

$D_{\text{agg } ij}$ is a dummy variable that takes on a value of 1 if the ith response of person j is to an item that assesses aggression and 0 if not, while $D_{\text{del } ij} = 1 - D_{\text{agg } ij}$ takes on a value of 1 if the ith response of person j is to an item that assesses delinquency;

$\pi_{\text{agg } 0j}$ is the latent aggression level of child j and $\pi_{\text{del } 0j}$ is that child's latent delinquency level;

X_{mpij} is a dummy variable that takes on a value of 1 if the response is to the pth item that measures trait m, 0 otherwise, for $m = $ agg or $m = $ del; and

π_{mpj} is thus the difference in log-odds of a correct response between item mp and a "reference item" for examinee j on trait m for $m = $ agg or $m = $ del.

(ii) Level-2 Model. The analysts first specified a bivariate unconditional model:

$$\pi_{\text{agg } 0j} = \beta_{\text{agg } 00} + u_{\text{agg } 0j},$$

$$\pi_{\text{del } 0j} = \beta_{\text{del } 00} + u_{\text{del } 0j}, \qquad\qquad [11.43]$$

$$\pi_{mpj} = \beta_{mp0} \quad \text{for } m = \text{agg, del}, p > 0.$$

Results of this analysis showed that aggression and delinquency were very highly correlated. The authors also fitted a model with covariates:

$$\pi_{\text{agg} 0j} = \beta_{\text{agg} 00} + \sum_{q=1}^{Q} \beta_{\text{agg } q} W_j + u_{\text{agg} 0j},$$

$$\pi_{\text{del} 0j} = \beta_{\text{del} 00} + \sum_{q=1}^{Q} \beta_{\text{del } q} W_j + u_{\text{del} 0j}, \qquad\qquad [11.44]$$

$$\pi_{mpj} = \beta_{mp0} \quad \text{for } m = \text{agg, del}, p > 0.$$

Here covariates W_{qj}, $1 = 1, \ldots, Q$, included age and indicators for gender and ethnicity. The authors found stronger effects of age and gender for delinquency than for aggression. This suggested that, though the aggression and delinquency traits are highly correlated, they cannot be viewed as tapping a single underlying dimension.

The authors extended this analysis to include a third level, the neighborhoods in which the children resided. They assessed the association between neighborhood disadvantage and both aggression and delinquency and found that this association was similarly positive.

Two-Parameter Models

The item response models discussed in this chapter are known as "one-parameter" models because each item is characterized by a single parameter: its difficulty. A key assumption of the one-parameter model is that the curves describing the association between the trait and the probability of a correct response are parallel. If this assumption is false, one might choose a two-parameter model, where the second parameter accounts for the differing slopes of the trait-probability curves (Birnbaum, 1968). These can be represented by a hierarchical model in which a factor analysis model is imposed on the random effects (Miyazaki, 2000). Such applications, however, are beyond the scope of the current chapter.

Summary of Terms Introduced in This Chapter

Missing Data Problems

Latent variables: Variables that cannot be directly observed. It is often useful to conceive of latent variables as missing data.

Complete data: Includes the observed data and the missing data.

Incomplete data: Includes only the observed data.

Data missing completely at random (MCAR): Occurs if the missing data are a random sample of the complete data. In this case, the probability that a datum is missing is independent of the value of that datum.

Data missing at random (MAR): Occurs if the probability that a datum is missing is independent of the value of that datum after taking into account all of the observed data.

Model-based imputations: Sampled from the distribution of the complete data given the observed data. Multiple model-based imputations produce multiple "complete" data sets in which the missing data have been replaced by model-based imputations. Appropriate analysis of the multiple data sets will produce consistent estimates of model parameters and standard errors under the MAR assumption. Even if the MAR assumption is false, the inferences will be robust if the fraction of missing information is small.

Efficient estimation: Uses all of the information in the observed data to estimate the parameters generating the complete data. Such efficient estimates will also produce consistent estimates of model parameters and standard errors under the MAR assumption. And, again, if the MAR assumption is false, the inferences will be robust if the fraction of missing information is small.

Measurement Error Problems

Measurement error models: Specify the distribution of observed data given latent variables and, possibly, other missing data.

Item response models: Represent conceptions of how latent person characteristics and latent item characteristics combine to shape the response of a given person to a given item.

Rasch model: An item response model that represents the response of a given person to a given item as a function of that person's value on the trait being measured and the difficulty or severity of the item. Given the person trait and item difficulty, the item responses are assumed independent.

Two-parameter item response model: Represents the response of a given person to a given item as a function of that person's value on the trait plus two item parameters: the item difficulty and the item discrimination. Given the person trait and these two parameters, the item responses are assumed independent.

Notes

1. With this distribution in mind, it is possible to estimate, for each participant, the conditional distribution of the missing values given the observed data and model parameters. The multiple imputations are sampled from this conditional distribution.

2. The methods described in this chapter are best suited to moderate- to large-sample data. We illustrate these methods with small-sample data, however, for clarity of exposition.

3. If, however, the outcome and explanatory variables are standardized, the regression coefficients will be estimated with bias.

4. The actual computations may be handled in various ways. For example, using the weighting option internal to HLM5.0 program of Raudenbush et al. (2000), one computes for each outcome the weight $W_{ij} = 1/V_{ij}$, which, in this case, would be $1/4.50^2$ for Z_j, $1/2.60^2$ for X_{ij}, and $1/4.90^2$ for X_{2j} (weights are the same for all j). Specifying the weights in this way will reweight the J variance-covariance matrices. This is equivalent to specifying a model having level-1 variances of 1.0 for each weighted outcome. Thus, after specifying the weighting variable, the user sets the level-1 variance to be 1.0. The level-2 model remains unchanged. See Equation 11.20 for an example.

5. The interpretation of social control as a "mediator" of the association between social composition and violence depends strongly on the adequacy of model specification. In particular, it requires the assumption that social control is not influenced by violence and that there are no omitted mediators related to social control. Such assumptions are difficult to defend with nonexperimental data. The results should therefore be viewed as suggestive results requiring further research.

6. Even if the direct association between gender and high school growth were null, one might fault high schools for failing to intervene effectively to ameliorate this growing gap. But such an assertion is quite different from the assertion that high school experience is actively widening the gap.

7. These students belong to the subset of NELS known as the High School Effectiveness Study (HSES). The students are representative of the 30 largest SMSAs (Standard Metropolitan Statistical Areas). Although the students are nested within schools, we ignore this for purposes of simply illustrating the application of latent variable analysis in growth models.

12 Models for Cross-Classified Random Effects

All of the applications discussed thus far in this book have involved a strictly hierarchical data structure. For example, in Chapter 5, we considered the case in which persons (level-1 units) were nested within organizations (level-2 units), and it was assumed that each person belonged to one and only one organization. Chapter 8 added a third level to the hierarchy (e.g., with children nested within classrooms nested within schools), and we assumed that each child belonged to one and only one classroom and each classroom belonged to one and only one school. We now consider a somewhat more complex data structure in which the lower-level units are cross-classified by two or more higher-level units. Models for such data have many interesting applications in social science.

Consider, for example, neighborhood and school contributions to children's educational attainment. We shall typically find that a given neighborhood will "send" its children to a variety of schools and that a given school will draw its children from a variety of neighborhoods. For example, Garner and Raudenbush (1991) studied a sample of 2,310 children within 524 neighborhoods and 17 schools. The structure of the data is displayed in Table 12.1. Each row is a neighborhood and each column is a school. The numbers in this matrix are the counts—the numbers of children who lived in a given neighborhood and attended a given school. For example, we see that six children living in neighborhood 259 attended school 10, one child in that same

373

TABLE 12.1 Organization of Data in the Scotland Neighborhood Study: Number of Observations in Each Neighborhood-by-School Cell

	School																	
Neighborhood	0	1	2	3	4	5	6	7	8	9	10	11	12	13	14	15	16	Totals
26																	5	5
27																	1	1
29															1		8	9
30																	2	2
31															1		1	2
32															1		5	6
33															1		2	3
35																	3	3
36																	2	2
38															1		4	5
.																		.
.																		.
.																		.
251														4	1			5
252													1	3		1		5
253														3				3
256																	2	2
258												4						4
259											**6**	**1**					**2**	**9**
260											6							6
261											3						3	6
263											14					1	1	16
.																		.
.																		.
.																		.
793									6									6
794		1		1					11									13
795			2						1									3
796			9						1									10
797			3			1												4
798								10										10
799			1							1								2
800			3	1														4
801			1	1														2
803									3									3
Totals	146	22	146	159	155	101	286	112	136	133	92	190	111	154	91	102	174	2,310

neighborhood attended school 11, and two children in that neighborhood attended school 16. Note that the row totals give the number of children in each neighborhood, while the column totals give the numbers of children in each school.

One might pursue a variety of goals in analyzing data of this sort to:

- estimate components of variance in outcomes that lie between neighborhoods, between schools, and between children (within neighborhood-by-school "cells");
- identify neighborhood and school characteristics associated with children's outcomes;
- estimate residual components of variation in outcomes that lie between neighborhoods, between schools, and within cells after taking into account student, neighborhood and school characteristics;
- assess the extent to which the associations between child characteristics and outcomes vary over neighborhoods, schools, and cells;
- assess the extent to which neighborhood characteristics have effects that vary across schools (and the extent to which schools have effects that vary across neighborhoods); and
- estimate unique effects ("random effects") associated with particular neighborhoods or schools.

Of course, the data in Table 12.1 do not reflect the balanced two-way design of the classical analysis of variance. Sample sizes per cell vary greatly and many of the cells in the matrix are empty. Moreover, some predictors may be continuous and others may be discrete. Thus, classical approaches to the analysis of two-way data will not easily apply. Raudenbush (1993) reanalyzed the data using a cross-classified random-effects model, and we expand on this analysis later in the chapter.

Another prominent example of cross-classified structures is the case in which each student is classified by the middle school and the high school attended. Goldstein (1995) used a cross-classified random-effects model to assess the relative importance of the two types of schools in understanding student differences in educational attainment. A similar structure might involve the cross-classification of workers by occupation and industry. One could thus consider occupational differences in earnings controlling industry effects and industrial differences in earnings controlling occupational differences. Interesting applications also arise in the context of repeated-measures studies, as illustrated in our second example below.

It is important to distinguish a cross-classified random-effects structure from other closely related structures that are more appropriately treated using the hierarchical models described in previous chapters. Consider, for example, an experiment in which persons are assigned to an experimental or

TABLE 12.2 Cross-Classification of Jn Children by Treatment and Site (N Children in Each of J Sites)

	Site 1	Site 2	$\cdots$	Site J	
Experimental	$\dfrac{n}{2}$	$\dfrac{n}{2}$	$\cdots$	$\dfrac{n}{2}$	$\dfrac{Jn}{2}$
Control	$\dfrac{n}{2}$	$\dfrac{n}{2}$	$\cdots$	$\dfrac{n}{2}$	$\dfrac{Jn}{2}$
	n	n	$\cdots$	n	Jn

NOTE: Site is a random factor, treatment a fixed factor.

control treatment within a site (e.g., school or clinic), and this experiment is replicated in many sites. Thus, treatments and sites create a cross-classification as illustrated in Table 12.2. Each column is a site and each row is a treatment condition. While the structure of the data are similar to that in Table 12.1, there is a crucial difference. In the neighborhood-by-school case, the investigator would typically seek to generalize from the sample to populations of neighborhoods and schools. Hence, both neighborhood and school effects would typically be regarded as random effects. However, in the treatment-by-site case (Table 12.2), the goal would typically be to make specific statements about the treatment of interest (not to generalize to some "population of all possible treatments"). Yet one *would* want to generalize the findings to a population of sites. Thus, in Table 12.2, treatment effects would typically be regarded as fixed effects and site effects as random effects. This scenario can be handled by means of a two-level hierarchical model, in which participants are the level-1 units and sites are the level-2 units. Treatment group membership would be represented by a level-1 variable—a dummy variable or a contrast code. The current chapter is concerned with cases in which two or more random effects are cross-classified.[1]

Formulating and Testing Models for Cross-Classified Random Effects

Unconditional Model

Using Table 12.1 as an example, one might be interested in simply estimating components of variation that lie between neighborhoods, between schools, and within cells. The model would be unconditional; that is, it would include no predictor variables at any level.

Level-1 or "Within-Cell" Model. A unique set of children is nested within each cell of the cross-classification, and the within-cell model describes variation among these children. In the unconditional case, we have

$$Y_{ijk} = \pi_{0jk} + e_{ijk}, \qquad e_{ijk} \sim \mathrm{N}(0, \sigma^2), \qquad [12.1]$$

where

Y_{ijk} is the attainment of child i in neighborhood j and school k;

π_{0jk} is the mean attainment of children in cell jk, that is, children who live in neighborhood j and attend school k; and

e_{ijk} is the random "child effect," that is, the deviation of child ijk's score from the cell mean. These deviations are assumed normally distributed with mean 0 and a within-cell variance σ^2.

The indices i, j, and k thus denote children, neighborhoods, and schools, where there are

$i = 1, \ldots, n_{jk}$ children within cell jk;

$j = 1, \ldots, J = 524$ neighborhoods; and

$k = 1, \ldots, K = 17$ schools.

Level-2 or "Between-Cell" Model. Variation between cells is attributable to neighborhood effects, school effects, and (possibly) a neighborhood-by-school interaction effect:

$$\pi_{0jk} = \theta_0 + b_{00j} + c_{00k} + d_{0jk},$$
$$b_{00j} \sim \mathrm{N}(0, \tau_{b00}),$$
$$c_{00k} \sim \mathrm{N}(0, \tau_{c00}), \qquad [12.2]$$
$$d_{0jk} \sim \mathrm{N}(0, \tau_{d00}),$$

where

θ_0 is the grand-mean attainment of all children;

b_{00j} is the random main effect of neighborhood j, that is, the contribution of neighborhood j averaged over all schools, assumed normally distributed with mean 0 and variance τ_{b00};

c_{00k} is the random main effect of school k, that is, the contribution of school k averaged over all neighborhoods, assumed normally distributed with mean 0 and variance τ_{c00}; and

d_{0jk} is the random interaction effect, that is, the deviation of the cell mean from that predicted by the grand mean and the two main effects, assumed normally distributed with mean 0 and variance τ_{d00}.

In many applications, the within-cell sample sizes are not sufficient to distinguish the variance attributable to τ_{d00} from the within-cell variance, σ^2. We would have to drop the interaction effect from the model, knowing that the within-cell variance and interaction-effect variance are confounded. Such would be the case for the data in Table 12.1, which has very small cell sizes.

Combined Model. Substituting Equation 12.2 into Equation 12.1 yields the single combined model

$$Y_{ijk} = \theta_0 + b_{00j} + c_{00k} + d_{0jk} + e_{ijk}, \qquad [12.3]$$

which is recognizable as a two-way analysis of variance with random row effects, b_{00j}; column effects, c_{00k}; two-way interaction, d_{0jk}; and within-cell deviation, e_{ijk}.

Variance Partitioning and Reliabilities. The two-level model described in Equations 12.1 and 12.2 partitions the total variance in the outcome into a within-cell component, σ^2, and a between-cell component. The between-cell component is further partitioned into three components: variance between neighborhoods, τ_{b00}; variance between schools, τ_{c00}; and a residual variance between cells, τ_{d00}, that is, variance between cells that is not accounted for by the row and column variances. This setup generates three kinds of intraunit correlation coefficients:

1. the correlation between outcomes of two children who live in the same neighborhood and attend the same school:

$$\text{corr}(Y_{ijk}, Y_{i'jk}) = \rho_{bcd} = \frac{\tau_{b00} + \tau_{c00} + \tau_{d00}}{\tau_{b00} + \tau_{c00} + \tau_{c00} + \sigma^2}; \qquad [12.4]$$

2. the correlation between outcomes of two children who live in the same neighborhood but attend different schools:

$$\text{corr}(Y_{ijk}, Y_{i'jk'}) = \rho_b = \frac{\tau_{b00}}{\tau_{b00} + \tau_{c00} + \tau_{d00} + \sigma^2}; \qquad [12.5]$$

3. the correlation between outcomes of two children who attend the same school but live in different neighborhoods:

$$\text{corr}(Y_{ijk}, Y_{i'j'k}) = \rho_c = \frac{\tau_{00c}}{\tau_{b00} + \tau_{c00} + \tau_{d00} + \sigma^2}. \qquad [12.6]$$

One might wish to assess the reliability with which neighborhood effects can be distinguished for individuals who attend a particular school:

$$\text{reliability}[(\hat{b}_{00j} + \hat{d}_{0jk})|c_{00k}] = \frac{\tau_{b00} + \tau_{d00}}{\tau_{b00} + \tau_{d00} + \sigma^2/n_{jk}} \qquad [12.7]$$

versus the reliability with which school effects can be distinguished for individuals all coming from the same neighborhood:

$$\text{reliability}[(\hat{c}_{00k} + \hat{d}_{0jk})|b_{00j}] = \frac{\tau_{c00} + \tau_{d00}}{\tau_{c00} + \tau_{d00} + \sigma^2/n_{jk}}. \qquad [12.8]$$

Conditional Models

The fully unconditional model of Equations 12.1 and 12.2 specifies variability associated with students, neighborhoods, schools, and neighborhood-by-school interaction effects. Presumably, part of each source of variability can be accounted for by measured variables. That is, student characteristics, neighborhood characteristics, school characteristics, and relevant interactions among them could be predictors.

The two-way model for cross-classified random effects permits an extraordinarily rich class of modeling possibilities. For example, a neighborhood characteristic might have an effect on an outcome under study. This effect, in turn, could be fixed, random, or nonrandomly varying over schools. For example, Garner and Raudenbush (1991) found that neighborhood social deprivation had an effect on educational attainment. The magnitude of this effect might depend on the social organization of the school a student attends. Similarly, a school characteristic might have an effect that varies over neighborhoods. Next, consider the association between a child background characteristic, such as ethnicity or social class, and educational attainment. Such an association might depend on measured or unmeasured characteristics of neighborhoods, or schools, or of interactions between neighborhood and school characteristics.

The richness of modeling possibilities makes it difficult to write down a general model without resort to rather complex notation. Therefore, to clarify the logic of the model, we shall consider a scenario with three level-2 variables: a single neighborhood characteristic, W_j, a single school characteristic, X_k, and their interaction term, $W_j^* X_k$. These three explanatory variables can be used to account for variation in any level-1 coefficient, π_{pjk}, defined by cell jk of the neighborhood by school matrix.

To make the presentation even simpler, let us consider the hypothetical data structure of Table 12.3 with balanced data. Here we have $J = 6$ neighborhoods randomly assigned to an experimental treatment ($W_j = \frac{1}{2}$) or the control treatment ($W_j = -\frac{1}{2}$). We also have $K = 4$ schools, with two assigned at random to an experimental treatment ($X_k = \frac{1}{2}$) or a control treatment ($X_k = -\frac{1}{2}$). Thus, there are $JK = 24$ cells, and, within each cell, we randomly sample $n_{jk} = n = 20$. The students are half female ($a_{ijk} = \frac{1}{2}$) or male

TABLE 12.3 Layout of Hypothetical Data from an Experiment Conducted in
Neighborhoods and Schools, Both Viewed as Random Factors

			School-level variable, X				
			Experimental Group, $X = \frac{1}{2}$		*Control Group,* $X = -\frac{1}{2}$		
			$c = 1$	$c = 2$	$c = 3$	$c = 4$	
	Experimental	$r = 1$	n	n	n	n	$4n$
	group	$r = 2$	n	n	n	n	$4n$
Neighborhood-	$W = \frac{1}{2}$	$r = 3$	n	n	n	n	$4n$
level							
variable, W	Control	$r = 4$	n	n	n	n	$4n$
	group	$r = 5$	n	n	n	n	$4n$
	$W = -\frac{1}{2}$	$r = 6$	n	n	n	n	$4n$
			$6n$	$6n$	$6n$	$6n$	$24n$

NOTE: Experimental treatments X and W are fixed factors.

$(a_{ijk} = -\frac{1}{2})$. Such a design would likely afford little statistical power, and
we employ it here strictly as a device for clarifying the logic and notation.

Within-Cell Model. Within each neighborhood-by-school cell, the model
specifies a cell mean achievement and a gender gap:

$$Y_{ijk} = \pi_{0jk} + \pi_{1jk}a_{ijk} + e_{ijk}, \qquad e_{ijk} \sim \mathrm{N}(0, \sigma^2), \qquad [12.9]$$

where

Y_{ijk} is the attainment of student i in neighborhood j and school k;

π_{0jk} is the intercept, in this case, the mean attainment for cell jk;

a_{ijk} indicates the gender of student ijk (female $= \frac{1}{2}$, male $= -\frac{1}{2}$);

π_{1jk} is the regression coefficient relating a_{ijk} to Y_{ijk}, in this case, the "gender gap"
or mean attainment difference between females and males in cell jk; and

e_{ijk} is a within-cell random effect that represents the deviation of student ijk's
outcome from the predicted outcome based on student gender. This random
effect is assumed normally distributed with mean 0 and variance σ^2.

Level-2 or "Between-Cell" Model. The level-1 model defines two cell-
specific coefficients, π_{pjk}, $p = 0, 1$, the mean attainment and the gender gap
in attainment, respectively. These level-1 coefficients become outcomes in a
level-2 model that represents the variation between the cells created by the

crossing of the two random factors (i.e., neighborhoods and schools). This variation can be modeled as a function of level-2 predictors that describe the neighborhoods, the schools, the interactions between neighborhood and school predictors, and other attributes that characterize distinctive combinations of neighborhoods and schools. In addition, row effects (i.e., effects of neighborhood predictors) can vary randomly across the columns, and column effects (i.e., effects of school-level predictors) can vary across the rows. Because the modeling framework is quite rich and flexible, we begin by considering some simple cases and gradually work up to the more complex full model.

(i) Fixed Effects of a Level-2 Row Predictor and a Level-2 Column Predictor. Here a neighborhood variable W_j and a school-level predictor X_k are both hypothesized to have main effects on π_{pjk}. The level-2 equation would be

$$\pi_{pjk} = \theta_p + \beta_p X_k + \gamma_p W_j + b_{p0j} + c_{p0k} + d_{pjk}, \quad p = 0, 1, \quad [12.10]$$

where

θ_p is the model intercept, the expected value of π_{pjk} when all explanatory variables are set to zero (in this instance, θ_p is the grand mean);

β_p is the fixed effect of X_k (assumed constant over all neighborhoods in the population);

γ_p is the fixed effect of W_j (assumed constant over all schools in the population); and

b_{p0j}, c_{p0k}, and d_{pjk} are residual random effects of neighborhoods, schools, and neighborhood-by-school cells, respectively, on π_{pjk} after taking into account W_j and X_k.

(ii) Randomly Varying Effects of a Level-2 Row and a Level-2 Column Predictor. In the model above, the effect of school characteristic X_k was assumed constant across all neighborhoods. Similarly, the effect of neighborhood characteristic W_j was assumed fixed across all schools. Either or both could randomly vary. The extension of the level-2 equation to the model is

$$\pi_{pjk} = \theta_p + (\beta_p + b_{p1j})X_k + (\gamma_p + c_{p1k})W_j + b_{p0j} + c_{p0k} + d_{pjk}, \quad [12.11]$$

where

θ_p is again the model intercept, the expected value of π_{pjk} when all explanatory variables are set to zero;

β_p is the fixed effect of X_k (averaged over all neighborhoods in the population);

b_{p1j} is the random effect of neighborhood j on the association between X_k and π_{pjk};

γ_p is the average effect of W_j (averaged over all schools in the population);

c_{p1k} is the random effect of school k on the association between W_j and π_{pjk}; and b_{p0j}, c_{p0k}, and d_{p0jk} are residual random effects of neighborhoods, schools, and neighborhood-by-school cells, respectively, on π_{pjk}.

(iii) Explaining Randomly Varying Effects of Level-2 Row or Column Predictors. Equation 12.11 is analogous to an unconditional level-2 model in regular two-level analysis. We can see this clearly if we rewrite the combined formulation of Equation 12.11 in hierarchical form:

$$\pi_{pjk} = \theta_p + \beta_{pj}X_k + \gamma_{pk}W_j + b_{p0j} + c_{p0k} + d_{pjk}$$

with

$$\beta_{pj} = \beta_p + b_{p1j}, \qquad\qquad\qquad [12.12a]$$

$$\gamma_{pk} = \gamma_p + c_{p1k}. \qquad\qquad\qquad [12.12b]$$

Notice that Equations 12.12a and 12.12b are unconditional models; that is, they include no level-2 predictors. Given that β_{pj} and γ_{pk} vary randomly across neighborhoods and schools, respectively, this leads naturally to consider whether measured characteristics of the neighborhoods (i.e., other W_js) might be introduced as predictors in Equation 12.12a. Similarly, measured characteristics of schools (i.e., other X_ks) might be introduced in Equation 12.12b. There is, however, one complication to consider. The introduction of W_j as a predictor in Equation 12.12a is formally equivalent to introducing X_k as a predictor in Equation 12.12b. That is, they yield the same combined model:

$$\pi_{pjk} = \theta_p + (\beta_p + b_{p1j})X_k + (\gamma_p + c_{p1k})W_j + \delta_p X_k * W_j$$
$$+ b_{p0j} + c_{p0k} + d_{pjk}, \qquad\qquad [12.13]$$

where δ_p is the regression slope for the W by X interaction.

For this reason, it makes most sense to use the combined model formulation of Equation 12.13 as our basic modeling framework for cross-random effect applications. In addition, it allows for another novel possibility—the inclusion of predictors of a cell-level effect, π_{pjk}, that is defined only at the cell level. For example, the mean attainment of students from neighborhood j who attend school k, π_{0jk}, might be affected by how far this home neighborhood is from the school attended. The value for such a variable, say Z_{jk}, depends on the particular combinations of neighborhoods and schools and is not a simple cross-product of some W_j and X_k. Such a variable could simply be added to Equation 12.13 to yield an additional fixed δ_p effect.

Table 12.4 summarizes the sources of variation for a level-1 coefficient, π_{pjk}, as specified in Equations 12.9 and 12.13, respectively. In addition to the

TABLE 12.4 Sources of Variation in a Level-1 Coefficient, π_{pjk}, Based on Equation 12.13

Source of Variation	Contributor	Degrees of Freedom
(1) Mean	θ_p	1
(2) Neighborhood treatment	$\gamma_p W_j$	1
(3) Unexplained neighborhood effects	b_{p0j}	$J - 2 = 4$
(4) School treatment	$\beta_p X_k$	1
(5) Unexplained school effects	c_{p0k}	$K - 2 = 2$
(2) × (4)	$\delta_p X_k W_j$	1
(2) × (5)	$c_{p1k} W_j$	$K - 2 = 2$
(4) × (3)	$b_{p1j} X_k$	$J - 2 = 4$
(3) × (5)	d_{pjk}	$(J - 2)(K - 2) = 8$
Total		$JK = 24$

mean (1), there are three fundamental sources of variation: variation between neighborhoods, variation between schools, and school-by-neighborhood variation. Variation between neighborhoods is partitioned into a component that is explained by the neighborhood-level fixed effects (2) and another component left unexplained (3). Variation between schools is similarly partitioned into a component explained by fixed effects (4) and a component that is unexplained (5). Each of the two neighborhood components interacts with each of the two school components to form four sources of neighborhood-by-school variation: a component that is explained by the fixed effects [(2) * (4)], a component that accounts for the fact that the effect of the neighborhood-level treatment varies randomly over schools [(2) * (5)], a component that accounts for the fact that the effect of the school-level treatment varies randomly over neighborhoods [(4) * (3)], and a residual between-cell component unrelated to the treatments [(3) * (5)].

A similar table can readily be constructed to represent variation among students within the cells of the matrix. That table would show that student-level variation is partly explained by the fixed effect of the student covariates; by the interaction between these covariates and each component of school, neighborhood, and school-by-neighborhood variation in Table 12.4; and, finally, by a residual within-cell component unrelated to the student covariates or any of their interactions with components.

A Full Combined Model. Substituting the level-2 model (Equation 12.13) into the level-1 model (Equation 12.9) yields a combined "mixed model" equation

$$Y_{ijk} = \theta_0 + \theta_1 a_{ijk} + \beta_0 X_k + \gamma_0 W_j + \delta_0 X_k * W_j + \beta_1 X_k * a_{ijk}$$
$$+ \gamma_1 W_j * a_{ijk} + \delta_1 X_k * W_j * a_{ijk} + b_{01j} X_k + c_{01k} W_j$$
$$+ b_{10j} a_{ijk} + c_{10k} a_{ijk} + d_{1jk} a_{ijk} + b_{11j} X_k * a_{ijk} + c_{11k} W_j * a_{ijk}$$
$$+ b_{00j} + c_{00k} + d_{0jk} + e_{ijk}. \qquad [12.14]$$

Two comments are essential:

1. With only two cross-classified factors and with only a single covariate for each level (students, schools, and neighborhood), the sources of variation are already quite numerous and the corresponding modeling possibilities extensive. The model expands dramatically as more cross-classified factors (e.g., time) or nested factors (e.g., school districts) are added and as more covariates are added.

2. Given the fact that these models can rapidly become complex and that the data in any application may not be extensive at every level, some attention to the principle of parsimony is needed. That is, certain covariates must be constrained not to have random effects, at least not at each level, and it will often be impossible to estimate random row-by-column interaction effects because cell sizes are insufficient. Indeed, the full model of Equation 12.14 would not be estimable given the data in Table 12.3 without imposing constraints on the covariance structure of the random effects. Constraints imposed to simplify the model are best based on theory. The two examples that follow illustrate the kinds of constraints that one might impose to achieve a reasonably simple representation of the variation that nonetheless is arguably justifiable on the basis of available theory.

Example 1: Neighborhood and School Effects on Educational Attainment in Scotland

The design of the study was previously depicted in Table 12.1; descriptive statistics appear in Table 12.5. The 2,310 students were nested within 524 neighborhoods and 17 schools. The outcome variable is total attainment ($m = 0.116$, sd $= 1.00$), a composite measure constructed on the basis of a series of national examinations (called *O levels* and *Highers*) administered in Scotland during the later secondary years. These examination results are highly influential in decisions regarding employment and entrance to universities. Covariates included Primary 7 VRQ (verbal reasoning quotient administered at primary school, Grade 7; $m = 0.51$, sd $= 10.65$), a Primary 7 reading test score ($m = -0.04$, sd $= 13.89$), and a variety of social-demographic indicators, including father's employment status and occupation and father's and

TABLE 12.5 Descriptive Statistics from the Scotland Neighborhood Study

Variable	n	Mean	sd
(a) Neighborhood level			
Social deprivation	524	0.04	0.62
(b) Student level			
Total attainment	2,310	0.09	1.00
Primary 7 VRQ	2,310	0.51	10.65
Primary 7 reading	2,310	−0.04	13.89
Dad occupation 29	2,310	−0.46	11.78
Dad education			
(1 = Schooling past 15; 0 = No)	2,310	0.22	0.41
Mom education			
(1 = Schooling past 15; 0 = No)	2,310	0.25	0.43
Dad unemployment			
(1 = Yes; 0 = No)	2,310	0.11	0.30
Sex (1 = M; 0 = F)	2,310	0.48	0.50

mother's education. Table 12.5 shows that only 22% of the fathers and 25.0% of the mothers continued in school past the age of 15 and that 11% of the fathers were unemployed. The key predictor variable of interest was a 20-item indicator of neighborhood social deprivation attached to each enumeration district in the educational authority under study (enumeration districts are similar to census tracts in the United States). The scale incorporates information on the poverty concentration, health, and housing stock of a local community, $m = 0.04$, sd $= 0.62$ (see Garner & Raudenbush, 1991, for details).

Unconditional Model

Let us first consider a decomposition of variance using an unconditional model. At level 1, we have

$$Y_{ijk} = \pi_{0jk} + e_{ijk}, \qquad e_{ijk} \sim N(0, \sigma^2), \qquad [12.15]$$

where Y_{ijk} is the attainment of student i in neighborhood j and school k; π_{0jk} is the "cell mean," that is, the mean attainment of students who live in neighborhood j and attend school k; and σ^2 is the within-cell variance.

At level 2, we consider only a "main effects model." That is, we omit the random effect associated with the neighborhood-by-school interaction because the cell sizes are too small to reliably distinguish this source of variation from the within-cell error. Thus, we have

$$\pi_{0jk} = \theta_0 + b_{00j} + c_{00k},$$

$$b_{00j} \sim N(0, \tau_{b00}), \qquad c_{00k} \sim N(0, \tau_{c00}). \qquad [12.16]$$

TABLE 12.6 Modeling Results for Scotland Neighborhood Data

(a) Fixed Effects

Predictor	Model 1 Unconditional Model			Model 2 Conditional Model			Model 3 Conditional Model, with Social Deprivation Effect Random		
	Coeff.	se	t Ratio	Coeff.	se	t Ratio	Coeff.	se	t Ratio
INTERCEPT	0.075	0.072	—	0.100	0.021	—	0.098	0.021	—
VRQ				0.028	0.002	11.59	0.028	0.002	12.21
READING				0.026	0.002	14.68	0.026	0.002	14.99
DAD OCC				0.008	0.001	5.80	0.008	0.001	5.96
DAD EDUCATION				0.144	0.041	3.54	0.142	0.041	3.50
MOM ED				0.059	0.038	1.59	0.060	0.037	1.63
DAD UNEMP				-0.121	0.047	-2.58	-0.120	0.047	-2.57
SEX				-0.056	0.028	-1.97	-0.056	0.028	-1.98
NEIGHBORHOOD DEPRIVATION				-0.157	0.025	-6.22	-0.159	0.027	-5.94

(b) Variance Components

Parameter	Estimate	Estimate	Estimate
Neighborhoods $\mathrm{Var}(b_{00j}) = \tau_{b00}$	0.141	0.000	0.004
Schools $\begin{pmatrix} \mathrm{Var}(c_{00k}) & \mathrm{cov}(c_{00k}, c_{01k}) \\ \mathrm{cov}(c_{01k}, c_{00k}) & \mathrm{Var}(c_{01k}) \end{pmatrix} = \begin{pmatrix} \tau_{c00} & \tau_{c01} \\ \tau_{c10} & \tau_{c11} \end{pmatrix}$	0.075	0.004	$\begin{pmatrix} 0.004 & 0.002 \\ 0.002 & 0.001 \end{pmatrix}$
Students $\mathrm{Var}(e_{it}) = \sigma^2$	0.799	0.459	0.455
Model df	4	12	14

The analysis (see results in Table 12.6, Model 1) enables us to estimate three interesting intraunit correlations. The intraneighborhood correlation is the correlation between outcomes of two students who live in the same neighborhood but attend different schools. It is estimated to be

$$\widehat{\mathrm{corr}}(Y_{ijk}, Y_{i'jk'}) = \frac{\hat{\tau}_{b00}}{\hat{\tau}_{b00} + \hat{\tau}_{c00} + \hat{\sigma}^2}$$

$$= \frac{0.141}{0.141 + 0.075 + 0.799} = 0.139. \qquad [12.17]$$

Thus, about 13.9% of the total variance lies between neighborhoods. Similarly, the intraschool correlation is the correlation between outcomes of two students who attend the same school but live in different neighborhoods:

$$\widehat{\mathrm{corr}}(Y_{ijk}, Y_{i'jk'}) = \frac{\hat{\tau}_{c00}}{\hat{\tau}_{b00} + \hat{\tau}_{c00} + \hat{\sigma}^2}$$

$$= \frac{0.075}{0.141 + 0.075 + 0.799} = 0.074. \qquad [12.18]$$

That is, about 7.4% of the variation lies between schools. Finally, the "intracell" correlation is the correlation between outcomes of two students who live in the same neighborhood and attend the same school:

$$\widehat{\mathrm{corr}}(Y_{ijk}, Y_{i'jk}) = \frac{\hat{\tau}_{b00} + \hat{\tau}_{c00}}{\hat{\tau}_{b00} + \hat{\tau}_{c00} + \hat{\sigma}^2}$$

$$= \frac{0.141 + 0.075}{0.141 + 0.075 + 0.799} = 0.212. \qquad [12.19]$$

Thus, according to the fitted model, about 22.0% of the variance lies between cells. Note that $\hat{\tau}_{d00}$ from Equation 12.4 does not appear in Equation 12.19 since the main effects model assumes $\tau_{d00} = 0$.

Conditional Model

Garner and Raudenbush (1991) sought, within the limits of nonexperimental data, a stringent test of the hypothesis that neighborhood social deprivation undermines educational attainment. Available were two prior measures of cognitive skill, verbal reasoning quotient ("VRQ") and reading achievement ("Reading"), both measured at primary grade 7, just before entry to secondary school (see Table 12.5). These two measures provide substantial information on a student's verbal skill. Thus, controlling for these covariates, any neighborhood effect on verbal skill occurring prior to the end of primary school was virtually eliminated. When demographic background variables are also included as additional level-1 predictors, the model is

$$Y_{ijk} = \pi_{0jk} + \pi_{1jk}(\text{VRQ})_{ijk} + \pi_{2jk}(\text{READING})_{ijk}$$
$$+ \pi_{3jk}(\text{DAD OCC})_{ijk} + \pi_{4jk}(\text{DAD ED})_{ijk}$$
$$+ \pi_{5jk}(\text{MOM ED})_{ijk} + \pi_{6jk}(\text{DAD UNEMP})_{ijk}$$
$$+ \pi_{7jk}(\text{SEX})_{ijk} + e_{ijk}, \qquad [12.20]$$

where all the level-1 predictors are grand-mean centered and the residual within-cell variance is $\text{Var}(e_{ijk}) = \sigma^2$.

The level-2 model for the intercept is simply

$$\pi_{0jk} = \theta_0 + \gamma_{01}(\text{DEPRIVATION})_j + b_{00j} + c_{00k}. \qquad [12.21]$$

In the interest of parsimony (given the small cell sizes and within-neighborhood sample sizes), all other level-1 coefficients are fixed:

$$\pi_{pjk} = \theta_p, \qquad p > 0. \qquad [12.22]$$

Several features of the results (Table 12.6, Model 2) are remarkable:

- Several level-1 covariates are significantly related to educational attainment, with especially large effects for READING and VRQ.
- The residual level-1 variance is estimated to be 0.459, implying that 46% of the unconditional level-1 variance (estimated at 0.799) is accounted for by the covariates.
- Controlling these level-1 effects, a highly significant negative effect of social deprivation appears ($\hat{\gamma} = -0.157$, $t = -5.94$).
- The residual variation between neighborhoods, τ_{b00} (estimated at 0.000), and between schools, τ_{c00} (estimated at 0.004), are close to zero; compare to the unconditional variance estimates (0.141 and 0.075). These level-2 variance components were substantially reduced.

Estimating a Random Effect of Social Deprivation

In the analysis just completed, the relationship between neighborhood social deprivation and attainment was assumed invariant across schools. It is of substantive interest to test this assumption. Moreover, if that association does vary over schools, the standard error will be underestimated when that association is assumed fixed over schools. We therefore expand Equation 12.21:

$$\pi_{0jk} = \theta_0 + (\gamma_{01} + c_{01k})(\text{DEPRIVATION})_j + b_{00j} + c_{00k},$$

where

$$\begin{pmatrix} c_{00k} \\ c_{01k} \end{pmatrix} \sim N \left[\begin{pmatrix} 0 \\ 0 \end{pmatrix}, \begin{pmatrix} \tau_{c00} & \tau_{c00,01} \\ \tau_{c01,00} & \tau_{c01} \end{pmatrix} \right].$$

Thus, c_{01k} is the unique contribution of school k to the association between neighborhood deprivation and attainment. This effect has variance τ_{c01} and it also covaries with the school random effect c_{00k}.

The fitted model reveals no evidence, however, that the deprivation effect varies over schools. The point estimates were

$$\begin{bmatrix} \hat{\tau}_{c00} & \hat{\tau}_{c00,01} \\ & \hat{\tau}_{c01} \end{bmatrix} = \begin{bmatrix} 0.004 & 0.002 \\ & 0.001 \end{bmatrix},$$

yielding a model deviance of 4,768.51. A comparison with the deviance of 4,769.60 associated with the model in which deprivation had a fixed effect (Table 12.6, Model 2) yielded the difference $4,749.60 - 4,768.51 = 1.09$. This difference can be compared to percentiles of the χ^2 distribution with $df = 2$, supporting retention of the null hypothesis $\tau_{c01} = \tau_{c00,01} = 0$. Not surprisingly, the standard error for $\hat{\gamma}_{01}$, the social deprivation effect, remained nearly unchanged, as did all inferences about the fixed effects.

Example 2: Classroom Effects on Children's Cognitive Growth During the Primary Years

Chapter 8 considered the estimation of contextual effects on individual growth using a three-level model. The example involved repeated measures on children who were nested within schools, yielding inferences about school differences in children's rates of learning. Other examples include the progress of patients nested within therapists and neighborhood influences on changes in criminal propensity during adolescence (Raudenbush, 1995). A limitation of the three-level hierarchical model in assessing such contextual effects on individual change is that the model applies only to those persons who remain in a single context during the course of the investigation. When persons cross contextual boundaries during the study, the data no longer have a nested structure. Rather, the structure involves cross-classification of persons by social settings.

   Just such migration occurs when one attempts to study the effects of classrooms on children's cognitive growth during the primary years, as the data
in Table 12.7 illustrate. The data constitute a subsample from the Immersion
Study (Ramirez et al., 1991), a national evaluation of alternative programs for
children in the United States having limited English proficiency. The example appears in Raudenbush (1993), though our treatment of it here, based on
a cumulative effect model, is new. Each row in Table 12.7 is a child and each
column is a teacher. For brevity, only the first and last 10 children are listed.
The histories of children 5009 and 5010 illustrate the shifting social memberships that characterize many elementary schools: These children share
membership during grade 1 in the classroom of teacher 10 but were split
apart in grade 2, when child 5009 was assigned to teacher 17 and child 5010
to teacher 11. During grade 2, child 5009 became a classmate of child 5011
for the first time, when they both had teacher 17.
   The level-1 model[2] assumes straight-line growth trajectory in mathematics
for each child during these elementary years (an assumption that appears
sensible based on examination of residual plots):

$$Y_{ijk} = \pi_{0jk} + \pi_{1jk}a_{ij} + e_{ijk}, \qquad e_{ijk} \sim \mathrm{N}(0, \sigma^2), \qquad [12.23]$$

where

   Y_{ijk} is the math outcome at time i for child j in classroom k;

   a_{ij} takes on values of $0, 1, 2, 3$ in grades $1, 2, 3, 4$, respectively; thus,

   π_{0jk} is the expected math outcome for child j at first grade;

   π_{1jk} is the annual rate of growth in math for child j; and

   e_{ijk} is a random within-subject residual assumed normally distributed with mean 0
        and variance σ^2.

At level 2, we begin by specifying an unconditional model. We again
omit the random interaction effect associated with cells. Given at most one
observation per cell (no child is observed more than once while in a given
classroom), it is impossible to disentangle the person-by-classroom variance
from the within-cell variance. We conceive of teacher effects on pupil growth
as "deflections," either positive or negative, from each child's specific growth
trajectory.
   A problem now arises with the cross-classified model as presented so far.
Suppose we view c_{00k} as the "deflection" created by encountering teacher

TABLE 12.7 Organization of Data in a Subsample from the Immersion Study: Each X Indicates an Observation

Grade	Grade 1												Grade 2							Grade 3					Grade 4			Totals
Teacher / Student	1	2	3	4	5	6	7	8	9	10	11	12	13	14	15	16	17	18	19	20	21	22	23	24	25	26	27	
5003									X		X																	2
5005				X										X														2
5006									X																			1
5007					X						X																	2
5009										X						X						X					X	4
5010										X	X																	2
5011									X								X				X							3
5013					X																							1
5014																			X		X							2
5015		X																X			X							3
·																												·
·																												·
5232								X																				1
5234						X								X										X				3
5236													X							X				X	X			4
5237			X												X					X								3
5238												X																1
5241	X																											2
5242							X						X															2
5243				X									X															2
5245						X																			X			2
5246		X																	X		X				X			4
Totals	5	13	15	18	14	15	13	13	13	10	7	11	9	10	11	13	4	6	15	11	12	12	3	3	2	11	2	250

k. Child j's trajectory would then be described by the simple model:

$$\pi_{0jk} = \theta_0 + b_{00j} + c_{00k},$$

$$\pi_{1jk} = \theta_1 + b_{10j},$$

$$\begin{pmatrix} b_{00j} \\ b_{10j} \end{pmatrix} \sim N\left[\begin{pmatrix} 0 \\ 0 \end{pmatrix}, \begin{pmatrix} \tau_{b00} & \tau_{b00,\,10} \\ \tau_{b10,\,00} & \tau_{b10} \end{pmatrix} \right],$$ [12.24]

$$c_{00k} \sim N(0, \tau_{c00}),$$

where

θ_0 is the average math achievement at grade 1;

θ_1 is the average learning rate;

b_{00j} is the random effect associated with child j on grade 1 achievement;

b_{10j} is the random effect associated with child j on the math learning rate;

c_{00k} is a random teacher effect, that is, an expected deflection to the growth curve associated with encountering teacher k.

Here the notation $\tau_{b00,\,10}$ denotes a covariance between b_{00j} and b_{10j}. Thus, a child's grade 1 status and growth rate are presumed correlated.

The problem with this model is that teacher contributions would disappear at the end of each year. To see this, consider a hypothetical case in which student j encounters teacher 1 at grade 1, teacher 2 at grade 2, and teacher 3 at grade 3. The predicted values for that student, given that student's growth parameters and the teacher effects, would be

Predicted value at grade 1: $\widehat{Y}_{1j1} = \theta_0 + b_{00j} + c_{001}$,
Predicted value at grade 2: $\widehat{Y}_{2j2} = \theta_0 + b_{00j} + c_{002} + \theta_1 + b_{10j}$,
Predicted value at grade 3: $\widehat{Y}_{3j3} = \theta_0 + b_{00j} + c_{003} + 2(\theta_1 + b_{10j})$.

Here the gain from grade 1 to grade 2 would be $\theta_1 + b_{10j} + c_{002} - c_{001}$; the predicted gain from grade 2 to grade 3 would be $\theta_1 + b_{10j} + c_{003} - c_{002}$. A more natural model is to specify *cumulative* teacher effects, so that the predicted values would be

Predicted value at grade 1: $\widehat{Y}_{1j1} = \theta_0 + b_{00j} + c_{001}$,
Predicted value at grade 2: $\widehat{Y}_{2j2} = \theta_0 + b_{00j} + \theta_1 + b_{10j} + c_{001} + c_{002}$,
Predicted value at grade 3: $\widehat{Y}_{3j3} = \theta_0 + b_{00j} + 2(\theta_1 + b_{10j}) + c_{001} + c_{002} + c_{003}$.

Now the gain from grade 1 to grade 2 is $\theta_1 + b_{10j} + c_{002}$, while the gain from grade 2 to grade 3 is $\theta_1 + b_{10j} + c_{003}$. For each year, the gain is the student's rate of growth plus a teacher deflection.

To incorporate such cumulative effects, we rewrite the level-1 model (Equation 12.23) as

$$Y_{jt} = \pi_{0jt} + \pi_{1jt}t + e_{jt}, e_{jt} \sim N(0, \sigma^2) \qquad (12.25)$$

where $t = 0, 1, 2, 3$ denotes time elapsed (in years) since child j was in grade 1. This model allows the intercept and slope to change with time, though only the intercept will do so in the current application. At level 2, we have

$$\pi_{0jt} = \theta_0 + b_{00j} + \sum_{k=1}^{K} \sum_{h=0}^{t} D_{hjk} c_{00k},$$

$$\pi_{1jt} = \theta_1 + b_{10j},$$

$$\begin{pmatrix} b_{00j} \\ b_{10j} \end{pmatrix} \sim N \left[\begin{pmatrix} 0 \\ 0 \end{pmatrix}, \begin{pmatrix} \tau_{b00} & \tau_{b00,10} \\ \tau_{b10,00} & \tau_{b10} \end{pmatrix} \right],$$

$$c_{00k} \sim N(0, \tau_{c00}).$$

$$[12.26]$$

Here $D_{tjk} = 1$ if student j encounters teacher k at time h, 0 otherwise. The double summation in Equation 12.26 "cumulates" the teacher effects c_{00k} over time.

Results. Table 12.8 compares the crossed random-effects model, which includes the cumulative teacher effects c_{00k}, with a standard two-level growth model (see Chapter 6) that ignores the clustering of children within classes. The comparison of results between the two-level hierarchical model that ignores classrooms (Table 12.8, Model 1) and the crossed random-effects model (Table 12.8, Model 2) produces some obvious similarities. Estimates of mean initial status (mathematics proficiency at grade 1) are nearly identical (256.58 versus 256.60). The estimated average growth rates (47.11 points per year versus 47.13 points per year) are also similar and indicate that children are growing at quite a rapid rate (approximately one standard deviation per year averaged over the four years of the study).

However, there are differences between results as well. Estimation of the teacher effect variance of $\hat{\tau}_{c00} = 106.16$ in Model 2 is accompanied by reductions in the estimates of variance among children in intercepts ($\hat{\tau}_{b00}$ of 398.27 for Model 2 versus 478.74 for Model 1). Thus, part of the variability that had been attributed to individual differences is now attributed to classroom experience. Also, the variance within children is reduced ($\hat{\sigma}^2$ of 273.07 versus 329.06), indicating that part of the variability attributable to temporal instability in Model 1 is accounted for by classroom experience in Model 2. We

TABLE 12.8 Modeling Results for Immersion Study Data

| (a) Fixed Effects | Model 1 Classroom Variance Ignored | | | Model 2 Classroom Variance Estimated | | | Model 3 Classroom Variance Predicted | | |
Predictor	Coeff.	se	t Ratio	Coeff.	se	t Ratio	Coeff.	se	t Ratio
Expected First-grade status	256.58	2.51	—	256.60	4.00	—	251.62	5.08	—
Expected linear Growth rate	47.11	2.22	21.19	47.13	3.53	13.36	41.39	5.22	7.94
Effect of master's degree							7.64	5.45	1.40

(b) Variance Components Parameter	Estimate	Estimate	Estimate
Initial status $\mathrm{Var}(b_{00j}) = \tau_{b00}$	478.74	398.27	395.65
Growth rate $\mathrm{Var}(b_{10j}) = \tau_{b10}$	122.72	128.01	125.01
Covariance, initial status and growth rate $\mathrm{cov}(b_{00j}, b_{10j}) = \tau_{b00,10}$	35.85	75.90	79.24
Teacher effect $\mathrm{Var}(c_{00k}) = \tau_{c00}$		106.16	81.97
Residual error $\mathrm{Var}(e_{ti}) = \sigma^2$	329.06	273.07	278.62
Model deviance	2,332.09	2,295.75	2,294.01
Model df	6	7	8

note that the variance attributable to teacher-specific deflections is part of the "within-child" variation in a two-level hierarchical model but is associated with teachers in the cross-classified model.

To examine the statistical significance of the classroom effects, one can compare the fit of Models 1 and 2, yielding a difference between deviances of $2,332.09 - 2,295.75 = 36.34$, which, when compared to the critical value of χ^2 with df $= 1$, leads us to reject the null hypothesis $H_0: \tau_{c00} = 0$, $p < .001$.

How can we interpret the size of the classroom effects? The estimated variance $\hat{\tau}_{c00} = 106.16$ is equivalent to a standard deviation of $\sqrt{106.16} = 10.30$. Now the average growth rate is 47.13, so that the expected learning gain in a given year for a classroom having an effect one standard deviation above average would be $47.73 + 10.30 = 57.43$, while the expected gain in a classroom with an effect one standard deviation below average would be 36.83. This would seem a nontrivial difference, especially given the possibility that it could be compounded by a run of good or bad luck—that is, a series of good or bad teachers. Another way to gauge the magnitude of classroom effects is to compare their variance to the variance of individual-level growth differences. We compute $\tau_{c00}/\tau_{b10} = 106.16/128.01 = 0.83$. Thus, the classroom contribution is estimated to be about 83% of the individual component of the variance of increments to learning per year, a seemingly fairly large component.

Conditional Level-2 Model. To illustrate the process of modeling the teacher effects, we now expand the level-2 model to incorporate teachers' postgraduate education as a covariate:

$$\pi_{0jt} = \theta_0 + b_{00j} + \sum_{k=1}^{K}\sum_{h=0}^{t} D_{hjk}[\beta_{01}(\text{Degree})_k + c_{00k}],$$

$$\pi_{1jt} = \theta_1 + b_{10j},$$

$$\begin{pmatrix} b_{00j} \\ b_{10j} \end{pmatrix} \sim N\left[\begin{pmatrix} 0 \\ 0 \end{pmatrix}, \begin{pmatrix} \tau_{b00} & \tau_{b00,\,10} \\ \tau_{b10,\,00} & \tau_{b10} \end{pmatrix}\right],$$

$$c_{00k} \sim N(0, \tau_{c00}).$$

Here $(\text{DEGREE})_k$ takes on a value of unity if teacher k has a master's degree, 0 otherwise, so that β_{01} is the adjusted mean difference in teacher effects between those who do and do not have such degrees. Here c_{00k} is the residual effect for teacher k after controlling that teacher's post-graduate education level. The addition of the teacher education indicator to the model (Table 12.8, Model 3) resulted in a reduction in the estimated teacher-level variance component of τ_{c00} from 106.16 to 81.97. The effect of teacher education was in the expected direction, $\hat{\beta}_{01} = 7.64$, but failed to achieve conventional significance levels as judged either by the ratio of the coefficient to its standard error, $t = 1.40$, or by a comparison of fit between Model 2 and Model 3, which yields a difference between deviances of $2,295.75 - 2,294.01 = 1.74$, df $= 1$.

Summary

Purely nested structures occur when each lower-level unit (e.g., a student) belongs to a single unit at the next level (e.g., a classroom), which, in turn, belongs to one and only one unit at the next level (e.g., a school). More complex nested structures involve cross-classification. A cross-classification arises when lower-level units (e.g., students) share memberships in a unit of one factor (e.g., a neighborhood) and can belong to different units of a second factor (e.g., different schools). This chapter has considered two-way cross-classified models, where level-1 units are nested within "cells" defined by the cross-classification of two higher-level factors and where the higher-level factors are conceived as random rather than fixed. We have labeled the higher-level factors as "rows" and "columns" for ease of communication. Two-way cross-classified models begin with a level-1 or "within-cell" model. The level-1 coefficient can vary over rows, columns, and cells, partly as a function of predictor variables defined as rows, columns, and cells. Effects of predictors defined on rows can vary randomly over columns, and effects of predictors defined on columns can vary randomly over rows.

Summary of Terms Introduced in This Chapter

Two-way cross-classified data: Involve basic observations or "cases" classified into a matrix having J rows and K columns.

Cross-classified random-effects model: Conceives of the effects associated with the rows and columns in a two-way cross-classified data set as *random*, that is, sampled from a distribution of possible effects.

Level-1 or "within-cell" model: Describes sources of variation in outcomes among observations found in the same cell of a two-way cross-classified random-effects model:

$$Y_{ijk} = \pi_{0jk} + \sum_{p=1}^{P} \pi_{pjk} a_{pijk} + e_{ijk}, \qquad e_{ijk} \sim \mathrm{N}(0, \sigma^2).$$

The level-1 outcome is Y_{ijk}, that is, the value of the outcome variable Y for case i nested within row j and column k of the two-way array, with

$i = 1, \ldots, n_{jk}$ cases in cell jk;

$j = 1, \ldots, J$ rows;

$k = 1, \ldots, K$ columns.

The level-1 predictors are a_{pijk} for $p = 1, \ldots, P$.

The level-1 coefficients are π_{pjk} for $p = 0, \ldots, P$.
The level-1 random effect is e_{ijk}.
The level-1 or "within-cell" variance is σ^2.

The level-1 coefficient, π_{pjk}, is the outcome at level 2.
The *level-2 or between-cell model* is

$$\pi_{pjk} = \theta_p + \sum_{q=1}^{Q} (\beta_{pq} + b_{pqj}) X_{pqk}$$

$$+ \sum_{r=1}^{R} (\gamma_{pr} + c_{prk}) W_{prj} + \sum_{s=1}^{S} \delta_{ps} Z_{psjk}$$

$$+ b_{p0j} + c_{p0k} + d_{pjk}.$$

Column-specific predictors are $X_{pqk}, q = 1, \ldots, Q$.
Row-specific predictors are $W_{prj}, r = 1, \ldots, R$.
Cell-specific predictors are $Z_{psjk}, s = 1, \ldots, S$.
Column-specific predictors have fixed effects β_{pq}, but column-specific predictors can also have effects b_{pqj} that may vary randomly over rows $j = 1, \ldots, J$.
Row-specific predictors have fixed effects γ_{pr}, but row-specific predictors can also have effects c_{prk} that may vary randomly over columns $k = 1, \ldots, K$.

Cell-specific predictors have fixed effect δ_{ps}.

After taking into account all row and column covariates, row random effects b_{p0j}, and column random effects c_{p0k}, the cell-specific random effects d_{pjk} contribute independently to the level-2 outcome π_{pjk}.

The components of covariance include:

1. the variances and covariances defined on rows,

$$\text{Var}(b_{pqj}) = \tau_{bpq}, \qquad \text{cov}(b_{pqj}, b_{p'q'r}) = \tau_{bpqp'q'};$$

2. the variances and covariances defined on columns,

$$\text{car}(c_{pqk}) = \tau_{cpq}, \qquad \text{cov}(c_{pqk}, c_{p'q'k}) = \tau_{cpq,p'q'};$$

and

3. the variances and covariance defined on cells,

$$\text{Var}(d_{pjk}) = \tau_{dpp}, \qquad \text{cov}(d_{pjk}, d_{p'jk}) = \tau_{dpp'}.$$

When time-series data on persons are nested within cells defined by the cross-classification of persons and social settings, a *cumulative effects* model may be appropriate to describe the constributions of the social settings.

Notes

1. From a Bayesian point of view, the distinction between fixed and random effects is not salient. Raudenbush (1993) given a Bayesian interpretation of the cross-classification model. See Chapter 13 for a detailed presentation of the Bayesian perspective.

2. To be consistent with the notation in Chapter 8, we might formulate the model as

$$Y_{tij} = \pi_{0ij} + \pi_{1ij}a_{tij} + e_{tij}$$

for child i who encounters teacher j at time t. However, we use the notation in Equation 12.23 to emphasize continuity with the first example in the current chapter.

13 Bayesian Inference for Hierarchical Models

- An Introduction to Bayesian Inference
- Example: Inference for a Normal Mean
- A Bayesian Perspective on Inference in Hierarchical Linear Models
- The Basics of Bayesian Inference for the Two-Level HLM
- Example: Bayes Versus Empirical Bayes Meta-Analysis
- Gibbs Sampling and Other Computational Approaches
- Summary of Terms Introduced in This Chapter

Throughout this book, interest has focused on three types of quantities: randomly varying regression coefficients, fixed regression coefficients, and variance-covariance components. Our approach to inference has been based on a combination of maximum likelihood and empirical Bayes. As we discussed in Chapter 9, this approach works well when the number of higher-level units is large. Moreover, the approach will be quite robust even when the number of higher-level units is small if the data are not too unbalanced and interest focuses on the fixed regression coefficients or the variances and covariances.

In some applications, however, these conditions will not hold. The number of higher-level units may be small and the data may be unbalanced. In these settings, there are distinct advantages in becoming "fully Bayesian" rather than "empirical Bayesian." The purpose of this chapter is to clarify the logic of the fully Bayesian approach in application to hierarchically structured data. We use examples to demonstrate when and why the fully Bayesian approach will be advantageous.

Although Bayesian methods are becoming increasingly popular in applications, many quantitative social scientists do not yet understand the Bayesian logic. This is not surprising, as graduate course work has not traditionally emphasized the Bayesian approach. We find it necessary, therefore, to begin this chapter with an introduction to Bayesian inference in the simple setting of single-level data and very simple models. Next, we apply the logic to a comparatively simple application to two-level data. This enables us to compare and contrast Bayesian methods with empirical Bayesian methods using either full or restricted maximum likelihood estimation of variance components. Finally, we consider application of the Gibbs sampling method to obtain Bayes inferences for a broader class of models. We restrict attention here to linear models at each level for simplicity.

This introduction to Bayesian inference for hierarchical models is necessarily brief. We refer the interested reader to Seltzer, Wong, and Bryk (1996), Gelman et al. (1995; see especially chaps. 5 and 13 to 15), and Carlin and Louis (1996) for more comprehensive treatments.[1]

An Introduction to Bayesian Inference

A model represents an investigator's current belief about the process that generates the data to be analyzed. The aim of statistical analysis is to make inferences about the parameters of the model. Such inferences include point estimates, interval estimates, and hypothesis tests. Two quite different approaches to inference have emerged in statistical theory, and these have special relevance for hierarchical models.

The first is generally known as the "classical" or "frequentist" approach. In this tradition, parameters are fixed constants. The data of interest represent a probability sample from a population characterized by these parameters. The probability of a given sample result is its relative frequency of occurrence over many independent probability samples from the population. The laws of repeated random sampling underlie the machinery of inference in classical statistics.

The second, the Bayesian approach, is quite different. Probability is no longer viewed as relative frequency over many repeated samples. Instead, probability quantifies an investigator's uncertainty about some unknown. The unknowns of most interest are the parameters of the distribution generating the data. Bayesians view these parameters as themselves having probability distributions. These distributions describe the investigator's uncertainty about the parameter values.

These contrasting notions of probability have far-reaching implications for how classical and Bayesian statisticians think about point estimation, interval estimation, and hypothesis testing.

Classical View

Point Estimation. A point estimate is a real number that represents a good conjecture about the value of an unknown parameter. What makes the conjecture "good" in the eyes of the classical statistician is that the method of obtaining it, known as the "estimator," produces, over many repeated samples, results that have good properties. Such properties include unbiasedness, consistency, and minimum variance.

Interval Estimation. An interval estimator states a rule for computing a lower and upper bound for an unknown parameter and a degree of confidence that the unknown parameter lies in the interval. The validity of the interval estimator depends on its sampling properties: A rule for computing a 95% confidence interval should produce an interval that will include the unknown parameter in 95% of infinitely many repeated random samples. The classical statistician cannot speak about the probability that an unknown parameter is contained in any one interval. The parameter is not a random variable and therefore cannot be assigned a probability between 0 and 1. One can say only that the method of computing the interval will capture the fixed unknown parameter with a given probability, such as .95.

Hypothesis Tests. A test statistic is evaluated similarly: When the null hypothesis is true, the test should produce a rejection of the null hypothesis 5% of the time at the 5% significance level. The classical statistician will not say "the probability that the null hypothesis is true is less than .05." In the classical view, the null hypothesis is not a random event and cannot be assigned a probability. If the sample result can arise with small probability when the null hypothesis is true, we tend to view the null hypothesis as implausible and we reject it. We speak about the probability of a given event under the null hypothesis, not the probability that the hypothesis itself is true.

Bayesian View

Bayesian statisticians use different language in describing point estimates, interval estimates, and hypothesis tests. All unknown parameters are assumed to have some probability distribution and inferences are based on this. A "prior distribution" describes the investigator's beliefs (possibly based on results from prior studies) about a parameter before any new data are collected. Once the new data become available, the prior distribution is revised in light of these data to produce a "posterior distribution," that is, a distribution for the parameter that combines the new evidence with the prior view.

Point Estimation. In the Bayesian view, the point estimate for an unknown parameter is some indicator of the central tendency of the posterior distribution of that parameter, typically its mean, median, or mode. A "good" point estimator minimizes the expected distance between the unknown parameter and the estimator. For example, an estimator that minimizes mean-squared error minimizes the expected squared distance between the parameter and the estimator based on the posterior distribution.[2]

Interval Estimation. A confidence interval, often referred to as a "credibility interval" (or "highest posterior density interval") by Bayesians, is a range of plausible values of an unknown parameter. A Bayesian credibility interval estimate defines the posterior probability that a parameter lies in such an interval. For example, one might conclude that an unknown parameter lies between two numbers with posterior probability of .95.

Hypothesis Testing. Like classical statisticians, Bayesian statisticians often use data to choose between two hypotheses, a null hypothesis and an alternative hypothesis. However, unlike classical statisticians, Bayesians compute the probability of the null hypothesis, using the posterior distribution to do the calculations.

Example: Inference for a Normal Mean

Suppose Y_i represents the score on the Graduate Record Exam (GRE) of applicant i to graduate school at a given university. Our aim is to estimate the mean GRE score, μ, at that university and to compare it to the national average score of (say) 500. For simplicity, assume we know the variance, σ^2. We also assume $Y_i \sim N(\mu, \sigma^2)$ independently; that is, Y_i has a normal distribution with mean μ and variance σ^2 for persons $i = 1, \ldots, n$.

Classical Approach

Point Estimation. The classical statistician computes the point estimate $\hat{\mu}$ of μ:

$$\hat{\mu} = \overline{Y} = \sum_{i=1}^{n} Y_i/n, \qquad [13.1]$$

that is, the sample mean. He or she defends this point estimate by referring to its behavior over many samples. It is unbiased, that is, $E(\hat{\mu}) = \mu$, so that the expected value of the estimator is equal to the unknown parameter. It is also efficient; that is, its variance, $\text{Var}(\hat{\mu}) = \sigma^2/n$, is a minimum within the class of unbiased estimators (see Stuart & Ord, 1995). It is, of course, consistent as well (i.e., as n increases, the variance of $\hat{\mu}$ goes to zero): $\lim_{n \to \infty} \text{Var}(\hat{\mu}) = \lim_{n \to \infty} \sigma^2/n = 0$.

Interval Estimation. The classical statistician computes the 95% confidence interval

$$95\% \ \text{CI}(\mu) = \hat{\mu} \pm 1.96 * \sigma/\sqrt{n} \qquad [13.2]$$

and justifies this choice by noting that, over repeated random samples, intervals computed by this formula will capture the true value of μ 95% of the time.

Hypothesis Testing. To test the null hypothesis $H_0: \mu \leq 500$ against the alternative hypothesis $H_a: \mu > 500$, the classical statistician computes

$$p = \text{Prob}\left(\overline{Y} \geq c | H_0 \text{ true}\right), \qquad [13.3]$$

that is, the probability that the estimator $\overline{Y}$ will equal or exceed c, the value of the statistic computed in the current sample, given that the null hypothesis is true. If p is sufficiently small ($p < \alpha$), the null hypothesis is rejected. This approach to hypothesis testing is justified by the assertion that, over infinitely many samples, if the null hypothesis is true, the estimator $\overline{Y}$ will equal or exceed the computed value c with $p \geq \alpha$. Again, the frequentist behavior of the statistical estimator provides its justification.

Bayesian Approach

According to the Bayesian approach, all inferences about μ will be based on its posterior distribution after collecting the data, Y. This also requires the investigator to specify some prior distribution for μ.

Prior Distribution. Suppose that the investigator believes, in advance of collecting the data, that μ is normal with mean γ and variance τ^2. That is, a priori, $\mu \sim N(\gamma, \tau^2)$. The prior mean, γ, specifies the investigator's prior belief about the location of μ, while τ^2 reflects that investigator's uncertainty about the location of μ. Thus, if τ^2 is small, the investigator is quite sure that μ is near γ. However, if τ^2 is large, the investigator has little confidence in the belief that μ is near γ.

Posterior Distribution. After the data, Y, are collected, one can compute the posterior distribution, $p(\mu|Y)$, by means of Bayes theorem:

$$p(\mu|Y) = \frac{p(Y, \mu)}{h(Y)} = \frac{f(Y|\mu)p(\mu)}{h(Y)}. \qquad [13.4]$$

In words, the posterior distribution of μ, given Y, is the ratio of the joint distribution of Y and μ, $p(Y, \mu)$, divided by the marginal distribution of Y, that is, $h(Y)$. Standard calculations[3] (Lindley & Smith, 1972) reveal that μ, given Y, is normal with mean μ^* and variance V_μ^* where

$$\mu^* = \frac{n\sigma^{-2}\overline{Y} + \tau^{-2}\gamma}{n\sigma^{-2} + \tau^{-2}},$$

$$V_\mu^* = \frac{1}{n\sigma^{-2} + \tau^{-2}}. \qquad [13.5]$$

Point Estimation. The Bayesian would likely choose as the point estimate of μ the posterior mean, μ^*. This choice minimizes the squared distance between the true μ and the estimator (see note 2). That is,

$$E\left[(\mu - k)^2|Y\right] \qquad [13.6]$$

achieves a minimum when $k = \mu^*$. Let us investigate μ^* in some detail.[4]

First, in Equation 13.5, we see that μ^* is a weighted average of the prior mean, γ, and the sample mean, $\overline{Y}$. As noted in Chapter 3, the precision of an estimator is the inverse of its variance. The weights associated with the prior mean and the sample mean are proportional to the precisions of each. Specifically, the precision of the prior mean is τ^{-2}, the inverse of its variance, τ^2. If the prior precision is large, heavy weight will be assigned to the investigator's prior belief, γ, in estimating the true mean. Similarly, the precision of the sample mean is $n\sigma^{-2}$, the inverse of its variance. The precision of the sample mean will be large when the sample size, n, is large.

Note that the posterior precision of μ (the inverse of its variance) is the sum of two precisions: the prior precision, τ^{-2}, and the precision of the sample mean, $n\sigma^{-2}$. It is clear that the posterior precision $n\sigma^{-2} + \tau^{-2}$ will always exceed the precision of the sample mean alone, implying, of course, that the posterior variance will never be larger than the variance of the sample mean, that is, $(n\sigma^{-2} + \tau^{-2})^{-1} \leq \sigma^2/n$.

Second, note that as the sample size increases, the Bayesian posterior mean will converge to the classical estimator. That is, $\lim_{n\to\infty}(\mu^*) = \overline{Y}$.

Third, suppose that the prior precision is essentially zero. In that case, τ^{-2} approaches zero (meaning, of course, that the uncertainty associated with the prior belief that μ is near γ is very large). In that case, the Bayesian posterior mean will coincide with the classical estimator. That is, $\lim_{\tau^{-2} \to 0}(\mu^*) = \overline{Y}$.

Fourth, suppose that the investigator really does have useful prior information. For example, he or she may know from prior research that the national mean GRE is γ and that the variance across universities $j = 1, \ldots, J$ of their means, μ_j, is approximately τ^2. In the absence of any data from our university, we would be inclined to suspect that μ_j for any university j would be near γ. How near is specified by τ^2, the variance between universities on μ_j. With no data available, our posterior would equal our prior. However, after collecting n cases and computing $\overline{Y}_j$, the sample mean for university j, we can compute a posterior estimate based on Equation 13.5. Note, we can also calculate the "reliability" of $\overline{Y}_j$, that is, the ratio of the variances of the true means, μ_j, to the variance of the sample means, $\overline{Y}_j$, over many schools, yielding

$$\text{Rel}\left(\overline{Y}_j\right) = \lambda_j = \frac{\text{Var}(\mu_j)}{\text{Var}(\overline{Y}_j)} = \frac{\tau^2}{\tau^2 + \sigma^2/n_j}. \quad [13.7]$$

This leads to a new expression for the posterior mean and variance of μ_j, namely,

$$\mu_j^* = \lambda_j \overline{Y}_j + (1 - \lambda_j)\gamma,$$
$$V_\mu^* = \lambda_j \sigma^2/n_j. \quad [13.8]$$

As n_j increases, the sample mean becomes a more reliable estimate of μ_j and the posterior mean is more strongly influenced by the sample mean. When the sample mean becomes perfectly reliable ($\lambda_j = 1$), the posterior mean and variance become $\overline{Y}_j$ and σ^2/n_j, respectively, in agreement with classical theory. However, until perfect reliability is achieved, the Bayesian posterior variance will be less than σ^2/n_j because λ_j cannot exceed 1.0.

Interval Estimation. (We drop the subscript j now for simplicity.) The Bayesian statistician is comfortable stating the posterior probability that the unknown parameter μ lies in a given interval. This probability is calculated from the posterior distribution. Given Y,

$$\text{Prob}\left(\mu^* - 1.96\sqrt{V^*} < \mu < \mu^* + 1.96\sqrt{V^*}\right) = .95. \quad [13.9]$$

From the previous discussion, we can see that the Bayesian credibility interval never exceeds the classical interval in width. If the prior precision is zero, $\mu^* = \overline{Y}$ and $V_\mu^* = \sigma^2/n$ and the Bayesian and classical intervals coincide. But if the prior precision τ^{-2} exceeds zero, the Bayesian interval is shorter.

Hypothesis Testing. To test the null hypothesis H_0: $\mu \leq 500$ against the alternative hypothesis H_a: $\mu > 500$, the Bayesian statistician computes

$$p = \text{Prob}(\mu < 500|Y), \qquad [13.10]$$

that is, the posterior probability that μ lies in the region defined by the null hypothesis. If p is sufficiently small ($p < \alpha$), the null hypothesis is rejected. Once again, if the prior precision, τ^{-2}, is null, the p value so computed will duplicate the p value of classical statistics, though its interpretation as $p =$ "the probability that H_0 is true" will differ from the classical statement that $p =$ "the probability of obtaining a sample mean as large or larger than that obtained in this sample under the null hypothesis."

Some Generalizations and Inferential Concerns

In the example above, the Bayesian and classical results coincide numerically if (a) the prior precision is zero, or (b) the sample size increases without bound. This convergence will generally hold in more complicated examples. Similarly, if the prior information is nonnull and the sample size moderate, the Bayesian results will be more precise than those based on the classical method *as long as the prior distribution is sound.*

A popular argument against the Bayesian viewpoint is that science frowns on an inference that reflects an investigator's personal prior beliefs. Thus, the frequentist argument goes, point estimates, interval estimates, and tests should be determined only by the data. The Bayesian counter-argument is that one can always allow the prior belief to have zero or near-zero precision, in which case the Bayesian analysis will closely (in many cases exactly) reproduce the classical results. This simply makes explicit the fact that no prior information is available or useful. However, even in such applications, the Bayesian prefers the probabilistic interpretation that can be assigned to all unknowns based on the calculus of probability. There is no need to invoke the intellectual construct of "repeated random samples from some population" to justify inference.

Bayesian Methods, Classical Evaluation. It is possible to use Bayesian methods and interpretations while still relying on classical methods to evaluate the adequacy of point estimates, interval estimates, and tests computed from posterior distributions (Gelman et al., 1995, chap. 4). For example, given a Bayesian point estimator, $\hat{\theta}$, one can evaluate its classical properties (e.g., efficiency) over many repeated samples. Some studies have shown Bayesian estimators to have good properties over many samples when applied to hierarchical models (Carlin & Louis, 1996, chap. 4).

Multiple Parameters. In our simple example, only one parameter, μ, needed to be estimated. For simplicity, we assumed σ^2 to be known. This, of course, is unrealistic. When more than one parameter is unknown, the Bayesian strategy remains straightforward: Specify a prior probability distribution for all parameters, collect data, then use Bayes theorem to compute the "joint posterior." For example,

$$p(\mu, \sigma^2|Y) = \frac{f(Y|\mu, \sigma^2)p(\mu, \sigma^2)}{h(Y)}. \qquad [13.11]$$

Now suppose our aim is to make inferences about μ. Though σ^2 may be of less interest, our lack of knowledge of σ^2 must be taken into account in making inferences about μ. Our inferences about μ will then be based on the "marginal posterior distribution," that is, the posterior distribution of μ after "integrating out" σ^2:

$$p(\mu|Y) = \int p(\mu, \sigma^2|Y)\,d\sigma^2$$

$$= \int p(\mu|\sigma^2, Y)p(\sigma^2|Y)\,d\sigma^2 \qquad [13.12]$$

$$\approx \sum_{m=1}^{M} p(\mu|\sigma_m^2, Y)p(\sigma_m^2|Y) \Big/ \sum_{m=1}^{M} p(\sigma_m^2|Y).$$

To understand this last expression, suppose that we choose M possible values of σ_m^2 between 0 and some very large number. At each value of σ_m^2, we compute the posterior density of μ, that is, $p(\mu|\sigma_m^2, Y)$. We now compute a weighted average of all of these, where the weights are $p(\sigma_m^2|Y)$, that is, the posterior density of σ_m^2. The idea is that the posterior distribution of $\mu|\sigma^2, Y$ can be evaluated at every possible value of σ^2. Such a "conditional posterior" is a good representation of the marginal posterior, that is, $p(\mu|Y)$ only if the σ_m^2 value on which we are depending is a plausible value of the unknown σ^2. In constructing the marginal posterior for μ, we therefore weight each conditional posterior $P(\mu|\sigma_m^2, Y)$ by the "plausibility" of that σ_m^2 value, where the plausibility is $p(\sigma_m^2|Y)$.

This example shows that when an "auxiliary parameter" (here σ^2) is unknown, Bayesian methods provide inferences about the "focal parameter" of interest (here μ) that take into account uncertainty about the auxiliary parameter. This is achieved in the example by averaging over all possible values of the auxiliary parameter. This way of accounting for uncertainty about auxiliary parameters in making inferences about focal parameters turns out to be an important strength of the Bayesian method in applications of hierarchical models, as we shall see below.

A Bayesian Perspective on Inference in Hierarchical Linear Models

In the previous chapters on two-level models, for normally distributed outcomes, we have sought inferences about three kinds of unknown parameters: level-1 random coefficients, $\boldsymbol{\beta}$; level-2 fixed coefficients, $\boldsymbol{\gamma}$; and variance-covariance parameters, such as the variance-covariance matrix of the level-1 coefficients, $\mathbf{T}$, and the residual level-1 variance, σ^2. We have employed two general strategies to obtain these estimates. The first is based on full maximum likelihood (ML) estimation of $\boldsymbol{\gamma}$, σ^2, and $\mathbf{T}$ and empirical Bayes estimation of $\boldsymbol{\beta}$. The second is based on restricted maximum likelihood (REML) estimates of $\mathbf{T}$ and σ^2 and empirical Bayes estimation of $\boldsymbol{\gamma}$ and $\boldsymbol{\beta}$. We briefly review the logic of these approaches and consider how a Bayesian approach can add inferential strength. Although ML and REML are classical procedures, we shall show that REML may also be viewed as a "partially Bayesian" departure from full ML. Moreover, even ML itself has a certain Bayesian flavor in the case of hierarchical models.

Full Maximum Likelihood (ML) of $\boldsymbol{\gamma}$, $\mathbf{T}$, and σ^2

The full ML approach chooses as estimates of $\boldsymbol{\gamma}$, $\mathbf{T}$, and σ^2 the set of values $\hat{\boldsymbol{\gamma}}$, $\hat{\mathbf{T}}$, and $\hat{\sigma}^2$ that maximize the joint likelihood of these parameters for a fixed value of the sample data, $\mathbf{Y}$ (see Chapter 14 for details). Given these ML estimates of $\boldsymbol{\gamma}$, $\mathbf{T}$, and σ^2, we compute empirical Bayes estimates of the level-1 coefficients, $\boldsymbol{\beta}$.[5] This approach has several key strengths:

1. Under very general conditions, ML estimates of $\boldsymbol{\gamma}$, $\mathbf{T}$, and σ^2 are consistent; that is, they converge to the true parameter values as the level-2 sample size, J, increases. This implies also that they are asymptotically unbiased; that is, any bias vanishes as J increases.

2. Moreover, these estimates are efficient, meaning that, in large samples (i.e., large J), no other unbiased estimates have smaller variance.

3. For large J, the sampling distributions of these estimators are approximately normal, provided that the ML estimate of $\mathbf{T}$ is positive definite (which requires, for example, that variance estimates are not zero and that the ML covariance estimates do not produce correlations equal to -1.0 or 1.0). These large-sample normal sampling distributions have variances and covariances that are known even for very complex models. This means that, for large J, the normal distribution can be used for constructing confidence intervals and testing significance, and this is very convenient.

4. Again assuming large J, the empirical Bayes (EB) estimates of the level-1 coefficients will also have good properties. Most important, they will tend to be more accurate (i.e., they will have a smaller mean-squared error), on average,

than estimates based on alternative methods (cf. Morris, 1983; Raudenbush, 1988). One source of strength of these EB estimates is that they depend on ML estimates of γ, $\mathbf{T}$, and σ^2. The excellent large-sample properties of these ML estimates thus strengthen inference about β.

The reader will have noted that the favorable properties described above all depend on "large J," that is, having a large number of level-2 units. The question that arises concerns the problem of "small J": Will these estimates be trustworthy if the number of level-2 units is small?

The answer to this question depends on other aspects of the design, especially the degree to which the design is balanced. It depends also on which parameters are of most interest. Key concerns are as follows:

1. Estimates of γ and $\mathbf{T}$ may be quite inaccurate in small samples. Moreover, the estimates of both, and especially of the variance elements in $\mathbf{T}$, will not have normal sampling distributions. Assuming that a particular variance estimate, $\hat{\tau}_{qq}$, is nearly normal, for example, can lead to serious errors in statistical inference, as we shall illustrate in a simple application to small-sample data.

2. If the data are unbalanced, estimates of γ will depend on weights that are functions of the ML estimates of $\mathbf{T}$ (see Chapter 3 for several simple examples and Chapter 14 for the general case). Random errors in these weights will lead to uncertainty about γ that will not be reflected in standard errors routinely printed out in software using the ML approach. Thus, confidence intervals for γ will be shorter than they should be and tests of significance will be more liberal than they should be. The more unbalanced the data, given small J, the more serious the problem is likely to be because the weights will be more highly variable when the design is unbalanced. This is a case where uncertainty about an auxiliary parameter ($\mathbf{T}$ in this application) can produce misleading inferences about a focal parameter, γ. The Bayesian approach can address this problem.

3. Similarly, inferences about $\mathbf{T}$ will not take into account the uncertainty about γ. In some applications, $\mathbf{T}$ itself may be the focal parameter and we want to ensure that our inferences about it are not distorted by uncertainty about other, auxiliary parameters.

4. Because the EB estimates of β also depend on ML estimates of γ, σ^2, and $\mathbf{T}$, errors in these ML estimates will also produce extra uncertainty about β. Yet this extra uncertainty will not be reflected in the standard errors associated with the EB approach. Again, confidence intervals for β will be too short and tests for β will be too liberal. This problem, which is consequential only when J is small, will tend to diminish when n_j, the sample size for level-2 unit j, is large because, in that case, the EB estimate of β will depend mostly on the data from that unit. However, for small J and small to moderate n_j, the dependence of the EB estimates on possibly inaccurate estimates of auxiliary parameters (here γ, σ^2, and $\mathbf{T}$) is undesirable.

In contrast, ML inferences about σ^2 will generally not be sensitive to small J or the unbalanced nature of the data. This is because the accuracy of estimation of σ^2 depends essentially on the entire sample size of level-1 units, $N = \sum n_j$. In most applications, N will be large enough to support firm inference about σ^2.

The key problem with the ML-EB approach, then, is that inferences about focal parameters depend on point estimates of other unknown, auxiliary parameters, and that these inferences do not fully take into account the uncertainty about these other unknowns. This problem is most significant when J is small and the level-1 data are highly unbalanced. The REML approach partially addresses this problem.

REML Estimation of T and σ^2

For any possible value of $\boldsymbol{\gamma}$, say $\boldsymbol{\gamma}_m$, we can define a likelihood of $\mathbf{T}$ and σ^2, say $L_m(\mathbf{T}, \sigma^2 | \boldsymbol{\gamma}_m, \mathbf{Y})$. If we average over all possible values of $L_m(\mathbf{T}, \sigma^2 | \boldsymbol{\gamma}_m, \mathbf{Y})$, we have a likelihood of $\mathbf{T}$ and σ^2 given $\mathbf{Y}$ alone. This is called the restricted likelihood, $L(\mathbf{T}, \sigma^2 | \mathbf{Y})$, since it does not include $\boldsymbol{\gamma}$.[6]

The REML approach chooses as estimates of $\mathbf{T}$ and σ^2 those values that maximize the joint likelihood of these parameters given the observed sample data, $\mathbf{Y}$. Conditioning on these ML estimates, we compute generalized least squares estimates of $\boldsymbol{\gamma}$ and empirical Bayes estimates of the level-1 coefficients, $\boldsymbol{\beta}$.[7] This approach has several key strengths.

Like the ML estimates, the REML estimates of $\mathbf{T}$ and σ^2 are consistent and efficient; and, for large J, the sampling distributions of these estimators are approximately normal, again provided that the ML variance estimates are not zero and the ML covariance component estimates are in the acceptable range (e.g., the REML estimates of $\mathbf{T}$ must be positive definite). However, unlike the ML approach, the REML estimate of $\mathbf{T}$ does take into account the uncertainty about $\boldsymbol{\gamma}$. We can view the REML estimate of $\mathbf{T}$ as a weighted average of the possible ML estimates of $\mathbf{T}$, where each possible ML estimate is calculated at one possible value of $\boldsymbol{\gamma}$. By averaging over these possible estimates rather than conditioning on a single estimate of $\boldsymbol{\gamma}$, the REML estimate of $\mathbf{T}$ effectively takes into account the uncertainty about the unknown $\boldsymbol{\gamma}$.

Again, as in ML, the EB estimates of the level-1 coefficients will also have good large-sample properties. These EB estimates will depend on REML estimates of $\mathbf{T}$ and σ^2, and the excellent large-sample properties of these ML estimates thus strengthen inference about $\boldsymbol{\beta}$.

The limitations of the REML-EB approach are closely related to those of the ML-EB approach. Once again, estimates of $\mathbf{T}$ may be quite inaccurate in small samples. Moreover, in most applications, the estimates of the variances in $\mathbf{T}$ will not have near-normal sampling distributions unless the same size is exceptionally large. And once again, if the data are unbalanced, estimates of γ will depend on weights that, in turn, depend on REML estimates of $\mathbf{T}$ so that random variation in these estimates of $\mathbf{T}$ will lead to uncertainty about γ that will not be reflected in standard errors routinely computed. Thus, confidence intervals for γ will be shorter than they should be and tests of significance will be more liberal than they should be. Again, the more unbalanced data, given small J, the more serious the problem can be.

Because the EB estimates of β also depend on REML estimates of $\mathbf{T}$ and σ^2, errors in these REML estimates will also produce extra variation in these EB estimates. Yet this extra uncertainty will not be reflected in the standard errors associated with the EB approach. Again, confidence intervals for β will be too short and tests for β will be too liberal. Unlike the ML case, however, the EB point estimates depending on REML estimates of $\mathbf{T}$ and σ^2 will accurately reflect uncertainty about γ.

In sum, in the ML-EB approach, inferences about key parameters depend on point estimates of other unknown auxiliary parameters, and these inferences do not fully take into account the uncertainty about these other unknowns. The REML approach partially addresses this problem, by allowing estimates of $\mathbf{T}$ and β to take into account uncertainty about γ. In that sense, the REML approach may be thought of as "partially Bayesian," as we shall illustrate below in the context of an example.

In contrast, a "fully Bayesian" approach would ensure that inference about every parameter fully takes into account the uncertainty about all other parameters. The price to be paid is that the fully Bayesian approach requires specification of prior distributions for all parameters. These "priors" reflect the investigator's prior knowledge of these parameters. Typically, investigators have little knowledge about γ, σ^2, and $\mathbf{T}$, and will therefore construct a "vague prior" that is intended to have little influence on the inferences drawn. However, in the context of the applications of concern in this volume, it is impossible to construct a perfectly noninformative prior; that is, any choice of a prior will have some effect on inferences. So some steps must be taken to assess the sensitivity of inferences to the choice of prior, especially in the case of small sample sizes (that is, especially, small J in the two-level case), when the prior becomes comparatively important in affecting the posterior (Seltzer, Wong, & Bryk, 1996).

The Basics of Bayesian Inference for the Two-Level HLM

In the Bayesian view, the data to be observed arise from a probability distribution defined by certain unknown quantities. Prior distributions must be assigned to all of these unknowns. Combining the data with the prior leads to a joint posterior distribution of all of the unknowns given the data. Inference about specific unknowns (e.g., focal parameters) is achieved by averaging over the possible values of other unknowns (e.g., auxiliary parameters). We now apply this logic to the hierarchical linear model for two-level data.

Model for the Observed Data

The Bayesian model for the observed data coincides with the standard level-1 model used elsewhere in this book. We have an outcome Y_{ij} for level-1 unit i in level-2 unit j

$$Y_{ij} = \beta_{0j} + \sum_{q=1}^{Q-1} \beta_{qj} X_{qij} + r_{ij}, \qquad r_{ij} \sim N(0, \sigma^2). \qquad [13.13]$$

In Bayesian notation, the observed data, $\mathbf{Y}$, are distributed according to $f(\mathbf{Y}|\boldsymbol{\beta}, \sigma^2)$, where f is the normal density. Here $\mathbf{Y}$ is a vector containing elements Y_{ij} for all level-1 units $i = 1, \ldots, n_j$ within each level-2 unit $j = 1, \ldots, J$. Similarly, $\boldsymbol{\beta}$ is a vector containing the elements β_{qj}. The outcomes Y_{ij} are assumed independently normally distributed with mean

$$E(Y_{ij}|\boldsymbol{\beta}, \sigma^2) = \beta_{0j} + \sum_{q=1}^{Q-1} \beta_{qj} X_{qjk} \qquad [13.14]$$

and variance σ^2. We must specify a prior distribution for the unknowns, $\boldsymbol{\beta}$ and σ^2. This entails a two-stage prior.

Stage-1 Prior

The first stage of the Bayesian prior coincides with the standard level-2 model used elsewhere in this book:

$$\beta_{qj} = \gamma_{q0} + \sum_{s=1}^{S_q} \gamma_{sq} W_{sqj} + u_{qj}, \qquad [13.15]$$

where $u_{qj}, q = 0, \ldots, Q - 1$, form a Q-variate normal distribution with variances $\text{Var}(u_{qj}) = \tau_{qq}$ and covariances $\text{Cov}(u_{qj}, u_{q'j}) = \tau_{qq'}$. In Bayesian notation, this specifies the first-stage prior $p_1(\boldsymbol{\beta}|\boldsymbol{\gamma}, \mathbf{T})$ where $\boldsymbol{\gamma}$ is a vector containing elements γ_{qs} and $\mathbf{T}$ is a matrix containing elements $\tau_{qq'}$. This is often called an "exchangeable" prior. The vectors $\mathbf{u}_j$ containing elements u_{qj} are exchangeable in the sense that we have no prior information that would lead us to believe that the elements of the vector $\mathbf{u}_j$ from group j would be larger or smaller than the elements of a vector $\mathbf{u}'_j$ obtained from some other level-2 unit j'. Exchangeability is, in Bayesian terms, similar to the notion that the vectors $\mathbf{u}_j, j = 1, \ldots, J$, constitute a simple random sample from a population of such vectors. If the investigator does have prior information about the likely values of $\mathbf{u}_j$, that information should be incorporated in the model, for example, by adding explanatory variables W_j to account for these differences.

Stage-2 Prior

To complete the Bayesian specification, a prior distribution must also be specified for γ, σ^2, and $\mathbf{T}$. Without such a prior, it would be impossible to construct a posterior for these parameters and, hence, impossible to make probability statements about them. (Recall that the aim of the Bayesian is to make valid probability statements about all unknowns.) We therefore specify a prior $p_2(\gamma, \sigma^2, \mathbf{T})$. For now, we shall leave the exact form of this prior unspecified. It will take on specific forms in different applications, though, in most cases, the prior will be chosen to reflect "prior ignorance," meaning that the investigator has little or no prior information about these parameters.

Posterior Distributions

Inferences about all unknowns are derived from their joint posterior distribution given the data. In this case,

$$p(\boldsymbol{\beta}, \gamma, \sigma^2, \mathbf{T}|\mathbf{Y}) = \frac{f(\mathbf{Y}|\boldsymbol{\beta}, \sigma^2)p_1(\boldsymbol{\beta}|\gamma, \mathbf{T})p_2(\gamma, \sigma^2, \mathbf{T})}{h(\mathbf{Y})}. \qquad [13.16]$$

Here $h(\mathbf{Y})$, the marginal distribution of $\mathbf{Y}$, is a normalizing constant that ensures that the posterior is a proper probability distribution.[8]

Inferences about focal parameters of interest are obtained by averaging over auxiliary parameters. For example, if γ is of focal interest, we compute

$$f(\gamma|\mathbf{Y}) = \iiint f(\boldsymbol{\beta}, \gamma, \sigma^2, \mathbf{T}|\mathbf{Y})\partial\boldsymbol{\beta}\,\partial\sigma^2\,\partial\mathbf{T}. \qquad [13.17]$$

Relationship Between Fully Bayes and Empirical Bayes Inference

Empirical Bayes Inference for $\boldsymbol{\beta}$ Using ML Estimates of γ, σ^2, and $\mathbf{T}$. Suppose γ, σ^2, and $\mathbf{T}$ are known. This is an extreme version of the second-stage prior $p_2(\boldsymbol{\gamma}, \sigma^2, \mathbf{T})$ in which the investigator's prior knowledge is certain. In this case, the only unknown is $\boldsymbol{\beta}$, so that only the first-stage prior is needed. Inference about $\boldsymbol{\beta}$ would then be based on its probability distribution given the data and the known parameters, that is, $p(\boldsymbol{\beta}|\boldsymbol{\gamma}, \sigma^2, \mathbf{T}, \mathbf{Y})$. Empirical Bayes inference operates in just this way, with one caveat. Rather than assume $\boldsymbol{\gamma}, \mathbf{T}$, and σ^2 to be known, the empirical Bayes approach substitutes the ML estimates $\hat{\boldsymbol{\gamma}}, \widehat{\mathbf{T}}$, and $\hat{\sigma}^2$ for the true values of $\boldsymbol{\gamma}, \mathbf{T}$, and σ^2. For purposes of inference about $\boldsymbol{\beta}$, the true values of $\boldsymbol{\gamma}, \mathbf{T}$, and σ^2 are assumed equal to these ML estimates.

Empirical Bayes Inference for $\boldsymbol{\beta}$ *and* $\boldsymbol{\gamma}$ *Using REML Estimates of* σ^2 *and* $\mathbf{T}$. Now let us assume that $\boldsymbol{\gamma}$ is unknown (along with $\boldsymbol{\beta}$) but that $\mathbf{T}$ and σ^2 are known. A Bayesian would then specify a prior distribution for $\boldsymbol{\gamma}$, that is, $p_2(\boldsymbol{\gamma}|\mathbf{T}, \sigma^2)$. If this prior had a precision of zero, inference about $\boldsymbol{\beta}$ and $\boldsymbol{\gamma}$ would be equivalent to empirical Bayes inferences discussed elsewhere in this book (Chapters 3, 5, 7, and 14) except that REML estimates of $\mathbf{T}$ and σ^2 would be substituted into the posterior distribution $p(\boldsymbol{\beta}, \boldsymbol{\gamma}|\mathbf{T}, \sigma^2, \mathbf{Y})$. Thus, the true values of $\mathbf{T}$ and σ^2 would be assumed equal to the REML estimates and inferences about $\boldsymbol{\gamma}$ and $\boldsymbol{\beta}$ would be based on their posterior distribution given these REML estimates of $\mathbf{T}$ and σ^2.

In sum, the empirical Bayes procedures described elsewhere in this book can be viewed as Bayesian procedures in which certain auxiliary parameters are set equal to their point estimates and assumed known. In the ML-EB case, the focal parameter is $\boldsymbol{\beta}$, and auxiliary parameters $\boldsymbol{\gamma}, \sigma^2$, and $\mathbf{T}$ are set equal to their ML estimates. In the REML-EB case, focal parameters are $\boldsymbol{\beta}$ and $\boldsymbol{\gamma}$, and auxiliary parameters σ^2 and $\mathbf{T}$ are set equal to their REML estimates. As discussed earlier, these procedures work well when J is large and the ML or REML estimates of the auxiliary parameters are quite precise. However, in general, when J is small and the data are unbalanced, there is a good argument for using fully Bayesian procedures. We illustrate these principles in a series of examples below.

Example: Bayes Versus Empirical Bayes Meta-Analysis

To illustrate the Bayesian approach and to compare it to the more familiar results in this book based on empirical Bayes with ML or REML inference, we return to the simple example of data from 19 experiments assessing teacher expectancy effects on student IQ. The example is described in Chapter 7 and the data are displayed in Table 7.1. Each study produces an effect size estimate, d_j, and a squared standard error, V_j. The aims of the inquiry are threefold: (1) to estimate the average effect size, γ, across all 19 studies; (2) to assess the effect-size variability, τ; and (3) to use the information from all 19 studies to identify improved estimates of the true effect size, δ_j, in each of the 19 studies.

Bayes Model

Observed Data. The first level of the Bayesian linear model for the observed outcomes coincides with the standard level-1 model

$$d_j = \delta_j + e_j, \qquad e_j \sim N(0, V_j). \qquad [13.18]$$

In Bayesian notation, the observed data, d, are distributed according to a distribution $f(d|\delta, V)$, where f is the normal distribution. Here d is a vector containing elements d_j for all units $j = 1, \ldots, J$. Similarly, δ is a vector containing the elements δ_j, and V is a diagonal matrix with entries V_j. The outcomes d_j are assumed independently normally distributed with mean $E(d_j|\delta_j) = \delta_j$ and known variance V_j. We must also specify a prior distribution for the unknowns, δ. This will be a two-stage prior.

Stage-1 Prior. The first stage of the Bayesian prior coincides with the standard level-2 model used in Chapter 7:

$$\delta_j = \gamma + u_j, \qquad u_j \sim N(0, \tau), \qquad [13.19]$$

where $u_j, j = 1, \ldots, J$, are independently distributed as normal with mean 0 and variance τ. In Bayesian notation, this specifies the first-stage prior $p_1(\delta|\gamma, \tau)$.

Stage-2 Prior. To complete the Bayesian specification, a prior distribution must also be specified for γ and τ. We shall consider a prior in which these parameters are assumed independent and uniformly distributed on their parameter spaces ($-\infty < \gamma < \infty; 0 \le \tau$). Such a "flat" prior conveys that we have essentially no a priori knowledge of the parameters. For each of the two parameters γ and τ, all possible values are equally likely.[9] One of the advantages of this prior is that the posterior will be proportional to the likelihood $L(d|\gamma, \tau)$, which facilitates comparison with inference based on maximum likelihood. Technically, we write

$$p_2(\gamma, \tau) \propto C_\gamma C_\tau, \qquad -\infty < \gamma < \infty, 0 \le \tau, \qquad [13.20]$$

where C_γ and C_τ are arbitrarily small constants.

Posterior Distributions. Inferences about all unknowns are derived from their joint posterior distribution given the data using Bayes theorem. In this case,

$$p(\delta, \gamma, \tau | d) = \frac{f(d|\delta)p_1(\delta|\gamma, \tau)p_2(\gamma, \tau)}{h(d)}$$

$$\propto \left(\prod_{j=1}^{19} (v_j \tau)^{-1/2} \right)$$

$$\times \left(\exp\left[-\frac{1}{2}\sum_{j=1}^{19}(d_j - \delta_j)^2 / V_j - \frac{1}{2}\sum_{j=1}^{19}(\delta_j - \gamma)^2 / \tau \right] \right). \quad [13.21]$$

Here $h(d)$, the marginal distribution of d, is a normalizing constant that ensures that the posterior is a proper probability distribution.[10]

Inferences about the focal parameters of interest are based on averaging over auxiliary parameters. Let us begin by supposing that γ and τ are jointly of focal interest, while δ_j, $j = 1, \ldots, 19$, are auxiliary. We are therefore interested in

$$g(\gamma, \tau | d) = \int f(\delta, \gamma, \tau | d) \, \partial \delta. \quad [13.22]$$

Using standard calculations, we see that this expression becomes, for our data,

$$g(\gamma, \tau | d) \propto (2\pi)^{-19/2} \left[\prod_{j=1}^{19}(V_j + \tau)^{-1} \right]^{1/2} \exp\left[-\frac{1}{2}Q \right]$$

with

$$Q = \sum_{j=1}^{19}(V_j + \tau)^{-1}(d_j - \gamma)^2. \quad [13.23]$$

Parameter Estimation and Inference

Joint and Marginal Posteriors for γ and τ. Figure 13.1 displays the joint posterior density of the mean, γ, and the variance, τ, given the teacher expectancy data, d. The posterior for γ is unimodal and nearly symmetric with most of the posterior density located between -0.10 and 0.20 with the central tendency in the neighborhood of 0.10. In contrast, the posterior for τ is also unimodal but quite positively skewed with most of the posterior density between 0 and about 0.08. The mode is at $\tau = .013$. We can obtain

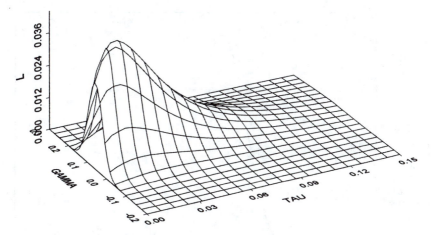

Figure 13.1. Joint Posterior Density of γ and τ Given d

a clearer graphical view by displaying the marginal posterior densities for each:

$$p(\gamma|d) = \int p(\gamma, \tau|d)\, \partial\tau,$$
$$p(\tau|d) = \int p(\gamma, \tau|d)\, \partial\gamma. \qquad [13.24]$$

These are displayed in Figures 13.2 and 13.3.

Inferences About γ. Because of the near symmetry of the posterior density of γ (Figure 13.2), the central tendency of γ is similarly represented by the posterior mean, $E(\gamma|d) = 0.096$, or the mode 0.078. Most of the plausible values of γ are positive, but small negative values are not entirely implausible. We formalize this visual insight by computing an approximate 95% posterior credibility interval

$$\text{Prob}(.096 - 1.96 * 0.0656 < \gamma < .096 + 1.96 * .0656)|d)$$
$$= \text{Prob}(-0.033 < \gamma < 0.225) = .95. \qquad [13.25]$$

Clearly, we cannot reject the hypothesis H_0: $\gamma \leq 0$ against the alternative H_0: $\gamma > 0$. Indeed, we can compute

$$\text{Prob}\,(\gamma \leq 0|d) = \int_{-\infty}^{0} p(\gamma|d)\, \partial\gamma \approx .063, \qquad [13.26]$$

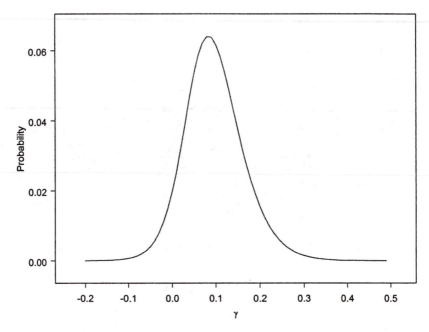

Figure 13.2. $p(\gamma|d)$

suggesting that negative values of γ, while less likely than positive values, cannot be ruled out. Note that uncertainty about γ is substantial. While negative values of the mean effect size cannot be ruled out, values as large as 0.23 are also possible.

Inferences About τ. Because of the positive skewness of the posterior for τ (Figure 13.3), the central tendency of τ is quite differently represented by the posterior mean, $E(\tau|d) = 0.047$, versus the mode 0.019. The most probable values of τ, those around the posterior mode, are positive. However, a value of zero for τ appears possible based on a visual inspection of Figure 13.3.

Inferences About δ_j. Suppose now that our focal interest is in the effect size of a particular experiment, say, δ_4. All other parameters are auxiliary. Thus, we average over all of them and over γ and τ to obtain the posterior for experiment 4:

$$p(\delta_4|d) = \iint \left(\int_1 \int_2 \int_3 \int_5 \cdots \int_{19} \right) p(\gamma, \tau, \delta|d)$$
$$\times \left(\partial\delta_1\, \partial\delta_2\, \partial\delta_3\, \partial\delta_5 \cdots \partial\delta_{19} \right) \partial\gamma\, \partial\tau. \qquad [13.27]$$

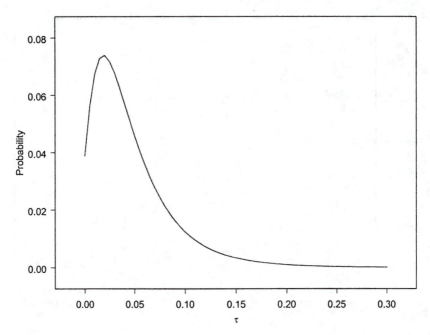

Figure 13.3. $p(\tau|d)$

The marginal posterior density for experiment 4 is displayed in Figure 13.4. It is unimodal and roughly symmetric about its expectation, $E(\delta_4|d) = 0.336$. The 95% probability interval is $(-.022, 0.694)$.

Similarly, Figure 13.5 displays the posterior density for experiment 17. Note that this posterior is much less dispersed than that for experiment 4 (Figure 13.4) because experiment 17 used a much larger sample and therefore yielded a much smaller standard error: Compare $V_4 = 0.139$ versus $V_{17} = 0.019$. Table 13.1 (panel b) provides the posterior mean $E(\delta_j|d)$ and standard deviation $S(\delta_j|d)$ of each $\delta_j, j = 1, \ldots, 19$. Note the shrinkage of $E(\delta_j|d)$ as compared to the least squares estimates d_j (panel a). Note also that the posterior standard errors are considerably smaller than the least squares standard errors. These differences reflect the fact that the Bayes inferences take into account prior information about each δ_j provided by all other effect sizes.

Summary. Using the Bayesian approach, we first specified a model for the data given the unknowns (Equation 13.18). We then specified a two-stage prior for the unknowns (Equations 13.19 and 13.20). To obtain inferences

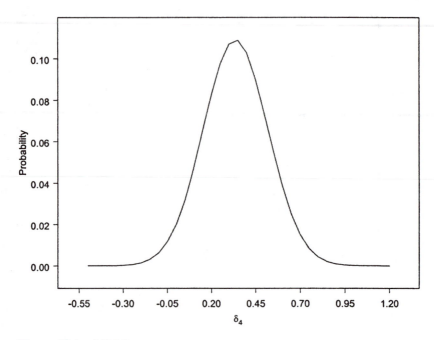

Figure 13.4. $P(\delta_4 | d)$

about any focal parameter, we integrated the joint posterior distribution of γ, τ, and $\delta_1, \ldots, \delta_{19}$ with respect to the auxiliary parameters. For any focal parameter, we can compute the probability that the parameter lies in a given interval. Inferences about any focal parameter fully take into account the uncertainty about the remaining auxiliary parameters. We found that the posterior density of the variance, τ, was quite positively skewed, while all other posteriors were nearly symmetric. This fact is consequential as we turn to a comparison between these fully Bayesian results and results based on empirical Bayes, either EB-ML or EB-REML.

A Comparison Between Fully Bayes and Empirical Bayes Inference

We consider inference about the three types of unknowns of interest here, that is, the level-1 coefficients, δ_j, the level-2 coefficient, γ, and the level-2 variance, τ, using ML or REML estimation in conjunction with empirical Bayes. We are especially interested in comparing these results to the Bayesian results just obtained.

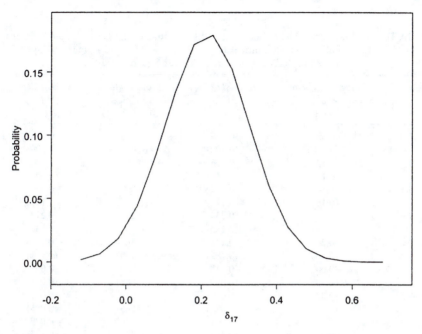

Figure 13.5. $P(\delta_{17}|d)$

Inference Based on ML for γ and τ and EB for δ. The likelihood for γ and τ is given by

$$L(d|\hat{\gamma}, \hat{\tau}) = \int f(d|\delta) p_1(\delta|\hat{\gamma}, \hat{\tau}) \, \partial \delta. \qquad [13.28]$$

Because our Bayesian analysis above was based on a uniform prior for γ and τ (see Equation 13.20 and discussion below it), this likelihood is proportional to the joint posterior (Equation 13.23) graphed in Figure 13.1. ML estimation takes as a point estimates of γ and τ their joint modal values (note the joint mode in Figure 13.1).

(i) Inference for γ. Under ML theory, the large-sample distribution of the ML estimate, $\hat{\gamma}$, given the true γ, is normal with a mean of γ and a standard error that is computed from the Fisher information matrix (see Chapter 14). Our results, $\hat{\gamma} = 0.078$, with standard error $S_{\hat{\gamma}} = 0.048$ enable us to compute what we shall describe as an "estimated sampling distribution" for $\hat{\gamma}$, treating γ as equal to $\hat{\gamma}$ (see Figure 13.6). This is equivalent to the posterior distribution of γ given $\hat{\tau} = 0.013$, that is, $p(\gamma|\tau = \hat{\tau}_{\text{ML}} = 0.013)$. It is a way of conveying plausible values for γ according to the logic of ML.

TABLE 13.1 Posterior Means and Standard Deviations of the Effect Size δ_j Under Fully Bayes, Empirical Bayes Based on ML, and Empirical Bayes Based on REML Compared to Least Squares Estimates

Study	(a) Least Squares d (s_d)	(b) Fully Bayes $E(\delta\|d)$ $[S(\delta\|d)]$	(c) EB-ML $E(\delta\|d, \hat{\tau}, \hat{\gamma})$ $S(\delta\|d, \hat{\tau}, \hat{\gamma})$	(d) EB-REML $E(\delta\|d, \hat{\tau})$ $S(\delta\|d, \hat{\tau})$
1	0.03	0.050	0.054	0.054
	(0.125)	(0.102)	(0.093)	(0.096)
2	0.12	0.106	0.101	0.100
	(0.147)	(0.115)	(0.101)	(0.104)
3	−0.14	−0.033	−0.007	−0.006
	(0.167)	(0.125)	(0.106)	(0.111)
4	1.18	0.334	0.216	0.214
	(0.373)	(0.183)	(0.129)	(0.137)
5	0.26	0.131	0.105	0.105
	(0.369)	(0.182)	(0.129)	(0.137)
6	−0.06	−0.018	−0.009	−0.008
	(0.103)	(0.089)	(0.083)	(0.085)
7	−0.02	0.010	0.017	0.017
	(0.103)	(0.089)	(0.083)	(0.085)
8	−0.32	−0.081	−0.030	−0.029
	(0.220)	(0.146)	(0.117)	(0.123)
9	0.27	0.186	0.161	0.160
	(0.164)	(0.122)	(0.106)	(0.110)
10	0.80	0.350	0.250	0.249
	(0.251)	(0.156)	(0.121)	(0.127)
11	0.54	0.224	0.163	0.162
	(0.302)	(0.169)	(0.125)	(0.133)
12	0.18	0.127	0.110	0.110
	(0.223)	(0.147)	(0.117)	(0.123)
13	−0.02	0.057	0.065	0.065
	(0.289)	(0.166)	(0.124)	(0.131)
14	0.23	0.135	0.111	0.110
	(0.290)	(0.166)	(0.125)	(0.132)
15	−0.18	−0.060	−0.029	−0.023
	(0.159)	(0.121)	(0.104)	(0.108)
16	−0.06	−0.010	0.026	0.026
	(0.167)	(0.125)	(0.106)	(0.110)
17	0.30	0.216	0.191	0.190
	(0.139)	(0.110)	(0.098)	(0.101)
18	0.07	0.074	0.074	0.074
	(0.094)	(0.082)	(0.078)	(0.080)
19	−0.07	0.007	0.025	0.025
	(0.174)	(0.128)	(0.108)	(0.113)

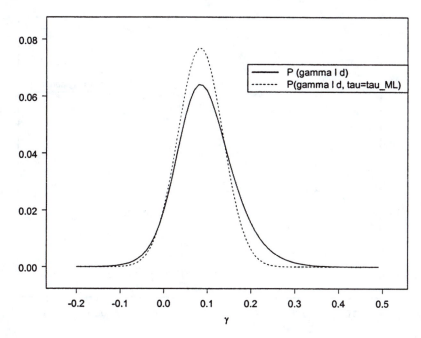

Figure 13.6. Plot of $P(\gamma|d)$ and $P(\gamma|d, \tau = \tau_{ML})$ Versus γ

We superimpose this distribution on the marginal posterior $p(\gamma|d)$ computed earlier (Figure 13.2). While the ML estimate of γ and its estimated standard error condition on $\tau = \hat{\tau}_{ML}$, the posterior distribution averages over possible τ values (Equation 13.24). The two views of plausible values for γ overlap considerably. However, the marginal posterior is somewhat more dispersed than is the conditional given $\hat{\tau}_{ML}$. This is not surprising as the marginal posterior takes uncertainty about τ into account while the conditional posterior of $\gamma|\hat{\tau}_{ML}$ does not.

  (ii) Inference for τ. Under ML theory, the large-sample distribution of the estimate $\hat{\tau}$, given the true τ, is normal with a mean of τ and a standard error that is computed from the Fisher information matrix. Our results, $\hat{\tau} = 0.013$, with standard error $S_{\hat{\tau}} = 0.012$ enable us to sketch this normal approximation as "estimated sampling distribution" for $\hat{\tau}$, treating τ as equal to $\hat{\tau}$ (Figure 13.7). This can be viewed as a first-order approximation to the true marginal posterior $p(\tau|d)$. We superimpose this approximation on the true marginal posterior $p(\tau|d)$ computed earlier (Figure 13.3). Clearly, the approximation is poor. It is unimodal and near symmetric, while

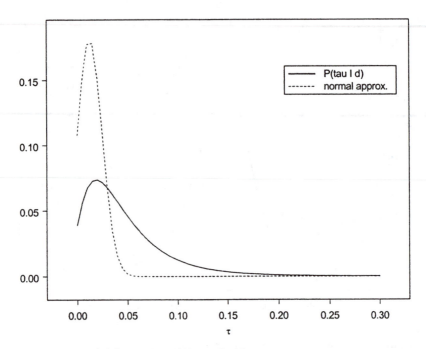

Figure 13.7. $P(\tau|d)$ and Normal Approximation

the true posterior is highly positively skewed. The approximation includes many negative values, which are inadmissible, and excludes many positive values that are clearly plausible given the marginal posterior.[11]

Empirical Bayes Inference for δ Using the ML Estimates of γ and τ. The ML-EB approach to inference about δ_j treats γ and τ as known and equal to their ML estimates. Under these assumptions, inferences about δ_j are based on conditional normal distributions

$$\delta_j|\gamma, \tau, d_j \sim \text{indep } N(\delta_j^*, V_j^*), \qquad [13.29]$$

where

$$\delta_j^* = \lambda_j d_j + (1 - \lambda_j)\gamma,$$
$$V_j^* = \tau(1 - \lambda_j) \qquad [13.30]$$

with $\lambda_j = \tau/(\tau + v_j)$. The posterior mean of δ_j, given γ, τ, and d, is a weighted average of two components: the treatment effect estimate, d_j, which uses only the data from study j; and the mean γ, assumed known, but, in fact, estimated by ML from the data provided by all 19 studies. The posterior variance $\tau(1 - \lambda_j)$ does not depend on J, the number of studies, even though the accuracy of estimation of γ does depend on the number of studies. Thus, the posterior variance does not take into account the uncertainty associated with estimation of γ. The weights λ_j are also assumed known, though they depend on τ. Here τ is also assumed known though it must, in reality, be estimated from the data.

Panel c of Table 13.1 displays the means $E(\delta_j|d, \hat{\tau}, \hat{\gamma})$ and standard deviations $S(\delta_j|d, \hat{\tau}, \hat{\gamma})$ for the treatment effects based on this EB-ML method ($\hat{\tau}$ and $\hat{\gamma}$ are the ML estimates). Note first that the EB-ML posterior standard deviations are considerably smaller than those computed under the fully Bayes method (panel b). This discrepancy arises because, unlike the fully Bayes method, the EB-ML approach does not take into account the uncertainty about τ and γ. For this reason, the fully Bayes standard deviation must be regarded as more accurate than those yielded by EB-ML. The latter are negatively biased.

Second, the EB-ML posterior means experience more severe shrinkage than do the fully Bayes posterior means (note the greater dispersion of the fully Bayes posterior means). The EB-ML posterior means are computed based on the assumption that $\tau = 0.013$. This is a modal value of τ (based on Figure 13.1), but given the positively skewed character of the posterior for τ (Figures 13.1 and 13.3), it is clear that much larger values of τ cannot be ruled out. The fully Bayes approach averages over all possible values of τ in calculating these posterior means of δ. A lucid illustration and discussion appears in Rubin (1981). This fact inclines us to view the fully Bayes posterior means as more credible than those based on EB-ML.

REML Inference for τ. The restricted likelihood for τ is given by integrating the likelihood for γ and τ with respect to γ:

$$L(d|\tau) = \int L(d|\gamma, \tau)\partial\gamma = \iint f(d|\delta)p_1(\delta|\gamma, \tau)\partial\delta \, \partial\gamma. \qquad [13.31]$$

Because our Bayesian analysis above was based on a uniform prior for γ and τ (see Equation 13.20 and accompanying discussion), this likelihood is proportional to the marginal posterior of τ (Equation 13.24) graphed in Figure 13.3. REML estimation takes as a point estimate τ its modal value (note the mode of Figure 13.3) of 0.019.

Under REML theory, the large-sample distribution of the REML estimate, $\hat{\tau}_{\text{REML}}$, is normal with a mean of τ and a standard error that is computed from the Fisher information matrix. Our result is $\hat{\tau}_{\text{REML}} = 0.019$, with standard error $S_{\hat{\tau}} = 0.015$. As in the case of ML, the approximation is poor and for similar reasons.

Empirical Bayes Inference for γ and δ Using the REML Estimate τ. The EB-REML approach to inference about γ and δ_j treats τ as known and equal to its REML estimate. Under this assumption, inferences about γ and δ_j, $j = 1, \ldots, J$, are based on their joint conditional normal distributions

$$\begin{pmatrix} \gamma \\ \delta \end{pmatrix} \Big| \tau \Bigg) N\left[\begin{pmatrix} \gamma^* \\ \delta^* \end{pmatrix}, \begin{pmatrix} V_\gamma^* & C_{\gamma, \delta}^* \\ C_{\delta, \gamma}^* & V_\delta^* \end{pmatrix} \right],$$ [13.32]

where V_γ^* and V_δ^* are posterior variances and $C_{\gamma, \delta}^*$ is the posterior covariance.

Inferences about γ are based on its marginal posterior distribution given τ and d, that is,

$$\gamma^* = \frac{\sum_{j=1}^{19}(\tau + v_j)^{-1}d_j}{\sum_{j=1}^{19}(\tau + v_j)^{-1}},$$

$$V_\gamma^* = \frac{1}{\sum_{j=1}^{19}(\tau + v_j)^{-1}}.$$ [13.33]

The estimate γ^* is the precision-weighted average of the treatment effect estimates from the J studies and its precision is the sum of those precisions, $\sum(\tau + v_j)^{-1}$. The expression for γ^* has the same form as does the ML estimator for γ, but it uses the REML estimate of $\hat{\tau}_{\text{REML}} = 0.019$ rather than $\tau_{\text{ML}}^* = 0.013$. Computations for our data lead to $\gamma^* = 0.084$ with standard error $S_{\gamma^*} = 0.052$ and a 95% interval $(-0.018, 0.185)$. This interval is slightly wider than that for the EB-ML estimator. This is because $\hat{\tau}_{\text{REML}}$ is a bit larger than $\hat{\tau}_{\text{ML}}$ as is generally the case. This occurs because $\hat{\tau}_{\text{REML}}$ takes into account the uncertainty about γ.

Inferences about δ are based on the conditional distribution given $\hat{\tau}_{\text{REML}}$ and d (lower right entries of Equation 13.32). For each δ_j, we have

$$\delta_j^* = \lambda_j d_j + (1 - \lambda_j)\gamma^*,$$

$$V_j^* = \tau(1 - \lambda_j) + (1 - \lambda_j)^2 V_\gamma^*,$$ [13.34]

where λ_j has the same form as in the ML case (Equation 13.30), though $\hat{\tau}_{\text{REML}}$ rather than $\hat{\tau}_{\text{ML}}$ is used. The posterior mean of δ_j, given τ and d, is the same weighted average as in the case of ML except the formula now acknowledges that an estimate, γ^*, is used in place of the true value. Similarly, the posterior variance has an additional piece, $(1 - \lambda_j)^2 V_\gamma^*$, that does represent the uncertainty about the γ (compare Equations 13.30 and 13.34) for V_j^*. Thus, inferences about δ_j based on REML-EB should be somewhat more realistic than those based on ML-EB, especially when J is small and uncertainty about γ is therefore appreciable.

Table 13.1 (panel d) displays the means and standard errors for the treatment effects based on this EB-REML method. Note that the EB-REML posterior means experience somewhat less shrinkage than do the EB-ML posterior means. This is because the EB-REML posterior means are based on the assumption that $\tau = 0.019$, a larger value than the EB-ML estimate of 0.013. To the extent one believes the δ_j to be heterogeneous, less shrinkage to a common mean will occur. As expected the standard errors are, indeed, a bit larger than under EB-ML (compare panels c and d of Table 13.1). However, neither the EB-ML nor the EB-REML standard errors take into account uncertainty about τ, as the fully Bayes standard errors do. Note that the fully Bayes standard errors for δ_j are larger than those based on REML or ML.

Model Checking and Sensitivity Analysis. The validity of the results for the teacher expectancy data hinges on the validity of key assumptions. First, we assumed the estimated effect sizes, d_j, given the true effect sizes, δ_j, are normally distributed with mean δ_j and variance V_j. This assumption ought to be reasonable, based on the moderate to large samples used in the teacher expectancy research and based on the central limit theorem. Second, we assumed that the true effect sizes were themselves normally distributed over studies. This assumption can be checked graphically as described in Chapters 4 and 9. Seltzer (1993) provides a sensitivity analysis based on a family of t distributions for the true effect sizes. Third, we formulated a uniform prior distribution for the variance, τ. A further sensitivity analysis ought to be conducted by comparing our results to results based on alternative noninformative priors. The exact nature of these analyses would depend on the focal parameter of interest. See Gelman et al. (1995, chap. 2) for a clear discussion of sensitivity analyses and model checking using the posterior predictive distribution.

Gibbs Sampling and Other Computational Approaches

The computations used in the last section were based on a simple but very accurate approach to numerical integration. According to that method, we took the following steps:

1. Select M equally spaced possible values of τ, that is, τ_m, $m = 1, \ldots, M$.
2. Program calculations for the restricted likelihood (Equation 13.31).

3. Base inferences about τ on this likelihood. For example, the mode is found by finding the τ value that produces the largest value of $p(\tau|d)$ in the last example. The posterior mean is calculated as

$$E(\tau|d) \approx \frac{\sum_{m=1}^{M} \tau_m p(\tau_m|d)}{\sum_{m=1}^{M} p(\tau_m|d)}. \qquad [13.35]$$

Choose M to be large enough to ensure acceptable accuracy.

4. Compute other posterior densities similarly. For example, compute

$$p(\gamma|d) \approx \frac{\sum_{m=1}^{M} p(\gamma|\tau_m, d) p(\tau_m|d)}{\sum_{m=1}^{M} p(\tau_m|d)}. \qquad [13.36]$$

5. Compute means and variances of interesting quantities, as needed.

This method works well when the problem is quite simple and when uniform priors are chosen for τ and γ. However, in most cases, τ and γ will be multidimensional. Moreover, it is important to be able to investigate the sensitivity of inferences to the prior chosen for τ and γ. The simple graphical methods described so far, while useful for understanding the logic of Bayesian inference, become unworkable as the models become more complex and as it becomes necessary to investigate a wide range of prior distributions.

During the past 15 years, statisticians have developed an ingenious family of computational approaches that closely approximate posterior distributions by augmenting the observed data with simulated data based on current parameter estimates. These methods are generally referred to as data augmentation (Tanner & Wong, 1987) and a special case of that method known as the Gibbs sampler (Geman & Geman, 1984; Gelfand & Smith, 1990). We illustrate how this approach can be applied in the simple case of the vocabulary growth data previously introduced in Chapter 6.

Application of the Gibbs Sampler to Vocabulary Growth Data

These data are especially appropriate for Bayesian analysis because there are comparatively few higher-level units (22 children) and because the data are somewhat unbalanced. Indeed, half of the children participated in the first study and were observed on six or seven occasions, while the other half of the children participated in a second study and were observed on only three occasions. Given the small sample size and unbalanced nature of the data, our worry is that imprecise estimation of the level-2 variance may translate into imprecision in estimation of level-1 and level-2 regression coefficients. Under REML, which was illustrated in Chapter 6, this imprecision would not be represented in the reported standard errors for these regression coefficients.

TABLE 13.2 Bayesian Model for Vocabulary Growth Data (Seltzer, 1993)

Level-1 Model (Likelihood)

$$Y_{ti} = \pi_i a_{ti} + e_{ti}, \qquad e_{ti} \sim N(0, \sigma^2)$$
$$\text{for } t = 1, \ldots, T_i; i = 1, \ldots, n$$

Level-2 Model (First-Stage Prior)

$$\pi_i = \beta_0 + \sum_{q=1}^{3} \beta_q X_{qi} + u_i = X_i^T \beta + u_i, \qquad u_i \sim N(0, \tau)$$

Second-Stage Prior

$$p(\beta) = c_\beta, \qquad -\infty < \beta < \infty$$
$$p(\tau) = c_\tau, \qquad 0 \le \tau < \infty$$
$$p(\sigma^2) = c_{\sigma^2}, \qquad 0 < \sigma^2 < \infty$$
$$p(\beta, \tau, \sigma^2) = p(\beta)p(\tau)p(\sigma^2)$$

Joint Posterior

$$
\begin{aligned}
p(\pi, \beta, \tau, \sigma^2 | Y) &\propto p_\pi(\pi | \beta, \tau, \sigma^2, Y) r_\pi(\beta, \tau, \sigma^2 | Y) \\
&= p_\beta(\beta | \tau, \sigma^2, \pi, Y) r_\beta(\tau, \sigma^2, \pi | Y) \\
&= p_\tau(\tau^1 | \beta, \sigma^2, \pi, Y) r_{\tau 1}(\beta, \sigma^2, \pi | Y) \\
&= p_{\sigma^2}(\sigma^2 | \beta, \pi, \tau, Y) r_{\sigma^2}(\beta, \pi, \tau | Y)
\end{aligned}
$$

Model. The model is summarized concisely in Table 13.2. We use a slightly more succinct notation than used in Chapter 6 to simplify the presentation here. At level 1, there is a single predictor variable, $a_{ti} = (\text{age} - 12)^2$. There is no intercept in the level-1 model. (Recall that both the intercept and the linear coefficient for age were zero when children were 12 months of age.) Thus, the only level-1 coefficient is π_i, the acceleration rate.

At level 2, the acceleration rate is predicted by three child-level predictors: X_{1i} is the group (X_{1i} takes on a value of zero for children in study 1 and a value of unity for children in study 2); X_{2i} = maternal speech, the natural logarithm of the total number of words the mother used when the child was 16 months; and X_{3i} is an indicator for child's gender ($X_{3i} = 1$ if female, 0 if male). These predictors may be usefully collected into a vector

$$X_i^T = (1, X_{1i}, X_{2i}, X_{3i}).$$

Similarly, β is a 4 by 1 vector of level-2 regression coefficients.

As in the case of the teacher expectancy data described earlier, a Bayesian would describe the level-1 model as the likelihood, which describes the distribution of the observed data Y given the parameters π and σ^2. More formally, this likelihood is given by the normal density

$$f(Y|\pi, \sigma^2) = (2\pi\sigma^2)^{-T/2} \exp\left\{-\sum_{i=1}^{n}\sum_{t=1}^{T_i}(Y_{ti} - \pi_i a_{ti})^2/(2\sigma^2)\right\},$$

where $T = \sum T_i$.

In Bayesian terms, the level-2 model is the first-stage prior and is also normal with density

$$p(\pi|\beta, \tau) = (2\pi\tau)^{-n/2} \exp\left\{-\sum_{i=1}^{n}(\pi_i - X_i^T\beta)^2/(2\tau)\right\}.$$

The second-stage prior is $p(\beta, \gamma, \sigma^2)$, a product of priors spelled out in Table 13.2.

Gibbs Sampler. The joint density of all quantities is the product of the likelihood, the first-stage prior, and the second-stage prior. The posterior density of the unknowns given the data is proportional to this density (see Equation 13.16). Thus, we have

$$p(\pi, \beta, \tau, \sigma^2|Y) \propto f(Y|\pi, \sigma^2)p(\pi|\beta, \tau)p(\beta, \tau, \sigma^2).$$

However, the density of the unknowns can also be written as a product of conditional densities. Gibbs sampling exploits this fact, capitalizing on the equivalence of four representations of the joint density:

$$p(\pi, \beta, \tau, \sigma^2|Y) = p_\pi(\pi|\beta, \tau, \sigma^2, Y) * r_\pi(\beta, \tau, \sigma^2|Y)$$

$$= p_\beta(\beta|\tau, \sigma^2, \pi, Y) * r_\beta(\tau, \sigma^2, \pi|Y)$$

$$= p_\tau(\tau^1|\beta, \sigma^2, \pi, Y) * r_\tau(\beta, \sigma^2, \pi|Y)$$

$$= p_{\sigma^2}(\sigma^2|\beta, \pi, \tau, Y) * r_{\sigma^2}(\beta, \pi, \tau|Y).$$

In particular, Gibbs sampling exploits the fact that we can readily sample from the full conditionals p_π, p_β, p_τ, and p_{σ^2} because each of these has a known form. The form of each is specified in Table 13.2. The ingenuity of Gibbs sampling lies in the fact that we can approximate the posterior density of all unknowns even though the corresponding densities r_π, r_β, r_τ, and r_{σ^2} have an unknown form.

The Steps. We start with initial estimates $\beta^{(0)}$, $\tau^{(0)}$, and $\sigma^{2(0)}$, based, for example, on REML. Using these initial estimates, we sample from p_π to obtain $\pi^{(1)}$. Next, we use this value of $\pi^{(1)}$ in conjunction with $\tau^{(0)}$ and $\sigma^{2(0)}$ to sample from p_β to obtain $\beta^{(1)}$. Next, we plug $\sigma^{2(0)}$, $\beta^{(1)}$, and $\pi^{(1)}$ into p_τ to obtain $\tau^{-1(1)}$. The reciprocal of this quantity is $\tau^{(1)}$. Next, we plug $\tau^{(1)}$,

TABLE 13.3 Conditional Distributions Needed for Gibbs Sampling

Distribution	Distribution Type	Parameters[a]
$p_\pi(\pi_i \mid \beta, \tau, \sigma^2, Y)$	$N(\pi_i^*, V_{\pi_i}^*)$	$\pi_i^* = \lambda_i \hat{\pi}_i + (1 - \lambda_i) X_i^T \beta$
		$V_{\pi_i}^* = \lambda_i \sigma^2 / \sum_{t=1}^{T_i} a_{ti}^2$
$p_\beta(\beta \mid \tau, \sigma^2, \pi, Y)$	$N(\beta^*, V_\beta^*)$	$\beta^* = \left(\sum_{i=1}^{n} X_i X_i^T \right)^{-1} \sum X_i \hat{\pi}_i$
		$V_\beta^* = \tau \left(\sum X_i X_i' \right)^{-1}$
$p_{\tau^{-1}}(\tau^{-1} \mid \beta, \sigma^2, \pi, Y)$	gamma(a, b)	$a = n/2 + 1$
		$b = 2 / \sum_{i=1}^{n} (\pi_i - X_i^T \beta)^2$
$p_{\sigma^{-2}}(\sigma^{-2} \mid \beta, \pi, \tau, Y)$	gamma(c, d)	$c = T/2 + 1$
		$d = 2 / \sum_{i=1}^{n} \sum_{t=1}^{T_i} (Y_{ti} - \pi_i a_{ti})^2$

[a] $\lambda_i = \tau / (\tau + \sigma^2 / \sum_{t=1}^{T_i} a_{ti}^2)$

$\hat{\pi}_i = \sum_{t=1}^{T_i} a_{ti} Y_{ti} / \sum_{t=1}^{T_i} a_{ti}^2$

$\beta^{(1)}$, and $\pi^{(1)}$ into p_{σ^2} to obtain $\sigma^{-2(1)}$. The reciprocal of this quantity is $\sigma^{2(1)}$. This completes the first iteration of the Gibbs sampler.

This process is repeated until we reach stochastic convergence.[12] Seltzer et al. (2001) and Cowles and Carlin (1996) describe approaches to monitoring convergence. At that point, data from an additional m iterations are saved. The empirical distributions of these m values of the unknowns may be regarded as an approximation to the true joint posterior. Assuming m is large, the marginal posterior for any unknown may be approximated by the empirical distribution of the m values of that unknown produced by the Gibbs sampler. In this example, $m = 19{,}000$. See Seltzer (1993) for details.

Results. Table 13.4 compares results for the level-2 coefficients based on Bayes estimation via the Gibbs sampler to the results based on REML (latter

TABLE 13.4 Inference for Level-2 Coefficients, REML Versus Bayes

	REML			Bayes via Gibbs		
Model Parameter	Coefficient	se	95% Interval	Coefficient	se	95% Interval
INTERCEPT, β_0	−4.92	2.84	(−10.50, 0.66)	−4.89	3.22	(−11.25, 1.50)
GROUP, β_1	−1.11	0.30	(−1.81, −0.40)	−1.11	0.41	(−1.94, −0.30)
MATERNAL SPEECH, β_2	0.89	0.36	(0.18, 1.59)	0.88	0.41	(0.07, 1.70)
FEMALE, β_3	0.80	0.38	(0.06, 1.55)	0.80	0.43	(−0.07, 1.68)

results were presented in Chapter 6). The point estimates are nearly identical. However, the Bayes 95% intervals are somewhat wider in each case than are the intervals based on REML. This increase occurs because the REML intervals do not reflect the uncertainty about β that arises because τ is unknown. The Bayes intervals reflect this extra uncertainty. Seltzer provides a graph of the posterior for τ. It is somewhat positively skewed, so that a fairly large range of plausible values of τ lie to the right of the mode (which corresponds to the REML point estimate). This fact is ignored by REML but is taken into account in the Bayes approach. Interval estimates for the acceleration rates, π_i, are also larger under Bayes than under empirical Bayes conditioning on REML estimates of τ.

Summary of Terms Introduced in This Chapter

In prior chapters, inferences for hierarchical models were based on EB-ML or EB-REML. The EB-ML approach to hierarchical models bases inference about variance-covariance components and fixed regression coefficients on maximum likelihood. EB inferences about random coefficients are based on their conditional distributions given the data Y and the ML estimates of the other parameters. The EB-REML approach is closely related. Here inference about the covariance components are based on REML and EB inferences about the fixed and random regression coefficients are based on their conditional distribution given the data and the REML estimate of the covariance components.

EB-ML and EB-REML work well when J (the number of higher level units) is large. Even when J is small, the approaches work well for estimating fixed effects and covariance components as long as the data are not too unbalanced.

However, when J is small and especially when the data are unbalanced, there are distinct advantages in using a fully Bayes approach. Using this approach, inference about any unknown takes fully into account uncertainty about the other unknowns. Results may, however, be sensitive to choice of the prior distribution.

Prior probability distribution: Expresses an investigator's belief about the plausible values of some unknown parameter before collecting new data.

Likelihood: Specifies the likelihood of the sample data as a function of the value of an unknown parameter.

Posterior probability distribution: Specifies the investigator's belief about the plausible values of the unknown parameter after observing the data. The posterior probability distribution combines prior information with the information from the sample.

Posterior interval or **credibility interval:** Specifies the probability that an unknown parameter lies in a given interval, after taking into account the observed data.

Null hypothesis: Can be tested by computing its posterior probability and comparing that to the posterior probability of some alternative hypothesis.

This chapter has considered four approaches to statistical inference:

1. *EB-ML (empirical Bayes with maximum likelihood)*. A prior distribution is specified for the random coefficients given the fixed coefficients and covariance parameters. But no prior is specified for the fixed coefficients or covariance components. Instead, these are estimated via maximum likelihood (ML). Inference about random coefficients is based on their posterior distribution, assuming that the unknown fixed coefficients and covariance components are equal to their ML estimates.

2. *EB-REML (empirical Bayes with restricted maximum likelihood)*. Prior distributions are specified for both the random coefficients and the fixed coefficients. However, no prior is specified for the covariance components. Rather these components are estimated via REML. Inferences about the random and fixed coefficients are based on their joint posterior probability distribution where we assume that the unknown covariance components are equal to their REML estimates.

3. *Fully Bayesian inference*. Prior distributions are specified for all unknowns, including not only the random and fixed coefficients but also the covariance components. Inference is therefore based on the joint distribution of all unknowns given only the data.

4. *Gibbs sampling* is a strategy for approximating posterior distributions when they cannot be evaluated directly, which is virtually always the case for hierarchical models. By sampling from a sequence of well-defined conditional distributions, it produces, on each iteration, draws from the approximate joint posterior. After many iterations, the process is said to converge stochastically, and subsequent draws may be collected and described as representing the posterior distribution of interest.

Notes

1. We wish to thank Mike Seltzer for his numerous helpful comments on an earlier draft of this chapter and for his permission to reproduce his analysis of the vocabulary growth data.

2. More precisely, a good estimator minimizes Bayes risk: the expected value of a "loss function." A loss function defines the penalty to be paid when the true parameter is θ and the estimator is $\hat{\theta}$. For example, a squared error loss function would be $L(\theta, \hat{\theta}) = (\theta - \hat{\theta})^2$. Squared error risk is $E[(\theta - \hat{\theta})^2|Y]$, and this is minimized by choosing as $\hat{\theta}$ the posterior mean of θ.

Other loss functions can be defined, leading to other point estimators. For example, to minimize expected absolute error loss, that is, $E[L(\theta, \hat{\theta})|Y] = E(|\theta - \hat{\theta}| |Y)$, one chooses the posterior median as the point estimator.

3. With $f(Y|\mu)$ and $p(\mu)$ assumed normal, $p(\mu|Y) \propto \exp[-\frac{1}{2}\sum(Y_i - \mu)^2/\sigma^2 - \frac{1}{2}(\mu - \gamma)^2/\tau^2]$. Algebraic simplification leads to $p(\mu|y) \propto \exp[-\frac{1}{2}(\mu - \mu^*)^2/V_\mu^*]$ as defined in Equation 13.5.

4. Taking the first derivative of Equation 13.6 with respect to k and solving for k yields $k = E(\mu|Y) = \mu^*$, thus minimizing Bayes risk.

5. As shown in Chapter 14, these ML and empirical Bayes estimates are computed simultaneously in each set of iterations. However, they are conceptually distinct, as one might construct empirical Bayes estimates that depend on some method of estimation of γ, T, and σ^2 other than ML.

6. The average of $L_m(T, \sigma^2|\gamma_m, Y)$ should be a weighted average where the weights are proportional to the likelihood of γ_m. Suppose that γ is scalar, and we choose γ_m, $m = 1, \ldots, M$, such that γ_1 is a very much less than zero and γ_M is very much more than zero, with the spaces between successive values of γ_m equal. As the number of terms in the sum increases without bound (with the distance between successive values of γ_m diminishing without bound), this weighted average converges to an integral

$$\lim_{m \to \infty} \sum_{m=1}^{M} p(\gamma_m|Y) * L_m(T, \sigma^2|\gamma_m, Y) = \int p(\gamma|Y)L(T, \sigma^2|\gamma, Y)\, \partial\gamma$$

$$= \int L(\gamma, T, \sigma^2|Y)\, \partial\gamma$$

$$= L(T, \sigma^2|Y).$$

Thus, the restricted likelihood, $L(T, \sigma^2|Y)$ is the full likelihood, $L(\gamma, T, \sigma^2|Y)$ with γ integrated out.

7. The generalized least squares (GLS) estimates of γ under REML may be viewed as empirical Bayes estimates. They are based on $p(\gamma, \beta|T, \sigma^2, Y)$, the conditional posterior distribution of γ, β, given the REML estimate of T, σ^2 and the data, when the prior precision of γ is null (see Chapter 14 for details). Specially, the GLS estimation of γ, given T, σ^2, Y, is the posterior mean $E(\gamma|T, \sigma^2, Y)$.

8. To be proper, the posterior density must integrate to 1.0. The marginal density

$$h(Y) = \iiiint f(Y|\beta, \sigma^2)p_1(\beta|\gamma, T)p_2(\gamma, T, \sigma^2)\, \partial\beta\, \partial\gamma\, \partial\sigma^2\, \partial T$$

is the normalizing constant that ensures integration to 1.0.

9. This prior density is known as an "improper prior" because it does not integrate to 1.0 as is expected of a proper probability distribution.

10. The marginal density of d is $h(d)$, where

$$h(d) = \iiint f(d|\delta)p_1(\delta|\gamma, \tau)p_2(\gamma, \tau)\, d\tau\, d\gamma\, d\tau$$

is the normalizing constant that ensures integration to 1.0.

11. One advantage of using a uniform prior for τ is that the marginal posterior for τ is then proportional to the likelihood. This provides a way of checking the validity of the normal

approximation. However, Seltzer (personal communication—see also Seltzer, in press) has comments that there are also some disadvantages. He has found in simulation that the 95% posterior intervals for γ have greater than 95% coverage over repeated samples. Moreover, there does not seem to be a prior that will ensure exact 95% coverage from a frequentist perspective.

12. Stochastic convergence occurs when subsequent cycles of the algorithm are deemed random draws from the joint posterior. Monitoring a Gibbs sampler for convergence is currently a topic of intense research, and a discussion of rules for assessing convergence is beyond the scope of this chapter.

14

Estimation Theory

- Models, Estimators, and Algorithms
- Overview of Estimation via ML and Bayes
- ML Estimation for Two-Level HLMs
- ML Estimation via EM
- ML Estimation via Fisher Scoring
- ML Estimation for the Hierarchical Multivariate Linear Model (HMLM)
- Estimation for Hierarchical Generalized Linear Models
- Summary and Conclusions

Models, Estimators, and Algorithms

In making methodological choices for hierarchical models, it is essential to keep in mind the distinctions between the *model*, which defines the population parameters of substantive interest, the *estimation theory*, which enables us to make statistical inferences about those population parameters based on sample data, and the *computational algorithm*, which implements the estimation theory. Specification of the model entails several key choices: the number of levels in the hierarchy, the explanatory variables at each level, the probability distributions of quantities that vary at each level, and the most appropriate link function, which relates the expected outcome to a set of explanatory variables (see Chapter 10). Given the model, we may consider alternative approaches to estimation. These include, among others, full maximum likelihood (ML), restricted maximum likelihood (REML), and Bayesian methods (see Chapter 13). These three methods will give convergent results in large samples but will produce somewhat different results in small samples.

Finally, given the choice of estimation theory, we need a computational algorithm. If we have chosen ML as the method of estimation, we need to maximize the likelihood. In some cases, this can be accomplished by simply evaluating a formula. But, in most cases, there is no closed-form expression for the maximizer of the likelihood, and some iterative scheme is required. Popular choices include the "expectation-maximization" (EM) algorithm (Dempster, Laird, & Rubin, 1977; Dempster, Rubin, & Tsutakawa, 1981), Fisher scoring (Longford, 1987), and iterative generalized least squares (IGLS) (Goldstein, 1986). In principle, any of these algorithms applied to the same data and the same model should produce identical results. However, the performance of an algorithm, including its rate of convergence and the reliability of convergence across difficult applications, can vary.

Table 14.1 summarizes the models, estimation approaches, and computational algorithms illustrated in this book. Consider, for example, the two-level hierarchical linear model (HLM) described in detail in Chapters 1–7. We may wish to estimate the parameters of this model via full ML or restricted ML. (See discussion in Chapters 3 and 4.) To accomplish either goal, we may choose the EM algorithm or Fisher scoring. Alternatively, we may choose the Bayesian approach to inference. In this case, EM or Fisher scoring would not apply. The most common Bayes estimation algorithm uses Gibbs sampling as described in Chapter 13. The same choices are available for three-level and multivariate models, though we illustrate only the full-ML approach in this book. Chapter 10 considers hierarchical generalized linear models, estimated via penalized quasi-likelihood and full ML.

In this chapter, we consider estimation methods and computational algorithms for two-level models based on maximum likelihood estimation. Our

TABLE 14.1 Models, Estimators, and Computational Algorithms Considered in this Book

Models	*Estimation Theory*	*Computational Algorithm*
Hierarchical linear models (two level)	Full ML	EM algorithm or Fisher scoring
	Restricted ML	EM algorithm or Fisher scoring
	Bayes	Gibbs sampling
Hierarchical linear models (three level) Cross-classified, multivariate models	Full ML	EM algorithm or Fisher scoring
Hierarchical generalized linear models (two- and three-level models)	Penalized quasi-likelihood	EM or Fisher scoring with iteratively reestimated weights
	Full ML	Laplace approximation with Fisher scoring

major aim for this chapter is to clarify some of the key distinctions that commonly arise in discussing how to choose methods for analysis of hierarchical data. Our discussion will consider applications selected to illustrate key principles. A more comprehensive account, including all of the models and methods listed in Table 14.1, is available on line at www.ssicentral.com. Even that more comprehensive account, however, does not exhaust the possibilities. For example, it does not discuss Newton-Raphson algorithms for maximizing likelihoods; see Lindstrom and Bates (1989). Nor does it consider Bayesian inference for hierarchical generalized linear models; see Zeger and Karim (1991). However, the on-line document does cover all of the examples in this volume and thereby provides a reasonably broad survey of approaches to estimation and computation.

We begin with consideration of the general problem of estimation for hierarchical models. This general problem is much easier to solve for HLMs than for HGLMs (Chapter 10), and we consider standard two-level HLM cases first. Next, we consider HLMs with multivariate outcomes. Finally, we take on the more challenging task of estimating the parameters of the HGLM.

Overview of Estimation via ML and Bayes

The HLMs considered in this book involve identity link functions at level 1 and multivariate normal distributions at each level. In contrast, the HGLMs involve nonlinear link functions and nonnormal data at level 1, with multivariate normal distributions of random effects at higher levels. Finding good algorithms is considerably simpler in the case of HLMs than in the case of HGLMs. This is true for ML and Bayes estimation alike.

ML Estimation

To maximize a likelihood in the context of a hierarchical model requires two steps: first, evaluating an integral and, second, maximizing that integral. For HLMs, the integral can be easily evaluated in closed form, whereas, for HGLMs, this integral must be approximated. The accuracy of the approximation will affect the performance of the algorithm chosen to maximize the likelihood.

Let Y denote a vector of all level-1 outcomes, let u denote the vector of all random effects at level 2 and higher, and let ω denote a vector containing all parameters to be estimated (i.e., all variance and covariance elements and any fixed regression coefficients of interest)[1]. Then we can denote as $f(Y|u, \omega)$ the probability distribution of the outcome at level 1, given the random effects and parameters. The higher-level models specify as $p(u|\omega)$ the distribution of the random effects given the parameters. The likelihood of the data given only the parameters is then

$$L(Y|\omega) = \int f(Y|u, \omega)p(u|\omega) \, du. \qquad [14.1]$$

The aim of ML is to maximize the integral in Equation 14.1 with respect to ω in order to make inferences about ω. The integral is easily evaluated for HLMs, so that the remaining problem is maximization. For HGLMs, both integration and maximization are more challenging.

Empirical Bayes estimation of the random effects u is based on their conditional posterior distribution given the data Y and ML estimates $\hat{\omega}$ of the parameters ω. Applying Bayes theorem, we have

$$p(u|Y, \hat{\omega}) = \frac{f(Y|u, \hat{\omega})p(u|\hat{\omega})}{\int f(Y|u, \hat{\omega})p(u|\hat{\omega}) \, du}. \qquad [14.2]$$

Bayesian Inference

The Bayesian method combines prior information with information from the data to support statistical inference. Using the Bayesian method, all information about the unknowns of interest is contained in their joint posterior distribution, that is, the conditional distribution of the unknowns given the data. We now modify Equation 14.2 by adding a prior $p(\omega)$ for the parameters (rather than conditioning on a point estimate $\hat{\omega}$) and again applying Bayes theorem:

$$p(u, \omega|Y) = \frac{f(Y|u, \omega)p(u|\omega)p(\omega)}{\int\int f(Y|u, \omega)p(u|\omega)p(\omega) \, du \, d\omega}. \qquad [14.3]$$

Inferences about subsets of the unknowns of focal interest are obtained by integrating Equation 14.3 with respect to auxiliary unknowns. If the parameters ω are of primary interest, we have

$$p(\omega|Y) = \int p(u, \omega|Y) \, du. \qquad [14.4]$$

If the random effects u are of primary interest, we have

$$p(u|Y) = \int p(u, \omega|Y) \, d\omega. \qquad [14.5]$$

The integrals in Equations 14.3, 14.4, and 14.5 cannot, in general, be evaluated for either HLMs or HGLMs. However, they can be approximated via simulation using Gibbs sampling. Because we describe this approach in Chapter 13, we shall not consider Bayesian inference or Gibbs sampling further in the current chapter.

ML Estimation for Two-Level HLMs

In this section, we consider ML estimation for two-level univariate HLMs, that is, models, with a single outcome at level 1, with an identity link function at level 1, and with multivariate normal random effects at level 2. To maximize the likelihood, we face a choice of algorithm: We consider the EM algorithm and Fisher scoring. We show that Fisher scoring is equivalent to iterative generalized least squares (IGLS) for these models.

The EM algorithm and Fisher scoring are intimately related for these models. Each EM step requires sums of squares and products of the conditional means of the random effects (given the data and current parameter estimates) as well as the conditional variances and covariances of these random effects. A Fisher iteration will be shown to involve a transformation of the EM step and, therefore, to depend on the same conditional means and covariance matrices.

ML Estimation via EM

In this section, we consider full-information maximizing likelihood estimation for two-level HLMs. To see how this method compares to restricted maximum likelihood, we refer the reader to www.ssicentral.com. The EM algorithm addresses the problem of maximizing the likelihood by conceiving of this as a problem in missing data.

The Model

Consider the level-1 model

$$Y_j = X_j \beta_j + r_j, \qquad r_j \sim \mathrm{N}(0, \sigma^2 I), \qquad\qquad [14.6]$$

where Y_j is an n_j by 1 vector of outcomes, X_j is a known n_j by Q matrix of level-1 predictors, β_j is a Q by 1 vector of level-1 coefficients, and r_j is an n_j by 1 vector of random effects assumed multivariate normal in distribution with mean vector 0 and covariance matrix $\sigma^2 I$, where I is the identity matrix, here n_j by n_j. Level-2 units $j = 1, \ldots, J$ are independent.

At level 2, the level-1 coefficients become outcomes:

$$\beta_j = W_j \gamma + u_j, \qquad u_j \sim \mathrm{N}(0, T), \qquad\qquad [14.7]$$

where W_j is a Q by f vector of known level-2 predictors, γ is an f by 1 vector of fixed effects, and u_j is a Q by 1 vector of level-2 random effects assumed multivariate normal in distribution with mean vector 0 and covariance matrix T.

Substituting the level-2 model into the level-1 model yields a combined model

$$Y_j = X_j W_j \gamma + X_j u_j + r_j, \tag{14.8}$$

a special case of the mixed model

$$Y_j = A_{fj} \theta_f + A_{rj} \theta_{rj} + r_j,$$

$$\theta_{rj} \sim N(0, T), \tag{14.9}$$

$$r_j \sim N(0, \sigma^2 I),$$

where $A_{fj} = X_j W_j$, $\theta_f = \gamma$, $A_{rj} = X_j$, $\theta_{rj} = u_j$. The mixed model is more general than the combined model of Equation 14.8 because it does not require every level-1 coefficient to have a random component. Thus, in many applications, A_{rj} will be a subset of X_j having random effects, whereas, in other applications, A_{rj} may contain variables that have no fixed effect.

M Step

EM conceives Y_j as the observed data with θ_{rj} as the missing data. Thus, the complete data are (Y_j, θ_{rj}), $j = 1, \ldots, J$, while θ_f, σ^2, and T are the parameters to be estimated.

If the complete data were observed, finding ML estimates would be simple. To estimate θ_f, we would simply deduct $A_{rj} \theta_{rj}$ from both sides of Equation 14.9, yielding

$$Y_j - A_{rj} \theta_{rj} = A_{fj} \theta_f + r_j,$$

and justifying the ordinary least squares (OLS) estimate

$$\hat{\theta}_f = \left(\sum A_{fj}^T A_{fj} \right)^{-1} \sum A_{fj}^T (Y_j - A_{rj} \theta_{rj}) \tag{14.10}$$

as the "complete-data" ML estimator of θ_f.

Complete-data ML estimators for T and σ^2 are similarly straightforward:

$$\hat{T} = J^{-1} \sum \theta_{rj} \theta_{rj}^T,$$

$$\hat{\sigma}^2 = N^{-1} \sum \hat{r}_j^T \hat{r}_j, \tag{14.11}$$

$$= N^{-1} \sum (Y_j - A_{fj} \hat{\theta}_f - A_{rj} \theta_{rj})^T (Y_j - A_{fj} \hat{\theta}_f - A_{rj} \theta_{rj}),$$

where $N = \sum n_j$.

This reasoning defines certain complete-data sufficient statistics (CDSS), that is, statistics that would be sufficient for θ_f, T, and σ^2 if the complete data were observed. These are

$$\sum A_{fj}^T A_{rj} \theta_{rj}, \quad \sum \theta_{rj} \theta_{rj}^T, \quad \sum Y_j^T A_{rj} \theta_{rj}, \quad \sum \theta_{rj}^T A_{rj}^T A_{rj} \theta_{rj}. \quad [14.12]$$

E Step

The CDSS are not observed, but they can be estimated by their conditional expectations, given the data Y and parameter estimates from the previous iteration. In their seminal paper, Dempster et al. (1977) showed that substituting the expected CDSS for the M-step formulas would produce new parameter estimates having a higher likelihood than the current estimates.

To find $E(\text{CDSS}|Y, \theta_f, T, \sigma^2)$ requires deriving the conditional distribution of the missing data, θ_r, given Y θ_f, T, and σ^2. From Equation 14.9, it follows that the joint distribution of the complete data is

$$\begin{pmatrix} Y_j \\ \theta_{rj} \end{pmatrix} \sim N \left[\begin{pmatrix} A_{fj}\theta_f \\ 0 \end{pmatrix}, \begin{pmatrix} A_{rj}TA_{rj}^T + \sigma^2 I & A_{rj}T \\ TA_{rj}^T & T \end{pmatrix} \right], \quad [14.13]$$

from which the conditional distribution of the missing data given the complete data follows:

$$\theta_{rj}|Y, \theta_f, T, \sigma^2 \sim N(\theta_{rj}^*, \sigma^2 C_j^{-1}), \quad [14.14]$$

with

$$\begin{aligned} \theta_{rj}^* &= C_j^{-1} A_{rj}^T (Y_j - A_{fj}\theta_f), \\ C_j &= A_{rj}^T A_{rj} + \sigma^2 T^{-1}. \end{aligned} \quad [14.15]$$

Proof. Standard normal distribution theory (cf. Morrison, 1967, p. 88) derives the conditional distribution of θ_{rj} given Y_j from their joint distribution (Equation 14.13) as

$$E(\theta_{rj}|Y_j) = \theta_{rj}^* = TA_{rj}^T (A_{rj}TA_{rj}^T + \sigma^2 I)^{-1} (Y_j - A_{fj}\theta_f) \quad [14.16]$$

and

$$\text{Var}(\theta_{rj}|Y_j) = T - TA_{rj}^T (A_{rj}TA_{rj}^T + \sigma^2 I)^{-1} A_{rj}T. \quad [14.17]$$

However, by Theorem 3 in Smith (1973),

$$(A_{rj}TA_{rj}^T + \sigma^2 I)^{-1} = \sigma^{-2}I - \sigma^{-2}A_{rj}(A_{rj}^T A_{rj}\sigma^{-2} + T^{-1})^{-1} A_{rj}^T \sigma^{-2}. \quad [14.18]$$

Following Dempster et al. (1981), we define

$$C_j^{-1} = \left(A_{rj}^T A_{rj}\sigma^{-2} + T^{-1}\right)^{-1}\sigma^{-2}$$

$$= \left(A_{rj}^T A_{rj} + \sigma^2 T^{-1}\right)^{-1}, \qquad [14.19]$$

thus revealing

$$A_{rj}^T\left(A_{rj}TA_{rj}^T + \sigma^2 I\right)^{-1}A_{rj} = \sigma^{-2}\left(A_{rj}^T A_{rj} - A_{rj}^T A_{rj}C_j^{-1}A_{rj}^T A_{rj}\right)$$

$$= \sigma^{-2}\left(I - A_{rj}^T A_{rj}C_j^{-1}\right)A_{rj}^T A_{rj}$$

$$= T^{-1}C_j^{-1}A_{rj}^T A_{rj}. \qquad [14.20]$$

Substituting Equation 14.20 into Equation 14.17 yields

$$\mathrm{Var}(\theta_{rj}|Y_j) = T - C_j^{-1}A_{rj}^T A_{rj}T$$

$$= \left(I - C_j^{-1}A_{rj}^T A_{rj}\right)T$$

$$= \sigma^2 C_j^{-1}. \qquad [14.21]$$

Similarly, defining $d_j = Y_j - A_{fj}\theta_f$ and using Equation 14.18 and Equation 14.16, we find

$$\theta_{rj}^* = TA_{rj}^T\left(\sigma^{-2}I - \sigma^{-2}A_{rj}C_j^{-1}A_{rj}^T\right)d_j$$

$$= \sigma^{-2}T\left(A_{rj}^T d_j - A_{rj}^T A_{rj}C_j^{-1}A_{rj}^T d_j\right)$$

$$= \sigma^{-2}T\left(I - A_{rj}^T A_{rj}C_j^{-1}\right)A_{rj}^T d_j$$

$$= C_j^{-1}A_{rj}^T d_j. \qquad [14.22]$$

This completes the proof.

Putting the Pieces Together

Having identified the CDSS needed for the M step, we are now ready to define the EM algorithm.

1. Estimate the CDSS. We find

$$E\left(\sum A_{fj}^T A_{rj}\theta_{rj}|Y, \theta_f, \sigma^2, T\right) = \sum A_{fj}^T A_{rj}\theta_{rj}^*,$$

$$E\left(\sum \theta_{rj}\theta_{rj}^T|Y, \theta_f, \sigma^2, T\right) = \sum \theta_{rj}^*\theta_{rj}^{*T} + \sigma^2 \sum C_j^{-1}, \qquad [14.23]$$

$$E\left(\sum r_j^T r_j|Y, \theta_f, \sigma^2, T\right) = \sum r_j^{*T} r_j^* + \sigma^2 \, \mathrm{tr} \, \sum C_j^{-1}A_{rj}^T A_{rj},$$

where $r_j^* = Y_j - A_{fj}\theta_f - A_{rj}\theta_{rj}^*$. These expectations are evaluated at the estimates of θ_f, σ^2, and T based on the previous iteration.

2. Substitute the estimated CDSS into the M-step formulas (Equations 14.10 and 14.11) to obtain new estimates of the parameters.

3. Feed these new parameter estimates into step 1.

4. Continue until (a) changes in the log-likelihood become sufficiently small or (b) the largest change in the value of any of the parameters is sufficiently small.

The convergence of the algorithm may be monitored by computing the log-likelihood at each iteration.

ML Estimation via Fisher Scoring

The EM algorithm, as applied to the maximization of likelihoods for HLMs in the previous discussion, has several advantages. First, it reliably converges to a local maximum within the parameter space. This means that it will not produce negative variance estimates or estimates of covariances and variances that imply non-positive-definite covariance matrix estimates, unless the model is so badly overfit that the computations become numerically unstable. Second, the computations are easy to derive and check. Third, the computational effort per iteration is small.

The main disadvantages are two. First, EM can be slow to converge. This is especially true when the likelihood is flat, meaning that there exists substantial uncertainty about the parameters given the data. Indeed, the rate of convergence of EM is a direct measure of the fraction of "missing information" (Schafer, 1997, Chapter 3). Second, EM iterations do not produce, as an automatic by-product, estimates of the asymptotic standard errors of the ML estimates.

A useful alternative algorithm for maximizing the HLM likelihood is Fisher scoring (Longford, 1987, 1993). The key advantages of this approach are two: (1) It will converge rapidly in most applications, and (2) it produces, as an automatic by-product, standard errors of all parameter estimates. Its disadvantages are as follows: (1) It can produce non-positive-definite estimates of variance-covariance matrices, for example, unacceptable negative variance estimates and correlations outside the interval $(-1, 1)$, and (2) computations become intensive in complex models (e.g., three-level models).

Given the comparative advantages and disadvantages of EM versus Fisher scoring for ML estimation, a sensible approach is to combine the two methods (Raudenbush, Bryk, Cheong, & Congdon, 2000). One begins with a small number of EM iterations, which generally produce estimates in the neighborhood of the ML estimate. One then computes a Fisher estimate. If the Fisher estimate lies within the parameter space, one accepts the estimate and computes one or more EM estimates. One then reapplies Fisher scoring. This process continues until convergence.

Application of Fisher Scoring to Two-Level ML

Notation. Before providing computational formulas, let us clarify the notation. First, the "vec" operator stacks the columns of a matrix. For example, if T is 2 by 2,

$$\text{vec}(T) = \text{vec} \begin{pmatrix} \tau_{00} & \tau_{01} \\ \tau_{10} & \tau_{11} \end{pmatrix} = \begin{pmatrix} \tau_{00} \\ \tau_{10} \\ \tau_{01} \\ \tau_{11} \end{pmatrix}. \qquad [14.24]$$

Second, the Kronecker product (sometimes called a "direct product") works as follows. Consider

$$A \otimes B, \qquad [14.25]$$

where

$$A = \begin{pmatrix} a_{11} & a_{12} \\ a_{21} & a_{22} \end{pmatrix}. \qquad [14.26]$$

Then

$$A \otimes B = \begin{pmatrix} a_{11}B & a_{12}B \\ a_{21}B & a_{21}B \end{pmatrix}. \qquad [14.27]$$

Note that if A is m by n and B is p by q, their direct product is mp by nq.

Third, we need the structure of key derivatives. Let φ denote the unique parameters in T, σ^2. Suppose T is 2 by 2. Then we have $\varphi = (\tau_{00}, \tau_{10}, \tau_{11}, \sigma^2)^T$,

$$E = \frac{\partial \, \text{vec}(T)}{\partial \varphi^T} = \frac{\partial \begin{pmatrix} \tau_{00} \\ \tau_{10} \\ \tau_{01} \\ \tau_{11} \end{pmatrix}}{\partial(\tau_{00}, \tau_{10}, \tau_{11}, \sigma^2)}$$

$$= \begin{pmatrix} 1 & 0 & 0 & 0 \\ 0 & 1 & 0 & 0 \\ 0 & 1 & 0 & 0 \\ 0 & 0 & 1 & 0 \end{pmatrix}, \qquad [14.28]$$

and

$$F = \frac{\partial \sigma^2}{\partial \varphi^T} = \frac{\partial \sigma^2}{\partial(\tau_{00}, \tau_{10}, \tau_{11}, \sigma^2)}$$

$$= \begin{pmatrix} 0 & 0 & 0 & 1 \end{pmatrix}. \qquad [14.29]$$

Fisher scoring for T, σ^2. To apply the Fisher-scoring methods, we write the model for level-2 unit j as

$$Y_j = A_{fj}\theta_f + d_j, \qquad d_j \sim N(0, V_j), \qquad [14.30]$$

where Y_j is the n_j by 1 outcome vector, A_{fj} is the n_j by f matrix of known predictors, θ_f is an f by 1 vector of fixed effects, and $d_j = A_{rj}\theta_{rj} + e_j$, with

$$\theta_{rj} \sim N(0, T), \qquad e_j \sim N(0, \sigma^2 I), \qquad V_j = A_{rj}TA_{rj}^T + \sigma^2 I. \quad [14.31]$$

Here A_{rj} is an n_j by Q matrix of known predictors, θ_{rj} is the Q by 1 vector of random effects, T is the Q by Q random effect covariance matrix, and I is the n_j by n_j identity matrix. Let φ be a vector containing the unique elements of σ^2, T. Then, using the results of Magnus and Neudecker (1988), we find the score vector, S_j, to be

$$S_j = \frac{\partial \log[L(Y_j; \theta_f, \sigma^2, T)]}{\partial \varphi^T}$$

$$= \frac{1}{2}\left(\frac{\partial \operatorname{vec}(V_j)}{\partial \varphi^T}\right)^T (V_j^{-1} \otimes V_j^{-1})\operatorname{vec}(d_j d_j^T - V_j), \qquad [14.32]$$

where

$$\frac{\partial \operatorname{vec} V_j}{\partial \varphi^T} = (A_{rj} \otimes A_{rj})E + (\operatorname{vec} I)F \qquad [14.33]$$

and

$$L(Y_j; \theta_f, \sigma^2, T) = (2\pi)^{-n_j/2}|V_j|^{-1/2} \exp\left\{-\frac{1}{2}d_j^T V_j^{-1} d_j\right\}. \qquad [14.34]$$

We now apply a standard algebraic identity (Magnus & Neudecker, 1988):

$$\operatorname{vec}(ABC) = (C' \otimes A)\operatorname{vec} B \qquad [14.35]$$

for conformable matrices A, B, and C.

Applying this identity to Equation 14.32 yields

$$S_j = \frac{\partial \log\left[L(Y_j; \theta_f, \sigma^2, T)\right]}{\partial \varphi^T}$$

$$= \frac{1}{2}\left[E^T \text{vec}\left(A_{rj}^T V_j^{-1} d_j d_j^T V_j^{-1} A_{rj} - A_{rj}^T V_j^{-1} A_{rj}\right)\right.$$

$$\left. + F^T\left[d_j^T V_j^{-2} d_j - \text{trace}(V_j^{-1})\right]\right]. \qquad [14.36]$$

The Fisher scoring approach also requires the expected matrix of second derivatives $E(H) = E(\sum H_j)$, where

$$E(H_j) = \frac{\partial^2 \log L(Y_j; \theta_f, \tau, \sigma^2)}{\partial \varphi \partial \varphi^T}$$

$$= -\frac{1}{2}\left(\frac{\partial \text{vec } V_j}{\partial \varphi^T}\right)^T \left(V_j^{-1} \otimes V_j^{-1}\right)\frac{\partial \text{vec } V_j}{\partial \varphi^T}$$

$$= -\frac{1}{2}\left[E^T\left(A_{rj}^T V_j^{-1} A_{rj} \otimes A_{rj}^T V_j^{-1} A_{rj}\right)E\right.$$

$$+ E^T \text{vec}\left(A_{rj}^T V_j^{-2} A_{rj}\right)F + F^T \text{vec}\left(A_{rj}^T V_j^{-2} A_{rj}\right)E$$

$$\left. + \text{trace}\left(V_j^{-2}\right)F^T F\right]. \qquad [14.37]$$

Computations. Computational formulas for the pieces of H (Equation 14.37) are the following:

$$A_{rj}^T V_j^{-1} A_{rj} \otimes A_{rj}^T V_j^{-1} A_{rj} = A_{rj}^T A_{rj} C_j^{-1} T^{-1} \otimes A_{rj}^T A_{rj} C_j^{-1} T^{-1},$$

$$\text{vec}\left(A_{rj}^T V_j^{-2} A_{rj}\right) = \text{vec}\left[T^{-1} C_j^{-1} A_{rj}^T A_{rj} C_j^{-1} T^{-1}\right], \qquad [14.38]$$

$$\text{trace}\left(V_j^{-2}\right) = (n_j - Q)\sigma^{-4} + \text{trace}\left(C_j^{-1} T^{-1}\right)^2,$$

where Q is the number of random effects per cluster in the model. The asymptotic standard errors for the elements of T and σ^2 are the square roots of the diagonal elements of the inverse of the information matrix, that is, the square roots of the diagonal elements of $-[E(H)]^{-1}$.

The Fisher scoring algorithm works by computing the correction factor $\varphi_{\text{new}} - \varphi_{\text{old}}$ as

$$\varphi_{\text{new}} - \varphi_{\text{old}} = -[E(H)]^{-1} S, \qquad [14.39]$$

where $H = \sum H_j$ and $S = \sum S_j$. This correction factor is added to φ_{old} to obtain φ_{new}.

Relationship between Fisher and IGLS.   Define

$$Y_j^* = \text{vec}(d_j d_j^T - V_j),$$

$$X_j^* = \frac{\partial \, \text{vec} \, V_j}{\partial \varphi^T},$$

$$V_j^* = \text{Var}(Y_j^*) = 2(V_j \otimes V_j),$$

$$\beta^* = \varphi_{\text{new}} - \varphi_{\text{old}}.$$

[14.40]

Then the Fisher scoring algorithm is equivalent to an iterative generalized least squares (IGLS) algorithm aimed at minimizing

$$Q^* = \sum (Y_j^* - X_j^* \beta^*)^T V_j^{*-1} (Y_j^* - X_j^* \beta^*).$$ [14.41]

The minimization is accomplished by computing at each iteration

$$\beta^* = \left(\sum X_j^{*T} V_j^{*-1} X_j^* \right)^{-1} \sum X_j^{*T} V_j^{*-1} Y_j^*$$ [14.42]

and then using $\beta^* + \varphi_{\text{old}} = \varphi_{\text{new}}$ to update Y_j^* and hence V_j^*. Note that X_j^* does not depend on φ in the case of the linear model at each level.

Fisher Scoring for θ_f.   The ML estimates of φ and θ_f are asymptotically independent. Thus, the Fisher steps for each component can be computed separately. For θ_f, we have

$$S_{\theta_{fj}} = \frac{\partial \, \log[L(Y_j; \theta_f, \sigma^2, T)]}{d\theta_f}$$

$$= A_{fj}^T V_j^{-1} Y_j - A_{fj}^T V_j^{-1} A_{fj} \theta_f = A_{fj}^T V_j^{-1} d_j$$ [14.43]

and

$$E(H_{\theta_{fj}}) = E\left(\frac{\partial S_{\theta_{fj}}}{\partial \theta_f^T} \right) = -A_{fj}^T V_j^{-1} A_{fj}.$$ [14.44]

Set $H_{\theta f} = \sum H_{\theta_{fj}}$ and $S_{\theta f} = \sum S_{\theta_{fj}}$. We now apply the Fisher scoring algorithm to obtain

$$\theta_{f \, \text{new}} = [-E(H_{\theta f})]^{-1} S_{\theta f} + \theta_{f \, \text{old}}$$

$$= \left(\sum A_{fj}^T V_j^{-1} A_{fj} \right)^{-1} \sum A_{fj}^T V_j^{-1} Y_j.$$ [14.45]

Once again, we see the equivalence of Fisher scoring and iterative generalized least squares.

The standard errors of the elements of $\hat{\theta}_f$ are computed as the square roots of the diagonal elements of D_{ff} at convergence where

$$D_{ff} = \sigma^2 \left(\sum_{j=1}^{J} A_{fj}^T A_{fj} - \sum_{j=1}^{J} A_{fj}^T A_{rj} C_j^{-1} A_{rj}^T A_{fj} \right)^{-1}. \qquad [14.46]$$

Relationship between Fisher and EM for Variance-Covariance Components. The components of S_j are

$$A_{rj}^T V_j^{-1} d_j d_j^T V_j^{-1} A_{rj} = T^{-1} (\theta_{rj}^* \theta_{rj}^{*T}) T^{-1},$$

$$\text{trace}(V_j^{-1}) = (n_j - Q)\sigma^{-2} + \text{trace}(C_j^{-1} T^{-1}), \qquad [14.47]$$

$$d_j^T V_j^{-2} d_j = \sigma^{-4} (Y_j - A_{fj}\theta_f - A_{rj}\theta_{rj}^*)^T (Y_j - A_{fj}\theta_f - A_{rj}\theta_{rj}^*),$$

and

$$A_{rj}^T V_j^{-1} A_{rj} = A_{rj}^T A_{rj} C_j^{-1} T^{-1}.$$

Combining the pieces of Equation 14.47 yields the useful insight that the Fisher-IGLS step for φ represents a transformation of the EM step. To see this, note first that

$$\sum A_{rj}^T V_j^{-1} d_j d_j^T V_j^{-1} A_{rj} - \sum A_{rj}^T V_j A_{rj}$$
$$= T^{-1} \sum \theta_{rj}^* \theta_{rj}^{*T} T^{-1} - \sum A_{rj}^T A_{rj} C_j^{-1} J^{-1}$$
$$= JT^{-1} (\widehat{T}_{EM} - T) T^{-1}. \qquad [14.48]$$

This last step is based on the identity

$$A_{rj}^T A_{rj} C_j^{-1} = I - \sigma^2 T^{-1} C_j^{-1} \qquad [14.49]$$

and the definition

$$\widehat{T}_{EM} = J^{-1} \left(\sum \theta_{rj}^* \theta_{rj}^{*T} + \sigma^2 C_j^{-1} \right). \qquad [14.50]$$

Using a similar logic, we find

$$\sum [d_j^T V_j^{-2} d_j - \text{tr}(V_j^{-1})] = N\sigma^{-4} (\hat{\sigma}_{EM}^2 - \sigma^2), \qquad [14.51]$$

where

$$\hat{\sigma}_{EM}^2 = \frac{1}{N} \left[\sum (d_j - A_{rj}\theta_{rj}^*)^T (d_j - A_{rj}\theta_{rj}^*) + \sigma^2 \text{tr} \sum A_{rj}^T A_{rj} C_j^{-1} \right]. \qquad [14.52]$$

ML Estimation for the Hierarchical Multivariate
Linear Model (HMLM)

We now consider estimation of multivariate normal models from incomplete data. These models can be represented as hierarchical models in which the first level describes the association between the observed data and the complete data. Higher levels describe the distribution of the complete data. Chapter 6 illustrated application of these models to repeated-measures data. Chapter 11 illustrated application to the problem of estimating linear regressions from incomplete data. We consider computation of ML estimates via the EM algorithm and via Fisher scoring.

The basic problem of estimation for these multivariate models is often similar to—or even simpler than—estimation of two-level, three-level, and cross-classified models. However, a variety of interesting covariance structures can be estimated, and they are of special interest in the case of repeated-measures data, as illustrated in Chapter 6.

Below we consider estimation for the basic hierarchical multivariate model. This work builds on Jennrich and Shluchter (1986). This approach may be extended to a two-level multivariate linear model, in which we might have, for example, multiple outcomes measured on persons who are, in turn, nested within social contexts such as schools, neighborhoods, or firms. Thum (1997) describes such cases in detail and Chapter 8 illustrates the method.

The Model

In Chapter 11, we described a multivariate normal model as a special case of a two-level HLM. The model accommodates data missing at random (MAR) in the sense of Little and Rubin (1987). The level-1 model simply identifies which of the complete data have been observed. We have

$$Y_j = M_j Y_j^*, \qquad [14.53]$$

where Y_j represents an n_j by 1 vector of the observed data, Y_j^* represents a T by 1 vector of the complete data, and M_j is the n_j by T matrix of indicators. At level 2, we have a standard multivariate model for the complete data:

$$Y_j^* = A_{fj}^* \theta_f + \theta_{rj}. \qquad [14.54]$$

After substituting Equation 14.54 into Equation 14.53, we have

$$Y_j = M_j A_{fj}^* \theta_f + M_j \theta_{rj}, \qquad \theta_{r_j} \sim N(0, \Delta), \qquad [14.55]$$

a special case of the general two-level model $Y_j = A_{fj}\theta_f + A_{rj}\theta_{rj} + e_j$, with $A_{fj} = M_j A_{fj}^*$, $A_{rj} = M_j$, and $e_j = 0.^2$

Thus, marginally, $Y_j \sim N(A_{fj}\theta_f, V_j)$ with $V_j = A_{rj}\Delta A_{rj}^T$. The joint distribution of Y_j, θ_{rj} is thus multivariate normal:

$$\begin{pmatrix} Y_j \\ \theta_{rj} \end{pmatrix} \sim N\left[\begin{pmatrix} A_{fj}\theta_f \\ 0 \end{pmatrix}, \begin{pmatrix} A_{rj}\Delta A_{rj}^T & A_{rj}\Delta \\ \Delta A_{rj}^T & \Delta \end{pmatrix} \right]. \qquad [14.56]$$

It follows that the conditional distribution of $\theta_{rj}|Y_j, \theta_f, \Delta \sim N(\theta_{rj}^*, D_j^*)$, where

$$\begin{aligned} D_j^* &= \Delta - \Delta A_{rj}^T (A_{rj}\Delta A_{rj}^T)^{-1} A_{rj}\Delta, \\ \theta_{rj}^* &= \Delta A_{rj}^T (A_{rj}\Delta A_{rj}^T)^{-1} (Y_j - A_{fj}\theta_f). \end{aligned} \qquad [14.57]$$

EM Algorithm

The M step for an EM algorithm follows directly. If θ_{rj} were observed, the ML estimators would be

$$\hat{\theta}_f = \left(\sum_{j=1}^{J} A_{fj}^T V_j^{-1} A_{fj} \right)^{-1} \sum_{j=1}^{J} A_{fj}^T V_j^{-1} (Y_j - A_{rj}\theta_{rj}),$$

$$\hat{\Delta} = J^{-1} \sum_{j=1}^{J} \theta_{rj}\theta_{rj}^T. \qquad [14.58]$$

The E step computes the CDSS as

$$E\left[\sum_{j=1}^{J} A_{fj}^T V_j^{-1} (Y_j - A_{rj}\theta_{rj}) | Y_j, \theta_f^0, \Delta^0 \right] = \sum_{J=1}^{J} A_{fj}^T V_j^{-1} \left(Y_j - A_{rj}\theta_{rj}^{*0} \right),$$

$$E\left(\sum \theta_{rj}\theta_{rj}^T | Y_j, \theta_f^0, \Delta^0 \right) = \sum_{J=1}^{J} \theta_{rj}^{*0}\theta_{rj}^{*0T} + \sum_{J=1}^{J} D_j^{*0}, \qquad [14.59]$$

where θ_f^0, Δ^0 are current estimates.

Fisher-IGLS Algorithm

The Fisher scoring iterations involve

$$\Delta(\text{new}) - \Delta(\text{old}) = -[E(H)]^{-1} S, \qquad [14.60]$$

where $S = \sum_{j=1}^{J} S_j$ and $E(H) = \sum_{j=1}^{J} E(H_j)$, with

$$S_j = \frac{\partial L(Y_j; \Delta, \theta_f)}{\partial \varphi}$$

$$= \frac{1}{2} \left(\frac{\partial \operatorname{vec} V_j}{\partial \varphi^T} \right)^T (V_j^{-1} \otimes V_j^{-1}) \operatorname{vec}(d_j d_j^T - V_j), \qquad [14.61]$$

$$E(H_j) = E \left(\frac{\partial S_j}{\partial \varphi^T} \right) = -\frac{1}{2} \left(\frac{\partial \operatorname{vec} V_j}{\partial \varphi^T} \right)^T (V_j^{-1} \otimes V_j^{-1}) \frac{\partial \operatorname{vec} V_j}{\partial \varphi^T}.$$

Here $d_j = Y_j - A_{fj}\theta_f$.

Substitution for V_j and algebraic simplification parallel to the approach of the previous section lead to

$$E(H_j) = -\frac{1}{2} E_\Delta^T \left(A_{rj}^T V_j^{-1} A_{rj} \otimes A_{rj}^T V_j^{-1} A_{rj} \right) E_\Delta,$$

$$[14.62]$$

$$S = \frac{J}{2} E_\Delta^T [\Delta^{-1} (\widehat{\Delta}_{\text{EM}} - \Delta) \Delta^{-1}],$$

where $E_\Delta = \partial \operatorname{vec} \Delta / \partial \varphi^T$ and $\widehat{\Delta}_{\text{EM}}$ is the EM estimator of Δ given by Equations 14.58 and 14.59. Thus, we see again that the Fisher step is a transformation of the EM step.

The Fisher scoring algorithm for θ_f leads to standard generalized least squares:

$$\hat{\theta}_f = \left(\sum_{j=1}^{J} A_{fj}^T V_j^{-1} A_{fj} \right)^{-1} \sum_{j=1}^{J} A_{fj}^T V_j^{-1} Y_j.$$

Estimation of Alternative Covariance Structures

Within the framework of Fisher-IGLS, it is quite straightforward to estimate a number of submodels of HMLM as illustrated in Chapter 6. Each submodel involves the imposition of a structure on Δ (Jennrich & Shluchter, 1986). Interesting examples include the following:

- a random coefficient structure with homogeneous level-1 variance;
- a random coefficient structure with heterogeneous level-1 variance; and
- an autocorrelated level-1 (AR1) variance structure.

To apply Fisher to these applications requires in each case

- specification of the unique elements of φ of Δ under the specified model, and
- computation of the derivative matrix $E_\Delta = \partial \operatorname{vec} \Delta / d\varphi$.

To illustrate, we show how the random coefficient structure can be estimated as a special case of the HMLM (as long as the complete data are balanced). Readers interested in the other cases (AR1, heterogeneous level-1 variances) may refer to www.ssicentral.com for a full discussion of these models.

Suppose now that the complete data Y_j^* are repeated measures in a study of growth, as in Chapter 6. More specifically, the design calls for observations at the same set of T occasions for each participant, but the data Y_j are missing at random. The complete data Y_j^* are balanced. We have, at level 1,

$$Y_j = M_j Y_j^*,$$
$$Y_j^* = A\pi_j + r_j, \qquad r_j \sim N(0, \sigma^2 I). \tag{14.63}$$

Here A is the level-1 design matrix and is invariant across participants. At level 2, we have

$$\pi_j = X_j\beta + u_j, \qquad u_j \sim N(0, T).$$

The combined model for the complete data is thus

$$Y_j^* = AX_j\beta + Au_j + r_j, \tag{14.64}$$

a special case of a multivariate model (Equation 14.54) with

$$\theta_f = \beta$$
$$A_{fj}^* = AX_j,$$
$$\theta_{rj} = Au_j + r_j, \tag{14.65}$$
$$\text{Var}(\theta_{rj}) = \Delta = ATA^T + \sigma^2 I.$$

For example, in the case of the data from the National Youth Survey (Chapter 6), we have five time points per person. The unrestricted HMLM would have a Δ with $5(5+1)/2 = 15$ unique elements $(\varphi_1, \ldots, \varphi_{15})$, and $E_\Delta = d \text{ vec } \Delta/d\varphi^T$ would be a 25 by 15 matrix. In contrast, a linear growth system with homogeneous variance might have

$$A = \begin{bmatrix} 1 & -2 \\ 1 & -1 \\ 1 & 0 \\ 1 & 1 \\ 1 & 2 \end{bmatrix}, \qquad T = \begin{bmatrix} \tau_{00} & \tau_{01} \\ \tau_{10} & \tau_{11} \end{bmatrix}, \tag{14.66}$$

giving us

$$\varphi_1 = \tau_{00}, \quad \varphi_2 = \tau_{01}, \quad \varphi_3 = \tau_{11}, \quad \varphi_4 = \sigma^2.$$

Thus, E_Δ will be 25 by 4. Here we have

$$E_\Delta = (A \otimes A)E_\tau + \text{vec}(I)F, \qquad\qquad [14.67]$$

where $E_\tau = \partial \text{vec}(T)/\partial\varphi^T$ and $F = \partial\sigma^2/\partial\varphi^T$.

This two-level growth model can be estimated as a special case of the general HMLM. Given the current estimates of T and σ^2, compute Δ as in Equation 14.65. Now define E_Δ as in Equation 14.67 and apply the standard Fisher algorithm of Equation 14.62.

Discussion

As noted above, the HMLM can be tailored to handle a great variety of covariance structures. These are specified by Δ, which is a function of unique elements in the vector φ. The standard algorithm applies, but the parameter vector φ is tailored to the specific covariance structure of interest. The derivative matrix $E_\Delta = \partial \text{vec}\, \Delta/\partial\varphi^T$ is also tailored to the particular covariance structure of interest. Extension to higher levels follows. For example, suppose the aim is to study the distribution of the complete data Y_{jk}^* for person j nested in cluster k. The within-cluster covariance matrix would then be $A_{rjk}\Delta A_{rjk}^T$. The estimation problem then resembles a three-level problem with level-1 variance set to 0. We refer the interested reader to Thum (1997), who also provides a variety of interesting applications, and to www.ssicentral.com for further discussion.

The key assumption underlying this approach is that the missing data are missing at random. This means that the missing data $(I - M_j)Y^*$ are independent of M_j given the observed data Y_j. This assumption will often be plausible. While this assumption may be technically incorrect, results will nonetheless be robust if the fraction of missing information is small. The fraction of missing information will be small when few cases have missing data or when the observed data are strongly associated with the missing data. Schafer (1997) provides an extensive review and discussion of this assumption.

Estimation for Hierarchical Generalized Linear Models

As described in the beginning of this chapter, obtaining maximum likelihood (ML) estimates for hierarchical models is a two-step problem (see "Overview of Estimation via ML and Bayes"). The first step is to find the likelihood. This requires integration of the random effects from the joint distribution of the data and the random effects (Equation 14.1). The second step is to maximize that likelihood. The first step is easy when the model is linear with normally distributed random effects at each level. The only difficult problem is the maximization.

We now consider the more difficult estimation problems that arise when the level-1 model is nonlinear and the level-1 random effects are nonnormal in distribution. Application of such models was described in Chapter 10. Examples of nonlinear, nonnormal level-1 models included the logit link for binary outcomes, the log link for count data, the cumulative logit link for ordinal outcomes, and the multinomial logit link for multicategory nominal-scale outcomes. In each of these cases, the level-1 sampling model was nonnormal, while the random effects at higher levels were assumed multivariate normal in distribution.

In terms of the general notation introduced in Equation 14.1, we have a data vector, Y, a vector of random effects u, and a vector of parameters ω. The parameters include variance-covariance components and fixed regression coefficients. The distribution of the data given the random effects, that is, the level-1 model, is denoted $f(Y|u, \omega)$, while the distribution of the random effects is denoted $p(u|\omega)$. The joint distribution of the data and random effects is thus

$$g(Y, u|\omega) = f(Y|u, \omega)p(u|\omega), \qquad [14.68]$$

while the likelihood of the data given the parameters ω is the marginal density of Y, that is, the integral of this joint distribution over the space of the random effects:

$$L(Y|\omega) = \int f(Y|u, \omega)p(u|\omega) \, du. \qquad [14.69]$$

When both $f(Y|u, \omega)$ and $p(u|\omega)$ are normal, the marginal $L(Y|\omega)$ is also normal and can be derived analytically. The computational problem is to maximize $L(Y|\omega)$ with respect to ω.

The problem we face now is that $f(Y|u, \omega)$ is perhaps binomial, or Poisson, or multinomial, but it is not normal. In this setting, we might choose $p(u|\omega)$ to be a conjugate prior for the random effects. Then the integral of Equation 14.69 would be available analytically. For example, if f were binomial, p would be the beta distribution; if f were Poisson, p would be gamma; if f were multinomial, p would be Dirichlet. We could then move immediately to the problem of maximization as in the "normal-normal" case.

The difficulty with such an approach arises because we are generally interested in multivariate random effects. While the conjugate priors are convenient when each higher-level unit has only one random effect, these nonnormal priors do not readily represent the joint distribution of multivariate random effects. We turn to the multivariate normal as our prior primarily because of its utility as a model for multivariate distributions.

We are therefore confronted with joint distributions that are nonconjugate mixtures: "binomial-normal," "Poisson-normal," and "multinomial-normal" mixtures, for example. In these cases, the integration required to obtain the likelihood (Equation 14.69) is not available in closed form. We must turn to a numerical approximation to solve the integration problem. Of course, the problem of maximization must then also be tackled.

We first provide a brief overview of approaches to the problem of numerical integration. Next, we present the method of Laplace. This method helps clarify the nature of the integration problem. It also provides a general and computationally feasible numerical strategy for hierarchical models with multivariate random effects of arbitrary dimension. We illustrate how this approach applies in the case of binary data and then generalize it to a broader class of models.

Numerical Integration for Hierarchical Models

Stiratelli, Laird, and Ware (1984) estimated the parameters of a logistic regression model with nested, normally distributed random effects by approximating the density of $u|Y, \omega$ with a multivariate normal density having the same mode and curvature at the mode as the true posterior. Wong and Mason (1985) used essentially the same approach. Direct maximization of this approximate joint distribution avoids the difficult integration of Equation 14.69. Lee and Nelder (1996) refer to the integrand of Equation 14.69 as the "h-likelihood" and discuss properties of estimates of u, ω based on its direct maximization.

Several authors have extended the approach in different ways, for example, see Belin, Diffendal, Mack, Rubin, Schafer, and Zazlavsky (1993), Breslow and Clayton (1993), Gilks (1987), Goldstein (1991), Longford (1993), McGilchrist (1994), Schall (1991), and Wolfinger (1993). Following Breslow and Clayton (1993), we term this approach penalized quasi-likelihood (PQL). However, Breslow and Lin (1995) have shown that for logistic regression models with nested random effects, PQL estimates of the normal covariance matrix and, hence, of the regression coefficients, are biased and inconsistent (see also Goldstein & Rasbash, 1996). Bias is most serious when the random effects have large variances and the binomial denominator is small.

Application to Two-Level Data with Binary Outcomes

Consider now a level-1 outcome Y_{ij} taking on a value of 1 with conditional probability φ_{ij}. The combined model is

$$\log\left(\frac{\varphi_{ij}}{1 - \varphi_{ij}}\right) = \eta_{ij} = X_{ij}^T \gamma + Z_{ij}^T u_j \qquad [14.70]$$

for level-1 unit i nested within level-2 unit j. At level 1, we assume Y_{ij} conditionally distributed as Bernoulli (given the Q by 1 random effects vector u_j), while the random effects vector u_j is Q-variate $N(0, T)$ across the level-2 units. At times, it is useful to work with the model that eliminates the subscript i:

$$\eta_j = X_j \gamma + Z_j u_j, \qquad [14.71]$$

where η_j is an n_j by 1 vector with elements η_{ij}, and X_j and Z_j are matrices of predictors having rows Z_{ij}^T and X_{ij}^T, dimensioned n_j by f and n_j by Q, respectively.

Penalized Quasi-Likelihood

The PQL approach can be derived as a nonlinear regression model (Seber & Wild, 1989). In the case of binary outcomes with logit link, we start with the level-1 model

$$
\begin{aligned}
Y_{ij} &= \varphi_{ij} + e_{ij}, \\
E(e_{ij}) &= 0, \qquad\qquad [14.72] \\
\text{Var}(e_{ij}) &= \varphi_{ij}(1 - \varphi_{ij}).
\end{aligned}
$$

This is a nonlinear model which we "linearize" by means of the first-order Taylor series expansion. At this iteration s, we have

$$\varphi_{ij} \approx \varphi_{ij}^{(s)} + \frac{d\varphi_{ij}}{d\eta_{ij}}\left(\eta_{ij} - \eta_{ij}^{(s)}\right). \qquad [14.73]$$

We evaluate the derivative

$$\frac{d\varphi_{ij}}{d\eta_{ij}} = \varphi_{ij}(1 - \varphi_{ij}) = w_{ij} \qquad [14.74]$$

at $\varphi^{(s)}$. Substituting the linear approximation for φ_{ij} in Equation 14.72 yields

$$Y_{ij} = \varphi_{ij}^{(s)} + w_{ij}^{(s)}(\eta_{ij} - \eta_{ij}^{(s)}) + e_{ij}. \qquad [14.75]$$

Algebraically rearranging this equation so that all known quantities are on the left-hand side of the equation produces

$$\frac{Y_{ij} - \varphi_{ij}^{(s)}}{w_{ij}^{(s)}} + \eta_{ij}^{(s)} = \eta_{ij} + \frac{e_{ij}}{w_{ij}^{(s)}}. \qquad [14.76]$$

This equation has the form of the familiar two-level hierarchical linear model

$$Y_{ij}^{*(s)} = X_{ij}^T\gamma + Z_{ij}^Tu_j + \varepsilon_{ij}, \qquad \varepsilon_{ij} \sim N(0, w_{ij}^{(s)-1}),$$
$$u_j \sim N(0, T) \qquad (14.77)$$

where

$$Y_{ij}^{*(s)} = \frac{Y_{ij} - \varphi_{ij}^{(s)}}{w_{ij}^{(s)}} + \eta_{ij}^{(s)},$$
$$\varepsilon_{ij} = \frac{e_{ij}}{w_{ij}^{(s)}}. \qquad [14.78]$$

The estimate $\eta_{ij}^{(s)}$ is

$$\eta_{ij}^{(s)} = X_{ij}^T\hat{\gamma}^{(s)} + Z_{ij}^Tu_j^{*(s)}, \qquad [14.79]$$

where $u_j^{*(s)}$ is the approximate posterior mode

$$u_j^{*(s)} = (Z_j^TW_j^{(s)}Z_j + T^{(s)-1})^{-1}Z_j^TW_j^{(s)}(Y_j^{*(s)} - X_j\hat{\gamma}^{(s)}) \qquad [14.80]$$

for $W_j^{(s)} = \text{diag}\{w_{ij}^{(s)}, \ldots, w_{n_j j}^{(s)}\}$

The penalized quasi-likelihood (PQL) algorithm works as follows:

1. Treat Equation 14.77 as a standard hierarchical linear model, using the methods of EM or Fisher scoring to maximize the likelihood with respect to the level-2 variance-covariance components T and the fixed effects γ, based on some initial estimates of η_{ij} and w_{ij}.

2. Based on the new estimates, $\gamma^{(s+1)}$, $T^{(s+1)}$, compute new weights $w_{ij}^{(s+1)} = \varphi_{ij}^{(s+1)}(1 - \varphi_{ij}^{(s+1)})$. Also compute new values of the linearized dependent variables, $Y_{ij}^{*(s+1)}$.

3. Go back to step 1. Iterate until the parameter estimates converge to some pre-assigned tolerance.

This algorithm treats the linearized dependent variable (Equations 14.77 and 14.78) as approximately normally distributed, in which case the integral in Equation 14.69 has closed form. The algorithm is very reliably convergent and produces sound estimates so long as the level-2 variances are not too large, in which case the variance estimates and fixed effects estimates are negatively biased (see Breslow & Lin, 1995). The PQL algorithm produces excellent starting values for the more accurate Laplace approximations discussed in the next section.

The marginal quasi-likelihood (MQL) algorithm is identical to the PQL algorithm except that the Taylor series is expanded around $u_j = 0$ rather than around the approximate posterior mode $u_j = u_j^{(*)}$ (Breslow & Clayton, 1993). The weights and linearized dependent variable are computed from

$$\eta_{ij}^{*(s)} = X_{ij}^T \hat{\gamma}. \qquad [14.81]$$

The MQL estimates are more severely biased than are the PQL estimates (Breslow & Clayton, 1993; Breslow & Lin, 1995; Rodriguez & Goldman, 1995). We have also found these MQL estimates to be less reliably convergent than the PQL estimates.

Closer Approximations to ML

An alternative approach that will produce consistent and asymptotically unbiased estimates is to approximate ML estimates by approximating the integral in Equation 14.69 as closely as desired and then to maximize the approximate integral. Anderson and Aitkin (1985) applied Gauss-Hermite quadrature to evaluate the likelihood and maximized that likelihood in the case of a logistic regression model with one random effect per cluster of observations. Hedeker and Gibbons (1994, 1996) applied Gauss-Hermite quadrature to evaluate the required integral for ordinal probit and logistic models with multivariate normal priors. See also Tsutakawa (1985) for the case of a Poisson-normal mixture.

Pinheiro and Bates (1995) used adaptive Gauss-Hermite quadrature to approximate ML estimates for a nested random effects model with normal data and nonlinear link. Using the adaptive approach, the variable of integration (the random effect u) is centered around its approximate posterior mode rather than around its mean of 0. In principle, this approach will produce more accurate results than nonadaptive quadrature, especially when the dispersion of the random effects is large. Chan (1994), Karim (1991), and

Wei and Tanner (1990) used Monte Carlo integration to evaluate integrals such as that in Equation 14.69. Numerical integration via Gaussian quadrature becomes progressively difficult as the number of correlated random effects per cluster increases, while Monte Carlo integration is computationally intensive and provides stochastic rather than numerical convergence. Stochastic convergence can be difficult to assess.

An alternative approach to the approximation of integrals uses Laplace's method. Breslow and Lin (1995) used a fourth-order Laplace approximation to correct the bias associated with PQL in the case of nested random effects models with a single random effect per cluster. Lin and Breslow (1996) extended this bias-correction strategy to the case of multiple independent random effects per cluster. Raudenbush, Yang, and Yosef (2000) extended this logic to higher-order approximations and to multiple dependent random effects per cluster. Rather than using the method to correct bias, they viewed the approximated integral as the likelihood and maximized it to make inferences about ω. The approach has the following advantages: (1) Integration per cluster is fully multivariate with arbitrary dimension; (2) the approximation is accurate to any degree required; (3) convergence is numerical rather than stochastic; and (4) computations are remarkably fast.

Representing the Integral as a Laplace Transform

The problem of numerical integration becomes clear if we rewrite the integrand of Equation 14.69 using the method of Laplace. Because the integration proceeds cluster by cluster, we shall consider a single generic cluster and, for simplicity of presentation, drop the j subscript. First, we rewrite the natural log of the integrand as

$$h(u) \equiv \log[f(Y|u, \omega)] + \log[p(u|\omega)]. \qquad [14.82]$$

Next, assuming that $h(u)$ and all its derivatives with respect to u are continuous in the neighborhood of $\tilde{u}$, we expand $h(u)$ as a Taylor series about an estimate $\tilde{u}$:

$$h(u) = h(\tilde{u}) + h^{(1)}(\tilde{u})(u - \tilde{u})$$
$$+ \frac{1}{2}(u - \tilde{u})^T[h^{(2)}(\tilde{u})](u - \tilde{u}) + \sum_{k=3}^{\infty} T_k. \qquad [14.83]$$

Here $h^{(m)}(\tilde{u})$ is the mth derivative of $h(u)$ evaluated at $\tilde{u}$ and T_k is the kth term of the Taylor series.

We select $\tilde{u}$ to be the maximizer of $h(u)$. Then $h^{(1)}(\tilde{u}) = 0$ and the desired integral (Equation 14.69) becomes

$$L(Y|u, \omega) = \exp\{h(\tilde{u})\} \int \exp\left\{\frac{1}{2}(u - \tilde{u})^T[h^{(2)}(\tilde{u})](u - \tilde{u})\right\} \exp\left\{\sum_{k=3}^{\infty} T_k\right\} du$$

$$\propto |V|^{1/2} \exp\{h(\tilde{u})\} E_{N(0, V)}\left[\exp\left\{\sum_{k=3}^{\infty} T_k\right\}\right], \qquad [14.84]$$

where $E_{N(0,V)}$ denotes an expectation taken over a normal density with mean 0 and variance

$$V = -[h^{(2)}(\tilde{u})]^{-1}. \qquad [14.85]$$

If $h(u)$ were a quadratic function, all derivatives higher than 2 would be 0 so that $\exp\{\sum T_k\} = 1$, and the integrand of Equation 14.84 would be a joint normal density. This is the form of our integration problem in the case of the HLMs considered earlier.

If $h(u)$ is approximately quadratic, meaning that terms T_3 and higher are negligible, maximization of Equation 14.85 with $\exp\{\sum T_k\} = 1$ is a normal approximation that is referred to as the "conventional" Laplace approximation. Suppose, for example, that $f(Y|u, \omega)$ is binomial, but is based on a large number of trials. It is well known that the binomial distribution converges to the normal as the number of trials increases. Therefore, with $f(Y|u, \omega)$ being an approximately normal density and with $p(u|\omega)$ being normal, $h(u)$ will be approximately quadratic, and the conventional Laplace approximation will be accurate. We shall denote the conventional Laplace approximation as L_2, the second-order Laplace approximation, because it is founded on the assumption that $h(u)$ is approximately quadratic.

However, if $f(Y|u, \omega)$ is not even approximately normal, $h(u)$ will not likely be approximately quadratic and the correction term $\exp\{\sum T_k\}$ will be substantially different from unity. We may therefore write the Kth-order Laplace approximation as

$$L_K = L_2 * E_{N(0, V)}\left(\exp\left\{\sum_{k=3}^{K} T_k\right\}\right). \qquad [14.86]$$

Setting $S_K = \sum_{k=3}^{K} T_k$, we define a second series as $\exp\{S_{KM}\} = 1 + S_K + S_K^2/2! + \cdots + S_K^M/M!$, where we have represented the exponential function as a Maclaurin series with M terms. Thus, we have

$$L_{K, M} = L_2 * E_{N(0, V)}(1 + S_K + S_K^2/2 + \cdots + S_K^M/M!). \qquad [14.87]$$

This leads to a family of approximations of ever-increasing accuracy as K and M are increased.

Raudenbush, Yang, and Yosef (2000) describe this approach to approximation for a broad class of level-1 model known as the "generalized linear model" (McCullagh & Nelder, 1989). They show how to derive these approximations to the likelihood for random effects of arbitrary dimension and illustrate the speed and accuracy of the computations in the case of two-level models with binary outcomes. While referring the interested reader to that article for computational details, we illustrate how the methodology applies in the case of binary outcomes.

Application of Laplace to Two-Level Binary Data

Level-1 Model. We drop the j subscript for simplicity here. Translating to the binary case (Equations 14.70, 1471), we have, at level 1,

$$f(Y|u, \omega) = \prod_{i=1}^{n} \varphi_i^{Y_i}(1 - \varphi_i)^{1-Y_i} \qquad [14.88]$$

so that

$$\log[f(Y|u, \omega)] = l(u) = \sum_{i=1}^{n}[Y_i\eta_i + \log(1 - \varphi_i)]. \qquad [14.89]$$

Level-2 Model. The density of the random effect, u, given the data are normal, can be written as

$$p(u|\omega) = (2\pi)^{-n/2}|T|^{-n/2} \exp\{-u^T T^{-1}u/2\}. \qquad [14.90]$$

Combined Model. Combining the level-1 and level-2 models produces the joint distribution $p(Y, u|\omega) = (2\pi)^{-n/2}|T|^{-1/2} \exp\{h(u)\}$, where

$$h(u) = l(u) - u^T T^{-1}u/2. \qquad [14.91]$$

Maximizing $h(u)$. The Laplace transform requires maximizing $h(u)$ with respect to u. Equating the first derivative to 0 yields Q equations:

$$h^{(1)}(u) = l^{(1)}(u) - T^{-1}u$$
$$= Z^T(Y - \varphi) - T^{-1}u = 0. \qquad [14.92]$$

Let W be a diagonal matrix having elements $d\varphi_i/d\eta_i = w_i = \varphi_i(1 - \varphi_i)$. Define the linearized dependent variable of McCullagh and Nelder (1989) as

$$Y^* = W^{-1}(Y - \varphi) + \eta. \qquad [14.93]$$

Substituting $W(Y^* - n)$ for $Y - \varphi$ in Equation 14.92 yields

$$Z^T W(Y^* - X\gamma) = (Z^T WZ + T^{-1})u. \qquad [14.94]$$

This equation can readily be solved by means of a Newton-Raphson algorithm. We need the matrix of second derivatives

$$h^{(2)} = -(Z^T WZ + T^{-1}). \qquad [14.95]$$

The Newton-Raphson algorithm computes, at iteration $s + 1$,

$$\begin{aligned}
u^{(s+1)} &= u^{(s)} - [h^{(2)}(u^{(s)})]^{-1} h^{(1)}(u^{(s)}) \\
&= (Z^T W^{(s)} Z + T^{-1})^{-1} Z^T W^{(s)} (Y^{*(s)} - X\gamma). \qquad [14.96]
\end{aligned}$$

In sum, for any value of the unknown parameters ω, we can choose u to maximize $h(u)$ using a Newton-Raphson iterative scheme. This maximizer $\tilde{u}$ of $h(u)$ becomes the centering constant for the Taylor series that defines the Laplace-based approximation to the log-likelihood, defined as the sum of the log-likelihoods for each cluster. We then maximize the log-likelihood with respect to ω using Fisher scoring. Computational details appear in Raudenbush et al. (2000).

Comment. The Newton-Raphson step defined by Equation 14.96 has an extremely interesting form: $u^{(s+1)}$ is identical to the estimated posterior mean or "empirical Bayes residual" of the random effect u in a two-level model with continuous outcome Y^* and level-1 covariance matrix W^{-1}. This makes sense. If $h(u)$ were quadratic, $u|Y, \omega$ would be normally distributed, and the mode of u given Y, ω would be equal to the mean. This relationship between normal-theory hierarchical linear models and the nonnormal hierarchical generalized linear model is crucial to simpler approximations to maximum likelihood, including PQL (see Equation 14.80).

Generalizations to Other Level-1 Models

While we have illustrated the approximate ML approaches and the quasi-likelihood approaches in the case of binary data, these approaches extend readily to a broad class of level-1 models known as the exponential family, which includes as special cases the normal distribution, the binomial, the Poisson, the gamma, and others. Our level-1 model, generalized to include the exponential family, becomes

$$f(Y_j|u_j, \omega) = \exp\{l_j\},$$

with

$$l_j = \sum_{i=1}^{n_j} \{[Y_{ij}\eta_{ij} - \delta(\mu_{ij})]/\alpha(\theta) + \kappa(Y_{ij}, \theta)\},$$

where α, δ, and γ are arbitrary functions of their arguments, and $E(Y_{ij}) = \mu_{ij}$. Note that μ_{ij} and η_{ij} are implicitly functions of the random effects u_j.

To get the marginal likelihood, we wish to integrate out u_j from the joint density of Y_j and u_j, $j = 1, 2, \ldots, J$:

$$L = \int \prod_j f(Y_j|u_j, \gamma) p(u_j|T) \, du_j$$

$$= \prod_{j=1}^{J} \frac{1}{(2\pi)^{Q/2}} |T|^{-1/2} \int \exp\left(l_j - \frac{1}{2}u_j^T T^{-1} u_j\right) du_j. \qquad [14.97]$$

To apply Laplace's method, we regard $l_j - \frac{1}{2}u_j^T T^{-1} u_j$ as $h(u)$ in Equation 14.83 for $u = (u_1, \ldots, u_J)^T$ and, given a maximizer $\tilde{u}(\gamma, \tau)$ of $h(u)$, find derivatives up to the sixth order:

1. $h_j(\tilde{u}_j) = \tilde{l}_j - \frac{1}{2}\tilde{u}_j^T T^{-1}\tilde{u}_j$, where $\tilde{l}_j$ is l_j evaluated at $\tilde{u}_j$.
2. $h_j^{(1)}(\tilde{u}_j) = \tilde{l}_j^{(1)} - \tilde{u}_j^T T^{-1}$, where

$$\tilde{l}_j^{(1)} = \left.\frac{\partial l_j}{\partial u^T}\right|_{u=\tilde{u}} = (Y_j - \tilde{\mu}_j)^T Z_j/\alpha(\theta) = (Y_j^* - \tilde{\eta}_j)^T \widetilde{W}_j Z_j/\alpha(\theta).$$

Here $Y_j^* = \widetilde{W}_j^{-1}(Y_j - \tilde{\mu}_j) + \tilde{\eta}_j$, the linearized dependent variable (McCullagh & Nelder, 1989); $\widetilde{W}_j$ is diag$[\tilde{w}_{ij}]$, with $\tilde{w}_{ij} = d\tilde{\mu}_{ij}/d\tilde{\eta}_{ij}$, the derivative of μ_{ij}, with respect to η_{ij}, evaluated at $\tilde{u}_{ij}$.

3. $h_j^{(2)}(\tilde{u}_j) = \tilde{l}_j^{(2)} - T^{-1}$, with $\tilde{l}_j^{(2)} = -Z_j^T \widetilde{W}_j Z_j/\alpha(\theta)$, the second derivative of l_j, evaluated at $\tilde{u}_j$.

4. For $k \geq 3$, $h_j^{(k)}(\tilde{u}_j) = \tilde{l}_j^{(k)}$ is the kth derivative of μ_j, with respect to η_j, evaluated at $\tilde{u}_j$. In the case of binary Y_{ij} with logit link, $w_{ij} = \mu_{ij}(1 - \mu_{ij})$ and the third to the sixth derivatives are

$$\tilde{m}_{ij}^{(3)} = \tilde{w}_{ij}(1 - 2\tilde{\mu}_{ij}), \qquad \tilde{m}_{ij}^{(4)} = \tilde{w}_{ij}(1 - 6\tilde{w}_{ij}),$$

$$\tilde{m}_{ij}^{(5)} = \tilde{m}_{ij}^{(3)}(1 - 12\tilde{w}_{ij}), \qquad \tilde{m}_{ij}^{(6)} = \tilde{m}_{ij}^{(4)}(1 - 12\tilde{w}_{ij}) - 12\tilde{m}_{ij}^{(3)2}. \qquad [14.98]$$

In the case of count data ($Y_{ij} \in \{0, 1, \ldots\}$) drawn from a conditional Poisson distribution with log link, $w_{ij} = m_{ij}^{(k)} = \mu_{ij}$ for all k. When Y_{ij} is conditionally gamma-distributed with reciprocal link, $w_{ij} = \mu_{ij}^2$, $m_{ij}^{(k)} = (k-1)!\mu_{ij}^k$. In the normal case, $w_{ij} = 1$ and $m_{ij}^{(k)} = 0$ for $k > 2$. The constants $\alpha(\theta)$, as is well known, are unity for the binomial and Poisson, var$(Y_{ij}|u_j) = \sigma^2$ for the normal, and $-1/v$ for the gamma, where var$(Y_{ij}|u_j) = \mu_{ij}^2/v$. All derivatives of l_j are evaluated at $\tilde{u}_j$.

Summary and Conclusions

In general, the likelihood for a hierarchical model is an integral. For hierarchical models that are linear at each level with normally distributed random effects, this integral is easily evaluated by analytic means. The remaining problem is to maximize the likelihood. We showed how this can be done for two-level models using the EM algorithm and Fisher scoring. However, when the level-1 link function is nonlinear and the level-1 model is nonnormal, the required integral must be approximated.

A simple approximation known as "penalized quasi-likelihood" constructs a linear approximation of the level-1 model, assumes the "linearized dependent variable" is approximately normal, and proceeds much as in the case of HLM. This approach is reliably convergent but produces seriously biased estimates if the higher-level variance components are large. More computationally intensive approaches, based on more accurate approximations, are then required. These include Gauss-Hermite quadrature, Monte Carlo integration, and high-order Laplace approximations.

It is useful to note that the integral of interest is an infinite-order Laplace approximation. This insight defines a family of approximations and explicitly defines the error of each approximation. Raudenbush et al. (2000) find that the conventional Laplace approximation has error of order $O(n^{-1})$, where n is the number of level-1 units per level-2 unit. Typically, n must be at least moderately large to facilitate estimation of random slopes as well as intercepts. The Laplace approach works well here, as it is accurate and allows an arbitrary dimension of the random effect. For random-intercept models, however, n may be small and adaptive Gauss-Hermite quadrature is more accurate (Yosef, 2001).

Note

1. In previous chapters we have used bold face type to denote vectors and matrices. We depart from that convention in this chapter.

2. We use Δ rather than T for the covariance matrix here, reserving T to represent parameters of more specific models in the next sections, for example, Equation 14.65.

References

Achenbach, T. (1991). *Manual for the child behavior checklist/4–18 and 1991 profile*. Burlington: University of Vermont.

Adams, R. J., Wilson, M., & Wu, M. (1997). Multilevel item response models: An approach to errors in variables regression. *Journal of Educational and Behavioral Statistics, 22*(1), 47–76.

Agresti, A. (1996). *An introduction to categorical data analysis*. New York: John Wiley.

Aitkin, M., & Longford, N. (1986). Statistical modeling issues in school effectiveness studies, *Journal of the Royal Statistical Society, Series A, 149*(1), 1–43.

Anderson, D. A., & Aitkin, M. (1985). Variance component models with binary response: Interviewer variability. *Journal of the Royal Statistical Society B, 47*(2), 203–210.

Arbuckle, J. (1994). *AMOS3.5: Analysis of movement structures*. Chicago Smallusters Corporation.

Bartlett, M. S., & Kendall, D. G. (1946). The statistical analysis of variances-heterogeneity and the logarithmic transformation. *Journal of the Royal Statistical Society*, (Suppl. 8), 128–138.

Belin, T., Diffendal, J., Mack, S., Rubin, D., Schafer, J., & Zazlavsky, A. (1993). Hierarchical logistic regression models for imputation of unresolved enumeration status in undercount estimation. *Journal of the American Statistical Association, 88*(423), 1149–1159.

Bentler, P. M. (1983). *Theory and implementation of EQS: A structural equations program*. Los Angeles: BMDP Statistical Software.

Bentler, P. (1995). *EQS structural equations program manual*. Encino, CA: Multivariate Software.

Berkey, D., Hoaglin, F., Mosteller, F., & Colditz, G. A. (1995). A random effects regression model for meta-analysis. *Statistics in Medicine, 14*, 395–411.

Birnbaum, A. (1968). Some latent trait models and their use in inferring an examinee's ability. In F. Lord & M. Novick (Eds.), *Statistical theories of mental test scores*. Reading, MA: Addison-Wesley.

Bock, R. (1989). Addendum-measurement of variation: A two-stage model. In R. Bock (Ed.), *Multilevel analysis of educational data*. New York: Academic Press.

Bowles, S., & Gintis, H. (1996). *Productive skills, labor discipline, and the returns to schooling*. Unpublished manuscript.

Braun, H. I., Jones, D. H., Rubin, D. B., & Thayer, D. T. (1983). Empirical Bayes estimation of coefficients in the general linear model from data of deficient rank. *Psychometrika, 489*(2), 171–181.

Breslow, N., & Clayton, D. (1993). Approximate inference in generalized linear mixed models. *Journal of the American Statistical Association, 88*, 9–25.

Breslow, N., & Lin, X. (1995). Bias correction in generalized linear mixed models with a single component of dispersion. *Biometrika, 82*, 81–91.

Bryk, A. S., & Driscoll, M. E. (1988). *An empirical investigation of school as a community.* Madison: University of Wisconsin Research Center on Effective Secondary Schools.

Bryk, A., Lee, V., & Holland, P. (1993). *Catholic schools and the common good.* Cambridge, MA: Harvard University Press.

Bryk, A. S., & Raudenbush, S. W. (1987). Application of hierarchical linear models to assessing change. *Psychological Bulletin, 101*(1), 147–158.

Bryk, A. S., & Raudenbush, S. W. (1988). On heterogeneity of variance in experimental studies: A challenge to conventional interpretations. *Psychological Bulletin, 104*(3), 396–404.

Bryk, A. S., & Thum, Y. M. (1989). The effects of high school on dropping out: An exploratory investigation. *American Educational Reserach Journal, 26*, 353–384.

Bryk, A. S., & Weisberg, H. I. (1977). Use of the nonequivalent control group design when subjects are growing. *Psychological Bulletin, 84*, 950–962.

Burstein, L. (1980). The analysis of multi-level data in educational research and evaluation. *Review of Research in Education, 8*, 158–233.

Carlin, B. P., & Louis, T. A. (1996). *Bayes and empirical Bayes methods for data analysis.* New York: Chapman & Hall/CRC.

Carter, D. L. (1970). The effect of teacher expectations on the self-esteem and academic performance of seventh grade students. *Dissertation Abstracts International, 31*, 4539-A. (University Microfilms No. 7107612)

Carter, L. F. (1984). The sustaining effects study of compensatory and elementary education. *Educational Researcher, 13*(7), 4–13.

Chan, W. (1994). *Toward a multilevel generalized linear model: The case for Poisson distributed data.* Unpublished doctoral dissertation, Michigan State University, East Lansing.

Cheong, Y., & Raudenbush, S. (2000). Measurement and structural models for children's problem behaviors. *Psychological Methods. 5*(4), 477–495.

Claiborn, W. (1969). Expectancy effects in the classroom: A failure to replicate. *Journal of Educational Psychology, 60*, 377–383.

Cochran, W. (1977). *Sampling techniques* (3rd Ed.). New York: Wiley.

Coleman, J. S., Hoffer, T., & Kilgore, S. B. (1982). *High school achievement: Public, Catholic and other schools compared.* New York: Basic Books.

Conn, L. K., Edwards, C. N., Rosenthal, R., & Crowne, D. (1968). Perception of emotion and response to teachers' expectancy by elementary school children. *Psychological Reports, 22*, 27–34.

Cook, T. D., & Campbell, D. T. (1979). *Quasi-experimentation.* New York: Rand McNally.

Cooper, H., & Hedges, L. (Editors). (1994). *The handbook of research synthesis.* New York: Russell Sage Foundation.

Cowles, M. K., & Carlin, B. P. (1996). Markov chain Monte Carlo convergence diagnostics: A comparative review. *Journal of the American Statistical Association, 91*(434), 883–904.

Cronbach, L. J. (1976). *Research on classrooms and schools: Formulations of questions design and analysis.* Occasional paper. Stanford, CA: Stanford Evaluation Consortium.

Dempster, A. P., Laird, N. M., & Rubin, D. B. (1977). Maximum likelihood from incomplete data via the EM algorithm. *Journal of the Royal Statistical Society, Seires B, 39*, 1–8.

Dempster, A. P., Rubin, D. B., & Tsutakawa, R. K. (1981). Estimation in covariance components models. *Journal of the American Statistical Association, 76,* 341–353.

Diggle, P., Liang, K., & Zeger, S. (1994). *Analysis of longitudinal data.* New York: Oxford University Press Incorporated.

Elliot, D., Huizinga, D. & Menard, S. (1989). *Multiple problem youth: Delinquency, substance abuse, and mental health problems.* New York: Springer-Verlag.

Elston, R. C., & Grizzle, J. E. (1962). Estimation of time response curves and their confidence bands. *Biometrics, 18,* 148–159.

Englert, C. S., Raphael, T. E., Anderson, L. M., Anthony, H. M., Fear, K. L., & Gregg, S. L. (1988). *A case for writing intervention: Strategies for writing informational text.* East Lansing: Michigan State University, Institute for Research on Teaching.

Erbring, L., & Young, A. A. (1979). Individuals and social structure: Contextual effects as endogenous feedback. *Sociological Methods and Research, 7,* 396–430.

Evans, J., & Rosenthal, R. (1969). Interpersonal self-fulfilling prophecies: Further extrapolations from the laboratory to the classroom. *Proceedings of the 77th Annual Convention of the American Psychological Association, 4,* 371–372.

Fielder, W. R., Cohen, R. D., & Feeney, S. (1971). An attempt to replicate the teacher expectancy effect. *Psychological Reports, 29,* 1223–1228.

Fine, L. (1972). The effects of positive teacher expectancy on the reading achievement of pupils in grade two. *Dissertation Abstracts International, 33,* 1510-A. (University Microfilms No. 7227180)

Firebaugh, G. (1978). A rule for inferring individual level relationshps from aggregate data. *American Sociological Review, 43,* 557–572.

Fleming, E., & Anttonen, R. (1971). Teacher expectancy or my fair lady. *American Educational Research Journal, 8,* 241–252.

Flowers, C. E. (1966). Effects of an arbitrary accelerated group placement on the tested academic achievement of educationally disadvantaged students. *Dissertation Abstracts International, 27,* 991-A. (University Microfilms No. 6610288)

Fotiu, R. P. (1989). *A comparison of the EM and data augmentation algorthims on simulated small sample hierarchical data from research on education.* Unpublished doctoral dissertation, Michigan State University, East Lansing.

Frank, K., & Seltzer, M. (1990, April). *Using the hierarchical linear model to model growth in reading achievement.* Paper presented at the Annual Meeting of the American Educational Research Association, Boston, MA.

Fuller, B. (1987). Raising school quality in developing countries: What investments improve school quality? *Review of Educational Research, 57,* 255–291.

Garner, C., & Raudenbush, S. (1991). Neighborhood effects on educational attainment: A multi-level analysis of the influence of pupil ability, family, school, and neighborhood. *Sociology of Education, 64*(4), 251–262.

Gelfand, A., & Smith, A. (1990). Sampling based approaches to calculating marginal densities. *Journal of the American Statistical Association, 85,* 398–409.

Gelman, A., Carlin, J. B., Stern, H. S., & Rubin, D. B. (1995). *Bayesian data analysis.* New York: Chapman & Hall.

Geman, S., & Geman, D. (1984). Stochastic relaxation, Gibbs distributions and the Bayesian restoration of images. *IEEE Transactions on Pattern Analysis and Machine Intelligence, 6,* 721–741.

Gilks, W. (1987). Some applications of hierarchical models in kidney transplantation. *The Statistician, 36,* 127–136.

Ginsburg, R. E. (1970). An examination of the relationship between teacher expectations and student performance on a test of intellectual functioning. *Dissertation Abstracts International, 31*, 3337-A. (University Microfilms No. 710922)

Glass, G. V. (1976). Primary, secondary, and meta-analysis of research. *Educational Researcher, 5*, 3–8.

Goldstein, H. (1986). Multilevel mixed linear model analysis using iterative generalized least squares. *Biometrika, 73*, 43–56.

Goldstein, H. (1991). Nonlinear multilevel models with an application to discrete response data. *Biometrika, 78*, 45–51.

Goldstein, H. (1995). *Multilevel statistical models.* (2nd ed). New York: John Wiley.

Goldstein, H., & Rasbash. (1996). Improved approximations for multilevel models with binary responses. *Journal of the Royal Statistical Society, 159*(part 3), 505–513.

Gottfredson, M., & Hirschi, T. (1990). *A general theory of crime.* Stanford: Stanford University Press.

Greiger, R. M., II. (1970). The effects of teacher expectancies on the intelligence of students and the behaviors of teacher. *Dissertation Abstracts International, 31*, 3338-A. (University Microfilms No. 7114791)

Harris, C. W. (1963). *Problems in the measurement of change.* Madison: University of Wisconsin Press.

Heagerty, P. J., & Zeger, S. L. (2000). Marginalized multilevel models and likelihood inference. *Statistical Science, 15*(1), 1–26.

Hedeker, D., & Gibbons, R. (1994). A random-effects ordinal regression model for multilevel analysis. *Biometrics*, 993–994.

Hedeker, D., & Gibbons, R. (1996). MIXOR: A computer program for mixed-effects ordinal probit and logistic regression analysis. *Computer Methods and Programs in Biomedicine, 49*, 157–176.

Hedeker, D., & Gibbons, R. (1997). Application of random effects pattern mixture models for missing data in social sciences. *Psychological Methods, 2*(1), 64–78.

Hedges, L. V. (1981). Distribution theory for Glass's estimator of effect size and related estimators. *Journal of the American Statistical Association, 74*, 311–319.

Hedges, L., & Nowell, A. (1995). Sex differences in mental test scores, variability, and numbers of high scoring individual. *Science, 269*, 41–45.

Hedges, L. V., & Olkin, I. O. (1983). Regression Models in research synthesis. *American Statistician, 37*, 137–140.

Henrickson, H. A. (1970). An investigation of the influence of teacher expectation upon the intellectual and academic performance of disadvantaged children. *Dissertation Abstracts International, 31*, 6278-A. (University Microfilms No. 7114791)

Horney, J., Osgood, D., & Marshall, I. (1995). Criminal careers in the short-term: Intra-individual variability in crime and its relation to local life circumstances. *American Sociological Review, 60*, 655–673.

Hunter, J. E., & Schmidt, F. L. (1990). *Methods of meta-analysis: Correcting error and bias in research findings.* Newbury Park, CA: Sage.

Huttenlocher, J. E., Haight, W., Bryk, A. S., & Seltzer, M. (1991). Early vocabulary growth: Relation to language input and gender. *Developmental Psychology, 27*(2), 236–249.

James, W., & Stein, C. (1961). Estimation with quadratic loss. In J. Neyman (Ed.), *Proceedings of the Fourth Berkeley Symposium on Mathematical Statistics and Probability* (Vol. 1, pp. 361–379). Berkeley: University of California Press.

Jennrich, R., & Schluchter, M. (1986). Unbalanced repeated-measures models with structured covariance matrices. *Biometrics, 42*, 805–820.

Joreskog, K., & Sorbom, D. (1989). *LISREL 7: User's reference guide.* Mooresville, IN: Scientific Software.

Joreskog, K., & Sorbom, D. (1996). *LISREL 8: Structural equation modeling with the SIMPLILS command language.* Hove and London: Scientific Software International.

Jose, J., & Cody, J. (1971). Teacher-pupil interaction as it relates to attempted changes in teacher expectancy of academic ability achievement. *American Educational Research Journal, 8,* 39–49.

Kalaian, H., & Raudenbush, S. (1996). A multivariate mixed linear model for meta-analysis. *Psychological Methods, 1*(3), 227–235.

Kamata, A. (1998). *A generalization of the Rasch model by the hierarchical generalized linear model.* Unpublished manuscript.

Karim, M. (1991). *Generalized linear models with random effects.* Unpublished doctoral dissertation, Johns Hopkins University, Baltimore, MD.

Kasim, R., & Raudenbush, S. (1998). Application of Gibbs sampling to nested variance components models with heterogenous with-in group variance. *Journal of Educational and Behavioral Statistics, 20*(4), 93–116.

Keshock, J. D. (1970). An investigation of the effects of the expectancy phenomenon upon the intelligence, achievement, and motivation of inner-city elementary school children. *Dissertation Abstracts International, 32,* 243-A. (University Microfilms No. 7119010)

Kester, S. W., & Letchworth, G. A. (1972). Communication of teacher expectations and their effects on achievement and attitudes of secondary school students. *Journal of Educational Research, 66,* 51–55.

Kirk, R. E. (1982). *Experimental design: Precedures of the behavioral sciences.* Belmont, CA: Wadsworth.

Kirk, R. E. (1995). *Experimental design: Procedures for behavioral sciences,* 3rd edition. Wadsworth Publishing.

Laird, N. M., & Ware, H. (1982). Random-effects models for longtitudinal data. *Biometrics, 38,* 963–974.

Lee, S. (1990). Multilevel analysis of structural equation models. *Biometrika, 77*(4), 763–772.

Lee, V., & Bryk, A. (1989). A multilevel model of the social distribution of educational achievement. *Sociology of Education, 62,* 172–192.

Lee, Y., & Nelder, J. (1996). Hierarchical generalized linear models. *Journal of the Royal Statistical Society, Series B, 58,* 619–678.

Liang, L., & Zeger, S. (1986). Longitudinal data analysis using generalized linear models. *Biometrika, 73,* 13–22.

Lin, X., & Breslow, N. E. (1996). Bias correction in generalized linear mixed models with multiple components of dispersion. *Journal of the American Statistical Association, 91*(435), 1007–1016.

Lindley, D. V., & Smith, A. F. M. (1972). Bayes estimates for the linear model. *Journal of the Royal Statistical Society, Seires B, 34,* 1–41.

Lindstrom, M., & Bates, D. (1989). Newton-Raphson and EM algorithms for linear mixed-effects models for repeated measures data. *Journal of the American Statistical Association, 84,* 1014–1022.

Littell, R., Milliken, G., Stroup, W., & Wolfinger, R. (1996). *SAS system for mixed models.* Cary, NC: SAS Institute Incorporated.

Little, R. J. (1992). Regression with missing X's: A review. *Journal of the American Statistical Association, 87*(420), 1227–1237.

Little, R. (1995). Modeling the drop-out mechanism in repeated measures studies. *Journal of the American Statistical Association, 90,* 1112–1121.

Little, R., & Rubin, D. (1987). *Statistical analysis with missing data.* New York: John Wiley.

Little, R., & Shenker, N. (1995). Missing data. In G. Arminger, C. Clogg, & M. Sobel (Eds.), *Handbook of statistical modeling for the social and behavioral sciences* (pp. 39–75). New York: Plenum.

Long, J. S. (1997). *Regression models for categorical and limited dependent variables.* Thousand Oaks, CA: Sage.

Longford, N. (1987). A fast scoring algorithm for maximum likelihood estimation in unbalanced models with nested random effects. *Biometrika, 74*(4), 817–827.

Longford, N. T. (1988). Fisher scoring algorithm for variance component analysis of data with multilevel structure. In R. D. Bock (Ed.), *Multilevel analysis of educational data* (pp. 297–310). Orlando, FL: Academic Press.

Longford, N. (1993). *Random coefficient models.* Oxford: Clarendon.

Magnus, J. R., & Neudecker, H. (1988). *Matrix differential calculus with applications in statistics and econometrics.* New York: John Wiley.

Mason, W. M., Wong, G. M., & Entwistle, B. (1983). Contextual analysis through the multilevel linear model. In S. Leinhardt (Ed.), *Sociological methodology* (pp. 72–103). San Francisco: Jossey-Bass.

Maxwell, M. L. (1970). A study of the effects of teachers' expectations on the IQ and academic performance of children. *Dissertation Abstracts International, 31,* 3345-A. (University Microfilms No. 710125)

McArdle, J. (1986). Latent variable growth within behavior genetic models. *Behavior Genetics, 16,* 163–200.

McCullagh, P., & Nelder, J. (1989). *Generalized linear models* (2nd ed.). London: Chapman & Hall.

McDonald, R. (1994). The bilevel reticular action model for path analysis and latent variables. *Sociological Methodology and Research, 22*(3), 399–413.

McGilchrist, C. (1994). Estimation in generalized linear mixed models. *Journal of the Royal Statistical Society, Series B, 56,* 61–69.

Meredith, W., & Tisak, J. (1990). Latent curve analysis. *Psychometrika, 55,* 107–122.

Miyazaki, Y., & Raudenbush, S. W. (2000). A test for linkage of multiple cohorts from an accelerated longitudinal design. *Psychological Methods, 5*(1), 44–63.

Morris, C. N. (1983). Parametric empirical Bayes inference: Theory and applications. *Journal of the American Statistical Association, 78,* 47–65.

Morris, C., & Normand, S. (1992). Hierarchical models for combining information and for meta-analysis. *Bayesian Statistics, 4,* 321–344.

Muthén, B. (1994). Multilevel covariance structure analysis. In J. Hox & I. Kreft (Eds.), *Multilevel modeling, a special issue of Sociological Methods & Research* (pp. 376–398).

Muthén, L., & Muthén, B. (1998). *Mplus user's guide.* Los Angeles: Muthén and Muthén.

Nye, B., Hedges, L. V., & Konstantopoulos, S. (2000). The effects of small classes on academic achievement: The results of the Tennessee class size experiment. *American Educational Research Journal, 37*(1), 123–151.

Orchard, T., & Woodbury, M. (1972). A missing information principle: Theory and applications. *Proceedings of the Sixth Berkeley Symposium on Mathematical Statistics and Probability, 1,* 697–715.

Pellegrini, R., & Hicks, R. (1972). Prophecy effects and tutorial instruction for the disadvantaged child. *American Educational Research Journal, 9,* 413–419.

Pinheiro, J., & Bates, D. (1995). Approximations to the log-likelihood function in the nonlinear mixed-effects model. *Journal of Computational and Graphical Statistics, 4*(1), 12–35.

Pinheiro, J. C., & Bates, D. M. (2000). *Mixed-effects models in S and S-PLUS*. New York: Springer.

Ramirez, D., Yuen, S., Ramey, R., & Pasta, D. (1991). *The immersion study: Final report*. Washington, DC: U.S. Office of Educational Research and Improvement.

Raudenbush, S. W. (1988). Educational applications of hierarchical linear models: A review. *Journal of Educational Statistics, 13*(2), 85–116.

Raudenbush, S. W. (1993). Hierarchical linear models and experimental design. In L. Edwards (Ed.), *Applied analysis of variance in behavioral science* (pp. 459–496). New York: Marcel Dekker.

Raudenbush, S. (1993). A crossed random effects model for unbalanced data with applications in cross-sectional and longitudinal research. *Journal of Educational Statistics, 18*(4), 321–349.

Raudenbush, S. W. (1995). Hierarchical linear models to study the effects of social context on development. In J. Gottman (Ed.), *The analysis of change* (pp. 165–201). Hillsdale, NJ: Lawrence Erlbaum.

Raudenbush, S. W. (1984). Magnitude of teacher expectancy effects on pupil IQ as a function of the credibility of expectancy induction: A synthesis of findings from 18 experiments. *Journal of Educational Psychology, 76*(1), 85–97.

Raudenbush, S. (1997). Statistical analysis and optimal design for cluster randomized trials. *Psychological Methods, 2*(2), 173–185.

Raudenbush, S. W. (2000). Marginalized multilevel models and likelihood inference [Comment on article written by Patrick J. Heagerty and Scott L. Zeger]. *Statistical Science 15*(1), 22–24.

Raudenbush, S. W. (2001). Comparing personal trajectories and drawing causal inferences from longitudinal data. *Annual Review of Psychology, 52*, 501–525.

Raudenbush, S. W., & Bhumirat, C. (1992). The distribution of resources for primary education and its consequences for educational achievement in Thailand. *International Journal of Educational Research,* 143–164.

Raudenbush, S. W., & Bryk, A. S. (1985). Empirical Bayes meta-analysis. *Journal of Educational Statistics, 10*, 75–98.

Raudenbush, S. W., & Bryk, A. S. (1986). A hierarchical model for studying school effects. *Sociology of Education, 59*, 1–17.

Raudenbush, S. W., & Bryk, A. S. (1987). Examining correlates of diversity. *Journal of Educational Statistics, 12*, 241–269.

Raudenbush, S. W., Bryk, A. S., Cheong, Y., & Congdon, R. T. (2000). *HLM 5: Hierarchical linear and nonlinear modeling*. Chicago: Scientific Software International.

Raudenbush, S., & Chan, W. (1993). Application of hierarchical linear model to the study appendix of adolescent deviance in an overlapping cohort design. *Journal of Clinical and Consulting Psychology, 61*(6), 941–951.

Raudenbush, S., Fotiu, R., & Cheong, Y. (1999). Synthesizing results from the Trial State Assessment. *Journal of Educational and Behavioral Statistics, 24*(4).

Raudenbush, S. W., Kidchanapanish, S., & Kang, S. J. (1991). The effects of pre-primary access and quality on educational achievement in Thailand. *Comparative Education Review, 35*, 255–273.

Raudenbush, S. W., & Liu, X. (2000). Statistical power and optimal design for multisite randomized trials. *Psychological Methods, 5*(2), 199–213.

Raudenbush, S. W., Rowan, B., & Cheong, F. Y. (1991). *Teaching for higher-order thinking in secondary schools: Effects of curriculum, teacher preparation, and school organization*. East Lansing: Michigan State University, College of Education.

Raudenbush, S. W., Rowan, B., & Kang, S. J. (1991). A multilevel, multivariate model for school climate with estimation via the EM algorithm and application to US high school data. *Journal of Educational Statistics, 16,* 295–330.

Raudenbush, S. W., & Sampson, R. (1999a). Assessing direct and indirect associations in multilevel designs with latent variables [Sociological Methods and Research]. *Sociological Methods & Research, 28*(2), 123–153.

Raudenbush, S. W., & Sampson, R. (1999b). Ecometrics: Toward a science of assessing ecological settings, with application to the systematic social observation of neighborhoods. *Sociological Methodology, 29,* 1–41.

Raudenbush, S., & Willms, J. (1995). The estimation of school effects. *Journal of Educational and Behavioral Statistics, 20*(4), 307–335.

Raudenbush, S. W., Yang, M., & Yosef, M. (2000). Maximum Likelihood for hierarchical models via high-order, multivariate LaPlace approximation. *Journal of Computational and Graphical Statistics, 9*(1), 141–157.

Reardon, S. F., Brennan, R., & Buka, S. L. (In press). Estimating multi-level discrete-time hazard models using cross-sectional data: Neighborhood effects on the onset of adolescent cigarette use. To appear in *Multivariate Behavioral Research.*

Rivera-Batiz, F. (1992). Quantitative literacy and the likelihood of employment among young adults in the United States. *Journal of Human Resources, 27*(2), 313–328.

Robinson, W. (1950). Ecological correlations and the behavior of individuals. *American Sociological Review, 15,* 351–357.

Rodriguez, G., & Goldman, N. (1995). An assessment of estimation procedures for multilevel models with binary responses. *Journal of the Royal Statistical Society, Series A, 56,* 73–89.

Rogosa, D. R., Brand, D., & Zimowski, M. (1982). A growth curve approach to the measurement of change. *Psychological Bulletin, 90,* 726–748.

Rogosa, D. R., & Willett, B. (1985). Understanding correlates of change by modeling individual differences in growth. *Psychometrica, 50,* 203–228.

Rosenberg, B. (1973). Linear regression with randomly dispersed parameters. *Biometrika, 60,* 61–75.

Rosenthal, R. (1987). Pygmalion effects: Existence, magnitude, and social importance. *Educational Researcher, 16,* 37–41.

Rosenthal, R., Baratz, S., & Hall, C. M. (1974). Teacher behavior, teacher expectations, and gains in pupils' rated creativity. *Journal of Genetic Psychology, 124,* 115–121.

Rosenthal, R., Jacobson, L. (1968). *Pygmalion in the classroom.* New York: Holt, Rinehart & Winston.

Rosenthal, R., & Rubin, D. B. (1982). Comparing effect sizes of independent studies. *Psychology Bulletin, 92,* 500–504.

Rowan, B., Raudenbush, S., & Cheong, Y. (1993). Teaching as a non-routine task: Implications for the organizational design of schools. *Educational Administration Quarterly, 29*(4), 479–500.

Rubin, D. B. (1980). Using empirical Bayes techniques in the Law School Validity Studies. *Journal of the American Statistical Association, 75,* 801–827.

Rumberger, R. W. (1995). Dropping out of middle schools: A multilevel analysis of students and schools. *American Educational Research Journal, 32*(3), 583–625.

Sampson, R., Raudenbush, S., & Earls, T. (1997). Neighborhoods and violent crime: A multilevel study of collective efficacy. *Science, 277,* 918–924.

Schafer, J. (1997). *Analysis of incomplete multivariate data.* London: Chapman & Hall.

Schall, R. (1991). Estimation in generalized linear models with random effects. *Biometrika, 40,* 719–727.

Seber, G. A. F., & Wild, C. J. (1989). *Nonlinear regression*. New York: Wiley.

Seltzer, M. (1993). Sensitivity analysis for fixed effects in the hierarchical model: A Gibbs sampling approach, *18*(3), 207–235.

Seltzer, M., Novak, J., Choi, K., & Lim, N. (2001). *Sensitivity analysis for hierarchical models employing t level-1 assumptions*. Los Angeles: UCLA Department of Education.

Seltzer, M., Wong, W., & Bryk, A. (1996). Bayesian analysis in applications of hierarchical models: Issues and methods. *Journal of Educational and Behavioral Statistics, 21*(2), 131–167.

Singer, J. D. (1998). Using SAS PROC MIXED to fit multilevel models, hierarchical models, and individual growth models. *Journal of Educational and Behavioral Statistics, 23*(4), 323–355.

Smith, A. F. M. (1973). A general Bayesian linear model. *Journal of the Royal Statistical Society, Series B, 35*, 61–75.

Snijders, T., & Bosker, R. (1999). *Multilevel analysis*. London: Sage.

Spiegelhalter, D., Thomas, A., Best, N., & Gilks, W. (1994). *BUGS: Bayesian inference using Gibbs sampling, version 0.30*. MRC Biostatistics Unit: Cambridge.

Stiratelli, R., Laird, N., & Ware, J. (1984). Random effects models for serial observations with binary response. *Biometrics, 40*, 961–971.

Strenio, J. L. F., Weisberg, H. I., & Bryk, A. S. (1983). Empirical Bayes estimation of individual growth curve parameters and their relationship to covariates. *Biometrics, 39*, 71–86.

Stuart, A., & Ord, J. K. (1995). *Kendall's advanced theory on statistics*. New York: Halsted.

Tanner, M. A., & Wong, W. H. (1987). The calculation of posterior distribution by data augmentation [with discussion]. *Journal of the American Statistical Association, 82*, 528–550.

Thissen, D. (1982). Marginal maximum likelihood estimation for the one-parameter logistic model. *Psychometrika, 47*, 175–186.

Thum, Y. (1997). Hierarchical linear models for multivariate outcomes. *Journal of Educational and Behavioral Statistics*.

Tsutakawa, R. (1985). Estimation of cancer mortality rates: A Bayesian analysis of small frequencies. *Biometrics, 41*, 69–79.

van der Linden, W. J., & Hambleton, R. K. (1996). Item response theory: Brief history, common models, and extensions. In W. J. van der Linden & R. K. Hambleton (Eds.), *Handbook of modern item response theory* (pp. 1–28). New York: Springer-Verlag.

Wei, G., & Tanner, M. (1990). A Monte Carlo implementation of the EM algorithm and the poor man's augmentation algorithms. *Journal of the American Statistical Association, 85*, 669–704.

Willett, J. B. (1988). Questions and answers in the measurement of change. In E. Rothkopf (Ed.), *Review of research in education (1988-89)* (pp. 345–422). Washington, DC: American Educational Research Association.

Willett, J., & Sayer, A. (1994). Using covariance structure analysis to detect correlates and predictors of individual change over time. *Psychological Bulletin, 116*(2), 363–380.

Willms, J. D. (1986). Social class segregation and its relationship to pupils' examination results in Scotland. *American Sociological Review, 55*, 224–241.

Wineburg, S. (1987). The self-fulfillment of the self-fulfilling prophecy. *Educational Researcher, 16*(9), 28–37.

Wolfinger, R. (1993). Laplace's approximation for nonlinear mixed models. *Biometrika, 80*, 791–795.

Wong, G., & Mason, W. (1985). The hierarchical logistic regression model for multilevel analysis. *Journal of the American Statistical Association, 80*(391), 513–524.

Wright, B., & Masters, G. (1982). *Rating scale analysis: Rasch measurement*. Chicago: MESA Press.

Yosef, M. (2001). *A comparison of alternative approximations to maximum likelihood estimation for hierarchical generalized linear models: The logistic-normal model case.* Unpublished doctoral dissertation, Michigan State University, Department of Counseling, Educational Psychology and Special Education.

Zeger, S., & Karim, M. (1991). Generalized linear models with random effects: A Gibbs sampling approach. *Journal of the American Statistical Association, 86*, 79–86.

Zeger, S., Liang, K.-Y., & Albert, P. (1988). Models for longitudinal data: A likelihood approach. *Biometrics, 44*, 1049–1060.

Index

About the Authors

Stephen W. Raudenbush is Professor, School of Education, Professor, Department of Statistics, and Senior Research Scientist, Survey Research Center, at the University of Michigan. His research focuses on statistical methods for multilevel and longitudinal research.

Anthony S. Bryk is the Marshall Field IV Professor of Urban Education in the Department of Sociology at the University of Chicago. He directs the University's Center for School Improvement and is Senior Director of the Consortium on Chicago School Research. His research interests include school organization, urban school reform, accountability and educational statistics.